W9-CXY-969

4.40

COST_____ BOOK NO._ 7

Property of

ROMULUS CENTRAL SCHOOL

ROMULUS, NEW YORK

DATE	PUPIL'S NAME (IN INK)	CONDI-TION
5/10/60	Pancy Brown	New
9/7/61	Sue Brodnick	New

The pupil to whom this book is issued will be held responsible for reasonable care of it and must replace if lost or damaged.

NEW - GOOD - FAIR - POOR

CLOTHING CONSTRUCTION AND WARDROBE PLANNING

1960 Edition

Clothing Construction

CLOTHING CONSTRUCTION AND WARDROBE PLANNING

and Wardrobe Planning

1960 Edition

DORA S. LEWIS

Chairman, Department of Home Economics
Hunter College, New York City

MABEL GOODE BOWERS

Director of Clothing, Textiles, and Applied Art,
Department of Home Economics
New York University

MARIETTA KETTUNEN

Associate Professor of Art
Alabama Polytechnic Institute

THE MACMILLAN COMPANY : NEW YORK

© *The Macmillan Company 1960*

All rights reserved—no part of this book may be reproduced in any form without permission in writing from the publisher, except by a reviewer who wishes to quote brief passages in connection with a review written for inclusion in magazine or newspaper.

First edition Copyright The Macmillan Company 1955

The Macmillan Company, New York
Brett-Macmillan, Ltd., Galt, Ontario

PRINTED IN THE UNITED STATES OF AMERICA

INTRODUCTION

The Educational Department of The Macmillan Company now makes available a series of five textbooks for the home economics department. The authors and editors have taken into account the dramatic changes that have taken place in home and community living in the past decade. They have carefully selected subject matter and experiences to prepare young people for the responsibilities they face in their families and which they will eventually encounter in homes of their own.

Tomorrow's Homemaker, the first book in the series, is planned to meet the needs and interests of students both as individuals and as members of families. It provides information for a general introductory course in home economics. Each of the other four books deals comprehensively with a specific area of home economics. *Family Living* presents personality development, family relationships, child development, and the establishment of constructive relationships between the family and the community. *Housing and Home Management* presents the home in the community as the setting for the life of the family. It deals with the selection, arrangement, and use of furnishings and equipment and gives guidance for developing skills to extend resources and to achieve the important goal of a smoothly run home.

This book, *Clothing Construction and Wardrobe Planning,* helps students to appraise clothing needs, to develop good taste and the ability to buy wisely, and to develop skills in constructing the garments they want to make. *Family Meals and Hospitality* gives guides to good nutrition at different cost levels in line with advances in knowledge about nutrition and the many new developments in food products. The social aspects of skillful and creative food management are emphasized.

In each of the books in this series the students are encouraged (1) to think critically and to apply principles of science, art, economics, and human relationships to the problems of personal and home living; (2) to make decisions and choices in the light of values that are important to family and community living; (3) to learn to work competently in homes by developing essential homemaking skills; and (4) to make long-range plans for personal and family living based on thoughtful consideration of what life can be if the resources now available are used effectively.

The authors of *Clothing Construction and Wardrobe Planning* have sincere convictions about the personal, social, and economic significance of clothing. Equitable sharing of the family's clothing money and the responsibilities of the consumer-buyer are both stressed throughout the text. Careful and detailed instruction is given for developing and enjoying the skills needed to construct garments of good design, material, and workmanship.

Marietta Kettunen is a teacher of fine arts and costume design. Beginning with the interests of high-school girls in making the most of their personal appearance, Miss Kettunen gives practical guidance (1) for art expressoin through pleasing combination of color and design, (2) for definite planning of personal wardrobes, (3) for wise handling of the economic aspect of clothing. Good grooming and clothing care are given due emphasis. The chapter on careers in clothing and fashion fills a need deeply felt by inquiring high-school girls.

Mabel Bowers draws on many years of experience in teaching at both secondary and college levels, including the instruction of home economics teachers and the supervision of student teachers in junior and senior high-school home economics classes. Her specialization in clothing, textiles, applied art, and economics gives her writing unusual validity. Her sections on the selection and use of sewing tools, patterns, fabrics, processes of clothing construction, and the management of all of these for developing good construction techniques should lead to enjoyment of clothing construction. Important construction processes are clearly illustrated in her own line drawings.

Mrs. Bowers encourages the use of quick construction methods wherever they can be used without sacrificing good results. While the garments suggested for construction in the book are for the girls themselves, the principles learned can be applied to selecting, constructing, and caring for garments for other members of the family, both children and adults.

Clothing is a persistent interest in everyone's life, and this interest is at its peak during adolescence when the need for social acceptance is great. This is the time to present this important subject. In most families more money is spent for clothing than for anything else except housing and food. Clothing education should help young people to appraise their clothing needs and wants and should develop the ability to select clothing that enhances the personality of the wearer. It should aid them to find good values at all price levels and to use good judgment about what to buy and what to make. If the course arouses the student's interest in becoming skilled in constructing, altering, and caring for clothing, it can be of inestimable value to individuals and families. All these aspects of clothing have been considered in this book from the point of view of high-school girls. Teachers and students who use the book will find sound guidance for creative and practical handling of both personal and family clothing problems.

DORA S. LEWIS

PREFACE

Every girl wants to be attractive. In this book we have capitalized on this motivation to help girls develop skills of lasting value to themselves and to their families. Starting with simple grooming procedures and the art of choosing becoming lines, textures, and colors, we have gone on to show how to choose clothes and accessories that create harmonious costumes. Most families have limited funds for clothing, and girls must be resourceful and intelligent in meeting their clothing needs if they are to be well dressed. It is quite a trick for them to assemble a wardrobe that provides plenty of changes for school wear, for working or lounging at home, for parties, and for other occasions. We have suggested ways to co-ordinate color schemes and choose interchangeable garments that provide variety at reasonable cost. In this new edition, we have added a section on planning travel wardrobes for trips by land, sea, and air.

A girl should understand the clothing needs of the entire family—not only now while she is a member of a family group but later, when she must plan for a family of her own. To help her do this, we have included new material on budgeting, planning, and assembling wardrobes for men, women, boys, and girls. The influence of differing incomes and occupations on clothing plans is also discussed.

Because no wardrobe can be better than the materials from which it is constructed, whether garments are purchased readymade or made at home, we have included a section on textiles. The advent of numerous man-made fibers and new finishes makes it increasingly important for the consumer to understand the strengths and weaknesses of materials and how to care for them. A certain amount of background knowledge is essential to an understanding of the labels on fabrics and clothing. In this edition, the chapter on textiles has been reorganized; textiles have been placed into related groups which share similar properties, thus simplifying their study. The chapter has also been expanded to include new and up-to-date textile information. Detailed definitions of numerous special finishes applied to fabric have been added.

After textiles, we discuss wise buying practices, such as how to decide what to buy readymade and what to make, where to shop, and what size to buy. Altering ready-to-wear, mending, and caring for clothing are covered. For the career-minded girl, there is a section on professional opportunities in the clothing field.

A large part of the book is devoted to actual sewing. While we do not recommend that girls make all their own clothing or that every girl should continue to sew in later life, we do believe that anyone can profit from a chance to make several garments under expert guidance. Even the girl who has never sewed before, or the one who has been unsuccessful in past attempts, is likely to enjoy sewing by the methods outlined here.

This book is planned to make sewing as easy as possible. Because the attention span of high-school girls is short, every unnecessary step is omitted; yet because their skill is limited, every possible aid is provided. The unit method of construction is followed; that is, units are completed, then assembled into the whole. Many original techniques are included and many commercial techniques, observed first-hand in New York's garment district, have been borrowed and adapted to the abilities of students. All "shortcuts" advocated recently by educators, pattern companies, and commercial firms have been tried—then accepted, rejected, or adapted. No method or practice is included that has not proved successful in classroom situations.

This book represents a new approach to clothing construction. In the main body of the book, step-by-step instructions are given for making four garments, each representative of those worn by high-school girls today. Another one-hundred-and-sixty-page section, devoted to special techniques, discusses the various steps in greater detail, and includes additional processes. New material on inserting zippers and lining dresses and skirts has been added in this section, and many of the other techniques have been revised. This technique section is printed on buff paper for convenience, since frequent cross references are made to it.

Although the patterns which students select for their four garments will vary from the exact designs described here, the over-all plans are so basic that with slight variations they can be used for any similar pattern. Girls who follow the detailed directions given for making the first simple garments will be ready to launch into styles requiring more complicated processes. The technique section on buff paper will provide ample help for these more adventurous stylists.

While we have concentrated on girls' own clothing problems, the skills developed will be equally useful in planning and making clothing for other members of the family.

Mabel Bowers
Marietta Kettunen

CONTENTS

PART V—CARE OF CLOTHING

SEWING TECHNIQUES

PART VI—CAREERS IN CLOTHING

PART I

PERSONAL GROOMING

CHAPTER I · *BODY BEAUTIFUL*

It really goes without saying that a good posture is the key to charm and beauty. Squared shoulders and a head held high give a girl confidence in herself; and she in turn will inspire confidence in others. A slouch conveys an "I-don't-care" attitude, or worse yet, an "I-can't" impression. When a girl *cares* and when she *can,* she perks up and shows her enthusiasm.

The girl "who's got style all the while" has a spring in her step. She draws admiration whether she appears in a three-dollar cotton dress or the smartest linen. On the other hand, round shoulders and a protruding stomach can spell doom even to the dress that cost a small fortune.

THE BACKBONE OF BEAUTY

The backbone of beauty, of course, means the spine. It is your chief building material. Remember, your body is in the making. The spine will bend at your will. If you would build of it an arch, it will eventually set that way. If you would build a graceful Grecian column, it will do that, too. Let's build the latter!

Head high. We could learn something from the native or peasant who balances her basket on the top of her head. Her spine is so aligned that her body is a perfectly balanced column of support. She stands with her shoulders back, her chest out, her head high. If she should slouch, that perfect balance would be destroyed and the basket would come tumbling down.

Could you trust yourself to carry a basket of eggs on your head? Fortunately, we don't have to go around supporting such loads. All we are asked to do is to hold up our heads!

Think of your spine as a type of accordion. When it is extended to its full height, you look your best, whether you are tall, short, or medium. When you droop, that spinal accordion collapses. No one wants to be caught in a state of collapse, so test yourself to see how you stand.

Look at your side view in a full-length mirror. Do you see telltale "wings," a sagging stomach, or a protruding derrière? Usually, if you see one, you see all three. Whenever a girl lets her "middle" sag, the shoulders slump, the abdomen bulges, and the hips are thrown back. Not a pretty picture!

To correct it, back up to the wall. Stand with your feet about 2 inches apart, your heels 1 inch from the baseboard. Bend your knees but keep your head against the wall. Place the back of your waistline against the wall. Press it back so that you know it is there. Now slowly push up to a standing position, keeping your spine in contact with the wall.

When you have reached your full height, check these "points of contact." The back of your head should touch the wall, with your chin held in at a comfortable, relaxed angle. Your shoulder blades should be flat against the wall. There should be very little space between your waistline and the wall. The pelvic section of your spine should be against the wall.

Now step forward retaining the correct line. If you feel stiff, relax. Drop your shoulders, remembering to keep the blades flat. You don't want to look

Does your posture express confidence or gloom?

like the little boy who plays soldier by raising his shoulders back in a stiff, forced position. You can even shift more of your weight to one leg, still retaining that perfect balance in which your abdomen is flat.

Here is another way to find the correct position for that tummy and derrière. Pass sidewise through a narrow space. Instinctively you stand tall. In doing that, you are correcting the position of your pelvis. In turn, your abdomen becomes flat. Check and see!

Walk on air. Can you read character in a walk? Study the people around you. What comes to your mind when you see boys or girls slouch along in a disjointed manner? Do they look as if they had a purpose in life? Do they look confident? Happy? Eager?

Now consider the impression that you make on others. Check yourself as to how you walk in to breakfast. Does your buoyant step really mark the beginning of a "Good Morning"? Or does your Dad look up from his grapefruit to say, "For heaven's sake, hold yourself up"?

Don't slump. Walk head up, spine straight, chest lifted, all your weight on one foot, and your figure will look its best.

To stand correctly, keep your chin high and place one foot slightly in front of the other.

Don't twist your legs. Cross them if you like, but sit back gracefully.

Photos courtesy of Helena Rubinstein

Your way of walking tells people many things about you. A good walking posture is of vital importance to your appearance. With practice everyone can develop a fine walk. Here are a few pointers.

Wear properly fitted shoes. A painfully narrow shoe that cramps the toes not only creates that cringing step but also brings on corns, bunions, and a pained facial expression. Shoes that do not provide adequate support for the arches produce a flat-footed stomp. Extremely high heels encourage a sway-back and a mincing gait.

As you walk, remember the position of your shoulder blades, your abdomen, and your pelvis. Point your toes forward. When they point out, they encourage a side-to-side sway.

Move forward by walking "from the hips." Your body remains in perfect balance. When you walk "from the knees," your abdominal muscles sag and your hip muscles become flabby. When the leg swings forward from the hip, those muscles are kept trim and firm.

Test your balance and sway by carrying a book on your head. Before long you might be able to carry that basket of eggs!

Sitting pretty. Are you? Would you be pleased if a school photographer were to take a candid shot of you this very minute? Or would you wail at the thought of seeing it in the school yearbook?

Any girl is so much more attractive when she sits gracefully. She looks better and she actually feels better. When she hunches her shoulders, she is setting her spine into an arch. She tires more easily, too, because she is crowding her inner organs and is breathing incorrectly. Ask any stenographer or typist how she sits in order to work most efficiently.

So much of our time is spent in sitting that we should look at it from the angles of both health and beauty. Stop to think just how many hours you sit. Take a typical school day. You spend about five or six hours in the classroom or in study hall. You sit during your meals and snacks. At night you either sit doing your homework or at the movies, or you curl up to read, to sew, or to watch TV.

Whenever and wherever you sit, sit well back on the chair. Keep your shoulders back. Expand your chest as you breathe and you will find that your abdominal muscles will not sag. Shallow breathing develops a slump throughout the body.

Keep your knees quite close together at all times. If you cross your ankles, avoid that unbecoming triangular front view where the knees are spread apart. If you cross your legs, don't rest an ankle on the other knee—ever!

There are times when you must sit and just look or listen—to a lecture in the auditorium, to your teacher's explanation, to your classmate's recitation, to a movie, or to a social conversation. So sit back and relax—gracefully! Some people have annoying habits, such as picking at their nails, twisting rings and bracelets, tugging at stray locks, or constantly shifting their feet. A completely charming person avoids such nervous habits.

Then there are those times when you work at your desk or table. When you study your assignment, prop your book up and sit back, relaxed but straight! When you have to bend over your work, bend from the hips. Don't hunch your spine from the waist or from the shoulders.

From the time you were a two-year-old, you have been talked at, scolded, perhaps even punished, for the way you sat at table. So you are well-informed on that subject! By now you avoid further family glares by keeping your elbows off the table. You allow your free hand to rest in your lap, and you do sit up straight.

Which girl is sitting pretty?

"Sitting pretty," you see, does not mean that you look as if you had a ram-rod at your back. Neither does it mean that you look too prim and prissy. It does mean that you are more attractive.

THE ESSENTIAL "E's" OF BEAUTY

Have you noticed that, so far, you don't have to spend a penny in creating a "more attractive you"? Good posture is a *habit* which is free. And so it is with these four essential "E's of Beauty." You can't buy them at the cosmetic counter; nor can you pick them from a dress rack. Each is a *health habit* con-trolled directly by you alone. No one can be truly attractive unless she is healthy. In grandmother's day a languid miss might have been considered angelic. Today a girl's sparkling vitality puts her in the "heavenly" bracket. If she lacks it, she may turn out to be the "wet blanket" of the party. In these days we accept the fact that health habits and beauty walk hand-in-hand.

Early to bed. The first "E" stands for "early to bed." . . . "But," you might say, "my favorite orchestra doesn't broadcast until eleven o'clock," . . . or "When I get hold of a good story, I can't put it down till it's finished."

And so far into the night! Sleepily, you decide to skip your face and teeth. "One night won't matter." You even forget to raise the window.

The next morning your mother has to call you three times before she succeeds in arousing you. You crawl out "from the wrong side of the bed" into a hard world. Everything goes wrong—your slip strap breaks, your skirt zipper catches, you can't find a fresh blouse, and your mirror tells on you! You stand in the kitchen to gulp a glass of milk. You're still munching toast when the front door bangs after you.

What an eye opener! Oh, what a day! By nine o'clock that night you are too groggy and out-of-sorts to think of anything but bed. Your mother suggests a warm bath. Then how good it feels to snuggle down between smooth sheets for a full night's sleep! Soon you're breathing deeply—fresh, cool air from the open window.

The next morning when you awaken to sounds in the kitchen, you aren't the least bit irritated, because you've had your full quota of sleep. After a shower or sponge, you feel thoroughly refreshed. The mirror tells a different tale too. Your eyes have a sparkle and your skin glows. This time there is no need to rush haphazardly through your dressing. You feel decidedly presentable when you sit down to a well-rounded breakfast. It's a pleasant, unhurried meal that gives you a good start for the day.

Maybe this is your story, maybe it's not. But each of us has had days like those. We know from personal experience that we need eight or nine hours of sleep every night to *feel* our best, to *do* our best, and to *look* our best.

Wait for late hours until Friday and Saturday when you can sleep late the next morning. Select a reasonable bedtime hour for school nights and then abide by it. It is a habit that really counts. Your body needs regular rest—and plenty of it. Remember that it is your beauty sleep. It is essential in achieving sparkling eyes, a clear skin, and a sunny disposition with plenty of vim, vigor, and vitality!

Eat for beauty. Here is food for thought! A day doesn't pass that you don't hear or read terms like these—protective food, body-builder, energy food, bone-builder, blood-builder, or sunshine vitamin. If you have already studied foods, you know that such terms really describe what certain foods do for our bodies. If you have not made a study of foods as yet, ask your teacher what constitutes a well-balanced diet. In addition, she will be able to suggest books which will help you to plan your meals.

Remember that an automobile will not run unless it has its balanced quota of gasoline, oil, grease, and water. Similarly, your body demands different types of food *every day* to maintain a high level of health—and beauty. A car will not run on gas alone any more than your body can function perfectly if you overload it with carbohydrates (starch and sugar). Yet that is exactly what so many people select for their meals.

The next time you are in a cafeteria, glance at the trays around you. You will be shocked to see what some people are eating for lunch. One tray may contain a plate of mashed potatoes, spaghetti, and baked beans, a large white roll, a piece of fudge cake, and coffee. At the next table you may see a girl hurrying through a sandwich, a Danish pastry, and coffee.

These may strike you as far-fetched examples, but they happen to be true stories. No wonder that people have health complications, figure problems, and skin troubles!

If you are guilty of such selections, stick this beauty equation on your mirror for daily reference:

FOOD = HEALTH;   HEALTH = BEAUTY;   SO, FOOD = BEAUTY

And if you feel that you have developed an unwelcome bulge or a bad complexion, begin to do things about it.

First of all, good-bye to those between-meal snacks! Say "No" to that butterscotch sundae topped with pecans and whipped cream. Order an orange juice or limeade if you're with the crowd. Push away that dish of candy while you do your homework. Chew an apple instead. In short, don't be a "nibbler."

At mealtime, refuse second helpings. Avoid foods fried in fat or oil, or those drenched with butter. Eat bread that is low in calories and cut down on butter, although you should get two pats of butter or an enriched substitute daily. Eat lean meat, vegetables, and salad. Switch your desserts from rich pies and cakes to fresh or stewed fruit. Go slow on cream, but do drink at least a pint of milk a day. Milk is not fattening, and it does protect you from harmful deficiencies.

These are sensible suggestions. If you follow them, you won't suffer from weakness. In fact, you'll have more pep. You will be eating three well-balanced meals a day, minus the fattening trimmings.

At this point a warning should be sounded! Three well-balanced meals *include* breakfast. Never slight the meal that is your self-starter for the day. Weakness, dizziness, and sick headaches often result from an empty stomach. You can't do your best at school or any job if your body has no fuel to go on.

Doctors give us further warnings. It is not safe to lose more than ¼ pound a day. To lose more weakens a person. So avoid those "fad" diets that starve you for a certain number of days. Furthermore, never take any laxative reducing salts or "patent" reducing medicines. They are dangerous! When overweight is not the result of overeating, consult your doctor. If he diagnoses the case as a glandular disturbance, follow his prescription.

Elimination. "Early to bed" and "Eat for beauty" are habits which should become a matter of regular routine. But the "E's of Beauty" don't end there. You already realize the importance of regular elimination in preventing a sick headache! a grouch! an offensive breath! skin blemishes! and that all-around below-par feeling.

If irregularity is your trouble, check your daily diet to see whether it includes enough whole-grain foods, fruits, and vegetables. Make every effort to correct your trouble by eating foods that will encourage regularity. This suggestion may be your remedy. Start breakfast with a dish of stewed fruit—

THIGHS. Lie on stomach, elbows on floor under chest, weight on elbows. Bend knees, bringing heels up near buttocks. Raise right thigh, slap it to the floor. Alternate sides.

ABDOMEN. Lie on back, hands under buttocks, knees over chest, stomach pulled in. Point toes, bicycle with legs.

HIPS. Sit on floor, arms raised, elbows bent. Twist upper torso to right, place left leg forward. Then swing to left, extending right leg. Swing side to side, each time taking a larger step forward on buttocks.

CALVES. Sit on floor, weight on hands behind body. Pull knees toward chest with feet on floor near buttocks, toes turned up. Slide right leg forward with a slap. Repeat with left leg as you pull right leg toward chest. Alternate legs as you go.

BUTTOCKS, HIPS, THIGHS. Sit on floor, legs straight and together. Relax and roll to your right as far as possible, catching your weight on right hand with elbow bent. Alternate sides as you do this.

HIPS, WAIST, ABDOMEN. Lie on floor, arms out, palms up. Bend knees over chest. Drop knees to floor on left. Shoulder stays flat on floor. Pull knees up to elbow. Try to make them touch elbow. Raise knees over chest. Repeat to right. But take it easy.

applesauce, apricots, or prunes. Eat fresh fruit for those between-meal snacks. Drink from six to eight glasses of water daily. Set aside a certain time in your daily health program so that elimination becomes a regular habit. The morning is convenient for most people. You will feel better if you make elimination part of your regular routine—and what's more, you will look better!

Exercise. Exercise is the last but not the least of the "E's of Beauty." Exercise develops good posture and firm contours. It sets your skin atingle too because it sends the blood coursing through your veins. Girls of your age usually get plenty of exercise. In school you have regular gymnastics and recreational sports, like basketball or bowling and, of course, dancing. The outdoor sports are better for you, and they're more fun. In winter you can choose between skating, skiing, or sledding. In the summer there's a choice of bicycling, roller-skating, boating, swimming, or tennis. Each is an excellent body conditioner.

You may not have access to some of these sports where you live, or some physical condition may prevent you from any strenuous form of exercise. Even a plain, ordinary walk does wonders for a person. Enjoy a tramp through the woods, take a breather along the lakeshore, hike across the fields, or walk briskly through your neighborhood park.

From time to time you may think of exercise in terms of reducing. The sketches on page 9 illustrate a few "boudoir gymnastics" that are intended to trim down those problem spots.

"UNDER" STATEMENTS

The "Body Beautiful" is almost complete! Good posture and sound health habits went into its "building." But the body still needs support and protection. And that is where undergarments come in.

Foundation garments. Foundation garments may make you think of something stiff and stodgy. You think of them as something to poke you and pinch you with every move. Not at all! Think of girdles and bras in terms of smoothness, firmness, and flexibility. Every girl needs those qualities to appear at her best in everything that she wears.

Even though you are slim, wear a step-in, two-way-stretch girdle to control your lines. It will not hamper your movements. You will find that it improves your posture.

If you need more abdominal support or control, select a girdle that has a boned front. It will hold in that protruding stomach.

As for bras, select one that gives you a firm contour without constricting you. A bra that is too tight is injurious.

THE YEARLY PHYSICAL

Yearly physical examination is important for anyone at any age. It is a sensible way of protecting health. Once you have had your yearly examination and the report is safely tucked away in the doctor's files, you can settle back comfortably and enjoy your good health.

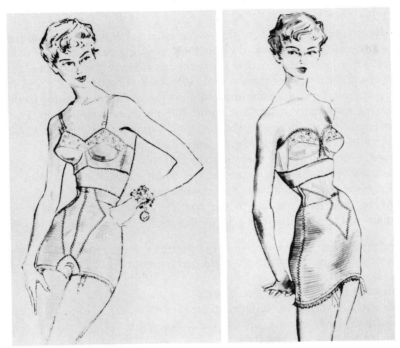

Warner's

Left, a good foundation for school clothes. Right, undergarments to wear with sun-back dresses and strapless evening gowns.

A visit to the doctor's office or to the school physician offers an opportunity to discuss certain aspects of your health that may be disturbing to you. You can rely on your physician's advice.

ACTIVITIES

For the class

1. **Maintain** a bulletin board and open reference files in the classroom. Bring in photographs that illustrate both good and bad posture as well as corrective exercises. Collect magazine or newspaper articles and booklets that have to do with good meal planning. All this material will be helpful in planning class discussions.
2. **Invite** the physical education teacher to address the class on good posture and corrective exercises. Ask her to suggest what individual pupils can do to improve posture and figure "problem spots."
3. **Ask** a foods' expert (a home economics teacher, a home demonstration agent, or the school cafeteria dietitian) to discuss well-balanced daily menus. She can also suggest safe, low caloric menus for reducing weight and high caloric menus for gaining weight.

For the individual

1. **Study** any recent snapshots that were taken of you before you became "posture conscious." How do you look standing and sitting? If there is room for improvement, decide how you can remedy your posture. Practice and check yourself constantly. Ask members of your family and friends to co-operate by calling attention to any sign of faulty posture. Good posture will eventually become a habit that needs no reminding. Then ask someone to take candid snapshots of you. Compare the "before and after" pictures to see the extent of your improvement.

2. **Record** your weight and measurements. If you are overweight or wish to reduce in "spots," start to exercise and count calories. Check your weight and measurements each week to see what progress you have made.

3. **Analyze** your living habits to see how they compare with the suggested routine for the essential four "E's of Beauty." (*Do not write in this book.*)

	YES	NO
Do you retire early enough to get eight or nine hours of sleep?		
Do you have fresh air while you sleep?		
Do you eat a wholesome, unhurried breakfast?		
Do you have plenty of milk, eggs, meat, whole-grain foods, fruits, and vegetables?		
Do you say "no" to excessive starches and sweets?		
Do you have regular elimination?		
If not, have you tried to correct the difficulty by eating more fruits and vegetables and drinking plenty of water?		
Do you have any exercise other than a lazy stroll down the street?		

If you can say "yes" to each of these questions, you
are a young lady with good health habits.

4. **Read** a good book on nutrition. See Bibliography, pages 555–557. Perhaps improving your diet is the best thing you can do for your appearance. If you find that your diet is inadequate, talk over the book with your mother and discuss how your family's meals can be improved.

CHAPTER 2   *STRICTLY PERSONAL*

By now you realize that beauty is not skin-deep. Your "inner" health is reflected in your skin, teeth, nails, and hair. Yet each of them demands regular external care too. Plan your day and your week so that no personal detail is slighted. That "bandbox" look begins with your boudoir-bathroom routine.

ATTENTION! THE BODY!

We know that one of the functions of the skin is to secrete and excrete both oil and perspiration. The sebaceous glands of the skin provide the oil which keeps the skin soft. The sweat glands carry off body waste matter in the form of perspiration. These processes do not stop for one minute; they go on night and day.

The skin must be cleansed regularly to keep the pores open and clean. Otherwise the oil in the pores attracts dirt. Clogged pores develop into blackheads. Then other blemishes or skin infections are more apt to develop. Furthermore, unless perspiration is washed off regularly, it mixes with the skin

Morning or evening, the daily bath is a pleasant part of the day's routine.

oils to produce that "hush-hush" condition known as *B.O.* And everyone surely wants to avoid that whispered criticism.

A daily bath. Just when you take your daily bath depends on you. Of course, you will have to adjust the time to the family schedule. Hot water and the bathroom itself may not be available at all hours.

You might prefer to take your bath before the evening meal. It would freshen you up after a day at school and a round of tennis or that after-school job you might have.

Or perhaps you're the girl who likes to do her school homework in lounging clothes. That means that you could take your bath before you get into your pajamas and robe. Besides, the bathroom might be more available at that hour.

Although a morning bath is a wonderful "eye-opener," it may not always fit in with your schedule. You have to make that eight o'clock class! Or perhaps you want to help Mother with several little jobs around the house before you leave for school.

Some people have the facilities and the type of daily schedule that allow for what might be considered the ideal bathing routine. This includes a warm tub at night before retiring. It does seem good after a grimy, strenuous day. Somehow it relaxes the whole system. However, the bath should not be too hot because that stimulates the body and might cause wakefulness. In the morning a quick shower perks one up for the day. This need not be a thorough soap-and-scrub affair because the evening bath took care of that. Start out with a warm shower and gradually turn on the cool. This closes the pores and prevents your catching cold from exposure.

Just when you take that daily bath does not matter so much; just *so* you

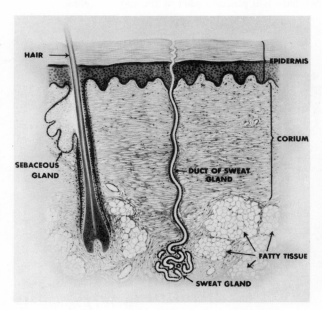

Bristol-Myers

The daily bath is necessary to wash off dried oil from the sebaceous glands as well as perspiration from the sweat glands. Under normal conditions the average human body gives off about a quart of perspiration a day.

take it is the important thing. The type of bath depends on the facilities in your home. It is possible to keep perfectly immaculate whether you take a tub bath, a shower bath, or a sponge bath. It is the warm water, soap, and scrubbing that count!

A bath does not mean just a dip in the tub, a dash under the shower, or a scanty sponging. It means a generous soaping and rubbing with a washcloth. A bath brush is ideal for those hard-to-reach places. Then the soap should be rinsed off with fresh water. Of course, the shower provides the ideal thorough rinse, but one can get rinsed thoroughly after a tub bath too. Fresh tap water can be splashed over the body. If a sponge bath is taken in a bedroom, it is a good idea to have two basins or containers—one for the soapy water and one for the fresh. If soap is not thoroughly rinsed away, it may result in chafing.

Finally, give yourself a brisk rubdown with your *own* Turkish towel. Be sure that all parts of your body are entirely dry. Moisture between the toes may lead to a painful condition in which the skin "cracks." Such lesions invite a variety of foot infections.

And of course you will slip on clean panties and hose each day. Change your bra and slip two or three times a week. If you wear a girdle, change that once a week. A pantie-girdle should be changed daily. You want to be dainty through and through.

Deodorants. A daily bath does not necessarily mean that a person is free from all perspiration odor. Further precautions should be taken.

If you are troubled by excessive perspiration, sprinkle a little baking soda into your bath water. This helps to counteract the odor of perspiration although it does not check perspiration itself.

Some commercial preparations, known as *deodorants,* both deodorize and check perspiration. You will find terms like "antiperspirant" or "nonperspirant" on some labels. There are cream, liquid, and powder varieties on the market.

Most people have to use some type of underarm deodorant. You cannot be sure that you are completely dainty and inoffensive unless you do. So select a deodorant to your liking, and apply it at least twice a week or more often when necessary. You can use a powder every day. Although most commercial preparations are guaranteed not to stain clothing, you can avoid any possibility of a stain if you apply cream or liquid deodorant at night before retiring. Wash under your arms before application. In the morning wash the deodorant off.

A deodorant that checks perspiration also prevents those embarrassing underarm stains on blouses, sweaters, and dresses. Many women who are troubled with excessive perspiration also wear dress shields as an additional protection against such stains. Remember that unless dress shields are laundered frequently, they can be offensive too.

During your menstrual period, you will also need a deodorant powder. Sprinkle this powder on the entire length of the napkin. It acts as a complete deodorant. In addition, you should be doubly careful about your bathing routine during your period. A warm bath or shower will have no ill effect on you. Avoid taking a chill afterwards. The belief that it is not safe to bathe at that time is an old-wives' tale. Modern hygiene stresses cleanliness.

Depilatories. Feminine daintiness has always been a matter of soft, smooth skin unmarred by superfluous hair. Fashions today make such daintiness a "must" with every girl. No one can afford to be careless when she wears sleeveless evening dresses, short-sleeved blouses and dresses, revealing play togs, and bathing suits. Sheer hosiery, "liquid" stockings, and bare legs call for smooth skin too. But don't remove downy hair unnecessarily.

Superfluous hair can be removed either by shaving, by specially prepared hair-eraser discs, by abrasive mittens, or by wax preparations. Follow the directions given on the product that you choose to use.

Words of caution! (1) Do not apply any deodorant to your underarms for twenty-four hours after hair-removal. You can apply it the night before. (2) Do not shave or use a depilatory on any part of the body that suffers from a skin disorder. A cut or abrasion may lead to a more serious skin infection. (3) Use extreme care in shaving! If you should happen to cut your skin, apply an antiseptic to it immediately.

Bleaching downy hair. Instead of removing hair from your face, arms, and legs, you may prefer to bleach it. Use 20 per cent peroxide of hydrogen (you may add a few drops of ammonium hydroxide). Apply the solution with cotton. Dilute the solution or discontinue it if your skin becomes irritated.

Sun baths. The subject of bared arms and legs and bathing suits naturally leads to sun baths. It seems that most people get reckless as soon as the sunning season rolls around. They want a glorious tan in such a hurry! Doctors say that sun baths are beneficial only when taken in the right doses. The first dose (to be safe) is a 5-minute exposure. The next time it may be increased to 8 minutes, then 15, and so on. It is wise to use an oil to prevent the drying out of the natural skin oils. An oil will also prevent a severe burn. There are several sun-tan oils on the market or you can use peanut or olive oil.

With such gradual sunning and oil treatment, you retain both your skin and your tan! And you won't suffer from headaches, nausea, or sunstroke. If you should get a burn, make a solution of very strong tea or a vinegar solution and apply it with cotton or a soft cloth as often as needed.

ABOUT "FACE"!

The first thing that perhaps enters your mind in a discussion about the face may be make-up. Yet we will leave cosmetics until later. The care of your "natural" face is the chief concern at this point.

Facial cleansing for normal skin. Here again beauty is achieved by clock-like regularity. Cleanse your face thoroughly before going to bed. Don't skip a single night! Select a mild facial soap. Some doctors recommend the untinted variety. If a soap leaves your face tight and burning, it is too strong. Find one that is mild enough for your skin. The face cloth should be soft and not too

Helen Pessl, Inc.
A clean, clear skin is attractive in itself. The girl with such an asset needs only a touch of make-up to look her best.

Bristol Myers
Feminine daintiness includes the removal of underarm hair and the use of a deodorant.

Pond's

Elizabeth Arden

Apply cream in the directions shown by the arrows. Be gentle with your face.

heavy. (It is more sanitary not to use the same cloth on your face that you have used on your body.)

First, apply plenty of warm water to your face and neck with your face cloth. The heat will open the pores. When your face feels steamy and looks rosy, apply a soap lather with your fingertips. With this lather massage your entire face and neck. Concentrate on the nose and chin area. That is where clogged pores develop into unsightly blackheads. This massaging may be done with a face cloth or with your hands as you prefer. If your skin is unusually sensitive or if it is broken out, a face cloth might be too rough. Some people scrub their faces when they use a cloth. Such scrubbing can bruise a skin that is broken out.

Use plenty of clean warm water to splash away every bit of soap. Follow it with a generous application of cold water. Pat the skin dry. Apply a cream if you have any tendency toward dryness. Then you can go to bed with a "clean" conscience!

Your face is no trouble at all in the morning. Wash it with warm water, followed by a dash of cold. It will then be ready for make-up.

Skin problems. So many girls (women too) have troublesome skin conditions. Most skin disorders can be improved by observing the essential "E's of Beauty" and by using proper cleansing methods.

Check and double-check the following suggestions if you have a skin problem. Get at the bottom of it. Of course, if you have a really serious condition, see your doctor.

If you have poor skin, avoid bruising the pimples with your face cloth or

SKIN PROBLEMS

Problem	Cause	Suggestion
Dry Skin	Inadequate diet—not enough milk, eggs, butter, fat	Eat a balanced diet. Increase protective foods: milk, eggs.
	Too many condiments	Say "no" to spices, vinegar, mustard, etc.
	Run-down condition—an aftermath of fever and illness	Build up strength by rest, food, and exercise.
	Dry climate, too much sun or windburn	Apply oil before exposure. Cleanse with cream. Use night cream.
	Lack of outdoor exercise resulting in sluggish oil glands	Exercise outdoors. Massage and slap your face to increase circulation.
	Improper cleansing—strong soap or cosmetics not entirely removed	Cleanse with cream. Use mild soap only twice a week. Use foundation cream. Use night cream.
	Hard water	Use the water softener that is recommended in your particular community.
Oily Skin	A "rich" diet—too many sweets, starches, and fats	Say "no" to candy, nuts, cakes, cream, fried foods. Eat lean meat, fruits, and vegetables.
	Faulty elimination	Become "regular." Drink more water.
	Improper cleansing leading to clogged pores and blackheads	Use soap and hot water twice a day. Rinse with cold. Apply astringent.
Pimples (*occasional*)	That favorite candy bar, etc.	Chew an apple instead of a sweet.
	Digestive upset or constipation	Check elimination. Drink more water.
	"Allergy" food. (Example: you break out if you eat strawberries)	Avoid a food when you are sure it causes your skin to break out.
	Oily scalp (may cause forehead pimples)	Shampoo hair once or twice a week.
	Nervous fatigue	Rest and exercise outdoors.
	Menstrual period	Rest and drink more water. Check elimination.

towel; use pressing and patting motions when washing your face. With cotton apply an antiseptic solution of hydrogen peroxide or alcohol to the pimples. Do not use any cream or powder until the condition improves. Never pick or pinch pimples or blackheads. You can get rid of them by following rules of health and cleanliness. If they should result in enlarged pores, an astringent will help to improve the texture of your skin.

Many chronic cases of pimples are the result of an oily skin. When the condition of the skin improves, pimples are more apt to disappear.

Severe, prolonged eruptions (acne) are the result of a glandular disturbance that may occur with the beginning of maturity. For this, consult your doctor. Follow the diet and facial care prescribed by him.

The girl with the smiling face stands out in a crowd.

Clear but dry skin is often improved by being cleansed with cream rather than soap and water. Work the cream into the skin with the finger tips. Use a firm upward motion on the neck, jaw, cheeks, and nose. A downward pressure would eventually create sagging muscles. Use an outward motion from the center of your forehead to the temples and down to the cheekbone. Then very gently pat in the cream under your eyes. The skin around the eyes is very delicate. If you cleanse it with a dragging pressure, you will develop eye wrinkles before your time! Remove the cream with cleansing tissue. Follow with a dash of cool water.

HAPPY FACES!

Happy faces! . . . Or are they? . . . Is yours? Stop reading this very minute. Are you frowning or squinting? Look at those about you. Do they look troubled? Some people screw up their foreheads when they try to concentrate. Others seemingly grit their teeth.

The next time you mingle with crowds in a shopping center, observe the people's faces. Study the expressions of travelers on buses and trains. Oh, such frowns, grimaces, and dogged expressions! Some of them look actually angry! It is always such a relief when your eyes fall on someone who looks pleasant and serene—yet very much alive. She is someone you would like to know.

Such a woman spells charm . . . she invites friends.

Personal charm is the aim of every girl—and the facial expression has a good bit to do with it. So it's best to "wipe off that scowl." Every bad facial habit that you form now will literally be carved on your face. It may be a thinking furrow between your eyes, stripes of wrinkles on your forehead, or a dissatisfied scowl. Of course, poor vision and bad lighting or even ill-fitting shoes can produce frowns and squints. If that is the reason, remove the source of the trouble. Otherwise, check your bad facial habits *now,* or they'll be with you for life.

Someone once said, "A charming woman looks as if something very nice had just happened to her." Try it and see. When you find yourself scowling, think of the very nicest thing that has happened to you lately. It works!

YOUR CROWNING GLORY

Truly beautiful hair is healthy and clean. How to keep it so is our chief concern here. Styling comes later.

Daily care. Each head has thousands and thousands of hairs, so they aren't asking too much when they beg for a meager "one hundred brush strokes" per night. Every head of hair—whether normal, oily, or dry—needs a regular brushing. It provides the "daily exercise" that is needed for good circulation of blood. When the scalp is tight and unexercised, the glands and nerves of each hair suffer from a lack of nourishment that the blood stream should provide.

Choose a brush with firm bristles—not metal. Brush up from the hairline all around the head. Then part the hair and brush again until every inch of the scalp is stimulated. This will remove the dust and dirt that have accumulated during the day. It also prevents dandruff from clinging to the scalp.

Shampoo. The normal scalp may be shampooed every one or two weeks. A weekly shampoo is necessary if the air is heavy with smoke and dust, or if the hair is light in color.

Commercial shampoos come in liquid, jelly, or cream preparations. Most of the shampoo solutions are based on olive oil, coconut oil, or palm-nut oil. Those with olive oil are generally best. Tincture of green soap and other shampoos that have a high percentage of alcohol should be used only for oily scalps, as they have a drying effect. So-called tar shampoos tend to darken light hair. In recent years, "soapless shampoos," or detergents, have been introduced. They are equally effective in hard or soft water which makes them quite desirable. The person with dry hair or an unhealthy scalp condition may find a standard shampoo less drying, however.

It is not advisable to use a bar of soap on the hair as it is so difficult to get the soap out. If you wish you may prepare your own shampoo jelly. Soak some shavings of Castile or some other mild soap in water. Slowly bring the solution to a boil and allow it to simmer until every chunk is dissolved. Keep it in a wide-mouthed jar. Soap flakes or beads dissolve in warm water without heating.

This is the routine for a shampoo:

1. Brush your scalp to remove dust and loosen possible dandruff.

2. Wash your brush and comb with warm soapy water, or use a synthetic detergent. Rinse and put aside to dry.

3. Immerse your head in warm water. (If the water in your community is hard, use a softener that is recommended for your particular locale. Or use rain water if you have access to a supply.)

4. Apply the shampoo. Rub thoroughly over your entire scalp. Apply lather to full length of hair.

5. Rinse in clean warm water.

6. Apply second lather. Rub vigorously as before. Usually two lathers are sufficient. Oily or very dirty hair may require a third.

7. Rinse three or four times, using clean warm water each time. When hair is thoroughly rinsed, it "squeaks."

8. Now prepare a rinse to which you add the juice of a lemon or a little vinegar. Lemon is recommended for blondes, vinegar for brunettes. This may be your final rinse, but some prefer to follow it up with a rinse of clear water.

9. Wrap a clean towel around your head to absorb most of the water.

10. With another clean dry towel rub your scalp until your hair is just damp enough to arrange into waves or curls.

11. Comb out and brush your hair bit by bit. Then comb the waves or curls in place. Pin and dry. If you are fortunate enough to have one available, use an electric hand dryer.

12. If your hair does not require a "set," rub it and brush it dry. Train the ends by slight moistening if necessary.

13. Never go to bed with a head of wet hair!

Oily hair. Excessive oiliness indicates that something is wrong. The scalp may need more exercise, so don't forget that nightly "hundred." Whenever possible, brush your hair in the open sunlight. An invigorating massage can also tone your scalp.

A lack of outdoor exercise and sunshine may encourage an oily condition. Hie to the beaches and open fields where the air and sun can get at your hair—and body. Go bareheaded as often as possible.

Oily hair—like oily skin—is often due to a diet too rich in fats and carbohydrates. So think twice before you ask for that pie à la mode! And do drink more water and avoid constipation.

Courtesy of Helena Rubinstein

Brush your hair up. A cape like this one will protect your clothes.

Although some hair tonics claim to lessen an oily condition because of their astringent action, their chief benefit lies in the fact that the scalp is stimulated when the tonic is rubbed into the scalp. If you do use a tonic, part your hair at one-inch intervals and apply tonic with absorbent cotton. Massage by rotating your scalp with your fingertips. Then brush your hair vigorously.

Shampoo your hair as often as necessary—it may be every four or five days. Try tincture of green soap or a soapless shampoo. Use a lemon or vinegar rinse.

Glandular disturbances, such as the one that causes acne, may result in an oily scalp. A general upset condition plays havoc with the glands. See your doctor when ordinary precautions don't bring results.

Dry hair. Dry hair often follows an illness. Your hair will have its natural luster when you regain complete health through proper rest and good diet.

Hair can also become dry and brittle if it is exposed to too much sun and dry, hot air. Permanents too have a drying effect on the hair.

Your diet should include sufficient fats and oils. "Inner" nourishment has the most beneficial effect on the health of the hair although an external application of oil helps. Give yourself this scalp treatment occasionally. Apply a *little* lanolin, castor oil, or olive oil to your scalp with your fingertips, parting your hair at one-inch intervals. Rub vigorously; follow by brushing. Any exercise you give your scalp will help to recondition the oil glands.

A hot-oil treatment can be beneficial also. Apply it the night before you shampoo your hair. First brush your scalp briskly. If you have dandruff, a fine comb will loosen it. Part your hair at one-inch intervals and apply warm olive oil to your scalp. Rub vigorously. Steam your scalp by wrapping hot towels around your head. Remove the towels and allow the steamy moisture to dry off. Wrap your head in a dry towel and go to bed. In the morning massage your scalp and apply hot towels as before. Next apply a generous amount of liquid shampoo. Rub thoroughly. Then immerse your head in warm water to remove this first oil lather. Proceed with the usual shampoo.

Dandruff. The scalp sheds tiny scales of skin just like any other part of the body. So a slight accumulation of such scales is quite normal and can be removed by thorough brushing and regular shampoos. If scales are permitted to remain on the scalp, they impair normal circulation and invite trouble. Any excessive scaling with itchiness is a real case of dandruff. The best remedy is cleanliness and stimulation of the scalp through brushing and massage. Tonics that claim to cure dandruff may dissolve the flakes or scales during the shampoo, but they do not prevent the condition from recurring. Some dandruff lotions contain ingredients that actually irritate the scalp. If a dandruff condition is severe or prolonged, consult a skin specialist.

Aside from keeping your scalp clean, you should take other precautions whether you have dandruff or not. Always use your own comb; do not lend it to others and never borrow one from somebody else.

THAT TELLING SMILE

There are smiles and smiles . . . and you know that the flash of sound, white teeth is the best part of a smile. But did you know that "twelve-to-eighteen"-agers reportedly have more cavity trouble than any other age group?

Why is this true? For one thing, by the age of twelve, baby teeth have given way to permanent teeth. If a child's diet has been wholesome, the new teeth grow in firm and strong. But if the diet has been deficient in bone-building foods, the new teeth may be weak and crumbly. Then cavity trouble begins.

What can you do about it? First, eat a well-balanced diet that includes a healthy share of vegetables, fruit, and bone-building milk foods. Second, cut down on "gooey" sundaes, candy, cakes, and pies.

This is only one side of the story. We are told that carbohydrates, left in the crevices between teeth, form acids which injure the tooth enamel. That is why some dentists recommend brushing teeth within ten minutes after eating, rather than merely on arising and retiring.

A recent study on tooth decay recommends the use of fluoride in the toothpaste formula or in the city water supply. Extensive experiments indicate that children who have had fluoridated drinking water during their early years have fewer cavities than children who have had ordinary water. Adults, however, receive little or no benefit from fluoridated water. On the other hand,

tests show that toothpaste which contains fluoride is beneficial to both adults and children.

You should have two toothbrushes and use them alternately so that the bristles have a chance to dry. Brush your teeth in the direction in which they grow: that is, away from the gums. Crosswise strokes wear away the enamel at the gum line and cause food particles to lodge between the teeth. Use dental floss to remove stubborn food particles. When necessary, freshen your breath with mouthwash.

Finally, see your dentist at least twice a year. August and February are as good months as any—before school begins and after the Christmas bills are paid! In addition, see him as soon as you even suspect a cavity or if you develop bleeding gums.

If your permanent teeth have grown in crookedly, do consult your dentist. Dentists and physicians alike stress the importance of correctly aligned teeth. Some cases of faulty alignment may correct themselves with the passage of years. Others may continue to be a real handicap to both health and appearance. Let your dentist decide. You may hate the idea of wearing braces for long months to come, but you may be glad that you did, in years to come!

FROM THE TIPS OF YOUR HANDS

Television, radio, and magazine advertisements have made everyone conscious of lovely hands these days. But lovely hands have been and always will be a part of perfect grooming. Chafed skin, grimy knuckles, and grubby nails will rate a minus score wherever you go.

This is what happens to skin when it gets dry and rough.　　　*Bristol-Myers*

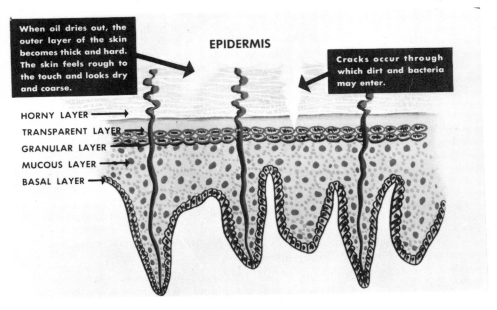

Daily care. Wash your hands as frequently as necessary, especially before meals. Always wash them as soon as you get home. Don't contaminate your food or your belongings with germs that you have picked up at school, on the playground, or in stores. After each washing, clean your nails with the pointed end of an orangewood stick. Then apply some hand lotion, always rubbing from the fingertips and over the wrist. While your skin is moist, gently push back your cuticle. A soft, loosened cuticle prevents those painful hangnails. Once a day smooth off any rough edges on your nails with an emery board. So much for daily care.

The manicure. Give yourself a manicure once a week. Learn to do it for yourself. Your left hand will soon learn "what thy right hand doeth."

1. Remove every trace of old polish with polish remover and cotton.

2. Shape each nail into an oval with the coarse side of an emery board. File from outer edge to tip. Smooth off all ragged edges of nail with the fine side of the emery board. Excessively long nails are not in good taste.

3. Scrub nails in warm, soapy water with hand brush. Dry thoroughly. Clean under nails.

4. Gently push back cuticle with the flat end of an orangewood stick. *Never* pull off ragged cuticle. Cut *only* when necessary.

5. Buff the nails with a chamois buffer.

6. Apply cuticle oil or cream to the cuticle with your fingertips.

The manicure is complete unless you wish to apply liquid nail polish. Colored polish is largely a matter of personal taste and custom. You are well-groomed without it. In fact, it is not exactly suitable for school. Unless you have time on your hands, you will not be able to manicure your nails each time the polish chips. Irregular blotches of red on your nails present a sorry sight.

If you wish to use polish, apply it after step 5 above. Apply the polish in strokes that lead from the base of nail to the tip of the nail. Hold back the side cuticle so polish will not adhere to it. Wipe off tip to prevent chipping. Allow the nails to dry thoroughly. Apply a second coat for that professional finish. Allow to dry. You may wish to brush on a transparent protective lacquer. Remove all specks of polish from surrounding skin with polish remover. Wash and dry hands.

Now go on to step 6 above.

Finally, apply hand lotion. Massage hands, wrists, and forearms thoroughly —elbows too!

Precautions. Hands are the most active part of our bodies—they get into everything. For that reason they seem to demand a good bit of attention. Protect them while you work around the house. Wear rubber gloves when you have to plunge your hands into strong solutions. Wear gardener's gloves when

Photo courtesy of Trushay

Finish up a manicure with hand lotion. In the summertime, a bit of the same lotion on your shoulders and elbows will help you look your best in a sleeveless dress.

you dig around in the soil. Use a stick mop when it's your turn to do the dishes. Dig your nails into a bar of mild soap before you start painting the porch furniture. The soap under your nails prevents the paint from seeping under them.

If after all these precautions you still have rough, scaly skin, try this. Rub a generous amount of vaseline or pure lanolin into your hands and arms before retiring. Protect the bedding by covering your arms and hands with long cotton gloves or cotton hosiery. You might look a sight, but it's your last resort.

When your nails chip and peel in layers, it may indicate a lack of calcium in your diet. Eat more milk foods. Continued use of polish may result in dryness and chipping; so forego polish. If the condition persists, see your doctor.

TO THE TIPS OF YOUR TOES

Elaborate pedicures with colored toenails have been on the upswing ever since stockingless feet and toeless sandals came into their own. You must decide whether you wish to go to such extremes. It does seem a bit unnecessary. A certain amount of regular foot care is necessary, however. You will be thankful in later years for every bit of attention you give your feet today. It is said that your disposition lies in your feet!

The pedicure. Give yourself a pedicure once a week after a warm tub. Soften and push back the cuticle as you do from your fingernails. Cut the nails and file off rough edges. Doctors recommend that toenails be cut straight across

Remington Rand

Good grooming is an everyday affair—not something that can be reserved for dates and special occasions.

rather than in an oval shape. If you have a painful ingrown toenail, file it thin across the center of the nail. Then place cotton beneath the nail at each side. This will force the nail to grow away from the side cuticle. Finally, apply some skin lotion or cream to your feet and massage thoroughly.

Danger spots. A calloused spot on your toe can develop into a painful corn. A callus on the ball of your foot will deepen and harden so that your foot will burn at every step. An ugly lump at the back of the heel, right above the shoe line, creates a painful rub when you walk, and it shortens the life of your hosiery.

If you develop any of these danger spots, go to work on them each night. Soak your feet in warm water. Then massage them with a generous amount of vaseline. Wear cotton anklets to bed. In the morning put a square of adhesive tape on the spot to keep the skin soft. Remove it before you take your foot bath. More than likely the calloused skin will come off with the plaster. *Never* cut a callous or corn with a knife or razor blade. If this care doesn't have rapid and permanent results, see a doctor. You may need to do foot exercises or wear special shoes as well as improve your walking habits.

An ordinary foot blister can lead to trouble. Give it immediate attention. Wash it thoroughly. Pat dry. Apply an antiseptic. When it is dry, place a folded square of sterilized gauze on it. Tape it in place with a strip of adhesive. Wear comfortable shoes that do not rub.

Other foot blisters are classified as skin infections. They are fungus growths. They demand medical attention; so do not experiment with home remedies.

If you get into the habit of good grooming the results in your looks and the way you feel will more than repay you for the time spent.

Plan your daily and weekly beauty schedule so that your skin, teeth, nails, and hair will reflect good care and beauty. You may have had a progress chart in the primary grades on which you marked an "X" every time that you brushed your teeth or washed your face and hands. This time, let it be a chart that you check mentally. There will be certain things to be done each morning and evening. Set some time each week for a shampoo, manicure, and pedicure. Once a schedule is established, beauty and cleanliness become a matter of routine and no one thing is slighted.

ACTIVITIES

For the class

1. **Invite** the school nurse or hygiene teacher to tell the class about the care of the skin and related subjects such as blemishes, depilatories, sunbaths, and foot care. Hers is the medical viewpoint, rather than "high-pressured" sales talk.
2. **Collect** for the class bulletin board and files any illustrations, magazine articles, and pamphlets that deal with the care of the hair, skin, nails, and teeth.

For the individual

1. **Give** your sister or friend a hot-oil scalp treatment some evening. Follow it with a shampoo the next morning.
2. **Give** a friend a manicure. The more you practice, the more professional your own manicures will be.

CHAPTER 3   *IN THE LOOKING GLASS*

Take a good, long look at yourself. Is your skin really clean and soft? Is it free of unsightly blemishes? Are your eyes clear and rested? . . . If you can honestly say "yes" to these questions, real loveliness is just around the corner. If you are forced to say "no," you cannot expect make-up to conceal a faulty skin condition or tired eyes. Make-up can accent loveliness, but by itself it cannot create loveliness. You cannot hide your real face behind a mask of make-up. And it should never be thought of as an artificial mask. Rather, it is that final touch that makes the most of your own true self.

BECOMING MAKE-UP

Beauty experts are agreed that a truly successful make-up should appear natural. It should make people say, "My, she looks lovely!" rather than, "I wonder what she looks like when she takes that stuff off!" That sounds like a catty remark, but there is more than a grain of sense in it if a girl's make-up is too obvious. Every girl should learn what constitutes a suitable and becoming make-up.

When? . . . What? . . . Where? More than likely you have already discussed the pros and cons of teen-age make-up. You have a good idea as to when girls should begin to wear it. At least, you're flabbergasted when you see a girl blossom out in lipstick at the ripe old age of twelve, because most of you think that fourteen or fifteen is the turning point.

Some people feel that it is not in good taste for girls to use any cosmetics until their late teens. Perhaps that idea is a carry-over from those days (not so long ago) when "nice girls did not paint." Instead, they pinched their cheeks to pinkness and bit their lips to rosiness! But times have changed and most people accept the fact that even "nice" young girls use cosmetics.

No one can set a definite age rule because it partly depends on where you live. Girls in larger cities are likely to wear make-up earlier and more regularly than girls in smaller communities. Then, too, it depends on what is the accepted thing among girls in your crowd.

At first, most teen-agers wear a touch of make-up just for special occasions. Powder and lipstick provide that dress-up feeling for gala hours. Gradually, however, make-up becomes a part of a girl's daily grooming. Then comes the question, "What make-up to use where?"

Most of you will grant that you would feel a bit silly using anything more than powder and lipstick during school hours. Somehow an elaborate make-up doesn't fit in with a schedule that includes a problem in frog dissection, an hour of x + y = z, a cooking session in the food lab, and a thorough workout in gym. Many girls even prefer not to use powder. The glow of smooth, healthy skin is so attractive that an accent of lipstick is make-up enough.

When a really BIG event looms up on the calendar, you will appreciate a few of those little extra touches. Light eyebrows may be touched up with *brown* eyebrow pencil—not too much, to retain that natural look. A bit of vaseline brushed on the edge of the upper eyelid and over the lashes gives your eyes a luminous quality. Such eye make-up is sufficient for social events.

When you do use make-up, apply it carefully and sparingly.

Remember that young, healthy eyes have a sparkle that can't be bought at any cosmetic counter! You may wish to use a touch of rouge, although in recent years it has not been considered a fashion "must." Women with dark skin tones (bronze, copper, or olive) seldom wear rouge. But it does seem to add a warm glow to a light skin that tends to look sallow.

Now when—if ever—may a schoolgirl use mascara? It is tabu during day-light hours certainly. It really should not make an appearance until, let us say, the **Junior Prom.** Save it for just such extra-special occasions.

This color? . . or that? The color of your skin may be described in two ways. First, it is *light, medium,* or *dark.* Second, it is *cool, neutral,* or *warm.* The cool skin has purple-pink tones; the neutral skin ranges from light, creamy tones to olive; the warm skin has a coral-pink or a light copper cast (orange-red).

One cannot say that all blondes have light, neutral skin tones; that all brunettes have dark, cool tones; or that all redheads have warm, coral tones.

There are some cool skins and warm skins in each group. There is no hard-and-fast rule as to which powder is best for each type. Each individual should be guided by her own particular skin tones when she selects her powder.

Cosmetic houses have prepared a wide range of colors to blend with every type of skin. Pool your pennies and buy samples of powder for class study. At first glance they may all look like a "sort of tan." Yet after careful comparison you will see that some have a hint of purple-pink; others are a creamy neutral with perhaps a faint trace of medium pink; while others have a definite copper (orange-red) cast. And, of course, they range from light to dark. By daylight try them in "patch tests" on your face. If you are pale and sallow, choose a powder that will give a slight pink cast to your skin.

You will also notice how important it is to select a powder of the correct lightness or darkness. If it is too light, you have that "dipped-in-flour" look. If it is too dark, it settles in dark splotches wherever there are oily spots—especially around the nostrils and chin.

Select your lipstick and rouge from the same color family as your powder. For example, if your powder has a definite copper cast, select an orange-red lipstick and rouge. A purple-red lipstick and rouge would look too harsh. However, it is possible to use either a purple-red or orange-red lipstick with a creamy, neutral powder. In this case, the final selection depends on the individual's costume.

The *darkness* of your rouge depends on the lightness or darkness of your skin. A dark rouge tends to create a hollow spot on a light skin because it looks like a shadow. The *darkness* of your lipstick is largely determined by the color of your hair and eyes.

For example, a dark lipstick would be too strong a contrast for the flaxen-haired blonde who has a pale, cool skin and light, gray eyes. Her powder should be light with a hint of purple-pink to give her color. Her lipstick should be a rather light purple-red; her rouge should repeat a faint flush of the same color.

On the other hand, a person with black hair, dark olive skin, and dark eyes needs the accent of a darker lipstick. Her powder should be a dark, creamy neutral and her lipstick a dark red or dark purple-red.

A girl of medium-dark coloring looks best in the medium-dark range. Let us say that she is a redhead with a coppery skin tone and hazel eyes. Her powder has a coral tint. Her rouge and lipstick should be a medium-dark orange-red.

There are a few other things to keep in mind. A change in season often demands a change of make-up. After you have developed a good sun tan and *if* you insist on covering it up, your new make-up should match it. A light make-up looks weird on a bronzed skin. Yet it does not look half so weird as the attempt to cover a "winter-white" skin with sun-tan make-up. The tell-tale white peeps through along the hairline and around the eyes.

The effect of artificial light on make-up must also be considered. Electric

What's New in Home Economics

No make-up . . . half make-up . . . ready for anything.

lighting casts a yellow light. When yellow is added to orange-red, it becomes more orange. This means that cosmetics in the orange-red family take on a yellowed, tawny look in artificial light. The person who uses orange-red cosmetics in the daytime should try medium-red make-up at night.

When yellow is added to colors in the purple-red range, they become slightly grayed. A person who uses a purple-red daytime lipstick should select a more intense purple-red for evening.

A medium-red lipstick appears lighter and slightly orange at night. The person who uses medium-red in the daytime should select an evening color that is a more intense red or one that is slightly purple-red.

When you use colored nail polish, select a color that is keyed to your make-up. Polish need not *match* your lipstick, but it should belong to the same color family. A dark purple-red polish would clash with an orange-red lipstick.

Here is a shopping hint. You are more likely to have a becoming make-up if all of your cosmetics are made by the same firm. The colors of powder, lipstick, and rouge have been keyed to one another.

Now just a word as to how you can key your make-up color to your costume color. Later, in Chapter 10 "Color and You," we shall discuss costume color in more detail. At this point we will insert this word of caution. You have already learned that nail polish should be in the same color family as lipstick. The same is true of costume color. An orange-red lipstick would clash with a "dusty" purple-pink sweater. And a purple-red lipstick would look horrid with a rust-colored suit! What to do about it?

Let us say that you are a medium brunette with a cool skin. Your usual powder has a faint purple-pink cast and you use a purple-red lipstick. You have glints of auburn in your hair that make rust a becoming color for you. To wear it successfully, you should use a creamy, neutral powder and wear lipstick that is slightly orange-red.

Many women prefer to use a medium-red lipstick because it is more likely to harmonize with costumes in either the purple- or orange-red color range. But it *is* fun to experiment!

In any event, whenever you use make-up, strive to create a well-blended, harmonious effect that accents your natural, teen-age loveliness.

How??? Even the simplest make-up should not be a hit-and-miss procedure. You cannot appear well groomed if you hurriedly rub your nose with a soiled powder puff and add a hasty dash of color to your lips. Take time to do it well so that you won't have to touch up your face at odd and improper moments. Always start off with a clean face. This does not apply only to the make-up which follows your morning wash-up. If you change your make-up during the day, the old make-up should be thoroughly removed first.

The following suggestions concern your daily make-up.

Foundation for daily use. First, apply a powder base to protect your skin from dust and extremes of temperature. It also provides a velvety surface for the powder. A good standard skin cream is recommended for dry skin; a non-oily skin lotion is suitable for normal or oily skin. A lotion is preferable for all skins during warm weather. (Heavy, colored foundation creams or lotions are not for regular, daily use.) Smooth a *little* cream or lotion on the skin with your finger tips. Blot off any excess with cleansing tissue. Special bases are made to cover birthmarks.

Powder. Pat the powder on lightly with a generous wad of cotton. Start at the hairline and work down under the chin and over the neck. Never rub in the powder; float it on. Now, take a fresh wad of cotton or a soft powder brush and whisk off the excess powder.

Eyebrows. After powdering, clean and smooth out your eyebrows. The hairs should be brushed up and out to follow the line of the arch. A touch of vaseline will keep them under control.

If you have stray hairs below or between your brows, attend· to them about once a week. Steam the brow with a hot cloth. Pluck the strays with tweezers. Apply a soothing witch-hazel pad. Do not trim above the brow line because that spoils the natural high arch of the brow. Don't pluck anything but strays. It's silly to pluck all but a few wispy hairs because you will then have to draw in a fake brow. Your natural eyebrows are a necessary frame for your eyes.

Lipstick. You may not be able to get a clean outline when you apply lipstick directly. Try a lip brush for a sharp outline. Open your mouth and hold the lips firm against your teeth. You have better control of the brush if you use your chin as a pivot for your little finger. Outline the "cupid's bow" of

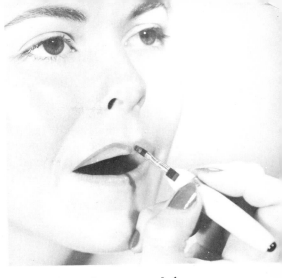

Martha Lorraine

Using a lipstick brush. Saturate the brush with lipstick . . . Then using your little finger as a brace, outline your lip . . . Finally fill in the outline.

the upper lip with two short strokes; another stroke marks the center of the color edge of the lower lip. Then, working from the center strokes to the corners of the mouth, finish both lip contours with clean lines. Now use the lipstick directly, applying the color up to the outline. Avoid lipstick on your teeth!

Press a tissue between your lips. Then blot them with tissue. Apply the lipstick directly a second time. Smooth the color by rubbing the lips together. It's that second time that counts. You won't have to touch your mouth for hours.

The preceding hints concern your regular daytime make-up. The following pointers are just for special occasions when or *if* you might want to try a few of those little extras.

Foundation for special occasions. For the season's big event you may wish to use a heavier, colored powder base that matches the color of your powder. If you have a dry skin, the foundations with an oil or cream base are best. If your skin is normal or oily, the nonoily lotion is preferable. Smooth the foundation on the skin with your fingertips to form an even film. Always use sparingly. Proceed with powder as described above.

If you use cake make-up, it does not require any other powder. Apply it evenly with a moistened pad of cotton or with a moist rubber sponge puff. The puff should be washed frequently with soap and water.

Rouge (if you use it). Rouge is applied before powdering. Apply three dots of cream rouge along the crest of the cheekbone. Place the first dot below the outer corner of the eye. The other two should follow the downward curve of the cheekbone about one-half inch apart. Blend the rouge into the cheek so that there is no visible edge. The "warm spot" should be on the highest point of the cheekbone, but it should never be aflame! Do not allow it to creep too close to the eyes.

Dry, cake rouge is applied sparingly. Merely create a natural flush on the cheekbone.

Eye make-up for special occasions. If your light brows need a dark accent, use brown eyebrow pencil. Create a natural effect by applying the pencil in short strokes rather than in one unbroken line. The strokes should follow the upward and outward lines of the hairs.

Eyelashes should never have a glued-bristle look. First brush a bit of vaseline on the edge of the lid and over the eyelash roots. Then with brown pencil outline the edge of the lid. The color melts with the vaseline to color the roots of the eyelashes. Wipe off excess vaseline. Finish off the eyelashes with a delicate touch of mascara. Avoid that beaded look! Blondes, redheads, and fair brunettes should use brown mascara; dark brunettes usually use black.

Your family will appreciate it if you groom your room as well as yourself. Good grooming has much in common with good housekeeping.

MAKE-UP MAGIC

There are many girls (and women too) who aren't too satisfied with the faces that they were born with. They look with envy at the perfect oval faces, widely spaced eyes, and nice noses of others! Perhaps you are foolishly self-conscious about something that is a very nice part of you. A little turned-up nose can have a certain gay air about it and a round, cherub face can be very appealing. So don't feel that all such distinguishing features are bad. This would be a monotonous world if all of us had perfect oval faces and delicately chiseled noses!

Nearly everyone has at least one redeeming feature. You may have a receding chin, but your eyes are lovely. Your nose is a mere button, but your smile and teeth would do justice to a toothpaste ad. The thing to do is to accent your best feature. Then improve the one that you think is a check against you. Make-up can do much to create an illusion of a narrower face, a firm chin, and so on. So let's see what can be done.

Powder can be used to modify the contours and features of the face. A dark powder tones down prominent features because it acts as a shadow. A light powder acts as a highlight; so it is used to accent a feature. In either case the powder should be of the same color family as the powder used on the rest of the face. Blend the powders to avoid a hard boundary edge.

The placement of rouge can also do much to modify the shape of your features and face. A wide face looks narrower when the "warm spot" on the cheekbone moves toward the front plane of the cheek. A narrow face will look wider when the "warm spot" moves further out on the cheekbone. A round face will look longer if the rouge is carried down diagonally on the cheek. A dab of very light rouge on a receding chin will tend to bring it forward. (Dark rouge would create a shadow that would make it recede still further.)

Because lipstick offers such a strong color contrast to the face, it can do much to change your appearance. A square jaw will look less severe if the lip color ends within the corners of the mouth and if the lip contour is curved. A full lower lip will look smaller if it is made up in a color darker than the upper lip. A large mouth appears smaller when the color is applied within the natural lip contour. Small, tight lips look fuller when the color is applied slightly beyond the natural lip contour. A light touch of color on the lips is best when a person has a receding chin. A strong color would stand out, only emphasizing the receding chin.

If eyes seem too close together, pluck your brows so that you have a one-inch space between. Then pencil in the outer ends of the brow line beyond their natural growth. Accent the outer corners of the upper eyelids with brown eyebrow pencil.

These are just a few of the illusions that can be created with make-up. They are simple enough for you to put into practice successfully if you so desire. Obviously, there are many of you who never need to make use of these "tricks." A few may wish to try them just occasionally. But even if you do not make use of them now, you may appreciate them in future years.

FRAGRANTLY YOURS

In addition to your cosmetics your dressing table is most likely graced by a bottle or two. One may be a bottle of cologne or toilet water and the other your favorite perfume.

There is an art to using them too. In the first place, you must select them carefully. It is far better to do without them than it is to use a cheap quality. The clean scent of a soap-fresh body is far sweeter than a harsh cheap perfume. If you can afford one bottle of scent, let it be a good cologne or toilet water. Later, when you can add perfume to your list, buy a tiny bottle of good perfume rather than a bigger bottle of something inferior.

Teen-agers should use the more delicate floral scents at all times. Even when you do begin to use the heavier scents, save them for the winter months.

The lighter floral fragrance is always best for spring and summer.

Cologne or toilet water is applied to the body after a bath when your skin is fresh. Apply it with an atomizer or dab it on your shoulders, arms, and chest. It literally bathes your body in a refreshing fragrance.

Perfume is far more concentrated; so do not use it lavishly. People will appreciate a whiff where they might resent a dense cloud! If you use an atomizer, spray under the chin and on the neck area before you put on your dress. If you apply it with your finger, dab it behind the ears, in the hollow at the base of your throat, and the inside of your elbows. Don't put regular perfume on your hair or clothing. You don't want a faded scent to linger about you. Whenever you use perfume, it should be fresh and sweet.

Perfume also comes in creams, pastes, and oils. These are very concentrated, so it is best to use them sparingly.

Here, too, it is good sense to match your scents! If you are going to use scented soap and bath talc, toilet water, and perfume, match them so that you carry one fragrance with you. Lavender soap, rose toilet water, and gardenia perfume can result in quite a jumble. Select one fragrance and let that be *you*.

Use whatever appropriate make-up you need—but remember it is still the natural you, the you behind the make-up that counts.

ACTIVITIES

For the class

1. **Collect** material for the class bulletin board and reference files which describes correct selection and use of cosmetics. Such articles appear in girls' and women's magazines from time to time.
2. **Let members of the class volunteer** to demonstrate:
   a. the proper application of cosmetics
   b. choice of color for each color type represented in class
   c. the application of make-up in suitable and unsuitable times and places. This could be shown in a humorous skit.

For the individual

1. **Arrange** a convenient place to keep and use your cosmetics at home. Perhaps you will want to build yourself a dressing table for your own room. If you prefer to put on your make-up in front of the bathroom mirror but the medicine chest is crowded, you may want to keep your cosmetics in a handy basket or box in your dresser drawer.

| CHAPTER 4 | *HEAD ATTRACTION* |

Most likely you have spent hours and hours experimenting with center parts and side parts. You have cut long bobs shorter and let short bobs grow out, all in a search for a hair style that will do something for you. You have noticed that even one tiny detail can spoil the effect. Then just another part, a twist, or a roll can change the whole picture. Your face and head really are the picture in this case. Just as the eyebrows frame the eyes, the hair forms a frame for the face and head. So it is up to you to find the perfect frame!

"HEADLINE" STORY

Speaking of pictures . . . you can have many a laugh looking through your family photograph collections. You will see the flapper of the 'twenties in a boyish, shingle bob. She may have a spiral spit-curl plastered to her cheek or forehead. You will howl at the huge ear puffs that girls wore at the close of World War I. People called the things "cootie garages"! At the turn of the

The elaborate hair style of the 1800's looks odd to us today whereas this simple Greek hair style from the fourth century B.C. is still beautiful.

Metropolitan Museum of Art　　　　　　　　　　*Museum of the City of New York*

century fashionable Gibson Girls piled their hair high and puffed it out with wads of stuff called "rats." But you will see other hairdos that really don't look too out-of-date. They don't stick out in lumps and bumps all over the head. They are soft and natural looking. And that is the real test of beauty in any hair arrangement. The Greeks knew all about it "way back when"!

Any style that distorts the natural shape of the head is more awkward than becoming. Clean, lustrous hair that softly frames the face has more feminine appeal (and comfort) than any artificial puff arrangement could ever offer.

The natural beauty of hair has really come into its own where the American girl is concerned. For years girls have worn bobs—either long or short—curled

Consider the over-all effect.

or just slightly waved. They have that well-cared-for look even though they appear casual. They are in step with the American girl's taste for simple, well-styled clothes. "Natural" seems to be the keynote for her hairdo.

Although teen-agers may all adopt one general type of hair arrangement, that does not mean that there are no variations in the style. Each type includes several possibilities. But you must know which particular details will make the style most becoming to you. It can be a bob—yes. But it can be long or short, whichever suits you better. It can be caught off the forehead or fall in bangs. It can be a center part or fall in a loose S-wave from a side part.

Whatever the current hairdo happens to be, adapt it to yourself by choosing the correct details. The same pointers hold true for the coiffure that you will select when you are twenty or thirty!

"FEATURE" STORIES

An egg-shaped head, a slim neck, an oval face, and regular features are the standard of perfection. Obviously, such a person can wear practically any hair style provided that her hair is of the right texture. But everyone is not that perfect. We have to think about short necks, long necks, stick-out ears, and those ticklish problem features.

"Overall" suggestions. First of all, if you are a tiny person, don't wear a hairdo that dwarfs you. Long bobs with stick-out frizz or massive roll arrangements make you top-heavy. Such a hairdo is out of proportion with your half-pint figure! A smooth, medium-length bob or a short-cropped, curly style is in key with your size. When your hair goes up, emphasize height with flat swirls or waves. Always keep the head contour small.

If you are a tall, buxom girl whose head seems small for the rest of you, do not wear a smooth, short style. It would create a pinhead effect that would emphasize your body contours. A medium bob is best for you. Loose waves—not tiny ringlets—should soften but not exaggerate the head contour. When your hair goes up, wear it rather low, with soft fullness at the crown and temple area.

Specific pointers. If your face is really too wide and round, let your hair softly frame your face without building it out. Use a high side part and form a wave up from the forehead. Do not draw your hair back skintight to expose both forehead and ears. That would surely create a full-moon effect. Avoid bangs because they create a horizontal line. When your hair goes up, try soft swirls that slant upward. Avoid encircling braids that go round 'n round!

If your face is definitely thin and long, build it out (not up) with soft rolls or waves at the temples and back of the ears. Yet do not build it out so much that your face seems pinched and even narrower by contrast. Rather full, soft bobs are good. Long, straight-hanging bobs are not for you. Too short a bob would tend to look like a pinhead. Part the hair low so that it falls softly over the forehead. A center part would emphasize a long, center line. If you want bangs, cut them low and curved. When your hair goes up, wear it soft and low.

If your neck is short and stocky, a medium-short bob that exposes the neck is best. You can wear a longer bob if the hair is worn over and behind the ears where it joins the ends of the swing-roll at the back. The uncovered ear and partially exposed neck have a lengthening effect. Since bangs cut height, use a high side part instead. When your hair goes up, wear it so that it sweeps upward from the neck and builds out the crown.

If your neck is too long and thin, rather long bobs are best. Let the hair fall softly around the face. Avoid exposing the ears. A low side part is flattering. When your hair goes up, choose a coiffure that partially covers the ears and fills out the area back of the neck.

If your jaw is decidedly square, soften the hair contour. A long, soft bob that covers the ears and falls over the back of the jaw line is a flattering camouflage. Avoid bangs because they would repeat the line of the square jaw. Try a high side part instead, but do not draw the hair back tightly. Introduce soft waves near the temple and forehead. When your hair goes up, continue to emphasize soft, irregular contours—no slick, flat arrangements!

If your jaw protrudes, try a loose arrangement of a roll, curls, or soft bangs on the forehead. You have to build out a forehead to balance that chin that

IF YOU HAVE A	DON'T	DO	
		WITH SHORT HAIR	WITH LONG HAIR
Round face			
Long face			
Short neck			
Long neck			
Square jaw			
Protruding jaw			
Receding chin			
Low forehead			
High forehead			
Large nose			
Big ears			

juts out. Yet do not build it out so much that it creates a dish-shaped profile. A long bob that covers the ears and conceals part of the jaw is a good style. When your hair goes up, continue the fullness over the forehead, keep your ears at least partly covered, and wear the hair rather low and full in back.

If your chin recedes, avoid the style in which the hair is drawn straight back from the forehead. That creates an unflattering arc of your profile. Yet don't pile too much hair on the forehead. That would tend to make a small chin look even smaller by contrast. A soft, upswept wave is best. Your profile should expose as much of the cheek and jaw as possible. So wear the hair rather full behind the ears, leaving them partly uncovered. When your hair goes up, wear it soft on the forehead and quite low and full in back.

If you have a shallow forehead, expose your hairline with an upswept wave or roll. Avoid bangs or dips that cover even a part of the forehead.

If you have a prominent, bulging forehead, cover it with bangs. Or try a soft diagonal wave from a low side part. Avoid center parts and slick effects.

If you have a long, prominent nose, avoid a center part. That would emphasize it. Wear hair slightly full to balance the size of the nose. If a nose profile forms a prominent arc, avoid the hairdo that sweeps back off the forehead. Build out the forehead contour slightly with some soft arrangement to check the line of the arc.

If your ears are large or if they stick out, they aren't worthy of exposure. Do cover them so that only the lobes show.

If one of your features is definitely irregular, stress irregular, soft contours in your hairdo. Avoid center parts and any equal arrangement of waves and rolls. For instance, when the bridge of the nose curves to the right, a left part helps to balance it. Likewise, if the mouth or jaw has a tendency to slant toward one side, part your hair on the opposite side. If you have a cowlick— and so many have—make it a part of your hairline. It can be the natural starting point for an upswept wave or two.

PERMANENT WAVES

If your hair has a natural wave, be thankful! No permanent could improve on it, so don't experiment. Simply encourage your own waves to do your bidding. The effect will be far more flattering.

If nature did not bless you with a curly top and your hair is as straight as sticks, avoid permanents that give you a tight mass of curls. The chances are that you look best with loose waves or smooth, straight hair. Many bobs are designed to be absolutely straight except for the hair ends which turn in a soft roll.

Make sure that your hair and scalp are in good condition before you have a permanent. Both the beauty and safety of a permanent wave depend on it. This is true whether you have a home permanent or have it done by a professional operator. If you even suspect an unhealthy condition, it is best to let a reliable operator decide whether you should have the permanent.

Seventeen. Photographs by Pellegrini

From one setting, shown at left, this girl is able to arrange her hair in five different styles.

Permanent waves are given by three different methods: (1) the "machine-wave" process depends on electrical heating units to curl the hair; (2) the "machineless-wave" process makes use of chemicals that generate heat to curl the hair; and (3) the "cold-wave" process is heatless and relies on the chemical action of solutions to curl the hair.

In general, the methods involving heat are most satisfactory for coarse and medium hair. The cold-wave method is usually most successful when used on fine and medium hair. A skilled operator is the best judge of which type of wave and solution and timing is suited to the texture of your hair. Even so it is wise to ask the operator for a test curl before your entire head is waved.

In recent years cold-wave "home permanents" have become increasingly popular. It is possible to give yourself a wave, but it is better to have someone

Procter & Gamble

To make a pin curl, lift a strand of hair straight up and beginning at the end of the strand, wind the hair toward your head. Hold it in place with a hair pin or a bobbi pin. Be sure to catch all of your hair up in pin curls. If some is left uncurled underneath, your hair will not comb out smoothly.

help you. Each product is accompanied by a step-by-step, illustrated procedure of the entire waving process: (1) preparation of the hair for the wave, (2) application of waving lotion, (3) winding of hair on curlers, (4) "time-check" tests to see whether wave has set, (5) application of neutralizer to check further action of wave solution, (6) unwinding of curls, (7) final rinse and setting of waves. The success of a home permanent depends on following directions very closely. So take time to study the process carefully and heed all words of caution concerning the use of solutions.

Seventeen. Photographs by Pellegrini

Do you change your hair style for different occasions or do you always wear it the same way?

HAIR ORNAMENTS

Many of you like to wear bows, flowers, and decorative clips in your hair. Solid-colored bows may be worn with solid-colored, floral, striped, or plaid costume fabrics. Bows of figured ribbon, such as a plaid, are best worn with solid colors unless you are able to match bows and fabrics exactly.

The style of the bow must also be in keeping with the whole costume. A small, flat bow that repeats the color of your anklets or sweater is best for a sports outfit. A perky, slightly larger bow can repeat the color of your blouse or gloves in a street outfit. A more elaborate bow is suitable with dress-up clothes or evening wear. Most girls prefer flower arrangements for those occasions anyway.

Your floral ornaments should be saved for your dress-up clothes. They don't belong with a sports outfit—ever! Try to imagine how a cluster of daisies

Procter & Gamble

Hair is naturally straight, wavy, or curly depending on the shape of the follicle from which it grows.

would look with a corduroy sport skirt, a T-shirt, a blazer, and sneakers. They would also look out of place with a strictly tailored costume.

In addition, you have to consider whether your particular dress-up outfit would look appropriate with a flower ornament in your hair. Your "Sunday best" might happen to be a gay, floral print or a colorful plaid taffeta. Flowers clash with plaids and stripes, and they are excessive with floral prints. They just don't "mix." It is best to reserve your floral accents for your solid-colored dress-up clothes.

Save your more elaborate hair clips and barrettes for your dressy clothes. Simple plastic or metal clips are more appropriate for general wear.

45

Do not wear your ornament low on the neck if you wish to add length to your face or your neck. Wear it high. When you wish to shorten a long face and a long neck wear your hair ornament low. Wear it high to lengthen a round face. An ornament at the earline would only tend to broaden the face.

You may not be able to afford Paris original gowns, but any girl can have well-groomed and well-styled hair—and that is a big step toward being well-dressed. Take time to brush your hair and give thought to its arrangement. You know that if your hair is dull and unkempt, you can't look attractive in the most becoming of dresses.

ACTIVITIES

For the class

1. **Collect** for the class bulletin board material on current hair styles, ways to set your hair, and ways to give a home permanent. Be sure you include photographs, cut from magazines, of hair arrangements that are becoming and unbecoming to the following types:
   a. wide, round face
   b. long, narrow face
   c. square jaw
2. **Invite** a trained beautician to discuss the proper care of hair and professional permanent waves. A helpful talk or demonstration on her part may prove to be a good advertisement for her shop.

For the individual

1. **Make a date** with a girl friend to experiment with various hair styles that are suitable for general daytime wear and for formal evenings. Let her dress your hair; then you arrange hers. The exchange of ideas and opinions is usually helpful in determining the becomingness of hair styles.
2. **Try dressing** your mother's hair. You will see how the suggestions for hair arrangements apply to mature as well as to youthful hair styles.

CHAPTER 5

PERSONALITY PLUS

Just what is personality? Is it a person's appearance? Disposition? Manners? The dictionary would tell you that it is "that which constitutes a person; that which distinguishes and characterizes a person." The definition is brief, but the subject is endless. The study of personality has challenged novelists, psychologists, educators, parents, and even song writers.

TYPE ANALYSIS

Technically speaking, there are as many different personalities as there are people. Each person is a blend of many different characteristics. Yet we do find that a person usually has some quality that dominates her other characteristics. We can divide those qualities into certain general groups to guide you in this matter of personality styling.

"Know thyself." This is where an honest self-analysis pays dividends. Every girl should learn how to select clothing which suits her type. Otherwise she will invest in some clothes in which she never feels "just right." As a result she seldom wears them. That is a sure sign that they do not suit her personality.

For example, let us say that you look your best and feel your best in sports suits and simple classic styles. Then one day you suddenly found yourself buying a peplum dress with rows of little ruffles edging the neck and sleeves. The saleslady told you that it was the very latest fashion. You took it home and wore it once but you felt uncomfortable in the fussy thing! So you hung it way back in the closet and returned to your favorite classics.

If you stopped to wonder why you never liked the dress, you may have realized that frilly things always did bother you. You may have learned a lesson, but it was an expensive way to learn!

Think about the clothes you like to wear and the ones you shove in the back of the closet and see if you can fit yourself into one of these types. A girl can be utterly charming as far as manners go. She may be faultlessly groomed. Yet she still runs the risk of not being becomingly dressed if her clothes do not express her personality. Moreover, becoming clothes can even *improve* a girl's personality!

DAINTY . . . opposite of . . .	STURDY
delicate, fragile, gentle, extremely feminine	athletic, rugged, strong, vigorous, "tomboyish"

DRAMATIC . . . opposite of . . . DEMURE

daring, extreme, striking, unusual, sophisticated	modest, retiring, shy, timid

DIGNIFIED . . . opposite of . . . VIVACIOUS

conservative, sedate, reserved, serious, deliberate	gay, sparkling, lively, flighty, impulsive

Each group represents a different type of individual. Note that each group in the left column is a direct opposite of one in the right column. That pair

If you are dainty . . . do   **. . . don't**

of opposites is not likely to appear in the same person. For instance, if you are a "dainty" lass today, there isn't much chance that you will be a "sturdy" tomboy tomorrow.

On the other hand, you may be classified as a "dainty," delicate type but have some of the shy quality of the "demure" type. You might even be quite conservative, which would put you into the "dignified" group. Usually, however, one group of characteristics dominates.

You yourself know that you have many moods. At times you may feel extremely feminine and "willowy," at other times you are gay and almost boisterous, and there may be occasions that bring on a sedate mood. You will have to find out which mood really describes YOU as you are most of the time.

But do not think that your type will never change. It most likely will. A girl of fifteen who is definitely "vivacious" today may be "dramatic" when she is twenty-five. Or a "demure" miss might easily become "dignified."

Personality styling. Now have you found yourself? If you are in doubt, talk it over with your friends. Classify each other. Then discuss the styling hints below.

But first you should realize that there are certain standard styles that are worn by all schoolgirls. You "live in" blouses, sweaters, and skirts. Sports suits and toppers with their casual accessories also follow a standard style. But you can express your individuality to a certain extent in your choice of color and texture. Your knowledge of personality styling is put to its real test when you select your street clothes, your "dress-up" outfits, and your evening clothes.

Dainty. If you are dainty, you enjoy wearing soft, smooth woolens because rough, coarse textures seem too harsh and bulky for your delicate tastes. You

If you are sturdy . . . do   **. . . don't**

lean toward sheer cottons—organdy, dimity, dotted Swiss—but you would feel right in almost any crisp, fresh cotton.

Usually you look and feel better in soft, pastel hues. Bright reds, intense blues, and greens tend to overpower a dainty girl unless they are used as accents. Select the more delicate prints and more subdued stripes and plaids. Big, bold stripes and vivid, splotchy prints would be a strike against you!

Try feminine details in a dress or blouse—frilly necklines, exquisite lingerie touches, and soft shirring. A severe, tailored style might be too "hard" for a dainty miss.

Adorable little hats were made for your type, because you can get away with flowers, froth, and frou-frou (for dress-up, of course—*not* with your plaid suit and sneakers).

You prefer smooth, lightweight leathers for your shoes and handbags. A heavier leather somehow looks clumsy on you.

Sturdy. If you are sturdy, you know that you feel right in rough tweeds and herringbones. But you look well in gabardine, flannel, and serge too. Most filmy fabrics and sheer cottons are "out" where you are concerned. Imagine yourself twirling around in a frilly organdy summer evening frock! Piqué, linen, or seersucker would be so much better.

You can wear strong colors—and you enjoy them. They suit your vigorous nature. Yet it's nice to own some pastel sweaters and classics—just for a change. Stripes and plaids appeal to you, but you are apt to feel overblown in most floral prints.

Fuss and frills are not for you, but take care that you don't look too masculine. Your dressier blouses can have simple but beautifully detailed collars— a fagoted edging, for instance. Your dress-up clothes should stress simple lines

If you are dramatic . . . do   **. . . don't**

that introduce some soft details. You can bring out some femininity without feeling "prissy," you know! It's the extreme ruffles, flounces, and lace inserts that you want to avoid.

Since you are not the flowery type, your hats are trimmed with ribbon, a perky feather, or a simple pompon. Good, simple styling in bags and shoes is important to you. Fussy detail and excessive strappings and perforations would bother you.

Dramatic. If you are dramatic, you may wear almost any fabric that suits your mood, although some sheer fabrics might seem too "pretty-pretty" to you. You like the novelty weaves that are the high fashion of the moment. The elegance, the drama, and the weight of velvet appeal to your luxurious moods. Perky taffeta with its sharp highlights and rustle accent your gay, brilliant moods. When you are older and feel sleek and suave, you may turn to satin.

Striking colors suit your extreme nature, but beware of peculiar color combinations that put you into the eccentric class! As you get a little older, you will have those sophisticated moments when you lean toward unrelieved black accented by a piece of unusual jewelry or a dash of color. You will love prints that are distinctive both in color and design. You can "get away with" bold, wide stripes and striking plaids.

You will feel wonderful in well-styled clothes that are unusual for their stark simplicity. They seem to form a "backdrop" for your own dramatic nature. Fussy details would only tend to clutter "your stage" with unnecessary "props." On the other hand, you're not afraid to appear in an extremely unusual style when the occasion demands.

When you select accessories, you don't look for just any hat, bag, and shoes. You react to simple, unusual styling in them too. Many extreme hats, distinc-

If you are demure . . . do   **. . . don't**

tive bags, and novelty shoes were designed with your dramatic type in mind.

Demure. If you are demure, you shy away from things that make you stand out. You feel safer in choosing conventional fabrics; so you usually end up in soft, plain materials. Novelty weaves "rub you the wrong way." Yet you should break away from the tried and true occasionally if only to develop a feeling for experimentation.

You naturally turn to subdued colors—powder blue, moss green, dusty pink, and aqua. They do suit your nature better than strong colors. As you get older, there is the danger that you might restrict yourself to brown, gray, navy, or black. Even now you may dislike to blossom forth in color. It's easier to remain unnoticed when you wear brown or navy. That does not imply that brown and navy are not good, wearable colors. They most certainly are! But there are so many other colors that are also becoming to a girl. Besides, color prevents you from getting that "mousey" look!

You may feel too conspicuous in gay plaids, checks, stripes, and splashy prints. But do wear them occasionally in subdued colors. Somehow, figured fabrics can have an enlivening effect without seeming brash.

You feel comfortable in simple styles with some soft detail. Severe tailoring would make you feel too aggressive, whereas fussy details would seem like too much. Daring, dramatic styles and strong color contrast in a dress would make you more conspicuous than you wish to be.

Select hats and other accessories that have that soft, feminine look. Your tastes will run to simple conservative styles in them too.

Dignified. Very few girls of your age are actually dignified as yet. However, you may have tendencies that will put you into this classification within a few

If you are dignified . . . do   **. . . don't**

years. The "demure" girl, for instance, is apt to find herself in this group when she develops more confidence and poise.

So—IF or WHEN you are dignified, you will *look* as self-controlled as you *are*. Perhaps we can say that in the matter of clothes you will be the "tailleur" type.

In fabrics your taste usually runs to suits of neat pin stripes, smooth serge, or firm gabardine. You veer away from the more casual, "roughish" fabrics. You prefer heavy crepes and velvet for evening clothes because they create a sedate silhouette. Filmy fabrics and billowy nets are too frothy for the serious type—and taffeta is too perky! The tailleur type likes firmness in cotton and linen weaves too.

You like positive colors because "baby pinks" and "sky blues" seem too anemic for your deliberate manner. Yet you are too conservative to enjoy intense hues in large areas. You use them for small color accents. When an entire garment is to be of one color, you prefer to have colors that are slightly grayed. And, of course, you lean strongly to black and navy ensembles. You stay away from startling figured fabrics—splashy prints and bold plaids.

Your clothes may have that tailored look, yet you aren't a bit masculine. You appreciate the "dressmaker" touch—beautiful, simple styling, restrained, lovely detail, and dainty lingerie accents. There is a look of quiet elegance about you.

Your accessories are "neat," well styled and more-or-less conservative. You don't feel right about a saucy hat, studded and perforated sandals, or an extreme novelty bag. Perhaps we can say that you have a rather "practical streak" in your nature.

Vivacious. A good many of you are vivacious. You have so many things

If you are vivacious . . . do   **. . . don't**

to do and so little time to do them that you rush from one thing to the next. That is why you like casual clothes. That is why you love sweaters that don't have to be pressed, blazers that stand up to wind and rain, and plaid skirts that won't show spots.

But you can't always afford to look too casual. There are times when you must put your best foot forward. Then especially your gay, lively personality asserts itself in the selection of your clothes. There isn't a trace of the "meek and mild" about you. You're not a tomboy, but you do like woolens that take a certain amount of knockabout wear. You look for materials that make up into perky, crisp outfits. Slinky, soft materials to some extent bother you. They aren't in step with your pep! You love faille, taffeta, piqué, and organdy for evening.

There will be nothing ultraconservative about your clothes. You like styles that have a direct quality—a ready-for-anything look. You don't like the type of dress that has to sit quietly in the corner so that it won't get mussed up.

Here are blouses which the dainty or the demure type might choose.

National Association of Blouse Manufacturers

You love tricky costume jewelry and fad accessories. You're happy when you have a drawerful of belts, collars, kerchiefs, clips, and bracelets to choose from because you crave frequent changes.

You really prefer to wear headgear that is the fashion of the moment—whether it is a hood or a headband arrangement. Of course, they can't "go" everywhere. When you must wear a hat, you feel best in one that isn't cluttered with "stuff." Your shoes and bags tend toward casual styles, but you enjoy novelty shoes and tricky bags too. In short, you thrive on endless variety.

As was mentioned earlier, perhaps most of you place yourselves in this group. The qualities do seem to describe what is known as our typical "American Girl." But remember, personalities do develop and change. In a few years you may find yourself in another group, which means that you will wish to revise your personality styling.

The above suggestions on fabric textures, fabric designs (stripes, florals, and so forth), and color pertain only to your personality preferences. Your final selection, of course, will also depend on physical characteristics—your build and your coloring. For that material, refer to Chapter 7, "Line and Shape," and Chapter 10, "Color and You."

THE KEY TO CHARM

Whether you are dainty or sturdy, dramatic or demure, dignified or vivacious, you may be a charming person or quite the opposite. Perhaps you know someone whom you consider "ideal." She may be a classmate, or she may be a bit older than you. What places her high on your list? Your answer might run something like this: "Well, I can tell her anything and she always listens and understands. And she always looks so nice too." That young lady has found the key to charm!

"Do unto others as you would have them do unto you," is your first guidepost. Of course, it's the basis of all good manners too. When you actually begin to feel a genuine consideration for others, you show it in your facial expression. There is a certain warmth to your smile. And gone is that faraway look from your eye! You look directly at your companion as if he or she really mattered. That is a big step toward a pleasing personality because your friends will feel that you are really interested in them.

Ask Connie how her art classes are coming along. Have Al tell you about his photography lab. Help Sis with her homework. Dad used to help you, you know! Don't wail when Mother asks you to dust the living room. Remember it's your home, too.

In other words, be helpful, considerate, and appreciative at all times. Try to act, think, and talk in terms of "you-you-you" rather than "I-I-I." Let the other person know that he is really worth your interest. Soon people will turn around and show interest in you too. And what's more, they'll call you CHARMING!

As soon as you learn how to get along with many types of people, you will feel more sure of yourself. You will be at ease in different situations. You will know what to say and what to do at the right moment. When that time comes, you can be sure that you have POISE!

Perfect grooming makes you more attractive and charming. Furthermore, when you know that you are spotless and pressed, you have more confidence in yourself. That feeling adds to your poise. A girl is judged by her grooming, you know; it tells a lot about her character. This is where we should mention

Charm, like charity, begins at home.

those personality traits, "orderliness" and "carelessness." The orderly girl usually has that bandbox look. The careless girl never! She is likely to look as if she had been thrown together.

Perfect grooming is a matter that involves a "top-to-toe" routine not just for a date or Sundays, but always. By now you realize that you cannot be well-groomed unless you give your clothing regular care. That involves mending, laundering, cleaning, brushing, airing, and pressing. We will go into detail about those subjects in Part V, "Care of Clothing."

Of course you must know what to wear for each occasion—whether it is a day at school, a shopping spree, a basketball game, or a home party. More about that in Chapter 11, "Wardrobe Requirements." Then you must check such things as your hair, your make-up, and your hands. You don't want to look tousled or grimy under any circumstances.

And remember, good grooming "lives at home" too. Members of your family enjoy seeing you in crisp house dresses or becoming play clothes with your hair neatly arranged. They hate to see you shuffling around in a shapeless robe spattered with toothpaste and egg yolk! Men, especially, appreciate a neat appearance about the house. It is a morale builder for both you and them.

Foreigners traveling in the United States often say, "Your American girls and women are so perfectly groomed." One woman even added, "Not just when they go out, but in the home as well." So you see we have to live up to that reputation. Not only is a single individual judged by her appearance, but the whole country is up for scrutiny!

ACTIVITIES

For the class

1. **Organize** a class "fashion show." Select a pair of girls to represent each personality type found in the class: dainty, sturdy, dramatic, demure, dignified, and vivacious. Arrange for one girl of each pair to appear in a costume in which each item is styled to suit her personality. Have the other girl in the pair wear a costume in which one or more items are not keyed to her personality. Let the class suggest how each inappropriate costume could be improved.

For the individual

1. **Find** full-length photographs of girls (preferably in black-and-white) in newspapers, catalogues, and magazines to represent at least three of the six personality types. Put yourself in the position of stylist and choose for each of the three types a complete winter costume that would be suitable for dress-up occasions. Find pictures of a dress, coat, hat, gloves, shoes, bag, and jewelry. Mount all illustrations on 9 x 12 manila paper or standard scrapbook paper. Give reasons for your selections.
2. **Classify** yourself as to personality type. Plan an Easter costume for yourself using photographs from magazines or catalogues to illustrate your choice of coat and dress or suit and blouse, hat, shoes, bag, gloves, and jewelry. Indicate your fabric and color preferences with actual swatches of fabric or pieces of colored paper. Mount all illustrations as above. Give reasons for your selections.

CONSTRUCTION ONE ▶

MAKING A BLOUSE AND SKIRT

There are many articles of clothing which a class might choose to make first. The experience the girls have had in sewing, their tastes, the kind of clothes they are in the habit of wearing, the equipment in the laboratory, should all be taken into consideration as a choice is made.

Classes with not much experience and few sewing machines may find it best to make small articles, partly by hand and partly by machine. Kerchiefs for their heads, colorful scarfs to wear around their necks, gay belts, linen or piqué collars to add a spring-like touch to dark dresses—these and many other small articles are easy to make, and add variety and charm to any girl's wardrobe. Often they can be made from scraps or remnants. Making such accessories provides valuable experience in handling material and doing certain kinds of sewing.

Girls with a bit more experience and sewing equipment usually want to start with a larger garment. Here, again, there are numerous choices. Blouses, skirts, waistcoats, boleros, jumpers, smocks, simple dresses, certain sports garments—any of these could be chosen.

Because we cannot be there to tell what choice you make, we shall assume that your choice will be similar to the choices of classes we have known. Since "separates" have become so popular, girls almost invariably choose a blouse and a skirt as their first project. The reason may be that no other wardrobe gives such variety at moderate cost. Carefully selected and co-ordinated skirts, blouses, sweaters, and jackets can be "mixed and matched" to give the right costume for both evening and daytime occasions. Let's assume that you start with a simple blouse. It is a very wise choice, because it is not too difficult, can be quickly made, and does not require too much material. Yet you learn many things as you make it.

Blouses similar to those illustrated here are always favorites because they are such useful garments to own. Styles change slightly from year to year, but some versions of these styles are always popular. Fashion experts call such styles "classics," because they remain in vogue for so long.

There is a becoming blouse style for every girl, if she selects the right neckline and the right color. The girl with a short neck will find that an open-neck style will tend to give her throat a long, slender appearance; while the girl with a longer neck may find the higher-neck styles more becoming. Colors should be tried for becomingness to both complexion and figure, and tried with other clothes for harmonious color effects. The girl who looks too short or too large when the upper and lower parts of her costume are sharply contrasted should select a blouse color to match some skirt she owns, or one she expects to make.

58

Blouses that are simple to make.

The all-over, one-color effect of blouse and skirt will tend to give her the tall, slender look her figure needs. Perhaps she will want to buy enough material to make a matching skirt and blouse, although she would learn more by using a different fabric for the skirt.

Remember that set-in sleeves, collars, and cuffs, can be quite troublesome unless you have had some experience with sewing. Leave such details for later problems if this is your first sewing project. Sleeves cut with the blouse are simpler than those that must be inset and short hemmed ones are less difficult than long, fitted, or cuffed ones. As to collars, the set-on, Peter Pan ones are the easiest to make. Convertible collars and the shawl varieties require greater skill.

SELECTING A BLOUSE PATTERN

If your class does decide to make a blouse, the next decision to make is whether all class members will use the same pattern style or whether each girl will make her own selection. The beginning class that wishes to make clothes quickly should take a tip from industry. Garment manufacturers gain much of their efficiency by making many dresses or blouses by the same pattern. They vary the fabrics, the colors, and the sizes, but they often make hundreds of dresses of one design. You should be able to find a pattern which pleases everyone in the class, especially since many patterns include two or three necklines or other slight variations that make the style becoming to different shaped faces. At most, two or three similar pattern styles should please every taste and suit every personality. Each student will need to buy a pattern in her size, but the one she buys should be a number approved by her class.

Girls in some classes prefer greater individuality. Each wants to have the privilege of selecting her own pattern style. This is a perfectly satisfactory plan for classes whose members have mastered many of the fundamental techniques of sewing, but it does slow down a class that has everything to learn at once. Even in an experienced class where different patterns have been agreed upon, it is best for students to select simple patterns with similar details until they have reached the point where they need little assistance from their teacher.

Blouse patterns are sized by bust measurements, but are cut for teens, junior misses, misses, and women. Take your measurements carefully as described in technique 4, "The Pattern." Then select a pattern designed for your build in your size. Starting with the right pattern size is half the battle. Before you shop for any pattern—whether you are buying the class-approved one or forging ahead on your own—be sure to read that technique. The techniques to which you will refer again and again, are on buff paper, pages 375–534. So that you can find the right one quickly, the number and name of the technique are given at the top of each page in the section.

SELECTING MATERIAL FOR A BLOUSE

For this first project, especially if you have sewed little, choose material that will be easy to handle. The cloth easiest to sew is firmly woven, medium-weight cotton. Recently, there has been a revival of interest in cottons of this texture, both for summer and for winter wear. You may have noticed a variety of lustrous cottons on the market, as well as new designs in madras, irridescent colors in chambray, and tiny checked gingham in unusual color combinations. Piqué, both the pinwale and the waffle weaves, is another cotton that is easy to work with. Birdseye piqué is a bit stiff but not too difficult to handle. Cotton broadcloth and poplin are excellent, especially the smooth, mercerized kinds. Percale is always good, and less expensive than some of the other cottons. Linen of medium weight is attractive, but expensive. And unless it has been treated to make it crush-resistant, linen wrinkles badly. While materials that crease readily are easy to handle during the construction of the garment, they are not so desirable to wear.

Of course there are other fabrics which would make attractive simple blouses. If you have had some experience in handling materials, you might try spun rayon, lightweight wool crepe, or wool jersey, for example.

Materials to avoid are those that are flimsy, stiff, or heavy. Avoid also transparent ones requiring special seams, and those that ravel easily, unless you are resigned to finishing the seams—a technique you may as well save for later.

Bold plaids, stripes, and large figured designs must be matched and carefully spaced to look their best. Those processes require time and skill and can well be postponed until you know more about how a blouse goes together.

Look for material that will hold its color and will not shrink appreciably. "Vat dyed" is a label which gives reasonable assurance of colorfastness. "Sanforized" and several other trademarked finishes guarantee that the material will shrink only a small percentage. Materials are sometimes given special finishes to reduce their tendency to wrinkle or to impart a crisp, starched finish. Look for information about these and other finishes on the end of the bolt, on tags, or along the edges of the fabric before you buy.

The best choice for your first blouse, if you want to use fast methods, is a medium or dark tone in a solid color, though figured materials with medium or dark backgrounds are satisfactory. The reason for the choice of a medium or dark color value is that construction details can be transferred from the pattern clearly, distinctly, and quickly on delft blue, dark green, rose, navy, and so on. Lighter colors and white require a more time-consuming method for transferring pattern markings to the fabric.

Besides keeping all these points in mind, give thought to selecting a material that is becoming to you and that will go with clothes you already have. You have two aims—to dress well and to learn to sew well. As you improve your sewing skills, you will have more choices in patterns and materials—and as you learn more about the principles of design and about your own individual self, you will find making a right choice easier.

When you have finally selected your material, look on the back of the pattern envelope to find out how much of it to buy. Notice that you must know which of the variations or "styles" of the pattern you expect to make, the

A high school class in Oshawa, Canada, made jumpers for their first project. Here the girls evaluate a finished jumper. This one rated high.

Modern Miss

Careful fabric selection is essential regardless of the type of garment you plan to make. For an initial project, choose a fabric that is easy to work with and that will present few sewing problems.

Young America Films

size of the pattern, and the width of the material. Most cotton materials are 35 or 36 inches wide. To be certain, however, check this measurement on the material.

Where it is necessary to increase the length of your pattern, or shorten it for a good fit, you may need a bit more or less fabric than called for. Be cautious about buying less, however, for yardage requirements are carefully calculated. Some people claim that they can cut from less than is called for on the pattern, but they can do so only by skimping or turning the pattern pieces incorrectly. Either practice gives poor results. It is often wiser to buy a few inches more than indicated, rather than less; for, unless material is torn or cut straight as you buy it, some is lost in preparing it for cutting. Also some may be lost in shrinking the material if you buy cotton that is not adequately preshrunk.

OTHER SUPPLIES AND NOTIONS

It saves time to buy everything you will need to make your blouse—and perhaps your skirt too—on one shopping expedition. Some pattern envelopes list on the back of the envelope the supplies and notions needed for the particular design. If your pattern doesn't carry such a list, you can easily figure out what you need yourself. It's a good guess that the list of notions for your blouse will call for thread and buttons. Often these supplies can be bought at the same store where you buy your pattern and material.

Thread. Thread is one notion you will always need. It should match both the color and texture of the material, so that stitching lines will blend inconspicuously with the fabric. For all colored cottons or linens of medium weight, mercerized cotton thread, size 50, is a good choice. You will find this size in a wide variety of colors, as well as in black and white. Mercerized cotton is not commonly found in other sizes. If you are making a black or white blouse, you may prefer to use regular sewing cotton which has not been mercerized because you can buy black and white in finer sizes than are available in mercerized cotton. Size 60 or 70 should be suitable for the type of cottons you will be using for your blouse.

To match your material, place one strand of thread directly on the fabric in good daylight, for that is the way thread will look when used. If the salesperson will not permit you to open the spool, buy thread that, on the spool, looks slightly darker than your material but has the same color tone. To go with a patterned material, thread should match the predominant color. This, in most cases, is the background color.

Notice that the yardage on spools varies. You will need about 100 to 200 yards of thread to make a blouse, ordinarily 2 spools. Get plenty. The cost is slight, and the inconvenience of running out of thread is annoying and wasteful of your time. Also, no matter how much thread on a spool, you need more than 1 so you won't have to unthread the spool on the machine if you have to rewind the bobbin or do some hand sewing.

Buttons. Most blouse styles call for several buttons. When you buy them, consider how they will launder. Pearl buttons, white, colored, and smoked, have been used on cotton clothes for generations and are proven durable.

Many cloth-covered buttons come apart when immersed in water, but there are gadgets on the market for making tubbable buttons of self material. They are quite easy to make and give a professional touch to clothes.

Test other types of buttons for washability before you use them. Glass buttons meet this test, but besides not looking appropriate on most cottons, they chip easily. They are best reserved for more delicate fabrics.

EQUIPPING YOUR WORKBOX

Of course you can't make a blouse or anything else without needles and pins and a few other pieces of equipment. Some of these your school will supply. (Your teacher will tell you which ones your school has on hand.) Others you may have at home, but some you may have to buy. Turn to technique 1, "Sewing Equipment," for a full discussion of workbox equipment. Here is a check list of the tools you will need to make a blouse, and to do other ordinary sewing.

Needles (size 7 or 8 for hand sewing)
Pins (dressmaker's or silk pins, sizes 16 or 17)
Pin cushion
Thimble (preferably metal)
Basting thread
Tape measure (reversible, 60 inches)
Ruler (12 inch transparent plastic, preferably marked in both directions)

Adjustable gauge (or plan to cut your own from cardboard)
Scissors and shears (sharp and of appropriate size)
Tailor's chalk
Tracing wheel
Tracing paper (white is safest)
Cardboard for mounting the tracing paper (which of course will be too big to fit into your workbox)

You will need a workbox or basket to hold all these tools. Workboxes may be purchased, or you may have on hand some wooden or cardboard box that will serve your purpose.

Label each piece of equipment that you buy or bring from home with your name or other identifying mark. Use ink for marking certain pieces; fingernail polish seems best for others; pencil, name tape, typed labels covered with plastic tape, and other methods should make it easy to label all articles. A permanent secret mark of identification is an added safeguard on expensive shears and scissors. Even mark your pattern envelope, guide sheet, and all sections of the pattern.

PREPARING TO WORK

Now that you have your pattern, material, and supplies, you are no doubt eager to start sewing. However, there are still a few things to consider first. You may as well stop and make some resolutions right now about the way you will work. Sloppy work results in garments that look homemade and that hang in your closet to discourage you each time you catch sight of them. Accuracy and good workmanship pay off. A really fine looking blouse that you enjoy wearing is not only a good result in itself, but will spur you on to greater triumphs.

The accurate way is the easy way too because in sewing each step follows another. Inaccurate cutting and marking make it almost impossible, try as you will, to do accurate stitching. On the other hand, if you cut and transfer markings accurately, accurate stitching is simple. Certainly your first resolution should be: Be accurate.

Another good resolution to make is to keep your work up-to-date. If you let several days go by after your teacher's demonstration of a process before you actually do it, you may be hazy on the best way to go about it. Keeping up-to-date is the easy way too. Of course, it goes without saying that you will work with clean hands and on clean surfaces. Dust tables if they need it. Wipe excess oil from the sewing machine. Use only clean, fine pins. Spread clean wrapping paper on the floor to protect skirts as you sew, fit, or press. Be sure that the iron is clean. In every way try to keep your material clean and unwrinkled. Delicate-colored fabrics may need to be wrapped in a clean cloth for storing and spread out on the cloth as you work. As soon as you are far enough along, hang up your unfinished garment between class periods.

Money Management Institute, Household Finance Corporation

This is an excellent set-up for sewing. You can make different groupings as your work progresses.

Large tables will probably be provided in your classroom for cutting, but when you are ready to stitch you should try to arrange a work center for yourself. The sewing machine in front of you, with an ironing board and heated iron nearby and a table or chair at your side is an ideal arrangement. Your workbox, pattern, and garment sections will be easy to reach on the table or chair and you won't skip that important during-construction pressing if an iron is ready for use. Have a well-filled pin cushion and a pair of scissors on the right hand side of the machine and keep other surfaces of the machine free from clutter.

That, in general, is how you will do your work if you are really going to learn to sew—accurately, promptly, and in a clean and orderly way. That is the efficient way which really means the easy way although it may not seem so at the moment. Now here are some specific hints for efficiency in putting a garment together (and incidentally in keeping it fresh looking by handling the material no more than necessary).

1. Check the fit of the pattern and make alterations in the pattern wherever possible, rather than waiting to make them in the cloth. Darts and most seam lines can then be stitched without basting and will not need to be ripped and restitched.

2. Plan your activities to save time. Do all your cutting at one time and all your marking at one time. You won't be able to do all the stitching before doing any pressing, but do what you can and then press all that you have stitched.

3. Leave the pattern pinned to the garment sections until you are ready to start sewing on each. Then it will be easy to identify parts.

4. Keep together cut-out pieces that will be joined; for instance, facings and the sections they will face.

5. Complete as much work as possible on the sections while they are small. Then join the small sections to form larger units.

6. Do as much work as possible while sections are flat. For instance, make darts before joining sections, complete necklines before closing side seams, and attach sleeve facings before stitching sleeve seams whenever that can be done.

There are a few additional tricks that make for professional-looking results. They are often overlooked by the beginner who may underestimate their real importance.

1. Use whatever aids to stitching you find most helpful, such as traced lines or a stitching guide, until you have learned to stitch accurately without them.

2. Use staylines, described later, to keep the structure of the cloth correct and the garment sections correctly shaped.

3. Always press a dart or seam line before crossing it with another seam. Unless you do, darts and seams will be hard to press and will not lie flat at stitching lines.

MAKING A BLOUSE

Successful sewing is done in orderly stages. One operation can't be done accurately until another is finished. For instance, the pattern had better not be laid on the cloth until the cloth has been straightened or the first washing will get the blouse permanently out of shape. Necklines are usually completed before sleeves are attached to prevent the neckline from stretching. Steps vary in some respects for different styles and materials, but the general procedure for making a blouse is as follows:

Prepare the material
Prepare the pattern
Check the fit of the pattern
Lay the pattern on cloth
Cut out the blouse
Mark construction details
Construct the blouse

Preparing the material. Some material is ready to cut when you buy it but unfortunately much is not. When you study Chapter 14, "Textiles," you will understand why this is so. In the meantime, you should merely satisfy yourself that the cloth you are using will not shrink excessively, that it is free from wrinkles, and that the structure of the cloth is true—not forced out of shape. When cloth meets these requirements, it is ready to cut.

The simplest way to prevent shrinkage is to buy material that has a shrinkage guarantee. It is a simple matter, also, to press cloth that has been creased too firmly or has become wrinkled through careless handling. It is not difficult to straighten cloth either, but it does require a little more explanation than the other processes, if you are to understand why it is necessary and how to do it.

Cloth is woven of two sets of yarns or threads which were originally set at right angles to each other. The directions in which the threads run are called *grain lines*. In material which is ready for cutting the crosswise grain runs at right angles to the lengthwise grain. When the angle is other than 90°, we say that the material is *off-grain*. Unfortunately during the finishing and pressing processes, yarns are often forced out of their original position, that is, the crosswise yarns no longer run directly across the cloth. It is the same thing that happens when a sheet or handkerchief is ironed crooked. You know that the sheet or handkerchief will return to its original shape when it is washed, and so will your cloth.

No harm is done to the handkerchief and none is done to the cloth. But here is the difficulty. If you cut the cloth while it is out of shape and make it into a garment, it is going to go back to its original structure when it is washed or cleaned. When it does, you can expect twisting to take place in the garment. The garment will feel uncomfortable as you wear it, and will never hang correctly on your figure. (The exceptions are the heat-set fabrics which you will learn more about later. These must be cut as they are because they will never, under ordinary circumstances, change their thread positions.)

Since it is difficult to follow the direction of the crosswise threads with your eye, you will need some other means of determining how they fall. Obviously, if you cut or tear along a thread at each end of the cloth, that will show you how the crosswise yarns at each end of the cloth are falling. Those between lie parallel to the end yarns. Now it is easy to see whether the crosswise yarns are running at right angles to the lengthwise ones. If they are, you need go no further. If they are not, you need to straighten the yarns—set the crosswise grain again at right angles to the lengthwise grain. Here in more detail is how you prepare cloth for use:

Cutting or tearing along a thread. Perhaps your material was torn from the bolt when you bought it. If so, you will be able to pick up a thread, or yarn, and pull it away from the cloth along the entire end. If not, test the material to see if it will tear satisfactorily. Most firmly woven, plain-weave cottons can be torn. At about ½ inch from the end of the cloth clip through the *selvage*— that firmly woven strip along both sides of material as it comes from the bolt. With a firm steady motion tear quickly across the cloth to the opposite selvage. Clip through that selvage, also. Prepare both ends in the same way.

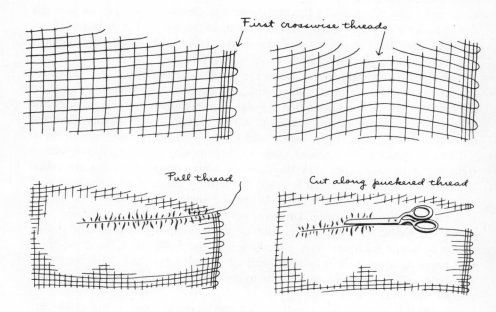

Ribbed materials, novelty weaves, loosely woven fabrics, linens, and many other kinds of cloth will not tear satisfactorily. To straighten these, you must pull a thread and cut along it. Pick up the first thread that goes all the way across the material if you can. The raveled thread ends will point to it. See diagrams above. Pull the thread until the material is gathered along the thread. Cut along the thread or puckered line. You do not need to draw the thread out of the cloth all the way across. If the thread breaks, pick it up again, or one beside it, and repeat the process until you have cut across the width of the fabric. Repeat at the opposite end of the cloth.

After tearing or cutting the ends of the material along crosswise threads, check to see if the ends of the cloth are square. Line up one selvage edge of the cloth along the side of a rectangular table. The cut ends of the cloth should be in line with the ends of the table.

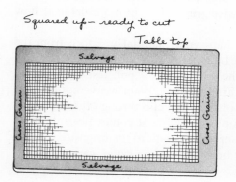

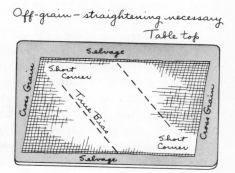

Restoring the right-angle structure of the cloth. When you find that the cloth is not square, you should straighten it. Untreated cottons can usually be straightened by pulling along a true bias from opposite sides of the material. A true bias is the imaginary line halfway between the lengthwise and crosswise grain—at an angle of 45° to each. Any direction that is not along a grain line is on a bias, but *true bias* is the term used for this exactly-in-between line— the direction in which material will stretch the most.

You can pull your material along a true bias by yourself, but it is easier if a classmate will help you. One of you should grasp the short corner firmly with both hands, the other should grasp the opposite edge just far enough from the end to pull on a true bias. Pull firmly and strongly and hold the cloth stretched for a few seconds before moving to the next positions a few inches away. Pull diagonally along the entire length of the cloth and across both ends. Never jerk the material.

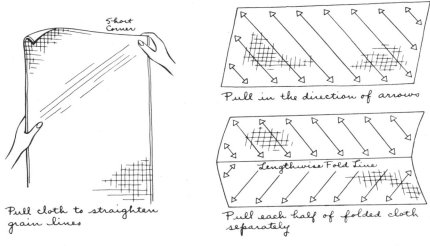

Pull cloth to straighten grain lines

Pull in the direction of arrows

Lengthwise Fold Line

Pull each half of folded cloth separately

This usually works but some cotton materials require more drastic treatment to straighten their grain lines. When they have been treated with a crush-resistant finish, it usually takes moisture in some form to relax the threads enough to change their positions. Try steam-pressing diagonally—in the same direction you would pull—to straighten fabrics of this kind. The procedure is the same as for straightening wool by pressing, described later in this construction. If this has no effect, the grains are probably permanently set and the fabric should be cut as it is. You should not attempt to straighten glazed and embossed cottons. If you have any trouble, refer to technique 6, "Materials that Require Special Handling."

Shrinking the material. Excessive shrinkage can ruin the fit of your garment. If there is danger of this, the only thing to do is to shrink the material by home methods, unless you are planning a loose fitting garment where a little shrinkage won't matter. Cottons have to be immersed in water, then partially dried and pressed. The only happy thought about having to do this is that you can square up the cloth at the same time. After wetting the cloth it is a simple matter to shift the limp cloth until all edges are square and then dry and press it that way. For more on shrinking cloth, refer to technique 6, "Materials that Require Special Handling."

Pressing. Whether you are pressing to remove excessive wrinkles and creases or because the cloth had to be wet to be shrunk or straightened, there are certain practices to follow. The general rule is to press on the wrong side of the material in line with the threads. The exception is when you must press diagonally to straighten the cloth—then always press toward the short corner. Refer to technique 12, "Pressing," for special pressing information.

Preparing the pattern. If you have never used a pattern before, it will pay you to carefully study this one and the guide sheet which accompanies it. Turn to technique 4, "The Pattern," for help. When you thoroughly understand the pattern and the meaning of all the markings used on it, select the pattern pieces you will need for the blouse style you have decided to make. Fold the other pieces together and put them back in the envelope where they can't get mixed in with the ones you are using. Some grain line markings, usually labeled "Place on the straight of the material," are too short for accurate placement. Extend lines on the pattern pieces you are using.

Checking the fit of the pattern. The simplest way to check the fit of the pattern is to pin it together as the blouse is to be made, and then try the half-pattern on. You will pin darts first, then join the blouse front to the back, always turning pins lengthwise along stitching lines. Be sure that the center lines of the pattern actually fall along the center lines of your figure as you try the pattern on. Probably the only measurements that you will have to check are the blouse length from neck to waistline, the width through the hips, and the positions of darts. The bust fit will be right if you bought the correct size. But you should make front darts point toward the high point of the bust. Frequently no alterations are needed for a blouse since it should fit rather loosely. To make sure, turn to technique 5, "Altering the Pattern and Fitting the Garment," for instructions on when and how to alter various pattern pieces.

Laying the pattern on the cloth. Your first step in laying the pattern on the cloth will be to find the right cutting diagram. It will be the one planned for the style you have decided to make, the width of your material, and the size of your pattern. Circle it with a pencil so that you can find it quickly and so that you will always refer to the right one.

From the diagram you can see how your cloth is to be folded. Notice where the selvages, folds, and cut ends of the material are indicated. A lengthwise center fold is the most common, but occasionally pieces are cut on a single layer or on other kinds of folds. Turn the right side of the cloth to the inside to keep it clean and to make the wrong side available for markings. As you make the fold indicated, you should realize that here is another place where grain lines can go awry if you are not careful. To avoid this, always measure folds carefully, then be certain that straightened ends are matched. To make

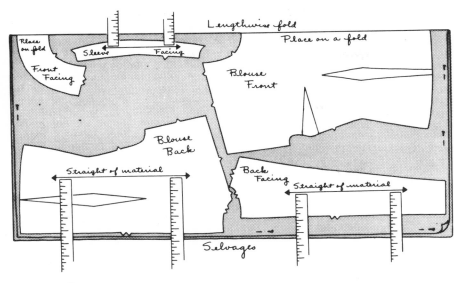

Lengthwise fold

Place on fold

Sleeve *Facing*

Front Facing

Place on a fold

Blouse Front

Blouse Back

Back Facing

Straight of material

Straight of material

Selvages

Measure, don't guess, in making a layout

sure that the fold stays in place, pin the layers together along their edges. Even now grain lines can get out of place unless you keep the cloth squared up. Line it up by the edges of the table or with a square. Refer to technique 7, "Laying the Pattern on the Cloth," for more detailed instructions on making folds.

After measuring and pinning the fold, you are ready to start laying the pattern pieces on. Notice that some have to be laid so that a center back or center front line falls exactly on a fold. This method is used to give you a whole back or front cut in one piece. All other pieces have to be laid so that their lengthwise grain lines actually fall along the correct grain.

Girls sometimes ask if it makes any difference whether they place pattern pieces along a lengthwise or a crosswise grain of the material. If you are tempted to ask this question, try gathering a piece of material along each grain. Or, try stretching the cloth between your fingers to test the amount of elasticity in each direction. Notice that the crosswise grain stretches more than the lengthwise one.

Material is stronger and stiffer in the lengthwise direction. Fabric falls much more gracefully when the lengthwise grain runs vertically on the figure. It wears better in that direction, too, and incidentally often shrinks more that way unless the cloth is properly pre-shrunk. Gathers fall more softly and evenly when gathering threads run along a crosswise grain.

It certainly does make a difference how you lay the pattern on the cloth. Follow your cutting diagram in this respect as well as in others.

As you put the pieces on, make a trial layout first. This means placing all pieces on before you pin any of them, just to see how they go and whether or not you have enough material. If you happen to have cuffs or a collar you will have to place these pattern pieces on more than once. Examine your layout to see how many times.

Start pinning the pattern on at one end of the cloth. Fit pieces together closely, but allow room enough to cut notches outward. Pin first along fold lines if you have any. Be extremely careful to match the fold line on the pattern to the edge of the cloth fold. Pin next at corners, then along edges, turning the pins diagonally at corners and at right angles to other pattern edges.

Work next on neighboring pieces. Straighten each pattern piece up as best you can, then measure from one end of the grain line to a selvage. Pin that end of the grain line in place. Next measure from the other end of the grain line to the selvage. Shift the pattern until both measurements are the same, then pin that end in place. It is easier if you take the first measurement at the broad end of the pattern. Then, you won't be so likely to have to shift the whole piece to fit it on the cloth. Refer to technique 7, "Laying the Pattern on the Cloth," for other helpful information on making layouts.

Cutting out the blouse. Be extremely accurate as you cut. Place your left hand on the pattern to hold it flat on the table as you cut with your right. Cut notches outward. Use ¼ inch clips into the seam allowance to indicate center lines. Refer to technique 8, "Cutting and Marking." Cut interfacings from interfacing material, if they are to be used. You won't need them for this blouse unless you are making collars or cuffs. Refer to technique 9, "Stay-lines, Interfacings, and Linings," for further instructions if you need them.

Marking construction details. Marks for darts, seam lines, buttonholes, center lines, and the like all have to be transferred from the pattern to the cloth

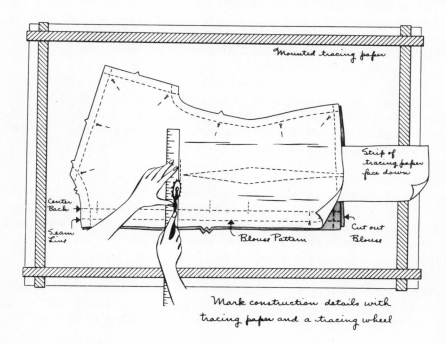

Mark construction details with
tracing paper and a tracing wheel

to be available where you need them. The easiest way to do this is to slip mounted tracing paper (white preferably) beneath the cut-out garment sections. For double layers of cloth remove a few pins at a time, then place a strip of the same paper, wax side down, between the pattern and the upper layer of the cloth. Lay a ruler beside all straight lines on the pattern and run a tracing wheel along each line once. Make a cross line at the tips of darts and across the ends of dart tucks. Mark curves free hand. Refer to technique 8, "Cutting and Marking," for further information.

Constructing the blouse. Instructions for this stage of making a blouse are best given in numbered sequence—as they are given on your pattern instruction sheet. Compare instructions given here to those on your pattern; if they differ, see if you can understand why. There may be a special problem in your blouse that requires an unusual order of work. Ordinarily the steps given here provide the easiest and fastest method for assembling a sleeveless blouse.

For the purpose of giving instructions simply, we will assume that you have chosen a style that opens down the back. If you have chosen one with a front opening, you should have no trouble in reading "front" for "back" in the steps involving the closing.

BLOUSE BACK

1. Set the machine for basting. Refer to technique 2, "The Sewing Machine." Use the longest stitch. Baste-stitch along fold lines, center back lines, and buttonhole markings to transfer the traced lines to the right side of the blouse.

2. Change the machine setting to about 14 stitches per inch, the size stitch you use for most sewing. Make staylines where indicated on the diagram. Stitch in the direction of the arrows and slightly closer to the edge of the material than the seam line. Refer to technique 9, "Staylines, Interfacings, and Linings," for more detailed instructions.

3. Stitch darts and dart tucks. Match dart lines, pin, and stitch from the wide end of the dart to the point. Clip threads, leaving ends ¼ to ½ inch long or, if you prefer, fasten the stitching line by tying the threads or by retracing. End dart tucks by turning a right angle and stitching across the edge of the fold. This holds the stitching line securely without further fastening. See technique 11, "Darts, Pleats, Tucks, and Gathers."

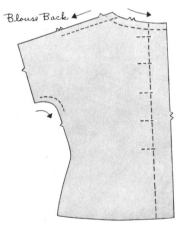

Blouse Back

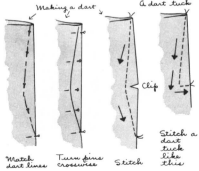

Making a dart   A dart tuck

Clip

Match dart lines   Turn pins crosswise   Stitch   Stitch a dart tuck like this

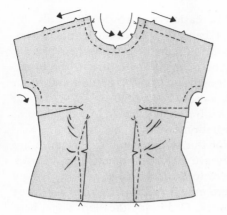

BLOUSE FRONT

1. Make staylines where indicated on the diagram as you did on the back.

2. Stitch darts and dart tucks as you did those on the back.

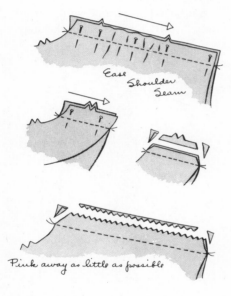

Ease Shoulder Seam

Pink away as little as possible

JOINING SHOULDER SEAMS

1. Pin the shoulder seams with the right sides of the blouse front and blouse back turned together. Match notches, first, then seam ends, and be sure that the stitching lines (not raw edges) match at the neckline. Stitch with the grain—that is, from the neckline outward.

2. Stitch the shoulder seams of the facing as you did those of the blouse.

3. Finish the blouse shoulder seam by pinking or another appropriate method. Trim the shoulder seams of the facing to about ⅜ inch. Then to reduce bulkiness clip away the corners of the seam allowances on seams that have been stitched on both blouse and facings.

Press crease in hem

PRESSING

Press darts, dart tucks, and seam lines. Refer to technique 12, "Pressing," for detailed instructions. Press darts toward center lines or downward. Press seams open, in the direction they were stitched.

FACING THE NECKLINE AND BACK CLOS-
ING

1. Stay-stitch around the unnotched outer edge of the neck facing, ⅛ inch from the raw edge. (This is especially helpful around curved edges.)

2. Edge-stitch the outer facing edge. To do this, fold under and crease the facing barely inside the stayline along its unnotched edge. Stitch on the right side quite close to the fold line.

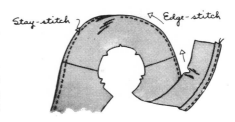

3. To join the neck facing to the blouse, match center lines, notches, and shoulder seams; then pin them together. Stitch in a continuous line around the entire neckline and along each side of the closing. (If your pattern calls for a Peter Pan collar, make and attach it before attaching the facing. See technique 13, "Neck Finishes," for instructions.)

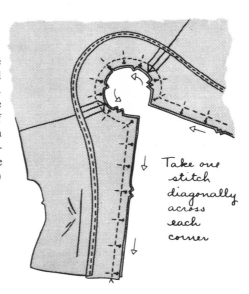

4. Trim seam edges to about ¼ inch in width. Cut away excess material at the corners. Clip partially through the remaining seam edge around the neck at ½ inch intervals. Now turn the facing into position and finger press to shape it. For more details turn to technique 10, "Seams and Seam Finishes," and read about enclosed seams.

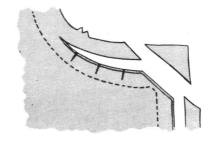

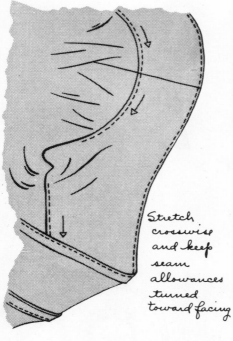

Stretch crosswise and keep seam allowances turned toward facing

5. Under-stitch facing edges to keep the facing from extending beyond the blouse edge. Do this by turning both seam allowances back against the facing; then with the facing side up stitch very near the neck seam through the facing and the seam allowances. Be careful to keep the facing smooth and perfectly shaped as you stitch. Under-stitch, also, along the closing edges where buttons and buttonholes are to be used. (Do not stitch along the lapel of the front closing if it is to be turned back as the blouse is worn.) Under-stitching is particularly helpful on washable and light-weight fabrics. See technique 10, "Seams and Seam Finishes" for other ways to treat enclosed seams.

6. Tack the edge of the neck facing in place by hand at the shoulder seams and perhaps at darts. Use several stitches to make each tack. It is not usually necessary to attach the entire edge of the facing to the blouse by hand, since buttons and buttonholes help to hold it in place.

PRESSING

Press the neckline and closing edges. If your pattern calls for sleeve hems, fold them back along the fold lines and press.

FINISHING THE SLEEVE EDGES

For hemmed sleeves edge-stitch the raw hem edges just as you did the outer edge of the neck facing.

For faced sleeves edge-stitch the un-notched facing edge. Then attach the facing to the sleeve with a plain seam. Under-stitch the facing edge as you did the neck facing, if desired. Press the facing back against the sleeve. (Shaped facings—those with curves or corners—have to be seamed to form a circle; then they are attached after the blouse side seams are made, not before.)

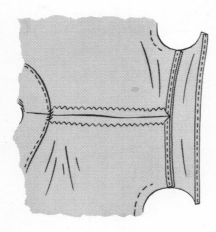

JOINING SIDE SEAMS

Stitch the side seams from the lower edge upward being careful to extend the sleeve hem or facing as you do. (When in doubt as to the fit, baste-stitch the side seams and try the blouse on before you stitch the seams.) Clip the seam allowances at the waistline so the seam can be pressed flat. Curved underarm seams need clipping, too, and always have to be reinforced. One way to do this is to stay-stitch each curve before stitching the seam. Then clip to the stay-line only. *Or,* another way is to baste folded seam binding beneath the curved seam just before it is stitched. Then, with seam binding down, stitch the seam and clip almost across the seam allowances. In either case, finish seam edges and press.

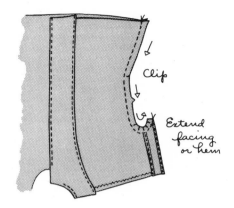

FINISHING THE SLEEVES

Turn the facings or hems under and, after pinning and basting, hand-hem them in place with a vertical hemming stitch. Refer to technique 19, "Hems."

FINISHING THE BOTTOM OF THE BLOUSE

Finish the lower edge of the blouse. Two rows of stitching ¼ inch apart just inside a pinked edge make the flattest finish. Be sure the closing facing is held in place and caught with the lines of stitching.

If you prefer, you may hem the edge. In that case, stitch across the lower facing edge at the time you attach the facing to the blouse, that is, with right sides together. You can still do this if you neglected the step earlier. (Do not hem the faced edge as the resultant bulk might show through a skirt.)

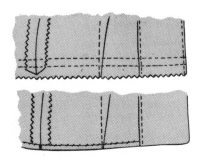

FASTENING

1. Use either machinemade buttonholes or make worked buttonholes by hand. Sew buttons on, being careful to form a shank or stem under each. Turn to technique 18, "Fastenings," for directions.

Button with shank

Worked buttonhole

Snap used with a button

2. When necessary, use either small snaps or tiny, flat buttons and thread loops to hold the upper part of the closing in place. Use snaps or buttons to hold the blouse closing together below the waistline also.

FINAL PRESSING

Press the blouse lightly from the right side. Your blouse is complete. Turn to technique 12, "Pressing," for directions.

PLANNING A SKIRT

As you made your blouse, you learned many techniques that you will use as you make a skirt. We will discuss here only the new things you must know for this garment. In planning a skirt remember that sharp contrasts, wide belts, and bulky effects are excellent for the tall slender girl. The not-so-tall girl who already has adequate or excessive curves will be wise to keep her silhouette streamlined. A slightly flared, gored skirt seems to take away pounds, especially when the blouse color is closely related in value to that of the skirt.

SELECTING A SKIRT PATTERN

For a class that has decided to use one pattern style, a simple, gored skirt is probably the best choice. Different fabrics, colors, and accessories can make it becoming to all figure types. Slender girls may want to use patch pockets to add width and bulk. When wide skirts are in vogue, some of the group may want to use a pattern style cut like the first choice, but with wider gores.

More advanced groups may prefer greater variety in patterns, or want to use materials that require special handling. Remember though that a gored or gathered skirt is easier to construct than one with yokes or pleats. If you do want some pleats, a few unpressed pleats are easier to handle than stitched or pressed pleats all around a skirt. Then, too, skirts cut on rather straight lines are easier to hem than those that are bias-cut or circular. They often require a lining, however. Patch pockets offer fewer problems than inset ones.

While blouse and dress patterns are sold by age or bust measurement, skirt patterns are sold by waist measurement. The chart on the next page gives the hip measurement for each waist size.

Waist	24	26	28	30	32	34	36	38½	41
Hips	33	36	38	40	42	44	46	48	50

Patterns for flared or full skirts should always be bought to fit your waist. However, for closely fitted, narrow skirts, your hip measurement is the more important one. Be sure your pattern is large enough to fit your hips—particularly if your hips are large in relation to your waist.

SELECTING MATERIAL FOR A SKIRT

Your choice of fabric should depend upon the season of the year, your experience in handling materials, and the design of the pattern, as well as upon your wardrobe needs. We think of cotton and linens as summer fabrics; of wools as winter materials; while acetates, rayons, and silks seem suitable the year around. These classifications are far from rigid. Dark cottons, cotton tweeds, and cotton suitings are often used for winter wear. Velveteen, a cotton fabric, is rarely used in summer, except in small amounts. Tropical worsteds and other lightweight wools make excellent skirts for fall, winter, or spring, and can sometimes be worn in the summer. In warmer climates, cottons in any color are worn in all seasons. Synthetics vary so much that there are some for every season.

Skirts are generally but not always made of materials that are somewhat heavier than those used for blouses. Consider the lines of the skirt as you choose the fabric:

Slim skirts retain their clear-cut, tubular lines best when made of firm, slightly heavy, resilient (springy) cloth. Wools and crush-resistant materials are excellent choices. Avoid flimsy, limp materials and those that pull at the seams.

Circular skirts should be made of materials that do not sag appreciably. Chintz, taffeta, faille, permanently starched materials, and other firm fabrics are excellent choices. Avoid jerseys, crepes, and fabrics that do not hold their shape well.

Flared skirts cut with numerous gores can be made of almost any fabric. The texture and the width of the skirt will determine the silhouette.

Skirts with pressed pleats are often made of wool, Acrilan, or Orlon, because these all hold creases well. Edge-stitched pleats are sometimes used on materials that resist creasing or that lose a crease easily.

Skirts with unpressed pleats look best in materials that are soft but have enough body and weight to fall in graceful folds. The cloth should not crease easily. Wool crepe, jersey, cotton suiting, ratiné, wool flannel, and some synthetics have the right textures for unpressed pleats.

Gathered skirts should be made of soft materials for a fairly slender effect, and of crisp or slightly stiff materials for a bouffant effect. All crepes gather well, as do most mediumweight cottons. Taffeta, shantung, and crisp cottons gather well, too, but give a wider silhouette.

These are just general suggestions, and you should test any material before deciding to use it for a particular pattern. Hold the material in folds or gathers to see how it falls. Press a sample into pleats, when these appear in your pattern. Pull the material on the bias or allow it to hang diagonally to test its tendency to stretch and sag. Until you have had quite a bit of sewing experience, you should avoid using velveteen, plaids, soft materials that do not hold their shape well, and other fabrics that are difficult to handle.

When you have decided on a material, refer to the chart on the back of the pattern envelope, as you did when you made the blouse, to see how much material you will need. You are more likely to be using material "with nap" this time, which means more material and a different pattern layout. Refer to technique 7, "Laying the Pattern on the Cloth."

Buy extra material if the fabric is likely to shrink, has designs that must be matched, or is off-grain so that several inches will be lost when you straighten it. Allow extra fabric, also, if you are taller than average or wear your skirts long. Buy slightly less material if you are short, or wear your skirts short. Beware of buying too little cloth, though, because having to skimp on material can cause you much trouble.

OTHER SUPPLIES AND NOTIONS

Thread. Mercerized cotton, size 50, may be used for any fabric except a very glossy one. Silk thread is stronger than cotton but is suitable only for garments that are to be dry-cleaned. Nylon and Dacron threads are strong but should be used only on synthetics since they may melt at regular pressing temperatures. Also, they are so elastic that seams sewn with them are likely to pucker and, in hand sewing, they are apt to twist and knot.

Zipper. Skirt placket zippers are 7 or 9 inches long and should match or blend with the color of the fabric. Be sure to select a skirt zipper that opens at the top and not a side seam dress zipper that is closed at the top.

Hooks and eyes, buttons, snaps. Either hooks and eyes or buttons are used to fasten the waistband above the zipper placket. Select black hooks and eyes for dark materials and bright metal-finished ones for light fabrics. Sizes 2 or 3 would be right for this purpose. Should you prefer to use a button, select one that is flat, of medium size, and of course, washable if the skirt is washable.

Whichever kind of fastener you use, you will need another type also—a snap or two to help hold the waistband in place. Again use black for a dark material and bright metal for a light one. The size of these snaps would be 2-0 or 3-0.

Interfacing. A lengthwise strip of muslin or tailor's canvas will be needed if the waistband is not firm without it.

Binding. Rayon ribbon seam binding gives a neat finish to hems of skirts that will be dry-cleaned. It is not essential unless the material ravels easily.

Lining. Some skirts require linings. Refer to technique 9, "Staylines, Interfacings, and Linings," for kinds and ways to attach them.

MAKING A SKIRT

Follow the general plan you used in making your blouse. Refer to other parts of the book for more detailed information wherever references are indicated.

Preparing the material. Straighten, remove wrinkles, and shrink the material as necessary. You learned how to prepare washable materials as you made your blouse, so if your skirt is cotton too, you know how to proceed. Wool and other fabrics are treated somewhat differently from cotton. To begin with, it is difficult to pull yarns in many wool materials. First try to tear the material. If you cannot, ask a classmate to help you. You will each grasp a selvage very close to the cut end of the material and stretch the material crosswise. Shift the position of your fingers until you find the line where the material stretches least. That will be along a crosswise thread. Each of you insert a pin where your fingers were. Fold back the edge of the material between these points and cut along the fold. Do this at each end of the cloth.

To "square up" or restore the right-angle structure of wool and similar materials, a thorough steam pressing may be the answer. At the same time the pressing removes wrinkles and is a satisfactory method for shrinking many fabrics that require dry-cleaning rather than washing. Note that you press on the bias toward the short corner to straighten cloth, instead of with the grain as usual. You will find instructions for steam pressing with and without a steam iron in technique 12, "Pressing."

When pressing alone does not give the results you want, there is still another method for straightening grain lines and shrinking the cloth. Sponging is particularly suitable for wool cloth. You will find instructions for this method in technique 6, "Materials that Require Special Handling."

Preparing the pattern. Study the pattern and select the pattern pieces that you need for the skirt you expect to make. Then check the fit of the skirt and make whatever alterations you need. If the pattern size was chosen carefully and your figure is fairly regular, you should have to do nothing but lengthen or shorten the skirt. For the sake of safety, however, add an extra ½ inch along the *side* seam lines—not elsewhere. These wide seam allowances will allow for minor alterations during fitting. They also provide material for making a placket and for future alterations. Refer to technique 5, "Altering the Pattern and Fitting the Garment."

Laying the pattern on the cloth. If you have any difficulty placing the pattern on the cloth, refer to technique 7, "Laying the Pattern on the Cloth." For designed and napped materials, refer to the same technique.

Cutting out the skirt and marking construction details. Cut out the pieces as you did the blouse. Mark with tracing paper and a tracing wheel, if traced lines will show on your cloth. Otherwise use tailor's tacks.

Mark all construction details, such as darts, pleats, gathers, pocket positions, the end of the placket, fold lines, center lines, and seam lines. If you prefer, you can leave the vertical seam lines unmarked except along the placket, and plan to use a stitching guide to keep seam lines straight.

Constructing the skirt. To make sure that you will join the correct sections, lay the gores side-by-side before removing the pattern from them. Place them in order from the center front to the center back, matching notches.

Next, separate the gores into two groups—one composed of the front gores, the other of the back ones. If there are to be seams down the center front and center back, turn the pattern back and pin those seams together right sides facing. Remove the pattern as you get ready to sew. Follow these steps:

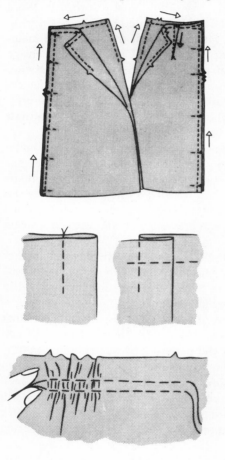

SKIRT BACK AND FRONT

1. Make staylines at the waistline and along side seams through the hip area. Stitch these about ⅜ to ½ inch from the cut edges on the extra wide side seam allowances the same as you do on other seams. This will make the staylines further from the stitching line than usual, but will save you from having to rip them out if you have to let the skirt out later. Stitch in the directions shown on the diagram, or with the grain.

2. Stitch center front and back seams. Sew from hem edge toward waistline.

3. Make darts.

4. When unpressed pleats are shown, baste-stitch along the pleat lines from the wrong side. After folding the pleats in the direction they are supposed to turn, stitch across the top of the pleat in the waistline seam allowances. Remove basting after attaching waistband.

When gathers are to be made, use machine gathering stitches between gathering marks. Stitch on the seam line or very near it and again ¼ inch away in the seam allowance. Refer to technique 11, "Darts, Pleats, Tucks, and Gathers," for instruction.

5. Join any remaining front gores to each side of the center section. Stitch from the hem upward. Join all back gores in the same way.

6. Finish seams by pinking or other means.

7. Press seams and darts. The general rule is to press darts toward the center and press seams open. Always press pleats in the direction they are to turn. Unpressed pleats are not pressed, of course.

POCKETS

Make and attach pockets if they are used. See technique 15, "Pockets."

JOINING SIDE SEAMS

1. Baste-stitch the side seams together, leaving the placket open above the placket marking.

2. Try on the skirt and the waistband to make sure of their fit. Make any necessary changes in darts and along the side seams. Refer to technique 5, "Altering the Pattern and Fitting the Garment." Then check the waistband length.

3. Stitch the right side seam, and then the left side seam up to the marking at the lower end of the placket. At that point fasten the line of stitching by retracing or by tying the thread ends.

ZIPPER

These instructions are for a slot placket. If you would prefer a placket with one overlapping edge, see technique 17, "Plackets." On materials that ravel at all, finish placket edges with seam binding before you start, or plan to overcast them later. Ravelings can play havoc with a zipper.

1. Baste-stitch the placket edges together as a continuation of the left side seam.

2. Press the seam open.

3. Turn the skirt right side out and place the zipper beneath the basted seam. Work with the zipper closed, right side up, and, of course, the pull at the top. Caution: place the top of the metal ⅛ inch below the waistline seam line—this will be about ¾ inch from the cut edge of that seam. Center the zipper so that the basted seam goes right down its middle. Be sure that the placket opening extends about ⅛ inch below the bottom of the zipper to prevent the zipper, as it is worked up and down, from catching the material at the end of the placket.

4. From the right side pin the zipper in place, pushing pins beneath the metal and as close to it as possible on both sides. Baste firmly by hand along each side of the zipper, then remove the pins. (You cannot stitch over pins with a zipper foot.)

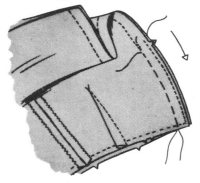

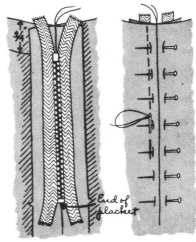

Wrong side   Right side

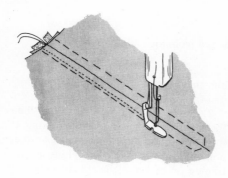

5. Stitch with the zipper foot attachment—the foot with just one prong, the left one. Stitch as a continuous seam. At the bottom be careful to go beyond the metal portion of the zipper before you pivot to stitch across the end and up the other side. Stitching should be ¼ inch from the seam line on each side.

6. Remove all bastings—both machine and hand.

WAISTBAND

If your waistband length needs adjusting, refer to technique 16, "Waistlines." Then, of course, you won't match notches as you join the waistband to the skirt.

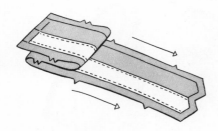

1. Cut an interfacing as long as the waistband and as wide as the distance from the fold line to the seam line of the waistband. That's the finished waistband width.

2. Pin this interfacing to the wrong side of the inside of the waistband. The inside is the side next to you as you wear the skirt.

3. With the interfacing up to guide you, stitch along each of its lengthwise edges to fasten it permanently to the waistband. Start stitching from the same end both times.

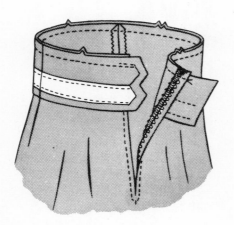

4. Now turn the waistband around and work with the side that will be away from you as you wear the skirt—the side without the interfacing. With notches and center lines matched, pin and stitch waistband to skirt, right side to right side. You may have to clip the waistline seam allowance on the skirt to make it fit the waistband.

5. Fold the waistband along its fold line, but with the right sides of the fabric facing each other. Pin raw edges together at each end.

6. Stitch the ends of the waistband. Follow the traced stitching line especially carefully around the overlap if it is pointed.

7. Trim the seams. At the ends of the waistband, trim seams to about ⅛ inch or in heavy material, layer them—that is cut one narrower than the other to keep them from being bulky. At the seam joining the waistband to the skirt, leave at least ⅜ inch seam allowance because of the strain imposed by the weight of the skirt. If your overlap is pointed, snip away most of the seam allowance at the point.

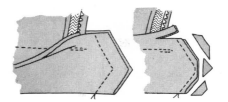

8. Turn the waistband right side out, then shape and press its ends. Also press the waistline seam edges up into the waistband, stretching crosswise slightly as you press.

9. Trim the unattached edge of the inside waistband so that its seam allowance is just ¼ inch. Turn the edge under and press along the fold or baste to keep the raw edge turned under.

10. Lay the skirt on a flat surface and pin the inside of the waistband to the stitching line. Match center lines. Check to see that no diagonal wrinkles appear in the waistband. If they do, shift the loose edge until they disappear. Baste and remove pins.

11. Hem the folded edge to the stitching line with slant hemming stitches, being careful to hide the stitches in the waistband. (If you do not know how to make slant hemming stitches, refer to technique 19, "Hems.")

Put over ironing board to pin

HOOKS AND EYES ON WAISTBAND

For the fastening given here, use 2 hooks with round eyes rather than straight ones. If you prefer, you may use a button and buttonhole instead.

1. Start with a round eye. Hold it on the under side of the underlapping edge near a corner with about half the eye projecting beyond end of waistband.

2. After fastening the thread inconspicuously, sew down first one loop end, then the other. When going from one loop to another, slip the needle between the layers of fabric to prevent long floating threads.

3. Make several stitches across each side of the eye just outside the loop ends to hold the eye against the cloth. This time they go on top of each other. Fasten the thread securely.

4. Now insert the hook in the eye with the hook itself turned toward the inside of the waistband.

5. Pin the waistband together, overlapping it as it will be worn. Then, with the hook and eye still fastened, sew the loops of the hook to the underside of the overlap. Allow the stitches to go through only one layer of the fabric so that they will be hidden from the right side of the garment.

6. Separate the hook and eye and slip the needle between the layers of fabric to come up beside the tip of the hook. Sew this to the garment and fasten the thread securely.

7. Sew the other hook and eye on to secure the other corner of the overlapping edge.

Wrong side

SNAPS ON WAISTBAND

One snap will do if the overlap is pointed, but you will need 2 snaps for a straight overlapping edge.

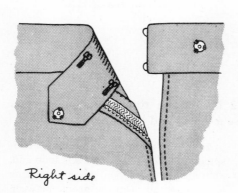

Right side

1. Sew the ball part of a snap onto the under side of the overlap about ⅛ inch from the point or one corner. Slip the needle into the cloth between holes.

2. Rub chalk on the ball part of the snap you have just attached. Fasten the hooks and eyes, then press the ball of the snap against the underlap.

3. Sew the socket half of the snap on top of the chalk mark. Go through both layers of cloth for added strength.

4. Sew on another snap if it is needed.

HEM

1. Try the skirt on and ask a classmate to turn the hem up roughly to help you determine the best length. Skirts that are even can be hemmed either on the line marked on your pattern or on a parallel line. For skirts that are uneven, your classmate will need to let the skirt down and mark the hemline all the way around the skirt after you have decided on a distance from the floor. See technique 19, "Hems," for more detailed instructions about marking uneven hems.

2. Take off the skirt and fold the hem over on the marked line. Put pins in at right angles to the hemline and enough above it so that you can press the fold. Adjust the pins slightly as necessary to obtain a smooth flowing curve at the fold.

3. Press the hem fold and shrink out as much fullness in the hem as possible. Remove pins. Then shrink by gliding the iron from the hem fold toward the cut edge.

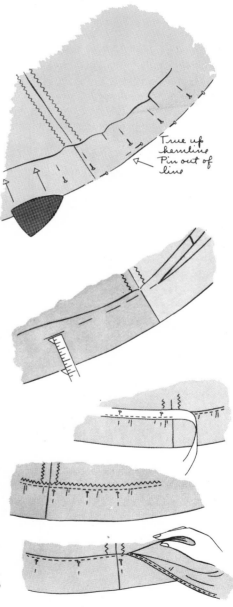

True up hemline
Pin out of line

4. Using a gauge, trim the hem to an even width. A straight skirt should have a 2½ inch hem. One and three-fourths inches is usually as wide as you can allow for a circular skirt.

5. Finish the raw edge. For a skirt that will be dry-cleaned, either pink it if the material is firm or sew on seam binding if the material is likely to ravel. If you couldn't shrink out most of the fullness, you will have to adjust it with a line of gathering. Always gather before putting on the seam binding. On a skirt that will be washed, don't use rayon seam binding. Edge-stitching provides a sturdier finish.

6. Pin and baste the hem in place. Lay the skirt flat on the table to keep your work accurate.

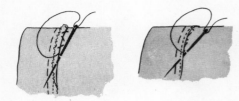

7. Hand-stitch the hem to the skirt. If the edge is pinked or finished with seam binding, use an invisible hemming stitch. If the edge is turned under and stitched, a vertical hemming stitch is easier to make. Refer to technique 19, "Hems," for more detailed instructions.

FINAL PRESSING

Press the hem from the wrong side. Then give the skirt a light over-all pressing from the right side. Press in the direction of the grain rather than on a bias. Use a press cloth on the right side if the iron would make it shiny.

PART II   *DESIGN*

CHAPTER 6 ·· ART IN DRESS

Some people have the idea that ART includes only such things as a painting that hangs on the wall, a beautiful church, or a statue in the city park. "Dress" is also an important art—and it always has been. There is art in the clothing which the Greeks designed two thousand years ago, in the jewelry and beaded moccasins of our American Indians, and in the fabric design of the primitive Fiji Islanders. Every article of clothing is the personal art expression of a people who created it. In addition to satisfying a specific need for body protection or decoration, each article reflects their feeling for suitability of design and their skill as craftsmen.

These are the basic standards by which we judge the art quality of clothing, whether it was created two thousand years ago, two hundred years ago, or today. A girl is artistically dressed when her costume is appropriate for a specific "need" or activity, when the various articles in her costume are nicely related and becoming in design, and when they are beautifully made.

FROM PAST TO PRESENT

Although these basic art standards have not changed with the centuries, we know that fashions have changed. Year by year, even season by season, some "new look" makes its appearance. Yet, is it so new? The well-worn phrase, "There is nothing new under the sun," certainly applies to fashions.

Fashion revivals. It is fun to compare the style of dresses that you see in old photograph albums, historic costume books, movies, and famous old portraits. You will often find that contemporary styles repeat certain features of some past mode of dress. For example, when the Gibson Girl shirtwaists and skirts staged a comeback, the girls who wore them looked very much as their grandmothers did at the turn of the century.

Fashions do have a way of repeating themselves because designers often refer to the past when searching for "new" ideas. They may use only one detail, such as the cut of a sleeve or the treatment of a neckline. Or they may borrow the entire silhouette. Throughout the years fashions have revolved around three basic silhouettes: (1) tubular, (2) bell, and (3) back fullness. Of course each has included many variations.

The tubular silhouette's basic feature is a narrow skirt. Some are pencil slim while others flare slightly at the hem.

The bell silhouette is full-skirted. There are really two kinds: (a) the rounded bell in which skirt fullness falls in gathers from the waist or hips and

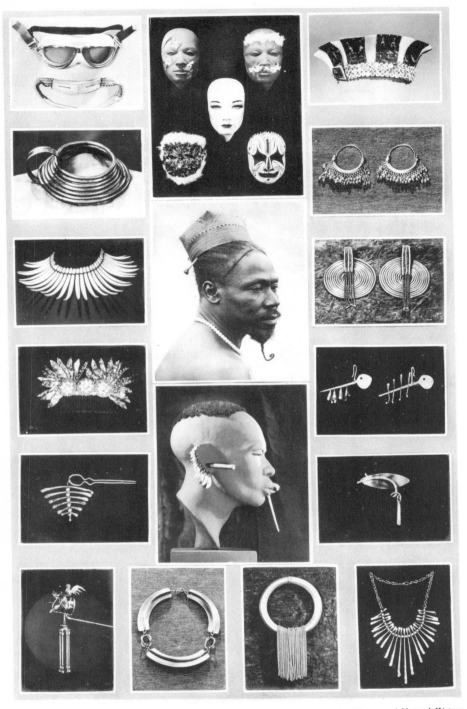

Museum of Natural History

Costume jewelry in a museum display shows that many of our modern designs have been inspired by jewelry from far away and long ago. Here the modern work is intermingled with decorative accessories from all over the world.

Modern Miss

Designers get ideas from national costumes. The Danish man's striped jerkin at left is almost literally translated in the girl's sport blouse above. Aprons such as the one at the right have been part of Dutch folk costumes for hundreds of years. The apron idea inspired the dress below.

(*b*) the cone-shaped bell in which a gored skirt flares from a fitted waist to extreme width at the hem.

The back fullness silhouette includes many variations of hip draping, bustles, and other "back interest."

Long ago when fashions changed slowly, a certain silhouette remained in vogue for many years. Now, with mass production and increased buying power, fashions change rapidly and each season may include several silhouettes. The fashions of the twentieth century have been basically tubular, but designers have introduced variations of other silhouettes from time to time.

The basic silhouettes tubular . . . bell . . . back fullness.

Sometimes a "big event" will bring about a fashion revival. In the spring of 1948 many designs were based on medieval styles of the fourteenth, fifteenth, and sixteenth centuries. How did that come about? At that time a wonderful collection of medieval French tapestries was exhibited in a few of our large cities. The long, flowing lines of the costumes depicted in those tapestries appealed to our designers.

But designers go back even farther than that in search of new ideas. Sometimes they are inspired by the costumes of ancient Egypt; at other times by those of ancient Greece. For example, the Greek sandal has been copied for many of our evening and play sandals.

National costumes. Often the contemporary costumes of people living in distant lands can be adapted to our specific needs. It may be an idea for the cut of a coat or dress; it may be an inspiration for headgear, belts, or other accessories; or it may be some decorative detail or fabric design.

We have worn hats and negligees that were patterned after the clothing of the Chinese coolies. We have seen dresses and coats that resembled Chinese mandarin coats. Ancient Chinese motifs have appeared on our boudoir slippers, on buttons, and in fabric designs.

At some time or other we have worn the boleros, the full skirts, and the mantillas of the Spanish peoples. And think of the fabric designs that are based on Mexican and South American motifs—cactus plants, donkeys, pueblos, pottery, and ancient Indian symbols.

The head kerchief that you wear has been worn by European peasants for centuries. Yet it did not become popular here until the late 'thirties. The hood of your raincoat or winter coat is patterned after the cowl of the monk's habit.

We could go on and on citing other examples, but perhaps you are convinced that the art of the past—the art of many peoples in many lands—contributes to our designs today. Fashions truly practice the "One World" creed.

Modern adaptations. It is obvious that our contemporary designs cannot be exact duplicates of any period or national costumes. If they were, we would look like so many masqueraders on parade! Designers borrow ideas insofar as they are practical for our modern needs.

You could not possibly wear the wide hoop skirt of Civil War days in crowded classrooms, busy offices, or in bus and subway jams. But you can wear modified adaptations of it at parties and dances.

Your mother would not like to shop or go calling in a cumbersome bustle and dragging train that was worn by a lady in the 'eighties. Yet a mild version of the back-fullness style is perfectly possible.

Most such period adaptations are found in designs for dressy afternoon or evening clothes. Adaptations of the more simple national or peasant costumes are more likely to be found in simple daytime or play clothes.

Whether our daytime and play clothes are adaptations or not, we can be sure that they are suited to the activities of this modern age. The girls and women of today are active. They are not the "sit-at-home" type of yesteryear. Think of yourself, for instance. You go to school, you participate in several sports, you help with the housework, and perhaps you even have a week-end job. As a result of such an active schedule, you want clothes in which you can comfortably work and play. Pinching 16-inch waistlines, bulky bustles, or expansive hoop skirts are not for you! You want clothing that is designed to suit the *functions* and *natural structure* of the body. In other words, the active girl or woman of today needs clothing that is truly functional in design—clothing that is suited to a specific activity—whether it is for work or play.

For example, the business girl knows that she can "function" best and look smartest in tailored suits, trim dressmaker styles, and simple classics. The exaggerated styles—bell skirts, extreme flares, and intricate back fullness—are saved for her dress-up occasions. They are not suited for working functions. Then, when she goes skiing, bicycling, skating, or swimming, she again finds just the right togs for her favorite sport. Each is functional in design.

By contrast the sports clothes of the past seem horribly cumbersome to us today. Girls of the 1860's actually appeared on skating rinks in hoop skirts that were raised by an elevator contraption to permit them to take a turn or two on the ice. Even as late as 1909 the fashionable skating costume consisted of an ankle-length street ensemble complete with hat, muff, and fur piece. Girls of

Museum of Natural History

In every age and every country people have used line and shape to fashion distinctive headgear. These hats come from Tibet, Africa, Mongolia, Siberia, the Philippines, Alaska, and New York.

the "gay nineties" went bicycling in long, full skirts. At the turn of the century girls tried to play tennis in long, swishing skirts and tight collars. And the poor dears tried to swim in long tunic blouses with elbow-length sleeves. Matching knee-length drawers and dark stockings went with the costume! All in all, aren't you glad you live today?

Costumes from our own past are adapted for modern use too.

YOUR PERSONAL DESIGN

Up to this point we have been taking a very broad view of clothing as a universal art. But clothing is also an art which every single individual can practice. Actually clothing is the most personal of all arts because it has to do with us directly. We are creating harmony and beauty in our appearance. *Art is harmony, fitness, and beauty.* So remember, each time that you plan an attractive costume, you are an artist creating a harmonious design. Each time that you succeed, your appearance reflects your good taste.

When a girl dresses attractively, you hear comments like: "She's always so well dressed" or "She has such good taste." These two comments should be combined . . . "She's well dressed because she has good taste."

Just what is good taste? Are people born with it? Are there certain rules about it? And last but not least, is it possible to acquire it?

First of all, good taste involves correct selection. This applies to every single article you buy or make—a dress, hat, scarf, jewelry, lampshade, or wastebasket. It is a matter of judging and selecting the good from the not-so-good.

In the second place, good taste involves the pleasing combination or arrangement of articles. That, too, applies to everything. It may be seen in the plan of a charming room, in the setting of a table, and, of course, in the various items that are used in the complete costume. Just one inappropriate item can spoil a costume. For example, let us say that a girl is all dressed up for an "extra special" occasion. She takes one last look in the mirror. She has a sneaking feeling that something strikes a wrong note. Perhaps it is that floral, figured scarf with her plaid coat. She decides to experiment . . . off comes the scarf. Then she replaces it with one of a solid color. That does the trick—the "noisy" effect disappears.

Sometimes you hear the remark that a person has instinctive good taste. In other words, she was born with it. To a certain extent that may be true. Just as one of your classmates naturally takes to music and another to poetry, the girl with instinctive taste is naturally more sensitive to fine qualities of design. She has that inborn "clothes sense" that tells her when an item is pleasing in design and appropriate in every respect. For instance, the girl who substituted a scarf of solid color for the scarf of floral design somehow *felt* that plaids and flowers should not "keep company" in the same costume.

To sum it up, good taste is a feeling for good design. It underlies all forms of creative art. It is based on fine artistic judgment. Everyone may not be born with it, but it is something that anyone can develop through study and observation.

First, you should try to develop that critical "sense" that will help you to tell at a glance whether an article or a complete costume is a pleasing design. If it happens to have some "trouble spots," your practiced eye will enable you to suggest an improvement. This critical analysis should take place whether you are buying or making a coat or a kerchief—a dress or a "doo-dad"!

Think of the times that you are undecided when selecting something in a store or in a pattern book. There are so many styles from which to choose.

How would you like to have to dress like this to go for a drive?

Celanese Corporation of America

First you want one thing—then another. You really do not know which is best. Perhaps your mother helps you to decide, but a time will come when you have to decide for yourself. That is why you should learn now to form your own basis for judgment. From now on you are the artist and the design is you!

DESIGN ANALYSIS

At this point we shall merely give a brief description of the *elements* and *principles* of design that will serve as an outline to the following chapters.

Like any other artist you will be combining (1) lines, (2) shapes, (3) textures, (4) colors, and (5) values. These are the ingredients, or *elements,* of any design. They are found in every form—in a building, in a piece of furniture, in a vase, and in every single article you wear or carry—a dress, a hat, a bag, or a shoe. And, of course, your entire costume is a combination of these elements. Let us identify them in the costume on page 99.

It is obvious that different *lines* define the various *shapes* in this costume. *Curved* lines outline the shoulders, the slightly rounded sleeves, the collar, the choker beads, and buttons. The pillbox conforms to the curves of the head. *Straight* lines are seen in the vertical closing of the jacket, in the tapering side seams of the jacket, in the horizontal band which creates a yoke effect, and in the hemline of the jacket. The skirt follows the hip curve and then tapers to the hem of the slim, straight skirt.

The *texture* of the suit is smooth, rayon-and-acetate flannel; the pillbox is firm, wool felt; the gloves are soft, dull-finished suede; the bag is of semi-glossy leather; the choker beads add a shiny accent. In each case, texture describes the appearance and "feel" of the material.

The *color* of the suit and hat is beige; the bag (and shoes, not shown) are British tan; the gloves are a creamy, egg-shell.

The suit, hat, bag, and beads are of a medium *value;* the gloves are of a light value.

Similarly you can describe any article about you. In fact, your own body includes every single one of these elements. You most certainly have line and shape! And your skin, hair, and eyes have definite texture, color, and varying values of light and dark. So you see how your entire body becomes the basis for your personal design. As a designer you will want to know what lines and shapes are flattering to your figure. You will want to know how to combine values, colors, and textures into an attractive costume that is becoming to you. And to do all of that you will need a few helpful guideposts.

This is where the principles of design come in. They will help you to achieve *harmony* in your costume. The principles of (1) unity, (2) dominance, (3) contrast, (4) proportion, (5) balance, and (6) rhythm apply to the assembling of an entire costume as well as to the combination of elements in a single item.

A design has *unity* when all lines, shapes, textures, colors, and values seem to belong together. No line or color strikes the wrong note because every element is an essential part of the design; nothing is superfluous. Each element should express a similar idea to give the design a well-related quality—a feeling of "oneness" or "completeness."

Landshoff: Reprinted from Mademoiselle;
© *Street & Smith Publications, Inc., 1959*

The elements of design in this outfit are analyzed on page 98.

The principle of *dominance* works hand-in-hand with the principle of unity to create this well-related effect. When one type of line, shape, value, color, and texture is allowed to dominate in a design, the design appears unified. It is not a hodgepodge of many lines, colors, and so on. In addition, a successful design allows one style note to dominate so that there is no "see-sawing" between points of interest or emphasis. There should never be a competition for interest between various parts of a design. For example, if the neckline is to be the dominating style feature of a dress, the effect should not be spoiled by an unusual treatment of the hemline, an elaborate belt, or tricky cuffs. They should be kept subordinate to the main feature. The same is true of accessories. If the neck and head area are to be emphasized with a colorful scarf or an unusual necklace, it should dominate other notes of color or jewelry that appear elsewhere on the figure. If a person wears a strand of pearls, a lapel pin, a fancy barrette, and a collection of rings and bracelets, she confuses her costume with too many points of interest.

The principle of *contrast* prevents monotony in a design. A contrasting line, value, color, or texture adds interest to a design. Care should be taken, however, to introduce contrasting elements that are similar enough to be pleasingly related. A sheer white batiste blouse trimmed with frilly lace would certainly contrast with a brown corduroy sport skirt, but would there be any relationship in style or texture? A light-colored tailored blouse of plain heavy cotton, rayon, or flannel would be nicely related to the corduroy skirt, yet it would offer pleasing contrast in both value and texture. A felt hat of vivid green is a definite color contrast to a flannel suit of pale pink, but it is too harsh a contrast to be a pleasing combination. A hat of dark brown or medium-dark soft blue would offer contrast and be nicely related to the pink suit.

A contrasting line, texture, value, or color is also used to direct emphasis to the dominating point of interest in a design. A note of contrast creates an accent. A dash of color, the glisten of metal, or light against dark will attract attention. Let one such note of contrast dominate. If they are used haphazardly the costume looks confused.

The principle of *proportion* concerns the relationship that exists between shapes, sizes, and amounts in a design. First, the design of every garment should be related to the structure and proportions of the body. Second, every article in the costume should be in *scale* with the figure—no top-heavy hats, enormous bags, or huge prints for the tiny miss, for example. Third, a design is more pleasing when unequal amounts of color or value are used. Equal amounts of anything produce monotony.

The principle of *balance* controls the placement of lines and shapes and the distribution of values and colors in a design to prevent top-heavy or lopsided effects.

The principle of *rhythm* controls the "eye movement" in a design. It refers to the way in which our eyes survey the design as a whole. When lines, shapes, textures, values, and colors are well organized, the eye movement is smooth. The eyes do not jump from spot to spot.

These, then, are the principles of design that help one to achieve harmony among the elements of a design. Using them as a yardstick of good taste, let us compare the costumes below.

In looking at the one on the left you might say, "No one would wear an out-fit like that." Unfortunately, too many do! In recent years, when short toppers have been so popular, many girls and women have been careless as to what they wore with them. But let us see *why* this costume is so unbecoming.

When a flaring skirt is worn with a hip-length flaring coat, the silhouette is monotonous because there is no contrast in lines or shapes. Such an arrange-ment of shapes produces a squatty, tentlike silhouette that drags your eye to the ground. Then the value scheme in this outfit is extremely confused because

The well-dressed girl displays her good taste.

both topper and dress are figured: one is plaid, the other floral. That in itself is a crime against good taste! Each fabric includes dark, medium, and light values and as many colors. It is a hodgepodge of unrelated fabric designs, mixed values, and colors. No single thing dominates. The only bit of relief is found in the solid color of the brown shoes and derby. Although this style of hat goes well with the topper, it is too severe in design to look well with the floral print. (But to wear this dress with this coat is out of the question if one is to be well dressed!) This costume could be vastly improved by one substitu-tion—a tubular, dark, solid-colored skirt should be worn. That would intro-duce the necessary contrast in silhouette and fabric. Only then would the attractive plaid coat dominate the design. The dark skirt, shoes, and hat would serve as controlling accents.

By now you should appreciate the fine design qualities of the costume that the girl on the right is wearing. You can see what a pleasing contrast the narrow skirt is to the flaring topper. The figure looks taller because the vertical lines of the tubular skirt lead the eye upward rather than downward as in the costume on the left. The proportion of the skirt to the coat is pleasing because they are unequal in both size and shape. The topper is the dominating item. The value scheme in the costume on the right is attractive and simple. The dominating light value is centered on the upper part of the figure. The darker value of the skirt and shoes brings a feeling of balance or stability to the figure. Although dark accents are repeated in the gloves and hat, they do not destroy the unity of the costume. In fact, such repetition unifies or holds the costume together because the eye moves rhythmically over the entire figure. The dark hat carries an accent of a contrasting light value, thus directing interest to the head area.

Perhaps this brief introductory analysis has shown you how the principles of art can be applied to the assembling of a harmonious costume. In the following chapters we shall deal with line and shape, texture, color, and value combinations in greater detail. When we apply the yardstick of good taste to single garments, you will learn that each well-chosen article adds to the success of your personal design.

ACTIVITIES

For the class

1. **Make a study** of historical costumes and accessories. Visit an art museum (if possible) to observe costumes pictured in old portraits. Some museums have rare collections of actual costumes on display. Study historical styles in costume books and in old photograph albums. Make a note to see any historical movies that may be showing.
2. **Organize** a costume exhibit in your classroom. Bring in items that have been stored away in family trunks and attics. Collect old photographs and reproductions of old portraits to mount on the bulletin board.

For the individual

1. **Choose** a costume from any period in which you see one or more distinct features that have been used as source material for the design of a contemporary garment. The feature may be a neckline, a shoulder treatment, a sleeve, a bodice opening, or a skirt style. Make a careful pencil tracing of the period costume and mount on manila paper. On an accompanying sheet, mount the illustration of the contemporary adaptation and give your reasons for believing that it has a kinship to the period costume.
2. **Design** a dress, suit, or blouse that is an adaptation of some traditional national costume such as Chinese, Mexican, Polish, Swedish, or any other you wish. Mount your sketch with an illustration of the national costume. Make a tracing of the latter if it cannot be mounted.

CHAPTER 7

LINE AND SHAPE

As you page through a fashion magazine or look at clothes in stores and shop windows do you ever wonder *why* one garment looks smart while another lacks "style"? Perhaps the basic cut annoys you, or the trimming appears excessive. Then, there are the clothes that look stunning on fashion figures in photographs, or on your best friend, but when *you* put them on, they don't look right on you!

This means that a garment must be judged in two ways. First, it should have fine design qualities; next, it should be nicely related to the figure. As a rule, however, *simple* styles, cut on good basic lines, look well on most figures. Troubles usually occur when a girl selects an exaggerated style or a garment with excessive, "gingerbread" trimming.

ANALYSIS OF LINE AND SHAPE

If good basic lines are the key to fine styling, you will want to learn how to analyze the "line arrangement" of a garment design. You may never have thought of a dress or coat as an arrangement of lines and shapes. Yet these two elements together create the pattern or plan of every design. For example, a gored skirt with an extreme flare forms a triangular shape that is defined by slanting lines. A puffed sleeve that is circular in shape is defined by curving lines. A square patch pocket is defined by vertical and horizontal lines. Every decorative detail and every article which you wear or carry are a combination of lines and shapes.

Types of line. Although all lines are either straight or curved, they create different effects depending on their direction. Lines can even create a mood. For example, in a trim, boxy suit, a girl can actually appear and *feel* very different than she does when she wears a ruffly, bouffant net evening dress.

Vertical lines stress an up-and-down movement, so they usually emphasize height. When verticals dominate a design, the effect is likely to be rather severe, dignified, or reserved.

Horizontal lines stress a side-to-side movement. When horizontals dominate a design, they tend to create an illusion of width. Because they repeat the ground line, they also tend to give a placid, stable effect.

Oblique lines increase or decrease width and height, depending upon the degree and direction of the angle. When oblique lines dominate a design, they tend to create an active, startling, or dramatic effect.

Curved lines can be long and flowing, large and full, or small and puffy. Long, flowing curves are the most rhythmic and graceful of all lines. Large,

The four kinds of lines and the effects they create.

Vertical

Horizontal

Oblique

Curved

rounded curves lend a dramatic air to a costume and tend to exaggerate size. Tiny, puffy curves are gay and definitely youthful.

Function of line. These, then, are the lines that are found in garment designs. In the outer or "silhouette" shape, skirts can be straight and slim, flaring and triangular, or rounded and full. Shoulder lines can be puffed, sloping, or squared. Waistlines can go up or down. Within the silhouette, other lines define the shape of collars, pockets, front or back closings, and so on.

Only in recent years have a woman's tennis clothes conformed to the shape of her body.

Do you realize what this means where Fashion is concerned? At the beginning of any season, advertisements call attention to the new *lines* that will be fashionable that season. Pencil-slim skirts are "good" one season; full, gathered skirts the next. Each time a major change takes place in the basic silhouette, a new style is born. Look at old magazines and snapshots to see how "lines" have changed through the years. Some clothes look quaint and lovely; others look awkward. Why? The lovelier clothes emphasize the structural form of the figure. Those which appear awkward ignore the figure. For example, the fashions of the mid-twenties ignored natural waistlines. These straight-hanging, box-like clothes did little to enhance even the loveliest of figures.

Despite this, these styles made a "come-back" in 1957–58. The chemise with its many versions was a revival of the mid-twenties styles. As the "latest" fashion, it was accepted by many people. But remember that the latest fashion is not necessarily a *pleasing* fashion.

Of one thing we *may* be sure: Dame Fashion will promote something new each season. It is up to us to make the final selection: a silhouette that is beautiful, functional, and that enhances the figure.

TYPES OF DESIGN

Before we begin to study various garments for their design qualities, let us make a distinction between structural and decorative design. *Structural* design refers to the *basic cut* or pattern of a garment. It includes all the various pattern parts and construction details which shape flat fabric into a garment that fits the contours of the body.

Decorative design refers to details that are used to *trim* the garment, such as braid, lace, edgings, and insertions. Decorative details are pleasing when they conform to the structural design of the garment. They may accent cuffs, neckline, or seams. Whenever and whatever decorative accent is used, it is wise to ask, "Is it really necessary? Is it in the right place?" If it looks excessive, or if it looks just as well elsewhere on the garment, discard it. Actually, a garment that has truly fine structural design seldom needs any trimmings other than an appropriate bit of jewelry or a color accent such as a scarf. All too often, a garment is completely ruined by "fuss and gingerbread." The ancient Greek maxim, "Nothing in excess," is still the standard of good taste.

The illustrations that follow should help you to analyze both the structural and decorative design of any article you wear. All the designs which are analyzed in the following discussion are sketched from photographs of actual garments.

STRUCTURAL DESIGN

First, let us recall the principles which contribute to the harmony of any design. These principles of unity, contrast, dominance, proportion, balance, and rhythm can be applied to the analysis of the following garments.

Distorted, unrelated shapes

Balanced, related shapes

Unity in a design. First, the various parts of a garment should be related to the structure of the figure. Line arrangements that distort or "cut up" the natural body structure destroy the feeling of unity that should exist between the figure and the garment. Secondly, all lines and shapes within the design should be sufficiently related to create a feeling of belonging together.

Compare the designs on page 106. The oblique line in the dress on the left divides the bodice into two unnatural shapes that are totally unrelated to the figure. The strong diagonal competes with the curving line of the pouch pocket. The light, contrasting bands only emphasize the lack of unity in this design.

Oblique lines are used effectively in the suit on the right. The diagonals, tapering from a broad shoulder line to a narrow waist, stress the natural converging shape of the chest area. The pockets form contrasting angles that accent the hip line. The use of line for accent is repeated in the collar. This jacket design has unity because it is a pleasing combination of diagonals, verticals, and horizontals, with the emphasis on diagonals.

    Jumpy design   **Unified design**

It is doubly important to have a fine structural design when the garment is made up of contrasting values. Compare the two dresses above. In the dress on the left, there is an attempt to balance a half-shoulder yoke with a half-hip yoke. This creates a jumpy, hopscotch arrangement that is totally unrelated to the figure. Although the dress on the right also uses two values, it appears unified because the design is divided into areas that stress the natural division of the figure: shoulders, waist, and hips.

Contrast and dominance in a design. Contrasting lines and shapes add variety and interest to a design. One type of line and shape should be allowed to dominate, however, so that the design is not a hopeless jumble of verticals, diagonals, and curves.

Now let us see how the principles of contrast and dominance apply to the dresses below. Both silhouettes are similar: flared skirts, fitted waistlines, and short sleeves. But there the similarity ends. The dress on the left is a jumble of oblique and curving lines. No one type of line or shape seems to dominate.

The dress on the right is a simple design with emphasis on the oblique lines of the flaring skirt and the pockets. The tie collar adds a pert accent at the neck. This design holds together as a unit.

Jumbled design   **Unified design**

Proportion in a design. Little tots who dress up in grown-ups' clothes look comical, for the hats and dresses are not in *scale* with their tiny bodies. Although this is an extreme example of poor proportion, it does prove that correct size relationships in a costume are important.

Since proportion is the principle of design that governs all size relationships, let us see how it applies to a few specific examples. You already know that the most pleasing and functional garment design conforms to the *structure* of the body. This same structural idea should govern the relationships that exist between the parts of a single garment. Compare the dresses on page 109, top. Both have two major areas—skirt and bodice. The dress on the left is a 1958 revival of the mid-twenties' style, with a belt at the hip line. This division creates two boxy shapes, too equal to be interesting. The belt in the dress on the right is at the natural waistline; this creates two unequal shapes that are not monotonous.

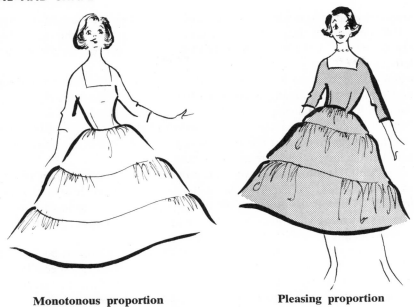

Monotonous proportion   **Pleasing proportion**

This is further proof that any design is more pleasing when its parts conform to the body structure.

This is true of a design that is divided into more than two major parts. In some dresses, the yoke marks the natural shoulder area, the belt is at the waist, and the skirt ends below the knees. The yoke, the bodice, and the skirt grow progressively larger. All pleasing size relationships are based on a natural progression.

Unpleasing proportion   **Pleasing proportion**

Designers employ this idea in many ways. In the dress at the bottom, right, page 109, the tiers of the skirt get narrower as they approach the waist. Such variety is lacking in the equal, monotonous division of tiers in the dress at the left.

Balance in a design. This principle brings over-all stability to a design through the satisfying arrangement of its parts. Balance plays a large role in life. In addition to balancing yourself when you walk, you have been balancing things all your life. As a child, you learned to balance a tower of blocks by placing the biggest blocks at the base. When you pile books or stack plates, you see that the largest ones are at the bottom.

It is natural, therefore, that we seek balance in a design. When the eye moves *up and down,* we generally want the larger or stronger shapes nearer the ground. Glance at the bottom right dress, page 109. The widest tier of the skirt is at the hemline; the other tiers grow successively narrower. Such a division gives a feeling of stability to the design.

We often find the larger shape at the top of the figure, however, because the shoulder area is the widest part of the normal figure. This is especially true of the jacket and "shortie" coat ensembles. In such costumes, the larger area at the top should be balanced by strong verticals in the skirt. A short, boxy jacket worn with a narrow skirt makes the figure seem taller and slimmer. If the shape at the top is too large, however, the figure looks top-heavy. Compare the two jacket ensembles below. The jacket on the left is so large and awkward that the figure fairly topples with the weight of it. The jacket on the right is loose, too, but it does not overpower the figure. Exaggerated styles, even though they are "high fashion," often destroy the balance in a garment.

Awkward shape   **Balanced shape**

What type of balance is most pleasing when we move our eyes from *side to side*? Take the human figure as an example. If a vertical line were drawn through the center front of the body, the lines and shapes on one side would be identical with those on the other side. This identical repetition of parts on either side of an imaginary center line is called *formal* balance. Look at the suit at the right on page 110.

A design can have balance without such equal divisions, however. An arrangement of lines and shapes on one side can balance a different arrangement on the opposite side, if correctly placed. This type of arrangement is called *informal* balance. It is neither the simple, horizontal, side-to-side movement of formal balance nor a vertical up-and-down movement. Informal balance involves both horizontal and vertical balance in a diagonal movement. A small area placed high on one side may balance a larger area placed lower on the opposite side.

Very often an accessory completes the feeling of balance in a costume. In the sketch of the ensemble at the left, below, the hanky in the slit pocket bal-

Informal balance   **Mixed formal and informal balance**

ances the feather on the hat. Occasionally one sees a garment in which both formal and informal balance are combined, as in the dress above, right. The dress looks lopsided because there is more weight on one side than on the other. Furthermore, the bodice and skirt are too unrelated to appear unified. Beware of this in separate blouse and skirt combinations, too.

Rhythm in a design. You are accustomed to think of rhythm in connection with music; you tap your foot or move your body in time with the music. In "art talk," rhythm refers to the way in which the eyes move from one part of a design to another.

Repetitive design   **Graduated design**

Rhythmic lines are found in the silhouette itself. Soft, clinging fabrics lead the eye along the flowing lines that sheathe the lithe body. Crisp or stiff fabrics lend a sharp, clean-cut movement to garments. Heavy, sturdy fabrics create a firm, restrained movement.

Within the actual silhouette, the eye is led from one part to another, following some dominating line in the structural design of the dress.

Rhythm is also based on *repetition*. This is certainly true of a musical theme. In dress design, rhythm is achieved by the repetition of tucks, pleats, scallops, buttons, and the like. (Notice the rhythm of tucks and buttons in the dress at the left, above.)

You have already seen how a designer may use the idea of progressive sizes in the flounced tiers of a skirt. Such a gradation in size contributes rhythm to a design. For example, the eye moves along the row of graduated buttons in the dress at the right, above, with the largest button focussing interest at the neckline.

DECORATIVE DESIGN

Garments with little or no decoration often have that "expensive look" because a truly becoming garment relies on simple structural lines and fine fabric for beauty. Yet, there are times when a decorative accent can be attractive. It may be an edging, a pattern of tucking, or braid. Whatever it is, it should accent the structural design of the garment.

Furthermore, a decorative accent should emphasize one part of the garment. Since the head is usually considered the center of interest, most accents are placed on the bodice to direct attention to the face. You instinctively wear contrasting collars, ties, or jewelry to "set off" your face. Of course, decoration is also used on cuffs and at the waist, hem, or other structural points. The able designer decides which point she wishes to emphasize and allows that one accent to dominate the garment. If she decides to create an unusual hemline, the rest of the dress is kept simple. Too many points of interest produce a cluttered effect.

Now let us compare examples of decorative design sketched from actual garments.

The coats below are actually similar in style, but the coat on the left is smarter because, unlike the other one, it is not overloaded with braid. The first coat can be dressed up or down with suitable accessories. It would look well with plaids or floral prints, whereas the other coat with its fussy braid would look too "noisy" with everything!

Simple design   **"Gingerbread"**

Study the blouses on page 114. The facings add just the right accent to the neckline and sleeves of blouse *a*. Blouse *b* has a turtle neck and is cut without set-in sleeves—an easy style to make. These are both simple blouses on which you could use a favorite pin. Graduated rows of tucking form an attractive yoke effect in blouse *c*; any jewelry would be excessive with the Peter Pan collar and pearl buttons. Blouses *d* and *e* have yokes. The V-yoke in blouse *d* is outlined by a narrow ruffle which is repeated at the neckline. Within the yoke, bands of eyelet embroidery harmoniously conform to the diagonal outlines of the yoke. Blouse *e*, on the other hand, looks confused because conflicting vertical bands of elaborate embroidery are crowded into a circular yoke. In blouse *f*, diamond-shaped insertions create a rounded yoke effect. They look out of place because diamond shapes, being angular, do not conform to a curved line.

The ever-popular jumper provides numerous changes when worn with different blouses and slip-overs. All too often, however, the blouses do not look as if they belonged with the jumper. This is especially true if the jumper itself is too ornate. A simple jumper forms a pleasing background for a greater variety of blouses and sweaters, either with or without collars.

Ornate styles are difficult to wear. Simple lines are always in good taste.

Compare the corduroy jumpers, page 114. The style on the left is too ornate
to be in good taste. The scalloped neckline of the jumper crowds the collar and
buttoned opening of the blouse which is worn with it. The corselette midriff
with its rows of nonfunctional buttons also adds to the confusion. The simpler
jumper on the right has a neckline that permits the wearing of collars or jewelry
without creating a crowded effect.

"Buttons and bows," strictly speaking, should be used only to serve a function. Buttons should button and bows should tie. When not actually used as
fasteners, they should at least be placed at structural points so as to appear
functional. Look at illustrations *a*, *b*, and *c* on this page. In coat *a*, the buttons
which emphasize the inverted pleat at center-back serve no function whatso-
ever; in fact, they would be uncomfortable when the wearer was seated. The
nonfunctional buttons in suit *b* create a spotty effect. This suit would be vastly
improved if the buttons (and the pouch pocket) were removed. In dress *c*, the
buttons are both functional and decorative.

The bows in *d* and *e* serve no purpose and appear to be afterthoughts. In
dress *f*, the bow actually serves a function; the drawstring at the neck ties in a
tiny bow.

Too much frosting spoils the cake. The simpler dress at the right is smarter.

And speaking of bows, compare the two evening gowns on this page. Both are similar in their basic design: a contrasting midriff ending in a bustle-like bow, a bodice with tiny straps, and a full skirt. The dress on the left goes further, however. Its festooned hemline is caught up with bows of self-material, with a similar bow tacked on the bodice. The scalloped bottom strip matches the midriff. There are enough ideas in this single dress for several evening dresses! The dress on the right has neither the bows nor the festooned hem, yet it is much more attractive with the single emphasis at the midriff. A single accent is far smarter and in better taste than several conflicting accents. That is an important thing to remember. (One can "dress up" apple pie with cheese *or* with ice cream—but never with both!)

Some garments involve another type of decoration—a design that is actually knitted or woven in. Apply the same principles to their selection that you do in the selection of other garments. Leaping deer, floating swans, and swaying palms have no place on sweaters—or any garments for that matter. Simple knits or cable designs are always in good taste. They look well with either plain or plaid skirts, and one does not tire of them as quickly as one would of a more pronounced design.

Figured fabrics. Up to this point we have been considering garments for which solid-colored fabrics are used. There are also things to consider when you select a stripe, a plaid, or a print for your patterns or readymades.

First, you might ask yourself whether a figured fabric is suitable for your particular pattern or whether it would be more attractive in a solid color. Often the basic style of a dress is so smart that it does not need the enlivening effect of a figured fabric. But if you decide on a figured fabric, plan the garment carefully before you make it (or examine a readymade before you buy it).

Every fabric design should bear a definite relationship to the various shapes that make up the garment design. Because stripes, plaids, and checks are based on straight lines, they lend themselves to designs in which straight lines, rather than curved lines, define the parts of the garment. (Remember that a square peg does not fit a round hole!) Print fabrics, especially medium or larger florals, are most suited to garment designs that have large unbroken areas and a minimum of construction details. Numerous seams, deep darts, and pleats obscure or cut up design motifs in the fabric. Small all-over prints, such as tiny floral sprigs, polka dots, and other small geometric designs, do not present such a problem.

Trimming for any figured fabric should be carefully chosen. Plain, solid-colored, ornamental details look best on figured fabrics. For example, a plaid garment would not look well with filigree buttons. Plain buttons or buttons covered with self-material are best. Edgings or ruffles of lace or embroidery are too fussy on figured fabrics. Use self-material, or a harmonizing solid color, to make bindings or edgings when a figured dress needs an accent.

Now that you have read these over-all suggestions, let us look at a few examples.

Stripes. Stripes may be used horizontally, vertically, or diagonally—sometimes singly but more often in combination. When used in combination, one line direction should dominate to avoid a restless effect. Seams should be planned so that the joining of stripes will create a harmonious pattern. The edge of a stripe may often define some area in the garment design.

In the dress on the left below, we see an unfortunate use of diagonal stripes. The stripes on the bodice and skirt do not follow either the structural

Poor use of line   **Good use of line**

lines of the dress or the structure of the human figure. Diagonal stripes are most successfully used when they appear "in opposition," as in the dress on the right where the diagonals meet at the center-front seams of the bodice and skirt, and on the pointed collar and cuffs. The stripes are not so bold that they create a restless effect, and they conform nicely to the structural design of the dress.

The dresses below are practically identical in their use of horizontal stripes for the bodice and vertical stripes for the skirts. The change in line direction occurs at the waist which is a structural point in the garment. In the dress on the right, the opposing diagonals on the pockets nicely span the vertical stripes to form a balanced design. Now compare these pockets with those on the dress at the left. The rounded contours of the pockets do not conform to the straight lines of a stripe! And the diagonal placement of these pockets does not create a pleasing pattern where the stripes on the pockets meet the stripes on the skirt.

Poorly placed　　　　　　　　　　　　　　　**Well placed**

Plaids. Whenever plaids are used for a garment, they, too, should be planned to conform to the structural lines of the garment. And every effort should be made to match plaids at the seams to form a pleasing design and a harmonious over-all effect.

In the dress on the right, page 119, the dark stripes of the plaid are well balanced on the bodice. The plaids in each sleeve are matched to correspond with the horizontal stripes on the bodice. The skirt pleats hide the dark stripes except when the pleats flare open. This dress shows careful planning, cutting, and stitching.

Poorly planned and matched plaid   **Well planned and matched plaid**

The dress on the left appears confused. The circular yoke does not conform to the straight lines of a plaid. A triangular or square yoke is always preferable to a curved yoke whenever stripes or plaids are used. This dress looks even more confusing because the vertical stripes of the waist are not carefully matched to the diagonals of the yoke and the pockets are "hit-and-miss" patches. There was not enough plotting and planning here! As a general rule, when pockets are used on a pronounced plaid, they look better if they repeat the line direction of the background plaid. On a less pronounced plaid, however, pockets may be effectively placed on the diagonal or at right angles to the main body of the garment.

STYLING FOR THE INDIVIDUAL

Now that we have studied the design qualities of specific garments, let us see how a girl can select garments that are becoming to her particular figure. Have you ever noticed that your friends (and you, too!) can appear quite different depending on the clothes they wear? A chubby miss can look slender in one costume and chunky in another; or a tall, thin girl may seem to "fill out" in one dress but look still lankier in another. Have you ever wondered what created these apparent changes?

Recalling the types of lines discussed at the beginning of this chapter, you will remember that a vertical emphasis can create an illusion of height; a horizontal emphasis an illusion of width; and curves an illusion of fullness. This means that the lines and shapes that create the silhouette and the other construction details of a garment can actually be used to improve the proportions of a figure or to camouflage certain "problem spots."

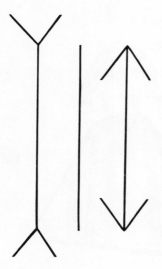

Here is a good example of the illusions created by lines. Compare the three lines at the left. The first line looks shorter than the second and the third line looks longer, yet all three are actually the same length!

The dresses below show what happens when these linear principles are applied to clothes. In contrast to the plain dress in the middle, the diagonals in the dress at the left create an illusion of height while the widely spaced horizontals in the dress at the right give an effect of breadth.

The becoming silhouette. The chances are that our modern styles will always include some variations on each of the basic silhouettes: bell, tubular, and back fullness. Such variety gives you the opportunity to select the silhouette that is most becoming to you.

There are a few things for you to keep in mind. First, the basic "over-all" silhouette of your dress, suit, or coat is the most important shape in your costume because it is directly related to your entire figure. People are more likely to see you as a "whole" before they notice details in your costume. Secondly, an extreme version of any silhouette is more difficult to wear than a more modified version. For example, suppose that an extremely flared skirt with a tiny waist and a full dolman sleeve with a sloping shoulder line are the height of fashion. A tall, slender person or a beautifully proportioned girl could wear such an exaggerated silhouette. But would it be so becoming to all other figure types? Consider it on a short, stocky girl. She is likely to appear even shorter and stouter in a dress that has decidedly sloping shoulders, full sleeves, and an extremely flared skirt.

As a rule, extreme versions of any silhouette are difficult to wear unless you are very nicely proportioned and slender. Furthermore, one tires of an exaggerated silhouette far more quickly than one does of a modified style. That is why most extreme fashions are short-lived. After one brief season they look out of date, whereas simpler styles are good for several seasons.

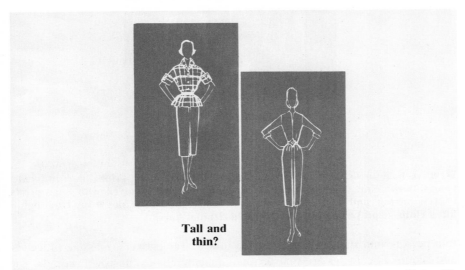

Tall and
thin?

Modern Miss

Wear loose or box coats and jackets. Try plaids, checks, horizontal stripes. Full sleeves and full skirts are right for you, as are dresses with contrast in skirts and tops. Don't be tempted by fitted coats or dresses or by straight, slim skirts. Tight sleeves, clinging fabrics, low waistlines, and single colors all make you look taller.

Figure types. Here are a few suggestions that may help you to determine what silhouettes, fabrics, and other details are becoming to your figure.

The *very tall, thin girl* should say "no" to all narrow "slinky" styles. Narrow tubular skirts, close shoulder lines, long, tightly fitted sleeves, long vertical openings, and deep V-necklines would only accent her extreme height. She should wear full skirts that give her softness and breadth—such as dirndl skirts, widely pleated skirts, circular or extremely flared skirts, gathered tiers, and perky bouffant styles. Flaring peplums over slim skirts help to cut her height. Boxy jackets, full capes, contrasting jackets and skirts are excellent. Large patch pockets, wide belts, and crushy girdle effects are good. Drawstring necklines, high collars, soft neckerchiefs, full gathered sleeves, dolman sleeves, or shirring all create soft flattering details. Pleated slacks worn with loose blouses are far more becoming than tight jeans and skimpy T-shirts. Better than any other figure types, the slender tall person can wear "splashy" prints, bold plaids, and heavy stripes. She is tall and thin enough to withstand the strong emphasis of such large fabric designs—provided, of course, they suit her personality. Long-haired or thick furs are more becoming on the tall

Short and
plump?

Modern Miss

Wear vertical tucks, seams, narrow stripes. Choose small prints, narrow center panels, dark colors, slightly flared skirts. Don't become involved with large prints, contrasting tops and skirts, bulky fabrics or too bright colors. Stay away from tightly fitted clothes and frilly trims. Avoid all horizontal lines.

thin person than slick or tightly curled furs. Large chokers, massive bracelets, and "chunky" earrings are smarter than delicate chains, narrow bracelets, and long, dingle-dangle earrings!

The *short, plump* miss can do without the added bulk and breadth of full, gathered skirts, extremely flared skirts, horizontal tiers and flounces. In general, trim tailored styles or simple clothes with a minimum of decorative detail are best for this type. Puffy or bell-type sleeves, large patch pockets, wide belts, bunchy bows, large collars, excessive gathers, and heavy trim only add weight to her appearance. Nor should her clothes be tightly fitted, for a narrow confining skirt, tight sleeves, and a smoothly fitted bodice would only emphasize her contours. Gored skirts with a slight flare and pleated skirts with their vertical emphasis provide flattering fullness without increasing the silhouette. A short stocky person appears taller and more slender when hemlines are slightly long—something to remember especially if Fashion favors knee-length skirts. A smooth shoulder line with a simple set-in sleeve or a plain raglan sleeve is good. Fitted sleeves that end above the elbow or at the wrist are better than three-quarter sleeves, especially if the latter are so wide that they increase the span of the figure at the hipline. Belts of self material are always preferable as they do not cut the height of the figure. For the same reason, matching skirts and jackets are better than contrasting ones. Slightly fitted tailored jackets are better than short boxy jackets or capes which would add too much weight to the upper part of the figure. Full-length coats cut on semi-princess lines are generally becoming. If the figure is definitely hip-heavy or full-waisted, a straight-hanging, full-length, slightly flared topper is more slenderizing. Fitted styles would follow the contours too closely. Large and "loud" figured fabrics are to be avoided. Inconspicuous, neat prints, small subdued stripes or checks are possible. If weight is a real problem, plain solid-colored fabrics are generally preferable. A short person should wear short or tightly curled furs rather than long or shaggy furs. She should use simple, medium-sized accessories. Large bags, hats, bracelets, and other items would appear bulky.

The *tiny,* "half-pint" young lady should select garments and accessories that are in harmony with her petite quality. Exaggerated flares, flounces, and extreme puffs are quite likely to dwarf her. Skirts with moderate fullness, simple sleeves and small collars are in scale with her proportions. She should avoid styles in which bodice and skirt areas are divided into many smaller areas, such as yokes, tiers, and panel effects. Decorative details should never be heavy. Use narrow edgings and small buttons, buckles, and bows. The strong horizontal emphasis that is found in the squared shoulders and wide hemline of boxy jackets appear awkward on her. Fitted jackets and skirts with a slight flare are more becoming. These should be of matching fabrics so as not to cut her height. She should always select small prints, checks or stripes in preference to larger motifs which are not in scale with her figure. Short or tightly curled furs are better than long shaggy furs. Small fur collars on coats look better than those which span the shoulders. Small or medium-size accessories are scaled for the tiny miss. Wide brimmed hats, large bags, and bulky jewelry are not meant for her!

The *tall, buxom* girl will want to avoid styles that increase her silhouette, such as bouffant or circular skirts or those with gathered tiers or bustle effects. Short puffy sleeves, wide flaring sleeves, built-out shoulders, peplums, and hip pockets also add pounds to her figure. She should never wear tight clothes, as narrow tubular skirts, tight sleeves, and fitted midriffs and bodices tend to emphasize her contours. She wants to introduce slight fullness by means of a few gathers and soft draping to camouflage her contours. A gored skirt with a slight flare gives her grace without adding either height or width. She does not accent a heavy waist with wide or contrasting belts, but uses belts of self material. She looks well in simple or tailored clothes, rather than those with fussy detail. Three-quarter length coats are better than hip length coats. Full length coats with a slight flare are better than those with an extreme flare. The large girl should avoid belted styles that create a "bunchy" look. She should select subdued prints in preference to large bold plaids and stripes and flashy prints. And if her size is a real problem she would do well to wear solid-colored fabrics. Smooth flat furs are more becoming than thick or shaggy furs. Medium-size accessories suit her best. A tiny hat or a small bag make her appear larger by contrast, whereas extremely large items would only add to her size.

The *lucky* girl who is neither too tall nor too short, neither thin nor plump, can wear any style that suits her fancy, provided the garments are attractive in design and are appropriate to the occasion. But even the well-proportioned girl has to be sure that her clothes fit well. That means that they should never be so tight as to appear skimpy or unpleasantly revealing; nor so loose as to look baggy and shapeless; nor so short as to be immodest. A perfect fit goes hand in hand with perfect styling *and* good taste.

Problem spots. Many girls and women may have just one little figure problem that annoys them. Whatever it is, it can usually be made less apparent by wearing the right style of garment.

A *long, thin neck* is concealed by high necklines with built-up collars, cowl necklines, or perky ruffly edgings. Wear soft kerchiefs or scarves with collarless sweaters, jackets, or coats. Collars of long-haired furs are good. Avoid deep V-necklines. Wear choker beads and chunky earrings rather than long beads, chains, or pendant earrings.

A *short, heavy neck* should not be crowded by built-up collars, cowl necklines, bunchy bows, large ties, shaggy fur collars, and heavy choker beads. Collarless V-necklines are good. Flat, narrow lapel collars on coats are more pleasing than wide lapels with a horizontal emphasis. Flat furs are better than thick or shaggy fur collars.

Sloping, round shoulders require building up. Set-in sleeves are always preferable to the sloping lines of raglan or dolman sleeves. Use shoulder padding or a puffy sleeve contour to create a squared effect. Deep V-yoke effects, with the diagonals rising from center front to shoulder lines seemingly lift the shoulders. Ruffly collar edgings will help to camouflage any roundness below the back of the neck.

Wide shoulders appear narrower in fitted or sloping raglan sleeves with little or no shoulder padding. Squared or puffy shoulder lines and heavy padding only accent wide shoulders. Avoid shoulder yokes and breast pockets with a horizontal emphasis. Balance the width of the shoulders by creating hip fullness with peplums, patch pockets, wide belts, and flaring hemlines. A tubular, pencil slim skirt only emphasizes wide shoulders unless there is a peplum to balance them. Avoid broad-brimmed hats or sailors. Wear soft crushy berets or small irregular brims instead.

A *large bust* requires moderate fullness in the bodice to conceal contours. In addition, a bodice that is divided into two or more areas or panels is more becoming than an unbroken waist front. Verticals in the front opening or rows of tucks break up the expanse. Diagonal draping on the bodice is also flattering but is more generally found in mature fashions.

A *heavy abdomen* and *waist* become less conspicuous if clothes are not tight. A moderately gathered skirt, slight front fullness, or diagonal draping on the skirt front help to camouflage the heavy abdomen. Plain gored skirts with a slight flare are more becoming than pencil slim skirts. Avoid contrasting and crushy belts. Avoid styles with a wide fitted midriff. Semi-fitted or straight-hanging coats and jackets are more slenderizing than form-fitting ones!

Wide hips appear narrower when balanced by a horizontal emphasis at the shoulder line by means of shoulder padding or softly draped sleeves. Confining, tubular skirts should be avoided as well as those with an extremely flared hemline. Gored skirts with a slight flare help to conceal the hips. Skirts

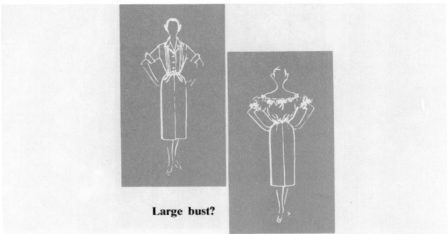

Large bust?

Modern Miss

Look for vertical lines if you have a big bust. Your neckline should be V- or U-shaped and your shoulder lines simple and plain. Single colors and loose, straight coats are your best bet. Don't go in for fancy, frilly clothes or blouses. Bows and pockets only emphasize the line of the bust. Cape collars, patterned tops, fitted coats, all should be avoided. Concentrate attention on whole figure.

with moderate waistline gathers, slightly flared peplums, or soft diagonal draping also camouflage hip contours. Introduce diagonal line direction at hips rather than horizontal. Wide sleeve openings and wide or contrasting cuffs should be avoided as they broaden the hipline.

Heavy legs become less noticeable when hemlines fall well below the knees. Narrow skirts emphasize heavy legs; skirts with a flare or fullness are more becoming.

HATS AND "HEAD LINES"

In Chapter 4, "Head Attraction," you learned that it was important to select a hair-do that was suited to the shape of the head as well as to the general proportions of the figure. The same basic principles apply to your selection of a hat. Most of you love to go hatless, or prefer a kerchief or a hood. Yet there are times when you do wear a hat. So here are a few general pointers to keep in mind as you browse around the millinery counters.

Select small hats that are simple in design because they are more youthful. Save the "chapeaux" with veils and an abundance of flowers until later. Hats with a simple ribbon trim, a small feather, or a perky flower are in better taste for a girl in her middle teens. You will find a variety of young styles from which to choose . . . snappy little pill-boxes, berets, or Breton sailors; tiny little skull-caps or petal arrangements to perch on the back of your head . . . any one of which will allow your hair to frame your face. More extreme hats are suitable after you pass the "twenty mark." And some of those extreme styles are never really smart. If they distort the shape of the head

Wide hips?

Modern Miss

Plan broad shoulder lines and fullness above the waistline if you are faced with the problem of big hips. Your skirts should flare, but not too much. Concentrate detail above the waist. Don't be lured by tight-fitting clothes or straight, narrow skirts. Skirts with an exaggerated flare or too-wide pleats also emphasize hip weight. Avoid sleeves that are too full, and tight, wide, fancy belts.

they are not good in design. They might be unusual . . . they might even make people turn around and stare! But something a bit less striking is likely to be in better taste.

In judging the suitability of any hat, always view yourself, standing, in a full-length mirror. Only then, can you see whether a hat is in scale with your figure.

Problem features. To further judge the becomingness of a hat, you should study your face and its relation to the hat in question. If you feel that you have some "problem feature," the right hat will help to correct it.

A *round face* looks even rounder in a hat with a circular crown or one with a regular, circular off-the-face brim. And a stiff squarish crown with a straight brim (like a sailor) would only call attention to the roundness of the face by its extreme contrast. An irregular crown with a diagonal tilt to the brim breaks the circular contours and gives a "lift" to the face.

A *square jaw* becomes more pronounced when a hat with straight hard lines is worn. Soft irregular brims worn at a tilt, soften the jaw line. Soft berets, crushy turbans and roll brims are also good.

A *long, thin* face looks even longer in a hat with a vertical emphasis. Narrow, pointed crowns, stick-up feathers and the like only add to the length of the face. Off-the-face brims that provide a wider frame for the face, soft irregular brims that cut the vertical line direction, or a low trim at the back of the hat are styles that will tend to shorten the face.

Profiles can also be improved by the correct hat. A receding jaw or an arched nose is emphasized by an off-the-face hat in which the brim sweeps back in line with the chin or nose to form an arc. A hat with a moderate brim that slants forward and upward or a soft rolled brim breaks such a line direction, and proves much more becoming. Protruding chins and large noses look more prominent in small, brimless skull-cap styles because the features appear even larger by contrast. Large or moderate brims with a forward, upward slant help to balance the size of large features.

You see, you need not be satisfied with what nature provided. You can do a lot with lines and shapes to enhance your appearance. It's just a question of knowing how.

ACTIVITIES

For the class

1. **Ask** members of the class to bring in various garments and accessories which, to them, are unsatisfactory in either structural or decorative design. In a class discussion, analyze each item and suggest how it could be improved.

2. **Organize** a class clothing demonstration. Let girls who represent various figure types volunteer to demonstrate the importance of selecting garments and accessories which are becoming to the proportions of their figures. First, have them model school or dress-up costumes which emphasize the very characteristics they wish to modify. (They may have to borrow items from friends or classmates to prove the point.) Then have the same girls appear in costumes which are becoming to them in every respect: in silhouette, in fabric design, and in choice of accessories. Clothing demonstrations in which "bad" is contrasted with "good" are valuable aids toward developing good judgment. In other words, "Seeing is believing."

For the individual

Select photographs of coats, suits, blouses, dresses, or evening clothes from magazines and catalogues which illustrate the following:

a. fine structural design with pleasing space divisions
b. poor structural design
c. decorative details that harmonize with the structural design
d. decorative details that are inappropriate or excessive
e. becoming designs for the short, plump girl
f. becoming designs for the tall, thin girl

Mount illustrations and give reasons for your selections.

CHAPTER 8 — *TEXTURE*

In describing a material—whether it is cloth, fur, leather, metal, rubber, or plastic—you would naturally consider it from several angles. Obviously, you would think of how it *looks*. Is it shiny or dull? Is it transparent or thick? Is it plain or does it have some surface design? Certainly you would think of how it *feels* to the touch. Is it smooth, rough, pebbly, ribbed, fuzzy, or clammy? In addition, you should be concerned as to how it *acts*. For example, does a dress fabric hang stiffly or does it drape in soft folds? Is a particular leather pliable enough to crease or fold, as suede, or is it heavy and stiff like calfskin? All of these qualities describe the *texture* of a material.

Each characteristic is important to you as a designer. In the case of fabrics, you will want to select textures that are becoming to your figure, whether you are buying a readymade garment or a dress length. When you sew, you want a fabric that will act or drape in a way that is suitable for your particular pattern. Then, too, you will want the material of each item in your costume to be appropriate for the occasions on which it will be worn. Last, but not least, you will want to make sure that the various textures that you combine in one costume really belong together. Remember that texture is one of the art elements with which you can create an attractive design.

FABRIC SELECTION

In Part IV you will study fabrics in more detail. In this chapter we will merely consider the various aspects of texture as they apply to the design quality of your costume.

How a fabric looks. Each fabric has a visual-surface quality which is largely determined by the fiber, weaving, and finishing processes used. A fabric can be shiny like satin, dull like velvet, shimmering like moiré, or glistening like metallic cloth. This particular quality depends on the amount of light that a fabric reflects. Satin is so smooth that it reflects light; velvet with its deep pile surface absorbs rather than reflects light. Other fabrics range between these two extremes. The surface quality of fabrics can also appear smooth or irregular. Cotton can be smooth as in chambray or ribbed as in dimity, corduroy, and some piqués. Wool can be smooth as in broadcloth or rough as in herringbone tweed. Then, of course, fabric can be transparent as in filmy chiffon, rayon sheer, organdy, nylon, net, and lace. Or it can be deep and thick as in

Lassie Coats

The fine texture of the lightweight wool used in the two coats above lends itself well to pastel coats for spring. In the winter coat at the right, the rough texture of the fabric adds richness to the color.

velvet, sturdy and firm as in whipcord, smooth and pliable as in batiste, challis, and chambray.

Some fabrics have an additional surface quality that has been achieved by a design woven into the fabric in contrasting colors. These include stripes, plaids, and figured fabrics like brocade. Other plain-woven fabrics, such as percale, rayon, or silk sheers and crepes, have designs printed on them after the weaving process. Still other plain-woven fabrics introduce some surface interest with the use of additional yarns. These include dotted Swiss and eyelet embroidered goods. Linens and cottons are often machine-stitched with a contrasting all-over floral pattern. Any one of these methods of decoration changes the visual effect of a fabric.

The fabrics described above are a few of the wide variety of textures that may be bought from the bolt. There are still other textural qualities that may be added to otherwise plain-surfaced fabrics during the sewing process. Unusual textural effects can be had by shirring, smocking, tucking, and pleating. Border designs or single motifs can be worked out in appliqué or in braid. In recent years various types of quilting have become popular. Fabric that is quilted into tiny, one-fourth-inch squares is used for collars, cuffs, and vestee effects on blouses and spectator classics. Cottons and sheer wool, such as challis, are quilted in larger squares and are used for jackets and skirts. Occasionally bands of this heavy quilting are used as decorative accents on the hem or collar of a dress. And, of course, quilted fabrics have long been used for lounging attire. Fabrics that are quilted in approximately one-inch squares may be bought by the yard. Of course, quilting is also found in shapes other than squares or diamonds.

How a fabric feels. The way a fabric feels to the touch is called its *tactile quality.* Most likely you could identify a dozen or more fabrics by their feel even if you were blindfolded. Some rayon or silk crepes and cotton seersuckers are pebbly to the touch; satins, sateens, and glazed chintz are slick. Pile fabrics, such as velvet or corduroy, produce a feeling of softness and depth as the hand passes over them. Organdy or cotton net feel crisp and brittle. Rayon taffeta or moiré and metallic cloth might feel cold and clammy. Chiffon feels airy and floating.

It is not surprising that such physical reactions influence people in their fabric selections. The *feel* of a fabric is more important than its appearance to many people. They love the softness of knitted sweaters; they feel good in fresh, crisp cottons; they adore the swish of velvet or the rustle of taffeta.

Knowing *if* and *how* you react to the tactile quality of a fabric should help you to select those in which you feel your best. You certainly would enjoy wearing such textures far more than those that "rub you the wrong way." And they are more likely to express your personality.

How a fabric acts. This, of course, is important to you as a seamstress. When you make your own clothes you learn a good deal about this textural quality. You probably already realize that you could not possibly use a heavy, clinging jersey for a dress pattern that calls for a full, bouffant skirt. Nor could you make a slim, tubular spectator frock of crisp organdy. Such examples may seem very obvious to most of you. But if you have not had much experience in using fabrics, try to find out how they act. Drape a length of fabric over your shoulder. Does it hang in heavy soft folds or does it stick out in sharp angles? Does a square of fabric float in the breeze or does it swish heavily? Does it form soft gathers when you crush it in your hands or is it too bulky to form gathers? Will it hold a firm pleat when pressed or will it spring open? These are qualities that should influence you in selecting a fabric for a particular pattern.

Every basic silhouette requires a certain type of fabric because each fabric drapes or hangs differently. Each has its own line quality—clinging jersey, perky taffeta, boxy tweed, flowing chiffon, and so on. So, in addition to selecting a pattern that has becoming lines for you, you must see that the fabric will form the lines of that particular silhouette. The following general suggestions for the basic styles may be of help to you.

For a rounded-bell silhouette with soft, full gathers at the hip or waist, select supple fabrics, such as rayon or wool crepe, firm but soft cotton, tie silk (surah), or rayon or wool jersey.

For a rounded-bell silhouette with a perky, bouffant hip fullness, select crisp fabrics, such as organdy, piqué, chintz, or taffeta.

For a cone-shaped bell silhouette with a decided flare, select firm, stiff fabrics, such as faille, moiré, taffeta, or piqué.

For a tubular silhouette with a slight flare, select firm yet supple fabrics, such as heavy crepe, heavy linen, tie silk, flannel, gabardine, corduroy, chambray, gingham, percale, or shantung.

For a tubular silhouette with straight vertical lines, select firm fabrics, such as tweed, serge, broadcloth, gabardine, or faille.

For a back-fullness silhouette with soft draping at hips or back, select supple fabrics, such as heavy rayon crepe, satin, tie silk, or lightweight woolens.

For perky bustle effects, select fabrics, such as moiré, brocade, or taffeta.

You will find that the general directions on most patterns suggest a list of fabrics that are suitable for the pattern in question.

TEXTURE AND FIGURE TYPES

You may have heard someone say, "I always feel as big as a house in this heavy tweed suit." Someone else might have said, "I feel like a beanpole in this jersey." If people feel that way, they probably create that impression.

The same dress can look radically different on different people. Avoid clinging fabrics if you are tall and thin.

Fabrics can reveal, increase, or camouflage the natural lines of the figure. Generally speaking, an average figure of good proportions may wear fabrics that reveal or emphasize figure contours; a thin person should wear fabrics that increase or build out her figure; and a heavy person looks best in fabrics that neither reveal nor increase the size of the figure, but softly camouflage it.

Although we have already discussed the selection of a becoming silhouette (Chapter 7, "Line and Shape"), and listed types of fabrics that are suited to each basic silhouette, you may want to have even a more definite idea as to what fabrics can do to the appearance of a figure.

The tall and thin girl. Heavy fabrics that add bulk are becoming to the tall lean figure. Tweeds, corduroy, shaggy coatings, butcher linen, and rough,

The same texture can be appropriate for one person, but inappropriate for another. The tiny girl is lost in a bulky textured suit; the stout one appears even bigger. The right texture is one which suits your build and personality as well as the occasion.

heavy cottons are all good. Fabrics that are quilted or shirred soften angular contours. Stiff fabrics such as organdy and other crisp cottons, taffeta, moiré, and faille that stand away from the figure are flattering. Supple fabrics such as velvet, heavy crepes, and challis that are easily draped or gathered soften the lean lines of a tall, thin figure.

Clinging fabrics that outline the figure closely are not becoming. For example, rayon jersey and some crepes emphasize a lanky look unless they are softly gathered. Satin, when closely draped, highlights bony spots and accents the figure contour. (Most likely you would not even wish to consider satin until you pass the twenty mark anyway.) Smooth, firm fabrics like serge or gabardine create a confining silhouette that makes the figure appear even narrower.

The plump girl. Whether tall or short, a heavy person should select fabrics that create a trim, unexaggerated silhouette. Firm yet supple fabrics that do not add bulk are best. Broadcloth, flannel, gabardine, wool or rayon crepe, chambray, or percale all lend themselves to simple, tailored styles. A few of them, notably the cottons and wool or rayon crepes, work up nicely into slightly gathered garments that conceal the contour of the figure without adding to its size.

Knitted garments, such as bouclé suits, dresses of rayon jersey—and yes, even most sweaters—follow the curves of the well-rounded person too closely to be becoming. Heavy knits also add to that bulky look, as do heavy tweeds, shaggy woolen coatings, and corduroys. And it goes without saying that the plump figure would look roly-poly in thick quilted or shirred fabrics. Such a person should also avoid shiny textures such as satin that would only highlight her roundness. Dull-textured fabrics help to tone down figure contours. Stiff fabrics, such as organdy, taffeta, or moiré that stand away from the figure increase its apparent size. Transparent fabrics that reveal parts of the figure are not becoming. Heavy hips, arms, and shoulders were not meant to be seen through peek-a-boo fabrics!

The tiny girl. The girl or woman of tiny proportions should select fabrics that are in scale with her petite quality. She needs textures that will build her up without weighing her down. Soft smooth woolens, lightweight corduroy, perky cottons, crepes of various fibers, taffeta, and faille all serve this purpose. Soft knitted garments provide flattering fullness.

Bulky, coarse, or heavy fabrics tend to overpower the tiny girl. Clinging fabrics, such as jersey, often follow her contours so closely that she looks even tinier though when softly draped, jerseys can be becoming.

The average girl. The person of average proportions has the whole range of textures from which to choose. The girl or woman with a lovely figure can wear clinging fabrics and shiny ones, heavy fabrics and filmy sheers, because she has no figure problem to hide. She can accent her good figure. Her chief concern is to select a fabric that is appropriate for a specific occasion and one that will harmonize with the textures of other items in her costume.

But that is the concern of everyone—regardless of figure—so we will take that up next.

APPROPRIATE USE OF TEXTURES

To begin with, here is a "true story." It was a cold and blustery afternoon in early spring. Several high-school girls had lined up at the edge of the baseball field after school to watch the boys at their spring training. It was a typical crowd of gay and chattering girls, but two of them who stood a bit apart from the others will be the theme of this texture story.

This is what one girl was wearing: a short swagger coat made of a green and brown plaid of four-inch squares; a dress of rayon sheer in a blue and yellow floral print. Her open coat exposed a slipover sweater of three-inch, red and white horizontal stripes. Her head kerchief was of multicolored floral chiffon, decorated with purple sequins. She wore brown mittens and carried a shoulder bag of brown calf. Her ballet-type shoes were of black kid. Does this conglomeration sound unbelievable?

Now let us look at her companion. She wore a full-length coat of brown herringbone tweed, a green corduroy skirt, a yellow cardigan, and a woolen head kerchief of green and yellow plaid. She carried yellow mittens. Her shoulder bag and brogues were of brown calf.

Obviously, the first girl had no idea as to how to go about assembling a costume. Or perhaps she did know, but did not think it was important to dress well on school days. There are girls, you know, who wear just anything at all on weekdays and leave their real planning for extra special events. They seem to forget that people often remember them at their worst rather than at their best. At any rate, her costume was a glaring example of inappropriate textures as well as a horrible combination of colors. But at this point we shall confine our discussion to texture alone. Comparing the costumes of the two girls, we can discover just what is meant by an appropriate use of textures.

In the first place the second girl had selected clothes that suited the weather. Her corduroy skirt and cardigan were ideal for a blustery March day, and so was her woolen kerchief. Second, her costume was completely appropriate for school and for the customary round of after-school activities. Finally, the texture of each item in her costume created a feeling of unity—of belonging together. The corduroy skirt, the sweater, and heavy sports coat were by no means matched or identical textures. The skirt was ribbed, the sweater was a soft knit, and the coat was a herringbone weave. There was plenty of variety and contrast there. Yet they are related textures; they all stressed a sporty *theme*—there was a *harmony of weight* among the three. The bag and shoes of calfskin with their durable quality were ideal for a sports costume. Her head kerchief and mittens repeated the texture as well as the color of the sweater. Incidentally, the plaid kerchief provided a single note of figured contrast to the solid colors of other items in her costume. All in all, this girl knew how to assemble an attractive costume that was appropriate in every respect.

Now, how about the first girl? First of all, that sheer dress! Spring may have been around the corner, but it was still too blustery to rush the season with a filmy sheer. Even the girl realized it, for she wore a heavy sport sweater with it for extra warmth. Aside from the weather angle, a dressy sheer is not appropriate for school, even on balmy days. And it certainly didn't belong on the baseball field! Her sequin-spattered chiffon kerchief was meant for dressy afternoon or evening wear. In fact, it seemed a bit old for her. The only items

Petti

The wool jumper is perfect for daytime wear—the silk print for late afternoon or evening.

Anne Fogarty—Couture Group, N. Y. Dress Institute

in her costume that really were appropriate for school and its related activities were the coat, the mittens, and the bag. Of course, sweaters are appropriate for school, but this particular one was too unrelated in both color and texture to the dress and to the coat to be a good choice.

Using her three suitable items as a starting point, let us try to improve her costume. First of all, the coat is of brown and green plaid; so she should not use any other designed fabric with it. If the girl preferred dresses to sweaters and skirts, she could wear a solid-colored dress of gabardine, flannel, or corduroy. Any one of these winter weights would be related to the coat fabric. Let us select a gabardine dress of green to match the green of the coat. A brown kerchief of sheer wool would repeat the color of her mittens and would also harmonize with the coat and dress. Brown calf brogues that matched her bag would look far better than her black kid ballet shoes! With such changes all of the textures would be nicely related to one another, and each item would be appropriate for school and its related activities.

No matter where you live or what your activities are, the textural quality of your clothing should be both weather-wise and appropriate in every other respect. Although the above "texture story" gave you an idea as to what such selection involves, here are a few additional pointers.

The weather. It stands to reason that certain costume materials are more appropriate for one season or climate than they are for another. You would not any more pull on a pair of fleece-lined boots during a sultry summer shower than you would wear open white fabric sandals with ice underfoot. This is an extreme example, but it points out what should be obvious to anyone selecting fabrics and accessories for a costume.

Heavy woolens, velvets, sturdy corduroys, firm thick knits, and similar fabrics are definitely "cold-weather weights," while lighter-weight woolens, thin cottons, rayon sheers, and linen belong to the balmier days. A fabric that is not in season looks out of place. That was one reason why the sheer dress of our first girl was inappropriate. This does not mean, however, that light cottons and rayon sheers must be worn only in summer. They are suitable when used for blouses that are worn under suit jackets. Then, too, sheer filmy fabrics are used for extremely dressy clothes and evening frocks throughout the year. But that involves appropriateness to occasion.

Every item in the costume may have its seasonal quality. Take your bags, shoes, and hats, for example. Raffia, washable fabrics, and light plastics are ideal for summer bags, but look inappropriate in winter when heavy, dark leathers, fabrics, and plastics are more suitable. Lightweight leather, fabric, and even straw are popular for summer footgear, but heavier leathers like calf-skin, reptile, or suede are introduced for winter. Straw, piqué, and linen are used for summer hats, but cold weather brings forth felt, velvet, corduroy, and wool-knit headgear.

Appropriateness to occasion. The girl with good taste has that "just right" look. She always wears clothes that are appropriate to the occasion. Each group really constitutes a "texture family" in which there is a harmony of ideas and a harmony of weights.

Generally speaking, three different types of costumes take care of the activities of most high-school girls. *Spectator sports* styles are ideal for school, sport events, streetwear, informal get-togethers, and travel. All items used in a sports costume should express a casual, durable, or knock-about theme. There should never be a frilly look to them. Sports styles include tailored toppers (short or long), sports suits, jackets, skirts, sweaters, simple blouses, and all standard classic sport dresses, together with simple hats, and plain, durable shoes, bags, and other accessories.

Write your own ticket in tweeds. These fabrics make it especially easy to pick attractive contrasting colors for accessories because you can match the colored flecks in the tweed itself.

American Woolen Company

SILK AND WORSTED TWEEDS

2 Lightweight, soft. Drapes well into suits

WASHABLE TWEEDS

3 Ideal for dresses and jumpers

BUG YARN TWEEDS

Heavyweight. Suitable for toppers and coats

ALL WOOL TWEEDS

4 Loosely woven. Suitable for heavy wear garments

Dressy clothes are meant for that special date, informal dinner parties and dances, holidays, or other special events. Clothes for such occasions generally stress a feminine, more or less individualized theme. Coats cease to have that standardized knock-about look. They are lovely both in fabric and detail. In winter, fur is often used for collars. Suits can be beautifully tailored or stress soft dressmaker details. Blouses are more delicate or frilly in styling. Dresses can be slim and sophisticated or softly gathered. Decorative, unusual details are found on necklines, cuffs, and belts. Hats may have a simple ribbon, flower, or feather trim. Shoes and accessories lose that practical, durable look, although they are still beautifully simple in design.

Evening clothes are for those red-letter occasions—school or club dances and formal banquets. They are chosen for beauty of color and texture rather than for practical reasons. Evening slippers and all accessories repeat the exquisite theme of fragile net, organdy, taffeta, or other fabrics used for formal occasions.

The texture of each item in any one type of costume should express the same idea or theme. If the textures in a costume are a mixture of two themes, the costume lacks a dominating idea—it looks confused and unrelated. A frilly, lace-trimmed batiste blouse is not related to a casual, plaid sports suit any more than sports moccasins and anklets are related to a dressy frock of velveteen or crepe. Such examples are in bad taste. Yet similar mistakes are made frequently.

ACTIVITIES

For the class

Organize a class fashion show to demonstrate the appropriate use of textures. Select four pairs of girls to appear in the following costumes for the current season:

a. school costume
b. active sports costume (tennis, bicycling, skating, et cetera)
c. dress-up costume suitable for dates, informal parties, and holidays
d. evening attire for formal occasions

Ask one girl of each pair to appear in a costume in which at least one item is inappropriate in texture. Let the other girl in each pair use a perfect combination of textures.

For the individual

Analyze your figure to decide what type of garment designs and fabrics are most becoming to you. Then select patterns from a pattern book for the following dresses: *a.* school dress, *b.* date dress, *c.* formal evening frock. (If you cannot cut out the pattern illustrations, make careful tracings of each dress and mount on manila paper.) Next, select a suitable fabric for each dress. Mount a small sample of the fabric with the illustration of each dress.

CHAPTER 9 | *QUALITIES OF COLOR*

Have you ever stopped to think how much color means to you? Do your spirits pick up when a drab room is redecorated with light, cheery colors? Do you feel like bubbling over with the first signs of spring—tiny, green shoots and sunny daffodils with a blue, blue sky overhead? Then think of the "lift" you get from wearing a dress of your favorite color.

THE POWER OF COLOR

Color has more power to affect us than many people realize. It can be exciting or relaxing. It can create a feeling of warmth or coolness. It plays tricks with size and distance. Sometimes we "see" color where there is none; some colors seem to quiver or dance. These qualities are important whenever you use color.

Color has emotional force. Experiments have shown that red, orange, and yellow have the power to stimulate or excite people whereas blue, green, and violet have a relaxing effect. A crowd at a football game would look drab indeed without the usual dashes of bright red, yellow, and orange. Even a rumpus room, to be successfully decorated, seems to need cheery red, yellow, or orange scattered about.

On the other hand, these colors can be too exciting. Large areas of bright color are too stimulating in a living room, bedroom, or any room where one wishes to relax. Hazy blue, soft green, or warm gray are much more restful. Smaller amounts of yellow, orange, and red can be used to add spots of cheer to a room.

Similarly, the colors you wear create your "personal setting." If red gives you a feeling of excitement and daring, wear it for that next ski meet. If yellow makes you feel gay and light as a canary feather, try it for that next dance. You may be surprised to discover how much colors can affect your mood and personality.

Color has warmth and coolness. We speak of red, orange, and yellow as warm colors, and blue, green, and violet as cool colors. From the beginning of time, man has associated red, orange, and yellow with heat. He saw them in the flames of his fire and in the sun. With twilight, he found coolness in blue and purple shadows. There was coolness, too, in the blue and blue-green of the sea and in the ice and snow of winter.

Even today we are influenced by those associations. In winter, we create the effect of warmth with cheery warm red, rust, gold, and yellow in our homes and clothing. But when the temperature lurks around the 90-degree mark, we crave frosty whites, crisp greens, and icy blues and blue-greens.

Colors advance or recede. Warm colors actually seem to come forward while cool colors seem to retreat. Paste a circle of bright yellow on a square piece of bright blue, and a circle of the same blue on a square of yellow. In either case, the yellow comes forward and the blue steps back.

However, the brightness of a color can change its advancing or receding quality. A bright blue can be more advancing than a dark, dull yellow. In addition, white and light colors are more advancing than black or dull colors. In a crowd the lighter colors pop out; the darker colors tend to blend with the background.

These illusions affect the choice of costume colors. Persons of large build should avoid advancing colors because they emphasize size. A heavy figure dressed in bright yellow or white stands out against any background. Receding colors of medium or darker tones are best for larger figures. A famous French designer noted that Nature used wisdom in clothing the tiny canary in yellow and the awkward elephant in dark gray!

Color may produce an afterimage. Stare fixedly at a one-inch circle of intense red placed on white paper. Then glance at a blank white paper and you "see" a green circle tinged with blue. This is an afterimage. You "see" green after staring at red because the eye reaction to these two colors is paired. Such color pairs are complements.

How can this "pairing" affect colors in clothing? Have you ever noticed that a bright red-and-green figured fabric seemed to quiver? This vibration of color is a strain on the eyes, so that a fabric of this sort would not make a becoming garment. When intense red and green are used in larger, solid-colored areas, such as a sweater and skirt, the vibration is not so obvious. Even so, the combination may become tiring unless one of the colors is quite dull in tone.

In addition, intense colors may produce either flattering or unbecoming afterimages on the skin.

DIMENSIONS OF COLOR

No color is completely described by its name alone. To say that a suit is *blue* gives no idea as to how bright or dull it is, nor how light or dark it is. A color has three qualities or dimensions by which it can be described.

Hue is the quality which distinguishes one color from another. It is the name by which we know a color—such as blue, red, or green.

Intensity, or *chroma,* is the quality of brightness or dullness of a color. Blue can be an intense royal blue or a grayed slate-blue.

Value is the quality of lightness or darkness in a color. Navy is a very dark blue, royal blue is medium, baby blue is light. Each color has a wide range or scale of value.

To have a better understanding of these three qualities of color, try mixing some paints. Opaque poster paints (tempera) are preferable as they produce a fabric-like surface. You will need jars of red, blue, yellow, white, and black.

Use clear plastic egg trays for mixing pans. Work with a medium-sized watercolor brush. Cut manila paper or heavy white drawing paper into three-by-five-inch swatches.

The *primary* hues are red, yellow, and blue. The *secondary* hues are orange, green, and violet. They are made by mixing equal parts of primaries: red and yellow make orange, yellow and blue make green, blue and red make violet. In arranging a color wheel (page 141), a secondary hue is placed between the primaries of which it is made. Orange belongs between red and yellow, and so on.

When a primary color is mixed in equal parts with its adjacent secondary, the result is an *intermediate* hue. For example, blue mixed with green produces a blue-green. There are six intermediate colors: yellow-orange, yellow-green, blue-green, blue-violet, red-violet, and red-orange.

Paint swatches of the primaries, secondaries, and intermediates and arrange them in color wheel sequence. These twelve hues which you have mixed are of fullest intensity because you have combined pure primaries and secondaries.

The majority of colors that you see are not so intense. Some, like mulberry, are deep and rich, others, like powder blue, are soft and subtle, or, like aqua, clear and light. Lower the *intensity* of a bright color by adding some of its *complement,* which is the color opposite it on the color wheel. Blue, for example, is the complement of orange, so you can neutralize orange with a bit of blue. The more blue you add, the less intense the orange becomes. First, it is a tile color, then dark rust, and finally it is a rich brown. Now, mix some neutralized hues for each of the primaries, secondaries, and intermediates.

Finally, mix a range of lighter hues by adding white in varying amounts. Add white to intense hues to obtain colors that are light and clear, such as peach, baby blue, or turquoise. Add white to hues that have already been neutralized by their complements to obtain light subtle hues such as beige or dusty pink.

Every time that you darken or lighten a color, you are changing its *value* as well as its intensity. When the value of a color is darker than the normal hue (the one that appears on the color wheel), it is called a *shade.* Navy is a shade of blue; rust is a shade of orange. When the value is lighter than the normal hue, it is called a *tint.* Pink is a tint of red, and lavender is a tint of violet. Every hue has a wide range of values. For example, violet can be so light that it appears to be practically white, or so dark that it approaches the darkness of black.

White and black represent the extremes of light and dark in the value scale. No color is as light as white or as dark as black. White mixed with black in varying proportions results in a wide range of grays that includes light, medium, and dark values. Because black, gray, and white have no actual hue, they are called neutrals. Include samples of them in your collection of swatches because they are important in planning a color scheme.

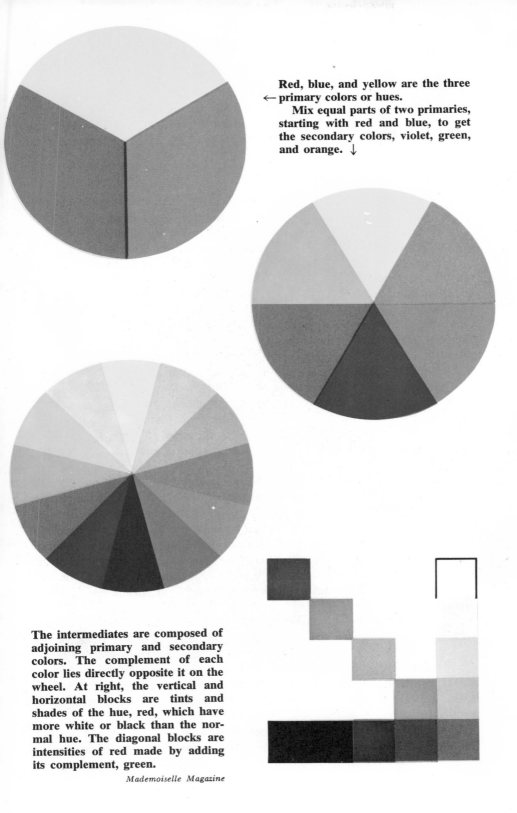

Red, blue, and yellow are the three ← primary colors or hues.

Mix equal parts of two primaries, starting with red and blue, to get the secondary colors, violet, green, and orange. ↓

The intermediates are composed of adjoining primary and secondary colors. The complement of each color lies directly opposite it on the wheel. At right, the vertical and horizontal blocks are tints and shades of the hue, red, which have more white or black than the normal hue. The diagonal blocks are intensities of red made by adding its complement, green.

Mademoiselle Magazine

"Why mix these color samples when I buy materials or garments already dyed?" you may wonder. Because by actually mixing colors, you can develop an appreciation for lovely color combinations. In addition, these swatches may be helpful in planning color schemes which you can use either at home or at school.

COLOR HARMONY

A lovely combination of colors can be as satisfying as a beautiful symphony. Just as surely, a badly chosen color combination can be as jarring as a melody played out of key. We can compare color to music still further. You know that the more you listen to good music, the more you appreciate truly fine music. Similarly, the more you study artistic color combinations, the more sensitive you become to color harmony.

Enjoyment of color. Increase both your knowledge and enjoyment of color by looking at paintings. If you cannot go to a museum, study good color reproductions. Observe the delicate tones in the paintings of Renoir, the vibrant colors of Matisse, the sunny hues of Van Gogh. See how the artist combines colors—cool with warm, light with dark, or intense with subdued.

The colors in a painting may even suggest a color scheme for a costume. One year, a New York shop displayed in its windows the work of several artists. Each painting was accompanied by a mannequin dressed in the colors that were dominant in the painting. Another year, spring fashions featured Renoir colors. And one autumn the fashionable color was Goya red, named for the famous Spanish artist who used that particular red a great deal in his paintings.

But do not stop with paintings; look at all objects of art. Beautiful rugs, especially authentic Orientals, are a gold mine to the colorist. Study the pattern of the rug, section by section. In one tiny spot you may discover two or three rich mellow colors that could be used for a costume. Look at treasured old French tapestries, early American coverlets, rich Chinese brocades, Mexican serapes, Navajo rugs, or Scandinavian wall hangings. Browse through the fabric department of various stores and study the lovely coloring of fine contemporary textiles. Beautiful china and pottery, both ancient and modern, can be an inspiration too.

Then, of course, the colors that you see in nature are the most varied and beautiful of all. They are the real source of all color harmony. Look at any one thing and you will see beauty—a pansy, blending from golden yellow to a velvety purple-blue; a butterfly, intricately patterned with rich glowing hues. Even the bark and moss on trees can provide a color scheme. The rich red-brown of the giant redwoods and the clinging, gray-green moss were featured one autumn as "Sequoia brown and moss green."

Color schemes. Along with such "color appreciation," you should become familiar with certain basic color schemes that are used as guides for combining colors. A successful color harmony is not always the result of a prescribed color scheme, however. An experienced artist whose color taste is highly developed chooses harmonious colors largely by instinct. The colors may or may not conform to any scheme. Even you may find yourself selecting colors because you *feel* that they are pleasing rather than because they fit into a definite scheme. Most beginning students, however, find that color schemes are helpful guides.

A color scheme merely suggests the hues to be used in a combination. You must decide in which value and in which intensity those hues would be most harmonious. There would be discord—not harmony—if each hue were used in its normal value and intensity. The following schemes are based on a twelve-hue color wheel that includes the primaries, secondaries, and six intermediates. Take out your swatches and sort them by hue, including all variations of any one hue in a single pile. Place the normal hue—the one that appears in the wheel—on top. Arrange the twelve piles in color-wheel sequence. As a scheme is described, pick up the specified colors and actually *see* how they look together. (Looking at a color wheel in a book or one that is posted on the bulletin board gives little idea of the effect that colors have on one another.) Shift your swatches so that you can judge which values and intensities of the particular hues create the most pleasing effect together. If one swatch is so intense that it seems to clash with another, a more subdued intensity or a lighter value of the same hue may be completely harmonious.

Color schemes are divided into two groups: related and contrasting.

Related color schemes. Related schemes are combinations that have one hue in common.

A *monochromatic* scheme is a one-hue scheme in which any one hue is used in different values and intensities. Examples: Orange, rust, beige, brown.

An *accented neutral* is another one-hue scheme in which a dash of color is used to accent a neutral costume. Example: Red with black; or navy with white.

An *analogous* scheme consists of two or more hues that are neighbors on the color wheel; they have a primary in common. Examples: A two-hue scheme might combine a dark red-violet (raspberry) with a grayed tint of violet. Or a three-hue scheme could include yellow, yellow-green, and green. Such a series includes a primary, intermediate, and secondary. Difficulties could arise if a primary and two intermediates were chosen, such as red-orange, red, and red-violet.

To use four or five analogous hues in one costume may create a jumble unless the hues appear in a print or plaid. In that case repeat one or two of the hues from the fabric in a coat and accessories. Example: A plaid dress includes red-violet, violet, violet-blue, and navy. Repeat the navy in the coat and all accessories; or if you wish, introduce an accent of red-violet in the hat or gloves.

Contrasting color schemes. Contrasting schemes combine hues that lie on opposite sides of the color wheel. They are a *balance* of unlike hues for they do not have a common primary. They include varying amounts of all three primaries, either in a mixture or as a separate hue.

A *simple complementary* scheme consists of two hues that are directly opposite on the color wheel. Examples: Yellow and violet; green and red; yellow-green and red-violet. (Note that each pair of complements includes all three primaries in some form.)

A *double complementary* scheme consists of any two pairs of complements. If used for a costume, it is generally advisable to select two pairs of neighboring complements. Example: Yellow and violet plus yellow-green and red-violet, a range most suitable for a print or plaid.

A *split complementary* scheme includes any hue plus the two colors lying on either side of its direct complement. Example: Blue-green plus accents of red and orange. (Red-orange is the complement of blue-green.)

An *analogous complementary* scheme is a combination in which a complement is selected for the dominant color in a group of neighboring colors. Example: If blue is the dominating hue in an analogous scheme of green, blue-green, and blue, orange becomes the complement for the series.

A *triad* scheme consists of three colors that are equidistant on the color wheel. Examples: The primaries are a triad; so are the secondaries; or any three equidistant intermediates, such as yellow-orange, red-violet, and blue-green.[1]

Color relationships. A color can appear quite different depending on the hue, value, and intensity with which it is combined. Perhaps you have already observed some of these varying effects as you combined your color swatches. If not, try them out now.

Related hues create a blended effect. The effect is not so startling as when contrasting colors are combined. Examples: Blue, blue-violet, and violet or yellow, yellow-orange, and rust appear to tie in well because of their common primary.

---

[1] The twelve-hue color wheel is not the only color wheel that is used for planning color schemes. Many commercial colorists prefer the Munsell ten-hue circle which consists of five principal hues and five intermediates. Technically, it is preferable to use the Munsell system to plan color combinations. But it might confuse you to use one color system for mixing colored pigments and still another to plot color schemes. For that reason it seems advisable to use the twelve-hue system for both. Furthermore, the twelve-hue color wheel is the one with which most people are familiar. Sometime you might wish to study the Munsell color system for it does give a slightly different set of complements and a detailed description of hue, value, and chroma.

Du Pont photo

Skillful use of accessory colors accents this plaid suit.

Complementary hues emphasize one another. Examples: Intense green seems even brighter when combined with red. Yellow appears brighter when combined with violet.

Cool hues and warm hues emphasize one another. Examples: Blue, blue-green, or violet accent warm yellow-orange tones. Red-orange, when combined with a cool gray, can make the gray seem quite blue.

A subtle hue may appear dull when combined with a similar hue of greater intensity. Examples: A subtle gold may look like a drab tan when combined with vivid yellow or yellow-orange. A delicate, hazy blue may appear faded and gray when combined with a more intense blue.

A hue seems more intense when combined with a neutral. Examples: Red takes on added sparkle when combined with black or white. Even delicate clear tints like pink or pale blue are emphasized by neutrals.

Contrasting values emphasize one another. Examples: Yellow appears even lighter when seen with navy or dark violet. Similarly dark brown or black are emphasized by light hues.

The value of a color can appear lighter or darker depending on the value with which it is combined. Examples: A medium-dark golden brown will look lighter with dark green but darker with a light pink or yellow.

Related hues of similar value and intensity are monotonous. Examples: A light brown would look quite drab with a taupe or dark tan. A navy blue combined with dark violet lacks interest. A contrast of value and intensity is especially necessary with large areas of related hues.

Learn to look for such effects whenever you combine colors. For example, you may wish to select a sweater to wear with a new sport suit of medium blue, but you also want to wear it with a brown skirt. A hazy blue would look well with the brown skirt, but it appears faded with the stronger blue of the suit. You decide on a soft shell pink that would be a nice warm contrast for the blue. The shell pink would also pep up the brown. Moreover, the shell pink would tie in perfectly with your warm skin tones.

You may have already guessed that these "color relationships" apply to the effects that costume colors have on personal coloring. For example, a girl with flaming red hair would know that bright contrasting colors would make it look altogether too fiery. Or a person with sallow skin tones and ash-blond hair knows that tans and beige do absolutely nothing for her!

In the following chapter you will learn how to select costume colors that flatter your personal coloring.

ACTIVITIES

For the class

1. **Collect** the following display for the class bulletin board:
    a. reproductions of paintings that create a definite mood or feeling by means of color: gay and depressed; warm or cool, et cetera.
    b. printed advertisements that attract attention by the correct use of advancing and receding colors.
    c. colored illustrations of flowers, fish, birds, and other natural forms.
2. **Ask** members of the class to bring in items which display a fine use of color: china, pottery, decorative tiles, small scatter rugs, Paisley shawls, bits of tapestry or brocade, and other art objects.
3. **Analyze** above color displays to see whether a definite color scheme has been used for any of the items.

For the individual

Plan a color harmony for a striped dress fabric using at least three colors found in any one flower, fish, bird, etc., on display. Mix colors to match those in the illustration. Make several trial color sketches until you arrive at a pleasing sequence of varying widths of stripes. Sketch final stripe on manila paper or heavy white drawing paper. Plan to have it cover a space of approximately 5 by 7 inches. Paint in stripes.

CHAPTER 10   *COLOR AND YOU*

You already know that the choice of costume colors is partly determined by personality or individual likes and dislikes. You have a good idea as to what colors harmonize with one another. But the final selection of costume colors should be determined by their becomingness to your natural coloring and figure. You may adore yellow, but cross it off your list if it makes your pale skin look ghastly. Beige may look stunning on your red-haired girl friend, but don't be a copycat if it makes your ash-blond hair look positively mousey. Red may give you a "lift," but use it in small accents if it calls attention to roly-poly dimensions. Build your costume around colors that bring out your attractive qualities.

COLOR TESTING

You may have grown up hearing that "blondes should wear blue, brunettes should wear red, and redheads should wear green." Color tests will show that color selection is not so simple (nor so limited) as all that! Each group or color type includes a wide range of coloration in skin, hair, and eyes. And every person within each group is an individual combination of different color traits. That is why it is not advisable to follow a ready-made list of colors that attempts to cover all blondes, all brunettes, or all redheads in one easy lesson! For example, three of your classmates may be classified as medium brunettes. One has brown hair with golden lights, a fair pink-and-white complexion, and blue eyes. Another has brown hair with an auburn glint, a warm coppery skin generously sprinkled with freckles, and mellow brown eyes. The third has dull brown hair with no glint, a dark sallow skin, and gray-green eyes. It is obvious that each girl will have a different list of becoming colors.

Similarly, you have your own coloring to consider. Actual color tests will help you to decide which colors are most flattering to your skin, hair, and eyes.

First, you will need a good mirror. Sit before it and drape colored fabrics over your chest or wear colored bibs made of fabric or colored paper. Or drape a piece of white fabric over your chest and pin your paint swatches one by one at the neckline. Test all colors in strong daylight and by artificial light as well. You will recall that artificial light changes cosmetic color by adding yellow to it. Costume colors are similarly affected. Colors that contain blue are somewhat neutralized; colors that contain yellow become more yellow in tone; reds tend to look more orange. Do not wear make-up during a color test. See how your natural skin tone reacts to color, whether it is a "winter white" or a deep sun tan.

Learn to think of your coloring as part of a color harmony which you complete by adding costume colors. Will you plan a related harmony in which costume colors *repeat* your loveliest "color feature"? For example, a dress of subtle blue would emphasize lovely blue eyes. Rust would accent the auburn lights of rich brown hair. Petal pink would bring out the delicate tones of a pink-and-white complexion. Or will you plan a harmony in which colors *contrast* your best color feature? For example, cool blues and violets would bring out the warm yellow tones of golden hair beautifully. Blue and blue-green would emphasize a becoming sun tan. Bright red would make black eyes seem more luminous.

From this you can see that it is possible to emphasize lovely coloring by either *repetition* or *contrast*. But just as similar or contrasting hues emphasize attractive qualities, just as surely they emphasize less attractive ones. Pink will bring out lovely pink cheek tones, *but* it can also call attention to pink skin blemishes! Blue and violet contrast golden hair beautifully, but, if they are too intense, they bring out a sickly pallor in yellow skin tones, and they may make blue eyes seem pale by comparison.

So you see how carefully you have to consider "color relationships," whether you are selecting colors to harmonize with your skin, hair, or eyes.

COLOR AND THE COMPLEXION

Before we discuss specific color types, here are some over-all suggestions for you to consider.

General pointers. Regardless of your color type, there are some rules that apply pretty much to everyone. For example, whites and light colors add radiance to most complexions. Because these colors reflect light, they lighten the skin and add vitality to the face. The following statements also have a general application.

SOME COLORS DRAIN THE FACE OF NATURAL COLOR.

1. Intense hues make light skin appear paler by contrast.
2. Black absorbs light, making sallow skin appear even duller.
3. Dark, somber colors and grays tend to drain the face of color.

FABRIC TEXTURE CHANGES THE EFFECT OF COLOR ON THE SKIN.

1. Shiny fabrics, such as satin, reflect more color on the face than rough or soft textures. (However, avoid satin in yellow tones if you are wan; avoid it in reds if you are florid; and avoid it in *any* tone if your skin is not flawless!)
2. A black dress in a sparkling or lustrous material (taffeta, moiré, etc.) will *not* drain the face of color as would a black dress in a dull fabric.
3. Soft, smooth textures are generally more becoming than shiny textures.

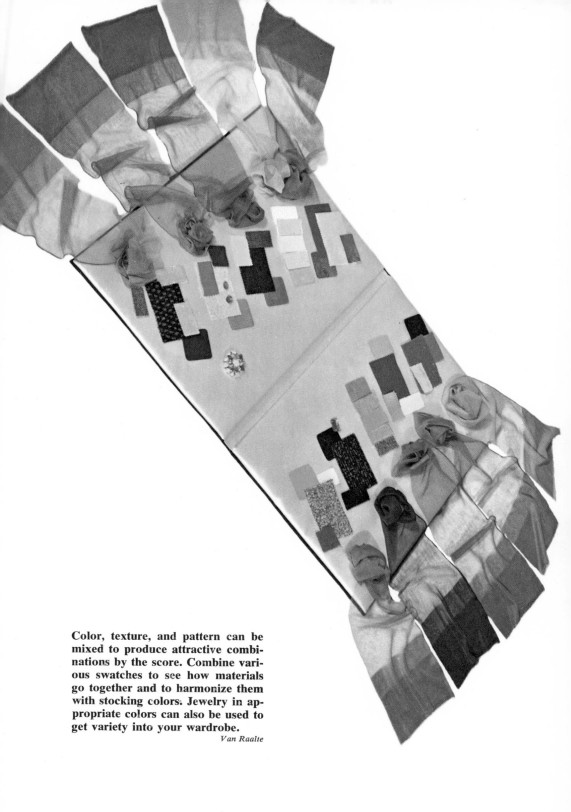

Color, texture, and pattern can be mixed to produce attractive combinations by the score. Combine various swatches to see how materials go together and to harmonize them with stocking colors. Jewelry in appropriate colors can also be used to get variety into your wardrobe.

Van Raalte

FACIAL BLEMISHES CALL FOR CAREFUL COLOR SELECTION.

1. Pink will emphasize pimples, and any intense hue calls attention to them. Subtle tints are better than clear tints; creamy white is better than pure white.

2. Intense blue or yellow will only emphasize any dark circles under the eyes because the repetition or contrast (as the case may be) acts as an accent. For example, a dress or blouse of intense blue accents the dark blue circles because it *repeats* the color; a garment of yellow or yellow-orange calls attention to the blue circles because it is a *contrast* to the blue.

3. The girl who dislikes her freckles even though they are *not* a problem should avoid tans, brown, or light, clear tints in her costume.

UNBECOMING COLORS CAN BE COUNTERACTED BY THE USE OF A FLATTER-ING COLOR AT THE NECKLINE.

1. If a dress or sweater is not very becoming in color, a collar in a be-coming color (that harmonizes with the garment) will flatter the face.

2. Wear a scarf, blouse, or hat in a flattering color to relieve the effect of a suit or coat that drains the face of color.

CAREFULLY SELECTED COSMETICS WILL RELIEVE THE EFFECT OF UNBE-COMING COSTUME COLOR.

1. A brunette with a neutral, creamy skin can offset the sallowing effect of a blue-violet dress by wearing a purple-red lipstick.

2. A blonde with a pale complexion will not appear drained of color in blue-greens if she uses orange-red rouge and lipstick.

3. A redhead with pale, creamy skin will not look ashen in grays if she uses rouge and lipstick in orange-red.

4. Black will not drain the sallow face of color when orange-red to me-dium-red lipstick and rouge are worn.

Color types. Although there are unlimited variations in skin coloring, com-plexions can be roughly divided into four main color groups, each of which has a basic, underlying color tone.

Group I   From "peaches-and-cream," to a deep, coppery suntan. (Skin has orange tones.)

Group II   From "petal-pink," to a deep, rosy flush. (Skin has red tones.)

Group III   From "creamy-ivory" to a "golden ivory" and on to dark, olive tones. (Skin has neutral, rather yellowed tones.)

Group IV   From yellow and tan skin tones to bronze and brown. (Skin has tan to brown tones.)

It is possible to suggest a becoming *range of color* for any one of these four complexion groups. However, each complexion group includes skin tones that may vary from light to dark, or from "delicate" to "high color." For this reason, you should try to use the recommended colors in *values* and *intensities* that are most flattering to your own particular coloring.

Group I Complexions that range from "peaches-and-cream" to a deep, coppery suntan are flattered by:

Related hues ranging on the color wheel from red-orange through yellow

Contrasting hues ranging from blue-violet to green

A. IF THE SKIN IS A FAIR AND DELICATE "PEACH"

Select:

1. Delicate, clear tints such as shell pink, pale yellow, peach, powder blue, or aqua
2. Soft shades of blue, blue-green, blue-violet, coral, rust, gold, and olive
3. Brown, beige, dark gray, white; black is possible

Avoid:

1. Intense colors which tend to overpower delicate coloring
2. All colors in the red to violet range

B. IF THE SKIN HAS A DARK COPPERY TONE

Select:

1. Subtle, grayed tints ranging from red-orange through yellow-green; and from blue-violet to green
2. Rich shades such as rust, burnt orange, tobacco, teal blue, olive green, moss green, mustard, and golden yellow
3. Brown, beige, and creamy white

Avoid:

1. Light, clear tints which may make a dark skin look muddy by contrast
2. Intense blue and blue-green which would make copper-toned skin appear harsh
3. All colors in the red to red-violet range

Group II Complexions that range from "petal-pink" to a deep, rosy flush are flattered by:

Related hues ranging from red through violet

Contrasting hues ranging from blue through green

A. IF THE SKIN IS PETAL-PINK (DRESDEN DOLL COLORING)

Select:

1. Delicate, clear tints such as pink, lavender, baby blue, light aqua, and pale green
2. Subtle, medium tones such as rose, mauve, powder blue, and teal blue
3. Darker shades such as plum, navy, and forest green for effective contrast
4. Black, brown, cool gray, and white

Avoid:

1. All intense colors which are too harsh for delicate coloring
2. All colors in the red to orange range unless considerably grayed

B. IF THE SKIN HAS MEDIUM RED COLORING

(Note: In general, this group has a wider range of hues from which to choose than any other complexion type. The final selection should depend upon hair color.)

Select:

1. Red-orange through yellow-orange if your hair is auburn
2. Red-orange *or* red-violet, even in quite intense hues, if you are a brunette; more subtle tones if you are a blonde
3. Cool colors for becoming contrasts for all types
4. Yellow-green and yellow, slightly muted, for all types, since the skin is rosy enough not to appear sallow

Avoid:

1. Red-violet and reds if your hair is auburn
2. All intense hues, whether warm or cool, if you have light hair as they tend to dull it by contrast

C. IF THE SKIN HAS A DECIDED ROSY FLUSH

Select:

1. Hazy, subtle tints ranging from blue-violet through green
2. Very grayed medium tones and shades from the above listing
3. Black, brown, navy, gray, and white

Avoid:

1. Intense red and red-violet which only add to the rosy flush
2. Bright blues and blue-greens which accent florid tones
3. Colors in the orange to yellow range

Group III   Complexions that range from "creamy ivory" to dark, olive tones are flattered by:

Warm colors, ranging from red-orange through red-violet
Cool colors, ranging from blue through green

A. IF THE SKIN IS CREAMY OR TENDING TO SALLOW (NO RED TONE)

Select:

1. Subtle tints and shades from either the red-violet or red-orange range (depending on hair color); try mauve, raspberry, or garnet or coral, russet, or henna to give warmth to the skin
2. Soft blues, blue-greens, and greens
3. Grayed hues from the yellow and violet range, such as dull gold, olive, or avocado; heather, plum, or wine

Avoid:

1. Intense orange, yellow-orange, yellow, and yellow-green
2. Intense blue, blue-violet, and violet

Note: The sallower the skin, the more these colors should be avoided.

B. IF THE SKIN HAS DARK OLIVE TONES

Select:

1. Rich hues from the red-orange, orange, yellow-orange ranges, such as scarlet, pimento, and tangerine
2. Dark shades in the above ranges, such as mahogany, tobacco, or rust
3. Rich, yet slightly grayed hues ranging from yellow-green through blue-green, such as olive, bottle green, or blue spruce

4. Dark shades of red-violet, such as mulberry or plum

5. Brown, warm gray, and creamy white

  Avoid:

1. Clear tints which cause dark skin to look muddy

2. Intense hues from the red-violet range, such as orchid or fuchsia

3. Intense blues or violets (they accent yellow tones)

Group IV Complexions that are included in the darker color range are flattered by:

Related, warm hues ranging from yellow-green through red-violet

Contrasting hues in rich, slightly grayed tones ranging from green through violet

A. IF THE SKIN HAS YELLOW, GOLDEN BROWN, OR BRONZE TONES

Select:

1. Rich, yet slightly grayed hues from the yellow-green and through red-orange range

2. Cool colors—green, blue-green, blue, and violet in slightly grayed tones to avoid harsh contrast

3. Brown, beige, tan, dull gold, and creamy white

Avoid:

1. Light, clear tints such as bright pink, fuchsia, baby blue, or aqua

2. Beige or tan of same value as skin tone (should be either lighter or darker for contrast)

B. IF THE SKIN IS BROWN WITH SLIGHT PURPLE CAST

Select:

1. Slightly grayed tints, either warm or cool

2. Warm, rich shades ranging from yellow-green through red-violet

3. Rich, yet slightly grayed, cool colors ranging from green through violet

4. Brown, beige, creamy white, or white

Avoid:

1. Light, intense tints

2. Intense, harsh blue, blue-green, or violet

COLOR AND THE HAIR

The skin color usually determines the choice of costume colors, but the color of the hair should also be considered. When a person's hair is her crowning glory, she generally thinks of it first when choosing colors. Even so, the colors should be in values and intensities that also flatter the skin tones. Emphasize the color of the hair by wearing colors that contrast it or colors that are related to it.

A contrast in color emphasizes the hair. The warm golden tones of blond hair are accented by its complement, blue-violet, and other cool colors. The warm coppery hue of red hair is emphasized by its complement, blue-green, and other cool colors. The blue-black sheen of glossy black hair may be empha-

Reprinted from Vogue © 1958, The
Condé Nast Publications, Inc.

**Delicate tints are particularly flattering to girls with petal-pink coloring. The
turquoise earrings provide an attractive accent.**

sized by intense warm colors. Medium-brown hair that has no definite red or
golden glints appears warmer when rich, cool hues are worn. Cool browns
and blue-grays also make it seem warmer. If the hair color is vivid, an intense
color may create a harsh metallic effect that is unbecoming. For example, vivid
golden hair tends to look cheap with extremely bright blue or green. The
orange-red tones of flaming red hair literally "shriek" when brilliant blue-
green or green are worn. Subtle tones would be so much more flattering.

A contrast in values is important too. Rich brown hair or glossy black hair
looks darker when light values are worn. Blond, red, or light brown hair
appears lighter when contrasted by dark values. A similarity in values looks
monotonous, especially if the costume color is closely related to the hair. For
example, blond hair fades away into nothingness with tan or beige. Likewise,
brown hair may look lifeless with brown or somber hues of identical value.
Even when it does not seem advisable to call attention to a less attractive
head of hair, a slight value difference relieves a drab effect.

There are times when it is effective to repeat the color of the hair in the
costume. Yet the color should not be so intense that it dulls the hair color by
comparison. Rich yellows will bring out the golden lights in blond or light
brown hair. Warm rust hues accent the auburn glint in brown hair nicely. If the
particular color (yellow, for example) does not look well next to the face, it
may be used as an accent in some accessory.

It may be interesting to wear a color that is not an exact repetition of the
hair color, but one which is related to it. For example, the rich tones of dark
red (orange-red) hair would be more pronounced when an analogous grayed
yellow is worn. The subtle dark yellow blends with, yet accents, the more intense red hair. The dark blonde who has yellow-green or "brass" tones in her
hair may wear subtle, analogous greens to emphasize it.

COLOR AND THE EYES

Have you noticed that eyes appear dark and luminous in some colors and paler in others? If your eyes are one of your best features, emphasize them by repeating their color in the costume.

When the eye color is repeated in a large area, such as a coat or dress, the costume color should be less intense and lighter than the eyes. A large area of similar intensity would weaken the eye color by comparison. Blue eyes seem brighter and darker in medium or light soft blues; gray eyes appear darker in light gray; dark brown eyes are accented by medium or light brown.

But repeat the eye color in an intense hue when using it for small accents, such as a collar, bow, scarf, jewelry, or hat trim. An intense color used in a small area does not overshadow the eyes; instead, it picks up the eye color. This is especially true of blue eyes.

Some eyes seem to reflect the costume color. For instance, gray eyes tend to look blue when blue is worn, but green when green is worn. So bring out what you wish!

Eye color can also be accented by contrasting hues. Black or dark brown eyes will look more luminous in poppy red, emerald green, and other intense or light colors. Green eyes are intensified by red and coppery tones. Violet or blue eyes may be accented by yellow and amber hues.

COLOR AND THE FIGURE

Before you begin to plan colors for a complete costume, you should also consider your figure. We have already mentioned that large persons should avoid advancing colors. But the arrangement of colors in a costume also has a good bit to do with the appearance of a figure. Here are a few suggestions as to how the proportions of a figure can be seemingly altered by the correct use of color. If you have no "problem spots" now, save these hints for the day when you may have one!

If "all-around" weight is a problem, avoid advancing colors and light or intense hues that only call attention to size. Select subtle, receding hues that minimize size. Avoid splotchy prints, stripes, and plaids with strong value and color contrast. Solid-colored fabrics are really best.

If you are short and plump, or just extremely short, do not cut the figure by a color or value contrast at the waist or hipline. A solid, unbroken color area adds height to the figure. That is why full-length coats are better than finger-tip length coats because they do not reveal a skirt of contrasting color or value. If you insist on a contrasting jacket, select a bolero or one that ends at a high hip line. This gives a longer unbroken line to the skirt and creates a vertical emphasis. A short person looks taller when her hat color repeats her coat color. Contrasting color accents should be kept high—in the scarf, collar, or jewelry.

If you are tall and thin, you may wear intense, advancing colors, provided they are otherwise becoming. Use color contrast in shoulder yokes, in belts, and at hips to cut height. Contrasting jackets and skirts are good; so are finger-tip length coats. Match scarf or blouse to handbag or gloves when using contrasting accessories.

If you are broad-shouldered or full-chested but of normal height or tall, wear dark solid colors for jacket or blouse and harmonizing plaids, stripes, or novelty weaves for skirt. Keep color accents away from chest area. Match hat to gloves or shoes to bag.

If you have a large abdomen, avoid contrast in skirts and waist or contrasting belts on dresses. Keep color accents high.

If broad-hipped but of normal height or tall, you should wear dark skirts and use lighter more intense colors for blouses or boleros. Keep color interest high, away from the hip line. Match hat to blouse or scarf rather than to gloves or bag which are on the hip level.

If heavy or bowed legs are a problem, avoid strong value contrast between hosiery and skirt area. Dark hosiery tones are best with dark skirts. Subtle, smoky tans are better than orange-tan hosiery with light-colored skirts. Avoid light or intense colors and contrasting combinations in shoes, for they also call attention to heavy legs and to large feet!

ASSEMBLING A COSTUME

When you have gathered all of this "personal color data," you are ready to plot and plan the colors for actual costumes. It might be easier if you could go out and buy a completely new outfit. But very few people can do that! More often the new color plan has to be built around a coat, a suit, or accessories left from the previous year. If you select colors to harmonize with that item, your costume will be a success. But if you buy a new dress, blouse, or shoes with no thought as to how it will look with other things on hand, you won't be happy with the result. A vivid brunette who buys a fuchsia dress that she must wear with her shortie of Kelly green, her rust hat, and brown accessories is not color-wise! Taken singly each color may be becoming to her; used together they create a riot of color. So, whatever you buy, be sure that the colors are harmonious with other colors in the costume as well as becoming to you.

PRINCIPLES OF DESIGN

Now just how do the principles of design apply to the color plan of a costume? Whether you have been conscious of it or not, you have already applied the principles of unity and contrast each time that you tested the becomingness of colors.

In the first place, you achieved *unity* when you selected colors that were becoming to you personally. You had a feeling that those colors were really *your* colors; they belonged to you. In addition, you combined colors that looked well together—whether you followed a definite color scheme or used your own personal judgment.

You have realized how a *contrast* of color can emphasize your best features. And you also learned that a pleasing contrast of hue, value, or chroma is the foundation of any successful color combination. Contrast adds sparkle or

Dress by L'Aiglon Apparel, Inc.

The slender black ribbon belt repeats the black of the delicate embroidery on this dress, creating a unified effect.

interest to a costume. A contrast in value or color is used to focus attention on the head area which is the most important part of anyone's personal design. It may be a light sweater or colorful scarf, a bit of jewelry, or a hat trim; whatever it is, the contrast makes the head the center attraction. It is obvious that there is also a contrast in areas or amounts of colors used in each costume, which brings us to other "principles."

You have already learned that a dress design is more pleasing when there is some variety in the sizes or areas of the design. The *proportions* are more satisfying. Similarly, there should be variety in the amounts of colors used in a costume. Equal amounts of anything are monotonous. Plan a costume so that there are a *dominating* hue and value. For example, if you plan to use three colors, let one appear in a large area, the second in a smaller area, the third as an accent. The dominating hue should set the *theme* for the costume. Will it be a gay bright costume? Will it be a subtle scheme? Whichever it is you will have to vary the values and intensities a bit. Three equally intense, vivid colors are likely to clash, just as three equally grayed colors would appear drab. In planning a gay costume, use one color in strong intensity with others that are slightly less intense and of darker or lighter values. The scheme is still spirited and gay; the colors are in key without appearing to clash.

Lassie Junior

By using different colored scarves and gloves with your basic coat, you can ring a change in your appearance. Try to choose for your coat, suit, and dress a color that will harmonize or contrast pleasantly with accessories.

Generally you will find that when you are combining warm and cool colors in a costume, a small accent of warm, more intense color will *balance* a larger area of subdued cool color. A belt of burnt orange is enough to accent a dress of cool green. When the entire suit or dress is of an intense color, an accent of contrasting neutral (black, gray, or white) or a dark grayed hue (brown or navy) is becoming. A sport suit of poppy red can be worn with a crisp white blouse and black shoes and bag. A date dress of chartreuse would look well with navy. A gabardine sport dress of burnt orange looks nice with brown and so on. Or if you should plan an all-navy or an all-black costume (later, if not in your teens), an accent or two of bright color in accessories will balance a larger area of the solid dark color.

Avoid the common mistake of overdoing a contrasting accessory color. If it is repeated too often, it creates a spotty, restless effect. In other words, the eye movement or *rhythm* is jumpy. A girl who wears a lovely beige suit and selects the identical green for her hat, blouse, bag, shoes, and gloves is really overdoing the color. Furthermore, she looks so obviously "matched." What to do about it? Let us say that she is a dark redhead. She could wear a blouse of creamy white, hat and gloves of green, and shoes and bag of brown. The creamy white and brown are related to beige, thus creating a rhythmic value sequence. The green provides the contrasting accent. To repeat an accent color three times is possible, but twice is always safe.

The same thing applies to white accents that are worn with dark colors. Take the typical navy-and-white costume which is popular in early summer. A girl has a navy street dress with a white collar. She feels that she should have a white hat, gloves, shoes, and bag. As a result, the eye jumps from white to white—tic-tac-toe! She would look far smarter if she used white for the collar and gloves and navy for the other items. Her hat might have a tiny touch of white.

Of course, when the dress color is very light, such as a pale green chambray, white may be used for all accessories. The value contrast between the dress and white accessories is so slight that the white items do not pop out in a jumpy sequence.

These suggestions should help you to assemble your best colors into an attractive costume. In Chapter 12, "Planning A Wardrobe," you will learn how to develop a color plan for your entire wardrobe.

ACTIVITIES

For the class

1. **Organize** an impromptu fashion show to demonstrate the becomingness of colors on each color type represented in the class. Select one girl of each type of skin coloring and hair coloring to model coats, jackets, or sweaters collected from class members for this purpose. The models should stand across the front of the classroom. After each has modeled a garment,

she should pass it to the model on her right so that the class can see the same coats and sweaters on each of the models. Which colors look best on which color models? Discuss.

For the individual

1. **Work out** an outfit for each of the following girls, starting with some clothes they already have. Work out each costume by yourself, pasting ads and color swatches on a piece of paper to illustrate your suggestions. Bring your paste-ups to class and discuss them. Choose some of the best to go on the class bulletin board.

   a. Rita has rich dark-brown hair, sparkling brown eyes, and a light creamy skin. She is of medium build with no particular problem spots. She classifies herself as "vivacious." She owns a crimson red sport jacket and black calfskin brogues and shoulder bag. She needs a spectator sports outfit for school and strictly casual activities.

   b. Lucy has ash-blond hair, a "petal pink" skin, and gray eyes. She is short and a bit heavy in the hips. She classifies herself as "dainty and rather demure." She has "best" pumps of light, warm brown calfskin. She also has white accessories for the summer. She wants an all-season suit for Easter that can be dressed up or down.

   c. Jean has red hair, medium-light coppery skin tones, and green eyes. She is tall and slender. She classifies herself as somewhat "dramatic." She has a camel's hair coat and brown calfskin shoes and bag. She needs an all-purpose dress to wear to school, for informal social get-togethers, and for a Saturday job that she has in a gift shop.

2. **Plan** a becoming spectator sports costume for yourself that consists of a plain topper, blouse or sweater, plain skirt, shoes, and bag. If you can't find the right colored pictures, find black-and-white ones in magazines to illustrate your choice of items. Mount them on manila paper and paste color swatches beside them. Indicate with arrows which color is to be used for each item in the costume.

CONSTRUCTION TWO ▶

MAKING A DRESS

And now you are ready to make a dress. What kind shall it be? A school dress? A dressy dress? What style? A classic? Or the latest fashion design? What materials and color? A soft green wool jersey? A blue taffeta? But wait a minute before setting your heart on a particular style and material. There are some other questions to ask yourself first. How much do you already know about making a dress? What will you need to learn? Again, your particular class with all of its interests and abilities should be kept in mind as you plan so that there won't be too many of you at a time who need individual help from your teacher before you can proceed with your work.

A dress is really a blouse and a skirt joined at the waistline. If you have made both garments, you already know how to make a simple dress except for the waistline joining. Perhaps you would enjoy making a dress with a few new details, but don't take on too many new problems in your first dress. Until you have acquired skill in sewing, avoid dress patterns with the right and left sides cut differently, and those with inset waistbands, gussets (those diamond-shaped inserts under the sleeves), or pressed pleats all around. Leave binding, cording, piping, and scallops for later problems, also.

SELECTING A DRESS PATTERN

A dress with a notched convertible collar and short set-in sleeves is such a classic that steps are given here for making that kind of dress. It is a good choice as a class project because some of you can wear your collars closed and some can wear them open, whichever is more becoming. Also, depending upon your figures and the dictates of fashion, skirts may be wide and billowy, pencil slim, or somewhere in-between. If you don't want your sleeves short, make them long or three-quarter length. Your pattern often gives all three styles. But perhaps your class has other ideas. If you decide on a shawl-type collar and raglan sleeves or any other variations, refer to technique 13, "Neck Finishes," and technique 14, "Sleeves" or to other appropriate techniques.

SELECTING MATERIAL FOR A DRESS

The material for a dress of this classic type should be firmly woven and of medium weight. Dress-weight flannel or crepe woven out of pure wool or wool blended with nylon, Orlon, or Acrilan would be a good choice. So would spun rayon in various weaves, cotton or silk shantung, denim, piqué, chambray, or dress linen. Fabrics used for sport and general wear are usually more suitable than dressy materials, though we do find this style made up for more formal occasions.

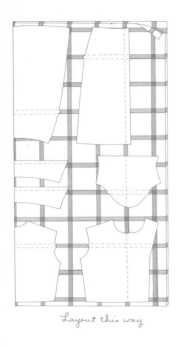

Layout this way

For this effect

Not this effect

Plaid materials require very careful layouts.

Avoid transparent materials, plaids, wide stripes, and other materials that require special handling until you have made several garments of plain color or of all-over designs. Silk crepe and other soft materials are difficult to handle, also. Of course, you will want to learn to use fabrics that require special treatment. A second skirt or dress could be made of one of them. Refer to technique 6, "Materials that Require Special Handling," for special instruction for using each type.

OTHER SUPPLIES AND NOTIONS

By this time you know how to buy the correct pattern size and the right amount of material. You must decide whether to buy buttons, have them covered from the fabric, or make self-covered buttons yourself with some of the button molds or gadgets on the market. Be sure the kind you use will stand the cleaning methods required for the dress, or select a type that can be quickly removed. There are tiny safety pins with humps on their backs for attaching shank buttons quickly.

What kind of belt are you going to use? Perhaps you have a leather belt that would be suitable. If you would rather have a self belt—one made of the same material as the dress—you may want to have it made. In most cities, you can have belts and buckles made from your material just as you can have buttons covered. You can also buy belt-making kits. These usually contain a plastic-treated strip of firm fabric, a buckle mold, patterns, and directions for completing the belt and buckle. If you would prefer to start from scratch, buy some cotton belting or some heavy grosgrain ribbon in a color that will harmonize with your dress. Don't forget to buy a buckle or a buckle mold too, unless you have an old buckle you can use as it is or cover.

A dress placket zipper is 12 or 14 inches long. Look on the back of the pattern envelope to see if the length you need is specified. Remember that dress-type zippers are closed at each end.

Set-in sleeves fit better with slight shoulder pads. Select a kind of pad that will clean as the dress is to be cleaned, or use a kind that snaps in. The pad should be covered with durable material, the stitching should be well done, and the padding should be smooth, not lumpy. Select the shape and size with fashion trends in mind.

Select matching thread and buy several spools. It will take approximately 200 yards for the dress, so look at the amount contained on the spools you buy.

Either buy, or have on hand, a firm interfacing material. You will also need tape to reinforce the waistline of your dress and make it conform to your figure. Buy a package of cotton twill tape for a washable dress. If your dress will be dry-cleaned, you can select ribbon seam binding in a harmonizing color. Buy enough for the hem too if the dress material ravels easily. For skirts or other areas that need to be lined or interfaced, refer to technique 9, "Staylines, Interfacings, and Linings."

It is a good idea to estimate the cost of all the materials you will need to make a certain dress before purchasing any of the materials. Compare the total cost with what you had planned to spend.

MAKING A DRESS

Cutting out a dress. Follow the same procedure as for making the other garments. Study the pattern, select the pieces you need, check the fit of the pattern, and make alterations, if they are needed. Prepare the material for cutting as you have done before. Make a careful layout. You may want to allow extra width along side seams as you did for your skirt. Add ½ inch to blouse side seams as well as to skirt side seams.

Cut and mark the pieces carefully. Sort them into units with the pattern still attached. Tear two lengthwise strips of pre-shrunk muslin to reinforce the facing beneath the buttonholes and buttons. These strips should be about 2 inches wide and long enough to extend beneath all buttonholes and buttons.

Constructing a dress. Occasionally dresses are made by attaching a completed front to a completed back with continuous side seams. The usual method, however, is to join a finished blouse unit to a finished skirt unit with a continuous waistline seam. The steps you follow are then similar to those for making a blouse and skirt. You can work first on the blouse, then on the skirt, or vice versa. Or you can carry both parts along at the same time.

The kind of buttonholes you plan to make will affect your construction order. For piped buttonholes, place the interfacing strips beneath the button and buttonhole positions on the blouse itself. Fasten these in place permanently with fine catch stitching that will not show from the right side. Proceed immediately to make the buttonholes as described in technique 18, "Fastenings." For worked buttonholes follow the steps as outlined below. Whatever plan you use, try to group your activities and work in an orderly way. Here is a suggested plan of work for constructing this typical dress:

BLOUSE BACK

1. Make staylines as you did on your blouse. In addition you will need them at the armscye (the armhole seam) starting at the shoulder and stitching downward.

2. Stitch darts.

BLOUSE FRONTS

1. Transfer traced markings for buttonholes and fold lines to the right side of the cloth. Use machine bastings. Mark both fronts in the same way.

2. Make staylines similar to those on the back.

3. Place the lengthwise strip of muslin on the under side of the facing beneath buttonhole markings. Keep the muslin strip about ¼ inch from the fold line, and not more than ½ inch above the top buttonhole position. Stitch continuously around both sides and ends. Repeat, on the opposite facing. Of course, you do not turn under its edges.

4. Edge-stitch the outer facing edges, or use another suitable finish.

5. Stitch darts.

JOINING SHOULDER SEAMS

Join shoulder seams and finish seam edges.

PRESSING

Press seams and darts.

MAKING THE COLLAR

1. Fold the collar with the right sides in.

2. Stitch the ends from the fold line toward the raw collar edges.

3. Trim, turn, and press.

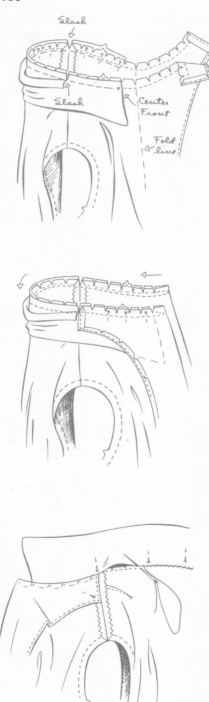

1. Since the neck is curved, clip almost to the stayline at about ½-inch intervals. It is not necessary to stay-stitch the collar edges or to clip them because they are cut on a straight grain.

2. Place the right side of the under collar against the right side of the garment, matching center backs, notches, and seam edges, and pin through both collar layers and the blouse neckline.

3. Slash through all seam allowances at each shoulder seam. End the slashes exactly at the stitching line.

4. Remove pins across the back of the neck and pin again, catching only the bottom layer of the collar. Baste.

5. Fold the facing back against the right side of the garment on both pieces of the blouse front. (In case a separate facing is used, place it against the garment with right sides facing.) Match and pin notches, shoulder seams, and raw seam edges along the neckline.

6. Stitch around the entire neckline seam. You will stitch through both collars as well as the garment and facing, but do not stitch through the upper collar between the slashes. Fasten thread ends by retracing at each end. (When separate facings are used, continue to stitch around the corners and on down the length of each front facing.)

7. Clip seam allowances enough to permit the collar to lie flat.

8. Trim all seams to ¼ inch and clip corners.

9. Turn facing to the under side.

10. Across the back of the neck turn and press the seam allowances up into the collar. At the same time, press the front collar. Then turn under the free edge of the top collar on the seam line. Hem it to the stitching line across the back of the collar with slant hemming stitches. Keep stitches hidden in the layers of the seam. Continue along the shoulder seam to catch the facing to that seam inconspicuously.

CLOSING BLOUSE SIDE SEAMS

When there is any doubt of the fit, baste-stitch side seams first, then try on the blouse. Check dart positions, shoulder length, and side seams. Refer to technique 5, "Altering the Pattern and Fitting the Garment."

1. Close blouse side seams, leaving the left side seam open below the placket marking. Fasten the stitching line at the top of the placket. Do this either by tying the threads or by retracing.

2. Finish seams and press.

MAKING THE SLEEVES

Regulation set-in sleeves are easier to make if they are completely finished before being attached to the blouse. All set-in sleeves are cut with the upper part of the sleeve (the sleeve cap) larger than the corresponding part of the armhole. In fitted sleeves this fullness is eased in so that the sleeve cap will fit smoothly over the curve of the upper arm with no gathers showing. Set-in sleeves are much easier to join at the armscye seam if the ease along the sleeve cap has been "shrunk out" before the sleeve is set in. Almost any material can be shrunk or shaped before the sleeve is attached. If your material cannot be shrunk, then fitted sleeves may not be a wise design for your garment. See technique 12, "Pressing," for full instructions on shrinking a sleeve cap.

As you "shrink out" fullness in the cap, you increase the width of the seam allowance. Therefore it is important to match the marked seam lines rather than the seam edges when you set in sleeves.

1. Starting at the notches on the lower armscye make staylines to the underarm seams.

2. Gather across the sleeve cap between notches. Make two rows of long machine stitching—one on the seam line and one in the seam allowance ¼ inch away.

3. Draw the gathering threads until the sleeve turns slightly and shrink out the fullness across the sleeve cap. Put the sleeve cap over the end of a sleeve board or over a tailor's cushion, wrong side out. Using a steam iron, press from the sleeve across the gathering lines in the cap. Pick up the iron at the end of each stroke and repeat. Do not allow pleats or creases to form. If creases seem to be forming, you have drawn the threads too tightly. Let them out a little and repeat the shrinking process. Do not be afraid of cupping the sleeve cap too much as long as the fullness shrinks out smoothly.

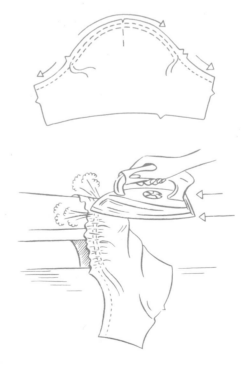

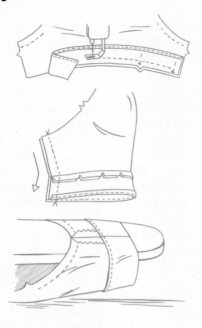

4. Edge-stitch the upper edge of the sleeve facing, or use another suitable finish.

5. Stitch the facing to the lower sleeve edge, right sides faced. Trim, and clip at intervals if necessary. Then press the seam toward the facing, or understitch it as you did the blouse sleeve facing.

6. With the facing extended, close the underarm seam through the facing. Fasten the end of the stitching line.

7. Place the sleeve wrong side out over a sleeve board and press the underarm seam open. Turn the facing up and press the lower sleeve edge from the wrong side.

8. Fasten the upper facing edge in place with a vertical or other suitable hand hemming stitch.

ATTACHING THE SLEEVES

The printed dot or mark at the top of the sleeve pattern is an aid in setting the sleeve into the armhole and distributing the fullness correctly. This mark or dot must meet the shoulder seam line to keep the center line of the sleeve straight. Notches are another aid. When they are properly matched you will notice that there is no fullness in the sleeve beneath the arm. Set-in sleeves are always attached to the blouse with plain seams. Armscye seams must be reinforced because of strain placed upon them as garment is worn. They must also be trimmed to ¼ to ⅜ inch so they won't cut into your arm.

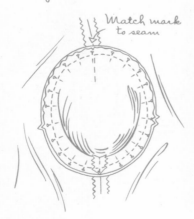

Attaching the sleeve

Match mark to seam

1. With both blouse and sleeve right side out, hold the right sleeve to the right armhole. Turn the blouse back over the sleeve and pin the mark at the top of the sleeve to the shoulder seam. Match notches and put pins there too. (Beware of notches that don't match. You are working with the wrong sleeve.)

2. Distribute fullness and pin between these points at 1-inch intervals. Pins should be placed at right angles to the seam line. Match seam lines, not raw edges in this case.

3. Baste the armscye seam, unless you have acquired some skill in stitching. Baste with the sleeve side up, using small stitches and keeping slightly outside the seam line. It is a good idea at this point to again try on the blouse, this time to check the set of the sleeves and the blouse length.

4. Stitch on the seam line with the sleeve side up. Start back of the underarm seam and overlap as you finish the line of stitching.

5. Stitch similarly ¼ inch away in the seam allowances.

6. Remove basting, if used, and trim the seam allowance away almost up to the second row of stitching. If any gathering stitches show on the right side of the garment, remove them.

PREPARING THE BLOUSE BOTTOM FOR JOINING

1. Pin the facings in position against the under side of the blouse. Trim the facing ¼ inch shorter than the blouse to reduce bulk. Baste-stitch in the seam allowance at the waistline ⅛ inch from the seam line.

2. Lap the right side of the blouse over the left side, with center lines exactly matched. Be sure that the two sides of the closing are identical in length and waistline seam edges are matched.

7. Materials which ravel excessively may require overcasting by hand. When necessary, overcast directly over the second line of stitching.

8. Press seam allowances toward the sleeve.

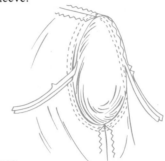

3. Baste-stitch near the seam line to hold the closing together. Continue the line of basting to hold darts or dart tucks in place along both front and back waistline.

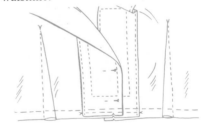

SKIRT

Follow instructions for making a skirt as far as joining gores and stitching the side seams are concerned. Do not insert the zipper, attach the waistband, or make the hem. Of course, you will check the fit of the skirt unless it is a full, gathered one.

JOINING THE SKIRT AND BLOUSE

To anchor the waistline of your dress to your own waistline, a tape is sewn below the waistline seam. Since the tape will probably be smaller around than the top of the skirt, the material must be eased onto it—and must be eased evenly. Getting it even would be no problem if the front of your waist were the same as the back of your waist. You could just start tape at zipper placket and see that its center point fell on the right side seam. However, such is not usually the case. Your waist front is probably larger than your waist back.

The solution is to put on your skirt (or your blouse if your skirt is to be gathered) and mark the tape as follows:

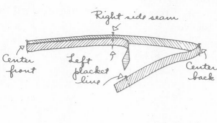

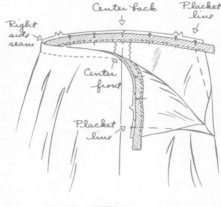

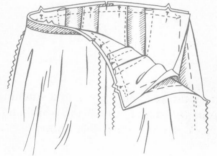

1. Put the tape around your waist and pin it together with the overlapping ends at the placket opening.

2. Place a pin in each end of the tape directly in line with the placket line.

3. Put another pin in the tape where it overlaps the right side seam line.

4. Take off the tape and find the center front and center back lines by folding the tape between the pins. These points will be on the folds.

5. Take the skirt off and pin the tape in place at these markings—the side seams and the center points. Be sure to place the tape beneath the seam allowance against the wrong side of the skirt. Caution: the end pins go to the placket line—not the placket edge. (If your skirt is gathered, it is easier to attach the tape to the waistline seam of your blouse. Follow the same procedure, sewing the tape to the blouse instead of the skirt.)

6. Finish pinning down the tape, easing in the skirt fullness if necessary. Then stitch the tape to the skirt. Stitch close to the inside edge of the tape. Remove pins.

7. Now, take the blouse and turn the skirt wrong side out over it with the waistlines matched. Match corresponding center lines and side seams, easing the blouse to the skirt evenly. Draw up the baste-stitching on the blouse to distribute ease evenly. Pin and stitch.

8. Finish the seam. Press it open or toward the plainer, flatter section whether that is the blouse or the skirt.

ZIPPER

Proceed as you did on your skirt, except that this time you will be using a zipper that is closed at the top. Before you start, be sure that the waistline seam is sewed only as far as the side seam line. Rip it, if it goes beyond. Check the length of the placket opening, also. If you had to change the blouse length, you will have to adjust the placket length.

HEM

Proceed as you did on your skirt or turn to technique 19, "Hems."

FASTENINGS

1. Make buttonholes, or have them made, and sew on buttons as you did on your blouse.

2. If you expect to wear the neckline closed, make a thread loop and sew on a small button to fasten the collar. See technique 18, "Fastenings," for instructions on making a thread loop.

BELT

Skip this section if you plan to wear a contrasting belt with your dress, to have your belt made, or to buy a belt-making kit. These instructions are for making your own belt stiffened with cotton belting or grosgrain ribbon.

1. Cut the belting or ribbon about 5 inches longer than your waist measurement. Make a point at one end.

2. If you have not already cut out the belt, cut a lengthwise strip of the dress material the width of the stiffening plus 2 seam allowances and ⅛ inch.

3. Turn under the seam allowance along the sides and point and trim corners. Finger press or baste.

4. Pin the fabric to the stiffening. The folded edge will extend ¹⁄₁₆ inch beyond the edge of the stiffening on both sides and along the pointed end. Baste in place.

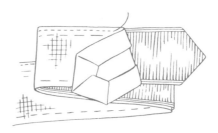

5. Stitch about ⅛ inch from the folded edge of the material around all edges except the end where the buckle is to be attached.

6. Remove basting and press lightly.

7. Sew on a buckle. Of course, you will have to cut a long narrow slot for the tongue of the buckle if there is a tongue. If you want to cover your buckle in the dress material, see page 172 for directions.

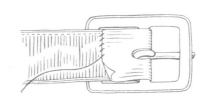

8. Measure your waist and make a hole in the belt that distance from the edge of the buckle. Make several more holes on each side of the first one. Use a stiletto, a nail, or an orangewood stick.

9. Hand-stitch over and over around the edge of each hole.

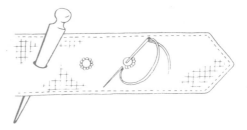

BELT LOOPS

To keep the belt in place over the waistline seam, belt loops are used at the side seams. They should be placed so that the belt will be held centered over waistline seam line. When there is a side placket, the left loop goes on the back of the dress along the placket edge. To make belt loops, use a double strand of sewing thread which matches your dress or the belt and make loops slightly longer than the belt width. Make a chain stitch, either with a crochet hook or with your fingers. Here's how you do it without a hook:

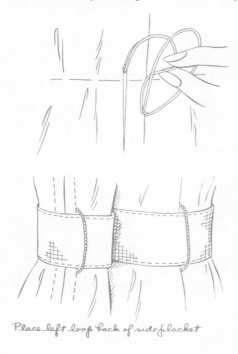

Place left loop back of side placket

1. Fasten the thread at the lower edge of the belt position on the wrong side of the side seam of the dress. Use several tiny stitches placed on top of each other.

2. Bring thread to the right side of the dress. Take a tiny stitch at that point but do not pull the thread tight; leave a loop large enough to get your fingers through.

3. Put your fingers through the loop and pull another loop through, closing the first loop. Pull a third loop through the second, closing the second one and so forth until you have a long enough chain. The needle is not used during this operation.

4. Draw the needle through the last loop to lock the chain.

5. Use the needle to fasten the end of the belt loop to the side seam of the dress above the belt. Fasten securely from the wrong side with several tiny stitches.

BELT BUCKLE

A stiffened belt calls for a buckle and you may use one that matches the buttons on your dress or cover one with the dress material. An old buckle can be re-covered or you can buy a buckle mold.

To cover a buckle:

1. Use the buckle mold as a pattern, but cut the cloth ¼ inch wider than the buckle on all edges.

2. Pry the top of the buckle mold from the under part gently.

3. Fit the fabric right side up over the top part of the buckle mold, slash- ing inside edges and cutting away corners or notching along the outer edges.

4. Join the raw edges together on the under side of this section of the mold with diagonal basting.

5. Press buckle top and lower sections back together again.

LINGERIE SLIDES

Lingerie slides are a "must" for wide-necked dresses and blouses if you wear undergarments with shoulder straps. Lingerie slides not only keep your straps from showing but also make the neckline of your dress lie smoothly across the shoulders. If you have sloping shoulders, you may want lingerie slides on all your dresses and blouses, for they will keep your straps from slipping off your shoulders.

Here is a simple way to make lingerie slides from thread. (Of course, if you prefer, you can use matching seam binding or narrow strips of the dress fabric.) In any event, put the dress or blouse on, adjust your shoulder straps, and mark on the dress shoulder seam the position and width of the shoulder straps beneath. Now, remove the garment.

Making a lingerie slide

1. Use a double strand of matching thread and knot the thread ends together.

2. Run the needle through one hole of the "socket" part of a small snap; draw the thread almost through the hole, then run the needle between the two threads near the knotted thread ends. Now draw up the thread, and the snap should be fastened to the thread with a loop.

3. To fasten the snap more securely, make several blanket (or buttonhole) stitches through that same hole, finally leaving a loop large enough to start a chain-stitch.

4. Make a chain-stitch (described earlier in this Construction for belt loops) just long enough to fit easily beneath your shoulder straps; then slip the needle through the final loop to fasten the chain-stitch.

5. Attach the end of the chain-stitch securely to the seam allowances of the shoulder seam at the outer mark you made earlier (the one that indicates the strap edge farthest from your neck). Clip away the thread.

6. Now sew the other part of the snap, the "ball" part, to the opposite (inner) side of the strap position.

7. Repeat on the opposite shoulder seam.

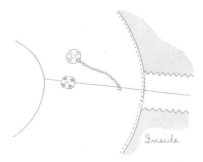

Inside

FINAL PRESSING

Even though you pressed carefully as you sewed, your dress will need a final pressing. This is a simple matter with a steam iron. Press large, flat sections with the dress turned inside out, using a sleeve board for sleeves. You will need no press cloth to press the under side of the cloth unless the material is extremely fragile. Now, turn the dress right-side-out to touch up collars, hems, pockets, and other bulky areas.

For top pressing, the rule is to use a press cloth because most materials become glazed or injured in some way without one. Although light-colored cottons are usually an exception to this rule, you should try the iron directly on a scrap to test its effect. A hot iron will flatten some textures and will nearly always glaze dark cottons. Silks, wools, and all thermoplastic materials also require a press cloth for top pressing. Use one or two layers of cheesecloth or, better still, a large scrap of the fabric itself. (Never use unbleached muslin. Gums from it stick to the iron, scorch, and are difficult to remove.)

Do not overpress. Use little or no pressure and keep the iron moving. For wools, especially, press with an up-and-down movement; that is, lift the iron instead of gliding it. For thick areas, use a deeply padded ironing board. Use a sleeve board for cuffs and a tailor's cushion for curved areas. And remember that thermoplastics tend to melt even at low temperatures!

Without a steam iron, you proceed in much the same way, except that you must dampen the fabric itself or use a dampened press cloth. You must also watch the temperature of the iron more carefully. For more detailed instructions, turn to technique 12, "Pressing."

PART III

PLANNING AND BUDGETING

CHAPTER 11 — *WARDROBE REQUIREMENTS*

So far we have been concerned mainly with the design quality of single garments or the plan of an individual costume. Now we face even a bigger issue—the requirements of a complete wardrobe, not merely for one season, nor even one year, but several years. Most of us have to wear coats, suits, dresses, and other basic items for two or three years or even longer. Many a college sophomore is still wearing a sports suit she had when she was a sophomore in high school. The trick is to select things that are so basic in style and good in design that they are appropriate for your present setup as well as suitable for a few years to come. Right now you are concerned with your needs today, but learn to look ahead too. Those needs are determined by climate and your activities in general, as we have briefly mentioned in the study of textures. But your particular community should also be considered. So let us see just how these various factors influence a wardrobe plan.

CLIMATE

It goes without saying that each weather zone has its own particular requirements. A winter coat means one thing to girls who live in the Great Lakes region and quite something else to those on the Gulf of Mexico. Girls who live in areas where snow and blizzards are a part of each winter have to plan for more seasonal changes in their wardrobes than girls who live in moderate climates where snow and a freeze are considered freaks of nature! Northerners really have to plan for the four seasons. First, there are the long months of frigid winter when thick woolen outer garments, heavy suits, sweaters, mufflers, and boots are in order. Winter is followed by a spring thaw and a couple of mild months when heavyweights are shed for lighter woolens, rayons, and even cottons. Then summer sets in—and it can be blisteringly hot even in the Midwest and far North. Finally, the crisp, snappy days of autumn roll around as a reminder of the coming freeze. Assembling a wardrobe for such extreme changes involves a great outlay of money. Anyone who has moved away from such a climate to an area where the seasons are merely either cool or warm will tell you that a mild climate is much easier on the clothes budget.

One way to cut down seasonal expenditures is to select clothes that are basic enough to be worn during both spring and autumn. This is especially true of a coat—a costly item. If it is to be your "one and only," do not consider a new spring coat of lush pink or daffodil yellow. Either might look lovely in the Easter parade, but how about the football games next fall? Choose a color that looks perfectly seasonal in either spring or autumn. Furthermore, unless you can afford more than one coat, a neutral shade has a more practical, all-purpose quality than a pastel tint. It permits you to introduce a wider range of colors in your dresses, suits, and sweaters.

COMMUNITY

You may live in a warm, sunny clime or in a wintry one—but wherever you live, the size of your community and its particular standards influence the exact type of your wardrobe still further. People in large cities dress differently from those in near-by towns. And in those towns people dress differently from their rural neighbors. This is obvious to anyone who has either visited or

Be prepared for bad weather.

moved from one place to another. To a certain extent it is a matter of "when in Rome, do as the Romans do." Of course, as teen-agers, you do find that girls throughout the states have more or less the same standards in styling, especially where spectator sports clothes are concerned. Even so, there are some differences, and they become increasingly apparent as you get older.

City standards. Girls and women who live and work in large metropolitan districts are more fashion-conscious. Because they live where fashions are born, made, and marketed, their styles are likely to be more extreme, unusual, and up-to-the-minute. Then too a city dweller who is just one in a milling crowd can wear a "high style" without fearing unfavorable comment from the neighbors. Yet she has to be practical too. City life with its rush and tear—and soot and grime—makes definite demands on her wardrobe. That is why she likes extremely simple clothes that are appropriate for a variety of occasions.

This suit is particularly appropriate for luncheons and late-afternoon engagements. The print blouse picks up the suit color and at the same time provides an accent for the outfit.

Herbert Sondheim—Couture Group, N. Y. Dress Institute

That is why black and dark colors are popular in the city during all seasons; they don't have to be forever laundered or dry-cleaned. Of course, this does not mean that light or bright colors and casual styles are not seen on city streets. They most certainly are! But on the whole, the typical metropolitan costume is far less casual, less colorful, and certainly darker than those seen in smaller communities. But even large cities can differ in their standards. Compare a city that is in the midst of a resort area with a city that is a center of big business and high finance. In the first the styles are decidedly casual—an informal, carefree attitude prevails. Play togs and slacks are often a part of the downtown scene. The tempo is entirely different in the second city where a person would feel horribly conspicuous strolling down the Avenue in slacks!

Town standards. Now, what is acceptable in most smaller towns? There tastes are generally more conservative. Casual clothes, modest tailored garments, and simple unaffected afternoon styles win favor. If a person wears the more extreme fashions, she is more than likely to be considered a "show-off." In a town where everyone knows most everyone else, that "big-city look" can result in making the wearer feel like an outsider. Group feeling is strong in most small communities. This is especially true of teen-agers who, year by year, evolve a new code of dress! If blue jeans, boys' shirts, and scuffers are the accepted garb for every activity except school and dress-up occasions, a girl feels out of things when she breaks the rule of the gang! It is really in the

For picnics or country wear in general, shorts and a blazer are the perfect answer. Here, the plaid is used as the basis of the color scheme: the blazer harmonizes with the greens of the plaid while the yellow sweater repeats the narrow yellow stripe.

Landshoff—Reprinted from Mademoiselle; © *Street & Smith Publications, Inc., 1958*

selection of dressy clothes that teen-agers break away from the group pattern. Even then they do not want to look too different from their friends. There is a certain similarity in style. Girls in small towns are apt to like fussier dress-up clothes than their city sisters.

Rural standards. Clothes in the country and scattered rural villages are usually even more conservative in taste. They stress the casual, wearable look that is in keeping with broad acres rather than a severe tailored look or extreme styling that goes with the city scene. A dark, dressy summer sheer that is ideal for a social engagement in the city would seem strangely out of place at a country church social where girls and women alike were wearing fresh, light informal cottons.

FAMILY CIRCLE

In addition to such community influence, you should plan your wardrobe so that it is in keeping with your home and family interests. Your home forms the background for many of your activities.

Consider the average American-town family of modest means. Dad works long and hard, and Mother's work is never done—perhaps she has an outside job. Even the children may have jobs after school. The family lives in a comfortable, small home in a modest neighborhood. They live simply and entertain informally. Everyone pitches in to help. Their friends entertain in the same way. Family outings include picnics, days at the beach, or long rides in the country. As a rule, such a family does not frequent show-place restaurants or sit in a box at the theater! All in all, their life and tastes are on a simple scale—and they dress accordingly.

Then, there is the family that lives on a farm. From dawn to dark there are endless chores for everyone in that family. Trips to town, church and school activities, and neighborly get-togethers make up the typical calendar of the average family in the country. Their clothes too are simple and practical.

Clothes which are fine for one activity . . .

A family whose income is in the upper bracket is apt to live on a more luxurious scale—whether in a city, in a suburb, or on a country estate. Servants and a large home permit them to entertain more frequently and lavishly and with greater variety—barbecue suppers, lawn parties, special teas, and formal dinners. Their day-by-day entertainment is not limited to movies and neighborly evenings; they include formal-dress affairs both in town and at the country club. Such a background demands a wardrobe of greater variety.

Because the vast majority of us belong to the more-or-less modest family circle, a wardrobe for the girl of such a family will be our chief concern.

ACTIVITIES

It does no harm to repeat what has been said earlier. "The girl with good taste always has that 'just-right' look. She wears a costume that is appropriate to the occasion." She does not make an appearance at a festive social event in casual sport togs, nor does she overdress for school, a ball game, or a class picnic.

School. Clothes for school should be simple in style and of durable, practical materials. That is why spectator sports styles are ideal. And, of course, all accessories should be in the same simple theme. Whenever possible, school clothes should be washable so as to save on cleaning bills. There are many new fabrics which make possible a washable wardrobe—particularly if you sew. As you know, most woolen skirts, jackets, and dresses are better dry-cleaned.

Street. Suits are ideal for street wear. A spectator suit with slipover sweater or a plain, tailored blouse, a simple felt hat, low pumps or oxfords, a bag of

. . . may not be suitable for another kind of activity.

calf, and short gloves is usually the favorite street costume of teen-agers. Although it is casual, it is appropriate for shopping, movies, or informal get-togethers in town or city. In colder weather it may be worn with an all-purpose coat or a fur coat.

Spectator sports dresses, tailored two-piece dresses, or simple, basic type afternoon dresses are also appropriate—in summer without a coat, but with hat, bag, and gloves. In other seasons an all-purpose coat looks well with any of these dresses. If you have a dressy coat, wear it with the afternoon dress. Accessories, of course, would be chosen accordingly. Your favorite knapsack shoulder bag and oxfords would be too casual with the afternoon dress. A word about hats—although a hatless vogue has swept the country in recent years, a street costume *does* look more complete when a hat is worn. Your dressy hat can afford to have a bit more trim than the one you wear with sports or tailored clothes. But if one hat per season is all your budget allows, choose a simple hat that is neither a strictly sport model nor definitely dressy. If it is a happy in-between, it does double-duty for both costumes. Or if you have an assortment of kerchiefs, berets, or knit caps for sport and school wear anyway, your one hat can be dressy. A final note about the street costume—

Kathryn Wilson

An evening dress above and an afternoon dress at right.

Simplicity Pattern Co. Inc.

it is always more appropriate to wear hosiery instead of anklets with a street outfit, even if it is a spectator sports suit.

Social events. Teen-agers have many casual social get-togethers for which their school or street clothes are perfectly suitable. They may even choose to appear in slacks or jeans for that potluck supper in the rumpus room or for a barbecue in someone's back yard. Yet everyone has a few occasions on the calendar that call for dress-up clothes. There are many festive "at-home" celebrations—a Thanksgiving family reunion, your birthday party, or just guests for Sunday dinner. There may be afternoons when your mother wants you to pretty up so that you can help to serve refreshments at her club meeting. The so-called afternoon dress with its soft styling and lovely detail is ideal for such occasions. It can be of sheer wool, velvet, or crepe; a rayon print, shantung, or faille; a dimity, chambray, eyelet material, and so on, depending on the season. If it is to be your only dressy frock for that particular season, select one that is so beautifully simple in style and detail that a change of jewelry, a sash, or belt will make it seem like a different dress. Call it your *basic* dress. In such a dress a solid color lends itself to more changes than a print. You are not likely to tire of a solid color so quickly either. If it is simple in line and of a fabric like sheer wool or heavy crepe, it might be worn to school the following year—and perhaps to business the year after—with appropriate accessories, of course. Another suggestion for the budget-minded girl is the always popular skirt and blouse. But this time let it be a full, swishy skirt of faille, taffeta, or jersey. Wear it with a dainty, frilly blouse or one that is striking in color or unusual in styling. Colorful crushed sashes, decorative belts, or interesting jewelry will dress it up still further. One such skirt and several blouses or boleros offer wide variety to a dress-up wardrobe. Shoes for dressy occasions are simple pump or strap styles with a medium-high, teen-age heel.

These same dressy clothes are suitable when you step out too—for those special movie or dinner dates or to a tea dance or informal school dance, or to someone's home party. Then you will have to think of your coat and accessories as well. Whether you have just one all-purpose coat or a special dressy coat, your dresses should be selected to harmonize with the color of your coat. If you can afford a dressy hat, select one with a simple flower trim or a puffy little pompon. But if your budget allows for just one all-purpose felt or straw that is also worn with street clothes, well and good. In summer many girls prefer to wear a flower arrangement in their hair instead of a hat. Your bag should be neat in design—not of the heavy knapsack variety. For instance, if your shoes are suede, a simple suede bag would be smart. It can double for street wear, too. Or, if your summer dressy shoes are white fabric sandals, a pouch bag of white fabric or plastic would look well. And, of course, you will wear gloves and hosiery—not anklets!

Now we come to the highlights in your social calendar—those special occasion school or club dances. For weeks, maybe months before each, you plot and plan as to what you will wear on that wonderful evening. All the girls in your crowd compare notes as to what *should* be worn.

If it is to be an informal class dance at the country club during the closing weeks of school, your escorts will appear in their Sunday best or wear white coats and flannels (if they have them). Such an informal summer dance means that the girls should not appear in their most elegant, frothy evening dresses. This is the time to use all those wonderful summer resort fashion ideas for gay, twirling plaid gingham, piqué, linen, embroidered cotton, sprigged dimity, floral chintz, batik, or India-print fabrics. They can be laundered, and what is more, they can be made at little cost. Wear them with a little jacket or stole

School clothes—an endless variety of shirts, blouses, and sweaters.

Martha Lorraine

in the same fabric or one that offers color contrast. Short, loose flannel coats are also smart. Gloves may be white or in a color to harmonize with the frock. Sandals may be low-heeled or high, of fabric or kid, as you prefer.

For informal dances during the fall or winter season, the typical dinner or theater type of dress is appropriate. Bodices are not cut very low and sleeves are in order. If the dress itself is sleeveless, a dinner jacket or bolero is worn. Heavy rayon or silk crepe, jersey, faille, or velvet are general favorites. In recent years the ballet-length skirt and blouse have been popular for informal dress-up occasions. Blouses vary from simple shirtwaist styles to frilly creations. Smart accessories would include a small pouch or clutch bag made of faille, velvet, or satin; evening sandals of fabric or kid; gloves of fabric or kid, either short or long. Recent fashions have used gold or silver kid for both bag and sandals. Delicate or unusual jewelry may be worn if the dress itself is simple. If it is trimmed with lace, embroidery, or the like, jewelry can appear excessive.

If the dance is to be a really formal occasion, such as the spring prom or a big New Year's Eve ball (when the men who have dinner jackets will wear them), you can come out in your frilly best! Such evening frocks are more luxurious and fragile in appearance than other dance frocks. Bodices are cut low and are usually sleeveless—even strapless. Delicate and more elaborate fabrics, such as tulle, chiffon, net, organdy, and taffeta, are seen on the dance floor. Rich brocades, sleek satins, elaborate lace, and luxurious crepes are likely to be favorites with girls over twenty.

Small evening bags of metal mesh, metallic cloth, bead, or sequin-trimmed fabric are smart—or the gold or silver kid with matching sandals is suitable. When a corsage is worn, the effect should not be spoiled by elaborate jewelry or artificial flowers in the hair!

Of course it is nice to own an evening coat for such occasions. But many girls have to make their one-and-only do. Fur coats are also suitable for evening attire. If or when an evening coat is within your budget, make it of velvet or soft, smooth wool. Interline it for winter comfort. In warmer weather, short loose coats of taffeta, satin, or brocade add a high fashion note.

Active sports. Active sports clothes are the ones that are truly functional. They are designed to suit the body movements involved in the particular sport. They make provision for snow, wind, and rain—and modesty. Summer sports clothes should be made of washable fabrics. Sports clothes are usually colorful; it's nice to see dashes of bright red and green whizzing over a white landscape, or brilliant blue, orange, and yellow dotting the beaches.

Slacks, shorts, or jeans worn with shirts or sweaters and jackets are best for all forms of boating. Full skirts present difficulties when you crawl over ropes, oars, and fishing tackle during a stiff blow!

Swimming, of course, means bathing suits. The firm, closely fitted one-piece variety is the choice of a real swimmer, while the bra and shorts variety in colorful, novelty fabrics is usually preferred by the "bather" who lolls on the sand a good bit of the time. Jackets, stoles, capes, or robes of terry cloth or

The wrong clothes can spoil the fun. Don't arrive for the outing club hike dressed in spectator, rather than active, sportswear.

other firm, gay cottons prevent sunburn as well as a chill. It is also nice to have a full skirt and a shirt, stole, or bolero to slip over the dry suit for the jaunt to the refreshment stand, the stroll along the boardwalk, or the trek back home through the village, as the case may be.

Divided, knee-length skirts, pedal pushers, or shorts worn with T-shirts or sports blouses are popular for bicycling. Some prefer to pedal in rolled-up overalls because they keep shirt tails tucked in place.

The short, full-skirted, one-piece dress is popular for tennis because it allows for quick leg action. With such a one-piece dress there are no hanging shirt tails or exposed midriffs when arms reach out this way and that. The tennis dress is white, although a colorful sweater may be put on after the game.

Full skirts are the favorite of ice and roller skaters too. They wouldn't get very far in narrow ones! If one goes in for fancy figure ice skating, a short circular skirt lined in a contrasting color is attractive. Of course, suitable tights should be worn with such a skirt. Jackets for ice skating are usually short and closely fitted at the waist to reveal the rhythmic movements of the body.

Ski pants and jackets should be lightweight but warm and windproof. Headgear is close fitting and often fastens under the chin in helmet fashion. Turtleneck sweaters are ideal because loose muffler ends could endanger vision.

Sturdy clothes are a must for "roughing it" in rugged country. Jeans or breeches, boots, sport shirt, and short jacket are best when clambering over mountain or forest trails. Waterproof fabrics make the ideal jacket, heavily lined or not, depending on the season. If a jacket is not needed for warmth, select a long-sleeved shirt of a firm fabric, such as flannel or gabardine. Sweaters snag in underbrush. Long sleeves prevent scratches and insect bites. It's a good idea to take along a kerchief to keep off those same mosquitoes! The wise woodsman always covers up.

Those who ride horses know that they need sturdy clothing, but the exact style selected depends entirely on the circumstances. The fashionable riding habit for a canter along the bridle path in a select neighborhood is a far cry from the outfit worn for a dash along country roads and over pastures and ranges. Jeans or breeches, boots, a sport shirt, and vest or jacket are ideal for the latter, while the former costume is complete only with white shirt, waistcoat, tie, bowler hat, gloves, and riding crop added to the jodhpurs and low boots. So—choose accordingly!

Then there are those lazy summer days when "activities" are limited to a bit of sunning, a book and the porch swing, or a snooze in the hammock. That's when sun clothes come into their own. They can be brief—shorts with a bra or halter. Or they can be longer—a dress with halter top or a low-cut bodice with or without straps. Such sun-back dresses often have boleros which make them ideal hot-weather dresses for town and country. Some play suits, either one-piece or separate shirt-and-shorts styles, include a skirt to provide cover for those strolls down to the corner for a soda or magazine.

House garb. One can't always loaf—even at home! There are chores to do, whether in or out—cleaning, cooking, laundering, gardening, and so on. If you are not already a member of the housework crew, you should become one. Experience *now* is the best teacher for those years that lie ahead. So, on Saturdays or when you come home from school, slip into washable house clothes when you attack a major job. Washables save wear and tear on your good school clothes, and help to hold down cleaning bills on woolens.

Not so long ago the one and only proper housedress was a Hoover apron or a trim little cotton print. Of course they are still appropriate. But housework garb has also taken on another look. Some homekeepers, the young moderns especially, have adopted slacks. One can see why! Running the vacuum under furniture, cleaning windows, wielding a paint brush, wiping up the floor, hanging clothes, dusting Venetian blinds, pulling weeds, hoeing in the garden, or a tussle with Johnny in his sandbox all involve bending, kneeling, stretching, stooping, and what not! Denim slacks or jeans worn with T-shirts or simple blouses seem ideal for such stunts. They are safer too—no bows or streamers to get caught in the clothes wringer, on doorknobs, or on pot handles. And they are so easily laundered. Knit shirts require no ironing and slacks are certainly more easily ironed than starched percales. Of course slacks look best on the trim figure. That in itself might prove an inducement to keep weight under control!

After the real work is done, it is refreshing to slip into a fresh cotton—and the menfolk appreciate a crisp look when they come home for supper. A clean dress also means you will be ready if company drops by for an evening's chat.

Lounging clothes. Every girl loves a lounging robe—the warm cuddly variety when temperatures are low and lighter weight for warm spells. Winter styles include tailored flannels, soft woolen plaids, and quilted fabrics. Summer weights come in terry cloth, seersucker, pongee, or poplin. Strictly speaking, robes are meant for the bedroom scene—for study hours or feminine bedtime powwows. As a general rule, they are not exactly the thing for a family breakfast. Some fathers frown on them. And they certainly are not meant for the morning's housework despite the fact that some women are caught in them!

Teen-agers seem to prefer the casual tailored styles for their lounging robes. The typical negligee or dressing gown with its soft, clinging lines and dressier feminine details may be a boudoir favorite later on.

Housecoats are a sort of combination robe and housedress and so are appropriate for "family-only" sessions. They are nice for those leisurely breakfasts when you don't have to dash off to school or business. Then there is also the shorter "brunch coat" that is usually worn with slacks. It is popular with many young business women who entertain a group of close friends for an informal Sunday brunch. And, of course, such an outfit is relaxing to put on after that hard day at the office.

Travel. Whether you are making a grand tour of Europe or spending a weekend in a nearby town as the house guest of a friend, the clothing you take along will partially determine the fun you will have. Poorly assorted, fragile clothing that comes from your suitcase crying for special attention is not the answer to how to have a happy holiday. A few rules may help, no matter where you are traveling.

Travel light; that is, severely restrict the quantity of clothing you take along. Take *only* what you need. You will have less to pack, carry, and keep in wearable condition. Today, the most experienced traveler may go around the world with no more than one or two lightweight suitcases. Air travel probably started this trend, because of its reduced baggage allowances and rather high charges for excess weight.

Include clothing for the life you will lead. List the activities in which you will take part. Will you travel in the family car, by train, plane, or perhaps by ocean liner or river boat? Will you do extensive sight-seeing in the traditional way or will you bicycle through some European country? Will you dance on shipboard or attend a formal party given by a friend? Tennis, hiking, swimming—will these be a part of your activities? Plan accordingly!

Take along clothing for the weather conditions you will encounter. (Travel books give the temperatures of important cities throughout the world.) Any extensive travel will require clothing for both hot and cool climates, even in summer. Remember that for varying weather conditions, several light layers are far better than one heavy one.

Take clothing that does not wrinkle easily, show soil too readily, or present a cleaning problem. Knit things seem made for travel. A jersey blouse, dress, suit, or even a firmly knitted jersey coat—any or all are happy choices. Or perhaps you would prefer a sweater or two, or a hand- or machine-knit dress or suit. None of these will ever need the touch of an iron. Figured materials show wrinkling (and spots) far less than plain colors do. Nubby or slightly rough textures are good choices, too, because they do not wrinkle easily. Wool and silk have always been good "travelers." Now the synthetics, blends, and wash-and-wear cottons have simplified clothing care en route even further.

Take clothing that will serve several purposes, for that is one way of streamlining your travel wardrobe. Your coat, if made simply of a smooth, plain colored fabric, will look right by both day and night. Have it treated, or treat it yourself, for water-repellency, and it may save you from a thorough drenching. A tailored suit is the backbone of many a travel wardrobe. You can wear it with a warm jersey blouse or a sweater on a cool day; take off the jacket and you are dressed for casual wear; then substitute a plain tailored blouse and a contrasting belt for a sudden rise in temperature.

A dark "basic" dress is a good choice, too, because you can wear it with a scarf or tailored pin for street wear. Substitute a strand of pearls and wear it to a luncheon, on a date, or to church. If you will need a late-day, low-necked dress, look for one with a matching jacket so that you can also wear the dress for daytime occasions. A white or pastel sweater could serve as a light evening wrap; then, with a matching, permanently pleated skirt, it would be perfect for resort wear. You will think of other multiple-purpose garments. If you take along shorts or slacks for active sports, be sure that they are acceptable attire before you wear them. In European cities, they are rarely worn.

Decide on a basic color scheme and stick to it! Plan everything to mix and match. That isn't an easy assignment, but it is possible and, oh, what a joy to be able to put on almost any garment and find that you are harmoniously dressed! If you have always planned your wardrobe in this way, you will not have too much trouble. You have probably already keyed your wardrobe to accessories in a good basic color—black, brown, or navy blue. If not, begin now, for it is doubly important for travel. Select your handbag, shoes, and perhaps, your gloves in that color. Your coat and hat could match or harmonize. Then key every garment to these ever-present articles—and to each other if they will be worn together.

Take comfortable shoes. In fact, take no other kind! It isn't wise to start out on a sight-seeing trip without well "broken-in" walking shoes. Take two pairs, if possible. One pair may get wet and, besides, a change rests your feet. Take a pair of dressier shoes for informal social occasions, and take evening slippers if you will need them. For hiking, shoes with thick spongy soles are a boon. Select bedroom slippers and rain shoes that fold to save packing space.

A tailored robe of dark, lightweight material, two sets of nylon or other drip-dry undergarments, and two sleeping garments of similar fabric will

This dress with a jacket would be a welcome addition to any summer travel wardrobe. Worn with the jacket, the dress is appropriate for traveling, sightseeing, and general daytime wear. Remove the jacket, change the belt, and the sheath dress is ready for late afternoon and informal evening wear.

Simplicity Pattern Co. Inc.

take up very little room. Perhaps you will need an extra slip or petticoat for a particular dress, but think twice before taking along bulky "crinolines." It is a good idea to buy all your nylon stockings in the same color; you might use the same rule for sport hose.

Of course, you will start out with everything in perfect condition. But for emergency repairs, take along a tiny, compact sewing kit with bits of thread to match your wardrobe colors, a snap or two, and any other items you might need.

For an extended trip or for air travel, transfer your cosmetics to plastic containers. Then make or buy plastic cases to hold your toilet articles and cosmetics. At the end of a grueling day, it is a relief to pick up one case with soap, washcloth, toothbrush, nail brush, and everything else you will need for your bath. Then, when you start your grooming, take out the case that has comb, brush, powder, lipstick, lotion—everything you need for face, hair, and nails. These are real time- and patience-savers and they also protect your clothing!

Girls who have carefully planned wardrobes usually find assembling a travel wardrobe is largely a matter of taking garments from the clothes closet, for they usually have on hand most of the clothing for their trip.

Sometime before you pack, spread out each suit, dress, and skirt that you plan to take and "ensemble" each. That is, bring out the shoes, gloves, belt, scarf, sweater, blouse, hat, or jewelry that you plan to wear with that garment. If your wardrobe is well planned, you will be able to shift blouses, sweaters, and accessories about. Some accessories will play a part in almost every complete costume. If you find any accessory that does not fit in, now is the time to eliminate it. While you still have things spread out, check them for cleanliness and repairs, too.

From now on, keep your travel things in a special place in your closet so that you will not be likely to forget anything. Any discussion of travel clothes leads finally to packing! Of course, when you are motoring, some garments can be carried in garment bags. The following hints are for those trips on which you will have no such conveniences.

First, select luggage which *you* yourself can carry. Porters and other strong arms are not always available! If you are planning a long trip which demands a more extensive wardrobe, do one of two things: send ahead any clothing that you will not need en route, or check baggage through to your destination, even if it means an extra fee.

Plan to carry no more than two pieces of luggage—and preferably one, if it will not be too heavy. Select a lightweight suitcase or perhaps one of the "flip-over" bags for hanging dresses full length. These bags fold for carrying, and have space for other things as well. A small "tote" bag holds the articles that you will need often and want to keep near you. In general, avoid special-purpose luggage such as cosmetic, hat, and shoe cases.

With clothes and luggage assembled, packing begins! First see that skirts are zipped and that blouses, dresses, and jackets are fastened.

Wardrobe cases, equipped with hangers, simplify packing. Arrange skirts and slacks over the hanger rod. In hanging jackets and dresses, fold sleeves to lie flat against the garment. All clothes become less creased if sheets of tissue paper are placed between garment folds.

Other traveling cases require "flat" packing, with garments folded to fit the case. Your aim is to have as few folds as possible, with the garment lying smooth and flat. Pack your heaviest garments on the bottom. Short, narrow skirts generally show less crease when folded once across the lap area. Long or full skirts are best folded lengthwise first, then folded back to fit the length of the case. To fold dresses, place them front down on the bed. Cover with sheets of tissue. Then fold back sleeves and sides of bodice to fit the width of the case. Fold the skirt back so that it fits into the case. If the case is long enough to accommodate the full length of jackets, fold them lengthwise (as you do a dress). If not, cross the jacket sleeves over the chest area; then fold back the lower part of the jacket crosswise to fit the width of the case. Blouses may be folded as the dress bodice above, or in the more compact, laundry-type of shirt fold.

Plastic envelopes provide a solution to the neat packing of blouses and sweaters. In fact, they have a multitude of uses. Lingerie, hosiery, hankies, gloves, and scarves don't become jumbled when packed in individual plastic cases. Set one aside for soiled items. You can use cases for shoes, which are often a real nuisance to pack. Wrap each shoe singly; then tuck it in a corner of your case. Hats can be a nuisance, too. Wear yours en route, and if it must be packed at some time, be sure it's a soft, crushable one so that you need not carry a hatbox.

All that remains now is to warn you *not* to forget your toothbrush!

ACTIVITIES

For the class

1. **Consider** the basic wardrobe needs in your community. List all the activities in which a typical girl takes part, including clothes for housework and lounging. Organize a class fashion show in which different girls will volunteer to wear appropriate attire for each type of activity.
2. **Select** a few volunteers to model street clothes which are suitable to wear to a job interview.

For the individual

1. **Pretend** that you have invited a cousin to spend Easter vacation with you. As she lives in a community very different from yours, she writes to ask you what type of clothes to bring. Write her a letter telling her what she will need.
2. **Pretend** that you are going by bus to a large neighboring city to spend a week end at the home of a friend. You plan to shop there on Saturday morning; to see a football game that afternoon; and to attend a formal school dance that same evening. Your Sunday program includes a church service, a dinner at the home of your friend, after which you board the bus for home. Plan a minimum wardrobe which involves little packing, but one which will see you well-dressed for each occasion.

CHAPTER 12   *PLANNING A WARDROBE*

There are times when everyone would like to discard every single thing in her wardrobe and start out with a fresh slate. Unfortunately such drastic renewals are not possible, except perhaps for a limited few. There are such things as family budgets! Some girls feel that they could dress well if only they had a lot of money to spend on clothes. Of course money does help. But it is possible for a girl from an average-income family to appear better dressed than a girl whose family is in the upper income bracket. It isn't the *money* you spend on a wardrobe but the *thought* you put into selecting it that really counts.

Wardrobe needs vary. Beth may need a variety of dressy clothes because she plays first violin in the school orchestra and appears in many programs both in church and in school. She does not participate in any active sports; so her sports clothes are limited to spectator styles and casual play clothes.

Beth needs dressy clothes for recitals.

Sally, on the other hand, follows up school hours with skating, tennis, and bicycling—and spends every nice summer Sunday at the lake shore with her family.

Because of these varying interests and because girls have different amounts of money to spend for clothes, it is impossible to give any specific over-all suggestions for a wardrobe that would suit every girl. But we can plan a minimum wardrobe that would answer the basic needs of a typical American girl like Sally.

MEET SALLY!

Sally is a high-school girl of fourteen who lives in a small city. Her father makes a moderate fixed income. Sally has a brother, Fred, who is sixteen and a sister, Midge, who is ten. She attends most class parties and dances. She has an occasional movie date but her parents prefer that she entertain her friends at home. Her favorite winter sport is skating; her favorite summer sport is tennis. She is a good swimmer and likes anything to do with boats.

Sally needs active sportswear.

Having a big brother and a little sister, Sally has learned to be unselfish when it comes to sharing things—including the family clothing fund. She knows that Dad has to dress well for business and she feels a bit selfish about begging for a new party dress when Mother has not had anything new in ages. Fred's clothes cost a lot, and he is constantly outgrowing everything. Her own clothes don't cost as much because Mother makes most of her dresses and blouses. Midge is not so much of an expense problem because Mother makes over some of Sally's clothes for her. Even so, there are new shoes and other things to buy for Midge.

During the past year Sally and Fred decided to earn their own spending money. She "baby sits" on week ends and runs daily errands for an invalid neighbor. That money really helps when it comes to hair trims, movies, and sodas. Once she even saved enough to buy some play sandals. Gradually Sally began to realize the value of a nickel—her own and her parents'!

One fall day Sally and her mother went shopping for a winter coat for her. They found a becoming brown, all-purpose coat that would look well with both her school clothes and Sunday best. It was marked $30. That seemed like a lot! It set Sally to thinking. If she had to pay for it, she would have to work for months to save for it. Finally she asked, "Mother, about how much do you and Dad spend on my clothes each year?"

"Well, we try to keep the family's clothing budget down to about $500. I expect your clothes cost around $85, but that covers everything, even underwear and hosiery," her mother replied.

Sally's Wardrobe

Coats + Jackets   Estimated cost

    1 Lightweight coat (autumn + spring)

 * 1 Heavy coat (winter) ————————————— $30.00

    1 Raincoat

    1 Corduroy jacket

Dresses + Skirts

    1 Woolen school dress

 *S 1 Heavy jumper

 *S 1 Light wool dressy frock ⎫ Autumn +

    1 Long dance frock (remodeled) ⎬ Winter

    1 Wool skirt (solid color)

    1 Wool skirt (plaid) ⎭

    3 Wash dresses for school + home

 *S 1 Two-piece cotton suit

    1 Dressy rayon frock (spring) ⎬ Spring + Summer

 *S 1 Dressy cotton (summer)

 *S 1 Cotton dance frock with jacket ⎭   Fabrics, patterns, thread, and notions for five new garments   25.00

    1 Full cotton skirt

Blouses + Sweaters

    2 Tailored sports blouses

 *S 1 Dainty blouse ————————————— 2.00

 * 1 Short-sleeved slipover sweater ————— 3.00

    1 Long-sleeved slipover sweater

    1 Cardigan sweater

Sportswear

    1 Blazer for skating with school skirt

    1 Denim slacks

    2 Denim shorts

    2 T-shirts

> *   Items to buy
> *S Items to sew

194

1 Tennis dress (remodeled piqué dress)
1 Bathing suit (had been gift)
1 Bathing cap _____ $ .50

Hosiery

* 2 (pr.) Sheer for dress (usually gift)
* 6 Service-weight for school + street _____ 6.00
* 6 Anklets _____ 3.00
2 Long, heavy skating socks

Shoes

* 1 (pr.) Heavy school shoes _____ 6.00
* 1 Low-heeled pumps for street + dress _____ 5.00
1 Dance sandals
1 Play shoes (bought with pin money)
1 Tennis shoes
1 Bedroom slippers (had been gift)
* 1 Galoshes or boots _____ 3.00
1 Rubbers

Hats

* 1 Felt hat for street + dress ⎫
1 Beret ⎬ Autumn + Winter _____ 6.00
1 Woolen kerchief ⎭
1 Straw hat (new ribbon, old one) ⎫
1 Cotton kerchief ⎬ Spring + Summer ____ .25

Accessories

* 2 (pr.) Mittens (Grandma knits them)
* 1 Dark fabric gloves (winter) _____ 1.50
1 Light-fabric gloves (spring + summer)
1 Leather bag for street + dress
1 Fabric bag (summer)
*S 1 Evening bag (make from old faille dress)

1 Sheer scarf for dress (gift)
1 Woolen scarf for school & street

Robes & Lingerie

1 Flannel robe (winter)
1 Cotton robe (summer)
2 (pr.) Pajamas (winter) (new last year)
2 (pr.) Pajamas (summer)
2 Rayon slips
*5 2 Cotton slips (material) —————————— $ 2.00
* 6 (pr.) Panties (3 new pr. @ 75¢) —————————— 2.25
* 3 (pr.) Snuggies (2 new pr. @ 75¢) —————————— 1.50
* 3 Brassieres (2 new @ $1.00) —————————— 2.00
1 Girdle (worn occasionally)
* 2 Garter belts (@ $1.00) —————————— 2.00

$ 98.00

Family allotment —————— 85.00

—$ 13.00

"After we pay $30 for the coat, there will be only $55 left for the rest of the year," Sally figured quickly and soberly.

"That's why you can't have a new suit this year," her mother said. "Next fall, when you don't have to buy a winter coat, you can get a new school suit. Then the year after that you could have a new spring coat. This winter coat is of better material than that cheaper $15 coat we saw, so it should hold up for three years if you take good care of it. It's good sense to buy good outer garments."

"But all that takes planning!" Sally exclaimed.

"Of course it does," her mother agreed, "but you'll have to learn sooner or later. When you buy a fall suit next year, you will choose one that looks well with this year's coat, just as this coat looks well with the things you have now."

"Maybe it would be kind of fun to work out a plan," Sally said. "Anyway, I'll try."

Her minimum wardrobe. With only $85 a year, Sally realized that she would first have to make a list of things that she must have each season. Without such a "must" list she might squander some of that precious fund on things she could really do without. In the end that would mean she would have to buy cheaper items of an inferior grade that would wear out sooner and not look too good to begin with.

Like every other girl, Sally had several things on hand from the previous year. But now that she was older, there were certain gaps in her wardrobe that she wanted to fill. All the girls in high school seemed to have so many changes —skirts and jumpers with many blouses and sweaters and jackets. Maybe a jumper would help to stretch her changes. Finally, after nights of figuring and looking through her favorite magazines and catalogues, Sally completed a list of what she considered to be her minimum wardrobe. The list included things that she already had and items which she would have to buy. Some items such as hats, shoes, hosiery, and undies that were left over from last year could still be worn but might have to be replaced during the year. Sally placed a * opposite each item that she planned to buy that year. If it could be made, she added an S to it—*S. That meant a big *S*aving if either her mother or she could *S*ew it. It was difficult for Sally to know how much the fabric for each dress would cost. Even her mother could not tell exactly. She said that woolen material for some dresses might cost $8.00, but some cottons could be made for as little as $2.00 or $3.00 if one took advantage of sales, which she did. So they decided that $5.00 would be a fair average per dress for Sally's plan. Gifts would also help out Sally's budget. She usually received hankies, scarves, gloves, undies, and hose for her birthday and at Christmas.

Sally's experiment really did not turn out too badly. It was only $13 more than the family budget provided for her. If she should buy her gloves and all

Find out what you have before you plan what you need.

Money Management Institute, Household Finance Corporation

of her hosiery and panties with her own earnings, she would break even. That would be easy, because some weeks she made as much as $2.00 from "baby-sitting." And, of course, she planned to use her own money for all cosmetic needs.

With a minimum plan for the current year, it was easier for Sally to plan for the coming years. Next year her fall suit would be the big item, but it would not cost so much as the coat. That would mean that she could have an extra "switch-about" skirt, a new wool school dress, a couple of blouses, two new summer cottons—and a new long dance frock! The third year she would buy a new spring coat; and the year after that she could have a new winter coat again. That would be timed just perfectly, because as a senior she would be looking forward to either college or business.

NOW YOUR PLAN!

Perhaps Sally's experiment has given you an idea of how to plan your wardrobe, even though her minimum requirements and her budget might be very different from yours. You may have much more than Sally to spend on your clothes—or then again you may have less. If most of your blouses and dresses are readymades, you will have to spend more for them than Sally had to allow for her materials. Whatever the case, it is a good idea to have a general plan for your wardrobe.

Family finances. First, determine your share of the family's annual clothing fund. If you are one of a large family, your share will be less than that of an only child whose father has a similar income. If your father has a fixed income, it will be easier to know how much is usually spent on family clothing. If his income fluctuates from year to year, the family clothing allowance may vary accordingly. Even so, it is possible to approximate how much your family spends on your clothing by adding up all items that were bought within one year.

Does your family tend to buy many things at one time or is the purchase of items distributed more or less evenly throughout the year because your father is on a monthly salary? If you intend to buy something in the near future, you should know how much your parents can spend at that time. If you can, make a practice of buying your clothes and fabrics after the peak of the season. You can realize substantial savings in seasonal clearance sales. Winter items are marked down in most stores in January, spring items are reduced after Easter, and summer sales are in full swing after the Fourth of July.

You may have a weekly allowance or you may earn your own pin money. In either case, learn how to spend that money wisely. It will help you with your budgeting later when you are completely on your own. Put aside a certain amount for things like hosiery, hair trims, shoe repair, and incidental needs. Spend the remainder on your pet extravagances—novelty jewelry, a gay kerchief, and, of course, your movies and sweets.

Taking stock. Stage a wardrobe inventory of the things on hand for a particular season *before* that season rolls around. As spring is approaching, look over the things that you wore last spring; and next fall look over the things that you have been wearing this winter. That is the best time to weed out your closet. If you discard things at the end of a current season, you may regret it next year. You are usually very tired of winter clothes by March. If you have an inventory then, you might discard a dress that really would seem perfectly all right to you by next October when it had been out of your sight for months.

The girl who can fill out her wardrobe with attractive hand-me-downs is lucky. She has a head start in assembling the clothes she needs.

Bring everything for the coming season out into the open. Otherwise you may overlook something in a garment bag or in some box stored in the attic. Your room will look like a ready-to-wear department. Warn your family that this inventory may take the better part of a week end! Hang up your coat, suits, jackets, skirts, blouses, and dresses; sort your sweaters; line up your shoes; lay out your hats, kerchiefs, bags, gloves, and undies. Consider each item carefully. Try it on. Can it be used as it is? Do seams or buttons need attention? Does it have to be lengthened or shortened? If you cannot use it as it is, could it be remodeled? Or is it so shabby, or of such a color, or so something else that you would not wear it more than once or twice? In that case, it is wiser to give it to someone who can make regular use of it.

Undoubtedly you will find that several garments can be used without any change. Set those articles aside as a nucleus for your wardrobe. Group them into school clothes, dressy clothes, and so on. Set aside all of the accessories that will be worn with each type of costume. Then you can see whether your best hat, your shoes, bag, and your one-and-only coat look well with each of your dressy frocks. For instance, a girl whose all-purpose coat is gray has a red felt hat, black calfskin pumps, and bag. These accessories look perfect when she wears her black velveteen jumper with its red belt and white crepe blouse, but the red felt hat does not look well with her latest date dress of rose wool crepe. That is her cue to plan for a new hat that will look well with either dress and her accessories. She could buy a gray felt with a black ribbon trim to match her coat, or a snappy little black felt would suit either her jumper or her rose crepe and would tie in with her accessories.

Many old items can be remodeled into attractive new-looking garments. It does take patience and a bit of imagination, but your efforts will pay good dividends. Read Chapter 16, "Altering Readymades and Remodeling Old Clothes" before you throw anything into the rag bag.

Decide what you need. Just as Sally found certain gaps in the wardrobe that she had on hand, your inventory will show you where your gaps are. Decide what replacements and which other items are necessary for each season during the year, just as Sally did. If your budget allows, you can then afford to consider items that you may want. What a girl wants is not always what she needs! She may want some dressy sandals that she might wear twice a week, when what she really needs is a new pair of moccasins for school.

Many girls (women too!) want a vast wardrobe. They are happy only when they have a half-dozen suits hanging in the closet, "umpteen" blouses and sweaters, several dressy frocks, and row upon row of shoes and as many hats and bags. Such a person may sacrifice quality for quantity, ending up with an odd assortment of cheap items from which it is difficult to assemble one decent outfit. Or she may be an impulsive shopper picking up a hat simply because she thinks it cute—not selecting it because it could be worn with a particular costume. She may pounce upon a bargain counter and grab two or three blouses—not because she needs them or even planned to buy them, but because she wants to get in on the bargain. When one does not need an article, even such a bargain is an extravagance.

So do not feel that you need a lot of clothes and accessories to be smartly dressed. It is far better to have a small, well-chosen wardrobe of good quality rather than a large motley assortment of cheap items that never do look presentable.

When you plan to wear some garments and accessories for more than one season, select a good basic style rather than an extreme fashion that might be "good" for only one season. For example, a flared coat with extreme back fullness might be the height of fashion one year, but out-of-date the year after. It would be wiser to select a more conservative flared model because it is likely to look up-to-date for several years. Confine your fashionable fads to inexpensive one-season items such as kerchiefs, novelty jewelry, or an extra hat.

A limited wardrobe includes garments and accessories that are planned to do "double-duty" with several costumes. Get variety from switching skirts, jackets, slacks, blouses, and sweaters. Select shoes, bags, hats, and gloves that look equally well with street clothes and rather dressy ones.

Jonathan Logan

Separates are especially practical for the girl with little money to spend. By mixing them she can have a variety of costumes. They have to be carefully selected to mix well, though.

Your basic color. A basic color makes such "switching" possible. It is the foundation or background color for a season's wardrobe. It is the color with which all of your favorite and becoming colors can be combined successfully. Obviously, the all-purpose coat is the one garment which appears with more costumes than any other single garment. Furthermore, it is the most expensive item in the wardrobe and cannot be discarded quickly. For those reasons the coat should be the basic color in your wardrobe. It should harmonize equally well with the colors of your school clothes, street clothes, and dress clothes.

If your present one-and-only coat is a bright red, a vivid blue or green, or a colorful plaid, you know how hard it is to combine it with some of your clothes. When you buy your next coat, select a brown, gray, beige, or navy. Such solid, neutralized colors permit you to wear a wider range of colors and figured fabrics in your dresses, suits, and sweaters. Black is the favorite basic color of many women, but it usually seems too old for teen-agers.

If your most becoming and favorite colors include green, yellow, rust, tan, light grayed blues, or pink, brown would be a good basic color for an all-purpose winter coat. A brown coat, bag, and shoes would tie in perfectly with all garments in those colors.

Gray would be a good basic color for winter or spring if you favor red, maroon, strong blue or green, or an occasional garment in black. Black shoes and bag would look well with the gray coat and garments in the colors listed. In winter, gray is often combined with dark brown; then brown bag and shoes are best. In spring gray is often combined with navy; then navy bag and shoes are best.

Navy, as a basic color, is used more often in spring and summer than in autumn or winter. It looks smart with gay prints, white, strong red, fuchsia, chartreuse, and most pastels. Navy shoes and bag are preferable to black when a navy coat or suit is worn with the colors listed.

Beige is also associated with spring and summer because light colors are not too practical for sooty winters. Beige looks well with most of the colors listed for brown. Bag and shoes could be dark or reddish brown or white. In addition, a very light beige looks smart with plain black dressy clothes. Then use bag and pumps of black patent leather.

White is often a basic color for summer in smaller communities or warm climates.

Of course, if your budget permits you to buy a coat for every type of occasion each season, you can afford to consider strong colors and figured coat fabrics if you wish. You might love a bright red coat for casual sports wear and school, a black-gray-and-yellow plaid for a street coat, and a royal blue, gray fur-trimmed coat for dress. In that case, red should look well with your sports clothes; the plaid coat should harmonize with all street clothes; and the blue should look well with your dressy clothes. Such variety generally involves many accessories. In the above examples, however, black would be smart with any one of the coats.

So far we have listed conservative colors for bags and shoes. Unless you can afford a great variety of them, it is safer to select conservative colors that can be worn with a number of costumes, even season after season. For instance, shoes and bag of green suede would look smart with a beige coat and harmonizing dress, but could they be worn with every dress or suit? Even if they could, it would be a bit tiresome to wear a strong color day in and day out.

Seasonal color transitions. Most girls do not like to use the same basic color for each season. A gray winter coat followed by a gray spring coat seems monotonous to them. On the other hand, many city women use black for each season of the year, year after year. It helps them to slide into the next season without changing all garments and accessories. Many of those items can be carried into the next year. It makes "cents" to the budget-wise!

But even when you have a different basic color for each season, it is possible to select colors that permit you to carry some of your blouses, sweaters, and accessories into other seasons. For example, if brown has been your basic winter color, a beige coat that you wear both for spring and for autumn would be a practical choice. If gray has been your winter color, navy blue would be possible for spring. Navy blue would not be so wise for the person whose winter coat has been brown. It involves a complete change of accessories. And if that navy blue coat was also the autumn coat, it would be difficult to swing into the winter season.

Perhaps the following suggestions will help you:

Winter	*Spring*
(Basic color, brown)	(Basic color, beige)
All-purpose coat: brown	All-purpose coat for both autumn and spring: beige
Suit: powder blue	Suit: gabardine, leaf-green
Extra plaid skirt: tan, brown, powder blue, and pink	Blouses: yellow, white
Extra jacket: solid brown	School dresses: (1) gingham plaid— brown, green, yellow, and white (nice with yellow cardigan) (2) chambray, aqua (3) piqué, powder blue
Sweaters (3): yellow, cardigan, dusty pink, ecru	
Blouses (3): cream, white, pink	
School dress: brown-and-yellow check	Dress-up frock: floral print—green and white predominating.
Dress-up frock: rose wool crepe	
School shoes: brown moccasins	School shoes: moccasins or saddle shoes
Street or dress shoes: low-heeled pumps, brown calfskin	Street and semidress shoes: spectator pumps—brown-and-white or all-white for summer.
All-purpose bag: brown calfskin	
Hats (2): brown felt, powder blue beret	Bags } Gloves } white for summer.
Gloves: brown fabric	If slacks are worn, brown ones would go with blouses or sweaters mentioned.
Mittens: powder blue	

Note: The suit, extra skirt and jacket, sweaters, blouses, and all accessory items from the winter column may be used in early spring with the beige coat. The new "springy" items added can carry over into summer. Although different colors have been introduced for variety, they still harmonize with some of the brown accessories.

WHEN A GIRL MARRIES

A girl can't help dreaming, can she? . . . There are times when she can almost hear the deep, full strains of "O Promise Me" and feel the swish of heavy satin. . . . She imagines how wonderful it would be to have whole suitcases full of heavenly new clothes for her honeymoon. . . . She literally glows when she thinks of *her* home—how she and her husband will plan it together, how they will entertain, how they will shop together. . . . And somewhere in the pink and blue future there will be babies to plan for.

Marriage can be a wonderful state, but it takes a lot of love and planning to make it so. And every girl should know how her share of planning can make a home and marriage a real partnership. She will have many responsibilities—including a plan for the family wardrobe within the family income.

At present, marriage may seem like a distant vision to you. It may be years before you can actually practice in your own home what you learn in school. Yet you can try some things out in your parental home even today—things such as unselfishness in sharing the clothing budget; not insisting on a new party dress when you know that your father needs a new suit for business; helping your mother to make playsuits and sleepers for your little brother. You can try stretching what you have—such as making a blouse out of your last summer's dress instead of putting it in the rag bag. All such things will train you for better home management and therefore less financial trouble and argument during the years that lie ahead.

The wedding. A wedding usually means weeks of planning. Will the ceremony take place at home or in church—or in the city hall? Will the bride wear the traditional bridal gown and veil or will she wear a lovely afternoon ensemble? Will the wedding be attended by hundreds of guests or only by relatives and very close friends? Will the ceremony be followed by an elaborate wedding reception at a hotel or by a simple home reception? These are decisions that involve both families and the bride and groom. They involve money as well as love! The more elaborate the wedding, the more it costs. Yet, because they think that a wedding is the most glorious event in a girl's life, her family will often sacrifice a great deal to make the day memorable. Sometimes, it is the girl's mother, rather than the girl, who wants to make it an elaborate occasion!

A formal wedding, followed by a large reception, involves endless details. Bridal consultants and bride books offer helpful advice as to costuming the bride, bridesmaids, and family, sending out invitations, and planning decorations and receptions, as well as details such as bouquets and gifts for the bridesmaids, best man, and ushers. Consultants plan a wedding to fit in with the family budget, unromantic as the term may sound. But budgets are budgets and formal weddings are likely to cost from $500 up—a fact which is important to the bride's family. Etiquette books are helpful in planning a smaller and a more simple wedding whether it takes place at home or in a small chapel.

Her wedding dress. "Something old, something new; something borrowed, something blue" has been the basis for planning many a bridal costume. Mother's own ivory satin wedding gown or Grandmother's veil of rose point lace may have been the "something old." A ruffly blue garter has often been the hidden "blue." A wedding is the time for many romantic traditions. The white bridal gown and veil is perhaps the outstanding one . . . and the cherished dream of most girls.

But even the loveliest of traditions and dreams have a way of giving in to changing conditions and ideas. Even girls who can well afford the loveliest of bridal costumes and a formal wedding often prefer to wear an afternoon dress or a simple going-away suit if the wedding ceremony is held either at home or in a chapel. Here are the reasons that a few recent brides gave for having a simple ceremony.

"When my sister was married, she had the whole family in an uproar for two whole months. It was a constant round of shopping, fittings, conferences with printers, photographers, florists, decorators, and hotel caterers. And then the showers and dinner dances! She was so worn out by her wedding day that her wedding trip was more of a rest cure than a honeymoon. I decided then and there to skip the fuss when I got married. I wore a simple suit and hopped into the car with Joe directly after a quiet ceremony for families only."

Another bride of one year said, "Mother wanted me to have a formal church wedding and a big reception at the country club. I was her only daughter and she wanted to do for me what some of her friends had done for their daughters.

Satin and lace symbolize the wedding ceremony. Many a girl has made her own wedding dress—but not as her first sewing project.

Tennessee Eastman Company

But I honestly think that she really wanted to see me married in shimmering satin and pearl-trimmed veil simply because she herself had not had them. So I gave in at first. Then we began working with actual figures. When I saw them mounting, I knew that Dad simply did not have that much money for a wedding. My two brothers were still in college. I had saved $200 toward my trousseau, but I wanted to spend it on suits and dresses that I could wear *after* my wedding day. So I finally convinced Mother that a small afternoon wedding at home with a wedding cake and punch for refreshments was all Dad could afford. I selected a floor-length dress of ivory crepe largely to please her. But I have been able to wear it as a dinner dress several times since then. I may have been too practical for a bride, but at least I knew that I wasn't depleting the family bank account."

Still another said, "Harry and I started married life 'on a shoestring' right after he had finished his internship. We had planned to wait until he had established his practice, but we suddenly decided not to wait any longer. My parents practically insisted on a big church wedding, despite the short notice, because formal weddings were the accepted thing in our family. Knowing about how much my folks would spend on such a wedding, Harry and I decided that it would be far better to use that amount to buy some equipment for his new office. So I meekly hinted to my parents that I would be happier if they changed the 'wedding fund' to an 'equipment fund' for Harry. Daddy thought we were very sensible. So we decided on a small garden wedding with my married sister and Harry's brother as sole attendants. I wore a white, ballet-length organdy dress and carried a bouquet of flowers from our own garden. After a very lovely reception on the lawn, Harry and I took off for the north woods in Maine, where I certainly did not need the usual trousseau finery. Our wedding fund actually went toward building our future . . . and I have never regretted it."

So you see, every girl has her very own reasons for doing as she does. Her wedding is "her day"—for her to plan and remember. For many, the traditional wedding gown is a symbol of true marriage, not to be changed. For others, a simpler way of getting married is wiser.

Her trousseau. Just what a girl buys for her trousseau depends largely on how much she can spend for new clothes and where she goes on her honeymoon. The lucky girl who has put aside something in her "hope bank" feels free to spend more on her trousseau than the girl who must rely on her parents to buy what she needs.

And the wise bride-to-be also selects her trousseau with a mind to the future because those same clothes may have to last her for several years. The average young couple establishing a home has to shoulder heavy expenses from the very beginning. New clothes necessarily become secondary when there are things like refrigerators, washing machines, cooking utensils, rugs, and furniture to buy. So even the trousseau involves long-range planning.

For the sake of example, let us consider the trousseau of Claire, the girl who had saved $200 toward buying new clothes that she could wear *after* her

Some girls get married in a simple suit

. . . that they can wear after the ceremony.

wedding. Claire was to be married in September. The newlyweds planned to motor to Quebec, Canada. After a few days there, they were going to tour the Gaspé Peninsula. In planning clothes for such a honeymoon, Claire knew that she would need a smart suit and coat that could be worn en route as well as in Quebec. She would need a dressy outfit or two for dining out and various evening occasions. So she decided to buy a lovely blouse to dress up her suit, plus a dressy afternoon frock. She would select a hat, simple pumps, bag, and gloves that would look well with all of these clothes. And she wanted to buy some lovely lingerie—a negligee and a couple of truly beautiful nightgowns. She already had several slips that she had received as shower gifts. Then, of course, warm sport clothes would be best for the trip around the Gaspé. These she already had. Her sport skirt, blazer, sweater, and sneakers would be just the thing for scrambles along the rocky coastline. Her last year's classic corduroy, comfortable brogues, felt hat, and shoulder bag would be ideal for browsing along some of the narrow cobblestone streets in old Quebec.

Knowing what she already had and what she wanted, Claire listed the things that she hoped she could buy with her $200. For weeks and weeks she shopped around during lunch hours and on Saturdays, looking for quality at a not-too-high price. She wanted her trousseau to be as lovely as her money could buy. After seeing what was available in various shops, she organized her shopping. For example, she did not buy her hat until she had bought all the clothes she would wear with it. The following list shows her "shopping sequence."

. . . .

An all-purpose basic coat	$ 55.00
A tailored suit	35.00
One dressy nylon * blouse	7.95
One tailored nylon blouse	6.95
Materials and pattern for an afternoon dress	10.47
One hat to go with above costumes	10.00
One pair of calf pumps, medium heel	13.50
One calf handbag to match	16.95
A pair of kid gloves	3.50
A negligee and nightgown ensemble	24.95
Another nightgown of nylon	10.95
Bedroom mules	3.00
Pantie girdle	2.50
Total	$200.72

* Claire selected nylon to eliminate ironing en route.

. . . .

Needless to say, Claire was prepared for a variety of occasions even with this minimum wardrobe. And what is more, everything she bought was exactly what she could wear back in her own home town. Nothing had to be packed away in tissues!

ACTIVITIES

For the class

1. **Invite** the buyer from a good local clothing store to come and talk to you about selecting a well co-ordinated wardrobe.
2. **Collect** for the class bulletin board and reference files any material which illustrates appropriate bridal attire for both formal and informal weddings.

For the individual

Collect and mount pictures of the garments and accessories you need to fill gaps in your wardrobe. Paste a color swatch beside each, choosing colors that will go with your basic color. Now make a price survey of these items, taking the prices from magazines, mail order catalogues, or the stores. Will you have to make some items in order to squeeze them into your clothing budget?

If you want to, make a similar collection of things you would like, but don't really need.

CHAPTER 13　　*CLOTHING THE FAMILY*

When a girl marries she is responsible not only for the selection and care of her own clothing but also, to a great extent, for the selection and care of her husband's clothing. And then comes the first baby . . . and later another. Through the early years she is in full charge of their wardrobes. Hers is a task that involves dollars, sense, soapsuds, and a ready thimble!

THE MAN OF THE HOUSE

Many a husband looks to his wife when he needs some suggestions in selecting his coats, suits, and other items of apparel. His sixth sense tells him that a woman knows good values in materials and workmanship. And he usually relies on her style sense in matters of color, line, and fabric selection. So the girl who has had training in clothing can give her husband and other menfolk some helpful pointers.

This does *not* imply that clothing selection should be left entirely to women. Clothing is *everybody's* business. How often we hear comments such as "Clothes make the man" and "He dresses the part." Every man—yes, even every high school boy—*can* develop that feeling of self-confidence which comes from being well-dressed. To do so, he merely has to learn a few fundamentals of clothing selection:

How to plan a wardrobe which meets the demands of his activities.

How to select styles, colors, and fabrics suited to him.

How to judge fabric for its suitability and wearing quality.

How to evaluate a garment for its fit and construction.

Planning a man's wardrobe. A man's work or profession, the community, the climate, and his outside interests determine the type of clothes he selects, just as they determine a girl's or woman's wardrobe.

The man who meets the public in banks, offices, stores, and classrooms generally finds that suits, shirts, ties, and socks which are more or less conservative in color and style are a wise choice. They are more practical and more "distinctive" than loud colors and flashy styles.

Conservative business clothes are also appropriate for such informal social occasions as dinners, club meetings, or theater parties. On these occasions, a man can introduce a "splash" of color in his tie. For informal social affairs, many men choose white shirts, and it is a wise choice if there is any doubt as to what will be proper.

In those circles where men and women "dress" for dinner and the theater, the dinner jacket with black tie is worn. Full-dress, formal balls and receptions call for white tie and tails.

Slacks and sport shirts (T-shirts, polo shirts, gay plaid, corduroy, and flannel shirts) are comfortable to wear around the house and garden. They are the perennial favorites for neighborhood gatherings where casual informality is the rule. In recent years, simple sport shirts with short sleeves and open collars have become acceptable even in some places of business, when summer temperatures begin to climb.

Countless occupations require special uniforms or standard work clothes. These may or may not be provided by the employer. The man who wears special clothes on his job has only to round out his wardrobe with clothes for his various social and community activities and for his leisure hours which may be spent in active sports or just plain loafing.

Today's trend toward outdoor living makes casual clothes essential to most wardrobes.

Evaporated Milk Association

Of course, a complete wardrobe for a man also includes such accessories as hats, shoes, socks, ties, and gloves plus nightwear and undergarments. (Refer to page 231 for the wardrobe inventory of a business man and to page 234 for the wardrobe of a young man of sixteen.)

Selecting styles, colors, and fabrics. A man's build largely determines the style and fabric of the suit or coat he should select; his personal coloring should influence his choice of colors.

A short man, whether he is slim or stocky, should avoid extremely built-out shoulders or too long jackets, for they create a squat appearance. Contrasting jackets and trousers cut height, too, so that matching tones are better. Solid colors, muted plaids, or pin stripes are better than pronounced checks, plaids, or widely spaced stripes. Smooth, firm fabrics tend to increase height, whereas bulky, coarse weaves tend to build out the figure.

The man who is very tall and lean will find that pleated trousers and rough tweedy textures build him out. Contrasting jackets and trousers cut apparent height. Jackets should not be so short, however, that they create an outgrown, "leggy" look.

The tall, stout man will find that firm, rather smooth fabrics in conservative solid colors do not emphasize his girth as much as rough, tweedy textures and pronounced colors and plaids would.

The man of average (or tall), strong build may wear contrasting trousers and jackets, smooth or coarse textures, and more pronounced figures, depending on his preference.

Whatever his build, every man should learn how to avoid "noisy" effects in fabric combinations. A plain, solid-toned garment can usually be combined with a plaid *or* a striped garment. For example, a solid-colored topcoat looks well with any suit fabric, whereas a coat of pronounced plaid would clash with another plaid or stripe. Plain trousers can be worn with jackets of striped, plaid, or checked fabric, while a plain jacket looks attractive with trousers of a striped or small checked fabric. Shirts of striped or checked material look best with solid-colored suits. Shirts in a solid color can be worn with either striped or checked jackets. Ties with a pronounced design should be reserved for plain shirts and suits or for those in which the pattern or weave is inconspicuous. Socks may either repeat the color of the tie or harmonize with the suit color. Some men prefer to repeat the shoe color, so that the socks seem less conspicuous.

Not so long ago, men's clothing was almost entirely limited to neutral or very muted colors, but with the growing emphasis on clothes for sports and casual living, men, too, have taken to color. Sport shirts, blazers, sweaters, and accessories come in a wide range of colors to provide the "punch" many men want for the casual hours of their work-a-day world. But pronounced color is not limited to casual clothes alone. Standard shirts now come in a wide range of colors, and many men prefer them for business and informal social wear, instead of the traditional white shirt.

In general, suits and topcoats are made in more conservative colors and rightfully so. They are long-term garments, selected to harmonize with a variety of shirts, ties, and sweaters. The topcoat should provide the basic color to which suit colors are keyed. In choosing his colors, a man should consider their effect on his personal coloring—hair, complexion, and eyes. Below are a few suggestions.

COLORS FOR MEN'S CLOTHING

HAIR COLOR	SKIN COLOR	SUITS AND COATS
Fair	Light and clear	Blues, grayed greens, slate gray
Sandy	Neutral, creamy	The above colors plus dark brown
Brown	Neutral to warm	Browns, tans, grayed greens, navy
Black	Warm, swarthy	Navy, all grays
Steel gray	Neutral to warm	Navy, dull blue-greens, all grays
Light gray	Neutral to warm	The above colors plus dark brown
Red	Neutral, creamy	Browns, tans, dull greens, grays, blues

Note: Black, so popular in recent years, looks well on most types.

Here are additional suggestions which apply more specifically to colors used for such items as sweaters, sport shirts, and ties. Generally, rich intense hues look striking on a man who has black or dark brown hair, swarthy skin tones, and dark eyes. The man with steel gray hair and warm skin tones also looks well in rather intense colors, ranging from cool to warm. More subtle tones, such as soft blues and grayed greens, rust, and maroon, look well on the man with fair, sandy, or gray hair, and fair or neutral skin tones. Red hair and warm skin tones are complemented by blue and green, and blend in nicely with tones ranging from gold and tan to rust and brown. The color of the eyes can be accented by repeating it in a tie, sweater, or sport shirt.

Judging fabric. In addition to selecting fabrics suitable for his various activities and for his figure type, a man will want to know how well a fabric will wear. Although tags and labels on ready-made garments identify the fabric and its fiber content, it is a good idea to know the properties of the fabric in question. (Refer to Chapter 14, "Textiles Used For Clothing," for more detailed descriptions.)

Suits and coats made of worsted hold their shape well. Because worsted yarn is made of long, straightened wool fibers, worsted fabrics are firm, smooth, resilient, and very durable. They hold a crease well and do not wrinkle easily. However, there is one drawback; some worsteds, such as *gabardine* and *serge* which have no nap, do become shiny with wear. On the other hand, worsted *sharkskin* with its variegated twill weave does not show shine. Worsted *cheviot, covert,* and *flannel* have a slight nap or surface fuzz which prevents a shine from developing. (These three fabrics are also woven of standard woolen yarns which are made of shorter, more crimped fibers than worsted yarns.)

Woolens are softer than worsteds because the short fiber ends project to provide a deeper nap. They are more flexible than worsteds because of the short fibers and also because woolens are often woven in looser weaves. For these reasons, they wrinkle more easily than worsteds do, but, in their favor, they do not get as shiny as the smoother worsteds.

In addition to cheviot, covert, and flannel (which may be made of wool as well as worsted), the following woolen materials are used for men's clothing. Wool *broadcloth* has a lustrous, napped surface, permanently brushed and pressed in one direction. It is used for dress suits and coats. *Homespun* is made of coarse, irregular, springy yarns which do not hold a crease, but which do not tend to wrinkle either. *Melton,* used for overcoats and sport jackets, is a heavy fabric with a thick, sheared nap. This is a durable fabric which looks like very heavy flannel. *Tweed* comes in a variety of weaves: flecked, striped, checked, or plaid. It ranges in texture from medium-rough to very rough and from lightweight for suits to heavyweight for topcoats.

A checked jacket, worn with trousers of a contrasting material, makes an attractive outfit for a man of average to tall height. The careful detailing and perfect matching of the checks on the jacket indicate a well-made garment.

Du Pont photo

Good-quality, firmly woven tweeds wear exceptionally well and hold their shape. A looser weave tends to get baggy. *Shetland* wool, a fine, strong, hairy type, produces high-quality tweed fabrics, sometimes referred to as "Shetlands." They are soft and spongy, and, like other tweeds, may lose their shape.

In addition to these standard worsted and woolen fabrics, many other fabrics and blends are · used for men's suiting, especially for summer or between-season wear. Tropical suits (traditionally made of worsted yarn) are now sometimes made of Dacron, or wool, rayon, and mohair. Silk is also used for men's suiting, by itself or in blends with wool and Dacron. Pure silk appears in many textures; used with other fibers, silk provides strength, light-weight quality, and freshness. Men's suits also come in wash-and-wear fabrics which are blends of Dacron and Orlon, Dacron and rayon, or 100 per cent Dacron. Cotton, by itself, comes in washable seersucker suits and sporty corduroys.

All of these fibers, from wool to cotton, also provide the finer yarns from which all men's shirts, underwear, and nightwear are made. (See Glossary of Fabrics, page 290.)

Checking fit and construction. Ready-made garments, especially the better brands, are now sized to fit the following figure types: average, tall, tall-stout, tall-thin, short-slight, and short-stout. Buy a suit or coat which requires a minimum of alterations. Sleeve and trouser lengths are easily altered, but try to avoid any alterations at the shoulder line because they seldom result in a perfect fit. If a man has difficulty in getting a good fit in a readymade, it would be wise to have the garment tailored-to-order. Even mail-order firms now provide this special service.

In trying on the coat and trousers of a ready-made suit, check these points for *fit:*

1. The coat should be long enough to cover the seat of the trousers.

2. The collar should lie smoothly with no gaping at the back of the neck. It should expose about ¼ inch of the shirt collar at the back.

3. The coat should hang straight and smooth from the shoulders with no diagonal "pull" at the shoulder blades or between the shoulders and neck; there should be no wrinkles under the arms, and no strain at the button closings.

4. Sleeves should be tapered and hang wrinkle-free when the arm hangs at the side. The sleeve should cover the bend of the wrist and may expose the edge of the shirt cuff.

5. Well-fitted trousers hang straight from the waist (at a point above the hipbone) with creases straight up and down both at the back and front.

6. There should be no strain at the seat or crotch. Trouser legs should be roomy enough at the thigh so that there are no "lap wrinkles" when the wearer is seated.

7. Trouser cuffs should barely cover the back of the shoe, leaving the shoe heel exposed, and should fold slightly over the instep.

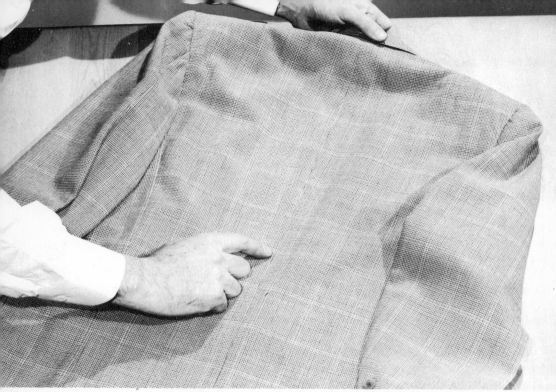

Money Management Institute, Household Finance Corporation

Use the same principles to judge men's clothing that you use to judge your own. The exact matching of the plaids in this jacket are a sign of good quality, but the poorly inset sleeves make it an inadvisable purchase.

In checking the fit of a topcoat or overcoat, use the same standards used for a suit coat. Try on the coat *over* a suit. Make sure that armholes are roomy enough to fit easily over a suit coat and that there is no feeling of strain at the button closings.

Check these points for *construction* of readymades:

1. Collars and lapels should be firm and spring back easily when folded back or "pinched." This indicates that good-quality tailor's canvas has been used for interfacing. Cotton interfacing does not hold its shape.

2. Garments lined with a strong twill lining will give better service than those lined with a plain weave lining.

3. If the garment is made of a plaid or other figured fabric, see that the patterns are perfectly matched at the seams.

4. Stitching should be close and even, with no sign of puckering.

5. Buttonholes should be smooth and firm.

Note: When ordering any of the above garments by mail, be sure to give all the measurements requested by the mail-order firm and be sure they are very accurate. When suits are to be tailored-to-order, fabric is selected from swatches sent to the customer.

Shopping for shirts. Whether shirts are for men or juniors, the basic style varies little. Collars may vary from soft, casual, roll collars to those with stays. They may have long or short points; the points may be buttoned or unbuttoned. Cuffs are either plain, barrel cuffs which button or French cuffs which fold back and fasten with links. Shirts come in a variety of fabrics depending on their use (see below). It is important to buy the correct size.

Men's *business* and *dress* shirts (broadcloth, Oxford cloth, cambric, madras, nylon crepe, and Dacron and its blends) are sized by neck measure and sleeve length. Before buying, measure the neck in inches and half inches; for example: 14, 14½, 15, 15½, etc. For the sleeve length, measure from the middle back of the neck, across the shoulder, over the bent elbow to the wrist.

Men's *sport* shirts (corduroy, cotton plaids, flannel, gabardine) are sized by neck measure, too, but are grouped under four basic sizes: small (S) 14–14½; medium (M) 15–15½; large (L) 16–16½; extra large (XL) 17–17½.

Men's *work* shirts (covert, drill, jean, and khaki) are sized as sport shirts, but often there is a choice of sleeve length, too.

Men's *nightshirts* and *pajamas* are "letter" sized according to chest measurements: A, 34–36; B, 38–40; C, 42–44; D, 46–48; E, 50–52.

Junior-sized shirts for boys are sold by *age*. The corresponding neck and chest measurements are as follows:

Age	6	8	10	12	14	16	18
Neck	11	11½	12	12½	13	13½	14
Chest	25	26½	28	29½	31½	33	34½

It is wise to buy cotton garments that are guaranteed against shrinkage. If there is no such guarantee, buy a size larger to ensure comfort and long wear even if the garment should shrink.

THE LADY OF THE HOUSE

The extent of a woman's wardrobe depends, of course, on her husband's income, their social activities, and her ability to sew for herself. The wife and mother of a modest-income family generally is willing to limit her wardrobe so that other members of the family are provided for. Growing children need new clothes frequently, and most mothers are inclined to make sacrifices. Yet, in all fairness to her, and to the others in the family, clothing budgets should be planned so that no one is slighted. Even children should learn that happiness in family living is largely due to fair sharing and unselfishness on the part of everyone.

The housewife. The average housewife generally needs more clothes for housework than for anything else. Her housedresses, skirts, slacks, and blouses should be washable. Knitted T-shirts or dresses and housecoats of seersucker and drip-dry fabrics which require little or no pressing are real time-savers. Neat, becoming, and appropriate house clothes are morale-

Some housewives think that what they wear around the house isn't important. Don't become one of them.

builders for everyone in the family. And certainly, if a mother is trying to instill good clothing habits in her children, she herself should dress well. Furthermore, most youngsters are quite sensitive about their parents' clothing. They fairly burst with pride when "Daddy looks nice" and "Mom looks pretty."

In addition to house clothes, the housewife should have at least one "town" costume for each season. This might be a suit which can be dressed up or down with suitable blouses and accessories for fall and winter wear. A simple, basic dress, either in a print or solid color with a harmonizing jacket or bolero, will give variety in warmer seasons. These costumes can be worn to church, luncheons, or for shopping. The housewife will also need at least one special-occasion dress per season. Her summer and winter·coats should be selected in a basic color which harmonizes with her suit and dresses.

Refer to pages 232–233 for the complete inventory of a typical wardrobe for a housewife in a modest-income family.

The "career-wife." Today there are an increasing number of women who have positions outside the home. In addition to the "house garb" which even these career-wives need, they must also have clothes for their jobs.

Since the career-wife meets the public in her job, she must have a greater variety of clothes and accessories than the housewife who has no job. Suits are perennial favorites both because they are appropriate for most jobs and because they can be easily varied with a simple change of blouse. Basic dresses with good classic lines are also a practical choice, for they can be varied with different collars and belts or with a suitable piece of jewelry. Such basic dresses can also be "dressed up" for an occasion after office hours when time does not permit a change of costume. Classic tailored styles are also favorites with all age groups. Some office or classroom jobs may permit the informality of casual spectator styles or sweater and skirt combinations, especially for the younger career-wife.

In assembling her clothes and accessories, the career-wife should select a basic color for her coat around which she will plan the colors of the other items in her wardrobe.

THE CHILDREN

The baby. Some young mothers tend to think of their first baby as a doll to be prettied up for exhibition purposes. But before long, they realize that clothes for the very young baby should be chosen with comfort and ease of laundering in mind. All baby's clothing should be washable. Mild soap and thorough rinsing prevent skin irritations. The wise young mother also selects clothing that needs no ironing. Knitted garments and soft cotton flannels may be neatly folded and put away when dry.

Select undergarments of soft material that will not chafe the baby's tender skin. Cotton, linen, and mixtures of wool with cotton, silk, or rayon are recommended. All-wool garments may feel prickly and harsh, especially when they shrink in laundering. All-wool fabric is generally reserved for outer clothing.

Select lightweight clothing for the young baby. Several layers of light fabric are warmer than a single thickness of heavy fabric, because the air spaces between the layers of clothing are non-conductors of heat. But do not "smother" the baby in excessive clothing. Being overdressed not only hampers the baby's freedom of movement, but also prevents radiation of body heat and keeps the infant unhealthily and uncomfortably warm.

Baby's clothes should be roomy to allow freedom of movement and prevent binding. Yet they must not be so large as to be bulky. Elastic bands on protective rubber panties should not be tight.

Nighties, shirts, and dresses that open down the front are easier for the new mother to put on a squirming infant than garments that have only a small neck opening. Tabs on shirts to which the diaper can be pinned at least double the life of the shirt. An infant is far more comfortable, and looks just as adorable, in a soft flannel nightie as in a fancy little dress that may bind at the neckline or armhole. But when the baby does wear a dress, be sure it is of soft material and has no bumpy seams or prickly lace edgings.

When the baby reaches the crawling stage, he can wear creepers or rompers of cotton knit or seersucker which are easily washed and require no ironing. Overalls of corduroy or denim are durable and may be worn with shirts of cotton knit. Doctors generally agree that a baby should not wear shoes until he starts to walk. These first shoes should have a hard but flexible sole and should be about one-half inch longer than the foot.

The young mother-to-be should seek advice as to how to clothe her baby. She should consult her doctor as to what constitutes an adequate layette. Hospitals in many communities have lectures for expectant mothers *and* fathers to advise them how to prepare and care for the baby. Other communities offer the services of a visiting nurse who is glad to give helpful advice to the young mother. Many women's magazines publish inexpensive but up-to-the-minute booklets on infant care and clothing. The Government Extension Division also prepares similar booklets. All such information is very helpful to the young mother.

The toddler. Youngsters from two to five years of age are gradually learning to dress themselves. It takes time and patience (on both the child's part and his mother's) before he can proudly say, "I can dress all by myself." When he can say that, he has observed the order in which clothes are put on; he knows back from front, wrong side from right side, and left from right, which is no small accomplishment; he has developed co-ordination by fastening his garments; and he has learned that he can finish the big job of dressing only if he concentrates on the task. Along with his sense of accomplishment he has developed independence, which is wonderful for his morale.

Children are proud when they can dress themselves. Select clothes for them that are easy to manage.

To help him during this complex learning process, his mother should select garments that are easy for him to manage by himself. Manufacturers of children's garments take this into consideration when designing self-help clothes. A decorative motif on the front of each garment helps a child to distinguish front from back. A mother who sews for her child (or buys plain garments) can appliqué or embroider an animal, a flower, or the child's initial on the front of both under and outer garments. Front fastenings on garments are easy for the child to handle. A single large button is easier than a row of tiny ones. Panties, union suits, and pajamas are designed to help the child through his bathroom "training" period. One-piece garments that have seats with elasticized waistbands can be managed by the young child far more easily than a seat that buttons across the back.

Toddlers belong to the "dirt age." They are drawn as if by a magnet to mud, sand, puddles, piles of overturned earth, and stacks of brush or leaves. It is their world so let them play in it without too much nagging. But clothe them in washables! Have plenty of seersuckers, cotton knits, and denim play clothes on hand. Dress them in sunsuits or briefs on warm, sunny days. Save linen suits and frilly dresses for summer dress-up occasions to cut down on ironing.

The standard outer garment for winter wear is the snow suit, often sold with matching cap or hat. This should be water-repellent and windproof on the outside and lined with another material for warmth. A color that will not show soil too readily saves many a washing. Be sure to buy it large enough to last the whole cold season. Winter festivities may call for dresses of flannel, challis, or velveteen. Little suits of pinwale corduroy are good for either boys or girls. Eton suits with short pants dress up the little boy for special occasions.

The selection of children's shoes is important. Growing bones must be allowed for. A young child generally outgrows his shoes before they are worn out. Never let a child wear shoes that cramp his toes. In buying a new pair, see that they are one-half inch longer than the length of the foot.

Even a four-year-old can be trained to put away his clothes. Low rods and hooks in the closet encourage him to hang outer garments. A child will take pride in having drawers and shelves for his own clothes. When taught, he can find such things for himself as underwear and socks. Good clothing habits can be started early!

The school-age child. Growing, active school children need durable and practical styles. At this stage, too, washables are best because they save on cleaning bills. Most woolen outer garments need dry-cleaning.

Little boys, like big ones, seldom like to wear a complete suit to school. They prefer corduroy trousers with which they can wear either a shirt or a T-shirt. A slip-over sweater, with or without sleeves, can be worn for extra warmth. Their choices of outer garments are likely to be mackinaws or jackets of wool or leather. Of course, some schools may specify the types of clothing which they want young boys to wear.

Play clothes include jeans, denim pants, T-shirts, and sneakers—all practical choices as far as the mother is concerned!

Standard suits and overcoats are generally saved for special events and holiday festivities. In buying these garments, allowance should be made for growth. Of course, they should not fit so loosely as to look awkward!

Little girls, like teen-agers, love jumpers and skirts of woolen plaid and pinwale corduroy to wear to school. These are worn with colorful sweaters and cotton blouses. Jumpers are a practical choice because shoulder straps may be adjusted when lengthening is necessary. Cotton dresses of gingham, percale, chambray, and the like are good the year around.

For winter dress-up events, velveteen, wool crepe, and challis are nice, if something warmer than cotton is needed. Summer dresses for parties and "Sunday best" can be of organdy, dimity, and other sheer perky cottons.

Full-length coats that can be worn with both party and school dresses are the most practical choice for the young girl. In buying or making dresses or coats, look for deep hems that can be let out.

Heavy sweaters or jackets are good for playtime along with jeans or overalls. Summer, of course, brings its own play assortment of sun clothes and pinafores.

Little girls can be quite clothes conscious, and their wishes should be considered as far as possible. If a child is not the "organdy and blue ribbon type," she should not be forced to wear such styles. Too many mothers disregard their child's personality in selecting her clothes. Naturally, the child rebels. Furthermore, little girls (and big ones too) like to wear what their friends are wearing.

Boys and girls of early school age should be required to hang up their clothes, to put away boots and galoshes, and otherwise keep track of their belongings.

Teen-agers. During the teen years, the "gang" spirit prevails among both boys and girls. This applies to activities, hobbies, and certainly to clothing. Teen-agers like to wear what the "gang" is wearing. This factor should be considered because no teen-ager likes to be set apart from others in the group. (Sally is a teen-ager and because her wardrobe needs were given complete coverage on pages 194–195, we shall confine the following discussion to boys of high school age.)

Calling all boys! You will agree that most boys have many things in common. Your parents may often think that you are a "race" apart. You leave your things scattered about; then you raise an alarm for your missing shoe or fuss because the shirt that you wore last week is not freshly laundered. Most of you rebel when your mother insists that you polish your shoes, take a shower, or clean and trim your nails. Some of you dislike the idea of wearing new clothes—or even the mention of shopping for them—unless, of course, they are the usual "cords," jeans, and blazers that "they" are wearing.

But times will change, and so will your attitudes. It is all a part of growing up. By the time you are in your late teens, you will probably want to maintain the standards held by your father or other men you admire. Gradually, you will realize that your "stature" is improved by the clothing you

Sybil Shelton from Monkmeyer

Dorothy Reed from Monkmeyer

Their interests and activities plus the fads of "the gang" influence teen-agers' wardrobes.

Sybil Shelton from Monkmeyer

select as well as by your day-to-day grooming. "As a man dresseth, so is he" is not just a meaningless saying. Your classmates, your adult friends, your prospective employers, and everyone along the way who can help you to move forward *are* impressed by the "total you," and that includes your appearance—posture, grooming, and clothing.

You needn't try to be a "Beau Brummel," but you can still be well dressed by selecting clothes that are suitable for school, dates, informal parties, formal dances, church, and other activities. You look better in colors, fabrics, and styles that suit *you,* and not everyone else in the block. And you can learn to shop wisely for *yourself* by analyzing the fit and construction of every garment before you buy it.

These are all basic factors with which every man and teen-age boy should be familiar. These factors are discussed on pages 210–217, and because they apply to men, they also apply to those of you who are approaching manhood.

Further information on a complete wardrobe for a boy of sixteen is found on page 234.

FAMILY FINANCES

Marriage is something like a business partnership. It takes wise planning and shrewd spending on the part of both husband and wife to meet the expenses of a home and family. Of course, family expenses vary a great deal and are determined by the following conditions.

Region. Living costs in the country differ from those in towns or cities. A farm family may spend comparatively little actual cash on food because it raises cows, hogs, and chickens and grows its own vegetables and fruits. Housing costs may be low. Simple work clothes cut down the clothing budget. As a rule, little is spent on paid entertainment unless the family goes to town. But farm folk have to spend a great deal on expensive farm equipment; and automobiles are practically a must.

A city family must buy all of its food. Apartment rents are high. "City" clothes are more expensive. There is a tendency to spend more on entertainment because the movie, the concert hall, and the theater are right there. But in contrast to the farm family, city folk do not have to buy expensive equipment such as tractors, reapers, milking machines, and separators. Those in the modest income group seldom own a car. Buses and other city transportation answer most of their needs more economically.

Climate also affects living costs. Those who live in wintry zones must spend more on fuel and heavy clothing than those in warmer areas.

Occupation. The occupation of the father (and the wife who works) also affects the way money is budgeted. A professional man or a "white collar" worker must spend more on clothes than the farmer, the factory worker, and others who need not "dress" to meet the public. Personal appearance can affect one's advancement in many types of work, so it is important to dress well.

The wife who has a job needs more clothing than the housewife who remains at home. In addition, working women may need extra help and services to run their homes. Some send out their laundry, others employ a cleaning woman, others eat out more often than they otherwise would. Food costs often run high because the working woman does not have an opportunity to shop for values and she tends to spend more on "prepared" foods. Clothing costs may run high because she has little time to sew and mend! Of course, her salary does increase the family income.

Children. The number of children in the family also affects the spending plan. Let us say that a man and wife have annual expenses of $1950. Another family with one child, living under similar conditions, will spend $2520. The family with two children spends $3000; the family with three, will spend $3450.

In other words, each child ups the family living expenses, but two don't cost quite twice as much as one and the third isn't quite as expensive as the second. Let 100 per cent stand for the amount spent by a family of four: father, mother, son, and daughter. Two people would need 65 per cent of that amount; three would need 84 per cent; and five would need 115 per cent.[1] So if you have several brothers and sisters, the percentage of the family income that can be spent for your needs is considerably smaller than the percentage of its income the family next door can spend on their only daughter.

Age of family members. Family spending is also directly influenced by the ages of both parents and children. Parents below thirty-five generally demand greater variety and more style in their clothes than parents who have passed the thirty-five-mark. They are also likely to want to spend more on entertainment, education, home improvements, and travel.

Young children and those of grade school age do not have as many expenses as teen-agers. At that age level, high school, social activities, and outside entertainment bring increased demands on both the clothing budget and the spending allowance.

Family tastes and interests. Even families in the same age and income group, in the same community, and with the same number of members spend their money differently. One family may spend a large proportion of its income on its home—replacing furniture as it begins to look worn, redecorating every few years, maintaining a perfect lawn and lovely garden. Another family may live in shabby and cramped quarters but take long expensive trips each year. Some families are "extravagant" about food (according to other families'

[1] *Worker's Budgets in the U. S.,* Bulletin No. 927 U. S. Department of Labor, Bureau of Labor Statistics.

A girl who makes some of the clothes she needs is helping out the family finances.
Money Management Institute, Household Finance Corporation

standards). Others will drink powdered skim milk, but drive a large impressive car. What one family considers essential to its well-being and happiness may not seem essential to another. Each has its own standard of living.

The family budget. As you can see, a budget is really a family affair . . . a spending plan that provides for the physical necessities of life and contributes to the general development and happiness of every member in the family. Budgets are not inflexible, rigid laws that say everyone must spend "thus and so." Each family must work out its own guide so that there will be enough money set aside for such basic physical necessities as *food, clothing, housing* (and its maintenance), and *medical care*. There must also be enough put aside for *miscellaneous* expenses such as transportation or automobile upkeep, taxes, education, recreation, gifts, insurance, and savings.

Without a carefully thought-out spending plan, a family may drift from one unpaid bill to another. Basic necessities are slighted in preference to things of lesser importance. If the family has extravagant tastes in clothes, doctor bills may go unpaid. If a disproportionate amount is spent on movies, sports, and luxury items, there will be nothing to deposit in the bank toward the insurance payment. If too much is spent on rent, the food budget may suffer.

A low-income family necessarily spends most of its income for food, shelter, and clothing. There is little or nothing left for recreation, education, insurance, and savings. A high-income family can allow a larger percentage for education, savings, home improvements, automobiles, and so on.

It is always easier to make a spending plan when your family's income is definite and regular than when it fluctuates from month to month or season by season. Nevertheless, it is possible for every family to make some kind of spending plan. Once the plan is down in black and white, it is important to spend according to that plan. The wise home manager keeps records of expenses. Then she studies those records to see if she can improve on her planning or spending. Of course, budgets are not rigid. They change with the times and with growing children and with new interests. A good spending plan allows for possible future demands as well as for current expenses.

The family clothing plan. From the preceding material, you can see how many factors influence a family's clothing budget. What is a reasonable budget for one family may not be for another. By and large, however, statistics indicate that the clothing costs of the average family range from 10 per cent of the total income in the lower income group, to about 17 per cent of the total income in the moderate income group.

The table on page 229 is based on a survey of clothing expenditures for families in Detroit, Michigan. The selection covers families of varying size and income. You will notice that the percentage spent on clothing gradually rises as the income rises, and as the size of the family increases.

Surveys made by the U.S. Commerce Department indicate that families spend an *average* of 13 cents out of every dollar (13 per cent) for clothing and accessories. This figure approximates the *average* of the percentages quoted in the table.

NUMBER IN FAMILY	INCOME	CLOTHING PURCHASES	PER CENT *
Husband and wife	$2,000–3,000	$298	9.9
With 1 child	3,000–4,000	399	9.9
With 2 children	4,000–5,000	500	10.0
With 3 children	5,000–6,000	813	13.5
With 3 or more children	6,000–7,500	1,285	17.1

Source: Monthly Labor Review, 1951

MEET THE BROWNS

In Chapter 12, you "met" Sally and learned how she planned her wardrobe for $85, which was her share of the family clothing fund. Now, let us go back to Sally Brown's family, so typical of many American families in the moderate-income group. Knowing how they planned a family clothing budget may help you to work out a budget for your family, either now or in the future.

You will remember that Mr. Brown is a business man, Mrs. Brown is a housewife with no outside job, Sally's brother Fred is sixteen, and her sister Midge is ten.

Mr. Brown's "take-home pay," after taxes and other deductions, is $4,165. The Browns try to keep the family's annual clothing purchases down to $500 which is 12 per cent of their cash income. Another 1 per cent (about $42) is spent annually on clothing maintenance—dry cleaning and shoe repair.

The Browns have kept records of clothing purchases for the entire family, including readymades, accessories, and sewing materials. They are able to estimate the annual requirements of each family member, allotting to each a certain percentage of the family clothing fund.

a.	Mr. Brown	28 per cent	$140
b.	Mrs. Brown	20 per cent	100
c.	Fred	22 per cent	110
d.	Sally	17 per cent	85
e.	Midge	13 per cent	65

a. Mr. Brown meets the public in his work, so he must "keep up" his appearance. His clothing costs run higher because he must purchase readymade clothing.

b. Mrs. Brown has no "outside job," so her clothing is largely limited to house clothes, plus a few tailored and dressier clothes, most of which she makes herself.

c. Fred, a junior in high school, is still growing, so his wardrobe needs frequent additions. Because his suits, slacks, and jackets are purchased readymade, his allotment is higher than Sally's.

d. Sally's wardrobe costs, as you know, were greatly lowered because her mother, and even she, could sew her clothes. (See page 197.) As she

* Percentage based on larger figure in each category.

grows older, her demands will be greater and her allotment will be larger, but by then, Fred will be more on his own.

e. Midge, at ten, has the lowest allotment. Her mother makes most of her clothes and occasionally remodels clothes which Sally has outgrown.

The above clothing budget of $500 for a family of five is made possible for the following reasons:

1. The Browns, whenever possible, take advantage of end-of-season sales, realizing substantial savings in the purchase of good merchandise. (They prefer *good* quality which has long-wearing value, even if it costs more than an item of *cheaper* quality which sells for less.)

Money Management Institute, Household Finance Corporation

A joint family planning session will help to produce a clothing budget which will meet everyone's needs. Apart from the money this family has to spend, many other factors will influence their clothing plan: the area in which they live, the father's occupation, the mother's occupation or her social interests, as well as the interests and activities of their teen-age children.

Dupont

2. The family buys basic items like coats and suits on a three-year-rotation system; for example, Mr. Brown buys an overcoat one year, a winter-weight suit the second year, and a spring-weight suit the third year. Additional slacks, jackets, and other items are purchased throughout the three-year period. The other members in the family follow this system (remember Sally's plan).

3. Mrs. Brown sews for herself and the girls. She buys yard-goods and remnants on sale whenever possible.

4. Both Sally and Fred earn pin money to supplement the amount their parents allot toward their clothing. These earnings go toward buying those cherished "extras."

The Browns' budget vs. the Whites'. Later, we shall analyze the specific clothing needs of each of the Browns. But here, let us point out that all family clothing budgets could not—and need not—be based on the same percentages as the Browns'. For the sake of comparison, let us briefly consider the Whites who live in the Browns' neighborhood.

Mr. White works for the same firm that Mr. Brown does, and their salaries are similar. However, Mrs. White is employed as a secretary, which brings their joint income, after deductions, to approximately $7,000. Their daughter Ann is seventeen and a senior in high school. Ted is fifteen and growing like a weed.

What factors influence the clothing budget for the Whites?

1. Because the Whites' joint income is larger than the Browns', they can afford to allot about 17 per cent of their total income to clothing. This leaves adequate funds for other current expenses as well as savings which include the children's college fund.

2. This larger percentage for clothing is necessary because both Mr. and Mrs. White must dress to meet the public.

3. The Whites have to spend more on readymade clothing because Mrs. White does not have time to sew for her family.

4. Ann's increased social activities and her "more adult" clothing requirements also raise the family's clothing expenses. Because her mother works, Ann assumes many household responsibilities which prevent her from earning pin money.

5. Ted, who is still growing, needs frequent additions to his wardrobe.

If the Whites spend 17 per cent of their joint income of $7,000 on clothing and its maintenance, they will have $1,190 to divide among the four members of their family. The following apportionment is suggested:

a.	Mr. White	22 per cent	$261.80
b.	Mrs. White	30 per cent	357.00
c.	Ann	28 per cent	333.20
d.	Ted	20 per cent	238.00

a. On a percentage basis, Mr. White is allotted less in his family budget (22 per cent) than Mr. Brown (who received 28 per cent), but in cash terms, he has more to spend.

b. Mrs. White is given 30 per cent of the family clothing fund, which is 8 per cent more than her husband's share. Statistics indicate that a woman in business spends as much as a third more on clothing than does a man, largely because a career woman requires more variety in clothing and a far greater number of accessories. Now let us compare Mrs. White's 30 per cent allotment with Mrs. Brown's 20 per cent share of the Browns' clothing budget. Mrs. White has a higher percentage, chiefly because she must dress to meet the public. In addition, she needs the house clothes which every homemaker needs. Mr. and Mrs. White also lead an active social life which requires a variety of dressy clothes. All of Mrs. White's clothing is bought readymade, whereas Mrs. Brown made many of her clothes.

c. Ann's allotment is 28 per cent of the family clothing budget. Some economists place the needs of a sixteen-year-old girl as high as 32 per cent of the family budget. Such a percentage, however, seems out of line for this family, inasmuch as there are four in the family, two of whom must dress well for business. Furthermore, Ann lives in a modest neighborhood, and her friends are from moderate-income families. Her allotment of 28 per cent is adequate even though her social needs are greater than those of a 14-year-old girl like Sally.

d. Ted's allotment of 20 per cent is adequate for a boy of his age. His preference for everyday wear runs to separates—slacks which can be worn with jackets and blazers. His one and only suit is worn to church and school parties. As Ted gets older and begins to participate in more "social" activities, he will need more suits.

The above comparisons prove what was said earlier: "A budget is really a family affair." Percentages and amounts vary according to the specific needs of families and their individual members. Furthermore, percentages will vary within any one family as conditions change and as the ages of family members change.

Individual clothing budgets for the Browns. Now let us go back to the specific needs of each member of the Brown family.

Mr. Brown, a man in his early forties, hopes to limit his clothing purchases to $140 for the current year. On page 231, you will find a list of all the items in his wardrobe.[1] Included are items already on hand, and those to be purchased. The latter are marked with a (*), accompanied by the price.[2]

[1] This inventory and those which follow are adapted from inventory data published in United States Department of Agriculture Bulletin No. 148: *Family Clothing Inventories and Purchases,* 1956. Survey of families in Minneapolis and St. Paul, Minnesota.

[2] Prices quoted are based on 1957–58 listings in mail-order houses and those chain stores which serve a national market.

Total Number		Item of Clothing	Description of Item	Quantity to Buy	Price
1	*	Overcoat	Winter, 100% wool tweed	1	$39.00
1		Topcoat	All-weather, rain repellent gabardine: rayon, Dacron, and nylon blend		
1		Toggle coat	Winter sport jacket with detachable hood; 100% wool		
1		Jacket	Corduroy, zipper closing		
2		Suits	Year-round weight: one, wool tweed; one, flannel		
1		Suit	Summer: Wash-and-wear tropical weave: Dacron and rayon blend		
1	*	Jacket	Suit-coat variety for business; 100% wool tweed	1	19.95
2	*	Trousers	Separates, to wear with above jacket; 100% worsted flannel	1 pr.	10.50
1		Work pants	Cotton, Army-type twill		
1		Slack suit	Summer casual wear; shirt and pants, matching denim		
1		Sweater	Coat-type, wool knit		
1		Coveralls	Cotton herringbone		
2		Shorts	Summer sports; cotton twill		
1		Swim trunks			
3	*	T-shirts	Cotton knit; short sleeves	3 @ $1.29	3.87
2		Work shirts	Cotton, Army-type twill		
3	*	Shirts	Summer, cotton, short sleeves	2 @ $2.29	4.58
2		Shirts	Winter, long sleeves, heavy cotton flannel		
7	*	Shirts	Business and dress	3 @ $3.95	11.85
6	*	Undershorts	Cotton broadcloth	3 @ $1.19	3.57
6	*	Undershirts	Knit lisle (cotton)	3 @ $ .98	2.94
3	*	Union suits	Winter weight; 10% wool, 90% cotton	2 @ $3.29	6.58
4	*	Pajamas	2 Winter, outing flannel 2 Summer, broadcloth	2 @ $2.95	5.90
1		Bathrobe	Terry cloth		
3 pr.	*	Socks	Winter; heavy sport boot socks	1 pr.	1.75
12 pr.	*	Socks	Business and dress: nylon; nylon-Orlon blends	6 pr. nylon @ 3 for $2.76	5.52
3 pr.	*	Shoes	Business and dress	1 pr.	12.00
1 pr.		Boots	Heavy sport type		
2 pr.	*	Shoes	Summer, sneakers	1 pr.	4.00
1 pr.		Slippers	House and lounging		
1 pr.		Overshoes	Arctics		
1 pr.	*	Rubbers		1 pr.	3.37
1		Cap	Leather sport cap		
2		Hats	Felt, snap brims		
1 pr.		Gloves	Wool knit		
1 pr.		Gloves	Leather		
1 pr.		Gloves	Work-type, canvas		
2		Mufflers	1 rayon; 1 wool knit		
20		Neckties	Variety; wool and silk		
24		Handkerchiefs	Cotton and linen		

Merchandise total	$135.38
3% State sales tax (if any)	4.06
Total amount with tax	$139.44

Mrs. Brown, a housewife in her late thirties, plans to limit her purchases of ready-made clothing, accessories, and sewing materials to $100 during the current year. Below is a list of what she considers an adequate wardrobe for her needs. Included are (1) items already on hand; (2) items to be purchased (*); and (3) items which she will sew for herself (*S). All clothing, accessories, and sewing materials to be purchased are accompanied by their price.

Total Number		Item of Clothing	Description of Item	Quantity to Buy	Price
1		Coat	Winter, heavy wool		
1	*	Coat	Between-season, all-purpose, full-length; blend of 85% wool and 15% nylon velour	1	$19.95
1		Raincoat	Water-repellent corduroy		
1		Mackinaw	Winter sport jacket, wool		
2		Suits			
		(a)	Winter, wool tweed		
	*S	(b)	All-season, 100% wool flannel	Fabric, lining, etc.	11.69
1		Jacket	Suit-type, wool plaid, worn with suit skirts and a & b below		
4		Skirts			
		(a)	All-season, Dacron and cotton blend		
	*S	(b)	All-season, corduroy	Fabric, zipper, etc.	3.25
		(c)	Summer, denim, sport		
		(d)	Summer, cotton print dirndl		
5		Blouses			
		(a)	Dressy nylon		
		(b)	Tailored nylon		
		(c)	Dainty Dacron and cotton		
		(d)	Dainty cotton batiste		
	*	(e)	Winter overblouse, Acrilan jersey	1	3.97
4		Shirts			
		(a) (b)	T-shirts, cotton knit		
		(c) (d)	Sport shirts, plaid gingham		
2		Sweaters			
		(a)	Pullover, short sleeves, Orlon		
		(b)	Cardigan, Orlon		
7		Housedresses	Miscellaneous cottons		
	*S 3		Percale prints	Fabric, etc.	5.40
6		Other dresses			
		(a)	Winter, dressy rayon crepe		
		(b)	Winter, sheer wool		
	*S	(c)	All-season, 2-piece faille	Fabric, etc.	6.78
		(d)	Summer, 2-piece butcher linen		
		(e)	Summer, dark cotton print		
	*S	(f)	Summer, dotted Swiss	Fabric, etc.	2.62
4		Aprons	Cotton		
2		Smocks	Cotton		
1		Swim suit			
3		Slacks			
		(a)	Winter, wool cavalry twill		
		(b) (c)	Jeans, heavyweight denim		
2	*	Play shorts	Cotton cavalry twill	1 pr.	1.98

Total Number		Item of Clothing	Description of Item	Quantity to Buy	Price
5		Slips	2 Nylon, full-length		
			1 Half-slip, cotton plissé		
	*		2 Full-length, cotton plissé	2 @ $1.98	3.96
8		Panties	2 Cotton-knit briefs		
			2 Knee-length snuggies		
	*		4 Nylon briefs	2 pr. @ $.79	1.58
4		Bras	2 Nylon		
	*		2 Cotton	2 @ $1.50	3.00
3	*	Girdles	2 Panty girdles	1	3.00
	*		1 Step-in girdle	1	4.95
4		Nightgowns	2 Winter, flannel		
			1 Nylon tricot		
			1 Cotton plissé		
1		Bed jacket	Nylon fleece		
1		Bathrobe	Chenille		
1		Housecoat	Cotton print plissé		
6 pr.	*	Hosiery	Nylon	3 pr. @ $.89	2.67
6 pr.		Anklets	Cotton		
2 pr.		Socks	Winter-sport boot socks, woolen		
1 pr.		Sport boots			
6 pr.		Shoes			
		(a)	Dressy kid pumps		
	*	(b)	Street shoes	1 pr.	7.95
	*	(c)	"Casuals" for housework	1 pr.	4.95
		(d)	Dressy summer sling-backs		
		(e)	Summer, leather sandals		
	*	(f)	Summer, play shoes, fabric	1 pr.	2.95
1 pr.		Bedroom slippers	Felt		
1 pr.		Galoshes			
1 pr.		Rubbers			
5 pr.		Gloves	1 pair wool knit gloves		
			1 pair wool knit mittens		
			1 pair nylon string gloves		
			2 pair cotton fabric gloves		
5		Hats			
	*	(a)	Dressy felt	1	3.95
		(b)	Casual felt		
		(c)	Dressy straw		
	*	(d)	Casual piqué	1	2.49
		(e)	Stocking cap for winter sports		
5		Scarves	Assorted; wool and silk		
4		Handbags	All-purpose calfskin		
			Velvet pouch for dressy wear		
			Summer, straw		
			Summer, white plastic		
24		Handkerchiefs			

Merchandise total		$97.09
3% State sales tax (if any)		2.91
Total amount with tax		$100.00

Fred Brown, a junior in high school, is allotted $110 or 22 per cent of the family clothing fund. At sixteen, he is suddenly shifting from boyhood to manhood. To a large extent, his likes and dislikes are still controlled by "what the gang wears." However, increased social life both in school and at church is making new demands on his wardrobe. So "the boy" becomes "a man" with a growing taste for men's clothes. The following list includes all the items in his wardrobe, those on hand as well as those to be purchased. The latter are marked with a (*), accompanied by the price.

Total Number		Item of Clothing	Description of Item	Quantity to Buy	Price
1	*	Coat	All-weather, 3-season, trench coat; water-repellent blend of rayon, acetate, and Dacron; zip-liner of 100% wool, quilted yoke and sleeves change topcoat into winter overcoat	1	$19.95
1		Mackinaw	Water-repellent cotton twill; sheepskin lined; mouton collar		
1		Jacket	Lightweight; athletic style; reversible, washable Dacron		
2		Suits			
		(a)	Winter, wool tweed		
	*	(b)	All-season, solid-tone, blend of 65% wool and 35% Orlon flannel, for dressy wear		27.95
3		Trousers			
		(a) (b)	Corduroy		
	*	(c)	Separate slacks; blend of acetate and rayon; crease-resistant	1	4.98
4	*	Jeans	Cotton denim	2 pr. @ $1.89	3.78
1		Swim trunks			
2		Play shorts			
7	*	T-shirts	Cotton knit, crew neck	3 for	3.40
5		Sport shirts			
		(a)	Corduroy		
		(b) (c)	Cotton plaid, short sleeves		
	*	(d) (e)	Cotton flannel, long sleeves	2 @ $2.29	4.58
3		Dress shirts	Combed cotton, solid colors and white	2 @ $2.89	5.78
3		Sweaters			
		(a)	Heavy wool, turtle-neck		
		(b)	Wool, long sleeves, V-neck		
	*	(c)	Wool, sleeveless, V-neck		1.95
5	*	Briefs	Knit underwear, cotton	3 for	3.40
5	*	Undershirts	Knit cotton, athletic style	3 for	3.40
3		Pajamas	Cotton		
1		Bathrobe	Heavy flannel		
3 pr.		Boot socks	Winter sport		
10 pr.	*	Socks	Regulation socks: cotton, wool, and nylon	6 pr. 3 pr. @ $1.99	3.98
1 pr.	*	Sneakers	Athletic shoe	1 pr.	4.77
1 pr.		Sport boots			
2 pr.	*	Shoes	Casual style for school, etc.	1 pr.	6.79
1 pr.	*	Dress shoes	Slip-on style	1 pr.	7.70
1 pr.		Arctics			
1 pr.		Rubbers			
1 pr.		House slippers			
3 pr.		Gloves	(a) Leather, fleece-lined mittens		
			(b) Wool knit gloves		
			(c) Work gloves, canvas		

Total Number	Item of Clothing	Description of Item	Quantity to Buy	Price
2	Mufflers	Wool knit		
6	Neckties	Assorted, wool and silk		
10	Handkerchiefs			
2	Caps	(a) Leather sport cap with turn-down ear flaps		
		(b) Hockey cap, wool knit		
1	* Hat	Wool felt snap brim for dress	1	3.95

	Merchandise total	$106.36
	3% State sales tax (if any)	3.19
	Total amount with tax	$109.55

Midge Brown, at ten, is allotted $65 or 13 per cent of the family clothing fund. At ten, Midge is emerging from "childhood" into those "sub-teen" years when girls become increasingly aware of clothes. As yet, her wardrobe consists mainly of clothes for school, active play, and Sunday best. Her mother makes all of her dresses and many of her play clothes. Below is a list of Midge's clothes. Included are (1) items already on hand; (2) items to be purchased (*); and (3) items which Mrs. Brown will make (*S). All clothing, accessories, and sewing materials to be purchased are accompanied by the price.

Total Number	Item of Clothing	Description of Item	Quantity to Buy	Price
1	Coat	Winter, all-purpose, 100% wool fleece; wool interlined		
1	* Coat	Between-season, all-weather, rain-repellent corduroy; quilted lining	1	$11.95
1	Jacket	Winter, sport; cotton twill; 100% wool interlining; collar converts into hood		
1 pr.	Pants	Winter sports; 100% wool		
8	Dresses	(One-piece styles)		
	*S (a)	Winter, printed corduroy	Fabric, etc.	4.55
	(b)	Winter, rayon-acetate plaid		
	(c) (d)	All-season, plaid gingham		
	*S (e) (f)	All-season, percale prints	Fabric, etc., for 2	3.69
	(g)	Winter, velveteen, for best		
	*S (h)	Summer, organdy, for best	Fabric, etc.	2.48
5	Separates	(Jumpers and skirts)		
	(a)	Jumper, rayon-wool plaid; re-modelled from Sally's dress		
	*S (b)	Jumper, pinwale corduroy	Fabric, etc.	3.28
	(c)	Winter skirt, pleated plaid; 65% Orlon, 35% wool; (Sally's)		
	*S (d)	Winter skirt, felt, 50% wool, 50% rayon	Fabric, etc.	2.54
	(e)	Summer skirt, denim		
5	*S Blouses	Cotton, worn with separates	Fabric, etc., for two	2.34

(Continued, page 236)

Total Number		Item of Clothing	Description of Item	Quantity to Buy	Price
3		T-shirts	Cotton knit, for shorts and jeans		
3		Sweaters			
	*	(a)	Pullover, turtle-neck, long sleeves; Orlon	1	3.29
		(b)	Short-sleeved pullover; wool, with matching		
		(c)	Cardigan		
2	*	Jeans	Blue denim	2 @ $1.57	3.14
4	*	Shorts	Sailcloth	Fabric, etc., for 2 pr.	2.04
3		Dresses	Play, sun-backs		
1		Swim suit			
4	*	Slips	Cotton, full-length	2 @ $1.39	2.78
2		Petticoats	Crinoline		
5	*	Undervests	Cotton knit	3 @ $.79	2.37
7	*	Panties	Cotton knit	5 for	2.98
4		Snuggies			
3		Pajamas	Cotton		
1		Bathrobe	Terry cloth		
2 pr.	*	Hosiery	Long, cotton	2 prs. for	1.57
8 pr.	*	Anklets	Cotton	6 pr.	
				3 pr. @ $.98	1.96
2 pr.	*	Socks	Knee-length, heavy cotton	2 prs. for	1.19
3		Hats, caps			
		(a)	Winter, beret, wool felt		
	*	(b)	Cuddle cap, wool knit	1	1.29
		(c)	Spring, straw		
6 pr.		Shoes			
	*	(a)	Winter school shoes; calf, moccasion style slip-ons	1 pr.	3.98
	*	(b)	All-season saddle shoes	1 pr.	3.77
		(c)	Dress shoes, patent leather		
		(d)	Dress flats, white kid		
		(e)	Beach sandals, fabric		
	*	(f)	Cotton shoes for play	1 pr.	1.97
1 pr.		Bedroom slippers	Felt		
1 pr.		Rubber boots			
1 pr.		Rubbers			
3 pr.		Gloves	Mittens, wool knit		
			Gloves, wool knit		
			Gloves, cotton string knit		
10		Handkerchiefs			
3		Scarves	2 silk squares		
			1 woolen muffler		
2		Purses	Clutch style, simulated leather		
			Basket style, woven reed		

Total from page 235		30.83
Merchandise total		$63.16
3% State sales tax (if any)		1.89
Total amount with tax		$65.05

Saks Fifth Avenue

Children's readymade clothes often provide the inspiration for clothes that can be made inexpensively at home.

STRETCHING THE CLOTHING DOLLAR

Women are the shoppers in the family. Surveys show that women actually spend the major part of the family income. Being entrusted with such a responsibility, the housewife has to know how to buy wisely.

The girl who has had some training and experience in selecting her own clothes is better able to judge family clothing for its design quality, appropriateness, and good value. It goes without saying that the mother who is needlewise can do much to stretch the family clothing budget. In addition to making many of her own clothes, she can make things for her children. Children's readymade garments of good quality are expensive. A mother can sew two or three dresses for a little girl for the same money that it would take to buy one readymade. She can make blouses, sun suits, slips, panties, and pajamas for her little boys and girls for a fraction of the price of readymades of similar quality. This is the time when short mill ends and remnants can be put to good use. The skillful sewer can even make her children's coats, snow suits, and heavy jackets. One mother learned that the snow suit which she wanted to buy for her five-year-old cost $25.00. Not wanting to spend that much money, she bought a lovely remnant of similar heavy, blue wool. The pattern, fabric, and three zippers for the front openings and ankles cost her exactly $4.21. The next spring, she also made the little girl a coat of pink flannel for which she bought a remnant, lining, and buttons for $2.43. Such savings on individual garments mean larger wardrobes for one and all!

Many adult clothes can be remodeled for children. Shirts, slacks, suits, and coats can be ripped, cleaned, and remade into attractive children's garments.

There are other saving ways that are part of the good homemaker's program. She knows the value of a stitch in time. She knows that collars and cuffs on men's shirts can be turned to give added wear, and that neat patches are a credit to anyone! She realizes that proper clothing care and laundering methods prolong the life of a garment. Such saving ways will be discussed in Part V, "Care of Clothing."

ACTIVITIES

For the class

Collect photographs and written material for the class bulletin board and files which illustrate correct clothing for:
   a. the infant
   b. the toddler
   c. the school-age child

For the individual

1. **Pretend** that you are actually going to help your father (or uncle, big brother, or some adult) to select a complete new business outfit. Keeping his build and coloring in mind, collect colored photographs to illustrate an appropriate topcoat, suit, shirt, tie, hat, socks, and shoes.
2. **Try to interest** your family in working out a budget, if they don't already have one. When you know the total amount your family budgets for clothes, use that figure to work out clothing budgets for several mythical families as well as your own.
   a. The Clarks who live on a farm. In addition to the mother and father there are boys eleven and fifteen years old and a girl thirteen years old.
   b. The Greens. Mr. Green works in a bank. Mrs. Green keeps busy taking care of twin girls three years old and a boy four. There is also a girl fourteen years old in the family.
   c. The Johnsons. Mr. Johnson and Mrs. Johnson are both teachers. Their children are girls, fourteen and sixteen years old.

CONSTRUCTION THREE ▶

MAKING A COAT

Perhaps you have always thought that only a professional could make a lined coat. If so, change your mind, for you, too, can achieve a smart looking coat by learning only a few new techniques. The secret, in case this is your first attempt, is to select a simple pattern and material that is not difficult to handle.

SELECTING A COAT PATTERN

The easiest-to-make coat styles are loosely fitted and have cardigan or collarless necklines. Obviously the fewer the seams, the more quickly finished. Raglan-type sleeves, sleeves cut-in-one with the body of the coat, and those with deep armholes or dropped shoulder lines are easier to make than those with standard armholes. Straight hemmed sleeves are simpler than those with cuffs. As you learned earlier, gussets are troublesome for the inexperienced seamstress. Vents (slits) and pleats complicate your problem somewhat, and so do pockets for that matter, but these latter are so important in a coat that you may not be willing to omit them. Machinemade buttonholes are easier, but carefully made piped buttonholes are attractive and perhaps worth the extra work. Of course, coats without buttons eliminate the need for buttonholes.

We have been speaking of a coat, but you may want to make a jacket of some type. As long as it is cut on lines similar to those described, you should have no difficulty following the instructions given here. With greater experience you may select a pattern with a collar or other more difficult details. In that case, turn for assistance to the appropriate technique in this book, and follow instructions on your pattern guide sheet. Steps are given here for a short coat with deep armholes.

In any event, buy a pattern by your measurements, just as you did for your dress and blouse and skirt. You will not need a larger size for the coat because coat patterns are cut fuller than dresses to provide ample room when worn over regular clothing. If the pattern is cut only in large, medium, and small, check the bust measurements indicated for each of these sizes before buying.

SELECTING MATERIAL FOR A COAT

Your best choice in material will be a slightly spongy, yet firm woolen of medium weight or a wool blend with these characteristics. Such a fabric is not too thick and cumbersome to handle during construction, yet is thick enough to hide hand-stitches within its depths. This weight material will make a coat for moderate weather. Turn to the "Glossary of Familiar Fabrics" at the end of Chapter 14, "Textiles Used for Clothing," for suggestions as to fabrics, then to Chapters 8 and 10 for color and texture suggestions.

OTHER SUPPLIES AND NOTIONS

Lining. Lining in a coat acts like a sheet on a bed—it keeps warmth in. Being smooth and slippery, it also simplifies pulling the coat on and off over suits and dresses. Linings usually match the coat in color but occasionally they are chosen to contrast or to harmonize with it.

There is a rayon twill made especially for linings. However, some of these twills are quite stiff and look bulky beneath mediumweight coat fabrics. In addition they often ravel excessively which makes them a poor choice. Instead you can use rayon or silk crepe, satin, or taffeta for a lining. The crepes are the softest of these and therefore interfere less with the outside appearance and hang of the coat. Wool jersey, flannel, and wool crepe are also sometimes used to line coats, especially sports coats. These fabrics are comfortable to wear, but are rather expensive, and not as easy to put on over heavy clothes. Milium linings, metal treated on the under side, reflect heat back to the body and thus add warmth. Light-colored linings show pin marks so work carefully if you decide on one of these.

Buttons. Buttons may be made of bone, mother-of-pearl, metal, or anything that dry-cleans successfully. They may also match the color of the coat, contrast, or harmonize with it. When using contrasting buttons, such as white pearl against navy, or silver on gray, consider whether such accents will be attractive with all of your accessories. Sometimes buttons covered in the coat material are your best choice. They do not wear particularly well, but it is usually not expensive to have two sets made at one time. Then you can sew on new buttons when the first set begins to look shabby.

Making a good-looking coat is a project anyone can be proud of. Here a student at Teacher's College, Columbia, is having her work inspected by her professor.

Modern Miss

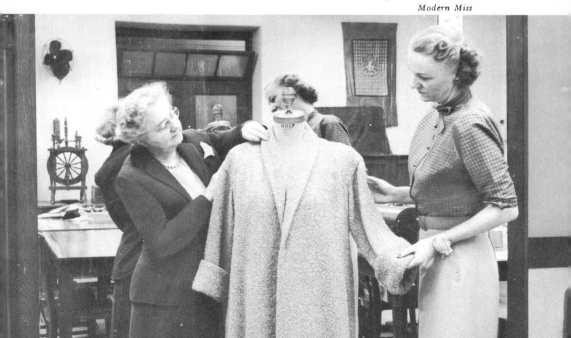

Interfacing. Every coat needs interfacing in certain areas to give it durability and a smart tailored effect. Interfacings are used along front closings, across shoulders, in collars and cuffs, and are generally needed in making any kind of pocket. Use firmly woven linen canvas, cotton drilling, firm muslin, or other similar fabric. For your first coat do not use mohair canvas because it is too stiff and springy to be incorporated in seams and therefore requires special techniques. Bias strips of muslin or wiggin should be used in sleeve and coat hems to keep them smooth and invisible on the right side. You will also need some cotton twill tape to reinforce the neckline.

Shoulder pads. You probably won't need shoulder pads in this style coat, but if you do want them, be sure you buy ones designed for coats, not dresses. They should have thin, rounded contours. Make certain that the pads can be dry-cleaned without injury.

Thread. Don't forget thread. Either silk or mercerized cotton is suitable for both the machine-stitching and the hand-stitching necessary. If you decide on decorative hand-stitched edges, select an embroidery floss too.

CUTTING AND MARKING

As always, prepare all cloth for cutting by shrinking, pressing, and squaring grain lines as necessary. Because the coat is to fit loosely, the pattern should need no alterations except perhaps in the sleeve or coat length. Darts occasionally need adjusting. Remember to alter the facing and lining patterns to correspond to any alteration that has been made in the coat pattern.

Ordinarily patterns include front and back lining and front interfacing patterns, though some do not. The sleeve lining is cut by the sleeve pattern. For lining and interfacing pieces that are not included in your pattern, use the coat pattern with a few minor changes. These changes are:

1. For the lining of the coat back add ½ to 1 inch at the center back to form a pleat. Mark the original center line so you will know how wide to make the pleat.
2. For the lining of the coat fronts, there is generally a line on the pattern showing you where to cut. Fold the pattern under on this line.
3. For coat interfacings use the coat front pattern for cutting the front interfacings. Use the coat back to cut back interfacings when they are used. Shape the lower edge of the interfacings as shown on page 246. Use muslin for the back interfacing since it should not be stiff.
4. For the pocket lining, cut by the pocket pattern but make the lining just long enough so that when it is joined to the hem with a seam, the two together will be the same size as the pocket.
5. For the pocket interfacing, cut a strip the width of the pocket and as deep as the hem at the top of the pocket will be.

In addition to cutting out all parts of the coat, lining, and interfacing, cut bias strips of muslin for the sleeve and coat hems. Cut them about ½ inch wider than the hems. Join the strips if necessary. Refer to technique 3, "Basic

Modern Miss

Clothing classes are not always just for girls. Most of the football team signed up at this high school. They made swimming trunks and slacks.

Sewing Techniques and Hand Stitches," if you need instructions on cutting and joining bias strips.

Also, to reinforce the cloth beneath each pocket, you will need a patch of muslin. Cut this patch by the pocket pattern and on the same grain.

Mark all construction details as usual. In addition, if you plan to make piped buttonholes by the patch method as described in technique 18, "Fastenings," mark buttonhole positions on the under side of interfacings.

ASSEMBLING AND CONSTRUCTING

There are numerous ways of assembling and constructing coats. The method we outline here is similar to methods used for many better quality readymade coats cut as this one is. Tailormade coats have more hand-work. Cheaper readymade coats usually have much less. In the method used here the coat is completely finished, except for the lining, the lining is made into a complete unit, and then attached to the coat by hand.

Notice that seams in coats ordinarily require no finishing to keep them from raveling since they will be enclosed between the coat and lining materials. However, to even up the seams, notches should be cut away after seams are stitched. Because coat materials are heavy, care should be taken to reduce bulk and keep the top surface smooth. This means opening wide darts, layering enclosed seams, and trimming away seam allowances at intersections, corners, and wherever needed. Of course, you will clip and notch curved seams as required. To prevent facings from extending beyond coat edges, the facing must be slightly reduced in size along curved edges. Refer to technique 13, "Neck Finishes."

Pressing should be done as work progresses, but several details can often be pressed on one trip to the ironing board. Always be sure to press darts and seams before they enter into any further construction.

COAT FRONTS

1. With a long machine-stitch, transfer to the right side of the coat center markings and markings for pockets.

2. If there are any darts that will be covered by the interfacings in the coat fronts, stitch and press them before applying the interfacings.

3. Stitch and press corresponding darts in the interfacings. These will be flatter if you slash down the center of the dart, overlap raw edges until dart lines match, and stitch. Lightweight interfacings can be stitched like any dart.

4. Lay coat fronts on a table with the wrong sides up. Place front interfacings over the coat fronts along the front closing, turning the side of the interfacing with the buttonhole markings up so you can see them. Match edges and pin facings in place. Clip away corners of the interfacing.

5. Baste-stitch the interfacings to the fronts along the front closing and the lower edges.

6. Make staylines at neck, shoulder, and armhole seams, stay-stitching through the interfacings to hold these permanently to the under side of the coat.

7. If you have decided to use piped buttonholes, make them through the coat and interfacing fabrics. (It is often wise to try your hand on a scrap before attempting to make them on the coat.) See technique 18, "Fastenings," for instructions for making piped buttonholes of several kinds.

8. Stitch and press other darts on the coat fronts.

9. Baste the muslin patch to the under side of the coat directly beneath the pocket markings.

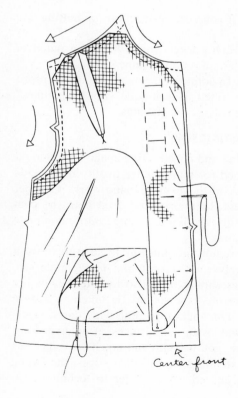

Center front

MAKING THE POCKETS

Instructions are given here for hemmed and lined patch pockets, an easy kind to make. If you would prefer another kind or if you want to face your patch pockets, refer to technique 15, "Pockets."

1. Baste the pocket interfacing to the wrong side of the pocket just below the hem fold line. Catch-stitch it to the fold line.

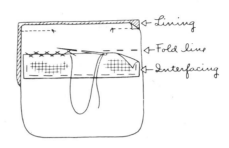

2. Pin the lining to the hem edge right sides together. Stitch a seam at each end, but leave a 3 or 4 inch opening in the middle part of the seam so that you will be able to turn the pocket right side out later.

3. Press both seam allowances toward the lining, carefully folding the lining along the seam opening.

4. To prevent the lining from showing beneath the finished pocket, trim away about ⅛ inch from all outer edges of the lining section and also from the two ends of the hem.

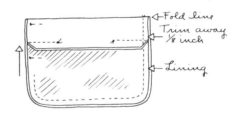

5. With the right sides of the pocket and lining turned together, fold along the hem fold line. Stretch the lining side so that all outer edges match as you pin, baste, and stitch around the entire pocket.

6. Trim, notch, and cut away corners as necessary to prevent bulky curves and corners.

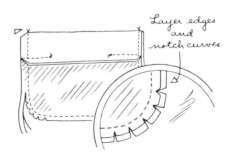

7. Turn the pocket right side out through the opening you left for that purpose.

8. Slip your fingers inside the pocket and carefully shape all outer edges. Baste the seam allowances to the lining side to hold the shape until you can press the pocket.

9. Press lightly, remove bastings, and press again.

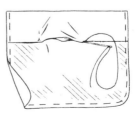

10. Slip-stitch the edges of the opening you left between hem and lining.

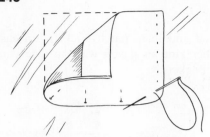

ATTACHING THE POCKET

1. Pin and baste the pocket in place on the coat.

2. Stitch, keeping the line of stitching at least ¼ inch from the pocket edge. Use a plain machine-stitch or a decorative stitch to correspond with other decorative stitching on the coat.

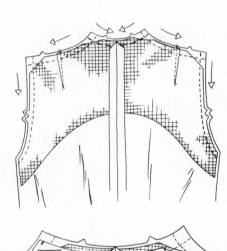

COAT BACK

1. Stitch darts on the coat back, then on the interfacing. Press, turning coat darts toward the center back and interfacing darts toward the sleeves.

2. Pin interfacing to each section of the back. Clip away corners.

3. Make lines of stay-stitching along shoulder and armhole seams. Baste-stitch to hold interfacing in position where staylines are not used.

4. Stitch center back and other seams within the back if there are any.

5. Reinforce the neckline with cotton twill tape, basting it over the neckline seam. Clip the tape at the lower edge to allow it to lie flat.

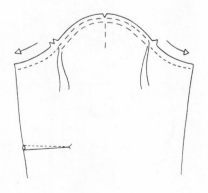

COAT SLEEVES

1. If the sleeves are cut separate from the coat, make staylines along their upper edges except where the sleeve is to be eased to the body of the coat.

2. Make a double row of large machine-stitches along the seams that are to be eased.

3. Stitch sleeve darts.

PRESSING

Press darts, seams, and other construction details not previously pressed on fronts, backs, and sleeves. Draw gathering threads along eased areas and shrink out the fullness as you did when you set in sleeves in your dress in Construction Two.

JOINING UNITS

1. Join front, back, and sleeve sections according to the cut of the pattern. The order of stitching will vary, but keep the coat flat—that is, do not stitch side seams yet.

2. Refer to technique 14, "Sleeves," and to the pattern guide sheet for the order of stitching. Clip as necessary and press the seams open.

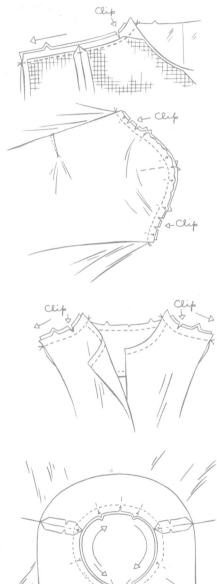

JOINING FACINGS

1. Stay-stitch facings at neck and the outside curved edge of the back facing.
2. Join the shoulder seams of facings. Press.

ATTACHING THE FACING

1. Spread the coat out flat on a table, right side up.
2. Place the facing over it, wrong side up. Match center back, shoulder seams, notches, and raw edges. Pin along neck and front closing edges.
3. With the coat (not the facing) turned uppermost, stitch around the neck, take two stitches diagonally across the corner, then continue to stitch the seam along the front closing.
4. Stitch the seam along the opposite front closing in the same way, starting by overlapping the stitching line along the neckline for a few stitches before stitching diagonally across the corner. This time the facing will be up.

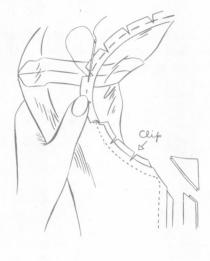

5. Trim corners and layer seam edges. Clip and notch seams as described for enclosed seams on heavy material, technique 10, "Seams and Seam Finishes."

6. Baste seam allowances to the facing around the neck. On the straight closing edge, press them toward the facing with a steam iron first. Always stretch crosswise carefully when opening up seams.

7. Turn the facing to the under side. Press and remove bastings.

SHOULDER PADS

Skip this if you aren't using shoulder pads.

1. Pin shoulder pads to the shoulder seam and try the coat on to check their position. When they are properly adjusted pin them along the shoulder seam from the right side of coat.

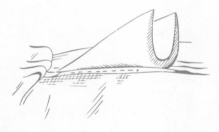

2. Fold the coat back to expose the shoulder seam allowance. Attach each pad to both front and back seam allowances of the shoulder seam with running stitches and a few back stitches for additional strength.

FASTENING THE REMAINING RAW EDGE OF THE FACING TO THE COAT

With the coat again placed flat on a table, facing side up, pin the raw facing edge to the coat. Attach permanently with an invisible hemming stitch. The stitches should go through the facing and interfacing but only partially through the coat material so that they will not show on the right side.

JOINING SIDE SEAMS

Close side and sleeve seams in a continuous line, stitching from the bottom of the coat upward. Press.

HEMMING SLEEVES AND COAT

1. After checking sleeve and coat lengths, fold hems to the under side along the hemline (original or adjusted) and press. In heavy materials trim away excess material that would be inside the hem at the bottom of the facing. Be careful to leave enough material to hide all raw edges when the hem and facing are in place.

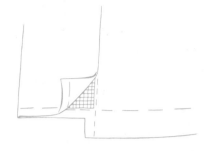

2. Place a bias strip of muslin or wiggin inside each hem. It should extend from the hemline to slightly outside the raw hem edge, perhaps ¼ to ½ inch. The strip in the coat hem should not go beneath the facing, except perhaps for a narrow overlap. With the coat flat on a table and the hems toward you, pin the strips to the hem edges stretching the bias strips slightly.

3. Open the hems out flat and stitch the raw hem edges to the strips, stretching the strips, if necessary, to prevent forming pleats in the hems. Press the hems back in place. (Notice how well the hems stay against the coat even before they are fastened there.)

4. Pin the hems in place while the coat is spread flat. Then attach the projecting edge of each strip to the coat with invisible hemming stitches about ⅜ inches apart. Stitches should not show on the right side.

5. Finish the bottom of the front facing by folding the edge under and slip stitching it to the hem along the hemline. Turn the facing under enough so that it will not show below the hem.

6. There is still one raw edge to be finished—the facing edge. Use slant hemming stitches closely spaced to fasten this to the hem.

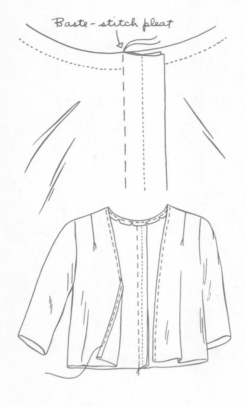

Baste-stitch pleat

MAKING THE LINING

1. Stitch staylines, darts, and seams in the front, back, and sleeve sections of the lining as you did those on the coat. (Sometimes darts are not stitched all the way to the point in the lining.) Press.

2. Baste-stitch the pleat at the center back. Press it toward one side—generally, it is pressed toward the right.

3. Join front, back, and sleeve sections as you did those of the coat. Press seams.

4. Stitch side and sleeve seams as on the coat. Press.

5. Fold under and hand-baste the seam allowance along neck and front lining edges, clipping as necessary.

ATTACHING LINING TO THE COAT

1. Lay the coat on a table with the back spread out flat wrong side up.

2. Spread the lining back over the coat back right side up. Place the sleeve linings inside the coat sleeves. Wrong sides will be together.

3. Match and pin center backs and shoulder seams. Along the lower edge of the back facing, overlap the lining an exact seam width. Pin and baste the lining to the back facing.

4. Match armhole and side seams. Place pins along them to hold the coat and lining backs together. Pins should go through the back of the coat about ¼ inch from the seam line and parallel to the line of stitching. If the seams have been properly pressed open, the pins will go through one seam allowance of the coat and one seam allowance of the lining. Ease the lining to the coat very slightly to keep it from drawing.

5. Turn the front sections of the lining back to expose the other seam allowances of coat and lining. Use a long hand running stitch to fasten these two seam allowances permanently, but loosely, together. Fasten shoulder and side seams, but stop 3 or 4 inches from the hemline. Then draw the sleeve lining out of the sleeve and fasten the armhole seams to those of the back in the same way.

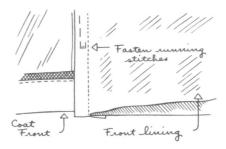

6. Spread one front of the coat out flat with the lining spread out smoothly over it. Start at the shoulder and pin the lining to the facing as you did across the back, easing the lining very slightly. Repeat on the opposite front.

7. Hand-baste the lining to the facings as you did across the back.

8. Permanently fasten the lining to the facing by hand, using a slip hemming stitch. Leave the last few inches above the hem until later.

FASTENING THE LINING TO SLEEVE AND COAT HEMS

1. Turn the sleeve and lining so the lining is on the outside over the coat sleeve. Fold the lining under with the fold line approximately ½ inch above the bottom of the sleeve. Pin about 1 inch above the fold line.

2. Form a pleat at the bottom edge of the lining to prevent the lining from drawing. Do this by making a line of slip-stitch hemming at least ¼ inch underneath the fold. To simplify this process turn the fold back slightly with your left thumb as you work. Be careful to catch only the layer of lining next to the coat and do not permit stitches to go through to the right side of the coat.

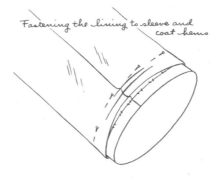

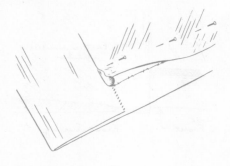

3. To finish the lining at the coat hem, spread the coat flat on the table with the lining toward you. Fold the lining under ½ inch above the coat hem and continue as you did when finishing the sleeve lining.

4. Now let the lining fall into place and finish slip-stitching it to the facing around the corner—those few inches you left undone.

BUTTONHOLES

If you have started to make bound buttonholes, slit the facing beneath them and hem the edges of the slit to the buttonhole. Otherwise, make or have made machinemade buttonholes.

BUTTONS

Sew buttons to the coat. This time you will need a longer shank than usual because the material is thick.

RELEASE BACK PLEAT IN THE LINING

Remove the baste stitching which holds the back pleat. Catch pleat at neck, waist, and hem with a catch stitch. See technique 19, "Hems" if you don't know how to make a catch stitch.

FINAL PRESSING

With the right sides of the coat up, press carefully any areas which seem to require it. Remember to use moisture and a press cloth, and never press the wool completely dry.

PART IV

CONSUMER INFORMATION

CHAPTER 14 | *TEXTILES USED FOR CLOTHING*

Cloth is the medium of the dressmaker, just as clay and stone are mediums of the sculptor. Like the sculptor, the dressmaker must understand her medium. She must know how fabric behaves, what she can do with it, and what its limitations are. Successful designers select their materials with care and handle them sympathetically.

With the many new materials being produced today and the changes taking place in familiar ones, it is increasingly difficult for the inexperienced shopper to choose materials wisely. This is true whether she is shopping for piece goods or for ready-to-wear. Labels give certain information, particularly as to fiber content and care, but are not nearly so complete or so ever-present as one might wish. Even when articles are thoroughly labeled, the shopper needs a basic knowledge of textiles to interpret some of the information. For instance, the term "vat dye" alone has no meaning to the shopper unless she knows that vat dyes are particularly fast to both sunlight and washing.

None of us starts the study of textiles without some knowledge of the way fabrics behave. You or some member of your family may have owned garments that lost their color, shrank, stretched out of shape, wrinkled badly, pulled into holes along seams, or wore out far too soon. Yet other clothing may have given excellent service and required a minimum of care. As you made garments in class, you learned that fabrics behave in different ways and have to be handled according to their particular characteristics.

You may ask why fabrics behave so differently. Think of a cotton dress you own, then of a fuzzy wool sweater that you may wear over it on a chilly morning. These two materials certainly look and feel different. One feels cool and smooth to the touch, the other feels warm and soft but perhaps slightly scratchy. One is firm, the other stretches and clings to the body. The fundamental difference, of course, is in the basic material—one is made of cotton fibers, the other of wool fibers. The next difference is in the way the fibers are made into cloth—one is constructed by weaving, the other by knitting. A last difference is in the way each is treated after the cloth is constructed—one is given a smooth finish, the other is napped to make it soft and warm.

Thus fabrics differ in three general ways, namely, in the *fibers* from which they are made, in the type of *construction* used to form the fibers into cloth, and in the various *finishes* applied to the cloth to improve its appearance and performance. While each of the textile fibers has specific characteristics of its own, these can be varied or changed to some extent by the way the cloth is

254

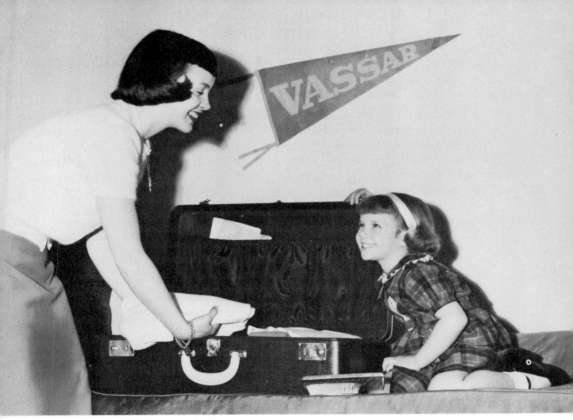

Luggage and Leather Goods

For the girl who goes away to school, wool skirts and sweaters are ideal because they come out of the suitcase unwrinkled. For her little sister, cotton is a better choice because it withstands frequent washing so well.

constructed and finished. That is why nylon can be made into sheer stockings or fluffy sweaters, and why cotton fabrics may be soft or crisp finished.

Some fibers are found in nature, some are made by man. Those made by man are sometimes called "modern" fibers. The principal *natural fibers* are wool, silk, cotton, and linen. Wool and silk come from animal sources and are called *animal fibers*. Cotton and linen come from plants and are called *vegetable fibers*. Important *man-made* fibers are rayon and acetate which are made from vegetable materials; and nylon, Dacron, Dynel, Orlon, Acrilan, and others which are created or *synthesized* from chemical elements. Hence the term "synthetics." Strictly speaking only a fabric made from chemical elements should be called a synthetic.

Textile fibers are also classified according to their chemical composition, the most useful classification of all, because fibers that are related chemically tend to react in the same way. All the fibers used extensively for clothing fall into three main groups: (1) protein, (2) cellulose, and (3) resins (which we shall call "thermoplastics"). Fibers within each of these groups have many characteristics or properties in common. But each fiber also has special or unique properties not common to the group as a whole.

PROTEIN FIBERS

Protein fibers are usually produced by animals, although certain plants produce a vegetable or incomplete protein. *Wool,* the hair or fleece of sheep, is used more extensively than any other of the protein fibers. It goes principally into winter-wear clothing to keep us warm. *Silk,* from the cocoon of the silkworm, appears in fashion apparel, luxurious robes, and fine lingerie.

Protein fibers have certain characteristics in common:

THE PROTEIN FIBERS: WOOL & SILK

CHARACTERISTIC	SIGNIFICANCE TO YOU
Elastic and resilient	Resist wrinkling and hold shape well. Wrinkled and stretched areas tend to hang out between wearings.
Hygroscopic (absorb moisture from the air without feeling wet)	Hanging over steam increases resiliency but relaxes pressed-in creases. Comfortable to wear in cold, moist climates because absorption of moisture actually creates heat.
Lose strength when wet (especially wool)	Have dry-cleaned or wash gently. Do not hang heavy, wet articles unless weight is evenly distributed.
Injured by alkalis	Use mild soap or detergent and rinse thoroughly. Protect from perspiration with dress shields.
Injured by oxidizing agents	Do not use chlorine bleach, boil, or hang in the sun. All weaken fibers and turn white articles yellowish.
Injured by dry heat	Press with moist heat to avoid harsh, brittle, scorched, or glazed fabrics.
Do not burn readily	Present little fire hazard. Tend to extinguish own flames.
Poor conductors of heat	Keep your body heat from escaping, hence they keep you warm.
Poor conductors of electricity	Build up static electricity, causing garment to cling to your figure. Wear over cotton or rayon rather than nylon.
Medium density	Are not heavy, hence comfortable to wear.

Wool. The first use of wool clothing probably occurred when cave men protected themselves from the elements with animal skins. Later, perhaps by accident, men learned that animal hairs would mat together to form felt. Eventually the processes of weaving and knitting became known, and from these the beautiful fabrics we know today were developed.

Production. When we use the term wool, we generally mean the hair of sheep, for sheep are our most important wool-producing animals. Other animals, however, such as the Cashmere goat, llama, alpaca, camel, and vicuña also produce hair fibers which are used for making fine clothing. These rarer wools are known as specialty fibers, and while related to wool, each has its own particular characteristics.

The fleecy coat of a sheep contains many millions of individual hairs. Each of these hairs is known in the textile world as a fiber. These hairs, or fibers, ranging from about 3 to 8 inches in length, are sheared from the sheep once or twice each year. The fleece from each sheep is sorted into various grades because the fibers from the different parts of the sheep's body vary in length,

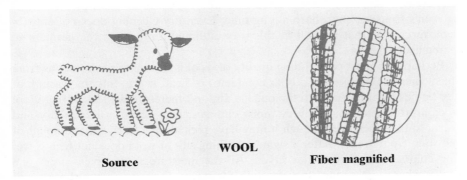

WOOL

Source   **Fiber magnified**

diameter, and quality. Also, the breed of the sheep, its health, and the way it is fed all affect the strength, texture, and length of the individual fibers. Once assorted, wool has to go through various cleansing processes to rid it of grease, dirt, and foreign matter. Next, the fibers are twisted into thread. In textile terminology the twisting process is called *spinning*. The thread is called *yarn*. Yarns are *woven* or *knitted* into cloth.

. Wool is made into two general types of fabrics, namely, *worsteds* and *woolens*. Worsted materials are made from the longer wool fibers which are straightened and laid parallel to each other as they are spun into yarn. This gives a firm, smooth, resilient fabric with little or no nap or fuzz on its surface. Worsteds hold their shape and retain creases especially well. They wrinkle even less than woolens, but some of them have the tendency to become shiny with wear. Examples of worsted fabrics are gabardine, wool sharkskin, and serge.

Woolen fabrics are made of the shorter wool fibers which are only partially straightened before they are spun and woven into cloth. With fibers lying at all angles, these fabrics are thicker, softer, and spongier than worsteds. Woolens are not generally so firmly woven either, and all have a slight nap caused by the projecting fiber ends. Some woolens go through an additional napping process which increases the softness and warmth of the material, and reduces its tendency to become shiny with wear. Woolens do not hold a press as well as worsteds, but they still surpass many fabrics in this respect. Examples of woolens are tweed, velour, and coating materials in general.

Performance. If you examine a wool fiber, you will notice that it looks wavy or crimped, and if it is of good quality, it is very springy. Notice how it returns to its original shape after you stretch it. Looking at the same fiber under a microscope you would see that its surface is covered with scales something like those of a fish. Wool's crimp and these scales have much to do with its peculiar characteristics or *properties,* so called by people working in textiles.

Wool is naturally crease-resistant because of the elasticity and resiliency of the fibers—its power to stretch, yet return to its original shape. Garments of wool ordinarily hold their shape well and do not wrinkle easily. When they do wrinkle, hang them for several days and most light wrinkles will disappear. Yet creases that have been pressed into wool, such as those in pleated skirts or men's trousers, stay sharp a long time. Even dry-cleaning does not entirely remove creases that are put in this way, although immersing the garment in water usually does.

Perhaps the most outstanding quality of wool is its ability to protect us from the elements. Because it is a poor conductor of heat, it prevents the warmth of our bodies from escaping to the outside air, and therefore we feel warm. Wool is comfortable to wear in very moist climates, too, because it feels dry and warm to the touch even though it may have picked up a fairly large amount of moisture from the air. After a swim, a bathing suit of wool does not feel as wet and cold as one of cotton or rayon. All the moisture seems to be inside the scales where you cannot feel its chill. Strangely, though, a light shower will roll off wool—again protecting us from the elements.

Wool can be dyed successfully, partly because it absorbs large amounts of water and partly because of its chemical nature. The dyestuffs penetrate the inner core of the fiber to react chemically with the protein of the fiber. Once dyed, the color of wool is usually permanent.

Wool is not as strong as many of the fibers, yet it usually wears well because it resists rubbing or abrasion. Where special strength and durability are required, as in wool hosiery, nylon and certain other of the synthetics are often blended with wool to increase its strength and wearing quality.

Since wool does not burn readily, it is safer for clothing and household articles than some of the other fibers. Wool will burn when in contact with a flame, but when the flame is removed, the fumes of combustion usually smother the fire and prevent further burning.

A unique characteristic of wool is its felting quality, no doubt a result of its scaly structure and the fact that the fibers become somewhat softened in the presence of heat and moisture. Under these conditions when wool is worked or manipulated, the fibers shrink, mat, and become firmly interlocked. Manufacturers make use of this property to produce felt from ordinary wool, as well as from beaver, muskrat, angora, rabbit fur, and other specialty fibers.

Unless care is exercised, wool fabrics do not generally launder well. Rough handling, hot or cold water, and strong soaps cause them to shrink and become harsh; that is, they tend to felt. For this reason wools are usually dry-cleaned or washed with special care. (See directions for laundering wool fabrics in Chapter 19, "Cleanliness is Next . . .") If you notice labels as you buy, you will find that some wool is treated to prevent excessive shrinkage during laundering. Look for such labels on articles that are to be washed frequently.

A

USDA photos

The longer, straightened wool fibers produce smooth, closely woven fabrics called worsteds (A). The shorter wool fibers which are not completely straightened produce fabrics called woolens which have a soft, spongy texture (B). The attractive suit at the right is made of woolen fabric.

The Wool Bureau, Inc.

Other wool materials should be thoroughly sponged by the manufacturer and so labeled. Otherwise you should sponge them yourself to control shrinkage before making them into clothing.

Another troublesome characteristic of wool is its tendency to retain odors. Unfortunately dry-cleaning may not remove perspiration odor entirely. To overcome this disadvantage, some wools are treated with a special finish which kills bacteria and therefore reduces odors.

Moths attack wool, causing much damage to clothing that is not properly cleaned and stored. A moth-resistant finish is being used on some wool fabrics with excellent results. Treatments are being given to wool fabrics, as well as to others, to make them more water-repellent. Some of these water-repellent finishes are permanent; others have to be restored by your dry-cleaner.

In 1939, Congress enacted the Wool Products Labeling Act, requiring that all fabrics containing wool (except upholstery materials and rugs) be labeled, showing the fiber content in percentage. This law divides wool fibers into three classes and requires that the percentage of each in a fabric be indicated on the label, as well as the percentage of any other fiber in excess of 5 per cent. Brief definitions of the three classifications are given on the next page.

Virgin Wool is new wool which has never been processed before.

Reprocessed Wool is usually obtained from clothing manufacturers' scraps. This wool was processed into cloth, but never used.

Reused Wool is made from rags, old clothing, and other used wool products.

These classifications are helpful, yet a label indicating "virgin wool" does not always insure fine quality. There is still much to learn from the feel and appearance of wool. Good quality wool feels light and springy when crushed in the hand. Stiff, heavy cloth that lacks resiliency is inferior in quality and will not be particularly warm or durable. Soft, silky wools are beautiful and luxurious, but do not wear as well as sturdier, harsher varieties of good quality.

Specialty Wools. These fibers come from various fur-bearing animals belonging principally to the camel and goat families. In appearance, they are much like wool, although some are coarser, some finer, some duller, and some more lustrous. Their characteristics are quite similar to those of ordinary wool.

WOOL SPECIALTY FIBERS

NAME OF FIBER	SOURCE	SPECIAL PROPERTIES	SIGNIFICANCE TO YOU
Camel's hair	Short, soft, undercoat of Bactrain camel	Soft, lightweight, high-insulating quality. Light tan in color.	Has warmth with little weight. Wears well. Natural color or dyed. Used for coats.
Cashmere	Downy undercoat of Cashmere goat	Extremely soft, fine, and smooth. Excellent insulator. Lightweight.	Very soft, lightweight, warm, and luxurious. Does not wear particularly well. Used for sweaters and coats.
Mohair	Hair of Angora goat	Coarse, strong, smooth, with almost no crimp. Most resilient natural fiber. Has fairly high luster.	Only the finer hairs used in clothing fabrics, often blended with wool or other fibers. Used for suits and dresses. Coarser hairs used for interlinings.
Vicuña	Undercoat of the vicuña, a small member of the camel family	Softest and finest of all textile fibers. Short, lustrous, and light cinnamon brown in color.	Rarest and most expensive textile fiber. Extremely lightweight, warm, and luxurious, but not sturdy. Natural color and dyed. Used for coats and sweaters.
Alpaca	Hair of the alpaca, tiny member of the camel family	Long fibers, 8 to 12 inches. Smooth and lustrous.	Only the fine hairs used in clothing. Makes smooth, lustrous fabrics. Used for suits and dresses.
Angora	Hair of the Angora rabbit	Fine, fairly long, soft, and smooth. White in color.	Makes warm, fluffy sweaters and heavily napped coat material. Sheds hairs and nap wears away at points where there is friction.

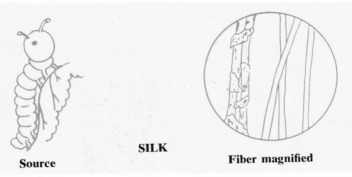

SILK

Source   Fiber magnified

Left: Gum-covered, Right: Degummed

Silk. Silk, often called the aristocrat of fibers, was produced first in China over four thousand years ago. Legend has it that a Chinese princess sitting in her garden dropped a silk cocoon into a cup of hot tea. When she removed it, she found that she could easily unwind the long continuous filament from the softened cocoon. Whether the tale is true or not, we know that long before the Christian era, silk cloth was being woven within the Chinese royal household. For hundreds of years the process was kept a carefully guarded secret, but finally knowledge of it leaked out to Japan and other Oriental countries, then later to Persia, Italy, and the rest of the world. The silk industry has never thrived in Western countries, however, partly because of the large amount of hand labor involved. The Orient still produces most of the silk fiber of the world.

Production. All silk comes from the cocoon of the silkworm, the larva of a moth. The growing of the worms is carried on in the homes of farmers today in almost the same way it was in ancient times.

One moth lays several hundred eggs. After the eggs are hatched, the tiny worms must be fed on tender young mulberry leaves. They eat greedily until they become large, pale gray caterpillars. At this stage each worm begins to spin its cocoon, ejecting two gum-covered filaments from an opening in its head. Within two weeks, if allowed to live, the worm changes into a moth and pushes its way out of the cocoon, breaking the fibers. To prevent this, the cocoons are bathed in steam or hot air to kill the worm. Then, by unwinding the cocoon, silk fibers from 800 to 1200 yards long are obtained.

Several of these fibers, or filaments, are reeled together to form one yarn. As they are reeled, varying amounts of twist are put into the yarn. Silk, taken in this way from the unbroken cocoons of cultivated worms, is soft, smooth, and lustrous. It is this silk that is used to make most handsome silk fabrics.

Silk reeled from the cocoons of the wild silkworm is called *tussah* or *wild silk*. This is coarser, stronger, stiffer, and more irregular than silk from cultivated worms. Because of the oak-leaf rather than mulberry-leaf diet of the wild worms, their silk is much darker than cultivated silk—an ecru or grayish brown color. This color is difficult to bleach in the manufacture, so it often appears in the finished material. The natural color and the uneven texture of wild silk are used to advantage in making pongee and shantung.

Spun silk is made from the broken cocoons and short fibers unsuitable for reeling. Instead, it must be spun with a fair amount of twist to hold the short fibers together. Spun silk is not as strong and elastic as reeled silk. It is duller in texture, also, because of the high twist and fuzzy projecting fiber ends. It is used principally in dull, textured fabrics, such as ratiné.

Performance. Under a microscope, silk looks like a glass rod with an irregularly shaped surface. It is this surface texture which gives it its luster. Though particularly valued for its beauty and luster, silk has other characteristics which are equally important. Nothing feels so luxurious to the touch as silk, partly

Ben Reig, Inc.—Couture Group,
N. Y. Dress Institute

The luxury look of silk makes it appropriate for dress occasions. Here the texture of the red silk organza lends a drifting airy quality to an evening dress.

because of its smooth texture and partly because, like wool, it absorbs a large amount of moisture without feeling wet. It is fairly warm, although it is the lightest of the natural fibers.

Silk is easy to care for. Because it is elastic and resilient, it resists wrinkles and when hung for several days sheds the light wrinkles it has acquired. On its smooth surface there is no fuzz to catch and hold lint, dust, and other soil. It can be dry-cleaned successfully and, if properly dyed and finished, can be washed with success too. Alkali injures it, however, so the soap used on it must be mild and must be completely rinsed out. Size for size, it is the strongest of the natural fibers, and it retains most of its strength when wet.

Because of its inherent properties, silk requires almost no special finishes. It will take dyes of any hue from palest tints to brilliant, vibrant tones found in no other fabrics. Silks can be fast dyed but unfortunately often are not.

To make it heavier and to give a firmer "feel," silk manufacturers sometimes use a metallic weighting on their silk. This means that a metallic salt is added to the dye bath and is absorbed by the silk as it is dyed. This type of weighting is permanent.

At one time, silks were so heavily weighted with metallic salts that they gave very poor service: the weighting weakened the silk fibers. Because of this, members of the Silk Association set up standards which limited the amount of weighting put into silk fabrics. Now, silk labeled "pure dye" means that not more than 10 per cent of any other substance has been added to the fabric. Fifteen per cent is permissible for black silks.

Instead of metallic salt, some manufacturers size their silks with starch to add stiffness and weight. Soluble sizing is what has given silk a bad reputation for water spotting. It also means a limp garment returned from the cleaner. Today most manufacturers avoid this by using a water-spot resistant finish.

Wonderful as silk is, it does have a few drawbacks. Sunlight weakens it very rapidly, and so do strong soap, chlorine bleaches, perspiration, and deodorants containing aluminum chloride. White silk is not only weakened by these agents; it is also turned yellow or cream colored by all of them. Silk can stand heat enough for careful pressing, but is injured by high temperatures and exposure to dry heat.

CELLULOSE FIBERS

Cellulose comes from plants and is composed of the fibrous part (the cell walls) that remains after the plant dies. Only certain kinds of cellulose are suitable for textile fibers. Of these, *cotton* is the most extensively used. The low cost and utilitarian nature of cotton largely account for its popularity. *Linen,* the fiber from the flax plant, commands a higher price, particularly in the United States. It is used for fine household textiles, for summer dresses and suits, and for draperies and upholstery fabrics. *Rayon* is made of regenerated cellulose, so called because cellulose material goes through a manufacturing process and then emerges as pure cellulose—re-formed and regenerated. Rayon is widely used for both clothing and decorator fabrics.

All cellulose fibers have certain characteristics in common:

THE CELLULOSE FIBERS: COTTON, LINEN, & RAYON

CHARACTERISTIC	SIGNIFICANCE TO YOU
Low in resiliency and elasticity	Wrinkle badly and remain wrinkled unless treated with crush-resistant finishes.
Absorbent	Absorb moisture from the body and give it off gradually, making fabrics feel cool in summer.
Withstand relatively high temperatures	Can be sterilized by boiling—cotton especially. Do not scorch easily when ironed.
Good conductors of heat	Feel cool because body heat is conducted away to the outside air.
Not greatly injured by alkalis	Can be washed in strong soap and detergents. Not weakened greatly by perspiration.
High density	Feel heavy in thick fabrics. A terry cloth robe, for instance, feels heavier than one made of wool.
Lack loft	Can be made into thin, sheer, fabrics, also compact ones.
Resistant to insects	Not likely to be damaged by moths, carpet beetles, or other insects.
Mildew easily	Do not leave clothes sprinkled too long before ironing, especially in warm weather. Dry articles before storing or putting in the clothes hamper.
Inflammable	Dangerous to wear near fires. Flannelette, net, and similar fabrics are very inflammable unless treated.

Cotton. Cotton, long known as "king" in the South, is the fiber most used throughout the world. It is a white or yellow-white vegetable fiber derived from the seed hairs of the cotton plant. The plant thrives in our South, in California, in Egypt, in India, in Peru, and in other areas with warm climates. Most of the plants are about 3 feet high, although heights range from 2 to 20 feet. After the plant flowers, the seed pods or bolls form. When the bolls are ripe, they burst open and expose the white fleecy cotton. These seed hairs range in length from about ¾ to 2½ inches, making cotton our shortest textile fiber.

There are many different varieties of cotton but all can be grouped into two main classifications: the *long-staple* varieties and the *short-staple* varieties. "Staple" is the term used in the textile world to designate textile fibers in their raw state. It is not used for all fibers, however, but only for the shorter ones which have to be spun into yarn. Cotton is commonly referred to as a staple fiber.

The long-staple varieties, Sea Island, Egyptian, and Pima, are all botanically related. Their fibers are relatively long, fine, silky, and strong—qualities which make them the finest of all cottons. These are the fibers used to make soft, lustrous cotton materials you sometimes see in men's shirts and women's silky cotton dresses. Unfortunately, the amount of long-staple cotton produced in this country and elsewhere is small.

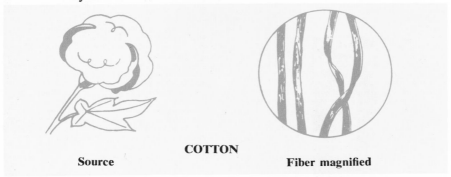

COTTON

Source   Fiber magnified

Left: Mercerized, Right: Unmercerized

Upland cotton is the principal source of the short-staple fiber. Its fibers are short (¾ to 1¾ inches in length), medium fine, and have little or no natural luster. Its quality, like that of the long-staple varieties, depends largely upon soil, climate, and growing conditions.

Production. Most cotton has to be planted each spring, although in especially mild climates some varieties grow throughout the year. Cotton takes about six months to develop and requires much labor to plant, thin, cultivate, and harvest. Mechanical cotton pickers have been developed in recent years, but most cotton is still picked by hand, a tedious job. Separating the fiber from the seed was another slow process until Eli Whitney invented the cotton gin in 1793. Then cotton production took a leap forward. After ginning, cotton is baled, graded, and shipped to the mill where it is processed into cloth.

One of the most important processes which cotton goes through is *carding*. Carding separates the fibers, partially straightens them, and removes any remaining bits of leaves or dirt.

All cottons are carded, but only the fibers for fine cotton materials are *combed*. *Combing* removes the short fibers and straightens the remaining long fibers so that they lie parallel to each other. These long fibers can then be spun and woven to produce a smooth, fine fabric.

Performance. Cotton fabrics are soft, smooth, and comfortable to wear. They have always been worn in warm weather because of their absorbency and cool feel. Now, more than ever before, they are being made into fabrics for winter wear as well.

Cotton is the most hygienic of fibers because it can be boiled during laundering, thus destroying bacteria. Not only can it stand high temperatures for a reasonable length of time, but the fiber is actually stronger wet than dry. Thus, frequent washings are practical, and ironing presents no special problem. Boiling bleaches white cotton as well as sterilizes it. Sunshine bleaches it, too. However, sunshine weakens cotton and hence clothing should not be exposed to it for too long a period of time.

Dress by L'Aiglon Apparel, Inc.

Here is further proof of the versatility of cotton. The same fabric is used in a shirtwaist dress for "nine to five" wear and in a sheath for "after five."

Despite its reputation for being extremely practical, cotton has certain disadvantages. The fiber is inelastic, which means it wrinkles easily. It shrinks, sometimes even after several washings. It soils easily. True, soap and water and ordinary ironing will not damage cotton, but it will need them often. Also, cotton mildews when left damp too long in warm weather. Another difficulty is that it burns readily.

More and more special treatments are being devised to alter cotton's appearance and improve its behavior. Mercerization—known for years—produces a sheen, and at the same time adds strength and improves the already good dyeing qualities of cotton. This caustic soda treatment actually alters the structure of the cotton fiber. Under a microscope, an untreated fiber resembles a twisted ribbon or a soft, deflated rubber hose. After mercerization, the fiber becomes plump and rounded like an inflated tube. It is this smoother surface which increases the luster of mercerized cotton.

Shrinkage control is treatment needed on any cotton fabric. Sanforizing shrinks cotton so that further shrinkage will be no greater than 1 per cent.

Beware of pre-shrunk claims which do not state the exact amount of shrinkage you may expect.

A crush-resistant finish not only reduces wrinkles, but at the same time reduces shrinkage, adds firmness, and prevents fabrics from soiling easily. A permanent starch finish is given organdy and other crisp fabrics. Water-repellency and fire-resistance are qualities imparted to some cottons, also. These two finishes are not always permanent but may be renewed by your drycleaner.

To produce chintz fabrics, cottons are given a temporary or permanent high glaze. Embossed cottons are first given a permanent glaze and then passed through engraved rollers to raise the designs.

In order to compete with the wash-and-wear thermoplastic fabrics, the cotton textile industry has developed a whole new concept in cotton finishing —the wash-and-wear cottons. Cottons are treated with chemical resins (similar to those used on crush-resistant, glazed, and embossed cottons) which reduce the need for ironing. Many of these cottons still need a touch of the iron to look entirely neat, but ironing time and effort have been effectively reduced. Resin finishes reduce the absorbency and cool feel of cottons to some extent, but they do add a high degree of firmness, crush-resistance, shrinkage-control, and soil-resistance—all this plus easier care!

Originally, the resins used were chlorine-retentive; that is, chlorine from the city water supply or from bleaching agents actually united chemically with the finish and could not be rinsed out. This chlorine build-up weakened fabrics, and with one type of resin finish, turned white fabrics a deep ivory color. Today non-chlorine-retentive finishes are available, but unfortunately some finishers do not use them. Until they do, buy cautiously or beware of chlorine bleaches in your wash.

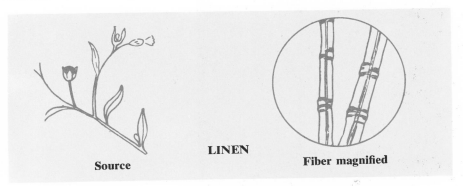

LINEN

Source **Fiber magnified**

Linen. Linen cloth has been respected throughout history for its strength and beauty. Prehistoric man used linen fibers to make cord and fish nets before he knew how to weave cloth. The ancient Egyptian Pharaohs were clothed in fine linens, and many of these fabrics are found still preserved in their tombs. Linen was known as a luxury fiber worn by the rich, and even today we cherish it as a symbol of elegance.

Production. Linen is a vegetable fiber obtained from the stalks of the flax plant. Because it is imbedded in the stalk, there are many processes necessary before the fiber is ready to be woven. A number of these steps are still done by hand. Hand labor and the long period of time needed for processing the fibers cause linen to be relatively expensive. In this country, Oregon is the only state in which flax for textile use is grown in quantity. Most of our linen is imported from Ireland, Belgium, and other European countries.

When harvested, the flax plants are pulled out of the earth, roots and all, to insure long unbroken fibers. The seeds are then removed, and the stalks of the plants are partially rotted, so that the fibers can be easily freed. This rotting, called *retting,* can be done by submerging the stalks in water, and may require from two to four weeks. *Dew retting* is still used in some countries. In this method the flax is spread on the ground and the moisture in the air causes the stalks to rot. Of course this takes longer than water retting. Chemicals have also been used to break down the flax stalk, but although they work faster, chemicals tend to weaken the fibers. After retting, the stalks are dried, then crushed, and the fibers are beaten free and combed. They are then ready to be spun into yarn, a process which is simplified because of the length of the fibers—from 18 to 20 inches.

Performance. Linen fibers are smooth, round, and lustrous. Under a microscope, you will see that each fiber resembles bamboo. The fibers are less elastic than any of the natural fibers and thus the material tends to wrinkle easily and requires frequent pressing. To eliminate this, many dress linens are now given a crease-resistant finish. This improves their behavior but also makes

Teena Paige

Linen, except when used in blouses, is strictly a summertime fiber. It is particularly effective in simple tailored dresses.

them warmer. Untreated linen clothes are cooler than those of cotton or any other fiber.

The lustrous smooth surface of linen resists soiling because dirt does not cling to it. Linen is strong and tends to be stronger when wet so that it washes well. It can be boiled but should not be boiled for long periods since high temperatures weaken it. Heavy bleaching also weakens the fibers. Therefore, white linens are not always the best buy.

Linen is the most difficult of all natural fibers to dye. For this reason it is often used in its natural color or is partially bleached. Darker colors sometimes lose enough dye after repeated washings to make them unattractive, but pastel colors are generally satisfactory.

Good linen is expensive, but with care it seems to improve with use, becoming softer. There are less costly linens on the market, but these cheaper fabrics are usually made from *tow* (the short fibers which are combed out of the better linens). Fabrics made from tow are neither as strong nor as smooth as good quality linens, nor do they last as well.

Rayon. Rayon was the first of the large group of man-made fibers which we now have on our market. It was originally produced as an imitation silk, but was not too well accepted in that role. Now, having outgrown many of its earlier disadvantages, it is accepted in its own right and for its own characteristics. Rayon is a relatively new textile fiber. Although there had been much thought about making imitation silk and many attempts to do so, the first commercial rayon plant was not set up until 1900.

Production. Rayon fibers are produced from cellulose found in plant tissue. It is usually obtained from wood pulp or cotton linters (the short fibers remaining on the seeds after ginning). Rayon is made by dissolving this cellulose in a chemical solvent, bleaching the solution, and forcing it through tiny holes in a nozzle, or spinnerette. The resulting filaments, hardened by air or by chemical means, form rayon. These filaments are naturally lustrous but can be delustered for dull effects. Rayon is made into yarns in two ways. Long filaments—they can be made any length—are twisted together, or short lengths are spun to form yarn.

Performance. Since rayon is made from cellulose, it generally behaves like other plant fibers—cotton and linen. It is cool to wear, carrying heat and moisture from the body and giving them to the outside air.

It wrinkles easily, too, unless given a crush-resistant finish. Also, it launders well. Water does not injure it though rayon is weaker wet than dry. Unlike the natural plant fibers, it should not be boiled. Sunshine, too, weakens it. It stands moderate temperature and can be pressed somewhat like cotton, but at lower temperatures.

Rayon takes dyes that are used on cottons and linens, vat dyes being the most permanent type. Recently, dyes have been added to the liquid solution before it is made into the filament; consequently, the color is locked in. Coloray and Jetspun are examples of solution-dyed rayon. White rayon re-

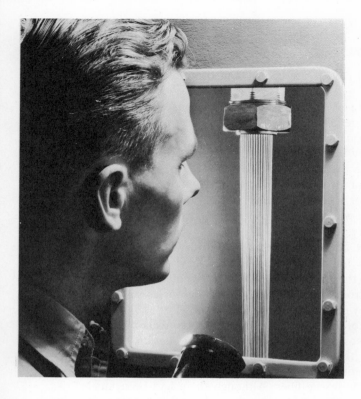

This is a spinnerette in action. The liquid forced out of the nozzle solidifies as it falls, forming filaments. These will be twisted together to form a single strand of yarn.

Eastman Chemical Products, Inc.

mains white—one advantage rayon has over silk, which is apt to become yellow.

Its disadvantages are that it shrinks or stretches out of shape unless it has been given a finish to stabilize its size. It has only fair strength and it burns rapidly unless especially treated. Napped rayons and sheer nets are dangerous to wear around an open fire because they are highly inflammable.

THERMOPLASTIC FIBERS

The thermoplastic fibers are all man-made, and most are true synthetics. From the housewife's standpoint, the thermoplastics' greatest asset is their ease of care: their drip-dry property alone has saved her countless hours of tedious ironing. When enough heat is applied to thermoplastics, they soften and will finally melt if the temperature is increased. It is this property that distinguishes the thermoplastics from all other fibers and accounts for many characteristics typical of the group.

Acetate and the tri-acetate fiber, *Arnel,* are both manufactured from cellulose but end as cellulose-acetate. *Celaperm* and *Chromespun* are trade names for acetate that has been solution- (or dope-) dyed and is consequently extremely colorfast to both washing and light.

Nylon was our first synthetic. Its phenomenal success spurred textile manufacturers on to develop numerous other synthetics, each under the company's own trade name. *Dacron, Orlon, Acrilan,* and *Dynel* are well known, but others are currently on the market and being promoted—*Creslan, Darvan, Zefran, Verel, Kodel,* and *Caprolan.*

All thermoplastic fibers have certain characteristics in common:

THE THERMOPLASTICS: ACETATE, ARNEL, NYLON, ORLON, ACRILAN, DYNEL, DACRON, ETC.

CHARACTERISTIC	SIGNIFICANCE TO YOU
Resilient and elastic	Do not wrinkle easily and wrinkles hang out. Some are so wrinkle-resistant that they require no ironing.
High tensile strength	Produce strong fabrics which give long service. Napped fabrics tend to pill because matted fibers do not break off.
Only slightly weaker when wet (except acetate)	Require no special care to prevent holes during washing.
Abrasion-resistant	Withstand rubbing and wear.
Absorb little moisture	Require special dyeing methods. Soil remains on surface; easily washed, dry quickly. Feel clammy if fabric is non-porous.
Build up static electricity	Cling to the body, may even cause electrical sparks. Not suitable for wear in an operating room because of the danger of igniting inflammable ether.
Soften and melt over a wide temperature range	Permits heat setting to stabilize size and shape. Gives permanent pleats and variety of textures. Do not wash or dry at high temperatures.
Heat sensitive (except Arnel)	Do not stand high temperatures. Pressing may glaze or melt fabric. Press at low temperature.
Resistant to insects and mildew	Little danger of damage by moths, carpet beetles, silverfish, or from mildew and mold.

Acetate. Acetate is a man-made fiber which, for a number of years, was classed as rayon. Like rayon, it starts out as cellulose, but the chemicals used to develop it are not entirely removed. The resulting fiber is a chemical compound quite different from the original material, with characteristics which are consequently different. Chemically it is cellulose-acetate.

Like all thermoplastics, acetate softens and melts at relatively low temperatures. It is naturally wrinkle-resistant, too, but not as resistant as the true synthetics. It has excellent draping qualities, and like the other thermoplastics, holds its size and shape well even when washed. It absorbs more moisture than the synthetics but less than cotton, linen, and rayon. Acetate absorbs enough moisture so that it is comfortable to wear. It is not as strong as the synthetics, and it loses some of its strength when wet, although not as much as rayon. Most stains stay on the surface and can be easily washed off. One stain to avoid, though, is nail polish remover because this often dissolves acetate. Acetate may be dry cleaned or washed. Avoid using chlorine bleaches on acetate; sodium perborate bleaches are preferable. Acetate is combined with rayon in many crepes made of filament yarns. The rayon yarns are tightly twisted to form the crepe; acetate yarns are added to lend texture and good draping qualities. Of course, acetate is also used alone or with fibers other than rayon.

Acetate dries fairly fast, and is ironed without difficulty if you use a barely warm iron on the wrong side of the material. At high temperatures this material melts or fuses.

Another troublesome trait of acetate is its tendency to change color. You may have wondered why some blue, gray, green, or brown dress—hanging unworn in a dark closet—should gradually lose its original color and take on a lavender, pink, or orange cast. Atmospheric gases reacting with the acetate dyes caused the difficulty. This kind of color change is known as *fume-fading*.

Chromespun and Celaperm were developed to overcome fume-fading. These fibers are made of acetate but instead of being dyed in the usual way, dye-stuffs are added while the acetate is still in a liquid form. Thus, the dye is mixed throughout the fiber. It is "locked" in where gases cannot reach it and consequently the colors of Chromespun and Celaperm are unusually fast to fumes, washing, and light.

Arnel. Arnel is a close relative of acetate because it, too, is made from cellulose, but whereas acetate has two acetate components in each molecule, Arnel has three. It is therefore called a *tri-acetate*. This greater saturation with acetate gives it special characteristics.

One characteristic, quite different from the other thermoplastics, is its resistance to high temperatures. It is machine-washable in hot water and is not damaged by ironing temperatures suitable for cotton. This is fortunate because Arnel usually requires a light pressing after laundering since it is not as wrinkle-resistant as the true synthetics. Like other thermoplastics, Arnel is susceptible to heat-setting, which gives it dimensional stability and enables it to hold permanent pleats.

Another important characteristic is Arnel's resistance to bacterial growth. Arnel has fair strength and its low moisture absorption causes it to retain its strength when wet. Of course it dries quickly. Black and navy Arnel are being solution-dyed, just as acetate is, even though Arnel does not gas- or fume-fade. It is used alone or in blends.

Nylon. Nylon was the first man-made fiber formed entirely from chemicals and hence was the first true synthetic. Rayon and acetate are made from a cellulose base which is changed or altered by chemicals, but nylon is built up entirely from four chemical elements: carbon, hydrogen, nitrogen, and oxygen. These elements are taken from coal, air, and water. It is a *polyamid*.

Nylon filaments are formed by forcing a thick solution through a spinnerette in much the same manner as rayon. The filaments are formed thicker than the finished fiber will be and are then stretched to the correct size. This stretching process not only produces a very fine fiber but increases its strength and elasticity.

Nylon yarns, like those of rayon and acetate, are made in two forms: filament yarns and yarns spun from fibers that have been cut into short lengths. Filament yarns are used for all smooth-surfaced hosiery and fabrics. Spun

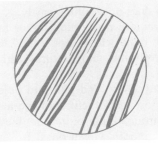

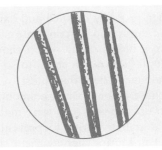

<table>
<tr><td>**Acetate fiber magnified**</td><td>**Nylon fiber magnified**</td></tr>
</table>

yarns, because of their tendency to mat or "pill," have restricted uses. "Pilling" means that little balls of matted fibers (pills) tend to cling to the surface wherever the fabric is rubbed or abraded.

Nylon and other true synthetics begin to soften or melt gradually as heat is applied. In this semimolten state, nylon can be shaped, pleated, puckered, or embossed. This process is called *heat-setting,* and once properly done, the fabric retains its size, shape, pleats, or surface design.

Extreme strength and elasticity are nylon's most unique characteristics, for no other fiber, natural or man-made, can surpass it in either of these respects. In fact, these qualities were "built" into nylon as it was created for women's sheer stockings, which must be strong enough to endure the strain put upon them and elastic enough to fit the leg closely. Another built-in quality of nylon is its resistance to abrasion.

Other virtues of nylon are that it is not readily flammable (although it will melt), and that it is moth-proof and mildew-resistant. It also does not lose strength when wet. However, strong sunlight and long exposure to heat will weaken it.

Nylon absorbs very little moisture which accounts for its drying so quickly, especially in the filament form. Spun nylon takes a bit longer to dry because water stays in the spaces between the napped fibers. Quick drying is an advantage, but the same reasons that account for that, make nylon difficult to dye. The dyes cannot penetrate the fibers. Also this lack of absorbency accounts for that sticky, uncomfortable feeling when you are wearing closely woven nylon garments on a hot day. Perspiration is held against the body instead of being absorbed and given off to the outside air. Porous fabrics such as tricot and sheer woven materials are more comfortable because air reaches the body directly to dry the moisture. Also, moisture is carried from the body outward on the fiber surfaces, a property called "wicking."

Washing nylon presents several problems. While it loses soil readily in cool, clean suds, it has a tendency to pick up color from other garments that may "run," and it becomes gray or discolored if washed with dirty clothing. It should not be wrung out vigorously, because the wrinkles formed are often permanent. Avoid hot water, for it drives oils and soil into the fibers and tends to set wrinkles permanently.

When properly finished and handled, nylon does not wrinkle easily. Knitted nylon fabrics and certain textured materials require no ironing; other fabrics require a little ironing which should never be done with a hot iron. Like all thermoplastics, nylon starts to soften at relatively low temperatures, although it stands more heat than most.

Because nylon fibers are smooth, seams used to slip and pull into holes regardless of the way they were made. Today, most manufacturers have learned to treat nylon fabrics to prevent slippage through dull or textured effects. Also, knit fabrics such as tricot slip less than smooth-woven ones. In sewing, nylon gives trouble because seams so often draw, causing the material on either side to ripple. The remedy is to use Dacron thread with loose tensions and a fine needle. In fact, unless Dacron or nylon thread is used, the seams are likely to give way before the garment is worn out. Seams not carefully finished ravel easily, too, especially when the fabric is smooth and made of filament yarns.

Nylon is added to other fibers in various blends. It adds strength and sometimes, as when blended with rayon, effectively reduces shrinkage. Caprolan is a "nylon type" fiber.

Dacron. Chemically speaking, Dacron is a *polyester* fiber. Extreme crease-resistance and stability of size are Dacron's unique contributions to the textile world. More than any other, it is the fiber that is responsible for clothing that really "drips dry." It holds its shape and rarely has to be pressed if carefully handled during washing or cleaning. Heat-set creases and pleats remain, but wrinkles disappear. Dacron softens at a slightly lower temperature than nylon and burns briefly when removed from flame.

Dacron is strong, although not quite as strong as nylon. Since it absorbs little moisture, it remains strong when wet and, of course, dries quickly. Its low absorbency gives it only fair dyeability but makes it particularly resistant to mildew and mold. Moths do not attack it. It resists all laundry bleaches—it is not sensitive to bleaches but neither is it whitened by them. Sunlight weakens Dacron gradually. It has a crisp texture and good abrasion-resistance in both the filament and staple (or spun) forms. "Pilling" is a problem with napped Dacron fabrics, however, just as it is with napped nylon. High twist and firm weave reduce this tendency, as do special finishes.

Dacron fiber magnified   Acrilan fiber magnified

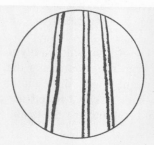 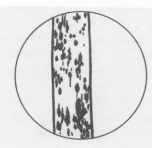

Du Pont photo

Synthetic fibers produce fabrics for every season. The winter dress above, a blend of Orlon and wool, combines warmth with ease of care. The all-Dacron dress at the right has the cool crisp appearance so necessary for summer clothes.

Dress by L'Aiglon Apparel, Inc.

The natural crispness or stiffness of Dacron may be altered by treating it with a non-static softener to make it softer, more absorbent, and less likely to cling to the body. Untreated Dacron attracts lint and soil because of its electrostatic property. The Taslan process for bulking yarns also alters Dacron's texture. All-Dacron fabrics made of bulked yarn are softer, more opaque, and more comfortable to wear than untreated Dacron fabrics, and they retain their crease-resistance!

Blended fabrics made of Dacron utilize Dacron's special characteristics, but other fibers are added to soften the texture, add absorbency, and reduce static electricity. Dacron can be blended with any fiber, but for optimum wash-and-wear performance, a definite percentage of Dacron must be present and should be carefully blended in both the warp and filling yarns. In Dacron-cotton blends, there must be at least 65 per cent Dacron. In Dacron-rayon blends, at least 55 per cent Dacron is needed. Kodel is a polyester fiber similar to Dacron.

Acrilan, Orlon, Darlan, Creslan. Acrilan, Orlon, Darlan, Creslan, and the more recent fibers, such as Darvan and Zefran, are all *acrylics,* although they differ slightly in their chemical composition. Accordingly, with a few exceptions, all react alike.

All acrylic fibers feel warm to the touch, are light and soft, and have high bulking qualities, particularly in their staple fiber forms. These are all qualities that make them resemble wool. Consequently, they are used in garments commonly made of wool. In the continuous filament form, the acrylics have entered the field traditionally held by silk, and are now being made into lightweight, silk-like fabrics which tend to drape very nicely. Other unique characteristics are Orlon's extreme resistance to sunlight, and Acrilan's excellent affinity for dyes and its resistance to matting.

In most other respects the acrylic fibers share the properties common to the thermoplastics. They are strong, absorb little moisture, are wrinkle-resistant, can be heat-set, and resist insects, molds, and mildew. They build up large amounts of static electricity, and some acrylic fibers have a tendency to pill. Acrylics generally are not readily flammable. They do have a tendency to "wick"; that is, water on the outside of a garment tends to penetrate through to the inside. Chlorine bleaches are neither particularly injurious to nor effective on the acrylics. The abrasion resistance of acrylics is fair—although somewhat less than that of nylon and Dacron.

Acrylic fibers blend readily. The blend of Orlon and wool has become a classic. Faille made of Acrilan and silk has excellent texture and drapes well. For wash-and-wear performance, however, at least 70 to 75 per cent Orlon is needed in blends with wool or rayon. With cotton, 80 per cent Orlon is required. Comparable percentages of the other acrylics are needed for drip-dry fabrics.

Dynel and Verel. Since these fibers are *acrylic and polyvinyl,* chemically speaking, they are related to the acrylic fibers. While Dynel and Verel are not identical in composition, they are "close kin" and therefore have characteristics in common. They are classified as *modacrylic* fibers.

One unique quality which both possess is that they are not affected by acids, alkalis, and other chemicals. Another quality is their flame-resistance; one type of Verel is especially resistant to flame. Both Dynel and Verel fuse and melt at lower temperatures than do nylon and Dacron. (In fact, Dynel is the most heat-sensitive of all fibers; it shrinks and hardens at 240°F.) For this reason, both fibers are used principally in knitwear, pile fabrics for coats

Orlon fiber magnified   **Dynel fiber magnified**

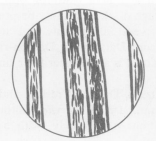

and coat liners, and for other fabrics that do not require pressing or ironing. When pressing is necessary, use the lowest heat setting, and for Dynel, particularly, use a press cloth. If you do not, the fabrics may stiffen noticeably.

Both fibers are used in the continuous filament and staple fiber forms. Like the acrylics, these fibers are soft and have good bulking properties. They retain their size unless too much heat is applied, and they also resist abrasion. They absorb very little moisture, although Verel absorbs slightly more than the other synthetics.

Like other thermoplastics, they dry quickly and resist moths, mildew, and mold. In fact, they resist weathering conditions generally, although Dynel is darkened by sunlight.

Dynel and Verel are used alone or in blends. Dynel and Orlon are blended to make fur-like winter coats, with such trade names as "Borgana," "Allegro," and "Glenara." (Special directions should be followed for the care of these pile fabrics.) Blends with cotton are also widely used for sport shirts. In fact, these fibers will blend with almost any other fiber.

FIBER IDENTIFICATION TEST

Of course, it is best to save the labels which identify the fiber content of materials and clothing you buy. However, if you do not have the label, you can at least determine from the following table whether the fabric is composed principally of protein, cellulose, or thermoplastic fibers. Since the fibers in each group behave in much the same way, knowing the group to which your fabric belongs, will enable you to care for it intelligently. Burn a small scrap or several yarns pulled from a wide seam, but be cautious of fire!

BURNING TEST TO IDENTIFY FIBER GROUPS

FIBER GROUP	WAY IT BURNS	RESIDUE	ODOR
Protein: Wool Silk	Burns with irregular flicker when in contact with a flame. Extinguishes itself quickly after flame is removed. (Does not support combustion.)	Forms crisp black, charred beads or thick mass along fabric edge. Easily crunched between fingers.	Strong odor of burning hair or feathers. Wool gives the stronger odor.
Cellulose: Cotton Linen Rayon	Burns readily with a bright, steady flame. (Supports combustion.) When flame is extinguished, an afterglow remains which smoulders for some time.	Forms a thin, flat, charred edge, jagged in shape. A white or gray feathery ash clings lightly to this narrow, black rim.	Odor of burning paper.
Thermo-plastics: Acetate Nylon Orlon Acrilan Dacron Dynel, etc.	When in contact with a flame, the edge of the fabric melts, rolls and twists, and forms droplets of hot, molten plastic. May or may not continue to burn after the flame is removed.	Forms hard, thick, black roll or mass along the fabric edge after molten plastic cools. Too hard to break between the fingers.	A chemical or acid odor.

YARN CONSTRUCTION

Before cloth is woven or knitted, the fibers must be formed into yarns—only felt fabrics and the large, rapidly developing class of non-woven fabrics are made directly from fibers. Yarns are of two main types, *spun* yarns and *filament* yarns, though there are many variations within each group.

Wool, cotton, and linen are short or staple fibers. To be made into yarns, these fibers have to be cleaned, laid in long, loose strands, and then spun together. Silk fibers too short for reeling are likewise spun. Also, to achieve a soft, dull effect, the man-made fibers are cut into short lengths and then spun like the natural fibers, except that they require no cleaning beforehand.

The creation of filament yarns is simpler. Long filaments of silk or man-made fibers are merely twisted together. Because filament yarns have almost no fiber ends extending from their surface, they are smoother, glossier, and often more regular in size than spun yarns. Unless fabrics made from filament yarns are firmly constructed, these smooth glossy yarns may shift position in the cloth causing holes or ugly spots.

Even by such a simple step as adding twist, it is possible to change the appearance and characteristics of both spun yarns and filament yarns and, consequently, of the fabric. A slightly twisted yarn is relatively glossy and soft, but is not especially strong. As more twist is added, the yarn becomes firm or even harsh and loses luster, but gains much in strength. If you cannot believe this, take any raveling and twist it first loosely, then tightly to see the difference.

Several stages in the production of spun yarns. Notice the fluffy look that even the finished yarns have.

Tennessee Eastman Company

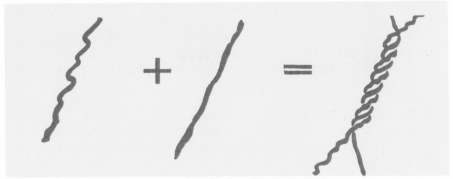

Yarns of different types are twisted together for texture effects.

Sometimes to make extra-strong yarns, two or more single yarns are joined together with additional twist. Yarns of this kind are called *plied* yarns and may be *two-ply, three-ply,* and so on.

Elastic fabrics are usually made of latex elastics. Latex, sold under the trade name Lastex, is natural rubber that has been forced through tiny holes while in a liquid state and then hardened and vulcanized. It is then covered with spiral yarns of cotton, rayon, or nylon, and woven into cloth for foundation garments.

Stretch yarns contain no rubber but get their elasticity from highly twisted, specially processed nylon yarns. Helanca yarns were the first of this type which made possible stretch socks, stockings, gloves, panties, and so forth.

Metallic yarns—Lurex yarns were the first—are usually made of aluminum or some other metal that is then coated with colored plastic to produce various effects. These yarns do not stand high pressing temperatures, but they do add life and sparkle to many fabrics.

Textured fabrics are usually made of special yarns developed to give a particular effect. Yarns that are thick in some spots and thin in others are used to simulate linen and wild silk, which are naturally irregular. Bouclé yarns are made with loops, and ratiné yarns have a nubby appearance. Yarns for tweeds and similar fabrics are often made of several colors; sometimes tiny flecks of many colors are used in the yarn. Different fibers are used together, different size strands, and so on. If you have never been conscious of yarn construction, you will be surprised at the number of variations which you find in your own wardrobe. Other sources of texture are the "texturized" synthetic yarns, Banlon, Tycora, Taslan, Agilon, and others.

FABRIC CONSTRUCTION

Weaving. Most fabrics used for clothing are woven into cloth. Weaving is done by interlacing two sets of yarns at right angles to each other. First, a set of *warp yarns* is threaded on a loom. These warp yarns must be as long as the piece of cloth that is to be woven. They are fastened parallel to each other on *beams,* really rollers, at opposite ends of the loom. During the weaving process, warp yarns have to stand much strain. Hence they must be firm, strong, and durable.

After the warp yarns are in place, a second set of yarns is woven directly across the first, over some warp yarns and under others. The second set of yarns is generally called *filling* or *weft yarns,* though you will occasionally hear this set called *woof* yarns.

Weaving takes place in this manner. The warp yarns are arranged so that part of them are raised, and part lowered at a particular time. A shuttle is shot straight across to lay the filling yarn in place between the raised and lowered warp yarns. When the shuttle reaches the opposite side, the warp yarns shift positions so that a different set of warp yarns is raised and a different set lowered. The shuttle then goes back again as before. This procedure continues over and over until the cloth is completed.

As you can tell, the filling yarns have to bear much less wear and tear than the warp yarns and therefore do not have to be as strong. This accounts largely for the difference in behavior of woven cloth in its lengthwise and crosswise directions.

Plain weave. The simplest weave is the *plain weave.* In this each filling yarn goes over one warp yarn and under the next alternately. Every second warp yarn is raised as the first filling yarn is shot across the loom. Then before it goes back, those warp yarns are lowered and all the remaining warp yarns are raised, and so on. Gingham, percale, voile, and many other materials are woven in this way. Plain-weave fabrics have no right and wrong sides unless they are printed or finished differently.

When closely woven, this plain weave is a strong weave. It wears best if the warp and filling yarns are approximately the same size and are about equally spaced in each direction. However, to achieve certain decorative effects, yarns of different sizes are used in one or both directions. Poplin, cotton broadcloth, and faille are made with large filling yarns to give a crosswise ribbed effect. Another variation is to group yarns together and weave them as one yarn. Dimity uses large yarns or groups of yarns more or less widely spaced to give a striped or checked effect. Some cloth, such as hopsacking, is woven in what is called a *basket weave,* which is really a variation of a plain weave. Two or more yarns are grouped side by side in each direction and woven as one. This produces a loose fabric that is not especially durable, though it may be interesting in appearance.

Twill weave. You can always identify a twill weave by its diagonal ridges. These ridges are formed by yarns which cross at least two other yarns before going under one or more yarns. Such yarns are called *floating yarns.* In a twill the floating yarns are arranged so that they fall in diagonal lines across the cloth. Some twills, such as gabardine, are more distinct on one side of the cloth than on the other. Flannel and serge are similar on both sides. Another variation among twills is the steepness of the twill. Gabardine has a steeper slant than flannel or serge. In *herringbone twill* the ridges produce a zigzag effect.

Westinghouse

Westinghouse

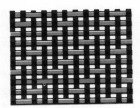

Plain weave

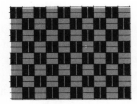

Basket weave

Twill weave

Twill fabrics are usually strong. The weave itself does not produce as strong a fabric as the plain weave, other things being the same, but twill fabrics are customarily woven so firmly of sturdy yarns that they give exceptional service.

Satin weave. In a satin weave, a yarn floats over at least four and as many as eight or ten cross yarns before passing under one. This throws many long floating yarns to the surface of the cloth. These floats may be either warp or filling yarns to produce warp-faced satins or filling-faced satins. These are arranged so that they form a smooth surface without any noticeable twill effect. Any satin tends to be lustrous, but when the float yarns are made of a lustrous fiber and are loosely twisted, satins have the highest sheen of any fabric.

Sateen, made of cotton, is made by the satin weave. Most sateens are filling-faced, although some fine ones are warp-faced.

Figure weaves. Various figures or designs can be woven in cloth by changes in the way the yarns are interlaced. Piqué and madras are formed by fairly simple manipulation of the yarns. Damask requires more complicated shifts and changes in the interlacing process.

Leno weave. The leno weave is similar to the plain weave except that pairs of warp yarns are crossed between the filling yarns. This separates the filling yarns and holds them in place. This weave is used principally to produce transparent fabrics though it is sometimes used for heavier ones. Marquisette is made by the leno weave.

Pile weave. Pile fabrics, such as velvet and velveteen, are made with either a plain weave or twill weave background. In addition a third set of yarns is introduced to form the pile which projects at right angles to the background.

Westinghouse

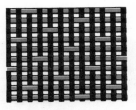

Satin weave

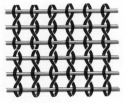

Leno weave

Corduroy is made in a similar way except that the pile forms lengthwise ridges. Terry cloth, another pile fabric commonly used for bath towels and beach wear, has pile on both sides of the cloth. Instead of being cut as it is in velvet, velveteen and corduroy, the pile of terry cloth is left in loose loops. A few rich velvets are made with part cut and part uncut pile to form designs.

Knitting. If you have ever knitted a sweater or a pair of anklets, you know that each new stitch forms a loop which is hung onto another in the preceding row. All knitting whether done by hand or machine is made similarly. Because of their loop construction, knitted fabrics are soft, elastic, and porous. This makes them comfortable to wear, particularly for underwear, hosiery, and other close-fitting garments. As you know, knitwear stretches with the movements of your body, yet clings close to your figure. Air passes through its openings freely to carry off perspiration, even when the yarn itself is not especially absorbent. That is why knitted nylon underwear is more comfortable than underwear made of closely woven nylon cloth.

Knitwear, like every other kind of fabric, has its limitations. Even if firmly constructed, knit fabrics do tend to lose their shape more readily than woven fabrics. This is a trait that is particularly objectionable in outer wear. Also, when a yarn is snagged or broken, some types drop stitches and develop runners or ladders. Even so, knit garments are favorites for sports, travel, and general wear, because they are so wrinkle-resistant and comfortable to wear.

You have, no doubt, noticed how easily nylon hosiery form runners. That is partly because of the simple knitting stitch used and partly because of the smooth yarns. Wool sweaters and cotton anklets made with the same stitch do not run so easily because their yarns are fuzzy. The same is true of wool jersey.

To prevent runners in glossy yarns a different stitch is needed. Tricot knitting is one answer. This complicated machine stitch is almost run-proof. Tricot-knit fabrics are slightly heavier than ordinary knit fabrics when both are made with the same yarn. It is less elastic, also. These qualities make tricot excellent for rayon and nylon underwear, but it does not meet today's demands for gossamer-sheer, form-fitting hosiery. You can learn to recognize tricot knitting easily. Its right side has rows of loops running lengthwise of the cloth

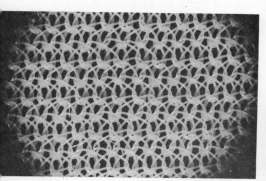

Tricot knit, left

Plain knit, below

USDA photos

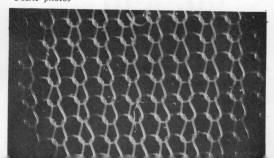

just like other knitting. Its wrong side has loops running crosswise, and that is its distinguishing characteristic.

Felting. As you studied about wool you learned that wool and hair fibers can be converted directly into felt by being pressed and worked under steam. Fabrics made by the felting process are fairly thick and firm. They hold their shape well, but are not especially strong. Air and water cannot penetrate felt easily, and thus felt protects the wearer from both cold winds and rain. These qualities account for the popularity of felt hats for both men and women, particularly for cool weather wear.

Wool felt, made entirely from wool, is stiff, weak, and dull in texture. This is the kind of felt that you ordinarily find in inexpensive hats, in yard goods, and in felt garments. Fur felt, made from rabbit, beaver, and muskrat fur, is softer, stronger, and finer in quality than wool felt. Fur felts have a leathery feel—firm, yet pliable. Some of these are given a smooth finish, some have a velvet-like texture, and still others have a napped, fur-like finish. In some cases the nap is left fluffy, in others it is flattened and polished to a satin-like sheen. Fur felts are usually made into medium-priced or expensive hats.

Non-woven or bonded-fiber fabrics are made directly from fibers, much as felts are. There is a difference, however, for fibers other than wool and fur. They require an adhesive or a bonding agent to hold the fibers together. Thermoplastics or resins frequently serve this purpose. For some types of fabrics, cellulose and thermoplastic fibers are blended together, then formed into a thin sheet or web. As heat is applied, the thermoplastic fibers melt slightly, thus fusing the web into a sheet or fabric. For other fabrics, the fiber web is impregnated with resin before it is heated. For still others, an adhesive is printed on in designs or stripes.

Pellon and similar non-woven interfacing and lining materials are fairly strong and durable. Disposable articles, such as handkerchiefs, towels, napkins, diapers, and washcloths, are stronger than paper and more clothlike, but they do not launder well. Their importance is increasing rapidly.

THE FINISHES

If you wonder what finishing does to cloth, look first at a piece of unbleached muslin and then at a colorful, smooth-textured percale. The percale has been singed (to remove fiber ends), bleached, dyed or printed, starched, and calendered—all finishing processes. Muslin, in contrast, is one of the few fabrics sold at retail in its unfinished state. Many fabrics look much like muslin or worse when they first come from the loom. It's the finishing processes that bring out fabric beauty and improve fabric performance.

Cleaning and bleaching. Except for the few fabrics that are sold as they come from the loom, cloth must be washed and treated to remove soil and natural gums. Bleaching further cleans and whitens fabrics and gives them a greater affinity for dyes. Cottons are always bleached, regardless of whether they are to remain white or to be dyed or printed. Wools (except white wool) are not bleached, and man-made fabrics usually need no bleaching.

Dyeing and printing. These finishes, which add color and design to fabrics, are of prime interest to the consumer, particularly insofar as their fading and discoloration properties are concerned. Today, as more and more fibers are being developed, no two of which take dye in exactly the same way, the demand for colorfastness poses a real challenge to textile colorists.

Even now, some dyes are affected by light, perspiration, laundering, or gas fumes. Consequently, you, as a consumer, should be concerned about guarantees of colorfastness. Of course, no color is absolutely fast. What you need to know is whether it will be fast to the conditions to which it will be subjected. Any clothing that will be constantly exposed to bright sunlight (beachwear, for example) should be guaranteed to be fast to the amount of sunlight it will receive, and clothing that will be washed repeatedly should be fast to the average laundering practices.

Dyeing can be done at various stages in the manufacture of the fabric. For mingled effects, such as those found in tweeds, dye is applied in the fiber stage; it is dyed in the yarn stages for iridescent effects (taffeta) or for checks, stripes, and plaids (gingham). If suitable dyes are used, fiber-dyed and yarn-dyed fabrics tend to retain their original colors because the dye has had a chance to thoroughly penetrate the fibers. The vast majority of materials, however, are dyed after they are woven or knitted—that is, in the piece. Piece-dyed materials can be colorfast, too.

This picture gives some indication of the wide variety of dye colors available today. Although some of them seem similar, each skein of yarn represents a separate dye color.

Du Pont photo

Vat-dyeing may be done at any of these three stages. It is extremely fast, especially to laundering, because the dye penetrates the fibers in a colorless, soluble form, then becomes insoluble as the color develops in the cloth.

A recent type of dyeing is done even before man-made fibers are completed. In this process, called *solution dyeing,* pigment is added to the spinning solution during the production of man-made fibers. Since the color becomes an integral part of the fiber, solution-dyed fabrics are highly resistant to fading. Solution dyes were originally designed to prevent acetate yarns from being faded by fumes, but they are now used in other man-made yarns as well. Chromespun, Celaperm, Jetspun, and Coloray are trade names for some of the solution-dyed fabrics.

Resin finishes, applied after fabrics are dyed, increase colorfastness in a similar way by sealing in the color. (Of course, resin finishes add other qualities. These will be discussed later.)

What has been said about the colorfastness of dyed fabrics is generally true of printed materials. *Vat prints* are extremely colorfast, and *resin finishes* improve the colorfastness of printed fabrics, just as they do dyed ones. Another form of printing is done with *resin-bound pigment* applied to the surface of fabrics. This process also imparts a resistance to fading. If improperly applied, however, color and finish both wear off.

There are several ways in which the dyes may be applied to printed materials. *Roller printing* is used to produce most patterned fabrics. It is done by passing cloth over an engraved roller which applies dye paste to the design areas only. A separate roller is needed for each color.

Screen printing is done with specially prepared screens, one for each color used. The design is transferred to the screens by a photographic method. Then the areas which are to remain undyed are coated over so that the dye paste is applied only to those areas of the cloth where the design is to appear. Screen printing produces large, very handsome designs.

Block printing is done by hand with carved wooden or linoleum blocks. These blocks are coated with dye, then stamped onto the fabric. Block printing is expensive but is highly prized for its irregular shading and hand-crafted designs.

Batik printing is also done by hand. The areas which are to remain undyed are coated with wax. Then the fabric is immersed in a dye bath. Light-colored areas are dyed first, and the process is then repeated for the darker colors.

Shrinkage and stretch control. During the entire finishing process, the cloth is under constant tension. It has to be stretched, or "tentered" as the trade terms it, to bring it to standard width and to square up its grain lines. It has to be pressed and stretched to remove wrinkles. Excessive tension during finishing can cause untreated cotton to shrink when it is laundered, and untreated wool to shrink when it is steam-pressed. Some of the shrinkage-control processes relax this tension to stabilize the size of the cloth. For example, *Sanforizing,* used on cotton fabrics, guarantees no more than 1 per cent residual shrinkage. Worsted materials are often *London Shrunk,* a slightly different process which produces similar results. On woolens, the label *Thoroughly Sponged* denotes reasonable stability of size.

Still another method for stabilizing fabric size was first used on rayon fabrics. It is a resin treatment which reduces both shrinkage and stretching, a fault to which rayon is subject. Resin finishes are now used on linens and cottons, too. The thermoplastic fabrics, being made of various kinds of resin, do not change size appreciably if they are properly heat-set during the finishing process.

Wools, especially the washable ones, are treated to reduce their felting quality and, consequently, their shrinkage. So far, the percentage of residual shrinkage on washable woolens has not been guaranteed, for, although great strides have been made, washing methods still affect to some extent the amount of shrinkage you must expect.

Texture. Before cloth is rolled on the bolt, it must be smoothed and processed by passing it between heated rollers. This finishing process, called *calendering,* is also used to produce the glazed finish found on chintz. In this case, wax or resin is applied. (Resin is preferable; wax glazes, though soft and beautiful, are lost in laundering.) Then one roller is revolved rapidly to polish the top surface of the chintz.

Smooth fabrics are *singed* to burn off fuzzy fiber ends. Fabrics to be *napped* are passed over brushes made of bent wires which pull fiber ends to the surface. Cotton fabrics to be *puckered* are printed with a caustic soda solution in certain areas only. These areas shrink, causing the other parts to pucker. Plissé crepe is made in this way. *Mercerization* (a process whereby fibers or fabric are treated with a caustic alkali solution) adds luster and smoothness to the texture of fine cottons, and also increases their strength and absorbency.

In addition to the traditional finishes of calendering, napping, puckering, and mercerizing, a whole new texture group was produced through the application of synthetic resins. These texture finishes are applied to cottons, rayons, and synthetics. Everglaze chintz, in 1938, was the first fabric with a durable resin finish. Then came embossing, with its replicas of piqué, seersucker, crepe, cord, and moiré. Embossed and sculptured effects are also found on jersey, corduroys, and velvets. Because the resin used for texture effects is similar to that used for wrinkle-resistance, most textured fabrics are also wrinkle-resistant. Some are even advertised as wash-and-wear materials.

Limp fabrics are made firmer in either of two ways—with *soluble starch sizing* much like the kind you use at home, or with a *durable starch sizing,* sometimes called a "starchless" finish. If a garment appears to be starched and you want it to stay that way, look for the label *Durable Finish.* It indicates durable crispness, such as that found on organdy. In contrast, soluble sizing vanishes after the first washing. A small amount of soluble sizing is not objectionable, but excessive amounts may be used to cover up poor quality fabric.

Other Special Purpose Finishes. Other special purpose finishes are added to fabric to give it various qualities. There are appropriate finishes for many purposes, so be alert to new developments and always read the labels.

Antiseptic. These are additives used on any fiber to inhibit the growth of bacteria. An antiseptic finish provides cleanliness, guards health, and prevents undesirable odors. It prolongs fabric life and prevents discoloration by combatting decay, putrefaction, mold, and mildew. It is a desirable finish for coat linings, lingerie, shoe linings, dresses, blouses, and other articles which come in contact with the body, and hence, perspiration. Some of these finishes are unaffected by washing and dry cleaning.

Antistatic. These finishes are used to reduce static electricity. Dacron, nylon, and other synthetics should be treated with a non-static softener to eliminate clinging. Such antistatic finishes increase absorbency, softness, and wearing comfort, and should be unaffected by washing or dry cleaning.

Fire retardant. This is a chemical treatment which reduces the flammability of fabric. With the passing of the "Flammable Act," fire laws became more stringent, and consequently, more and more apparel is being flame-proofed. Today there is no dearth of chemicals which retard fire. Several are unaffected by dry cleaning; however, washing is another matter! Washable fire-retardants *are* available but are still very expensive. Non-durable finishes may be renewed after dry cleaning.

Fuzz-resistant. This finish reduces matting and pilling of napped synthetic fibers.

Gas-fading inhibitors. These finishes are used on acetate to prevent the fading caused by gaseous elements in the air. Discoloration may be reduced or slowed down by these inhibitors.

Mildew-resistant. These are chemical finishes used to retard deterioration caused by the growth of mildew and mold. They are used on cellulose and protein fibers particularly and are similar to antiseptic finishes.

Moth-resistant. This treatment prevents moth and carpet beetle damage on wools. Some finishes are unaffected by dry cleaning and washing; others are removed by laundering or cleaning.

Spot-and-stain resistant. Finishes have been developed which impart to cloth both oil- and water-repellency, and consequently reduce spotting and soiling of treated clothing, upholstery, and drapery fabrics. Finishes of this type can be applied to wool, cotton, rayon, silk, and leather with little or no change in texture. Usually oils and liquids remain on the surface of treated materials and can be blotted away. More deeply imbedded water-borne stains are easily removed with a damp cloth, while the use of an ordinary solvent spot remover will usually remove oily stains without causing a ring. Scotchgard is a highly successful finish which is resistant to oil-, water-, and air-borne soil. It is abrasion resistant and is not affected by chlorine bleaches. Because this finish is both dry-cleanable and washable, it is being applied to all types of fabrics, including fabrics for wash-and-wear garments and for rainwear.

Water-repellent. These finishes resist wetting yet leave the fabric interstices uncoated. Such fabrics are said to "breathe." Some water-repellent finishes, such as the original Cravenette process, must be renewed after dry cleaning. *Durable* finishes impregnate the fibers with thermoplastic chemicals which make them resistant to proper cleaning and washing methods.

Weather-control. These are insulation finishes which protect body heat. Milium was the first trade-marked finish designed as a thermal barrier. These finishes consist of a thin coating of resin-bound aluminum particles applied

Labels give valuable consumer information as to the fiber content and the special finishes on garments. Her careful choice of fabrics will save this traveler much laundering and pressing time.

Lever Brothers Company

to the under side of lining materials. They add warmth but practically no weight, thus giving all-weather comfort. They can be dry-cleaned, but efforts to make them washable are still in the experimental stage.

Wrinkle-resistant. These are thermosetting resin finishes which add vitality and make wrinkles "hang out." They are used most frequently on cellulose fibers, although all fibers may be treated. Wrinkles tend to hang out because the finish makes the fabric resilient. Treated fabrics resist air-borne soil, wash easily, and dry quickly. They do not resist spots and stains but do have a limited resistance to mildew. The finish makes ironing easier, and sometimes unnecessary, and the garments remain well pressed. Chlorine bleaches can yellow and weaken wrinkle-resistant fabrics. The non-chlorine retentive resin finishes, which are now available, should eventually overcome these difficulties. Wrinkle-resistant finishes are a "must" for wash-and-wear cottons.

A GLOSSARY OF FAMILIAR FABRICS

The fabrics defined here are only some of the more common or standard materials found on the market today. A complete list would cover many pages. Each year the list grows, too, for new fabrics are introduced and old favorites come back in new guises. This has been especially true recently because of the rapid technological development in the textile field. Besides the regular fabric names, manufacturers often use trade names to designate some of these new fabrics, or to indicate their own particular version of some well-known material.

To further complicate textile terminology, fabrics that have for centuries been made of a particular fiber are now being made of some of the new synthetics or of blends of various fibers. An attempt has been made here to indicate fibers commonly used for each fabric. Changes are taking place so rapidly, however, that you should not be surprised to find favorite old materials being woven partially or entirely of the newer fibers. Already rayon and acetate have replaced much of the silk used a quarter century ago. Nylon, Orlon, Dacron, Dynel, Acrilan, and others are entering into the manufacture of more and more types of materials.

With the increased numbers of fibers to choose from, fabrics are being "engineered" with any desired characteristics. For instance, nylon is blended with wool to add the strength and other qualities of nylon to the warmth, durability, and texture of wool. Some fibers are introduced in blends to reduce the cost of the fabric, some to improve stability or texture, some to reduce the need for pressing. These and many other qualities are being produced in fabrics by blending and combining yarns. Not all such attempts will be successful, for we are still in an experimental stage where unexpected weaknesses may develop in even the best planned fabric. The complexity in textiles is recognized by our lawmakers. Recent enactments (see page 300) require that fabrics be labeled to indicate their fiber content. No such regulations yet apply to finishes, but for intelligent handling, those, too, should be identified. We are in a changing, exciting era as far as fabrics are concerned.

Batiste. A soft, sheer, slightly lustrous, plain-weave cotton fabric woven from fine combed yarns. Better qualities are mercerized. May be bleached white, dyed, or printed. (Nainsook is similar to batiste but slightly heavier.) Used for infants' wear, underwear, summer dresses.

Bengaline. A firmly woven, plain-weave fabric made of any fiber. It may be identified by the crosswise ribs or cords spaced at regular intervals. Ribs are formed by round filling yarns and hence ribs are not as flat as those in faille. Silk or rayon warp yarns are often woven with cotton or wool rib yarns, since these are completely covered by the more numerous warp yarns. Bengaline is used for dresses, coats, suits.

Bouclé. Any fabric knitted or woven with bouclé or loop yarn. Loops appear distributed over the surface of the cloth. The background of the cloth is visible between the loops, which gives the fabric an uneven texture. Bouclé is made of wool, rayon, cotton, silk, linen, and some of the newer fibers. Used for suits, dresses, coats.

Broadcloth. Cotton and wool broadcloth are two distinct fabrics. *Cotton broadcloth* is a closely woven, plain-weave fabric with the finest of all crosswise ribs. Better qualities are made of 2-ply yarns and are mercerized, soft, and lustrous. Used for men's shirts, pajamas, and women's dresses. *Wool broadcloth* has a twill weave and a lustrous napped surface, permanently brushed and pressed in one direction. Used for suits and coats.

Brocade. A rich fabric with an intricate pattern formed of floating yarns of one or more colors. Designs are raised slightly above the firmly woven background. Originally of silk, but today may be woven of cotton, rayon, or other fibers. Used for formal dresses and wraps, and for draperies and upholstery.

TEXTILES USED FOR CLOTHING

Challis. A lightweight, plain-weave fabric with a slightly napped, soft finish. Originally woven of closely spaced, fine yarns of worsted and silk. Now made of wool, rayon, or other fibers. Often printed with small floral designs. Used for children's dresses, babies' wraps, negligees, women's dresses.

Chambray. A plain-weave, cotton fabric with warp and filling yarns of contrasting colors. Or, may have small dobby design woven on plain ground. Originally, filling yarns were always white, but today may be of any contrasting color. This gives cloth a muted or changeable appearance, usually solid colors or stripes. Used for dresses, aprons, shirts, children's clothing.

Cheviot. Wool and cotton cheviot are two separate fabrics. *Wool cheviot* is woven of harsh, rugged wool in a twill or herringbone weave. Similar to tweed in construction, except that the yarns are not as large, wool cheviot has a rough, lightly napped surface. Very durable but may sag and shine with wear. Used for suits and coats. *Cotton cheviot* is a coarse, plain-weave fabric similar to coarse chambray. Used for men's work shirts.

Chiffon. A plain-weave, soft, sheer fabric of silk or similar fibers. Used for softly draped dresses. The term "chiffon" is sometimes used to describe softness or light weight in other fabrics, such as chiffon velvet. Used for blouses, dresses, and scarves.

Chintz. A gaily printed, plain-weave, cotton fabric, usually glazed. The glaze may or may not be permanent depending on the type. Used for dresses, curtains, draperies.

291

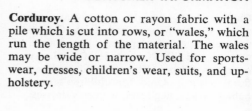

Corduroy. A cotton or rayon fabric with a pile which is cut into rows, or "wales," which run the length of the material. The wales may be wide or narrow. Used for sportswear, dresses, children's wear, suits, and upholstery.

Covert Cloth. A clear-finished medium- to heavyweight twill fabric, usually made from wool or cotton. The warp and filling are of different colors, which give the material a flecked or speckled appearance. Used for suits, coats.

Crepe. A crinkled surface, plain-weave fabric made from silk, nylon, rayon, cotton, wool, etc. The yarns are highly twisted, which gives the fabric an uneven surface. Used for dresses, underwear, suits.

Damask. A flat-surface, reversible, patterned fabric. The design is formed by reversing a satin weave on the right and wrong sides of the cloth. Thus, a design which appears in a satin weave on one side will be in a contrasting weave on the opposite side, and vice versa. Woven of any fiber or combination of fibers. May be of one or two colors. Used for women's evening wear, tablecloths, draperies, upholstery.

Denim. A heavy, coarse twill-weave cotton. Made in several weights, usually in solid colors or stripes, though lately in printed plaids also. White filling and colored warp yarns tend to give denim a faded look. It will shrink unless specially finished. Used for work clothes, dungarees, children's clothing, sportswear.

292

TEXTILES USED FOR CLOTHING

Dimity. A crisp, sheer, plain-weave cotton fabric with woven cords which form stripes or checks. It may be white, dyed, or printed. Used for dresses, blouses, lingerie, curtains.

Dotted Swiss. A crisp, sheer fabric with a plain-weave ground and woven dots. Ground and dots may match or be of contrasting colors. Sheer fabrics with paste or "flock" dots give a similar appearance, but are not true dotted Swiss. Used for women's and girls' dresses, aprons, curtains.

Faille. A fairly soft, ribbed fabric made principally from silk, rayon, or cotton. The rib is formed by using heavier yarns for filling than for warp. The ribs are rather flat —not so round and raised as those in bengaline. It is popular for dresses, suits, blouses, and draperies.

Felt. A fabric made directly from wool or hair fibers by the felting process. Sold by the yard or in shapes to be used for hats. When made of non-wool fibers, a cementing agent is required. Used for hats, skirts, sportswear, slippers.

Flannel. *Dress and suit flannel* is a soft twill fabric with a light nap. Formerly made of wool yarns, it is now sometimes blended with or made entirely of man-made fibers. *Outing flannel* of cotton, either plain or twill weave, is napped on both sides. *Canton flannel*, also cotton and twill weave, has a heavy nap on the under side. These two kinds are used for sleeping garments, linings. Wool-type flannel is used for suits, dresses.

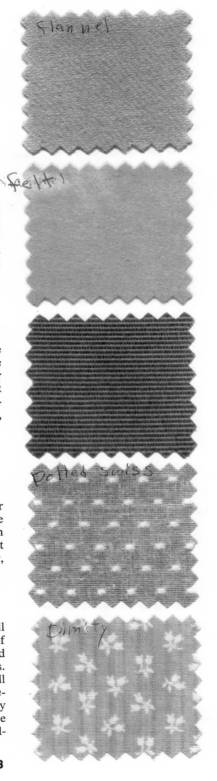

293

Gabardine. A twill-weave fabric usually woven of wool, rayon, cotton, etc., or a combination of fibers. It is tightly woven and has a fine diagonal twill, which is quite steep and much more prominent on the face than on the back. Wear and careless pressing cause the fabric to become shiny. Used for suits, coats, dresses, uniforms.

Gingham. A plain-weave cotton fabric in which the yarns are dyed before the fabric is woven. May be woven in solid colors, plaids, checks, or stripes. Comes in sheer or medium weight. Now gingham is made also of man-made and synthetic fibers. Used for dresses, play clothes, pajamas, shirts, curtains.

Grosgrain. A firm, fairly heavy, closely woven fabric with round cords or ribs running across the width of the material. It is heavier than bengaline. Made of silk, rayon, or cotton. Used for ribbons, dresses, suits, neckties.

Jersey. A fabric knitted with a plain-knit stitch. Wales extend vertically on the right side. Very elastic, but does not hold its shape as well as woven fabrics. It forms runners readily when made of smooth yarns such as rayon, acetate, silk. Wool, spun Orlon, cotton, and other rough or napped yarns do not run so readily. See "Tricot." Used for underwear, dresses, blouses.

Madras. A firmly woven, cotton fabric which may have a small woven design, a woven check, or a woven stripe running lengthwise of the cloth. It may be all white; or, like chambray, the warp may be colored and the filling white. Cords, stripes, and checks may be of contrasting colored yarns. Better qualities are made of combed yarns and are mercerized. It is used for men's shirts, women's dresses.

294

TEXTILES USED FOR CLOTHING

Marquisette. A sheer fabric, made in different weights of cotton, rayon, nylon, silk, and wool. May be dyed, printed, or have dots or figures woven in. Always made with a leno weave, it is used for curtains, evening wear.

Moiré. A finely ribbed fabric having a watermarked finish. Usually made of silk, rayon, or acetate. The design is pressed into the fabric, and is permanent only on acetate. Used for evening wear, robes.

Muslin. Firm, plain-weave, cotton fabric; sometimes used unbleached, but often bleached, piece-dyed, or printed. Yarns are carded and the fabric calendered for a smooth finish. Excessive sizing denotes poor quality and washes out. Sheets are made from heavier weight muslin, and often have the thread count indicated on the label. Dresses, underwear, uniforms, children's clothing are made from lighter weights.

Net. An open-mesh fabric formed of yarns which are twisted together. Mesh may be hexagonal or diamond shaped. Used for curtains, evening dresses, millinery.

Organdy. A thin, crisp, transparent cotton fabric. This plain-weave fabric may be bleached, dyed, or printed. Today a durable starch finish is usually applied. Silk and nylon organdy are similar to cotton organdy. Used for summer dresses, children's clothes, curtains, bedspreads, collars, and cuffs.

295

Percale. A firm, smooth, plain-weave, cotton fabric. Similar to muslin, but woven of finer yarns with a higher thread-count. It is calendered, but has little gloss. Fine percale sheeting is made of combed yarns, and has a very high thread-count. Bleached, dyed, or printed. Used for women's and children's dresses, men's and boys' shirts, aprons, curtains, sheets, pillowcases.

Piqué. A medium- to heavyweight fabric of cotton, rayon, or silk, made in several weaves. One variety has wales of various widths running lengthwise of the fabric. *Pinwale piqué* has very narrow wales. *Waffle piqué* has a woven check produced by the honeycomb weave. *Birdseye piqué* is woven with closely spaced, diamond-shaped designs. Used for neckwear, blouses, dresses, children's wear.

Plissé. A plain-weave cotton fabric on which the design (either a pattern or a stripe) is treated with caustic soda. This causes the treated section of the material to shrink, and the rest of the fabric to pucker. The finish is permanent, but may be flattened by pressing. Plissé is used for dresses, curtains, bedspreads, and lingerie.

Pongee. Similar to shantung, but lighter in weight. True pongee is woven in a plain weave of natural, ecru-colored, wild silk. The uneven, slub-like yarns give the characteristic texture. Used for dresses, shirts.

Poplin. A finely ribbed, mediumweight fabric, slightly heavier than cotton broadcloth, made from silk, cotton, wool, rayon. The ribs run across the width of the fabric. Cotton poplin may be made from combed or carded yarns, and is usually mercerized. Used for dresses, coats, suits, blouses, shirts, pajamas, boys' suits.

TEXTILES USED FOR CLOTHING

Ratiné. A nubby-textured fabric, usually in a plain weave, woven with ratiné warp yarns. The yarn, rather than the weave or knit, gives the characteristic spongy, knotty appearance. Made of various fibers. Used for coats, dresses, blouses, suits.

Sateen. A cotton fabric woven with a satin weave. Filling yarns usually form the loose floating yarns which extend crosswise of the cloth. It is calendered to produce a luster on the face, and better qualities are also mercerized. May be bleached, piece-dyed, or printed. Used for dresses, linings, draperies.

Satin. A lustrous material made with a satin weave. Usually of silk, nylon, acetate, rayon, or other fibers. The loosely twisted yarns float on the face of the cloth, which makes the right side much more lustrous than the wrong. Warp yarns usually form the floats which extend lengthwise of the cloth. Crepe-back satin is reversible with one crepe and one satin side. Used for women's wear, linings, draperies.

Seersucker. A plain-weave cotton, nylon, or rayon fabric with crinkled stripes running the length of the fabric. The stripes are produced by holding groups of warp yarns at different tensions, some tight, some loose. The loose threads form the crinkled stripes. Seersucker does not need ironing. Used for dresses, summer suits, bedspreads.

Shantung. A plain-weave fabric heavier than pongee. Its characteristic textured surface, originally produced by rough, irregular wild silk yarns, is now produced by filling yarns of uneven thickness (slub yarns). It is made of silk, rayon, acetate, nylon, cotton, and other fibers. Orlon and silk are combined in one version. It can be bleached, dyed, printed, or sometimes woven with a figured pattern. Used for dresses, suits, blouses.

297

Sharkskin. One type, made entirely of worsted yarns or blended with some of the newer synthetics, particularly Dacron, is clear-finished, and has a firm, twill weave similar on face and back. Both white and colored yarns are used in each direction. Another type, made of firm, rather heavy, acetate yarns in a plain or basket weave, is firmly woven, chalky in appearance, and rather stiff and firm. Both types used for suits, sportswear.

Surah. A broad term used to designate any lightweight, twilled silk or "silk-like" fabric. Sometimes called tie silk. Silk and rayon serge are similar to surah, but heavier. Foulard is similar, but was originally printed with colored dots on a white ground. Surah may be printed, dyed, or woven from dyed yarns to produce checks and plaids. Used for ties, scarves, dresses.

Taffeta. A crisp fabric which rustles, originally made of silk weighted with metallic salts. Today made of silk, acetate, nylon, rayon, and other lustrous fibers, and of cotton and wool. It has a firm close weave. Sometimes has a slight, crosswise, ribbed effect. It is semilustrous and comes in plain colors, woven designs, and in changeable effects. Used for dresses, evening wraps, millinery, negligees, draperies.

Terry Cloth. A very absorbent, pile-weave fabric of cotton. The surface is covered with uncut loops on one or both sides. These loops are formed by having two sets of warp yarns: one set woven tightly with the filling to form the ground, the other forming the loops. Also woven in designs. Used for towels, beach clothes and bags, slippers.

Tricot. A warp-knit fabric of silk, rayon, acetate, nylon, or other smooth fibers. Wales run vertically on the face, as in plain-knit jersey, but it can be distinguished by the crosswise wale-effect on the back. It is rather firm, fine, and close knit. It is almost run-proof, and only slightly elastic. Used for underwear, robes, dresses, gloves.

298

TEXTILES USED FOR CLOTHING

Tweed. A rough-surfaced, nubby fabric made from wool, in a plain, twill, or herringbone weave. Mixtures of "wool-like" yarns and cotton fibers are also used. *Harris tweeds* are hand-woven in Scotland. Tweeds range from light- to heavyweight, and are used for coats, suits, skirts, dresses.

Velour. "Velour," the French word for velvet, is used for two types of material. One is a heavy long-pile fabric, sometimes called plush. The other is a napped wool cloth made with a satin or twill ground. The nap is long and heavy but open enough to show the background weave. Pile velour is used for draperies, upholstery, coats. Wool velour is used for coats principally.

Velvet. A rich fabric, usually with lustrous, cut pile of medium length. Originally of silk, but now also of rayon, acetate, and nylon. The ground which supports the pile may be a plain, twill, or satin weave. Heavier types sometimes have the ground or back of cotton. Velvet has a shorter pile than plush. Used for dresses, suits, coats, robes, skirts, hats, upholstery.

Velveteen. Similar to velvet but made of cotton. The pile is short and closely spaced on either a plain or twill ground. The pile in better qualities is usually mercerized to give a slight luster. Used for dresses, robes, trimmings.

Voile. A sheer, transparent, plain-weave fabric made from tightly twisted yarns of silk, rayon, cotton, nylon. Better qualities are made from two-ply yarns. Used for dresses, blouses, curtains, lingerie.

299

The Textile Fiber Products Identification Act, which is expected to become effective March 1960, will be administered by the Federal Trade Commission. This law requires that the generic name must be used in conjunction with the fiber trade name in labeling and advertising textile products.

Wool, silk, cotton, linen, rayon, acetate, and nylon are well-known generic classifications for textiles. With this act, *acrylic, modacrylic, polyester, metallic,* and other generic terms are being added to classify the ever-increasing number of new (often synthetic) fibers being produced under individual trade names. These generic terms are based significantly upon the chemical composition of the fibers.

ACTIVITIES

For the class

1. **Arrange** a visit to a weaving or knitting mill, if possible. If there are no mills in your area, perhaps some local handicraft group will demonstrate weaving for you.
2. **Collect** swatches of as many different fabrics as you can and put them into a grab bag. Have a few class members, one at a time, pull out a swatch and tell as much as she can about the fabric and its characteristics.
3. **Divide** into groups to do experiments on shrinkage, colorfastness, and the permanency of starch finishes. Use some guaranteed and some unlabeled material for each experiment. Appoint someone from each group to give a report to the whole class when all the experiments are finished.

For the individual

1. **Do a few experiments** with off-grain material:
   a. take an old handkerchief or square piece of cloth and press it crooked or diamond-shaped. Then lay some square object on the cloth and draw a pencil line around it. Dampen and re-press the handkerchief so that it is again square. What has happened to the pencil line?
   b. press a piece of checked gingham off-grain. Cut out a simple doll dress from it and stitch up the seams. Now wash the doll dress and after it dries, press it. Notice the shoulder seams, the side seams, center lines, and the way the checks fall. Do you think the same things would happen to your own clothes if you cut them from off-grain material?
2. **Collect** swatches of as many different fabrics as you can. Put them in a notebook to keep for your own reference, and as you learn something about a fabric, make notes in your fabric notebook.

CHAPTER 15 — *BUYING READYMADES*

Every girl loves new clothes. From childhood on it is a pleasure no woman outgrows! It has never been estimated how many hours girls spend in planning wardrobes. Even a count of the hours actually spent in buying those wardrobes would be a startling set of figures. As a result, millions of people earn their livings each year from the garment industry—ranging from the manufacturing of textiles to their conversion into clothing. Clothing is a big business.

But what about *you*? Do you get a good return for the time and money you spend as a consumer in this vast market? Are you always satisfied with your purchases or would a little study and thought make you a better buyer?

TO BUY OR TO SEW?

For the girl who can sew, wise clothing management involves buying some articles and making others. No girl in these busy days has the time or inclination to make all her clothes—and there just isn't any reason, economic or otherwise to do so. If you want a man's plain white shirt, buy it. By the time you bought materials and perhaps had buttonholes made you would have spent more money for your shirt than you would for a perfectly good readymade— to say nothing of your time. And you would have just a plain white shirt— like a million others. Standard items that are mass produced offer very little incentive for the home sewer.

On the other hand, suppose you want an evening dress that you're sure you won't see on someone else at the dance. You want it to be "different," yet in the latest style and you want the color to be particularly becoming to you and the lines of the dress to enhance your particular face and figure. In that case, unless you can cheerfully pay a high price, you had better get out your sewing box. The more design interest in the garment, the more reason for you to sew. Not only do you save the most money that way but you have the most fun. Making clothes becomes an art.

Of course many garments fall between these two examples, the man's white shirt and the perfect evening dress. You don't want your school clothes to be startling in design and yet you do want them to be a little different. Just how much sewing versus buying you should do depends, among other things, on your ability and the time you have available. As you grow in ability you will be able to make a skirt or a simple blouse on a rainy Saturday.

Another element to consider is how easy it is to go shopping. If you live in a city where shopping is easy and the market unlimited, you would be wise to buy many items readymade. If you live in the country, shopping may be a semi-annual undertaking involving a long trip to the city. Of course in such a situation you would make more garments than your city cousin. An actual study shows that 96 per cent of the women who sew also buy readymade clothes. They buy more underwear than anything else, then coats, suits, separates, and dresses, in that order.

BUYING WISELY

After you have decided which articles of your wardrobe to buy, you still have some decisions to make before you find yourself going home with a dress box under your arm. Where will you shop? Some stores offer charge accounts and special services. Others offer very little service, but lower prices. Ask your friends where they shop and why. Compare similar products in different stores and in mail order catalogues to judge quality and price.

Cash-and-carry stores often offer the same quality for lower prices than stores which give you more service. However, the less help you get from salespeople the more you need to know about merchandise in order to buy wisely.

Become sale conscious. This does not mean that you must go out and buy something just because it is on sale whether you need it or not. It does mean taking advantage of a sale when the merchandise answers your present and future needs and is of good quality. Remember, a bargain is a bargain only if you needed the article anyway.

There are several types of sales. A store will often promote new merchandise by having a sale at the beginning of a season. Consider the August sales on winter coats. In September, the prices climb back to their usual levels. Seasonal sales are also designed to undersell the merchandise of a competitor. If one store sells a famous-make "town classic" for $14.95, another will try to sell similar merchandise for $13.95. Clearance sales usually occur at the end of the month or the season when a store wants to clear out its stock.

Pre-inventory sales occur before January, prior to the annual balancing of books. The store usually wants to reduce its old stock before the beginning of a new year and to make room for early spring merchandise.

"Special purchase" sales may occur from time to time when the store buys special "lots" of merchandise at reduced prices from manufacturers. It may be surplus stock which the wholesaler is forced to sell at a sacrifice. Merchandise that has manufacturing flaws is sold at reduced market prices to stores as "irregular" or "second." Such articles can be good buys when the flaw in the weave or knit is not visible and does not affect their strength or durability.

In fact there are many times when the old rule "Always buy the best" isn't the wisest guide in stretching your clothing budget. Long-term items—suits, coats, shoes—should be uncompromisingly good. But party clothes and novelty play clothes need not meet such high standards of quality since they will not get hard use. How they look at the moment is more important than how they will wear. Limit high style clothes to those that you don't expect to wear long.

When you shop for a coat or a suit, look for a basic conservative style and a color that will look as right in three years as it does on the date of purchase. Novelty designs and textures not only soon look dated, but also become tiresome to wear. In garments selected for hard wear, look for firmness of weave, generous seams, well-made buttonholes, and other finishing details.

Get the right size in any garment you buy. Alterations are troublesome or expensive. Unfortunately during the years sizing practices in the ready-to-wear industry have grown like "Topsy." For instance, a girl may wear a size 12 dress, a 32 bra, number 5 underpants, a 24 skirt, and a 36 sweater. Bust measurement, waist measurement, age, or mere arbitrary numerals—almost anything is used to designate sizes. To add to the confusion of the different sizing systems for different garments, even within one garment classification, sizes have not been sufficiently standardized so that you can safely buy without first trying the garment on. Not only are ready-to-wear sizes different from pattern sizes, but they also differ from one manufacturer to another. Some stores may not let you try on such garments as pajamas and slips before you buy them. In this case, be sure to hold them up against yourself to make sure they fit.

You undoubtedly learned long ago to look at the little tags that dangle from buttons or sleeves. There may be only one or there may be several but each has information upon it to guide you in making your selection. One tells size and price and there will probably be another which will give information such as fiber content, colorfastness, laundry or dry-cleaning information, type of finish, or treatment given (i.e., water-repellency, crease-resistance, or percentage of shrinkage expected). The brand name or manufacturer's name may be on this ticket or on a third tag. The latter tag is called the "prestige" tag because many commercial companies are proud of the quality of their merchandise and through advertising and earned performance have built a reputation which the shopper appreciates.

You have learned a great deal about clothing construction while doing the constructions in this book. If you have made dresses for yourself, you are alert at appraising the stitching, the allowance of material in the seams, the buttonholes, and whether or not the skirt hangs evenly or in uneven dips. You will also be able to recognize the use of a true bias where it is needed and the correct use of the grain of the fabric to assure good "hanging" qualities. Of course your knowledge of fabrics is important too, and the information you acquired in the chapter on fibers and fabrics will now be put to the test in making a choice!

One more thing to consider are the placket closings. Are they smooth, flat, secure, inconspicuous, and easy to operate? Are the fastenings suitable in color, and will they clean as the garment will be cleaned?

You are familiar with buttons, zippers, and such; now a more recent type of closure, called "Velcro," is appearing on brassieres, skirts, overshoes, and other apparel. It consists of two nylon tapes, one covered with minute hooks, the other with minute loops.

Velcro's adjustability offers advantages for wrap-around skirts, brassieres, and maternity garments, for the tapes will cling together wherever they are overlapped. This same adjustability, however, makes it difficult to close long Velcro plackets so that their two edges are properly aligned. Except for this difficulty, such closings are easy to operate. Unfortunately, however, as the tapes are peeled apart, they make a ripping noise. At the present time, the closing is fairly thick, which makes it more suitable for outerwear and sports garments than for sheer dresses.

Underwear. The wearing apparel which you will probably have to replace most frequently because you are growing and changing will be your underwear. Brassières are bought by both bust measurement—30, 32, 34, 36, and so forth—and "cup" size—AA for the very tiny bust, A for small, B for medium and C for the large bust. The larger sizes may have an extra band below the bra itself to make the whole structure firmer. Cotton (treated to prevent shrinkage), nylon, and rayon, either trimmed with nylon lace or plain, are comfortable to wear and easy to launder. The shoulder straps should be adjustable, and an inch or two of elastic in the back helps give firmness to the bust line and comfort and ease of arm movement.

For use with low-backed evening or sports dresses, there are strapless bras which depend upon bones or wires instead of shoulder straps to give support to the bustline. Some of these are combined with slips. Halter bras are also available for use with halter necklines.

Many girls do not wear girdles but there is no denying that their figures would be vastly improved if they did. If girdles are correctly fitted they will smooth figure irregularities and create a firm contour which will improve any dress or skirt.

For most girls your age a step-in, two-way-stretch girdle is sufficient. There are many models on the market without a single bone. You might select a pantie-girdle with detachable garters and crotch. It is an all-purpose foundation for the young girl. The garters are there when you wear long hosiery;

Lord and Taylor, New York

In addition to selecting the correct size, it is important to check the fabric, seams, and trimmings of any lingerie you purchase.

remove them when you wear anklets. Wear the crotch with your slacks and shorts. Remove the crotch when you wear separate panties.

If you need more support, select a girdle with a boned front. It will hold in that protruding tummy. Always try a girdle on at the shop to insure proper fit through waist and hips and proper length. Be sure to try it sitting as well as standing. You should have two girdles so that they can be laundered often.

Panties or "briefs" should be selected according to the silhouette you wish to create. Wear an untrimmed pantie that fits snugly under a smooth, clinging dress or slacks. Lacy ruffles would only create a bumpy line at your thighs. Full skirts permit the wearing of pants with ruffles or lace.

Panties are available in many fabrics: cotton, rayon, nylon, Dacron and cotton blends; and for cold weather, nylon and wool, or all-wool. Sizes are 5, 6, 7, and 8, and also small (33–34 inch hips), medium (35–36 inch), large (37–38 inch), and X for 40 plus. If you choose a rayon or nylon knit, be sure it is tricot and not plain jersey. There's a great deal of difference in the way these two knits wear. Be sure the seams are securely stitched, narrow, and tacked at points of strain to prevent rips and tears. The crotch should be of double thickness and the elastic at the waist should stretch to approximately twice its original size without strain. There should be ample room in the back to allow for sitting, bending, and stooping, and to prevent binding. Do without lace trimmings if you cannot afford a good quality. Cheap lace frays quickly and will soon look shabby. Only nylon lace is really durable.

In slips, rayon and nylon are the popular fibers although you will also find cotton and blends of nylon, Dacron, and cotton. Cotton makes a desirable summer slip because it is cool, absorbs moisture, and launders well. Blended with Dacron, it requires little or no pressing.

Nylon washes well too, but it does not absorb moisture. It attracts static electricity which causes it to cling to the body and pull some dress fabrics with it. Of all nylon slips, those made of a good quality tricot are the most satisfactory. Because tricot is rather porous, it does not make you feel as clammy in warm weather as closely woven nylon does. Tricot slips hold their shape very well and need no ironing.

Slips are designed to fit smoothly over the body. They are bought by bust size and there are brands which proportion their length to accommodate short, medium, or tall girls. The slender figure can wear either the bias or straight-cut models with equal ease. The stout figure will find less pull or "binding" in the straight-cut models.

Seams should be closely stitched and straps should be firm and securely attached to the garment. Examine lace trim carefully to determine its quality and the way it is stitched to the material.

"Fashion" determines the type of underwear which shall be worn. When the silhouette is smooth and sleek, then the undergarments are pencil-slim too. When flaring skirts are in style, then ruffled petticoats come into their own with a bounce and a flounce! Whatever the fashion, select your slip or petticoat accordingly. Certain standards remain constant, however. When you wear a sheer dress, see that there is no wide gap between the hemline of your dress and your slip hemline. Dark sheer dresses—and many light colors too— call for a slip of matching color, of course. Be sure that the top of your slip conceals your bra, including the back fastening. Prevent that "see-through-you" look by wearing a shadow-panel slip.

Nightclothes. Pajamas are the college classic and also the favorite of many high school girls. It's important to be sure you get plenty of room in the coat, waist, and crotch. Of course, any sleeping garment should be cut full.

Good quality fabric that will wash well should be one of the first things you look for in nightclothes. Just think how often you will throw them in the laundry hamper. Lace or other trimming had better be securely attached. Plissé-crepe, Dacron and cotton blends, or nylon for summer and cotton flannel for winter are particularly practical because they don't need to be ironed if they are straightened on a hanger while wet. If you don't mind ironing, you can have a wider choice in fabrics.

Pajamas and nightgowns are sized like dresses, 12, 14, etc., or by bust measure. You will find pullover or button-front styles in both. In nightgowns, you will have a choice of several lengths—to the ankle, just below the knee, or briefs with matching panties.

Socks and stockings. Correct size is important for comfort and wear in both anklets and hose. One-half inch longer than the foot is the general rule for fitting. Too long a sock or stocking forms uncomfortable ridges under your foot and too short a one will cramp your toe and cause holes in the toe of socks or stockings. It's improper fit of the shoe that causes holes in heels.

Cotton socks of good quality are strong, wear well, and will not shrink if properly treated. Woolen anklets can be treated to reduce shrinkage, also, but even then they must be washed with care.

Buying hosiery is something of a mystery to the average school girl as she wears socks to school and rarely needs to buy nylons. The few pairs she needs for dress occasion are likely to be gifts. When you do buy nylons there are several things to keep in mind. One blanket rule is to buy two or three pairs of socks or stockings the same color at the same time. This allows for re-pairing in case of rips or runs and therefore, longer wear.

To buy stockings wisely, you must understand the terms "denier" and "gauge." "Denier" indicates the thickness of the thread and affects the sheerness and wear of the stocking. "Gauge" means the number of loops to 1½ inches of the stocking fabric and determines the fineness of stitch and to a certain extent the elasticity. The more stitches the greater the elasticity and the better the fit.

Deniers range from 12 which is very fine to 75 which is quite heavy. Obviously it is possible to make more stitches to the inch when the thread is fine than when it is heavier. For this reason the denier (size of the thread) determines the gauge (number of stitches) within limits. If you need a dressy sheer stocking you might ask for a 15 denier, 51 or perhaps 60 gauge. Such a stocking is so sheer that it gives little service. A more durable stocking, still sheer enough for good looks, is 30 denier and perhaps 45 to 51 gauge.

"Full-fashioned" is another term you need to understand. It means that the stocking is knit to shape while flat, then seamed. "Fashion marks," dots on each side of the seam along the calf of the stocking, show that stitches have been decreased to shape full-fashioned hose. This type of stocking fits the curves of the ankle and calf of the leg. The seamless type of hose is knit on a circular or tubular machine and the shaping is done by means of heat when the stocking is on the metal drying form. Nylon can be permanently heat-set

Berkshire Knitting Mills

Both of these stockings have the same number of stitches per 1½ inch but the one on the right is made of sturdier yarns. It is a 51-gauge, 30-denier stocking. The one on the left is a 51-gauge, 15-denier stocking.

and therefore retains this shaping, but any seamless stocking will be heavier at the ankle than at the calf of the leg.

Mesh, or lace-like, stockings are knit on a special machine and cut to shape and sewn. They resist snags and will not "run" as other stockings will. However, they will tear and the tears make holes.

Always buy stockings which are the right length for you—a length which will not cut or bind because it is too short or cause wrinkles because it is too long. Stockings with extra wide tops are available for those who need them.

Shoes. Shoes present temptation to many women. They dream of a vast shoe wardrobe containing all kinds and colors of footwear. Even if your desires are most modest, shoes do take a good percentage of your clothing allowance. For her minimum wardrobe (Chapter 12, "Planning a Wardrobe") Sally felt she needed at least four pairs, plus tennis shoes, bedroom slippers, galoshes, and rubbers. This included one pair for school, one for street and dress, one pair of dance sandals, and a pair of play shoes. Many people would want an extra pair of school shoes as both shoes and feet wear better if shoes can be changed every day. And one pair might get wet some time.

Stick to your plan when you go shopping. Don't buy on impulse.

When you buy shoes, it is important for your health and disposition to get an accurate fit. Shoes that don't fit well cause trouble—if not now, then in later years. How many of your mother's friends have trouble with their feet? Keep them in mind as you pick out footwear.

Each time you buy new shoes, have your foot measured for both length and width. Don't tell the clerk your size. Let him tell you. Feet grow—or perhaps settle—after the rest of you has stopped growing. Test the fit of the shoes by standing up and walking around in them. You will find that your feet are longer when you are standing than when you are sitting.

Never even try on shoes that don't conform to the natural shape of the foot. You can tell by looking at them that they won't do you any good. Oxfords are a good choice for school because they have a thick sole which gives good wear and they have a little heel. Contrary to popular opinion, flat heels are not

Haymakers

Good leather shoes and gloves last a long time.

the most "sensible" kind of shoe. A heel of 1½ inches gives maximum comfort to the feminine arch. That may be a little higher than you want to wear to school, but keep it in mind for later, and come as close to it now as fashion will allow. Don't go clumping around, breaking down your arches in shoes with no heels. Ballerinas are a boon to foot doctors. If you must have them, keep them for an occasional party.

Loafers are another popular school shoe, but unless they are very well made, they stretch and loosen and give no support to the foot. The result at best is a run-down heel and a clattering walk.

Although you will find play shoes and dress shoes of fabric or novelty materials, shoes designed for hard wear are made of leather. Calfskin wears well and polishes easily. Patent leather, a varnish-like finish applied to calfskin or kid, will not stretch or "give" with the elasticity of an untreated hide. It will crack in cold weather and be hot in warm weather. However, in a moderate climate it is easy to care for, as it can be wiped off with a damp cloth. Dressed kid is attractive, but is softer, thinner, and therefore less durable than calfskin. Suede is a velvet finish given to calf and kid leathers. It has a fine nap which requires careful upkeep and is usually used for dress shoes.

It is difficult to judge the quality of a shoe because so much of its workmanship cannot be seen just by examining the finished product. However, there are certain signs which are an indication of quality:

The inside of the shoe should be smooth, with no wrinkles in the lining.

The insole (the part over the arch) should be smooth leather.

The rest of the lining should be closely woven drill or smooth leather.

The top edge of the shoe should be firm and should not stand away from the foot.

The leather should be soft and pliable—not stiff and unbending.

Rubber boots, rubbers, and toe rubbers protect your shoes as well as your health. Pulling and jerking weakens the rubber or boot and will cause tears. Buy boots and rubbers large enough to slip easily over your shoe and the kind in which any heel will fit.

Dresses. Fashion is perhaps the most important factor which influences the choice of a dress. To many women it gives much more satisfaction than the quality of workmanship used in the garment. However, remember that the "latest design from Paris" is usually extreme and expensive. The "classic" style, for instance, has been for many years the choice of women who like

Don't buy anything just because it's the latest fashion. Answer the questions below before you add anything to your wardrobe.

tailored clothes. Aim for good style rather than high style in most of the dresses you buy, unless you can afford to have a new wardrobe each season.

No matter how attractive a dress looks on a hanger or in an advertisement, try it on before you buy it if you possibly can. It's amazing how different a garment can look on the human figure. Model it before a three-way mirror. Take it over in front of a window and see what its color does for your complexion in natural light. As you peer at your reflection, consider these points.

Does this dress fill a definite need in my wardrobe?

Is it conservative enough to be worn for a long time if necessary without my friends and myself tiring of it?

Is the color becoming to my eyes, complexion, and hair, and is the silhouette "right" for my figure?

Does it go with my accessories?

Is the quality of the fabric as good as I can possibly buy for the price?

Is the workmanship good? Is there ample seam allowance and are the seams pinked, stitched, or finished in another way to prevent raveling?

Is the hem wide enough for lengthening, and is it smooth, flat, and suitably finished?

Are the fastenings and placket serviceable? Are the buttons made of a material that will not warp under heat or dissolve in cleaning fluid? Are the snaps and hooks adequate? Is the placket at least 12 inches long and finished invisibly with a self-colored zipper?

Are the buttonholes hand-bound or closely stitched by machine so that they will give long wear without becoming stretched?

Is the trimming of good quality and is the belt well made? Are the light-colored collar and cuffs detachable for ease in laundering? (Sometimes substituting a different belt or removing cheap trimming will improve the design of a dress.)

Is the dress cut correctly according to the grain of the fabric and are the plaids and stripes accurately matched?

Can it be washed or must it be dry-cleaned? What does the label tell about this fabric?

Last, but definitely not least, is it priced right for the product?

Dress buying is such an individual matter that the best one can do is to consider all these points. Then, if that "cheap little number" is still attractive and you prefer it, buy it even against your better judgment, and hold no one responsible but yourself.

Separates. Blouses, sweaters, and skirts are essentials in a girl's wardrobe and sometimes become collectors' items! It is sensible not to overstock, however, because each year the designers think up new and attractive articles and it is better to wear out the clothes you have and replace them with something new and fresh occasionally. The rules for shopping for blouses are much the same as for dresses. Look carefully at collar points to see that they are neatly finished and check lapels to be sure they lie flat. The bottom should have a smooth edge finish and the tails should be long enough to stay securely inside your skirt band. It is always wise to try on a blouse at the store to check the shoulder width, bust, and sleeve and tail length before you buy.

Sweaters are as much a part of school life as books and pencils. They are easy to care for and are good protection against uneven heating of classrooms. The use of synthetic yarns makes them easier than ever to launder. Signs of quality are softness of yarn, evenness and closeness of the knitted stitch, good quality ribbon along the edges of the cardigan, well-made buttonholes and pearl buttons, and taped or well-sewn shoulder seams. Like stockings, some sweaters are full-fashioned—sections are knitted to shape, then seamed together. Look for identifying fashion marks. Such sweaters are superior to the cut and stitched kind because they hold their shape better and do not tend to develop runs at the seams. Of course they cost more, too.

Skirts run the gamut of style, design, and fabric. Many smart girls buy the mix-match costumes of blouses, skirts, and jackets that can be worn together or interchanged. The new fibers and blends are a boon to skirt designers because many of them take permanent pleating which is really permanent in spite of repeated trips through soap suds. The cost of dry-cleaning which was once a price consideration need not exist any more when one can tub an accordion pleated skirt and have it look crisp without ironing. Quality signs in skirts are generous seams, well-placed, flat, and invisible zippers, inconspicuous hems of adequate width, and neatly stitched skirt bands. The grain of the fabric should run straight from the belt at the center front to the hem (unless the skirt is cut with center seams). All plaids or stripes should be carefully matched.

Coats and suits. Coats and suits take a big chunk of the wardrobe budget and are usually bought with the expectation of at least two years' wear and probably more. It is therefore wise to choose simple styling, good fabric, and good tailoring.

Woolen fabrics which are closely woven and firm and springy in hand make warm, durable coats and suits. Tweed, homespun, cheviot, and camel's hair are excellent coat fabrics for school and general wear. Velour and other solid color, smooth woolens are good for both school and dress occasions. Some napped fabrics wear quickly at the wrists and down the front where the button-holes are placed. Fur adds to the cost and limits the season in which you can wear the garment.

Buttons should be sewn with a long shank and an inner button to prevent tearing. Linings should be smooth enough to slip easily over other woolen garments. Rayon twill, satin, and crepe make serviceable and satisfactory linings. In well-made clothing the lining is hand-sewn around the edges and the shoulder and armhole seams of lining and coat are held together with hand-stitches. Lamb's wool interlinings and milium-treated linings add warmth.

Hats. When choosing a hat one good rule to observe for co-ordination of the ensemble would be to match it to the suit or top coat with which it is to be worn. However, your wardrobe plan may call for a neutral color or even a bright accent instead. Felts are more useful than straw because they are more adaptable. They may be worn comfortably at least nine months of the twelve. Fur felts retain their shape better than wool felts which are harsh and stiff. Fur felts feel leathery and pliable. Straws should be firmly woven. Choose one with simple trimming if you hope to wear it for more than one season.

Always be sure the hat you buy is suited *to you*. Try it on and look at it, with the help of mirrors, from all angles. Look in a full-length mirror—not just at your head. That's the way other people will see you, you know.

Du Pont photo

Whether you buy your dresses from a rack or have them made to order, you should inspect them carefully for workmanship as well as style.

The Adam Room, Saks Fifth Avenue

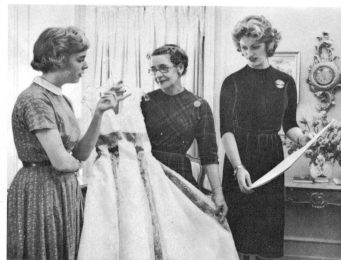

Gloves. Gloves are a nicety of dress which should not be overlooked. They certainly should be worn to church and on the street, and to school in cold weather. Sizes are obtained by measuring around the hand at the knuckles. Finger length is proportioned for long, medium, and short fingers, though you may have to try on the glove to find out which is which.

Gloves are made of various fabrics—cotton, rayon, wool, nylon—and of several leathers. Fabric gloves are cheaper than leather ones and have the advantage of washability. Nylon gloves are particularly practical because they wear well and dry quickly.

The leathers most often used are kid, chamois, doeskin, pigskin, and capeskin. Of these, chamois, pigskin and doeskin are sometimes washable—but do not attempt washing them unless they are so labeled. Then follow instructions carefully. The others are better dry-cleaned. Water would harden or spot them, or both. Unfortunately, dry-cleaning is not always successful either.

Handbags. A handbag—that article of feminine attire which takes the brunt of so many jokes—is really not a joking matter. Handbags are often the only pockets women have and it is no wonder that they are usually filled to capacity. The shoulder-strap bag is often a good choice for school because it leaves your hands free for books. However, the straps might wear the nap off your coat. Other good styles are the satchel and the envelope types. They are large enough to hold all the pencils and paraphernalia you need at school and of a shape that will stack with books and a notebook. For dressier occasions, you may want a smaller bag, perhaps a pouch or clutch style.

The same leathers that are used for shoes are used for bags—pigskin, patent leather, calf, alligator, and so forth. A wide variety of other materials from straw to plastics are used too. Velvet and metallic fabrics are charming for evening; faille makes a dressy afternoon bag. You can make or have made bags to match your dress or coat.

Costume jewelry. Be restrained in the purchase of costume jewelry. The displays in the shops are so attractive that many times we find ourselves buying a pin or a necklace for which we have no particular use. "Suitability" is the key-word when buying jewelry. Pearls are the classic accompaniment for nearly everything. Bracelets may be worn too if they do not make too much noise. Sometimes a pin is needed for a point of interest on a dress or suit. But for the most part, you will be wise to save your money for the important articles of your wardrobe.

Sportswear. Bathing suits, halters, shorts, pedal-pushers, and slacks could almost be considered a national summer costume for teen-age girls. Bathing suits are made of many different fabrics, both woven and knitted. Any attractive fabric which will not be injured by water is suitable. In the choice of style, the figure of the girl is the deciding factor. The girl with a good figure can wear almost any style—two-piece, snug one-piece, or dressmaker. The plump girl—even slightly plump—had better wear a dressmaker suit. Many girls make their own suits, especially if the dressmaker type is their choice. With a matching robe or a wrap-around skirt, such a suit makes an attractive beach ensemble. Suits of Lastex or other elasticized yarns for the slender or perfect figure must be purchased readymade.

Other sports apparel, such as pedal-pushers and slacks, are especially durable when made of denim, corduroy, or cotton gabardine. These fabrics are strong and will stand hard wear. Be sure to look for the label which states whether or not the garment has been treated to prevent shrinkage. Look also for sturdy seams, particularly crotch seams.

Raincoats. There are two types of raincoats: the waterproof and the water-repellent. The waterproof kind—the plastics, oiled silks, and rubber-treated materials—will shield you even in a downpour, but may make you uncomfortably hot. Air can't get through any more than water can and you may find yourself damp from perspiration if not from rain. A good waterproof raincoat has vents under the arms which help overcome this difficulty.

A water-repellent coat—of treated covert, gabardine, poplin, corduroy and other such fabrics—is sufficient protection for a light shower. In a heavy rain or during a long exposure it would get wet through. If you live in an area of light rainfall, this type of raincoat may be the best buy for you. It can double as a top coat in the spring and fall. Some water-repellent raincoats retain their finish through dry-cleaning. Others must be re-treated on each trip to the cleaners.

Umbrellas. Umbrellas can add a gay note to a somber rainy day. When buying one, however, consider the color of the garments with which it is to be carried. Another point which is frequently overlooked is the reflection of the color of the umbrella upon the face beneath it! Shades of rose or red cast a flattering glow upon the owner, while green produces unflattering shadows. Most people do not think of trying umbrella colors against their complexions, but it is a very good idea.

Umbrellas come in a variety of shapes and types: long handles, short handles, and folding ones for suitcases. The frames may have eight, ten, or sixteen ribs, the ones with less ribs being lighter, but possibly not as durable. A good frame should be made of rust-proof steel. The covers are made of cotton, silk, rayon, nylon, and plastic. The weave should be firm and close not only to keep out rain but because when the umbrella is open, there is quite a strain on the cloth.

Shopping manners. Knowledge of merchandise is part of what makes a good shopper, but there is more to it than that. Shopping involves dealing with people as well as with things. If you can enlist the co-operation of the sales-girl, you are more likely to find what you want. Courtesy really pays.

Always try to know what you want as nearly as possible before you go shopping and have a plan worked out as to price, size, and color before you leave home. In this way you will save much time—your own as well as the salesgirls'. "Just looking" is legitimate as long as you make it clear that you

Saks Fifth Avenue

Today's raincoats do more than keep you dry. They are styled and cut as carefully as regular coats and can often take the place of a lightweight coat in spring and fall.

Fashions by Peck and Peck

Money Management Institute, Household Finance Corporation

It isn't fair to the store to buy a garment and then return it simply because you have changed your mind. Make up your mind before you buy.

do not plan to buy and do not keep a clerk away from other customers who might. Do not handle anything more than is absolutely necessary and never touch perishable articles or articles that are easily snagged.

Of course neither your family nor the department stores would approve of your having merchandise sent home before you were quite sure you wanted to keep it. There are good reasons for returning goods, but changing your mind is not one of them. If you are not sure about a dress or coat, wait for another day and take your mother with you or a friend in whose judgment you have confidence. You will always be able to find something else just as pretty if the garment you were in doubt about is gone.

With all these points firmly in mind, you should make few shopping mistakes. Successful shopping requires a good deal of thought and preparation, but it is a stimulating task. Do it well and enjoy it.

ACTIVITIES

For the class

1. **Ask** for volunteers to give two skits: one of a girl with good shopping manners and another of a girl with poor shopping manners. The clerks should react as they would in such situations.
2. **Hold** a class discussion on the best shopping order for a girl who wants to buy a date dress, a coat, some costume jewelry, dress shoes, and a hat. Which should she buy first, second, et cetera? If she has a limited budget should the shopping order be different than if she can spend what she likes?

For the individual

1. **Explore** at least two clothing stores at which you do not ordinarily shop. Make a study of the kind of merchandise they carry and the kind of service they offer. Perhaps you can enlarge your shopping horizons or perhaps you will be better satisfied with your regular beat.
2. **Study** mail order catalogs, particularly if you live in a rural area, to see how much excellent information is given about each article.

CHAPTER 16

ALTERING READYMADES AND REMODELING OLD CLOTHES

Finding the perfect garment for what you have to spend is not always easy. If you find a dress, for instance, that fits, has good lines, and is made of good material in the right color, you have done well. Think twice before casting it aside. Perhaps the buttons are cheap and gaudy. Consider what it would cost to substitute others. It may be the belt that ruins the whole effect. Will your good leather one give the right accent? Perhaps it is a collar that needs to be replaced, or some cheap "do-dad" that should be eliminated. Again, it may be seams that show signs of raveling or dangling threads that make you hesitate. With your knowledge of sewing you can fix those things easily. Unfortunately you nearly always have to do some sewing anyway, because buttons and other fastenings are rarely sewn securely enough even on the most expensive dresses, and skirts invariably seem to be the wrong length. Of course, if there are many things to fix, you might do better to shop further.

Few of us escape alterations entirely unless we make all of our clothes or happen to have the standard fashion figure. Today most readymade feminine apparel is cut to fit the ideal figure of fashion, the well proportioned, 5 foot 7 inch figure. Studies show that the average American woman is not 5 foot 7, but more nearly 5 foot 3; and, as is quite evident, many of our figures do not conform to the proportions of the ideal whether we are tall or short.

There is reason for encouragement, however, for even now some clothing is being made for the 5 foot 4 figure; for the very tall girl; and in half sizes for the more mature, larger waisted, not-so-tall woman.

Realizing the cost and inconvenience of alteration to everyone concerned, mail-order houses, consumers, and leaders in the fashion business are working toward still more realistic sizing standards. As a result, there is already before the industry a set of proposed standards based on the actual body measurements of girls and women. Sizes under this system are determined not only by bust measurement, but also by height and body build. If the system is generally adopted, it is hoped that a high percentage of all women will be able to buy all of their apparel by one size. Already some of the mail-order houses are using the system successfully, and they have found that fewer garments are returned because of poor fit than ever before. Pattern companies are using this system, too, as are a few manufacturers, but it will take time for such a movement to become industry-wide.

ALTERING READYMADES

Until readymade garments are more accurately sized to fit women of various builds, many of us will have to make alterations. The important thing to know, at present, is what kinds of alterations to attempt. Obviously you cannot lengthen skirts if hems are skimpy or let out seams where there is not enough seam width to let out. Even when seam allowances are wide, look for clips or slashes that destroy their usefulness. Some fabrics are permanently marred by stitching lines and pressed creases. Avoid these materials if the garment will have to be let out. As a rule, taking up seams in any garment is safer than letting them out, but even this is not always successful.

Some alterations require so much time and skill that they are not practical. Those that involve the neckline, shoulder seam, and armhole are usually best avoided. Only an expert should attempt them. Even many professional alteration seamstresses do not have enough skill. If they do, such an alteration will be costly. Avoid, also, alterations which destroy the proportions of the garment. For instance, skirts with flounces often require an alteration in the depth of each flounce to retain a pleasing relationship of widths.

Your waist length often determines the cut of garments which can be altered successfully for you. For instance, the short-waisted girl who has to shorten the blouse length of every dress or suit she buys should look for garments with waistline seams. To alter such a style is simple enough even though it may be time-consuming. She should avoid princess dresses and fitted jackets where there is no crosswise seam to adjust. Of course, the waistlines of such garments cling to her waistline, causing the upper part of the dress or jacket to bag. If she rips the seams to allow the garment to fall into place, she finds insufficient width below the new waistline to cover her hip curve.

The problem for the long-waisted girl who cannot find a fit is reversed. The dress with a seam at the waistline is difficult for her to alter unless extra

Teena Paige

If you are short-waisted, don't attempt to alter a princess waistline. Such an alteration is strictly for long-waisted girls.

John Dritz & Sons

Adjusting the hem length is one of the commonest and easiest of alterations. A skirt marker makes the job easier. Chalk (above) will show on dark colored fabrics only. Pins can be used on any fabric. Have someone help you use the pin-it kind, for it will give you a more accurate line.

length has been allowed on the blouse. Often she is better off with a princess dress or fitted jacket provided it fits well above the waistline, because it is a simple matter to nip the seams in below the original waistline to fit her long-waisted figure.

SOME COMMON ALTERATIONS

Lest you begin to think that alterations are rarely worthwhile, we will tell you of a few that can be made, and quite successfully, too.

Changing hems. Changing the length of a skirt by adjusting the hem is undoubtedly the most common of all alterations. If the dress or skirt is one you are just buying, sometimes the alteration seamstress at the shop will mark your hemline for you free of charge. Naturally she doesn't take time to let the hem out. As soon as possible you should run a basting thread along the line she has indicated, through one thickness only, then let the hem down, press it thoroughly, and proceed as for a hem on a skirt you have made. Of course, if you are lengthening the skirt, you will have the hem let down and press it before it can be marked.

Unless the hem was marked at the shop, it is easier to let it down first, press it, and then get someone to mark a hemline for you. Creases that still show after ordinary pressing may be removed by wetting the crease line and allowing it to dry before pressing. Be cautious, though, for this may cause spotting.

Changing waist lengths. Should you want to lower the waistline of a dress with a waistline seam, look for an allowance on the bottom of the waist or blouse. If it isn't there, there is no simple way to make the blouse longer, although a matching belt can sometimes be ripped and inserted as a waistband. However, unless the belt is fairly wide, this adds very little length. Wide matching grosgrain ribbon can be inset, instead, if it harmonizes with the texture and design of the dress.

Whether you wish to lengthen or shorten the blouse, your first step is to take out the zipper and rip and press the waistline seam. Then try the dress on and ask someone to fit you. If the blouse is long enough, she should tie a string about your waist over the blouse to indicate your waistline. Next, she should mark the waistline on the blouse. Now remove the dress and stitch the skirt to the blouse along this line, being careful to match center lines and side seams. Then reset the zipper.

If the blouse is so short that it does not reach the waistline, the girl helping you can place the waistband or ribbon around your waist over the blouse and skirt with all openings matched. Pin the band to the blouse. Next pin the skirt to the band, being careful that center and side seams in the skirt are aligned with those in the blouse on the opposite side of the band. Remove the dress, stitch the band in place, then insert the zipper.

Altering the waist and hip sizes. Dresses without side plackets are simple to alter through the waist and hip areas. You merely rip the blouse and skirt side seams for the required distance above and below the waistline, press them to remove creases, then try the dress on, preferably wrong side out. Now ask someone to pin the side seams to fit you. The important thing to remember is to make identical alterations on each side of the dress, unless your figure is irregular. In that case, fit the dress right side out. Remove the dress, stitch along the fitted lines, and press. Caution: keep side seams straight from the hipline to the hem.

Dresses with side plackets are altered similarly, except that the placket must be ripped and remade on the left side along the newly fitted lines. Never attempt to fit the right side of a dress without fitting the left. Sometimes it is possible to alter the front and back seams, instead of side seams, to avoid remaking the placket. Be sure, however, that an alteration of this type will not destroy grain lines or change the design of the dress.

Changing the size of a skirt band. Separate skirts are altered like skirts of dresses, except that the waistband should be removed and pressed before the skirt is fitted. Fit both skirt and band, and attach the band as you would on a skirt you had made. See Construction One, "Making a Blouse and Skirt."

Changing the size or position of darts. Refer to technique 5, "Altering the Pattern and Fitting the Garment," to learn how to alter darts. A dart can be lengthened without ripping. It can be shortened without opening the dart completely flat, but it must be ripped. The original dart must be ripped and pressed flat before you attempt to relocate it.

SOMETHING NEW FROM SOMETHING OLD

Few families can afford to discard clothing just because it is outgrown or has worn shiny in a few spots. The unimaginative family usually has to continue to wear its outgrown, shabby clothing. The family with imagination and know-how, however, converts its worn clothing into garments of distinction that family members are proud to wear. Many a girl has more clothes, and prettier ones, just because she has learned to change and renew the clothing she has, or because a fond aunt sends her things that she can make over into skirts, jackets, party dresses, and the like.

Before starting any renovating project, ask yourself whether the material is worth the time you will spend on it. Test its strength by pulling it crosswise and lengthwise in several places, especially on the parts of the material you hope to use. Look for worn spots, shiny areas, discoloration, fading, and the like. Decide whether you can discard these areas. If not, look at the wrong side of the material to see if that side can be turned to the right. Tweeds, flannels, wool crepes, and other reversible materials often look like new on the under side. Consider tinting or dyeing cloth that is the wrong color or slightly faded. Sometimes a short length of new fabric for collars, cuffs, and facings will change the whole effect while covering worn spots.

Whatever you plan to do, you will want to start with clean, smooth material. It is pleasanter to work on, and you can tell how much usable material you have. Until it is cleaned, it is difficult to know which stains and creases are permanent and which ones will be removed by cleaning. For minor changes, such as shortening sleeves or turning a frayed collar, wash or have the garment cleaned and pressed as usual. For more extensive renovating jobs that require re-cutting the fabric, rip all sections apart first. Then have the pieces cleaned, or wash and press them yourself. To recut a garment, select a suitable commercial pattern. Then lay the pattern pieces on the fabric much as you would if the cloth were new. Of course, it is more difficult to find true grain lines, but

Mr. Mort—Couture Group, N. Y.
Dress Institute

An old dress might become an attractive jumper.

if you remember that the true lengthwise grain of cloth stretches less than any other direction, you should have no trouble You can find the true crosswise grain from the lengthwise one. Planning your own layout often means shifting pieces about several times. As usual, place large pieces first and do no cutting until you have laid all pattern pieces on the cloth correctly. Once you have planned and cut out a made-over garment, construct it as you would any other garment.

It takes ingenuity to make a stunning new garment from something old, but success brings enormous satisfaction. At little or no cost you have something you might not otherwise have had. Here are a few suggestions for making over particular garments. You can probably think of many other ideas.

Make a gay plaid woolen waistcoat and matching beret out of the too-short skirt or the dress that has worn thin at the elbows. Waistcoats are smart with skirts and blouses and with slacks or a riding costume.

Make a jumper out of your favorite wool or corduroy sport dress if it shows underarm stains. Face the edges with contrasting material or with bias seam binding to match.

Make a dress longer by adding a midriff or a band of contrasting fabric at the hem or partway down the skirt. Visualize a rayon print of navy blue, yellow, and green combined with several well-spaced bands of navy grosgrain or taffeta ribbon. Or use a single band of white embroidered cotton with designs to match the pale tints of chambray. Or if you prefer, combine two contrasting colors of the same fabric. For example, lengthen a dress of brown sheer wool with bands of burnt orange sheer wool; or combine navy with coral or red. There are many possibilities here.

If you have tired of the high neckline on your dressy dotted Swiss, cut it lower, either round or square, and edge it with a narrow ruffle of net or embroidery.

If some of your old white summer dresses seem a bit youngish by now, make them into blouses. If they are yellowed, tint them into your favorite pastels.

If you have tired of a full, gathered skirt, there is usually enough fabric in it to make a pencil slim skirt with a sleeveless bolero. Wear these with a contrasting blouse and a wide belt or sash.

If you wish to tackle really big remodeling jobs, ask your parents for their castoffs. One girl, with the help of her teacher, made a handsome winter blazer out of her father's blue top coat. It had frayed at the opening and cuffs and looked generally faded. Using the reverse side of the fabric, they cut off the frayed cuffs, because her arms were naturally shorter than her father's. They cut off the worn front edges, including the stretched buttonholes, and used a slide fastener for the front opening. The jacket was lined with a discarded red flannel bathrobe. All in all, it cost 75¢—25¢ for the pattern and 50¢ for the slide fastener.

Men's lightweight trousers and slacks of flannel or gabardine can be made into girls' slacks if the cuffs are frayed, or into shorts if the knees are worn thin.

Many women have learned that smart tailored suits with slim skirts can be made from men's tuxedos and other suits that are in good condition. If there is such a suit tucked away in your home because it no longer fits, take it out and see what you can do with it. Mother's winter coat, past its prime, may be just the thing for your new topper. In other words, in addition to finding possibilities within your own wardrobe, stage a salvage hunt throughout the house as a new season approaches. Also you may want to rejuvenate garments for other family members.

ACTIVITIES

For the class

Collect for the class bulletin board and files any illustrations, magazine articles, and pamphlets that deal with altering or remodeling.

For the individual

Think over the remodeling jobs that were done in your classroom. Consider the amount of time and the cost of the new material, if any, that went into each. Which kinds of alterations were most successful, in your estimation? Although making new clothes from old ones is sometimes an excellent practice, there is always the danger of putting more time into remodeling clothes than the wear they will give justifies.

 **PART V**

CARE OF CLOTHING

CHAPTER 17   *ROUTINE MATTERS*

A girl may select her clothes wisely, but if she does not care for them properly she will not be well dressed. A smart suit, a lovely sweater, and good shoes can soon look shabby if mistreated. All items in the wardrobe need regular care, so take time for daily and weekly checkups. A regular system for clothing care becomes a habit that saves both time and money. Furthermore, it is a habit that will carry over to those years when you will be managing your own home.

STORAGE SPACE AND EQUIPMENT

Before you can organize a satisfactory routine for the care of clothing, you should provide adequate space for it. This includes closets, shelves, and drawer space. There is nothing like having a place for everything and keeping everything in place!

Closets. The ideal house plan includes plenty of well-ventilated clothes closets. A family coat closet for outer wraps is near the entrance. Above the clothes rod is a shelf for hats. If there are small children in the family, a low clothes rod and low hooks are provided for them. Some arrangement, in this ideal home, is made for storing galoshes and rubbers. It may be a removable floor rack made of slats, or a ventilated boot chest in the entry. The coat closet is equipped with a supply of sturdy, shoulder-curve coat hangers that do not sag—and smaller hangers for children's garments. A whiskbroom or a large clothes brush can *always* be found on a hook in the closet. In addition to this coat closet, the family in the country needs another closet for chore clothes. That is ideally near the rear entrance and near a washroom. It is equipped with hangers for jackets, hooks for overalls, and floor racks for boots.

The ideal bedroom closet is tall enough to provide hanging space for full-length garments as well as shelves for hat boxes and miscellaneous articles. It may have a shallow area for jackets, skirts, and blouses over some built-in drawers. It would be fun to fix up such a closet with attractive garment bags, hat boxes, and shelf lining and edging. That would be an inducement to take perfect care of every item in the closet.

But too few people have such an ideal set-up. Many a bedroom closet has only a single clothes rod and is much too cramped by a low ceiling to permit even a shelf. Many old-time houses, small homes, and apartments do not even have a closet in each bedroom. In such a case it is generally possible to build

Modern Miss

A neat, well organized closet is the sign of a girl who takes care of her clothes.

a closet in some alcove or corner. If that is not desirable, there are portable wardrobe cupboards on the market. Some wooden models have either a shelf or drawer space or both, plus the full-length hanging area. Metal cabinets may have a shelf and the usual clothes rod. Full-length, sturdy cardboard models usually provide only the clothes rod. These wardrobes may be painted or papered to harmonize with the walls of the bedroom.

Each bedroom closet or wardrobe should have suitable hangers. Shoulder-curve hangers keep heavy garments in better shape than ordinary wire hangers do. For hanging garments made of sheer materials, velvet, or other delicate fabrics, padded hangers are best as they prevent shoulder marks. Spring-clamp hangers are ideal for skirts and slacks. If it is not possible to buy such an assortment, make them out of inexpensive wire or wooden hangers. Pad the shoulders of a hanger by wrapping strips of old sheeting around it; cover with cretonne if you like. Make a skirt hanger by bending the horizontal wire upward. Suspend skirt from lower ends of the hanger by safety pins or spring-clamp clothes pins. Make a slack or trouser hanger by padding the horizontal wire with paper or cloth. Slacks will not show a crease when placed over such padding.

Garment bags of plastic or glazed chintz are both protective and decorative. They come in a variety of lengths—for long evening dresses, daytime dresses, or short garments such as jackets and blouses. If your closet or wardrobe is too small for bags, you can use shoulder covers of plastic or cotton fabric instead to protect light-colored fabrics or garments that you seldom wear.

The following items are also closet equipment, but if your closet is too small for them, make provision for them elsewhere in your bedroom. You will need a shoe-pocket panel hung on the door or a built-in shoe rack. A towel rod attached to the door may also be used as a shoe rack. You will also need boxes or separate drawstring bags. Shoe trees are needed to keep shoes in shape. Set aside a box or shelf for shoe cleaning supplies: polish, cream, cleaner, sponge, brush, and shoe-shine cloths of flannel or soft wool. Have

Attractive closet accessories inspire you to keep your things in order. Perhaps you can make yourself some.

Princess House

hat stands and hat boxes. A swivel, three-branch kitchen towel rack on your closet door will keep your kerchiefs and scarves in press and within easy reach. Men's tie racks are ideal for your collection of belts. . . . And last, but not least, keep some brushes handy—a clothes brush with a long handle and fine bristles for dresses and suits, a flat brush for hats and stubborn spots, rubber sponge "brushes" for removing lint from woolens and keeping suede articles in good condition.

Drawer space. Every girl would love to have her very own chest of drawers and dressing table. Quite often, however, she has only a chest (or bureau) and sometimes shares even that with a sister. With such limited space, every inch must count. The only solution is to keep those drawers in apple-pie order. That means a convenient arrangement of all articles as well as frequent dusting and fresh lining papers.

Divided plastic utility trays are ideal for that top drawer in which you keep assorted pins, bobby pins, costume jewelry, manicure, and cosmetic items. It prevents them from scattering all over in a hopeless jumble. Small open boxes, placed side by side and clipped together, serve the same purpose.

Keep all lingerie in a separate deeper drawer. Fold lingerie neatly and arrange it in systematic piles. Careful ironing goes to waste when slips and pajamas are stirred up with bras, panties, hosiery and belts. If you want a perfumed scent in your lingerie drawer, insert an envelope or two of sachet between folds or in the corners of the drawer.

Your hosiery, anklets, gloves, and hankies might fill another drawer. Matched boxes are lovely in such a drawer—those covered with quilted satin or cretonne. Divided hosiery boxes protect hose from snagging and they keep anklets mated. Long boxes are nice for gloves, square ones for hankies. If you don't have such boxes, stationery or candy boxes will do.

When small drawer space is limited, cretonne-covered utility chests are an ideal solution. They come in models with three or more drawers and are convenient for hosiery, gloves, and those best shoes. Many college girls use them.

If you do not have a dressing table but would like one, here is a simple, inexpensive solution until you can get a real one. Nail together three orange crates—two of them standing vertically and the middle one lying on its side. Level off the table surface of each crate with layers of cardboard. Nail the top layer firmly. Pad the cardboard surfaces with several thicknesses of old sheeting. Cover table surfaces of each crate and short exposed sides of upright crates with one continuous strip of chintz or cretonne, allowing one inch overhang on all sides. Stretch the fabric taut and tack the overhang on the sides. Next line the six sections with heavy, glazed shelf or wallpaper to cover the slats. Use thumbtacks so that paper may be changed. Tack a pleated or gathered skirt of chintz around all exposed sides. Protect the fabric on the table surfaces from dust and spillage with mats of transparent plastic cut to size. An inexpensive closet-door type of mirror hung between the upright crates provides a good full-length mirror. Paint the frame to harmonize with the skirt. Tack a narrow ruffle of the skirt fabric to the back of the mirror frame if you want a frilly touch. If you don't want to invest money in cretonne or chintz, unbleached muslin or grain sacks can be dyed to match the bedroom scheme. The skirts can be dressed up with flounces or swags in contrasting color; or wide ruffles of embroidery add a feminine note. . . . Now you have a dressing table with six roomy compartments.

If you don't put your clothes away, getting them together is bound to be a problem.

Such decorating projects are a lot of fun, and they are real incentives toward keeping your room and clothes in order. You could also make a matching shoe-bag panel, a set of protective shoulder covers and even a laundry bag. Many girls cover old hat boxes with wallpaper or chintz.

DAY-BY-DAY

That well-groomed look is not the result of a casual "once-in-awhile" attitude. Clothes require a certain amount of attention from the time you put them on to the time you take them off. By taking care of your things *today* you ensure looking well *tomorrow*.

When you dress. The familiar phrase, "I tore into my clothes," too often means just that. Are you a "wear-and-wear" type or a "wear-and-tear" type? Getting good wear out of your things begins with how you put them on. Obviously, you must take certain precautions while wearing them as well.

Girdles. Never pull on a step-in girdle by tugging at the waistline. Fold over top of girdle about three inches. Step in and draw the garment up around your thighs. Grasping the fold, slowly ease the garment around your hips, keeping the garters in the correct position. Unroll the fold and adjust around the waist. In humid weather dusting yourself with talcum before you try to put the girdle on will make the process easier.

Hosiery. To begin with, see that your stockings are the correct size and length. A foot length that cramps your toes causes discomfort as well as holes. A short leg length causes strain and an excessively long leg length means that garters are fastened below the hem. Either causes runs. Another precaution: broken nails, hardened cuticle, or rough skin can spell doom to sheer hosiery, so see that your hands are not the cause of snags and runs.

In putting on hosiery, never thrust your foot into the leg part of the stocking. Always roll the leg of the stocking down past the heel so that your toes can slip into the toe section easily. Adjust the toe, foot seam, and heel. Line up the back seam with back of ankle. Then gently unroll the leg of the stocking, centering the seam as you draw it up. Fasten all garters within the reinforced hem, never below it. Fasten the front and side garters while you are seated to allow for the strain of knee action. Stockings that are fastened while you are standing may pop when you bend or sit down.

Shoes. Loosen ties or unfasten buckles before putting on shoes. Use a shoe horn so that you do not have to force your heel into the shoe. Such forcing breaks down the back of the heel. If the heel does not fit snugly enough, it rubs and creates holes in your stockings. Small heel pads of suede or sponge rubber can be glued within the heel to lessen such rubbing. Wear rubbers or boots in bad weather, to protect not only your health but also your shoes. Further, protect the nap of suede shoes by wearing heelless socks or shoe protectors when you wear rubbers or galoshes.

Slips. Many a day gets off to a bad start when a slip strap breaks! Straps that looked firm enough on mending day may rip if you yank the slip on carelessly over your elbows and shoulders. Instead, first insert your arms into the arm openings. Extend your arms straight over your head and let the slip fall easily into place over your shoulders. Unnecessary strain on both straps and seams can be avoided!

Skirts, Blouses, Dresses. Open all fastenings before you attempt to put on any garment. Pull your skirt down over shoulders rather than stepping into it whenever possible. It will mean less rearranging of your undies and less sweeping of floors! In putting on a dress with a small neck opening, slip your arms into the sleeves; extend your arms straight above your head and let dress fall over your shoulders. In this way protruding elbows won't strain the dress seams. Never attempt to fasten buttons, hooks, or slide fasteners until the garment is perfectly adjusted.

Arrange your hair and apply make-up before you put on a dress or blouse *if* the garment can be adjusted without disturbing make-up or hair-do. Otherwise arrange your hair and apply make-up after you are fully dressed to avoid getting make-up stains on your garment when putting it on. In that case protect your clothing with a make-up cape or hand towel. When finished, brush off stray hairs and powder. Do not flick off powder with your hand as the slight skin moisture only tends to smear powder into the fabric.

Hats. Never try to adjust a hat by tugging at the brim alone. Repeated pulling spoils the line of the hat. Shift the *whole* hat into the desired position. If you should later decide to carry your hat, don't play with it. Clutching and twirling only spoil its shape.

Coats. Put your arms in one sleeve at a time without flinging your coat overhead as many girls do. Adjust carefully before fastening. If the coat is close-fitting, unbutton it when you sit down whenever possible. Do not carry bulky or heavy articles in pockets, as they strain seams and stretch fabric.

Every school girl has to carry books. As most students tend to carry such loads always on the same arm, the coat begins to show signs of wear at that point. Try shifting the load from arm to arm, or better yet, carry your books by a strap or in a brief case. Any constant rubbing causes wear. This is especially true of fur coats. Books, sacks of groceries, shoulder-strap bags, or under-arm bags all leave their costly mark.

Gloves. Do not pull your gloves on by the cuff. Adjust the fingers first, one at a time; then the thumb. Avoid handling sooty or wet articles or banisters and the like if possible. Smudges may leave a permanent stain on leather or fabric gloves.

When you remove your clothes. What attention do you give the things you have worn during the day? If you drape your coat on the back of a chair, toss your hat on the dog's favorite window seat, or kick your shoes under the bed— you should change your habits! Compare your own routine to the following suggestions.

Hanging. As soon as you remove a coat, jacket, dress, or blouse, place it on a suitable hanger. Never hang any garment by its neck on a hook or nail as that pulls it out of shape and forms ugly, radiating folds at the back. Proper hanging keeps the garment in shape and, in the end, that means far less pressing. Select a hanger that conforms to the width and curve of the shoulders. If the hanger slopes too much, the shoulders of the garment are not properly supported. If the ends of a hanger extend too far beyond the shoulder seam, they poke bulges in the upper part of sleeves. A hanger that has a hook with a long shank is best for garments with built-up collars. If the shank is too short, the collar is crushed against the clothes rod. Such crowding is especially harmful to fur collars.

Arrange the garment so that it hangs straight. Fasten the top button, hook, or slide fastener. Remove stiff or heavy belts from dresses to prevent a strain at the side seams where the belt loops are inserted. Hang the belt by its buckle on the dress hanger. Hang skirts on clamp hangers (or on wire hangers as described) with the waistband pulled taut. Knit garments are never hung. Sweaters and knitted suits are aired, folded, and placed on a shelf or in a drawer.

Money Management Institute, Household Finance Corporation

This girl takes good care of her clothes. She has hung her jacket on a firm hanger and she is brushing it before putting it away.

Brushing. Well-brushed clothes go hand-in-hand with good grooming. Frequent brushing also prevents dust and grime from seeping into woolen fabrics where they could damage fibers. Correct brushing restores the surface of the fabric. So learn to brush your coat, suit, and dresses after each wearing—and before you put them in the closet.

Use long strokes on the body of garment, always brushing with the grain and nap of fabric. Thorough brushing both inside and outside of collars prevents that dingy, powdery look. Use a whiskbroom on coats and heavy fabrics; a finer bristled clothes brush on softer fabrics. If a coat has a fur collar, fluff the fur by shaking it before and after each wearing. See that the fur is not crowded between other garments in the closet because such jamming results in matted fur. If a coat or suit is damp from rain or snow, dry it away from heat in a well-ventilated room before brushing. When it is thoroughly dry, brush it and press it if necessary. When fur is damp, dry it thoroughly in a cool airy room; then brush lightly and fluff gently. If a fur coat is thoroughly soaked, it needs the expert attention of a furrier to prevent hardening of the pelts.

Make a habit of brushing your felt hats when you take them off. Flat brushes or small handled brushes are easiest to use. First brush the inner hatband, then all outer surfaces. Use a curved brushing motion that is in line with the nap of the fabric to keep the crown and brim in shape. Place everyday hats on hat stands and better hats in hat boxes away from dust.

Airing. After hanging and brushing your dresses and suits, air them overnight near an open window before putting them in the closet. Fresh air helps to remove body odors, and creases often vanish if the garment is allowed to hang freely overnight. It is wise to rotate the wearing of your dresses and suits. Odors and creases are less likely to "set" if the same garment is not worn on successive days.

Although your coats and jackets are exposed to air and sunshine while you wear them, it is a good idea to let them hang outdoors occasionally. Brush pockets, cuffs and all dust-collecting spots. Furs, silks, white wools, and garments that might fade should not be hung in the hot sun. Merely air them.

Lay your sweaters flat and let them air overnight, too. Occasionally turn them inside out for airing. Fold them and put them away in the morning. Slips and girdles that are worn for more than a day should also be placed near an open window until morning. When a washable blouse, dress, or some other garment cannot be worn another day, put it in the laundry bag or hamper. Do not clutter your closet with soiled clothes.

Nightly sudsing. Although the bulk of your laundry is postponed until "wash day" (see Chapter 19, "Cleanliness is Next . . ."), hosiery should be washed immediately after wearing because perspiration weakens the fibers. So allow a few minutes in your bedtime routine for that nightly sudsing. If you wear knit rayon or nylon panties or pantie girdle, you may as well wash them, too. (For complete washing directions, see Chapter 19, page 369.)

Shoes. Place shoe trees in your shoes as soon as you remove them. Shoe trees, or forms of the same shape as shoes, hold them in shape. If your shoes are of the heel-strap variety, standard trees cannot be used. In that case, stuff paper into the toe sections to keep them in shape. Air shoes for several hours or overnight because shoe leather or fabric and linings absorb perspiration. Then if your shoes do not need a thorough shine or cleaning, brush fabric or suede shoes and wipe smooth leather shoes with a soft cloth. Place everyday shoes on a rack or in a shoe bag and dressy shoes in boxes or bags. If possible, have two pairs of everyday shoes for general wear so that one pair can "rest" and regain its shape while the other pair is being worn.

Check heels frequently because a shoe loses its shape when the heel is run-down. Such shoes are harmful to your feet and they spoil both your posture and appearance. If the toes of your soles wear quickly, ask the cobbler to put metal toe taps on them to prevent scuffed toes.

When shoes get wet, shape them carefully by hand and stuff toes with paper. Do *not* put trees in wet shoes for they may force them out of shape. To prevent hardening of the leather as it dries, rub a little castor or neat's-foot oil on wet soles and uppers. Allow shoes to dry thoroughly *away* from heat before polishing. Wet shoes that are dried under radiators, on open hearths, or in warming ovens get stiff as boards!

When your shoes need more than a brush-off, use the right method to keep them in good condition. Clean them before putting them away as you don't always have time for such details during the early morning rush.

You're never too young to learn about proper shoe care. It makes a lot of difference in the way the shoes wear as well as how they look.

Esquire

Use an oily paste polish to lubricate and dress smooth leathers such as calfskin. Neutral paste polish may be used on all colors or, if you prefer, use brown paste for brown leather and black for black. Apply paste smoothly with cloth or brush. Buff vigorously with soft flannel or woolen shine cloth. A sheep's wool buffer is good, too.

Use a neutral, oily shoe cream to clean and polish reptile leathers and white or light-colored smooth leather such as kid. Apply with soft cloth and buff with shine cloth.

Wash elkskin with mild soap and water. Dry thoroughly. Lubricate with neutral cream or paste, and buff.

Wipe patent leather with damp cloth wrung out of mild soap solution. Rub a little vaseline on leather. After a few minutes, wipe it off. Extreme cold cracks patent leather, so avoid wearing it on cold days.

Use standard suede polish on suede shoes; follow directions on product.

Many light fabric shoes may be cleaned with soap and water. Ask the dealer when buying them. White fabric or white buckskin may be cleaned and whitened with white non-oily cake, paste, or liquid preparations. Follow directions on product.

Spots on fabric shoes may be removed with soap and water or cleaning fluid. Follow directions on product.

THAT WEEKLY CHECK-UP

Countless other little wardrobe jobs have a way of accumulating during the week. School girls and career girls who have a busy weekly schedule find that it is best to set aside a free morning or evening for small repairs, pressing, cleaning, and laundering. If you keep your entire wardrobe in wearable condition, you will have that many more things to wear. So plan to have an appointment with your wardrobe about once a week.

Repairs. Learn to look for weak straps, for ripped hems, pocket corners, and linings; ripped or frayed seams; broken belt loops; loose buttons, hooks, and snaps. Even new readymades often need such repairs. Examine hosiery and sweaters for thin spots, for a bit of reinforcing now will save a big darning job later. Make note of ripped glove seams and small tears or weak spots in your raincoats and rubbers. When an article needs attention, do not wear it until it is repaired. If you don't have time to take care of it that very minute, put it aside for your weekly "wardrobe appointment." It is wise to have a place to put things that need repair, just as you have a place to put things that need laundering. Otherwise you are bound to forget some of the repairs you have settled down to make.

Select a matching thread when you make repairs. If there are several weak spots in a hem, rip it and rehem. If a seam has ripped, restitch on the original seam. It may be advisable to restitch the entire seam to prevent further

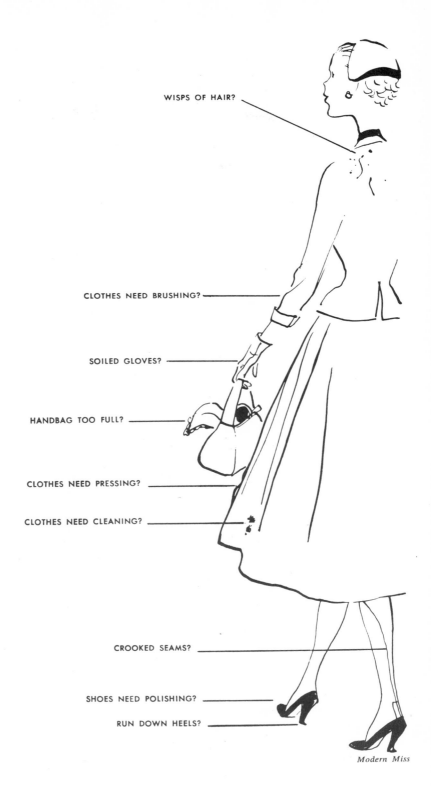

WISPS OF HAIR?

CLOTHES NEED BRUSHING?

SOILED GLOVES?

HANDBAG TOO FULL?

CLOTHES NEED PRESSING?

CLOTHES NEED CLEANING?

CROOKED SEAMS?

SHOES NEED POLISHING?

RUN DOWN HEELS?

Modern Miss

popping. If a seam has frayed, stitch within the original seam, then bind or overcast the seam to strengthen it. Sew up even the slightest rip in a lining or a pocket corner to prevent further ripping and possible tears. If a belt loop breaks or becomes loosened from the seam, it is often advisable to make a new loop.

When you reinforce a thin spot on a knitted article such as hosiery, a mitten, or the elbow of a sweater, select a yarn that matches the color and fiber of the yarn used for the article. The yarn should be a bit lighter in weight, however, to prevent a lumpy reinforcement. Stitch the yarn in and out in two directions over and a bit beyond the worn spot. Avoid pulling the yarn tight, as that creates a puckered reinforcement.

Resew loose buttons with strong thread—heavy linen for coat buttons and a firm but fine thread for lighter garments. Allow for a shank to permit the buttonhole to slip under the button without straining the cloth (see technique 18, "Fastenings"). A small button sewn on the back of a large one prevents strain on the fabric. Resew snaps or hooks securely with thread that matches the material.

Repair small tears or rips on raincoats and rubbers with adhesive tape. Ripped glove seams should be sewn with a stitch like the original seam. Use cotton thread on leather gloves, for silk or nylon may cut the leather.

These are just a few "ounces of prevention" that help to keep your clothes in good wearable condition. For major mending and darning jobs see Chapter 18, "A Stitch in Time . . ." For laundering and cleaning methods see Chapter 19, "Cleanliness Is Next . . ." They are all a part of that weekly wardrobe appointment.

Pressing. In some homes many clothes are sent out when they need pressing. In other homes mothers do the job. But every girl can and should learn how to press her clothes. It is an important part of personal grooming. In addition, proper pressing methods prolong the life of clothing.

When you decide that a garment is too wrinkled or mussed to look presentable, see whether it is clean enough to press, because badly soiled garments should not be pressed. If it is soiled throughout, it should be dry-cleaned or laundered. However, an otherwise clean garment may have just a spot or two. In that case remove the spot or stain before pressing because heat "sets" the spot.

Empty all pockets, remove lapel pins and detachable ties, belts, collars, and cuffs. Brush garment thoroughly, inside cuffs and pockets, too, as an accumulation of dust or lint may appear as a shiny ridge after pressing.

A good pressing job is the result of a correctly padded ironing board, a carefully regulated iron, the right press cloths, and a systematic procedure for pressing the parts of a garment. Refer to technique 12, "Pressing," when you are doubtful as to how to press a woolen skirt, a silk or rayon dress, a cotton or linen blouse; or how to remove wrinkles from a velveteen or corduroy garment. Carefully review the material on final pressing to help you during your "pressing engagement."

Monsanto Chemical Company

Putting moth crystals in your garment bags will help to keep moths away, but to ensure protection, clothes must be cleaned before they are stored.

SEASONAL CARE

If you have ever helped your mother to store the family's clothing at the end of a season, you have a good idea as to what measures should be taken to keep clothing in good condition for the following year.

Summer clothes. The storage of summer clothes is never a big problem. They must be clean, but that's about all. Don't starch them, add bluing or bother to iron them. The only washable material that requires special attention is acetate. If the garment is made of acetate, the final rinse water should contain a bit of washing soda to prevent fume-fading.

Turn garments inside out and pack them in clean boxes, suitcases, or trunks with layers of tissue between garments. Place a piece of heavier paper on top and tuck down around edges before closing the cover to keep the dust out. Since acetates should be stored in airtight containers, seal crevices with gum paper. Label all containers and store in a dry place to prevent mildew.

Non-washable garments should be dry-cleaned before storing. Hang them in garment bags to protect from dust and crushing. If there isn't room in the closet for that, fold each garment carefully, insert tissue between folds, and pack the garment in a box or chest as above.

Winter clothes. The care of woolens and furs is more of a problem than the care of summer clothes, as any homemaker knows. Every precaution must be taken to protect them from moths. A pair of wool socks left in ski boots or a sweater forgotten in some dark closet over the summer is likely to be moth-eaten by the time autumn rolls around! And worse yet, such neglected items can spread moth destruction to other woolen garments and furs, and even harm woolen rugs and furniture coverings.

At the outset it is good to know the habits of the clothes moth. The moth itself does not chew her way through woolen fabrics or furs. She deposits her eggs on wool or soft under-fur, seeking out the soiled spots, dusty seams, and hidden corners. These eggs hatch into small worms, or larvae, that feed upon the wool fiber or under-fur. It is the larvae, then, that are to blame for the holes you find in woolens, the bare spots on mohair furniture, and for the loosening of hairs in fur.

Consequently, when you get ready to store your woolen garments you want to do two things: destroy any larvae or moths that may already be in a garment and protect clothes while they are in storage from any possible invasion by moths.

Dry-cleaning and soap suds *destroy* all stages of moth life in a garment. Furthermore, moths are less likely to lay their eggs in a clean garment. For these reasons, if no others, see that your soiled woolens are clean before you store them. Wash all soiled washable woolens and have non-washable garments dry-cleaned. Garments that are worn but two or three times a year and do not really need cleaning should be aired in the sun and brushed inside and out. This includes pockets, cuffs, underseams, and other hidden places. The assortment of old clothes that most families collect through the years for sentimental reasons should also be aired and brushed every spring. If moths once establish themselves, even in an old attic trunk, they may spread to other parts of the home.

After garments are cleaned, washed, or brushed, prepare them for immediate storing. The use of moth-repellents, such as naphthalene (as flakes or moth balls) and paradichlorobenzene, will help to prevent moths from attacking clean woolens only when the garments are stored in airtight containers. A number of other products protect garments from moths. They all gradually lose their effectiveness when exposed to air. Mothproof sprays must be applied carefully according to directions to avoid spotting the garment. Washable garments may be rinsed in a solution containing a moth-resistant chemical compound. Some products guarantee permanence of moth treatment through dry-cleaning and washing for a year or even longer. It is wise to buy one that is so guaranteed. Follow all the directions that come with it carefully. Many dry-cleaning establishments now treat garments with moth-resistants for a small fee. Processes and guarantees of permanence vary.

Fold and wrap washed, unpressed woolens, such as sweaters, shirts, mufflers, socks, and undergarments in newspaper or heavy wrapping paper. Sprinkle the garments with flakes or insert moth balls between their folds. Tie securely and seal ends and open edges of the package with gum tape. Seal all crevices of boxes or chests used for such storage.

It is advisable to hang freshly cleaned and pressed woolen garments such as coats, suits, dresses, and skirts in clean, airtight garment bags. But make sure that the bags are free of dust and moths. If a garment has not been moth-proofed, it is wise to use some moth-repellent in the bag. Make small cheese cloth bags for moth balls or paradichlorobenzene nuggets or crystals and sus-

Time spent making a fancy, hard-to-keep-clean dressing table skirt might be better used in brushing your hair.

pend a bag from each hanger. Sprinkle flakes, crystals, or moth balls in any pockets. Seal the bags with gum tape. If a bag tears, repair it immediately. If you can't store pressed woolens in bags, store them as you do unpressed woolens. (Garments that have been treated with moth-repellents should be thoroughly aired and brushed when they are removed from storage, before you wear them.)

Cedar chests are safe for storing woolens only when garments are clean and free from moths. In themselves cedar chests or cedar-lined closets do not arrest moth life that is in progress. Cold storage, however, does arrest the development of larvae that may already be in the garment, but *only* while the garment is in cold storage. As soon as it is exposed to warmer air, the larvae may again develop.

Home storage of furs is not recommended. Summer heat dries out the pelts causing them to crack, and excessive humidity causes mold. Added to this is the danger of moths. Modern well-controlled cold storage plants offer protection against drying, excessive humidity, and development of moth larvae. So send fur garments to a reputable fur merchant who will insure the garment against moths, fire, and burglary while it is in storage. Follow his suggestions as to the cleaning and repair of the garment. Periodic cleaning and repair lengthen the life of fur.

If a fur-trimmed woolen garment is stored at home, it should be kept in an airtight container generously supplied with a moth-repellent. Sprays are not recommended for use on such a garment as some contain oil injurious to fur.

Closets. With each change of season, clean your closet thoroughly. Wash or wipe down the walls, shelves, and floor. When it is dry, spray all surfaces and crevices with moth or insect spray. Use a spray gun if your vacuum cleaner does not have a spraying attachment. Dust and air all hat boxes and shoe bags. Renew shelf linings and edgings when necessary. You will then be all set to greet a new season!

ACTIVITIES

For the class

1. **Ask** for two volunteers to give pantomimes:
   a. of how and how not to put on a girdle, hosiery, shoes, a slip, a dress, a hat, a coat, and gloves.
   b. of a well-groomed girl and a poorly-groomed girl removing and taking care of—and not taking care of—her clothes at night.
2. **Arrange** a display in the classroom of attractive closet accessories made by members of the class. These might include garment shoulder protectors, garment bags, shoe-pocket panels, laundry bags, covered hat boxes and storage cartons, and gathered shelf edging.

For the individual

1. **Make a survey** of closet and storage space in your bedroom. Could you improve the closet arrangement by:
   a. making shelves or shoe racks under short-hanging garments such as skirts, jackets, and blouses?
   b. making a shelf for hats above the clothes rod?
   c. attaching swivel towel rods on the door for your belts and scarves?
   Make a sketch of the closet plan as it now appears. Make another sketch with suggested improvements, or find pictures in home decoration magazines to illustrate your ideas.
2. **Discuss** with some friends in your class the best time for the weekly wardrobe check-up. Perhaps, if you live near each other, you might like to get together to do your mending.

CHAPTER 18

"A STITCH IN TIME . . ."

If you practice the "ounces of prevention" already suggested for the wardrobe checkup, your major mending will be cut to a minimum. Yet there are times when garments need darning or patching. And clever is the girl who knows how to make her clothing look practically new. A good mending job does just that. An inconspicuous darn or a patch carefully planned and neatly sewed does not spoil the appearance of a garment and certainly prolongs its wear. You may not know the difference between a darn and patch. A darn is a repair in which threads or yarns are worked into the weave or knit of the fabric. A patch is an additional piece of fabric that is used to replace or reinforce the torn or worn area. Both are methods of mending.

In deciding whether to use a darn or a patch to repair a garment, consider the size of the tear, the material it is in, and whether the garment will be washed or dry-cleaned. For a big hole, a patch is stronger than a darn and will withstand more wear and tear in laundering, but a patch would be too bulky in a thick material such as wool. Woolens are generally darned. Tiny holes, such as burns or snags in almost any fabrics can well be darned whereas big holes in most fabrics are better patched. Darning is also useful in reinforcing frayed lace and worn spots in any type of material before a sizeable hole has developed. If the worn spot is hidden, such as the base of a slip strap, a patch may be more effective in preventing a break-through.

Darn or patch garments before they are laundered or dry-cleaned. This prevents further tearing and raveling of both woven and knitted fabrics. Furthermore, if mending is done afterwards, the garment gets mussed up and needs another pressing. About the only mends taken care of after laundering are the holes in feet of stockings. And even they should be darned before washing if they show signs of running. All runs should be mended before sudsing.

In addition to your other sewing equipment (*see* pp. 63–64), you will need for mending:

a long-eyed darning needle that will hold several strands of thread

a blunt-pointed needle for darning heavy woolen knits

a darning egg for darning socks and stockings

embroidery hoops for machine darning

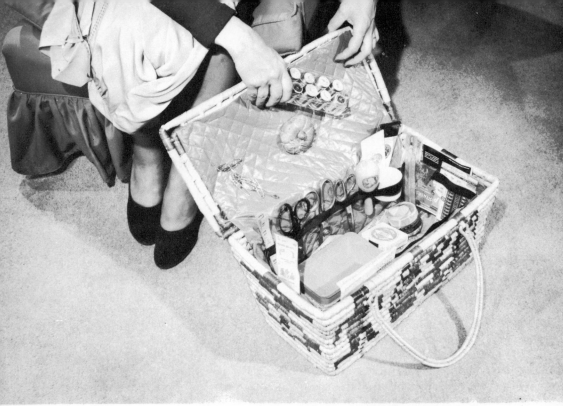

Money Management Institute, Household Finance Corporation

Having your equipment well organized is half the battle in mending.

darning cottons and embroidery floss in assorted colors

assorted buttons, hooks and eyes, and snap fasteners

seam binding and bias tape in assorted colors

assorted scraps of material: save scraps left from cutting out a garment or from altering a readymade; collect net and lightweight fabrics to be used for reinforcements

balls of woolen yarn left from sweaters, mittens, and socks knit at home, and other bits of yarn on hand

This is a starting point for your mending basket, but you will gradually find other items to include in your "bag of tricks." Such things as good zippers, garters, buckles, lace, braid, ribbon, and frogs can be removed from garments that otherwise are no longer wearable.

DARNING

Darns are less noticeable when the darning thread or yarn is the same as the original fabric or similar enough to blend well. When darning a woven fabric, either a tear or hole, ravel threads from scraps of left-over fabric or from seams or the hem of the garment. The warp and weft threads often differ in weight. If they do, use warp threads raveled from side seams for lengthwise darning and weft threads raveled from the hem for crosswise darning.

Some fabrics such as crepe or tweeds are not easily raveled. Then select a thread that is a bit darker than the garment because darning threads work up lighter. The thread should also be similar in texture: dull cotton thread or floss for crepes; strands of woolen yarn for heavy tweeds; mercerized or silk threads for shiny fabrics or silk lace. Hair is sometimes used to darn delicate sheers and laces.

Tears and cuts in woven materials. A tear or cut is easier than a hole to darn inconspicuously because you don't have to weave any new material. All you have to do is secure two edges neatly together. Work from the right side of the material, unless otherwise stated—and except on pile fabrics. If the tear is particularly large or if its edges are frayed, reinforce it with a piece of thin material or net on the under side. Darn through both layers of fabric. There are three kinds of tears and cuts requiring slightly different darning procedures.

Straight tear. A straight tear is a one-way tear or cut in which either warp or weft threads are broken. In other words, it is on a straight of the material, or on a grain line. To darn such a tear, work from the right side of fabric. Place the torn edges together. If the tear is frayed, keep yarn ends on under side. Do not knot the thread, but leave about six inches free on the under side. Begin darning about ¼ inch above and to the right of the tear. Use

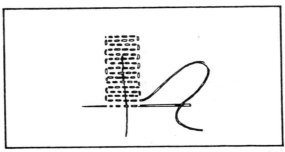

Courtesy of Coats & Clark's O.N.T.

Darning a straight tear

small running stitches spaced to resemble the span of the woven threads in the fabric. Stitch back and forth at right angles to the tear and parallel with the threads of the fabric. When crossing the tear, make a stitch in one row *span* the tear and a stitch in the next row go *under* it. Such alternation makes a firmer, flatter darn. Stitches should extend about ¼ inch beyond the tear, but the length of the rows should be varied a bit to avoid a conspicuous, clean-cut edge of darning. When beginning a new row, take a short stitch on the wrong side of the fabric. Leave a tiny loop at the turn to keep the darn flat and provide elasticity for strain. A thread pulled taut at each turn will pucker the darn. End the rows about ¼ inch below the tear. Draw the thread to the under side, catch the thread to last row, and clip. Now catch the six-inch thread at the starting point under first row of stitches and clip it.

Diagonal cut. In a diagonal cut both the warp and the weft threads are broken. Because the cut is on the bias of the goods, it is likely to stretch or fray badly. For this reason it is advisable to replace both crosswise and lengthwise threads. Always keep darning stitches parallel to the threads of the fabric. First darn lengthwise, then crosswise, allowing stitches to extend about ¼ inch on sides and ends of the tear. Alternate stitches over and under the tear as in darning a straight-cut tear. End the threads as above.

Three-cornered tear. The three-cornered tear is the common right-angle tear. Darn each side as for a straight tear, allowing the darns to overlap at the corner. Such crossing of threads adds strength to the corner.

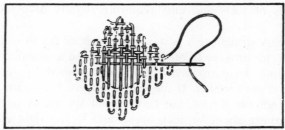

Courtesy of Coats & Clark's O.N.T.
Darning a hole

Holes in woven materials. Before darning a hole, trim only ragged or burnt edges. Leave the hole in its original shape. Keep the fabric flat. Do not knot the thread. First put in lengthwise threads. Use small running stitches parallel to the threads of the fabric. Work in a few rows of stitches beside the hole to reinforce its edge. Continue back and forth until the hole is spanned with evenly spaced lengthwise threads and there are a few rows of stitches on each side. Each row should extend far enough into the fabric to reinforce surrounding edges. Next put in crosswise threads weaving in and out among the lengthwise threads. This results in a plain-weave darn over the hole. Catch thread ends as in darning a tear.

When a hole in woven fabric is too large to cover with a plain-weave hand darn, a darned-in patch is used. This is especially advisable for heavy woolens or other rough textured fabrics. Cut edges of the hole into a square or a rectangle with the grain of the fabric. Cut a patch of matching material to fit the hole exactly; match the grain of the cloth and any figure in the fabric. Baste the patch to a piece of thin, firm material that is large enough to allow for darning on all sides. Fit the patch in place and baste the edges of the hole to the thin fabric. Darn each side of the patch as you would a straight tear. Overlapped stitches at the corners serve as a reinforcement. Remove the bastings and press.

Runs and holes in knitted materials. For a large hole in a sweater or another knit fabric, you may want to use a knit-stitch darn to match the knit of the garment. Refer to a knitting book for instructions.

If you want to mend a stocking run by hand, turn the stocking wrong side out and sew the edges of the run together with a whipping stitch. Be sure to catch the knit stitches at the ends of the run to prevent further raveling. There

Taking care of your own clothes gives you respect for them.

is a special hosiery hook on the market which enables you to knit the mend to match the stocking, but it takes considerable experience to do a professional-looking job with it. If you buy one, experiment on discarded stockings first.

Runs in hosiery may also be repaired on a sewing machine. Use mercerized thread for lisle and rayon, silk for silk or nylon. Turn the stocking wrong side out and fold on the run. Begin stitching slightly above the run; continue to stitch along the edge of the run as you would any seam. Be sure that the knit stitches at both ends of the run are caught to prevent further running. Leave the thread ends about six inches long. Tie them and then, with a short running stitch, work the thread ends back along the seam for a half inch or so before you cut them off.

There are shops that offer a special run-mending service. They reknit by machine to make the hosiery look practically new. The service cost depends on the width of the run, so it is not economical to have bad runs or old hosiery commercially repaired.

To darn holes in toes and heels of hosiery, use the same method that you use for holes in woven materials, but insert a darning egg into the foot of the stocking to make your work easier. Select a fine yarn to avoid creating a bumpy or uncomfortable mend. As you go back and forth be sure to catch each knit stitch to prevent running.

Machine darning. The hand-darning methods described above may be done on a machine when the appearance of a garment is not so important. This might be true of small holes, tears, or worn spots in lingerie, house dresses, and play clothes, for instance. Give added strength to the repair, if it is needed, by basting a piece of material (same as the garment, if possible) on the under side of the area to be darned. Hold the area taut with embroidery hoops. Use thread and machine needle suited to the fabric. Remove the presser foot so that you can manoeuvre the material manually. As you start to sew take a few stitches on top of one another to catch the thread in the fabric. Clip the thread ends out of the way. Continue stitching, slowly guiding the fabric forward and backward then from side to side until the hole or weak spot is covered. Always follow the weave of the fabric. Instruction manuals for different models of sewing machines usually include specific directions for machine darning.

Darned-in patches on heavy fabrics are more durable when stitched by machine. Baste the patch in position as described above. Proceed to stitch back and forth across each side of the patch until four sides are completed. Overlap stitching at corners.

PATCHING

To make a mend as inconspicuous as possible the patch should be of the same material as the garment. Always shrink new patch fabric when you are going to use it on a washable garment. If the garment is faded, take the patch from the hem or some other hidden or removable part of the garment—perhaps a sash end or the under side of the collar. If new scrap material must be used to patch a faded garment, wash it in hot soap suds and soda and dry in the sun until it is faded. If the fabric is figured, cut the patch to match the design perfectly. Such precautions are not so important in patching pajamas or other items that do not see the light of day. But even in such cases the patch material, to be durable, should be of the same weight and texture as the garment. Always cut a patch on the straight of the fabric and match the grain of the patch to the grain of the garment.

There are several kinds of patches. A *hemmed* patch is a durable mend that is used on washable cottons or rayons that get considerable wear and strain. An *inset* patch is generally used for dry-cleanable rayons on places that do not get much strain. *Shaped* patches are used to replace or cover worn areas under arms, on elbows, or on knees.

Hemmed patch. Trim edges of the hole or tear to form a square or rectangle. Cut along grain lines. Clip ⅜-inch diagonal cuts at each corner. Turn under the edges to the wrong side of the fabric. Be sure that the diagonal cuts are well tucked under. Press flat, being careful not to stretch the edges. Next cut a patch that is about one inch larger than the hole on all sides. If garment

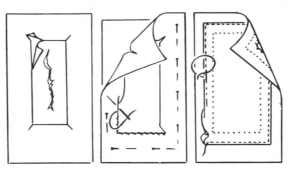

Courtesy of Coats & Clark's O.N.T.

Hemming a patch

is of figured fabric shift the hole over the patch fabric until the figures match perfectly. With both materials right side up and the patch underneath, baste the patch in position. Hem the folded edges of the hole to the patch with a slip hemming stitch. Space stitches very close at corners to prevent fraying of diagonal cuts. Next turn the garment wrong side out. Fold under the raw edges of the patch about ⅜ inch. Trim off the corners a bit so that the turned edges lie flat. Baste them in place. Hem carefully so that stitches will be invisible on the right side of the garment. Hand hemming of the patch is desirable when you do not wish the patch to show. Machine hemming is suitable for pajamas, house, and work clothes.

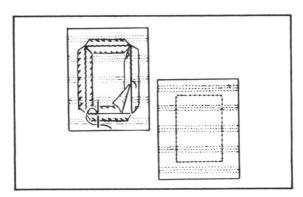

Courtesy of Coats & Clark's O.N.T.

An inset patch

Inset patch. The inset patch cannot stand as much strain as a hemmed patch, but it is less noticeable. Use it on silks and rayons that are not subjected to knockabout wear or frequent cleaning.

Trim and prepare the hole as for a hemmed patch. Cut the patch, allowing about ⅜ inch for a seam on each edge. Turn the seam edges of the patch to the wrong side and press. Measure carefully, so that patch fits the hole exactly. Snip off the tiny triangles where the folded edges overlap at the corners so that corners will lie flat. With right sides up, place the patch in position in the hole. Pin it in place with pins at right angles across the folded edges. Following the position of the pins, baste back and forth to hold the patch in position. Remove the pins. Turn the garment wrong side out. Sew the folded edges together with a tiny whipping stitch. Pink or overcast the raw edges to prevent fraying. Remove bastings. Press the seams open.

Darns and patches have extended the life of many a garment and eased the budget of many a family.

Shaped patch. There are two ways to use a shaped patch. The worn area may be cut out and replaced with an inset patch of new fabric; or a patch may be placed over a worn area. An example of the first type would be a shield patch under the arm and an example of the other type would be a leather patch over an elbow or knee.

Underarm patch. Use a shield-shaped patch to replace the worn or discolored underarm section of a set-in sleeve. Such replacement is generally needed on both waist and sleeve at the armhole seam. (But if the worn area is on the waist section only, omit the shield patch on under part of the sleeve.) Rip the armhole seam halfway around. Cut out the damaged areas on the sleeve and the waist in shield shapes. Use the cut-out pieces as patterns, but add double seam allowances on the outer curves that will be sewn to the waist and the sleeve. Although the armhole seam allowance is already included in the pattern, make it generous too. Cut patch on same grain as original, as always. Turn the garment wrong side out. Clip garment edges before matching raw seam edges. Baste as plain seams the outer curves of the shield patches to the waist and sleeve. Stitch by machine. Press. Then stitch the armhole seam.

To repair the frayed underarm seams of a set-in sleeve that is too snug use a square inset patch. Rip the four seams that meet at the underarm a bit beyond the damaged area. Spread this opening and trim irregular edges to form a square. The end of each ripped seam becomes a corner of the patch. Proceed as for an inset patch. If you wish to stitch seams by machine rather than overcasting by hand, this is the procedure. Turn and press the edges of the hole. From the right side baste these edges to the larger patch below with slip basting stitches taken directly on the folded edge. Now turn the garment wrong side out. Machine stitch along the basting line. Remove bastings and press the seams open.

Repair the underarm of a dolman or a kimono sleeve by inserting a square patch. Cut out the worn area so that opposite corners of the square fall on the underarm seam. Proceed as for an inset patch finished by hand or by machine.

To repair worn underarm areas on slips and sleeveless nighties, hemmed shield patches are used. On such garments, make a double thickness underarm patch and cover, rather than replace, the worn spot. Turn under the seam allowance around all edges of each shield patch and baste. Baste one patch on the right side of garment and the other on the wrong side directly facing it. Stitch all around the patch by machine.

Elbow and knee patches. The life of many a sport jacket, snow suit, and overalls has been doubled by the use of oval, square, or diamond patches on elbows or knees. These can be decorative as well as durable.

If the worn spots on any of these garments are already badly frayed, first reinforce by darning with a piece of lightweight fabric on the under side. The patch will cover the darn.

Leather patches are often used on heavy sport garments. You may be able to salvage some suede or some smooth but soft leather from old gloves or a purse. Often a leather dealer will sell odd scraps at a low price. First decide what shape will look best and make a paper pattern in that shape to extend well beyond the worn spot. Draw the outline of the pattern on the right side of the leather. Suede or thin leather may be cut with sharp scissors; heavier leathers, with a razor blade or sharpened knife. In the latter case, place cardboard or a breadboard underneath the leather to protect the table top. As it is not desirable to pierce leather with basting stitches, hold the patch in position for stitching with rubber cement. Let it dry thoroughly. It may be necessary to rip part of the sleeve or leg seam to place the patch in position for stitching. Use heavy cotton thread and a coarse machine needle. Adjust for a large stitch. Slowly stitch around the patch.

Elbow and knee patches on woolen garments may also be of felt (possibly from an old hat) or other heavy fabric that will not fray. Patches may be

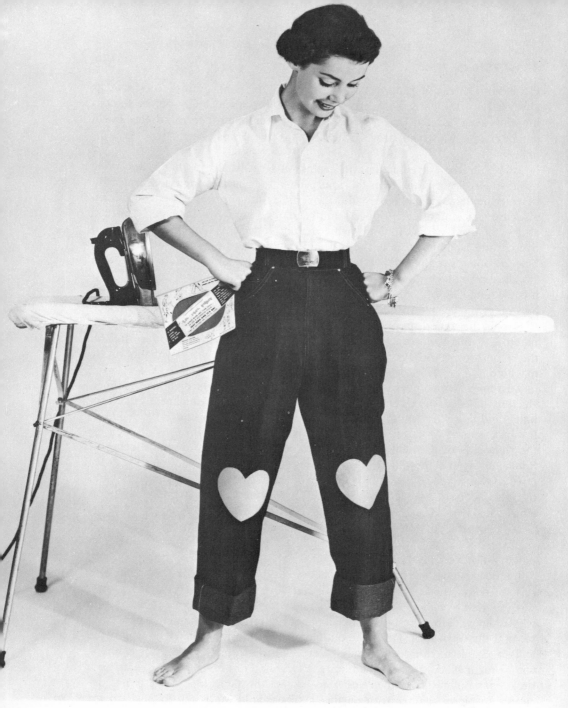

David Traum Co. Inc.

Iron-on patches are easy to use. Just cut to shape and then follow directions exactly for the length of time to hold the iron over the patch.

bought at some notion counters. Cut in the shape desired; baste in place. Stitch on the machine using a needle and thread suited to the weight of the material.

Overalls are patched with self material which may be purchased at notion counters. Turn under the raw edges of denim patch about ½ inch. Baste in place. Sew on the machine with a double row of stitching for extra strength.

Appliqué design patch. Small decorative patches are used to conceal burns, stains, or small tears. Solid colored fabrics may be trimmed with floral, fruit, geometric, or small animal motifs. Figured fabrics as a rule do not lend themselves to such appliquéd designs. Select a color that will contrast with the dress fabric. Draw design on paper; allow for a narrow hem. Pin the paper to the fabric you are using for the patch and cut through both paper and fabric at same time. Baste the appliqué motif in place and sew it with a button-hole stitch or simply hem it with tiny slip hemming stitches.

MISCELLANEOUS REINFORCEMENTS

There are numerous other things that you can do to prolong the life of a garment. A dress that fits too snugly across the back of shoulders may be kept from fraying at the armhole seams by an inner panel that takes the strain away from dress fabric. Cut the panel of lightweight cotton slightly narrower than the width of the shoulders of the garment. Cut the ends of the panel to conform to the curve of the armhole. Double stitch these ends to the armhole seams.

Sleeves that fit too snugly at the elbows and are beginning to show wear may be reinforced by a similar panel at the elbows. Cut a three-inch panel slightly shorter than the total width of the sleeve. Stitch it to the sleeve seam opposite the elbow.

When seams on skirts, dresses, housedresses, or lingerie *begin* to fray, reinforce them with tape or seam binding on the underside before they fray badly. First re-stitch the original seam line. Press the seam open. Baste the tape so that it covers both sides of the seam equally. Turn the garment right side out. Stitch along both sides of the original seam line. Stitch corresponding seams to match, if the double, outside-stitched seam is too apparent.

Pocket corners may strain garment, often causing tears. Sew tape across the under side of the pocket opening. Keep it within the top edge of pocket so that it will not show. From the right side re-stitch pocket corners, catching the tape in the new stitches. The tape gives added strength.

When the fabric under a button is torn, remove the button and trim the torn spot. On a cotton garment make a small hemmed patch, and on a woolen, silk, or rayon one make a small inset patch. At the point where the button will be attached, sew a piece of tape on the wrong side of the patch. Sew on the button with a shank. Reinforce large buttons on heavy garments with a small button on the under side of the garment.

Lingerie straps often break because of the strain caused when they fall over your shoulder. Hold your straps in place with tiny tapes attached to the shoulder seams of dresses and blouses. Use narrow tape or a folded and stitched strip of dress fabric about 1½ inches long and ¼ inch wide. Place on the shoulder seam in a position to hold your straps. Sew the outer end securely to the seam. Sew the socket part of a small snap fastener on the under side of the free end of the tape. Sew the ball part of the snap on the shoulder seam in line with the socket. With such tapes in your garments you no longer have to yank up shoulder straps! And you will do less mending of straps.

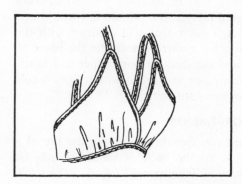 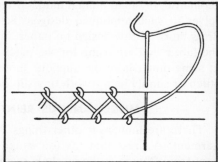

U.S. Department of Agriculture

Fagoting

Yet there will be times when straps on bras and slips need some attention. Replace worn out straps. Grosgrain or satin ribbon of good firm quality may be used on silk, rayon, or nylon undies. Sew in place securely. Or make straps of the same material as the slip if you have some on hand.

Ripped straps often need more than simple re-stitching. When the garment shows strain at the points where the strap is attached, tiny double patches are advisable. Semi-circular patches are nice on straight-edge bodices; triangular patches fit well into pointed slip bodices. Follow directions for double shield patch.

Re-work weakened or broken fagoting in blouses and lingerie with buttonhole twist, crochet cotton, or firmly twisted embroidery thread. Baste the two edges to be refagoted to a piece of firm paper allowing space for fagoting. Rip out all weak fagoting and re-stitch, working from left to right.

Lace on lingerie often wears out much sooner than the garment itself. As soon as lace shows weak spots, reinforce it with net footing. Baste the net to the under side of the lace and stitch it on the machine or by hand. Follow the contour of the pattern in the lace when possible. Net is also used to reinforce weak or torn spots in lace fabrics. Small holes or tears in delicate lace or filmy sheers may be darned with strands of human hair.

Replace weak elastic in garters with new elastic of the correct width. Stitch securely by hand. Avoid piercing the rubber "threads" with the needle as that cuts them.

ACTIVITIES

For the class

1. **Collect** *clean* discarded clothing that can be distributed to relief agencies such as the Red Cross, Salvation Army, European relief, community orphanages, and so on. Repair all garments so that they are in good, wearable condition before you turn them over to the agency.
2. **Ask** for volunteers to bring in garments that have been well patched or darned. Try to get examples of as many kinds of darns and patches as you can and arrange a display so that everyone in the class has a chance to examine them. Perhaps you will want to ask another class to see your display.

For the individual

1. **Go through** your closet and dresser for clothes you can put back in use once you have patched or darned them. If your own clothes are in perfect condition, you might do some mending for a small brother or sister.
2. **Refer** to special books on the subject of mending to learn even more about how to repair clothing. See Bibliography, starting page 555.

CHAPTER 19   **"CLEANLINESS IS NEXT . . ."**

"Cleanliness is next to Godliness"—so the old saying goes. At any rate, cleanliness is the very foundation of good grooming. That attractive "band box look" gives a girl a high rating wherever she goes. So it pays to know how to keep yourself fresh and spotless.

Until now you may have relied on your mother or someone else in the household to wash and iron all your nicer things that are not usually included in the regular family wash. When you wanted a particular blouse for the next day you had only to ask your mother. Presto—there it was, hanging crisply on its hanger when you came from school.

If you continue to rely on others to do these things for you, you will run into difficulties when you leave home and mother! Whether you go off to college or take a job in another town, you will be responsible for your own clothes. So get some experience now by including your personal laundry in that weekly checkup. Remember, too, that practice today will make you a more perfect homemaker tomorrow!

Of course, many of your washables will still be a part of the family laundry whether it is sent out or done at home. If you wash your clothes by machine at home, you can get instructions from the manual for that particular machine. Additional valuable information on home laundering may be found in pamphlets put out by the U.S. Department of Agriculture and by private industrial firms (see also the Bibliography, page 555). Although you yourself may not have occasion to do the regular family laundry, your mother may appreciate the suggestions in these pamphlets. And of course they will be helpful to you when you are managing your own home.

We will confine this discussion to hand-laundering methods. Certain items like dainty silk, rayon, or nylon lingerie, delicate blouses, sheer dresses, some washable gloves, sweaters and other woolens are not generally put into machines or sent out to commercial laundries. Because they are usually washed separately, they are the items that you can launder for yourself. Then, too, there will be times when you have to hand-launder a blouse or dress because you need it before wash day.

BEFORE YOU WASH

There are several things you should know even before you whip up a suds: the fiber content of the garment, its washability, and the actions of soap, detergents, and water.

Know the fiber content. Is the garment cotton, linen, wool, silk, one of the synthetics, or a mixture? The selection of soap, water temperature, method of washing, drying, and ironing—even stain removal—are determined by the fiber of the garment.

Don't be the girl who has just one dress ready to wear. Plans or the weather might change—or something might happen to your one outfit.

Be sure it is washable. Whenever possible buy products that have instruction labels or tags on them. Such labels are the result of special laboratory experiments and are meant to help you to care for your clothing. You will find them not only on garments but on gloves, fabric shoes, and purses. A good label identifies the fiber used; the kind or fastness of the dye; the process used to prevent excessive shrinking. It states whether a product should be dry-cleaned. If it is washable, the label includes laundering instructions. Save those labels and file them in a box for ready reference when laundering. Label each tag so that you won't forget which one goes with which garment.

When you buy washable yard goods, ask the sales person for any information that may be included with the bolt. Remember that vat dyed cottons, linens, and rayons are your best guarantee against color fading. If the fabric has no colorfast or tub-fast guarantee, ask for a swatch that you may test at home before you buy the fabric.

When a garment has no colorfast guarantee, test a sample of it before tubbing. Snip a piece from a generous seam and put it in a tumbler of *hot* soap suds. If the color in a piece of rayon or silk runs, it would be risky to wash the garment. Send it to a dry-cleaner. If the color in a piece of cotton or linen runs, wash the garment quickly in mild, *lukewarm* suds to prevent excessive fading. It should be washed separately so as not to discolor other clothing. Smooth, flat rayons and silks are likely to wash well, whereas crepe or pebbled textures are likely to shrink or stretch. If in doubt, send the garment to a dry-cleaner.

Know about detergents, soap, and water. Soft water, of course, is preferable to hard water for all household uses. It forms a good suds with standard soap products, whereas soap in hard water does not easily create suds. Furthermore, soap combined with hard water forms a scum which is often difficult to rinse from clothing. Detergents fall into two general classifications: the soap products, used for generations, and the newer synthetic detergents. The coined word "syndets" is applied to this latter group, but they are often merely referred to as "detergents" to distinguish them from soaps.

Because they do not generally react with the chemicals in hard water, synthetic detergents give better results than soap. They come in powder or liquid form. Synthetic detergents are almost as effective in hard as in soft water, creating a quick suds and leaving no scum. The mild, slightly alkaline type is excellent for fine fabrics, especially wool. Low sudsing detergents were developed especially for automatic washing machines.

Soap is a cleansing agent in which fat or oil is combined with an alkali and other substances. The so-called mild soap contains much less free alkali than the strong soap generally used for heavy-duty laundry. Laundry soap comes in bars, cakes, chips, flakes, beads or granules, and powders. Bars, cakes, and thick chips do not so quickly dissolve into suds as other varieties. For that reason, flakes, beads, or granules are generally recommended for laundry.

Whether you use a detergent or a standard soap product, you will generally need two types: a *mild* variety for delicate cottons, silks, thermoplastics, woolens, and non-fast colors; and a *stronger* variety for heavier white and colorfast cottons, linens, and thermoplastics, especially when they are quite soiled.

Hard water is not a laundry problem in your home if you live in a soft-water area, or if you use detergents exclusively. Yet, it is well to know what to do if or when it should be a problem. Hard water varies in mineral composition in different localities; therefore, a softener that is good in one district may not be effective in another. The local water department can advise as to which is the best softener. Or you can experiment with such well-known softeners as ammonia water, borax, washing soda, or trisodium phosphate. Water-softening compounds sold under various trade names are also popular.

Some people prefer to install a water-softening system in connection with the plumbing to treat all water used in the household. The salts or other softening agents must be checked and changed regularly.

Stain removal. Luckily, most spots caused by oily or sticky foods and general soiling disappear in warm sudsy water. A few are set by hot water and soap, though, and require special attention before the garment is washed.

Remove spots while they are fresh. Old stains or those that have been set into the fabric by washing and ironing are often impossible to take out.

You can also remove some stains from clothes that must be dry-cleaned if the garment is not soiled enough to require complete cleaning. Be sure to remove them before pressing garment or they may never come out! If you feel hesitant about removing a bad stain from a garment, let a dry-cleaner take

Test a spot remover on a hidden spot before you use it on the garment.

care of it. He has the equipment and skill to remove most stains from all types of fabrics. Stains that are incorrectly removed at home can be just as objectionable as the original spot.

Stain removers fall into three main groups: solvents, absorbents, and bleaches. Solvents are the most generally useful of the three. The best solvent for non-greasy stains like sugar or fruit is water. For grease stains, carbon tetrachloride, benzene, gasoline, naphtha, turpentine, and products made up of these are effective. *Caution:* Because carbon tetrachloride is non-inflammable, it is recommended for home use. However, its fumes are poisonous, and cleaning should be done with windows wide open. Most other solvents are inflammable, so use them in a well-ventilated room too, and *away from fire.* Always follow the directions on the product.

Absorbents must be sprinkled on a spot almost immediately if they are to be used effectively. Then they must be brushed out a few minutes later. Common absorbents used to pick up foreign matter from fabric are corn meal, cornstarch, French chalk, fuller's earth, and white talcum powder. There are commercial spot sticks, too, that are very effective on grease spots.

Commercial chlorine bleaches can be used to remove color stains from *white* and colorfast cotton, linen, or rayon *only*. But avoid using chlorine even on these fibers if they have been treated with resin to give them a permanent finish. Hydrogen peroxide, sodium perborate, or lemon juice may be used to bleach any fabric that is colorfast.

Here are a few general rules for successful stain removal.

1. Know the fiber content of the garment and any special finish used. A remover that is successful on vegetable fibers may ruin animal fibers or resin-treated cellulose fibers.

2. Always test any cleaning agent on a hidden part of the garment before you apply it to the stain, to avoid discoloration and water spots.

3. Try to remember what caused the stain: grease, fruit, coffee, et cetera. If you can't tell what it is, try removing it with water first.

4. Assemble all equipment within easy reach. Work on a clean table. Unless otherwise specified, you will need a pad of clean white cloth to put under the stain while you are working on it.

5. Work from the wrong side of the garment to avoid forcing the stain all the way through the fabric from the right side.

6. Use remover sparingly; repeated light applications are better than one single heavy dose.

7. Work *quickly*. Apply liquids with light brushing motions, using white lint-free cloth or a sponge. To avoid spots and rings, strokes should fan out over the spot. Use medicine dropper when "drops" are required.

8. Rinse cleaned area thoroughly, as bleaches and chemicals left in the cloth may rot the fiber.

9. Dry rapidly to prevent rings.

Here are some home methods for removing the more common stains. All cleaning agents mentioned may be bought at a drug store or grocery.

HOW TO REMOVE STAINS

STAIN	FIBER	DIRECTIONS
Acid	*Silk* *Wool*	Wash stain with cold water to stop action of acid. Sprinkle both sides with baking soda and moisten. Rinse with water when bubbling stops.
	Cotton *Linen* *Rayon*	Hold stain over open bottle of strong ammonia solution to neutralize acid; or apply a few drops of diluted ammonia (half-strength) to stain. If ammonia affects dye, apply white vinegar quickly. Rinse with water.

STAIN	FIBER	DIRECTIONS
Blood	*Silk* *Wool* *Rayon*	Sponge stain with cool water and let stand. (Hot water sets blood stains.) If fabric is washable, warm soapy water will then remove all stains. If fabric is not washable but is colorfast and stain remains after sponging, sponge with hydrogen peroxide. If fabric is not colorfast, moisten stain with water and bleach in sun wrong side out (except white silk or wool).
	Heavy Woolens	Apply thick paste made of raw starch and cold water to stain. Dry and brush off.
	Cotton Linen	Soak fresh stains in cold water until stain is light brown. Soak old stains in cold water to which ammonia water has been added—2 tablespoons per gallon of water. After soaking garment, wash in warm soapy water.
Candle Wax	*All Fibers*	Scrape off as much wax as possible without damaging fibers. Place clean white blotters on both sides of stain and press with warm iron. Next, with a clean cloth pad under stain, sponge off remaining grease with carbon tetrachloride. Remove any color stain that remains by sponging with a solution of 1 part denatured alcohol to 2 parts water. Rinse well.
Chewing Gum	*All Fibers*	Sponge with carbon tetrachloride or turpentine. *Washable* fabrics may be cleaned by another method as well. Soften gum with egg white; wash in warm suds; rinse well.
Cocoa	*All Fibers*	*Washables.* First rinse in cold water; then in warm suds. This usually removes all chocolate or cocoa stains. If stain remains, use the appropriate commercial bleach or sponge colorfast fabrics with hydrogen peroxide. *Non-washables.* First remove grease by sponging stain with carbon tetrachloride. When thoroughly dry, sponge with warm water to remove traces of starch and sugar.
Coffee and Tea	*Silk* *Wool* *Rayon*	Sponge stain with lukewarm water. Lightly rub glycerine into fabric and let stand for 30 minutes. Rinse with water. If oily cream spot remains, sponge with carbon tetrachloride.
	Cotton Linen	Fresh stains are often removed by washing in warm soapy water. To remove older stains, stretch fabric over a large bowl and tie securely. From a height of 3 feet, pour boiling water on stain. If stain remains, use the appropriate commercial bleach or sponge with hydrogen peroxide. If fabric is not colorfast, moisten stain with water and bleach in sun wrong side out.

STAIN	FIBER	DIRECTIONS
Fingernail Polish	*All Fibers*	Moisten stain with carbon tetrachloride; while wet apply a drop of banana oil. Pick up polish with clean, soft cloth. If color of polish remains, use a bleach. Moisten stain with water; sprinkle sodium perborate on stain; let stand 30 minutes; rinse well. (A commercial chlorine bleach may also be used on white cottons, linens, and rayons but *not* on silk, wool, or colored fabrics.) Nail polish may also be removed with acetone or nail polish remover from any material *except* acetate.
Fruit	*Silk Wool Rayon*	Sponge stain with cool water. Lightly rub glycerine into fabric and let stand for several hours. Then apply a few drops of vinegar on the spot. After 2 minutes, rinse with water.
	Cotton Linen	Stretch stained spot over a large bowl and tie securely. From a height of 3 feet, pour boiling water on stain. If stain remains on white goods, remove with commercial bleach. If stain remains on colored fabric, moisten with water and bleach in sun. Do not use soap until stain has disappeared. *Note:* If fruit acid has changed the color of fabric, color can often be restored with baking soda or ammonia water as described above under "Acid."
Grass	*All Fibers*	*Most washables.* Soap and hot water generally remove stain. If not, bleach with a sodium perborate bleach according to directions on the container, or bleach white and colorfast household cottons or linens with a chlorine bleach. *Non-washables and delicate washables.* Sponge with alcohol or benzene. When removing stains on colored fabrics and on acetate—whether colored or not—dilute alcohol, using 1 part denatured alcohol to 2 parts water.
Grease and Oils *(See "Lipstick" for Blackened Car Grease.)*	*Silk Wool*	Place stained area on top of clean blotter or absorbent paper towels. Cover with cornstarch, French chalk, fuller's earth, or talcum. Place absorbent paper on top on right side of garment and press with warm iron. Brush off powder. Repeat if necessary. Or spread a paste of cornstarch and carbon tetrachloride on spot. When dry, brush it off. Repeat until stain is removed.
	Cotton Linen Rayon	A synthetic detergent in hot water will remove grease and oil from washables. If grease has hardened, soften with lard before laundering. If not washable, sponge with carbon tetrachloride or benzene, or use cornstarch paste described above.

STAIN	FIBER	DIRECTIONS
Ink		Because inks differ so widely in chemical composition, let a dry-cleaner remove ink stains from non-washable garments.
	Washable Fabrics Only	Remove ink as soon as it is spilled when possible using clear water. Soap and warm water will then remove some writing inks. Another method is to saturate the stain with glycerine. Rub lightly and apply glycerine as long as any ink comes out on the rag. Rinse with clear water. If stain remains, bleach. Use a sodium perborate bleach or bleach cottons and linens (those without permanent finishes) with a chlorine bleach.
Lipstick and Blackened Car Grease	*All Fibers*	*Washables.* Rub lard, white vaseline, or glycerine into stain. Pick up with absorbent cloth or tissue. Wash in warm suds.
		Non-washables. Rub lard or white vaseline into stain. Pick up with tissue. Sponge spot with carbon tetrachloride. If color remains, sponge with denatured alcohol. When cleaning colored fabrics or acetate —whether colored or not—be sure to dilute the alcohol. To dilute the alcohol, use 1 part denatured alcohol to 2 parts of water.
Paint and Varnish	*Silk Wool Rayon*	Remove paint with turpentine or benzene as soon as possible to prevent drying. If hardened, apply benzene or turpentine to both sides of stain to soften paint. Rub lightly so as not to injure fabric. If some stain remains, sponge with carbon tetrachloride.
	Cotton Linen	Above method may be used on small spots. If stains are large and splattered, soak washables in equal parts of turpentine and ammonia water; follow with warm suds.
Rust	*All Fibers*	The following methods are safe on white fabrics but other fabrics should be tested for colorfastness before using.
		1. Sprinkle stain with salt, squeeze lemon juice on it, and dry in sun.
		2. Stretch stain over pan of boiling water, squeeze lemon juice on stain, and let stand 3 or 4 minutes. Rinse.
	Cotton and Linen Only	Boil white cotton or linen article in solution of 4 teaspoons cream of tartar and 1 pint water. Rinse in clear water.

STAIN	FIBER	DIRECTIONS
Scorch	*Silk* *Wool* *Rayon*	Little can be done to remove scorch from these fabrics. The appearance of wool can be improved by a light brushing with a very fine sandpaper.
	Cotton *Linen*	Light scorch is generally removed by a regular washing and bleaching in the sun. Commercial bleaches of the right type may be used on white and colorfast fabrics.
Water *Spots*	*Silk* *Wool* *Rayon*	Brush spot with piece of same fabric or soft brush. Or scratch ring around spot with finger nail. If spot remains, rotate that part of garment above steaming spout of tea kettle—first covering spout with cheesecloth. Press garment while still slightly damp. Send badly spotted or splattered garments to dry-cleaner.
	Cotton *Linen*	Dip entire garment in cool water; roll in towel until just damp enough to iron.

WASHING ROUTINE

In doing your personal laundry, follow the regular washday routine—sort, soak, wash and rinse, dry, and iron, if necessary.

Sorting. Remove detachable shoulder pads and any trimmings that might discolor the garment—such as cloth buttons, belts, and bows. Sort clothing according to fabric and colorfastness. You will want to wash similar items with the same kind of soap or synthetic detergent and in water of the same temperature. Make a separate pile for each of the following:

> White and light colorfast cottons and linens (Blouses, T-shirts, lingerie, hankies, all-fabric gloves, anklets, collars, and cuffs.)
>
> Dark colorfast cottons and linens (Blouses, dresses, slacks.)
>
> Wash-and-wear cottons (Dresses, blouses.)
>
> Rayons (Dresses, blouses, sport shirts, lingerie, slacks.)
>
> White and colorfast silks (Blouses, lingerie.)
>
> Woolens and part-wools (Sport shirts, "snuggies," hosiery, scarves.)
>
> Thermoplastics, such as nylon, Dacron, Arnel, acetate, etc. (Blouses, dresses, hosiery, lingerie.)
>
> Garments that require special handling (Non-colorfast dresses, blouses, gloves, socks; woolen sweaters, mittens, heavy socks; washable leather gloves; girdles.)

Soaking. Cottons and linens are the only fibers which can stand much soaking. If they are really dirty, soaking loosens the dirt, and saves time and rubbing. If they are just lightly soiled, it is not necessary. Use the stronger variety of soap or synthetic detergent and lukewarm water. Soak in separate containers: all-white garments for 1 hour or more; light colorfast garments about

15 minutes; dark colorfast garments about 5 minutes. Give stubborn spots such as necklines or cuffs an extra soaping.

Never soak non-fast colors. Do not soak silks or synthetics; if heavily soiled, two thorough sudsings are better than one soaking and one sudsing for such fibers. Heavily soiled woolens, especially shrink-resistant ones, such as blouses, or knitted undies may be soaked for about 5 minutes in tepid water and mild suds. Never soak sweaters or other outer wear. Do not soak girdles with steel stays, either, because the stays may rust.

Sudsing and Rinsing. Good suds. and thorough rinsing mean a clean wash. If clothes have been soaked, drain off dirty water and wash in fresh suds. Use enough detergent or soap product to whip up an adequate suds. Always sprinkle the flakes or granules into the water gradually to prevent forming a mass which is difficult to dissolve.

Heavily soiled garments may need two sudsings. Rinse thoroughly until last water is clear. Three or more rinses are recommended. Soap and detergents, if allowed to remain in fabric, will discolor and spot the garment, and may ruin the fabric. Here are a few suggestions for the various fabrics.

White and light, colorfast cottons and linens require *hot* water (130°) and strong soap or detergent. Rub soiled spots and squeeze suds through garment. Washboards are useful for rubbing heavier fabrics, but hand rubbing is safer for finer fabrics. Small hand brushes are good for removing stubborn soil. After rubbing, swish garment in suds, then rinse thoroughly. The first rinse water should be hot, because hot water removes soap best. The last two rinses should be lukewarm (110°). Wring dry. If garments are lacy or fragile, squeeze.

Note: Boiling of white cottons and linens is not necessary when garments are thoroughly sudsed and rinsed.

Wash *dark, colorfast cottons and linens* in *warm* water (120°). Use fresh suds for best results, rather than the suds from the white and light colors, because white lint may adhere to dark fabrics. After clothes are thoroughly rubbed and sudsed, rinse first in warm water and follow with two lukewarm rinses. Wring or squeeze dry.

Most of your *wash-and-wear cottons* (those treated with resin finishes) can go into the family wash. Once they are dry, undergarments and children's play clothes can probably be worn without ironing. Many outer garments, however, will need a touch of the iron, or more, for a really well-pressed look.

Although cottons are not as crease-resistant as the thermoplastics, many cottons can be worn without ironing if they are washed carefully by hand. Here's the way to proceed for that very special dress or blouse you hope to wear without ironing.

Wash glazed, embossed, and other wash-and-wear cottons in cool to lukewarm detergent suds. To avoid wrinkles, brush the soiled areas with a liquid detergent and swish the article up and down. Do not wring. Rinse thoroughly, place on a rust-proof hanger, shape by hand, and allow to drip dry. Avoid chlorine bleach since many of these fabrics are injured by chlorine.

Rayons, unlike cottons and linens, are weaker when they are wet. For this reason, you should wash them more gently than you do ordinary cottons. Rough handling can cause frayed seams and sometimes holes! Use lukewarm to warm suds, rub gently, and squeeze out water instead of wringing. Almost all rayons, especially the spun variety, have been treated for wrinkle resistance, but most still need to be ironed. Press them on the wrong side to avoid glazing or flattening the texture. Caution: do not use a chlorine bleach on permanently finished rayons because it may cause deterioration.

Washable silks should be laundered in lukewarm water (110° F.) and mild suds. Strong suds can injure silk. Squeeze suds through garments; do not rub. Do not wash white and colored garments together. If you want to use the same suds, wash white garments first, then fast-colored ones. (Darker silks should usually be dry-cleaned.) Rinse thoroughly, using lukewarm water for all rinses. Careful rinsing is especially important since silk is injured by any trace of alkali left from the soap or detergent. Caution: never hang silks in the sunlight. Sunlight weakens silk and turns white silks yellow. Roll silk garments in a towel until they are ready to be pressed or dry them in the shade.

Wash *wools* in tepid water (100° F.) and generous, mild suds. Hot water shrinks wools. Never rub cake soap on wool fabrics; make suds of special wool soap or mild detergent. Squeeze suds through the fabric; do not rub. Squeeze out suds. Rinse three or *more* times in water of the *same temperature.* This is important, for wet wool is sensitive to quick changes of temperature, and it is also extremely sensitive to alkali. Squeeze dry; do not wring. Use dry cloths or towels to absorb excess moisture. Dry indoors at a moderate, even temperature, or outdoors in the shade (if the weather is warm). White wool, like white silk, is yellowed by the sun. Even the shrink-resistant wools retain their original size, softness, and color better if they are washed and dried in this way.

To launder *thermoplastic* fabrics successfully, remember that body oils, dirt, face powder, and similar things tend to remain on the surface *unless* they are driven into the fiber by *warm or hot water.* Furthermore, some of these fabrics (nylon in particular) have a tendency to pick up dirt and dyestuffs from dirty, discolored suds. Once thermoplastics become dingy or discolored, it is very difficult—and sometimes impossible—to bleach them back to their original whiteness or color. Thermoplastics also tend to develop deep-set wrinkles when they are handled roughly or at high temperatures.

Cold-water washing with liquid detergents may revolutionize the laundering of synthetics both by hand and machine. It removes body oils and soil readily, and articles can be washed repeatedly with little need for ironing.

To prevent soil and grease from penetrating the fibers, wash articles often and "cold-spot" neckbands, cuffs, and any other areas where body oils and soil have accumulated. To "cold-spot" garments, wet the area with *cold* water, then pour on a liquid detergent, and rub or scrub with a brush until the dirt disappears. For girdles, brassières, and other articles worn next to the body, immerse the entire garment in cold detergent suds, then scrub the particularly soiled areas with a brush and more detergent.

To prevent discoloration, dinginess, and wrinkles, wash synthetics (after cold-spotting any articles that need it) in clean, cool or lukewarm detergent suds. Separate articles into color groups and wash each separately, light colors before dark ones. For instance, wash whites, then pinks, then medium blues or tans, then browns, and finally blacks. (Thermoplastics do not form lint, as cottons do, and hence dark colors may be washed after light ones.)

White thermoplastics, particularly nylons, stay a clearer, brighter white if they are bleached each time they are laundered. Use a mild sodium perborate bleach and follow the directions on the package (and those given later in this chapter).

Be careful not to wrinkle articles as you wash them. Swish them up and down, squeeze them, and use a brush on stubborn spots. After rinsing thoroughly several times in cool water, either blot excess water in a towel or allow garments to drip-dry. Do not wring them! Smooth collars, cuffs, and hems with your fingers; then dry on rust-proof hangers or spread out smooth on a rod or line.

Fabrics made of *blends* of the thermoplastics are usually washed as if they were all thermoplastic. However, the other fiber or fibers must be considered too. You can wash a Dacron and cotton shirt, for instance, as you would a thermoplastic, but you *can* use a chlorine bleach which is effective on cotton and does not injure Dacron appreciably. An Orlon and wool skirt should be washed as a thermoplastic, *except* that all waters must be the same temperature—that is, tepid (100° F.). You should also be very careful to rinse the skirt thoroughly, roll it in a towel, and dry it in the shade at room temperature —just as you would an all-wool skirt.

Garments that require special care. For non-fast colors use *tepid* water (100°) and mild suds. Wash each garment separately and *quickly*. Rinse three times in tepid water. If color runs badly, spread garment flat on dry cloth. Place more cloth between all layers of garment so that no parts touch. Cover with dry cloth and pat out excess moisture. Hang to dry so that parts do not cling together. Dry quickly until just damp enough to iron. If garment is too wet, a hot iron may cause colors to run.

Sweaters, heavy woolen socks, and mittens have to be stretched to shape after they are washed. The first step in laundering wool knits, unless you have wire drying forms, is to trace an outline of the garment on heavy wrapping paper or old sheeting. It's a good idea to make an outline of each new sweater as you acquire it so that you can shape it to its original blocking each time it is laundered.

Wash and rinse a wool sweater as you do other wools except turn the sweater wrong side out and be particularly careful in lifting it out of the water. Use both hands cupped under it to prevent stretching it. Wash an Orlon or nylon sweater the same way except that you should cold-spot the neck band, as described in the section on laundering thermoplastics. Rinse waters need not be warm for these, of course.

Roll the sweater in a bath towel just long enough to get rid of the excess water and then shape it, right side out, on the pattern. Dry away from heat.

HOW TO WASH
A SWEATER

Procter & Gamble

Wash a sweater before it becomes too soiled. Hold it under water and squeeze the suds through gently. When you lift it out, cup the whole sweater in your hands. Careless lifting can stretch it out of shape. After rinsing, squeeze as much moisture from the sweater as you can without twisting it and roll it in a towel to remove still more water. Block your sweater on a dry towel, shaping it from the center out.

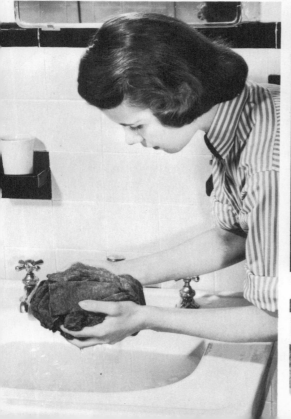

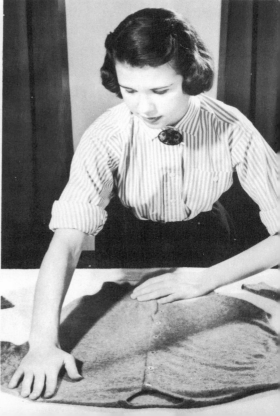

When dry, remove from pattern. Then, if necessary, press lightly, using a damp press cloth, or a dry press cloth and a steam iron. Brush lightly to restore nap.

Girdles should be washed frequently to preserve both their fabric and their shape. Cold-spot a thermoplastic one. Use lukewarm water and mild suds. Do not rub on a washboard. Brush soiled areas with a small hand brush. Rinse thoroughly in lukewarm water. Roll in Turkish towel to remove excess moisture. Dry flat or over towel rod away from heat. Do not clip garters on hanger as that stretches elastic. Press only lacy or fabric parts of garment; *never* elasticized parts. In fact, pressing is unnecessary.

Hosiery should be washed in mild lukewarm suds. Squeeze the suds through; never rub wool or nylon. Rinse two or three times in lukewarm water, squeezing the water through. Never wring water out of hosiery. Roll in a Turkish towel to absorb excess moisture. Gently shape the foot and leg of the stockings and place them over a smooth towel rod. Clothespins and metal clamps may snag or wear out sheer hosiery. Woolens and nylons should be kept away from heat. Nylons dry quickly, but allow from 24 to 36 hours for wool. Never wear any hosiery until it is thoroughly dry.

Leather gloves should never be washed unless they are marked "washable." Even then, once they have been dry-cleaned, they should not be washed. If you do wash your leather gloves, use tepid water and thick mild suds. Wash chamois and doeskin gloves off your hands, gently squeezing suds through the leather. Wash other leather gloves on your hands, gently massaging suds into the leather. Squeeze out the suds; rinse thoroughly in tepid water. Roll in a Turkish towel to absorb excess moisture. Remove immediately and shape gently. Blow into each glove to shape the fingers and then place the gloves on a clean cloth away from any source of heat. Before they are completely dry, soften them by gently massaging the leather between your thumb and forefinger. Rub and blow into the gloves alternately. Shape the cuffs, palms, and back of the gloves carefully. When all parts are soft and dry, crease the gussets between the fingers as in new gloves.

Bleaching, bluing, and starching. Although you may not often use any bleach, bluing, or starch for your personal laundry, it is a good idea to know something about them for the few occasions when you need it.

Bleaching is used principally on *white* cottons, linens, and thermoplastics, although other fibers may require bleaching at times. Do not bleach colored articles unless you know that they are "colorfast"; even then, use care and do not bleach them except when necessary.

Fortunately, really clean clothing needs little or no bleaching, for even the gentlest bleaching weakens fabrics slightly. To prevent excessive tendering (weakening), be sure the bleach is suitable for the fiber and finish. Use the minimum amount of bleach—no more than is recommended. Add it to sudsy water of the correct temperature and stir before adding the articles to be bleached. (Chemical bleaches are more effective in an alkaline solution than in plain water.) Leave the articles in the bleach solution only the prescribed length of time or until discolorations have disappeared; then rinse thoroughly. Never use bleach in the final rinse.

Bright sunshine bleaches cottons and linens beautifully, particularly if they are dried regularly outdoors in a sunny spot. Take cottons and linens indoors when they are dry, however, for long exposure to the sun weakens even these sturdy fabrics. White silks and wools must never be dried in the sun since sunlight yellows them. In fact, it is preferable to dry any protein fabric in the shade. You may dry thermoplastic fabrics in the sun although sunshine is not a particularly effective bleaching agent for them. Nylon, in particular, is actually weakened by exposure to sunlight.

Boiling suds have been used for generations to sterilize and bleach white cottons and linens. Cottons can stand 5 to 10 minutes of this treatment; linens should merely be scalded—that is, dipped in and then removed from the hot suds. These methods have been largely superseded today by other bleaching methods. Of course, you must never subject the protein or thermoplastic fabrics to boiling temperatures!

Chlorine bleach, the inexpensive household bleach and disinfectant that is sold under a variety of trade names, now comes in powder as well as liquid form. It is recommended for white and colorfast cottons, linens, and rayons. Follow instructions carefully, for chlorine is a strong chemical bleach. Here is an additional word of caution: Never use chlorine on any resin-treated fabric that is not guaranteed to be non-chlorine retentive. Some, but not all, resin finishes are chlorine retentive—that is, chlorine reacts chemically with them and cannot be rinsed out. The build-up of chlorine, especially in large quantities, weakens the fabric and in some cases will turn white garments yellow. Later, if the fabric is dried bone-dry, either by ironing or drying in a drier, it is likely to fall into shreds. Since polished, glazed, embossed, and wrinkle-resistant cottons and wrinkle-resistant linens and rayons are almost all resin-treated, chlorine is a questionable bleach for many of the cellulose fabrics. Of course, you must never use chlorine on protein fibers, such as silk and wool, for it will make them weak, harsh, and discolored. Chlorine is not particularly harmful to the thermoplastics, such as nylon and Dacron, but it also has little or no whitening effect on them.

Sodium perborate bleach, the powder that turns to peroxide of hydrogen when water is added, is also available under various trade names. It is a fairly gentle bleach recommended for white and colorfast materials made of *any* fiber. If used regularly, it will prevent the build-up of grayness or discoloration, since it not only bleaches, but also acts as a water softener for certain types of hard water. It is especially effective in keeping white nylon white.

Optical bleaches are fluorescent white compounds which are incorporated in soap and detergents to brighten white fabrics. They are not true bleaches but produce a whitening effect by emitting a bluish-white radiance which covers up the yellowish tinge.

Detergents with bluing and optical bleaches added have almost taken the place of a final bluing. However, some women still prefer the traditional method. Bluing actually does not whiten garments; it merely neutralizes yellowed fabrics causing them to appear less yellow. When white clothes are washed and rinsed properly, they require bluing only at rare intervals. Too much bluing can ruin the appearance of a garment; therefore, always test a sample before immersing it in the bluing bath. Prepare bluing water after garments have been thoroughly rinsed. Follow directions on product. Stir thoroughly to color water evenly. Immerse garments one at a time, stirring constantly. Remove and wring out.

Don't hang your pants like this unless you want puckers and rust spots.

Permanent finishes have made weekly starching almost a thing of the past; yet there are occasions when starch is needed. Starch is used to give cotton or linen garments a fresh or crisp look. You may wish to starch a blouse, dress, a piqué hat, or collars and cuffs. Clothes starch may be prepared as a cold solution or it may be cooked. The latter is more permanent and easier to iron. Either solution may be thin, medium, or thick, depending on the stiffness desired. There are also liquid preparations on the market, some of which contain a bit of bluing. Another variety, a "plastic starch," provides a starched finish that remains through several launderings. In using any one of these types of starches, follow directions on product. Because white starch often leaves light streaks on dark fabrics, use strained coffee to tint starch for all-brown garments, use bluing to tint starch for all-blue garments. Commercial dyes may be used to tint starches for other dark colors.

Drying. When possible, dry white cottons and linens in the sun and colored clothes in the shade or indoors. If you dry laundry indoors, hang it where air can circulate around it. Avoid extremes of temperature. Never dry garments near stoves or heaters, for heat can harm fibers. In freezing weather, hang the laundry indoors because stiff, frozen fabrics may tear easily.

Don't use clothespins to hang knitted garments or any delicate items, as pins tend to mat or stretch fibers, causing weak spots or tears. Hang knit lingerie carefully over a towel rod or a taut clothesline so that it will dry smoothly. Knit T-shirts retain their shape better when they are dried flat. Heavy woolens should also be dried flat to prevent sagging. Hang slips and nighties on wooden or rust-proof hangers, shaking them out for smooth drying. If they are hung on a clothesline, a clothespin, placed on either side of the hanger, will prevent them from sliding. Delicate items that need ironing should be rolled in a towel until they are dry enough to iron. Garments that must be ironed damp should be rolled in a towel until ironing time.

Hanger drying is advisable for all other blouses and dresses. This prevents pull or strain at hanging points and leaves few wrinkles to iron out. Arrange seersucker and chenille garments particularly carefully as these fabrics should not be ironed. (You can, if you like, press seams and hems in these materials from the wrong side when the garments are dry.) Before hanging a rayon jersey or crepe garment, roll it in a towel to absorb as much moisture as possible. Arrange the garment carefully on a hanger and shape it while it is drying so that it will not sag or stretch unevenly with the weight of the moisture. If water collects at the hemline, press it out with a towel. Blot up excess water from thermoplastics, too, if dripping water is a problem. Otherwise, shape them and let them drip dry.

Fabric gloves require no pressing when they are dried properly. Remove excess moisture by rolling them in a towel; smooth carefully to original shape. Blow into each glove to shape the fingers and dry them flat on a clean paper or towel. Clothespin hanging spoils the cuff line. Glove frames are convenient.

Ironing. Take down garments that are not colorfast when they are dry enough to iron and iron them right away. (You can protect the ironing board cover with a piece of old sheeting.) If a silk or rayon fabric is more easily ironed when bone dry (such as pongee or some lightweight spun rayons), leave the garment on a hanger until you are ready to iron it. Some wash-and-wear cottons and synthetics need "touch up" ironing. Iron them while they are slightly damp or with a steam iron.

White and colorfast cottons and linens may also be gathered when they are just damp enough to iron, if you plan to iron within the next few hours. If not, let them dry thoroughly. There is danger of mildew if damp clothes are covered for many hours unless you have room for them in your refrigerator. Dampen them for several hours before you iron them. Use warm, soft water. A bottle with a sprinkler nozzle dampens clothes more evenly than sprinkling them with your fingers does. Starched garments and all linens should be quite damp. Fold and wrap articles in a heavy towel or keep them in a plastic bag. Woolens should never be damp for pressing. When they are completely dry, press them with a steam iron or damp press cloth. For directions on ironing, refer to technique 12, "Pressing."

IRONING ROUTINES FOR TRICKY GARMENTS

Westinghouse

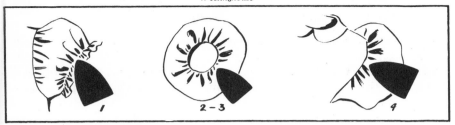

A CHILD'S PUFFED SLEEVE

1. Iron cuff first.
2. Fold sleeve back upon itself, matching cuff with armhole opening.
3. Iron sleeve, cuff side, first. Work point of iron into fullness at cuff.
4. Iron shoulder side, working point of iron into fullness at shoulder.

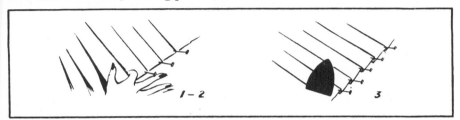

PLEATS

1. Work pleats into place with fingers, a few at a time.
2. Pin or even baste at hem if difficult to keep in place.
3. Iron hem first and work upward, pulling garment slightly against iron. Work on wrong side of fabric, if possible.

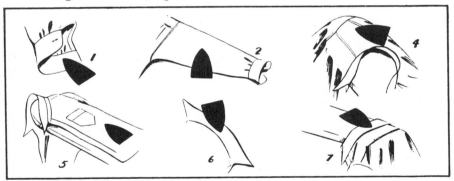

SHIRT

1. Iron cuffs first; inner surface first, outer surface second.
2. Iron body of sleeve, cuff opening side first.
3. Repeat on other sleeve.
4. Iron yoke. Slip one shoulder over end of board. Iron from center of back to shoulder. Reverse and iron other side of yoke.
5. Iron body of shirt beginning with one front and continuing to other front (or iron both fronts first if fabric is drying out quickly).
6. Iron collar, under surface first, upper surface second, working iron inward from edges.
7. Fold collar down, press over end of board.

HOME DRY-CLEANING

Garments that cannot be laundered should be sent to a reputable dry-cleaner. Home dry-cleaning is not recommended for several reasons. Many dry-cleaning solvents are inflammable and thus endanger the whole household. In addition, the solvents may create harmful fumes. They can injure the skin if they are not properly handled. And finally, the home process is never so thorough as that used by a professional cleaner who has special equipment and many kinds of solvents. A person working at home generally uses scanty amounts that cannot clean the garment thoroughly.

It is possible to dry-clean a few small, light-colored articles, such as gloves, blouses, or scarves, at home. Use a dry-cleaning fluid *only* outdoors or in a well-ventilated room *away* from all gas jets and any type of flame. Follow the directions on the product. Heavy or dark fabrics are not successfully cleaned at home because they require large amounts of solvent for good results. It is neither practical nor economical to dry-clean them at home.

ACTIVITIES

For the class

1. **Appoint** a committee to collect information for the class bulletin board about stain removal and laundering methods. They can send for pamphlets as well as collect articles from magazines and newspapers.
2. **Ask** for volunteers to demonstrate washing:
   a. a sweater
   b. heavy woolen socks
   c. washable leather gloves
   d. a girdle
3. **Appoint** one person to make arrangements for the class to visit a dry-cleaning plant.

For the individual

Collect swatches of different fabrics and stain them with the stains listed in the chart in this chapter. Remove the stains according to directions. It is better to practice on scraps of material than on actual garments.

TECHNIQUES ▶

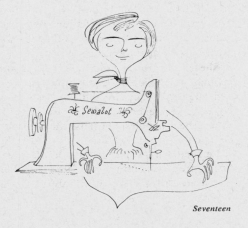

Seventeen

TECHNIQUE I   *SEWING EQUIPMENT*

Perhaps it is possible to learn to sew with makeshift tools, but the odds are against anyone who tries to do it. The girl with dull scissors, bent pins, and huge needles has to struggle every step of the way. Too often the dowdy garment which she makes seems to reflect the battle she has waged.

Borrowing from a neighbor is just as bad. The borrower must use whatever equipment is available whenever she can get it. Not only is she inconvenienced, but so is her neighbor. Borrowing is not one of the methods for becoming the most popular girl in a class.

It is not necessary for you to own everything you use. Your school will supply some equipment. Look around your clothing laboratory. You are likely to see sewing machines, ironing boards, cutting tables, mirrors, and perhaps low platforms for use in fitting. If you looked in closets and drawers you might find irons, yardsticks, skirt-markers, tracing wheels, pinking shears, and many other new gadgets which have recently appeared in sewing centers throughout the country.

Some schools furnish everything a girl needs in the way of sewing equipment. They furnish needles, pins, thimbles—everything. Others furnish only the larger, more expensive pieces. Whatever arrangement your school may have, you will need to know what equipment is available, how to use it, and how to care for it.

CUTTING DEVICES

All cutting tools should be of as fine quality as you can afford. Consider their purchase an investment, for with proper care scissors and shears should last for many years. Ideally you should have both shears and scissors, but there is an intermediate cutting tool that can substitute for both. This tool is called a pair of trimmers or light trimming shears.

Cut only cloth with your fine cutting tools. Have available old or cheap scissors for cutting heavy paper, string, and other harsh substances which make scissors dull.

Keep your cutting tools clean, dry, and stored away from the moisture of the air. Oil the blades and hinges occasionally, being careful to wipe away excess oil. This treatment will protect them from rust and make them easy to handle. Try oiling new scissors that seem stiff at the joint; you will be amazed at the improvement in their operation.

Shears. Shears are used for general cutting. They should be large enough, heavy enough, and have long enough blades to cut smooth straight lines but not so heavy and large that they are difficult to manage. Seven to 8 inches is a good length. Expert dressmakers usually prefer shears with handles at an angle to the blades, called "bent handles," because they permit the fabric to lie flat on the table as it is being cut.

Left-handed people require left-handed shears if they are to avoid blistered fingers from big cutting jobs. Notice the bevelled surfaces on the handles of shears which are planned for the comfort of right-handed people. Grasp a pair of such shears in your right hand, as if for cutting, and notice how smooth the handles feel to your thumb and fingers. Now switch them to your left hand and notice how sharp the handles feel.

The smaller handle on shears is for the thumb, and the larger one is for two or three fingers. Often the index finger is kept in front of the large handle to give better control; the little finger may, or may not, be kept inside the handle, depending upon which way seems more comfortable.

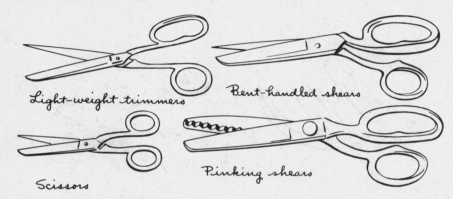

Light-weight trimmers

Bent-handled shears

Scissors

Pinking shears

Scissors. Scissors are designed for cutting threads, trimming, and slashing. They are smaller and lighter than shears. About 5 to 6 inches is a good length for a pair of scissors. When cutting around curves, or for other precision work, scissors are much easier to handle than shears.

The best kind of scissors for your purposes have blades of uneven width. They should be held so that the wider blade is above the narrower blade. Try inserting the narrow sharp blade in the central area of a piece of fabric. Notice that you can start cutting from this point in any direction. This is a useful technique for buttonholes and other details where you cannot cut from the edge of the fabric inward.

Pinking shears. Pinking shears are useful for finishing the edges of seams and other raw edges of fabric. The notched cutting line they produce discourages raveling, and is an adequate finish for most firmly woven materials. When cutting with pinking shears it is important that you exert pressure only in a vertical direction—never crosswise. To force the handles sidewise as you cut throws the edges out of line and prevents the proper operation of the shears.

SEWING TOOLS

Needles. The best quality sewing needles are made of hand-ground steel. Points are sharp, and eyes are smooth and well polished. *Sharps* are most commonly used for hand sewing. These are medium length needles with a short oval eye. *Crewel* needles, designed for embroidery work, have a long oval eye, and are, therefore, easily threaded.

Both styles of needles come in a variety of sizes—the smaller numbers indicating the larger needles. Some packages contain needles of one size only; others contain assorted sizes. The most suitable sizes for general hand sewing are 7's and 8's.

The paper used in needle packages is treated to prevent needles from rusting. It is wise, therefore, to store your needles in the package. When needles become dull from exposure, run them through an emery bag—that little strawberry attached to your pin cushion. This treatment will brighten and clean them. Needles should not be left in the emery bag, however, because it attracts moisture and causes them to rust.

Pins. Pins should be sharp, slender, and smoothly finished so that they will not injure delicate materials. Silk pins are the finest kind. Dressmakers' pins are a little

A "Sharp" and a "Crewel" needle
(Magnified)

Pin cushion with
emery bag

coarser, but are satisfactory for all but the most delicate fabrics. Sizes 16 or 17 (which refers to length) is an excellent choice. Pins which are purchased in paper folders are usually coarser than these, which come in boxes, but if carefully selected, may be satisfactory for use on sturdy materials.

Thimble. Your success in hand sewing depends largely upon your choice of a thimble, for, without a good one, you cannot develop the most efficient hand-sewing techniques. A metal thimble with well-formed markings, or indentations, is excellent. It is thin and sturdy, and the clear markings hold the eye-end of the needle firmly as you force it through the material.

Some people prefer plastic thimbles, claiming they are more comfortable to use over long periods of time. The disadvantages of plastic thimbles are their bulkiness and the shallowness of their markings.

Fit your thimble finger. This is the second, or middle finger of your right hand—unless, of course, you are left-handed. The thimble should cling, but not bind your finger. The tip of your finger should almost, but not quite, reach the thimble-end. Sizes commonly range from 5, which is small, to 12, which is large.

Pin cushion with emery bag. A pin cushion will keep your pins ready for use. Cushions filled with wool, sawdust, or many other materials are excellent because they will take pins readily. Avoid those filled with cotton for they are difficult to use. The emery bag, as noted under "Needles," is used for cleaning and sharpening needles.

Basting thread. For basting thread you may use thread which is especially made for basting, or any other medium weight thread. Silk thread is best for basting satins, velvets, and materials that mar easily. Partly used spools in different colors, left from other sewing, can be used for this purpose.

MEASURING TOOLS

Tape measure. The 60 inch tape measure is preferred for dressmaking. Numbers should start at opposite ends on reverse sides. Select a tape that is firm and will not

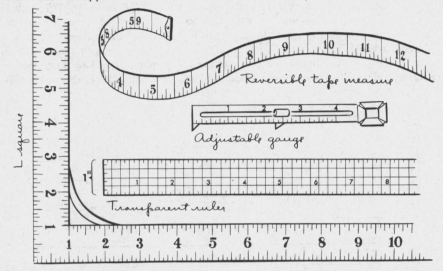

ravel at the edges. A plastic coating tends to prevent crushing, stretching, and shrinking. Keep your tape neatly rolled or folded and do not attempt to tie it into knots as you would a string.

Ruler. Rulers come in various lengths: 6, 12, 18, 36, and 48 inches. The 36 inch ruler is often called a yardstick because of its one yard length. Even though you have a tape measure, you will need rulers for marking straight lines. A small one is handy to have in your workbox. A transparent plastic ruler has the advantage of permitting you to see through it and its edges, like those of metal-edged rulers, remain smooth and true with continued use. A plastic ruler marked off across the end as well as lengthwise is a marvelous tool if you can find it. Perhaps your school supplies several yardsticks which will be enough for the whole class.

Square. Squares for dressmaking are L-shaped. They are used to draw perpendicular lines, and to obtain square corners.

Adjustable gauge. An adjustable gauge simplifies measuring hems, tucks, and other short distances. There is a metal gauge with adjustable pointer on the market today which measures distances up to 4 inches. However, you can always cut pieces of cardboard for gauges of different widths instead of buying one.

Skirt-markers. Skirt-markers are used to measure and mark the hemlines of skirts. One type makes a chalk line as it is moved around the skirt. This method is fast, but, unfortunately, chalk lines do not show on all fabrics and colors. Another skirt-marker requires pins instead of chalk. It gives a sharp, clear line on any material.

MARKING DEVICES

Dressmaker's tracing paper. Dressmaker's tracing paper is used with a tracing wheel to transfer markings from the pattern to the cloth. It may be bought in large sheets, either colored or white. White is the only truly safe tracing paper; colored papers often mar cloth permanently. On heavy fabrics you can sometimes use yellow, the palest of the colors, without injury—but test it first. As an added precaution, make all your markings on the wrong side of the material. The bottom piece of tracing paper should be mounted on heavy cardboard to protect the table or other surface from being marred by the points of the tracing wheel.

Tracing wheel. For transferring markings from pattern to cloth the saw-tooth tracing wheel gives the best results, except on heavy materials. These may require the longer spikes of a needlepoint tracing wheel. Occasionally oil the metal disk of your tracing wheel as you do your scissors.

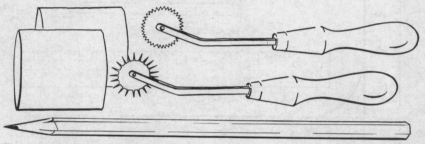

Tailor's chalk: cake + pencil ... Tracing wheels: saw-tooth + needlepoint

Tailor's chalk. Tailor's chalk is used for marking directly on the fabric, preferably on the wrong side. It comes in both cake and pencil forms, and with either a wax or a clay base. The wax type may be removed from wool by ironing. On other fabrics, however, it may leave grease marks. For cloth other than wool, clay-base tailor's chalk is the kind to use. Beware of strong colors in either type because the coloring matter from chalk, like that from tracing paper, is often difficult to remove and might mar the appearance of the finished garment. White chalk is the safest, but obviously will not show on white and light colored materials. If you must use colored chalk, test it on a scrap of your fabric before marking your dress with it.

MISCELLANEOUS SEWING AIDS

Loop-turner. A loop-turner facilitates turning belts, cloth loops, and strips of all kinds. It consists of a long wire rod with a hook at one end.

Point-turner. This is a little flat instrument with a pointed end, designed for turning the points of collars and such. It is very helpful.

Orange-wood stick. An orange-wood stick, the kind used in manicuring, is useful for turning and shaping points of collars, belts, and similar details if you don't have a point-turner.

Stiletto. A stiletto is a sharp-pointed instrument for punching holes in material. It is used for forming eyelets in belts and for embroidery work.

Bodkin. A bodkin resembles a large blunt needle. It is used to thread cord, tape, or ribbon through casings or eyelets.

Crochet hook. A crochet hook may be used to form chain-stitch loops, or to assist in making fringe.

Tweezers. Tweezers are a help in ripping bastings and machine stitching.

Ripper. Razor blade rippers with handles are effective, but dangerous to use for ripping.

Beeswax. Beeswax may be rubbed on thread to strengthen it for use in sewing on buttons or wherever thread needs strengthening. It is good for smoothing the surface of an iron also.

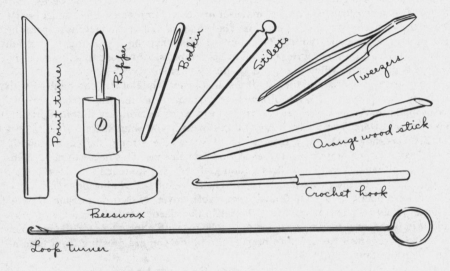

PRESSING TOOLS

Irons. Pressing has to be done throughout clothing construction so be sure that your equipment is convenient to use. Keep any type of iron clean at all times. Avoid pressing materials that may soil or stick to it. Wipe it with a clean damp cloth occasionally, and dry immediately. Run a warm iron over a piece of waxed paper now and then to smooth and polish its surface. Or, if you prefer, use beeswax. Place a small piece of the beeswax on several layers of paper or cloth, and run the warm iron over it until the surface of the iron is smooth.

When starch or other substances have stuck to an iron, scrubbing with an abrasive may be the only solution. Steel wool that is fine enough not to scratch the surface will remove such foreign substances. Remember that the sooner soil is removed, the easier the job will be.

Store a hot iron carefully. Never permit it to come in contact with anything that it might injure. Since heat injures an iron cord, don't wrap the cord around a hot iron. Neither should you take the cord from the outlet by pulling the cord. Grasp the plug instead.

Automatic iron. The automatic electric iron takes much of the guesswork out of pressing. By merely setting its heat control, you can maintain a suitable temperature for any fabric. Recent studies have shown that heavy pressure is not what does the pressing; it is moisture, and the smooth, heated surface of the iron. Manufacturers are, therefore, making lighter-weight irons, which are far less tiring to use than old-style, heavy irons.

Non-automatic iron. The non-automatic iron, whether heated on the kitchen stove or by electricity, must be constantly checked to see that the temperature is right. Irons without heat controls require more skill to use, but can give satisfactory results.

Steam iron. The steam iron contains a chamber where water is converted into steam. This flow of steam over the material makes a damp press cloth unnecessary. Since the iron can be used directly on the underside of most materials, pressing need no longer be done "blind." The operator sees what she is pressing. The steam iron can be used on any fabric, though napped fabrics, and those that shine easily, require a press cloth when you press on the right side.

Some steam irons require the use of distilled water while others can be used with ordinary tap water. Check the directions that come with the iron. Irons are also being made that can be used either as steam irons or as ordinary automatic irons. You just add water and make a simple adjustment if you want steam.

Other pressing tools. Any ironing board should be strong, flat, and smooth. Either wood or perforated metal gives a good firm surface. This needs to be padded. Old woolen blankets make excellent padding, if they are stretched free of wrinkles. Pads designed for the purpose can be bought for standard ironing boards.

Over the padding, a snug-fitting, removable cover of scorch-resistant cotton material is needed. This may have a drawstring or elastic around the outer edge to hold it in place, or it may be fastened on the board with clips made for the purpose. Keep the cover fresh and clean to prevent the fabric you are pressing from becoming soiled or stained.

A general-purpose standard ironing board. For general pressing and ironing use, a board should be about 15 by 54 inches. It should have one end and the space below it free so that skirts and other circular garments may be slipped over the board. Some boards are adjustable in height so that you may sit on an ordinary chair or stand and work comfortably. On some boards, a convenient device holds the cord out of the way above the board as you press.

Sleeve board. A sleeve board is almost a "must" for professional-looking pressing. Not only is it needed for sleeves, but it may be used for shrinking and shaping fabric, and for pressing "hard-to-get-at" spots. Whether it is purchased or made at home, a sleeve board should be about 20 inches long, narrow and tapered. Both ends should be rounded, or shaped to a curve.

Press cloth. Press cloths are essential for ironing some fabrics. They may be of cheese cloth, cotton drill, muslin, colorless wool flannel, or other similar materials. Chemically treated, heavy press cloths may be purchased ready to use. Never use unbleached muslin for a press cloth unless it has been washed numerous times, because the natural oils in new muslin stick to the iron. When this gummy substance is allowed to remain there, it scorches and discolors whatever is being pressed. To remove such gum from an iron requires thorough scouring.

Bowl and sponge: A slightly damp sponge or cloth is useful for dampening fabric or press cloth.

Tailor's cushion. Use either a tailor's cushion, a tailor's ham, or a press mitt for shaping fabric and pressing curved seams. The tailor's ham is especially useful in pressing suits and coats.

A needle board. A needle board, while expensive, does take the worry out of pressing velvet and other pile fabrics. It consists of many short erect wires embedded in a flexible back. Pile fabrics are turned right side down on the surface formed by the ends of the projecting wires, and are pressed on the wrong side.

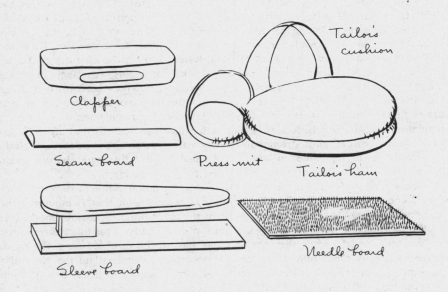

A seam board. A seam board consists of a half-round board or strip, padded and covered. You can buy a half-round stick at a lumberyard and cover it yourself. When you press a seam open on its curved surface you prevent an imprint of the seam edges showing on the right side of the garment.

Clapper. A clapper will help you give garments their final pressing. It is especially useful for suits or coats of wool or other heavy materials because it flattens top surfaces so that seams and heavy areas leave no imprint on the right side. After you get steam into the area (with a dry press cloth and a steam iron or a damp press cloth and an ordinary iron) clap the clapper—you see the reason for its name—on for a few seconds until the steam has left. You can make one very easily from a 2 by 4 board. Simply saw it off to 10 inches in length and sand it to smooth the rough edges and round the corners.

TECHNIQUE 2   *THE SEWING MACHINE*

        Sewing machines range in size from small toy and travel models, often operated by hand, to heavy power machines used in industry. For home use portable models are light and easily stored. Cabinet models are generally preferred, however, for large articles and where much sewing is to be done. Electric powered machines are less tiring to use than treadle machines, but well oiled and cared for foot-power models are not difficult to operate.

Some sewing machines form a *chain-stitch,* requiring but one thread. These are relatively inexpensive, but the stitch is not entirely satisfactory, since it rips too easily to be durable. Also, the stitch is different on the opposite sides of the cloth, which complicates stitching procedures. Sewing machines that make the *zig-zag stitch,* in addition to a regulation stitch, are now available for home use. These use one or two needles and various mechanical devices to help the operator make numerous embroidery stitches, buttonholes, finishes for seams, etc. Such machines are relatively expensive and complicated to operate, but they perform operations hitherto limited to industrial machines. By far the most popular type for general use is the sewing machine that makes the *lock-stitch,* or what we think of as a regulation machine stitch. It uses two threads which interlock in the fabric. When well adjusted, this stitch is strong and equally attractive on either side of the cloth. Since most sewing machines in homes and schools are of this type, the discussion in this book will be limited to machines that form a lock-stitch.

Even among lock-stitch machines there is great variation. Some have round bobbins, some have long ones. One bobbin case is separate, another is built into the machine. Devices for regulating the length of the stitch differ on various models, as do the mechanisms for regulating the tension on threads. You must thread one needle from the left, while the next one may have to be threaded from the right. These and many other differences make it necessary to understand the particular machine you are using. For this reason manufacturers supply instructions with each machine they sell. Some companies supply free student manuals [1] to classes.

Your teacher will probably show you how to operate the sewing machines in your laboratory. Nevertheless, you should keep a booklet of instructions or a student manual in a convenient place and refer to it for specific information. This textbook will give you general information which should help you understand and operate any machine.

PARTS OF THE LOCK-STITCH MACHINE

No matter how different they may seem, all lock-stitch sewing machines produce the same kind of stitch and operate on much the same principles. All require one thread above the cloth and one below and interlock these threads in the cloth at regular intervals. Here are some of the parts each sewing machine has and the function each part performs:

---

[1] The Singer Sewing Machine Company's *Student's Manual of Machine Sewing* is generally available. Other sewing machine companies may have something from time to time.

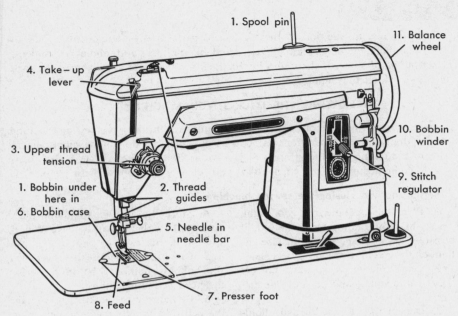

1. Spool pin

11. Balance wheel

4. Take–up lever

3. Upper thread tension

1. Bobbin under here in 6. Bobbin case

2. Thread guides

10. Bobbin winder

9. Stitch regulator

5. Needle in needle bar

7. Presser foot

8. Feed

Copyright © 1958 by The Singer Manufacturing Company
All Rights Reserved for All Countries

1. The *spool pin* with its spool of thread, and the *bobbin* filled with thread furnish the thread supply. Thread is fed from these two points to other mechanical parts as it is needed.

2. The *thread guides* hold the thread in position from the spool to the needle.

3. The *tensions*, upper and bobbin, hold the threads slightly taut. Without tension, threads would be fed so rapidly that loops would form along the surface of the cloth, as indeed happens when a tension is too loose or is bypassed in threading.

4. The *take-up lever* moves down to loosen the top thread as the stitch is formed and up to remove the slack as the stitch is completed.

5. The *needle* attached to the *needle bar*, pierces the cloth and carries the top thread below into the bobbin chamber.

6. The *bobbin case*, or *shuttle*, moves into position to catch the top thread and form the stitch as the needle is lowered into the bobbin chamber.

7. The *presser foot*, when lowered, holds the cloth firmly in position. Most new machines come with a hinged presser foot which makes it possible to sew over pins. For older models, hinged or flexible presser feet can be bought for a small price.

8. The *feed*, directly beneath the presser foot, pushes the cloth backward the required amount as each stitch is made. (The presser foot must be lowered for this operation.)

9. The *stitch regulator* controls the length of the stitch by regulating the stroke of the feed. Some regulators can be set to stitch in reverse.

10. The *bobbin winder* facilitates winding the thread on the bobbin. Some stop turning automatically when the bobbin is filled.

11. The *clutch* in the center of the *balance wheel* engages and disengages the stitching mechanism. (Refer to the picture above to locate these and other machine parts.)

Attachments. In addition to these essential parts, many attachments are available: hemmers, tuckers, seam guides, binders, quilters, buttonhole attachments. Descriptions of some of these and instructions for their use are given in the techniques to which they apply.

OPERATING THE LOCK-STITCH MACHINE

Success in sewing cannot be achieved without skill in using the sewing machine. Master the necessary operations as soon as possible, but do not be dicouraged if your first stitching is not as straight as you would like it to be. You will soon learn how to stitch accurately and efficiently if you practice and follow these suggestions.

Setting up and closing the sewing machine

1. Place the machine in a good light. The light should come from the left, if possible. Do not face the light. Use the light on the machine whenever necessary.

2. Learn the steps in their correct order for opening and closing the machine.

3. Detach the electric cord by holding the plug not the cord.

4. Store the cord in the same place each time so that it will be easy to find. Fold it, do not twist or knot it.

5. Close the bed slide (the cover over the bobbin chamber) before lowering the head of the machine.

6. Remember to loosen or disengage the belt of a treadle machine before attempting to lower the head.

Sitting at the machine

1. Use a comfortable straight chair, placing it squarely in front of the machine.

2. Sit upright with both feet squarely on the floor unless they are needed to operate a foot pedal or a treadle.

Learning to operate the power control of an electric machine

1. Bring either the knee lever or the foot pedal into a comfortable position.

2. Disengage the clutch.

3. Practice starting and stopping the machine by pressing and releasing the control. Notice that the amount of pressure you exert on the lever or pedal controls the speed of the motor. Learn to run the machine smoothly at both low and higher speeds. Do not grasp the balance wheel while still pressing the control although you may place your hand on it to stop the machine after releasing the pressure.

Learning to treadle a foot-power machine

1. Disengage the clutch.

2. Start the power wheel (the large one) in the correct direction, first by hand, then by treadling gently. This engages the belt and starts the balance wheel. To disengage the head of the machine, raise the belt shifter before you stop treadling.

Learning to "stitch" along lines. Engage the clutch. Leave the machine unthreaded and practice stitching on paper along lines of various shapes. Printed sheets can usually be obtained from sewing machine companies for school use. The needle perforates the paper, making it easy to tell how accurately you are stitching. Stitch on straight lines, curved lines, broken lines, and lines with corners until you can control the machine reasonably well.

Stitch around *curves* by turning the paper gradually as you stitch. Stitch more slowly than on straight lines. On extremely sharp curves raise the presser foot at intervals. To turn a *corner,* stop with the needle down. Raise the presser foot. Pivot the paper on the needle. Lower the presser foot; then stitch the other side of the corner.

Later when you are stitching on cloth instead of printed paper sheets, you can take your choice of several aids to keep your stitching straight and true. More and more teachers are having their students use guide lines or machine attachments for this purpose. Any of these stitching guides are helpful:

Traced lines, reproducing those on the pattern, are easy to follow when accurately made. (See the technique 8, "Cutting and Marking.")

The seam guide, an attachment which is furnished with most sewing machines, can be set at various distances from the presser foot. When the seam edges are kept against the guide, the stitching line is parallel to the edge of the cloth.

If you do not have a seam guide, you may use gummed, plastic, or contact tape pasted to the machine head to the right of the presser foot.

The edge stitcher, another attachment, is useful for stitching along the outer edge of facings, collars, cuffs, belts, and the like. It can be adjusted to stitch different distances up to about ¼ inch from the edge of the material.

Some machines have ruled lines beside the feed to guide you.

The presser foot itself has one wide and one narrow prong. Hence, it can guide you for two edge widths.

Threading the lock-stitch machine

Winding the round bobbin. (For long-bobbin machines refer to the instructions that come with the machine.)

1. Place the spool on the spool pin and draw the thread through the guide.

2. Thread from the inside of the bobbin outward. Turn the threaded side of the bobbin to the left to place it on the bobbin winder. (Start with a bare bobbin. Don't wind one color thread over another.)

3. Turn the bobbin on the winder until it clicks into place. (Do not force the bobbin winder enough to bend it.)

4. Press the winder until the rubber ring touches the hub of the balance wheel and is held there.

5. Disengage the clutch.

6. Hold the thread end loosely and start the power. When winding has been well started, pull the thread gently. The motion of the bobbin will cut it off quite clean.

7. Make sure that the thread winds on the bobbin evenly.

Under threading. Some bobbin cases are removable. Others are built into the bobbin chamber.

1. Insert the bobbin in the case so that the thread unwinds in the required direction, either clockwise or counterclockwise, depending on the model. Unless it is turned in the proper direction, the tension will be inadequate on the under thread, and the bobbin case may not remain threaded. See next page.

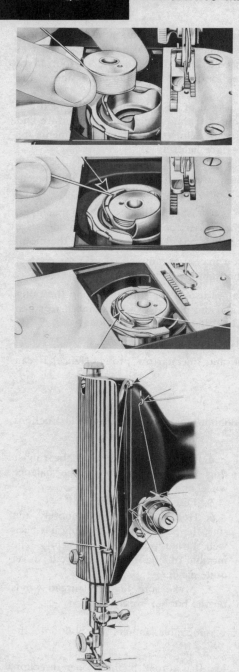

Copyright U.S.A. (July 26, 1935, and September 27, 1951) by The Singer Manufacturing Co. All Rights Reserved for All Countries.

2. Pull the thread through the openings and grooves, as directed for the particular model. Test the tension on the bobbin thread by pulling the thread end gently. There should be slight, but noticeable, tension and the bobbin should stay firmly in place. It should not bob up and down.

3. Leave a thread end 3 or 4 inches long extending from the bobbin case.

4. If your bobbin case is separate, now insert it in the machine.

5. Close the bed slide with the end of the thread drawn up through the slot or groove provided. (If no slot is provided, leave bed slide open slightly.)

Top threading

1. Raise the take-up lever to its highest point and keep it there throughout the threading operation as well as when the machine is not in use.

2. Place a spool of thread on the spool pin.

3. Thread through the guide above the tension.

4. Thread the tension, being sure that the thread goes through the tension spring correctly. There should be slight but noticeable tension. Some springs thread automatically, some must be threaded manually after you pull the thread between the tension disks.

5. Thread the take-up lever from the right or the side nearest the tension. (Notice that all machines require threading the tension before threading the take-up lever. If you remember that fact, you should be able to thread any sewing machine, because these are the only mechanical devices except guides between the spool pin and the needle.)

6. Thread the remaining guides which lead to the needle.

7. Thread the needle from the side on which the last guide appears.

8. Leave 3 or 4 inches of thread extending beyond the eye of the needle.

Bringing the bobbin thread up through the needle hole

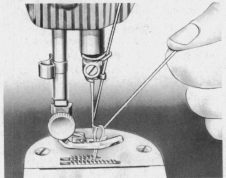

1. Grasp the end of the top thread with your left hand and hold it taut.

2. Turn the balance wheel with your right hand to make one complete stitch, stopping with the take-up lever at its highest position.

3. The bobbin thread will be pulled up through the needle hole in the form of a loop. Pull the loop to bring the end of the bobbin thread out.

Copyright U.S.A. (September 27, 1951) by The Singer Manufacturing Co. All Rights Reserved for All Countries

Starting to stitch

1. Have the presser foot raised.

2. Have the take-up lever at its highest position (as usual).

3. Draw the top thread downward between the prongs of the presser foot.

4. Pull both threads backward to prevent them from becoming knotted at the beginning of the stitching line.

5. Place the largest part of the material to the left of the needle.

6. Never start stitching without the cloth well under the needle. To do so would cause the threads to become entangled in the bobbin chamber, thus locking the machine.

a. For ordinary seams lower the presser foot so that it straddles the stitching line with the needle over the starting point.

b. For a seam which must start at a particular point, first lower the needle into the starting point by turning the wheel by hand. Then lower the presser foot.

Stitching. While you are stitching, guide the material with both hands, generally. There is a tendency for the lower layer to feed more rapidly than the upper one. For that reason it is wise to hold the two layers slightly taut, with the left hand holding the seam back of the needle and the right holding it in front. When stitching jersey or bias seams, stretch even a bit more. However, do not pull the material forward or backward as you guide it, because the machine feeds the cloth smoothly and regularly to form stitches of equal length. Any interference with this process will give uneven stitches.

Ending the line of stitching

1. Reduce the speed of the motor as you approach the end of the stitching line. As you bring the motor to a stop, place your hand on the balance wheel for better control. Do not sew beyond the cloth, as it dulls the feed and entangles the threads.

2. Stop with the take-up lever at its highest point.

3. Raise the presser foot.

4. Draw material back, being careful that both threads remain below presser foot. Hold balance wheel to prevent needle from being lowered as you do this.

5. Cut the threads on the thread cutter or with scissors. Leave several inches of thread extending from the machine or the needle will come unthreaded.

Testing and adjusting the stitch. Before starting to sew a garment, test the stitch on a scrap of the material you are using. Fold a rectangle of cloth crosswise so that grain lines match. Stitch a triangle through the two thicknesses, first along one grain, then along the other, and then on the bias. Mark the sides so that you will know which was on top as you sewed.

The thread. Notice the color, size, and texture of the thread. It should blend with the cloth inconspicuously.

THREAD AND NEEDLE CHART

FABRICS	THREAD TYPE AND SIZE	HAND NEEDLE SIZE	MACHINE NEEDLE SIZE	MACHINE STITCHES PER INCH
COTTON AND LINEN				
Heavy Coating Materials, Canvas, Denim, Duck, Drilling, Sail Cloth, Corduroy, Terry Cloth	Cotton 20–40, or Mercerized Cotton "Heavy Duty"	4, 5, 6	16, 18 or Medium Coarse	12–14
Gingham, Chambray, Madras, Poplin, Broadcloth, Percale, Velveteen, Dress Linen	Cotton 50 70, or Mercerized Cotton 50	7, 8	14, 16, or Medium	14–16
Voile, Dimity, Lawn, Batiste, Organdy, Marquisette, Handkerchief Linen	Cotton 80–150, or Mercerized Cotton "Sheer Fabric" (not often available) or Mercerized Cotton 50	8, 9, 10	9, 11, or Fine	16–20
WOOL, SILK, MAN-MADE FIBERS. AND BLENDS				
Coat and Suit Weights of Woolen, Worsted, and Blends	Silk A, B, or Mercerized Cotton 50	6, 7	14, 16, or Medium	12–14
Medium Dress-Weight Woolens, Worsteds, Silks, Rayons, and blends such as Crepes, Gabardines, Flannel, Taffeta, Satins, Velvets	Silk A, or Mercerized Cotton 50	7, 8	14, or Medium	14–16
Sheer Silks, Rayons, and Acetates such as Marquisettes, Ninon, Chiffon	Silk A, or Mercerized Cotton "Sheer Fabric"	8, 9, 10	9, 11, or Fine	16–20
Synthetic Fibers such as Nylon, Acrilan, Dacron, Dynel, Orlon and blends of these	Nylon (for durability), or Silk A, or Mercerized Cotton 50	7, 8, 9	Fine (to prevent holes, injury to yarns and drawn seam lines)	14–16

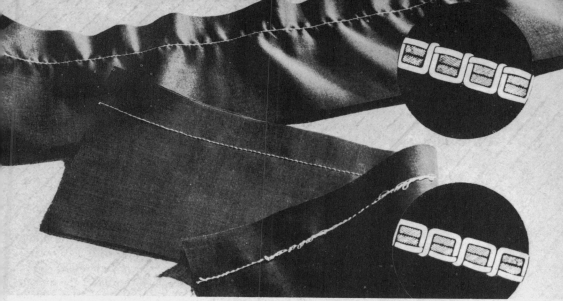

Copyright U.S.A. 1953 by The Singer Manufacturing Co.
All Rights Reserved for All Countries

When the upper tension is too tight, the seam puckers. When it is too loose, loops form on the under side.

The length of the stitch. Does the stitch seem to be the right length for the material you are using? Average weight fabrics require about 14 to 16 stitches to the inch. Fine and sheer fabrics, stitched with finer thread, may need 16 to 20 stitches to the inch. Coarser and heavier cloth should have fewer stitches to the inch. Refer to the chart on the opposite page for suggestions on the length of the stitch.

The tension. Notice the general appearance of the stitch. The stitches should form a continuous, straight, firm line along all sides of the test triangle. The stitching lines should not draw the cloth or form loops on either side of the cloth. The tension should be balanced so that the stitches lock together within the cloth. The appearance should be similar on each side of the fabric. When the cloth is stretched along the bias side of the triangle, the stitching should be somewhat elastic so as to give with the cloth. If the stitching at the corners of the triangle is not sharp, one of the tensions is wrong.

If the stitching does not meet these standards, try to correct it. Since very often it is the threading that is to blame, it is well to check that before changing the tension.

Either of the tensions can be too loose or too tight, but the upper tension is the one that usually requires adjustment. Avoid changing the lower tension, unless you are certain that the difficulty cannot be corrected by adjusting the top one.

One of the best ways to tell whether the tensions are balanced is to pull each end of the stitching along the bias of the cloth until a thread breaks. If the threads break together, you know that the tensions are balanced. If the top thread breaks, it is the tighter of the two and the top tension should be loosened. If the lower thread breaks first, the top thread is too loose and should, therefore, be tightened. Continue testing until the stitch is well balanced.

If after the tensions are balanced, the entire line of stitching is either too loose or too tight, the lower tension will have to be changed before you can get a perfect stitch. Make this change, then adjust the top tension to balance the lower one.

Changing a needle. Never use a needle that has become bent or blunt. Change it, using a needle especially designed for your machine. Select the correct size needle for your fabric and thread. Refer to the chart on the opposite page or on your needle package.

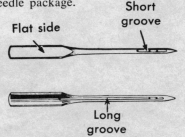

Flat side   Short groove

Long groove

Copyright U.S.A. (December 10, 1952) by The Singer Manufacturing Co. All Rights Reserved for All Countries

2. Loosen the thumb screw of the *needle clamp*.

3. Remove the old needle, noting the way it was turned.

4. Turn the new needle in the same direction. When there is no old needle to guide you, remember that the long groove should always be turned toward the side from which you thread. This groove is designed to protect the thread as the needle is lowered into the bobbin chamber.

1. Turn the balance wheel by hand until the needle is at its highest position. The take-up lever should, of course, be raised.

5. Insert the needle shank in the needle clamp, pushing it up into the hole as high as possible.

6. Tighten the clamp securely.

Stitching troubles. If the machines in your laboratory are kept in good condition and are carefully adjusted, and if you have tried to follow directions as to threading and stitching, not too many things can go wrong. However, there are certain difficulties which occur in clothing classes so often that it is just as well to tell you about them, so that you will know what to do to correct these minor troubles. Study the following chart.

STITCHING TROUBLES

SYMPTOMS	CAUSE	CURE
As you start to stitch, the machine may make a loud clucking noise. You stop and look on the under side of the cloth and find loops of thread in a matted, continuous mass along the stitching line.	You probably did not put the thread through the top tension correctly. Check your top threading. *or* Your top tension is extremely loose.	Re-thread correctly. *or* If you have the machine correctly threaded and still have trouble, then the top tension should be adjusted.
Suddenly you find that your machine seems to be locked. You cannot force the balance wheel to turn, and the needle bar will not rise and fall as it should.	You, or someone else, have allowed threads to become matted around the bobbin. Stitching without material, or the first trouble above, can cause this difficulty.	Rock the balance wheel back and forth until the threads have been dislodged; or pull the threads out of the bobbin enclosure with a pair of tweezers. In extreme cases you can remove the throat plate below the presser foot.

SYMPTOMS	CAUSE	CURE
The bottom thread seems loose and the top thread lies rather straight along the surface of the material. When you pull the top thread, you notice that it pulls out easily.	You may have improperly inserted the bobbin in the bobbin case and the bobbin has unthreaded itself. As a result, there is no tension on the bobbin thread. *or* The bobbin tension is too loose.	Re-thread the bobbin, turning it so that the thread unwinds in the correct direction. *or* Tighten the bobbin tension.
Your thread breaks at the eye of the needle.	You may have threaded the needle from the wrong side. *or* You have turned the needle in the wrong direction as you changed it.	Look for the last thread guide. Thread from that side. *or* Turn the needle around so that the long groove is turned toward the side from which the needle is threaded.
Your stitches are long in some places, and short in others.	You are pulling the material, or holding it back as you stitch.	Learn to guide the cloth under the presser foot with a lighter touch as you sew. Allow the machine to control the length of the stitch and stitches will be regular in length.
Your needle breaks or bends and the point becomes blunt.	The point of the needle has either struck the metal presser foot, or the metal around the needle hole. You may have pulled your material as described directly above, or you may have pulled the threads at the end of a row of stitching without first taking them beneath the presser foot and drawing them toward the back. Either practice bends the needle out of line; as a result, when it is lowered, it may strike metal. It either breaks or bends, depending upon the force of the impact.	Put in a new needle. Then avoid pulling this needle out of line in any way.
The yarns running more or less at right angles to the stitching line on the cloth you are sewing draw or pull, giving an unattractive, puckered appearance on either side of the stitching line.	Your needle has become blunted at the point, probably by striking metal as above or by striking a pin incorrectly used.	Change needles. Use pins only with a flexible presser foot. Place them across the seam with the head out of the way of the presser foot.

SYMPTOMS	CAUSE	CURE
Your machine skips stitches or you may even hear the needle strike metal in the bobbin case.	You did not use a needle designed for your machine when you replaced the broken or bent needle as directed above, or you set the right kind of needle too low.	Use the right make needle. If the needle is right and you still have trouble, see if the needle can be raised higher into the needle clamp. Push it as high as possible, then tighten the thumb screw.

If you will examine the chart you will see that all of the troubles listed there are caused by improper threading, tension adjustment, handling of material, or improper setting of the needle. None of these is a serious trouble, but knowing what causes it, where to look for the trouble, and how to correct it, can help you, your teacher, and all of your classmates. Machines do get out of order sometimes, but check the human element first, before attributing the trouble to the machine.

Caring for the sewing machine. A sewing machine really takes very little care. Keep it dusted and oil it at least once a week or oftener if the machine is in constant use. Put special sewing machine oil in all oil holes and where one part rubs against another. Be careful not to get any oil on the rubber ring on the bobbin winder as oil softens rubber.

If the machine becomes gummed with oil—this is especially liable to happen if it is idle for several months—put a drop of kerosene or gasoline in each oil hole and on working parts. Then unthread the machine and run it rapidly for several minutes. Wipe it off with cheese cloth and re-oil. It will need a second oiling within a few hours after this treatment.

The motor of the sewing machine requires grease—never oil. Follow the instructions in your manual or plan to have a serviceman grease the motor as he makes a periodic check-up.

These lines of stitching show the skipped stitches and swerving seam lines which may result when you set the needle in the machine incorrectly, or when you use a needle too short for the machine.

Copyright U.S.A. 1953 by The Singer Manufacturing Co.
All Rights Reserved for All Countries

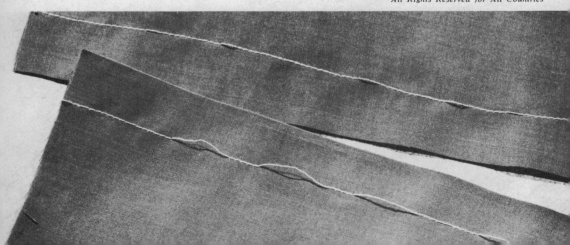

TECHNIQUE 3   *BASIC SEWING TECHNIQUES AND HAND STITCHES*

A number of processes are needed so constantly that everyone who sews should know how to do them. We sometimes assume that everybody knows how to thread a needle, knot a thread, pin, baste, rip, measure, and the like, but many of us can learn simpler and easier ways to do each.

All processes are described for the right-handed person. The left-handed person should substitute "left" for "right" and "right" for "left." She should also look at illustrations in a mirror to see the exact position for her hands and work.

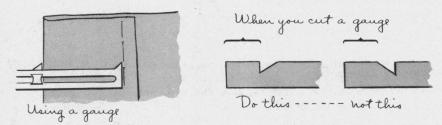

When you cut a gauge

Do this ------ not this

Using a gauge

Using pins. When you are fitting the pattern or fabric, place pins *lengthwise* along seam and dart lines like a line of stitching. When you are going to baste or stitch, place them *across* a seam line and at right angles to it. Turn the heads toward the cut edge of the material and keep them inside the raw edge. Then you can stitch over them. Lay large pieces of material on a flat surface before inserting pins. As you gain experience, you will need to use fewer pins to prepare for stitching seams, darts, and other details.

Measuring with a gauge. A gauge is more accurate and easier to use than a ruler for measuring hems, bands, bias strips, and the like. Set the pointer at the desired width. Place the pointer at the cut edge of the cloth and place a pin or a chalk mark at the top of the gauge. Repeat at intervals and connect these marks either with chalk or by folding on the line they make.

When a metal gauge is not available, cut a rectangular strip of cardboard several inches long. Measure the desired width from one end. Clip straight into the cardboard at this point and cut away a triangle on the handle side of the slash line, leaving the measuring area intact. See drawing above at right.

Threading a needle. For permanent stitches, the thread should not be longer than 24 to 30 inches. Longer threads are apt to snarl and knot. However for basting or tailor's tacks where it is used rapidly, thread can be cut longer. Cut diagonally across the thread with sharp scissors. This gives a clean, sharp point which you should have no trouble putting through an ordinary needle eye. When threading a very fine needle, moisten your finger tips and draw the thread between them to flatten the fibers and hold them together. Hold the needle in a good light and slip the flattened thread-end through the oval eye.

If you have difficulty in threading needles, try an inexpensive gadget called a needle threader. One kind has a wire loop which is much easier to get through the eye of the needle than a limp piece of thread. Once through, the loop opens up to provide a large hole for the thread. You pull the loop back through the eye, bringing the thread with it. The only trouble is that it can only be used for rather coarse needles.

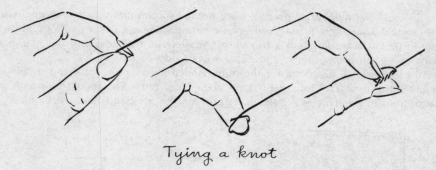

Tying a knot

Knotting the thread. A knot is ordinarily made in one thread end, since nearly all hand work is done with a single thread. If you do want a double thread, hold the two thread ends together as you tie the knot. Otherwise, the processes are the same.

Place the end of the thread across the tip of the forefinger of your left hand and hold it with your left thumb. Then wrap the thread around your finger tip, overlapping the end of the thread slightly. Next, roll the thread off your finger with your thumb, being careful to catch the thread end in the loop. As you roll the loop off, draw the thread up with your right hand. The knot should be small and at the end of the thread.

Fastening a line of hand sewing. Use several small stitches, one on top of the other, to end any line of hand sewing. The stitches should be made on the under side, or in some inconspicuous place. Start sewing this same way when you do not wish to use a knot.

Position of the needle and thimble. The needle is held between the right-hand thumb and the index finger. The thimble is worn on the second or middle finger of the right hand. Keep the thimble at the eye-end of the needle, so that the indentations on its side catch and hold the needle as you sew. For heavy going you will need to push the needle with the thimble end. It may help you to think of the second finger of your right hand as a motor which furnishes the power in hand sewing. The side is "high gear"; the end of it is "low gear."

Position of the fabric. Nearly all permanent hand stitches and much basting is done with the material held in the hands. The seam you are sewing should be uppermost, and the bulk of the material should fall downward in your lap or on a table. Hold the seam so that you sew from right to left when making ordinary basting stitches, running stitches, and similar stitches. Pinning the right end of the material to something firm and heavy so that you can hold the material taut facilitates the making of many hand stitches. Whipping and overcasting are easier to do that way, but you have to do several inches before you can pin the end.

Keeping the material flat on a table gives best results for two kinds of basting. These are uneven basting, generally used to transfer center line markings to the right side of the material, and diagonal basting which serves to keep two layers of fabric accurately matched.

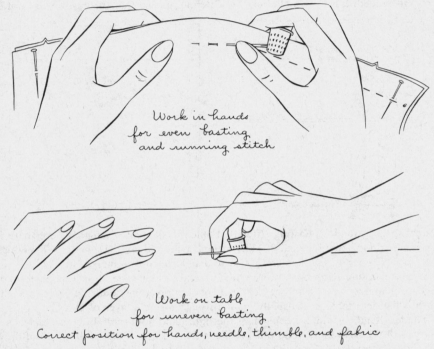

Correct position for hands, needle, thimble, and fabric

*Work in hands
for even basting
and running stitch*

*Work on table
for uneven basting*

Correct position for hands, needle, thimble, and fabric

Removing excess twist in thread. When mercerized or cotton thread begins to twist as you sew it, you can usually unwind it by allowing the needle to hang downward for a few seconds. This method will not work for silk and other glossy threads as the needle would slip off them. They must be untwisted by hand until the thread lies flat and relaxed.

BASTING

Once it was thought that every detail of a garment must be hand-basted before it was stitched. Now with accurate pattern alterations and the increased use of machine-basting, pins, staylines, stitching guides, and clearly marked construction lines, few details need to be hand-basted. And yet there are difficult spots where nothing takes the place of a row of well made hand-basting.

When basting is necessary, use thread of a contrasting color so that it can be easily seen and removed. Avoid dark colors which might discolor the fabric. Velvet and other materials that mar easily should be basted with silk thread. Start the line of basting as you end it or with a small knot. Form this fastening with small criss-crossed stitches. These hold firmly but are easier to remove than the usual ending in which stitches are placed on top of each other.

Even basting. Even basting, so-called because the stitches are of equal length on both sides of the material, is the most universally used of all temporary stitches. It is the one we use when basting seams and other details which must be held securely. Even basting is a simple in-and-out stitch. You work from right to left, unless you are left-handed. Baste ⅟₁₆ inch from the stitching line so that the basting will not be

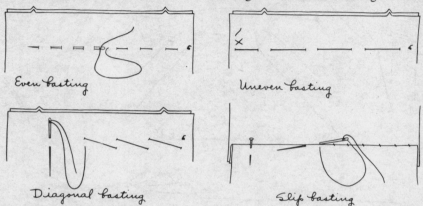

Even basting

Uneven basting

Diagonal basting

Slip basting

caught in the stitching. Basting stitches should be ¼ inch in length where there is strain, as along the hip area of skirt seams. Other areas may hold well enough with ½ inch stitches. Gathers and intricate details require ⅛ inch basting.

Uneven basting. Uneven basting (long stitches on top and short ones below) is used principally for marking center lines, pocket positions, and the like while the cloth is flat on a table. It is usually made through a single layer of cloth.

The left hand and the little finger of the right hand hold the fabric, as stitches are made with the right hand. You must make stitches one at a time, but need not draw the thread completely through until a number of stitches have been made.

Diagonal basting. Diagonal basting is particularly useful for preventing two layers of cloth from shifting position. It is made with crosswise stitches about ¼ inch wide, spaced ¼ to 1 inch apart. The stitches on the right side slant. The left hand and the little finger of the right hand hold the fabric flat on the table, as stitches are made with the right hand. You must make stitches one at a time, but this time you do have to draw the thread completely through at the end of each stitch.

Slip basting. Slip basting is most frequently used to match plaids and baste seam lines that have been fitted from the right side of the garment. You work from the right sides of the two pieces of material you want to join. Fold one seam edge under and pin it over the other seam edge along the stitching line. Bring the needle up very close to the folded edge through the three layers of cloth. As close to that point as possible go down through the single layer, and come up again between ¼ and ½ inch away through the three layers, as before. Continue. Stitches on the wrong side will be slightly diagonal but straight enough for your purposes. When you have finished, you will be able to open the seam out flat and stitch it as a plain seam.

Removing hand-basting. Clip away the knot if one was used and loosen the criss-crossed stitches. Cut the basting threads in short lengths. Use tweezers to remove basting threads. They are especially helpful for those that were accidentally caught by machine stitching. Never drag a knot through the material.

Machine-basting. To machine-baste, set the machine for its longest stitch. Ordinarily that is all you do, but you can also loosen the top tension slightly if you are basting heavy materials. Make note of the position of the tension before loosening it, so that you will have no trouble readjusting it when you have finished basting.

Ripping machine stitching. There are several ways to rip machine stitching. One of the best is to use tweezers to grasp one of the threads and pull that thread until it breaks. Then pick up the thread end again and repeat. If you are not successful when you pull the thread from the same side all of the time, alternate sides, pulling first from one side, then from the other.

Another way to rip machine stitching is to spread the seam as much as possible, then clip the threads between with sharp scissors. Continue to spread and clip, being careful to cut the threads only where the sides of the seam have been pulled apart enough to be safe. This method leaves short threads in the cloth which must be removed; the other method leaves no threads.

PERMANENT HAND STITCHES

The running stitch. The running stitch is used for handmade seams, tucks, gathering, and shirring. It is similar to even basting but the stitches are much smaller. The line of stitches should be straight, fine, and evenly spaced. Stitches should be $\frac{1}{16}$ to $\frac{1}{8}$ inch in length. To make this stitch:

1. Take a small stitch in the cloth at the right of the seam line, but leave the needle in the cloth.

2. Hold the cloth and the needle with your thumbs and index fingers. Your thumbs are on the side toward you, and one index finger is directly back of each thumb on the opposite side of the material. Leave about 1 inch of cloth between your hands and keep it stretched.

3. Guide the needle back and forth gently to make tiny stitches as you push the needle through the cloth with the thimble finger.

4. As you progress, shift your hands to the left and repeat the process. Allow the stitches to be pushed off the back of the needle, so that you need not draw the thread completely through until you reach the end of the stitching line.

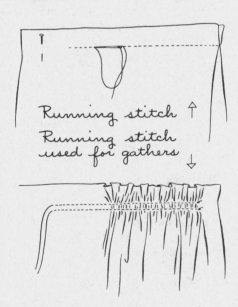

Running stitch

Running stitch used for gathers

This stitch requires practice. Therefore, do not be discouraged if you cannot do it correctly at first. Just remember that your thimble finger furnishes the "power," and keep practicing. Once you learn this technique, hand sewing will be quick and easy to do.

The back stitch. The back stitch is strong and is sometimes substituted for machine stitching, which it resembles, when a sewing machine is not available. However, it is time-consuming. Stitches should be about $\frac{1}{16}$ to $\frac{1}{8}$ inch long on the top side. To make the back-stitch:

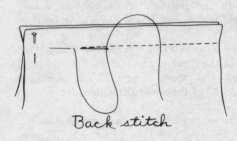

Back stitch

1. Push the needle up through the material about $\frac{1}{8}$ inch from the right end of the stitching line.

2. Take a stitch, inserting the needle $\frac{1}{8}$ inch back of the thread at the beginning of the stitching line and coming up an equal distance in front of the thread. For finer stitches use shorter distances.

3. Repeat, keeping stitches in a straight line, even in length, and barely touching each other.

The combination stitch. The combination stitch, used principally for hand-sewn plain seams, is faster than the back stitch and stronger than the running stitch. It is simply a combination of the two stitches. Make several running stitches and then take a back stitch.

The pin-point back stitch. The pin-point back stitch is used on hand-sewn zippers and the "hand-picked" lapel edges of tailored suits. It is made exactly like a back stitch, except that the stitches are almost invisible from the right side and are more widely spaced. Insert the needle just slightly behind the thread for each stitch and bring it up in front of the last stitch to make the stitches about $\frac{1}{8}$ to $\frac{1}{4}$ inch apart.

Pin-point back stitch

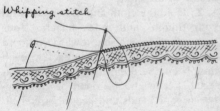

Whipping stitch

Whipping stitch. The whipping stitch is used for joining two finished edges such as lace on a handkerchief or slip. Hold the material with right sides together. Point the needle toward your left shoulder as you work. Insert the needle from the back and pull it through each time you take a stitch. Adjust the stitches so that they are firm but do not pucker the material. Keep the stitches close together and close to the edges of the materials—about $\frac{1}{16}$ inch apart and barely catching the two edges.

When this stitch is used on a seam allowance to prevent raveling, it is called *overcasting*. For this purpose, the stitches are longer and often go through only one layer of material. Refer to the technique 10, "Seams and Seam Finishes," for a quick way to do overcasting.

Hemming stitches. For hemming stitches, see the technique 19, "Hems."

CUTTING AND JOINING TRUE BIAS

Because bias is used for cording and around all sorts of curves, it is important that it be as elastic as possible. True bias, as you have no doubt discovered, stretches more than any other direction on cloth. For that reason you can see the importance of cutting your bias strips on a true bias.

Cutting bias. As you know, true bias falls on a diagonal line halfway between the two grainlines—at a 45° angle to each of them. If you fold a piece of cloth so that the lengthwise threads fall along the crosswise threads, the fold line will be a true bias. The most practical way to locate a true bias is first to measure and mark equal distances along each edge of a corner of a squared-up piece of material. Then with chalk or pencil, mark along a ruler to join the two points. (Be sure the cloth is spread out smoothly.) This line indicates one edge of a bias strip. Now if you can use a strip the width of your ruler—and you frequently can—just

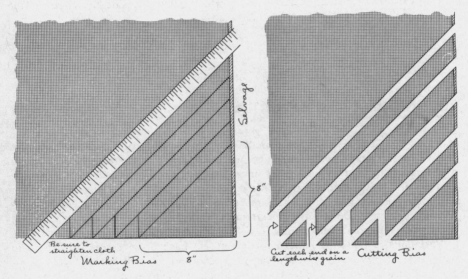

lay one edge of the ruler along the original line and mark along its other edge. It's as simple as that. With a wide transparent ruler marked off in both directions you can cut strips of various widths just as easily. If you don't have a transparent ruler and need a width other than that of your ruler, you will have to measure off the width you want with a gauge, then join points as you did before.

After you have marked enough strips, you will have to prepare them for joining. Mark all ends along a lengthwise thread, because joinings are much flatter and less conspicuous when joined along that grain. Do this before cutting the strips, while it is still easy to tell one grain from the other. After they are cut, each strip should be a parallelogram, that is, opposite edges will be parallel to each other.

Joining bias strips. Simple as joining bias is, it does give many people a bit of trouble at first. With properly cut strips half of your troubles are eliminated. Follow these steps and the rest will not be difficult.

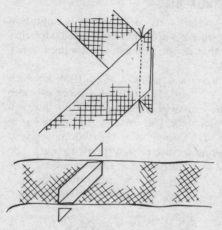

1. Place one bias strip right side up on a flat surface. Place another right side down over the end of the first but at an angle to it so that the end edges are in line with each other.

2. Shift the two pieces until a point extends about ¼ inch beyond each side of the joining.

3. Stitch parallel to the ends between the points where the sides meet—from one angle to another.

4. Open the strips out and press the seam open, then clip away the points which extend outside the edges of the strip.

TECHNIQUE 4   *THE PATTERN*

Today all large pattern companies print their patterns—quite a change from the time, not so long ago, when all patterns were merely cut to shape and perforated. Cutting lines, dart lines, center lines—every necessary construction detail—are printed on the pattern. Directions and explanations in English and sometimes in other languages are printed beside these markings. Patterns today are easy to understand and extremely accurate. Seam widths are true and darts taper to symmetrical points.

Variations in patterns. Pattern manufacturers have done a great deal to help make sewing easy. As you study patterns, however, you will see that each company has provided slightly different information and assistance.

Notice the length of the lines marked "Place on the Straight of the Material." These lines should extend almost all the way from the top to the bottom of pattern pieces in order to help you place the pattern accurately on the cloth.

Look for lines which show you where to lengthen or shorten pattern sections. On some patterns there is only a straight, crosswise line to indicate where to alter the length of each section. On others, you may find vertical breaks in the crosswise line to keep you from shifting cut sections out of line. Some patterns even go so far as to print measurements—little ruler-like diagrams—which help you to measure alterations.

Since it is better to cut "notches" so that they extend in peaks outside the seam line, it will be much simpler for you if your patterns are printed that way.

Fortunately, a number of patterns are. There may still be a notch printed inward, but there is also, on some patterns, a peak which extends outward.

It is not too difficult to cut one notch outward, but it takes time and skill to cut several distinct peaks. Realizing this, some pattern companies bracket multiple notches and suggest that you cut around the group rather than around each notch separately. When it is accurately cut, the length of the group projection will tell you how to match pattern sections just as accurately as do a definite number of separate notches.

Printing has also made possible the numbering of notches. Not only do numbers beside notches tell you which ones to join together, but they even tell you the order in which to stitch seams. You match notches numbered "1," then sew that seam. Next you match those marked "2," and so on.

Another helpful marking on some printed patterns is the line which runs down the center of darts. This line shows you where to fold so that you can be sure you will have matched dart lines and therefore true darts. Look for center dart lines.

Dart positions for very narrow darts are sometimes indicated by a single line— the fold line. This marking is inadequate, for you must then draw in stitching lines of your own—or guess. It takes practice to guess well!

A few patterns indicate the direction to stitch when you make staylines and seams—very helpful information because cloth (particularly certain kinds) does behave better if it is stitched in the correct direction.

Most patterns today are very carefully labeled. The pattern number, the size, and the company making the pattern are all given. In addition, each piece is labeled so that you know whether it is a collar, a sleeve, a blouse front, or some other part of the garment. There may be still further information on individual pattern pieces to tell you for which of the views or styles that particular piece is needed.

The instruction sheet. In addition to the pattern itself, examine the guide or instruction sheet. Does it suggest modern, time-saving techniques for constructing the garment? Are there clear, step-by-step directions for each process and are these directions supplemented by distinct diagrams of the processes being explained? Look at several guide sheets, if they are available, to see what information they give. As you do so, you will probably discover that some patterns have clearer directions than others.

The pattern envelope. Here is another place where it is wise to compare patterns. Are various kinds of fabrics suggested for the pattern, and do you find a list of supplies which will be needed to complete the garment? Most pattern envelopes give yardage requirements for various styles, sizes, and material widths, but is yardage given for material "with nap"? If not, there are probably no cutting charts inside for material of that kind either.

SELECTING PATTERNS TO FIT

For the first time in the history of pattern making, all the companies have agreed on complete standardization of pattern sizes. They are all cutting their patterns to fit the figure types and body measurements shown in the "Revised Measurement Chart for All Pattern Companies" which you will find in any large pattern book. Now, once you decide on the pattern classification and size that fits you best, you will be able to buy that type and size in any make of pattern. And as long as your proportions stay the same, your size in any make of pattern should fit you equally well.

First, decide on your figure type. You would hardly expect the same pattern to fit a mature woman and a ten-year-old girl, even if the chest measurements of the two were the same. The woman is likely to be taller and her figure more fully developed. Because figures vary so much in height, maturity, and general proportions, pattern companies cut patterns for various figure types. For your best fit, you should select patterns from the group cut for figures like yours. (In addition to the figure types shown here, patterns are cut for children, boys, young girls, men, and large women.) Here are the figure types which should fit most high school girls and average-size women.

Sub-Teen patterns are proportioned to fit the slightly developed growing girl in early maturity. They are shorter waisted and flatter through the bust than Teen patterns. They fit girls who are about 5 feet, 1 inch tall.

Teen patterns are proportioned for the high-bosomed, youthful figure which is taller than the Sub-teen but not as tall as the Junior Miss. Girls about 5 feet, 3 inches tall can wear these.

Junior Misses' patterns are proportioned for the fully developed figure which is shorter waisted than average and about 5 feet, 5 inches in height. These patterns are always cut in odd sizes (that is, size 11, 13, etc.) which fall between the sizes cut for Misses.

Misses' patterns are proportioned for the fully developed figure, slightly above average in height—the girl or woman who is about 5 feet, 6 inches tall. The waist length is normal for figures of that height.

Half-size patterns are proportioned for the figure that is about 5 feet, 3 or 4 inches tall, and is larger in the waistline and hips than the Misses' figure.

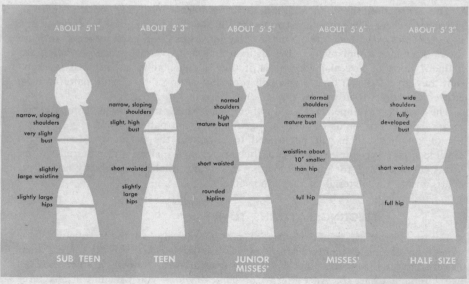

Adapted from McCall's Patterns

Second, take accurate measurements. It is difficult to take your own measurements. You may wish to work with a classmate and measure each other. Wear your regular foundation garments and remove heavy or bulky clothing. Take all measurements close, but not tight. Since you will be using a reversible tape measure, be careful to read it from the correct side. Record your measurements and keep the record in a convenient place, because you may need to refer to it later. Record these measurements:

Bust. Measure over the fullest part of the bust keeping the tape measure level or slightly higher in the back.

Waist. Measure around the smallest part of the figure. Work the tape measure back and forth to bring it to the smallest part of the figure.

Hip. Measure around the hips 7 inches below the waistline. Keep the tape measure level. Measure 7 inches. Do not guess.

Back waist length. Measure from the normal neckline to the waistline at the center back. (To do this, tie a cord tightly around the waist; then hold a cord around the neck as if it were a necklace. Measure from center back of one cord to center back of the other.)

Third, decide on your pattern size. Perhaps you already know that you should buy patterns by your measurements—not by the readymade dress size you wear or by the "bra" size, for these articles are not sized as patterns are.

For dresses, suits, and coats, your *bust* measurement is the most important one of all, although your other measurements should not be disregarded. (You need not buy larger sizes for suits, coats, and outer wear because adequate ease has already been provided.)

Purchase skirt patterns by your *waist* measurement if the skirt is designed with widely flared gores or has enough fullness so that very slim or larger-than-average hips will cause no fitting problems.

Select patterns for tubular skirts, slacks, and shorts by your *hip* measurement. (You will, of course, have to ask for them by the size indicated in the pattern book. Just be sure that the hip measurement is right for you.)

After you have determined your figure type, your next step is to select the best pattern size for your figure. The sizes in which each type is cut appear on page 406.

When you begin to compare your measurements with the measurements on the chart, you may find that yours vary from those given. For instance, let's say that you are tall and have a fairly well-developed figure. Because of your general build you know that you should use a Misses' pattern, but you don't know which size. Your measurements are: bust 36 inches, waist 25 inches, and hip 38½ inches, and that combination is not on the chart. Notice that your measurements are closest to those indicated for size 16. That will be the best size for you to buy, even though your waistline is smaller and your hips slightly larger than the measurements indicated for size 16.

Another girl in the class may be much shorter than you and her figure is perhaps only slightly developed. Her measurements, let's say, are: bust 31½ inches, waist 25 inches, and hip 33 inches. A Sub-teen pattern, size 12s, will be her best choice.

Still another girl who is not so tall as you but has a well-developed figure has the following measurements: bust 32½ inches, waist 25 inches, hip 35 inches. A Junior Miss pattern, size 13, would be her best choice, but if this is not available, she could use a Misses, size 12, realizing that she must make several alterations in the pattern before she uses it.

PATTERNS

FIGURE TYPE							
Sub-Teen Sizes							
	Buy Size	8s	10s	12s	14s		
	If Bust is	28	29	31	33		
	Waist	23	24	25	26		
	Hip	31	32	34	36		
	Back Waist Length	13½	13¾	14	14¼		
Teen Sizes							
	Buy Size	10	12	14			
	If Bust is	30	32	34			
	Waist	24	25	26			
	Hip	32	34	36			
	Back Waist Length	14¾	15	15¼			
Junior Misses' Sizes							
	Buy Size	11	13	15	17		
	If Bust is	31½	33	35	37		
	Waist	24½	25½	27	28½		
	Hip	33½	35	37	39		
	Back Waist Length	15¼	15½	15¾	16		
Misses' Sizes							
	Buy Size	10	12	14	16	18	20
	If Bust is	31	32	34	36	38	40
	Waist	24	25	26	28	30	32
	Hip	33	34	36	38	40	42
	Back Waist Length	15¾	16	16¼	16½	16¾	17
Half Sizes							
	Buy Size	12½	14½	16½	18½	20½	22½	24½
	If Bust is	33	35	37	39	41	43	45
	Waist	27	29	31	33	35	37½	40
	Hip	37	39	41	43	45	47	49
	Back Waist Length	15¼	15½	15¾	16	16¼	16½	16¾

UNDERSTANDING THE PATTERN

A wealth of information is provided with every pattern—important and valuable information—and yet many home dressmakers are unaware of much of it. Study any pattern you plan to use, because each new pattern is somewhat different. If you have never used a pattern before, there will be many things to learn.

The pattern envelope

Pattern styles. Notice the illustrations on the front of the envelope. There may be several styles showing variations of the design. If so, select the style you intend to use.

Yardage. Turn to the back of the envelope for information about the amount of material to buy. The style you have chosen, the width of your material, and the size of your pattern all affect the amount of fabric you will need. You may notice that different amounts are given for "material with nap" and for "material without nap."

As far as yardage for patterns is concerned, "material with nap" means any fabric that must be cut with the top parts of all pattern pieces turned in the same direction. This includes pile fabrics and some figured materials as well as the real napped materials such as wool. Nap is something like the fur on an animal and must run in the same direction on all parts of the garment. Velvet, a pile fabric, looks different from opposite ends of the cloth and must therefore be cut the same way. Some figured materials have a definite *up* direction, and a definite *down* direction. These too must be cut as if they had nap. You will notice that more yardage is required for materials "with nap" because the pattern cannot be laid on the cloth as economically as on cloth without nap.

Other information. You may also find on the envelope suggestions as to materials which are suitable for the pattern; the kind and amount of material to use for interfacings, linings, and trimmings; the kind and length of zipper required; the width of the skirt at the hem; and much other useful information.

The instruction sheet. The guide, or instruction, sheet explains the pattern and gives skeleton instructions for making the particular design. On it you are likely to find the following things:

A diagram of the parts of the pattern showing the pieces used for each style

Directions for making alterations in length of the pattern

Suggestions for preparing and handling the material

Cutting or layout charts for various views, sizes, and widths of material (both with and without nap)

Directions for transferring details from pattern to cloth

Step-by-step directions and diagrams for constructing the garment

The pattern itself. You may be surprised to find that the pattern seems to be for only half of a garment. Because most garments are alike left and right, pattern pieces for one side are enough. To cut a right and left side, simply cut through two layers of folded material or use each pattern piece twice. For some parts, such as cuffs, you may have to cut more than two pieces of material by a single pattern piece. On the other hand, for belts, waistbands, or other small parts, the pattern piece may be for the whole part. Examine one of the cutting charts to find out just how many pieces of material you must cut by each pattern piece.

Identifying pattern parts. It saves time, and sometimes costly mistakes, if you can tell at a glance where each part of the pattern fits into the whole. Most pattern companies make this easy by printing the name of the part on each piece, but even if this information isn't given on your pattern, you can identify standard pattern parts. Study their shape, size, darts, proportions, and construction details. Here are some hints to guide you:

A normal neckline is deeper in the front than in the back.

At the bust line, a garment is wider across the front than across the back.

The armhole is deeper on the blouse front than on the blouse back.

At the waistline, a fitted skirt is wider across the front than across the back.

At the hip line, a fitted skirt is wider across the back than across the front.

The front length of a skirt is shorter than the side and back lengths.

The back length of a long sleeve is greater than the front length. The underarm has a deeper curve in front than in the back.

With the diagram of the various pattern pieces before you, unfold the pattern and select the parts you will need. The style you have decided to use will determine this. Refold and return the remainder of the pattern to the envelope. Keep it handy though in case you made a mistake.

Details shown on the pattern. You will find various printed lines on all pieces of the pattern. These show how to lay the pattern on the cloth, where to cut, how to join darts and seams, and where to place construction details. All patterns identify these markings and sometimes tell how to use them with printing placed directly on the pattern.

Here are the directions which are given on the pattern for laying pattern pieces on the cloth correctly:

"Place on a lengthwise fold of material" or a similar instruction appears along the center line when an entire front or back is to be cut in one piece. The fold must be made on a straight grainline.

"Place on the lengthwise straight of the material" appears along lines on all other pieces. This line should be placed parallel to a selvage along a lengthwise grain.

Here is the line which is given on the pattern for you to cut by:

The outer printed line of printed patterns is the cutting line. Ignore the paper margin.

A printed pattern

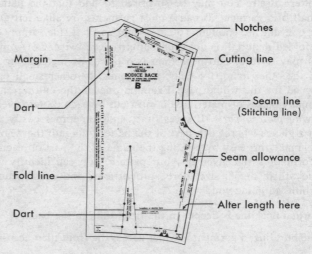

Notches

Cutting line

Margin

Seam line
(Stitching line)

Dart

BODICE BACK
B

Seam allowance

Fold line

Dart

Alter length here

Here are the construction details which are given on the pattern:

The seam line is the line where a seam is stitched, generally ⅝ inch inside the cutting line. It is the inside printed line. The seam allowance is the area between the cutting line and the stitching line.

Some patterns indicate with an arrow along the seam the direction in which you are to stitch.

Notches along seams show which seams are to be joined and where. These are often numbered to correspond so that there is no guesswork in assembling parts.

Center lines are the lines that are intended to lie on the center front and center back of the figure. They are sometimes shown as such on the pattern. When sections are "cut-on-a-fold," the fold is the center line. Center seam lines indicate the center front or center back of a pattern with such seams.

The waistline of the pattern is planned to fall exactly along the waistline of the figure. It is usually the narrowest part of the garment and the place where double-pointed darts are the widest. It may be indicated by a seam line rather than by actual markings.

Darts are indicated by two converging lines which meet to form a V-shaped point. Darts which extend both above and below the waistline are often pointed at both ends.

Dart tucks are indicated by two lines that do not come to a point.

Fold lines appear along hems and other details to show where the material is to be folded.

Buttonholes, pockets, gathering lines, pleats, tucks, and many other details are also indicated on the pattern.

TECHNIQUE 5   *ALTERING THE PATTERN AND FITTING THE GARMENT*

Your pattern was designed and cut by experts who know fashion and figure requirements. If you have chosen the correct size, few alterations, if any, should be necessary. Make those few changes carefully to retain the style of the original design.

Whenever possible, make alterations before you cut the material. It is often too late afterward. For instance, the waist length of a princess-line dress or jacket cannot be shortened satisfactorily after the fabric is cut. Neither can length be added to a blouse or skirt. If alterations will be extensive, cut the garment in a cheap fabric. Make the alterations in the cloth and then alter the pattern accordingly. Once you have a correct fit, make a record of the changes you have made because other patterns will have to be altered in a similar way.

Even if your pattern fits perfectly, it is an excellent safety measure to add an extra half inch along all *side* seams. Mark and use the original stitching line but leave a wider than usual side seam allowance. This extra material can be used for minor alterations during fitting. It is useful for plackets and later alterations as well. Do not make the mistake of cutting all seams wide—just side seams.

CHECKING THE FIT OF A PATTERN

You want your clothes to fit properly, yet it is difficult to say just what is a "proper" fit. Everybody realizes, for instance, that a coat has to be looser than a dress, but even dresses are not all designed to fit alike. In spite of these differences we can make a few generalizations about fitting which may help you. Here they are:

> Any garment should fit comfortably; that means not only enough room for body movement, but also some snug areas to hold the garment in place.

> Grain lines must be true or else the garment will twist on the figure or hang poorly. This again is difficult to pin down in words because designs vary so much. However, on a typical slender garment, lengthwise grain lines generally fall in a vertical direction and crosswise grain lines fall in a horizontal direction.

> Center lines and vertical seam lines should fall perpendicular to the floor when viewed squarely from in front of each.

> Darts, which are used to shape the cloth to the curves of the figure and keep grain lines in position, have to be carefully located and of the correct length and width. They should point toward the fullest part of the figure but should end just before reaching that point—perhaps ½ to 2 inches away. They should be the right width to give a perfect fit and to keep grain lines running in the correct direction.

> Fullness in the form of tucks, dart tucks, or gathers must be directed toward, but need not reach, the fullest part of the figure. This applies only to fullness used to shape the garment to the figure—not to ordinary skirt fullness.

> Jacket, sleeve, and skirt lengths should be influenced by the prevailing fashion, yet be appropriate to the figure of the wearer.

There are two ways of checking the fit of a pattern—pinning it together and trying it on, or measuring the pattern and comparing its dimensions with your own. You get a good general effect of style and fit by pinning the main parts of a pattern together and trying them on. In this way you can easily tell whether a sleeve is designed with a deep armhole or whether a neckline is the right depth for your figure. You are less likely to spoil original lines and more likely to see what changes are necessary with this method of fitting. On the other hand, waist measurements and hip measurements may be more accurately measured than fitted. Sometimes a combination of fitting and measuring is the best procedure.

Trying the pattern on for fit. Here is the way to assemble a pattern and prepare for a fitting. You don't need to try on all the pattern pieces—just the ones that form the basic garment, that is, the blouse, the skirt, and the sleeve. Don't bother with collars or facings or pockets yet.

1. Pin darts, pleats, and tucks according to the pattern instructions except turn them to the right side for easy adjustment. Place pins lengthwise along the stitching lines. Where gathers are indicated pin small pleats.

2. Assemble pattern parts. First pin any seams within fronts and backs, then join these sections. Pin along seam lines as you did along the other stitching lines, turning seams to the right side. To avoid tearing, do not pin the blouse side seam all the way to the top. Pin the sleeve for a fitting, but do not attempt to attach it to the blouse.

3. Get a pencil and paper to record any needed alterations.

4. Remove your outer garments and tie a cord tightly around your waist to indicate your true waistline. Attach shoulder pads to your shoulder straps if pads are to be used.

5. Put the pattern on, being careful not to tear it or injure it with perspiration.

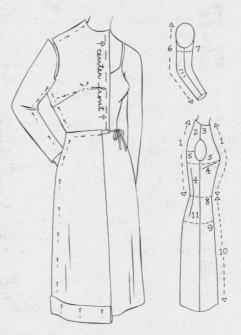

See pages 412–413 for explanation of numbers.

Now you will need someone to help you check the fit. She may hold the pattern gently in place as she fits it or she may prefer to pin it to your slip along center lines. She should start by locating on the pattern and matching to your figure the back neckline, the shoulder seam, the center back line, and the center front line. If the pattern is too small, she will have to unpin the side seam.

The skirt pattern can be pinned to its blouse or to the cord about your waist. A separate skirt should be pinned to its folded waistband. As soon as whoever is helping you has located the center lines on your figure, she is ready to start checking the fit of your pattern. Remind her to allow for whatever ease is required for comfort and body movement. The minimum amounts to allow wherever ease is needed are given in the list on the following two pages.

If your bust, waist, and hip measurements are exactly those indicated on the pattern, you won't have to worry about ease at those spots because the pattern allows ease for both style and comfort. Your partner should check the following places when fitting your pattern. Later in this technique, you will find instructions for the common pattern alterations keyed to this check list. The directions below are given to your helper as she fits your pattern.

BLOUSE

1. Length of blouse, back and front. Check by the cord at the waistline. Make no allowance for ease in princess garments, but allow ½ inch or more in dresses with waistline seams.

2. Width at shoulders. Check the shoulder seam length from the neck to the armhole. No allowance for ease is needed but the length will naturally vary according to the style.

3. Slope of shoulder seam. While you are holding one hand on the center front of the pattern and one on the center back, you pull the pattern down gently to see if the shoulder seam hugs the shoulder along its entire length. If it doesn't, don't change the seam at the neckline but pin a tapered line from there to the armhole, either taking it up or letting it out as necessary. Measure the change at the outer end of the shoulder seam. That is the measurement needed to make the alteration.

4. Position and size of darts. Crisscross pins to mark the high point of the bust. Then check to see whether darts point at these pins and stop ½ to 2 inches away from them. Check the widths of darts, also. Take them up or let them out as necessary for a smooth fit. Crisscross other pins over the tip of the shoulder blade. Keep vertical back darts well below these—about 2 inches away. Check their width also. You will find that full body curves require wider darts than slight body curves. For a princess-line dress, in addition, check to see that the fullest part of the side front pattern is centered on the crisscrossed pins.

5. Width across bust and back. Be certain that center lines are in place. Then check these measurements at the side seam. See that the seam falls in a vertical line directly beneath the arm, then check the amount of ease. There should be about 1 inch on either side of the side seam. In other words, you should be able to pinch up a 1 inch tuck there. Even though the pattern was bought by the correct bust measurement, a fuller-than-usual bust will require more width (and often more length) on the blouse front. Similarly, rounded shoulders or prominent shoulder blades will call for greater room on the back. In addition to checking the side seam, notice the upper back width from center back to the armscye seam. If one of the back measurements is too narrow, both are likely to be. Check the chest width similarly.

SLEEVE

6. Sleeve length. Match the armhole seam of the sleeve to that of the blouse at the underarm. Hold the sleeve in position and check its length. When fitting a long tight sleeve, bend the elbow slightly as you check the location of elbow darts. They should point toward the elbow.

7. Sleeve width. Even on a snug fitting sleeve you should be able to pinch up at least a 1 inch tuck at the upper arm and elbow positions while the arm is extended. Now bend the arm to see whether that much ease gives a comfortable fit at the elbow. At the forearm and wrist a sleeve may be fitted more closely. If you can pinch up a ½ inch tuck, that is sufficient. Push-up sleeves must be tight enough at their lower edges to stay pushed up.

SKIRT

If you are sure there is enough material, it is sometimes easier to adjust dart widths and seams in cloth rather than in the pattern. The hang of the skirt can best be adjusted as a garment is being fitted too.

8. Waist measurement. Almost no ease is necessary. The waist measurement should be snug but not tight. Use the waistband, folded lengthwise, to measure for skirt bands, because the wider the band the longer it has to be.

9. Hip measurement. At the hips a narrow skirt needs only slight ease. With centers in place, if you can pinch up a ½ inch tuck at the side seam, that is sufficient. Flared skirts fit the figure for only a few inches below the waist.

10. Length of skirt. Allow enough length for a good hem and remember that some length is likely to be lost when the hem is leveled.

11. The hang of the skirt. The hang of the skirt is controlled at the waistline. A high hip or a sway back will change the direction of seam lines and, in flared skirts, the placement of fullness.

Before you take the pattern off, also check the positions of pockets, buttonholes, and other details. After you have a list of the changes you think necessary, you may want to ask your teacher to approve the list. Then take the pattern off and remove the pins—except those crisscrossed ones if your darts need altering.

Checking by measurements. If you prefer to check the fit of the pattern by measurements rather than by trying it on, compare your measurements with those of your pattern at the places indicated on the diagram. Fold out any darts, tucks, or pleats in the pattern before taking measurements and measure inside the stitching lines, not the cutting lines. Add to your own measurements the allowances for ease given above for checking the pattern by fit. If the pattern seems too large, consider whether the style calls for large measurements.

In some cases it is easier to take your measurements on a garment that fits you correctly rather than on yourself—for one thing, you don't have to add ease. The garment should be one that is similar in line to your pattern.

MAKING ALTERATIONS

After deciding where the pattern needs to be changed and just how great the changes are to be, your next step is to decide where to make the alterations on the pattern. As a matter of fact, there are only three places where the proportions of a pattern can be changed successfully. Here they are:

1. One of the most common alterations is through the body of the pattern pieces. When alterations are made <u>across</u> an entire pattern section, they must usually be equal in width in order to keep closing edges straight and center lines true. When alterations run <u>up and down</u>, they can be tapered. Tapered insets need not be made in a straight line but they do have to extend from one outside edge to another to keep the pattern flat. This is true in theory. However, in practice you can stop an inch or so from one outside edge to keep the pattern pieces together. They need not extend quite all the way across a pattern piece but must extend far enough to allow the pattern to lie quite flat on a table after being altered. See drawing on next page.

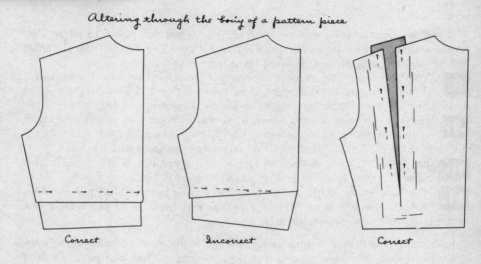

Altering through the body of a pattern piece

Correct   Incorrect   Correct

2. Adjusting darts is another important way of obtaining a perfect fit. It is a simple matter to change the position, length, or width of any dart. You can even add a new dart if you are sure it is needed. The important thing to realize is that it takes only 3 points to establish the lines of any simple dart. Then you can draw lines between these points to indicate the sides of the dart. Since any appreciable change in a dart disturbs the seam line where the dart appears, the seam line may have to be redrawn. Usually you have to add paper to the pattern edge before folding out the dart. Double pointed darts require four points and do not disturb any seam line since they do not enter a seam.

3. The only other place to alter is along pattern edges, either along seam lines or hemlines. Princess-line dress patterns are altered on seams for figures that vary from the pattern standard. Also, skirt patterns are sometimes changed at seams and hemlines rather than through the sections or gores. The important thing to remember, in this case, is to redraw both cutting and stitching lines accurately. When adding to any shaped pattern edge, it is easy to trace the pattern lines on another sheet of paper. Then shift them over the necessary distance before pinning the paper to the pattern. Straight lines may be easier to mark with a ruler, especially if you have the transparent kind marked in both directions.

Analyze your problem to decide which of these adjustments will give you just what you need. Don't rush in recklessly, and be sure that you are not making unintentional changes as well as those you have planned. For instance, don't alter along center lines generally because you may be changing the neckline size or the proportions of a center panel—changes you hadn't intended to make. The same holds true for alterations at the armhole. Don't change the blouse side seam at the armhole without making a corresponding change in the sleeve seam.

Remember that you are dealing with a whole garment rather than just one pattern piece. Alter adjoining sections so that seam lines will still match. Alter linings, facings, and interfacings when corresponding garment sections have been altered.

Equipment for altering patterns, beside your list of trouble spots, includes a pair of scissors, some light-weight paper, and pins. Heavy paper isn't suitable for making insertions. The light pattern attached to it is likely to tear. You will also need a ruler and a pencil to re-draw construction details that are interrupted by your alterations.

Some of the more common alterations are shown on the following pages. Their numbers correspond to those of the check list on pages 412–413. You need not be limited by these, however, once you learn how to analyze your problems and decide on the best type alteration for each. You may even work out other methods for the common alterations given here.

Paper is shown under seam edges that must be re-drawn, but often pattern margins are wide enough for this purpose. Notice that center lines and grainlines are kept in line across insets. That is important. To reduce pattern size, pleats are used instead of tucks because they are more accurate. In other words, you pin through three layers of the pattern instead of two. Notice that a pleat removes twice its width—a ¼ inch pleat across a pattern, for example, shortens it ½ inch. Alter both the front and back of a pattern similarly unless different methods are shown.

BLOUSE ALTERATIONS

1.   Length of blouse, back and front

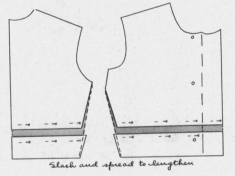

Slash and spread to lengthen

To lengthen a blouse (long waistline):

1. Cut across the pattern about 2 or 3 inches above the waistline at right angles to the center line.

2. Spread the pattern the necessary amount and pin each edge to a strip of paper.

3. Draw new side seam lines keeping them straight from armhole to waistline.

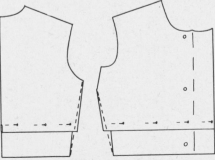

Make a pleat to shorten

To shorten a blouse (short waistline):

1. Make a pleat of the correct width across the pattern about 2 or 3 inches above waistline. Keep it at right angles to the center line. Pin.

2. Draw side seam lines, as above.

To shorten the blouse back more than the blouse front (flat back, erect posture):

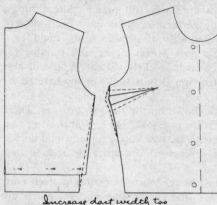

Increase dart width too

1. Shorten the back and front blouse patterns whatever amount is needed, using the methods described on page 415.

2. Increase the width of the underarm dart on the blouse front just enough to keep the front and back side seams the same length when the dart is folded out. In case there is no underarm dart, add one to shorten the front side seam. When the front is the correct length (as illustrated), this means that you have to take up exactly as much in the width of the dart as you do in the pleat.

2. Width at shoulders

To increase the shoulder width (broad shoulders):

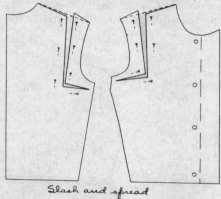

Slash and spread

1. Slash from the shoulder downward past the armhole, then across almost to the side seam.

2. Spread the slashed edges the correct amount and pin to a piece of paper.

3. Draw new shoulder seams making straight lines from the neckline to the armhole. (In case darts enter the shoulder seam, fold them out before drawing new shoulder seam lines.)

To decrease the shoulder width (narrow shoulders):

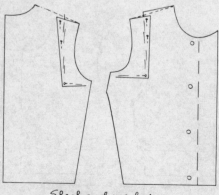

Slash and overlap

1. Slash as described above, but overlap the edges of the slash the necessary amount. Pin.

2. Draw new shoulder seam lines keeping them straight from neckline to armhole. (In case darts enter the shoulder seam, fold them out before drawing new shoulder seam lines.)

3. Slope of shoulder seam

To raise the height of the shoulder seam at its outer edge (square shoulders):

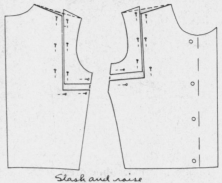

1. Slash from the shoulders downward, then across through the side seam.

2. Raise the entire armhole section and make a crosswise inset. Pin.

3. Draw new shoulder seam lines keeping them straight from the neckline to the armhole. (First fold out darts, as in step 3 under 2.)

Slash and raise

To lower the shoulder seam at its outer edge (sloping shoulders):

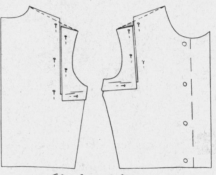

1. Slash as described above.

2. Lower the entire armhole section, overlapping along the crosswise slash. Pin.

3. Draw new shoulder seam lines from the neckline to the armhole keeping them straight from the neckline to the armhole. (First fold out darts, as in step 3 under 2.)

Slash and lower

4. Position and size of darts

To raise the dart positions (high bust):

1. Working from the crossed pins—those you used to indicate the highest point of the bust—find new positions for all dart points.

2. Draw new dart lines pointed toward these from the broad end of the original darts.

3. Pin paper to the side seam so that you can draw new seam lines.

4. Fold out the dart, turning it down as it will be pressed in the garment.

5. Draw new side seam lines using a tracing wheel so that all layers will be perforated.

Raise both dart points

To lower darts (low bust):

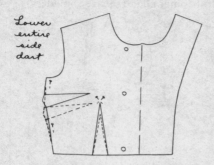

Lower entire side dart

Proceed as for a high bust, except that you lower all points. Also, you may wish to lower the wide end of the crosswise underarm dart to prevent a droopy, downward line. To do this:

1. Lower the point of the dart as needed.

2. Measure the distance between the original dart point and the new one.

3. Draw new dart lines parallel to the original ones.

4. Fold new dart and re-draw side seams.

To alter a princess-line dress at the bust (high or low bust):

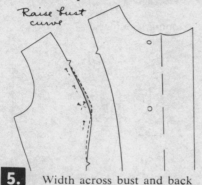

Raise bust curve

1. Working with the side front pattern, trace the bust curve on a strip of paper.

2. Raise the strip or lower it as necessary to center the curve on the crossed pins in your pattern which you used to indicate the high point of your bust.

3. Rule new seam lines from the new curve first to the shoulder line and then to the waistline.

5.   Width across bust and back

To increase the size of a blouse front (large bust):

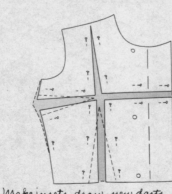

Make insets, draw new darts

1. Make slashes crosswise and lengthwise, cutting through the center of any darts. When there is no dart at the shoulder, slash almost to the shoulder line.

2. Spread the pattern and pin it to paper to add the necessary amount in each direction.

3. Locate new dart points halfway between the tips of the separated dart lines.

4. Draw lines from these points to the broad end of the original dart. (Notice that darts become wider, but that is what is needed.)

5. Draw new seam lines as described for raising dart positions for a high bust, steps 3, 4, and 5.

To increase the size of the back (full back):

1. Slash in both directions, as shown. If there is a dart on the shoulder seam, slash down the center of it.

2. Pin to paper, spreading the necessary amount—rarely more than ½ inch in either direction.

3. Locate a new dart point halfway between the tips of the original dart. Draw in the new dart from the broad end of the original dart. In the event that there was no shoulder dart in the pattern, add one the width of the slash and about 2½ inches long.

Make wedge-shaped slashes

To alter a princess-line dress at the bust (large or small bust):

1. Working with the side front pattern, trace the pattern curve at the bust line on a separate sheet of paper.

2. Move the traced curve in or out as necessary to increase or decrease the bust width.

3. Rule new seam lines from the curve to the shoulder seam and to the waistline.

4. Now take the front pattern piece and make a crosswise inset if you have increased the bust curve or a pleat if you have decreased it. This is necessary to keep seam lines equal in length.

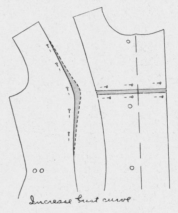

Increase bust curve

SLEEVE ALTERATIONS

6. Sleeve length

To lengthen a sleeve (long arms):

1. Slash directly across the sleeve above the elbow, and again below the elbow. Separate slash lines and make insets of correct widths to keep elbow darts or fullness properly located.

2. Straighten seam lines if necessary.

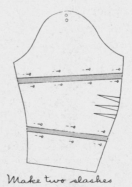

Make two slashes

To shorten a sleeve (short arms):

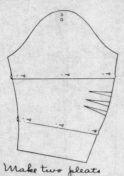

Make two pleats

1. Fold out pleats above and below the elbow to keep proportions correct.
2. Straighten seam lines if necessary.

7. Sleeve width

To increase the sleeve width (large arm):

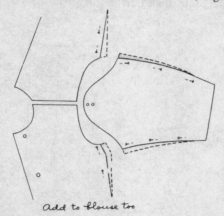

Add to blouse too

1. Add extra width on each side of the sleeve at the seam lines, tapering it off toward the wrist.
2. Add similarly to both front and back blouse side seams. At the armscye seam be sure that the alterations on blouse and sleeve are identical.

To decrease the sleeve width (slender arm):

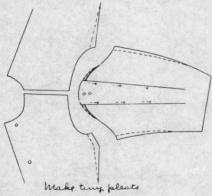

Make tiny pleats

1. Fold out tiny pleats (not more than ⅛ inch wide) on each side of the sleeve cap. Taper these off toward the wrist.
2. Redraw the sleeve cap.
3. For very thin arms, in addition, you may have to take out a small amount on both the sleeve and the blouse side seams. Do this in fitting preferably.

SKIRT ALTERATIONS

8. Waist measurement. Adjust the width of darts and the slope of seams to achieve a perfect fit. Generally it is better to do this during the first garment fitting rather than the pattern fitting.

9. Hip measurement

To increase the width (large hips):

1. Slash the side gore—both front and back—between the side seam and the dart position.

2. Make an inset of even width from waist to hem on both front and back. This alteration increases the size of the waistline but that can be adjusted above the hip line by taking up darts and seams, preferably at a fitting.

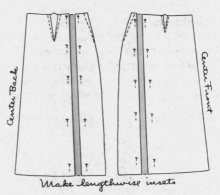

Make lengthwise insets

10. Length of skirt. Alter each gore equally

To lengthen a skirt pattern (tall girl):

1. Cut across the skirt pattern at right angles to the lengthwise straight-of-the-material line a few inches above the hemline.

2. Spread the slash the necessary amount and pin to a strip of paper.

3. Extend the seam lines and the hemline until they meet.

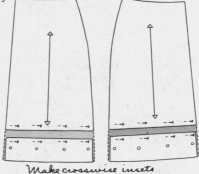

Make crosswise insets

To shorten a skirt pattern (short girl):

1. Fold a pleat of the correct width across each gore a few inches above the hemline. Fold at right angles to the grain line.

2. Straighten the seam lines by folding back the projecting edges below the crosswise alteration pleat. Keep each of the folded-back edges even in width.

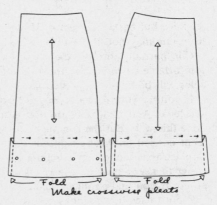

Make crosswise pleats

421

11. Hang of the skirt. Adjust the hang of the skirt at a garment fitting rather than in the pattern. See later in this technique.

FITTING THE GARMENT

Try the garment on when it is partially completed to check the fit and see whether the cloth falls as you want it to. Fabric conforms to the figure more readily, and falls more softly than the paper pattern; hence a few details may have to be adjusted as your work progresses.

Before you try the garment on for the first time, all staylines should have been made and all darts and vertical seams should have been either stitched or basted. The general rule is to stitch and press the darts and seams within front and back

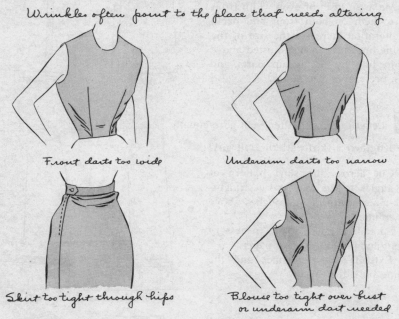

Wrinkles often point to the place that needs altering

Front darts too wide   *Underarm darts too narrow*

Skirt too tight through hips   *Blouse too tight over bust or underarm dart needed*

sections, but baste side seams. However, when you suspect that any dart, pleat, or seam line may not fit, baste it until after you have checked it.

Clip partially through the seam allowance of a snug fitting neckline to make it comfortable when you try the blouse on. Remember that the neckline and the armholes will be larger after their seams are stitched and finished.

If you try your garment on right side out, you can see how the finished garment will look. And for the figure that is different on the two sides, all fitting must be done this way. But the symmetrical figure is often more easily fitted when the garment is tried on wrong side out so that darts and seams are exposed. It is easier to place pins along new stitching lines from the wrong side. Also, alterations are easier to keep equal on the two sides of the figure when seams and darts are exposed. If you make radical changes, take the garment off and try it on again right side out to see how it looks before stitching the alterations.

When checking the fit of the garment, use the same standards as those you used when you checked the fit of the pattern. In addition, watch for any wrinkles because they are an indication that all is not well. The wrinkle itself often points to the place which needs altering. Here are a few examples:

A diagonal wrinkle that starts at the widest part of a dart often means that the dart is too wide.

A wrinkle that slants downward from the fullest part of a figure may mean that some dart is not wide enough.

A wrinkle that starts at a certain point on a seam often means that the seam is too tight there or too loose elsewhere.

A wrinkle directly across a skirt just below the waistband means that the skirt is too tight through the hips and should be let out, usually at the side seams.

If necessary, mark a new waistline

If necessary, mark a new waistline

Then, for dresses with waistline seams, trim to leave a seam allowance

For those without a seam, taper darts and seams from the new waistline

Fitting the blouse. Put the blouse on with closings accurately fastened. Fit over shoulder pads if they are to be used. Check the size of the neckline. Then check the slope of the shoulder seam. See if lifting the outer edge of the shoulder seam improves the set of the blouse. Go next to darts and other details within the front and back areas. Pin seams or darts that must be changed. Next, check the side seam, remembering to leave adequate ease through the bust. The side seam can be fitted snugly at the waistline, however.

Next, notice the armscye seam. Try to avoid any alteration that will change its size or position. When changes must be made, put a row of pins where you think the armscye seam stitching line should be. Then, after removing the blouse, fit the pattern to the armhole of the blouse, matching the stitching line of the pattern over the pin line as best you can. Recut the armhole along the cutting line of the pattern to retain the original shape.

After setting on the collar and basting in the sleeves, fit the blouse again to check the armscye seam. Check the waistline at this fitting also. To do this, tie a cord snugly around your figure at the waistline. Adjust the blouse. If the cord does not fall on the waistline of the blouse, mark a new line with pins or chalk along the cord. For a blouse that is to be attached to a skirt, trim below this line to leave a seam allowance. For princess-line blouses, darts and seam lines must be altered so that the waistline will be the smallest part of the blouse. This means that the widest part of double-pointed darts must fall exactly at the waist. Mark new lines along the side placket edges as well as other parts of the seam if side seams had to be changed.

Fitting the skirt. Before starting the fitting, the skirt should be pinned or basted to the blouse, the waistband, or a cord. Close the placket accurately and center the skirt on your figure. Adjust darts and seam lines, always working on the front and back, then on the side seams. If the skirt does not hang correctly, adjust the

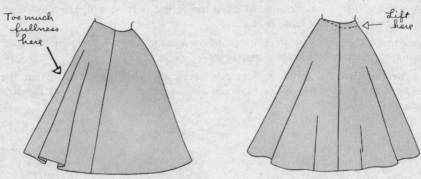

waistline seam. Lift the skirt wherever more fullness is needed. Lift it, also, at any low part of the waistline such as at a low hip or sway back to straighten seam lines. If the waistline has to be changed, mark a new one as you did the one on the blouse. Mark a new line on each side of the placket when the side seam has to be altered. Mark the hemline at the last fitting after other details have been stitched. See instructions in technique 19 "Hems" for making the hemline.

TECHNIQUE 6   *MATERIALS THAT REQUIRE SPECIAL HANDLING*

Some fabrics require special treatment at some stage of the construction. Some have a stubborn off-grain set that won't respond to ordinary squaring-up methods. Some have nap and require special cutting. Others are sheer and call for seams and finishes you wouldn't use on a sturdier garment. In this technique we will take up some of these special problems that you may not meet in the ordinary course of events, but will need help on if you do.

STRAIGHTENING AND SHRINKING STUBBORN CLOTH

Straightening the grain lines. Details on how to straighten ordinary cotton materials by pulling them are given as part of preparing to make a blouse in construction I, "Making a Blouse and Skirt." In the same construction, as you prepare to make a skirt, you are told how to straighten wool and similar fabrics by pressing them with a steam iron. These two processes ordinarily take care of straightening problems. Pressing used as the straightening method has the added advantage of shrinking wools and certain other fabrics if they happen to need it.

Some fabrics are more obstinate, however, and require greater moisture if their grain lines are to be straightened. Roll or fold these in a damp sheet and leave them for several hours. That makes them limp enough to straighten without difficulty. Keep them straight as you press. Follow the directions for "Shrinking wool" given later in this technique, because the procedures for straightening obstinate grain lines and for shrinking wool are the same.

You should realize that there are many fabrics that you should not attempt to straighten. Their grain lines are so permanently set that they will not change position even after they are cleaned. This group includes some—but not all—synthetic fabrics, and certain rayons, cottons, and linens with crush-resistant finishes, glazes, and plastic prints. These cannot be straightened and do not ordinarily shrink. Cut them as they come.

Shrinking materials. If you have no assurance that a fabric has been adequately pre-shrunk when you buy it, it may pay you to shrink it yourself, especially if you are making a garment where fit and length are important. The difficulty with most home shrinking is that cloth is likely to become wrinkled and misshapen if it is not carefully handled. Never shrink any fabric that has been properly shrunk during finishing, because it is a waste of time and often injures the appearance of the cloth as well.

You will never need to shrink "Sanforized" fabrics or others which are guaranteed to shrink not more than 1 percent. Neither will you need to shrink wools manufactured by well-established mills which invariably pre-shrink their fabrics adequately. "London shrunk" (on worsteds) and "Thoroughly sponged" are some of the labels to look for on wool.

Steam pressing as a shrinking process. Crepe materials, sheer materials, wools, and many other dry-cleanable fabrics need only careful steam pressing to shrink them sufficiently before they are used. This method preserves the original appearance of the cloth better than other methods and does not shrink the material excessively. Press with the grain except when attempting to straighten the fabric.

Shrinking washable fabrics. Cottons and linens have to be immersed in water to be shrunk, because that is the way they will be cleaned later. Proceed as follows:

1. Cut or tear both ends along a crosswise thread.

2. Fold the cloth lengthwise down the center, preferably right side in.

3. Fold several times crosswise and place the cloth in a basin of warm water. Soak several hours or overnight.

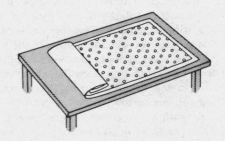

4. Lift the cloth and allow it to drip; do not wring it.

5. Spread an old sheet or other cloth on a table. Place the fabric on the cloth and fold both together. Leave them folded up for a short time.

6. Spread both out flat and straighten the material you are shrinking. Be sure that all edges are matched and the ends are at right angles to the sides. Allow to dry partially if too damp to press.

7. Press with the grain, but do not press quite to the fold. Open the material and press along the fold.

Shrinking wool. Wool may be shrunk much like a washable fabric, except that it is not immersed in water. Here is the procedure to follow:

1. Cut along a crosswise thread at each end of the cloth.

2. Fold the cloth lengthwise down the center with the right side in and place it on a table.

3. Wring an old sheet or other clean cloth from water (preferably warm).

4. Lay the sheet over the wool fabric. Fold the two together smoothly. The reason for folding rather than rolling is that you might roll wrinkles in. Cover with a dry cloth and leave several hours or overnight until the wool is damp through.

5. Spread the wool out on the cloth. Straighten the grain lines by matching the ends of the cloth and keeping them at right angles to the fold and to the selvages.

6. Allow the wool to dry thoroughly while flat.

7. Steam press.

TYPES OF MATERIALS THAT PRESENT SPECIAL PROBLEMS

Sheer materials. Your first consideration in planning a sheer dress or blouse is to select a pattern that will make up attractively. This means a pattern with some fullness since the material is so light. It also means a pattern that calls for garment edges that will look neat and attractive in sheer material. Narrow bindings of self fabric or grosgrain ribbon, for example, make an excellent edge finish and are infinitely more attractive than wide facings which would show through to the right side and spoil the transparent effect. In figured sheers, facings are even less attractive because of the blotches of confused design they create.

Seams, too, must be especially neat and narrow in sheer garments. There should be no ravelings. Even pinked edges are not attractive. Use French seams or plain seams double stitched and trimmed, as described in technique 10, "Seams and Seam Finishes." Turn hems a second time instead of finishing them with seam binding. Sheer materials such as nets, marquisettes, and laces, must be stitched over strips of light-weight paper to keep their seam lines from drawing. After stitching, tear the paper away.

Any sheer material is fairly difficult to work with, but some, such as chiffon, are so soft and flimsy that you should not attempt them until you have had years of sewing experience. Then pin or baste the fabric to thin paper and work with it that way as you cut and construct the garment.

Other sheer fabrics, such as net and lace, do not have grain lines. You cannot draw threads to straighten the cloth, yet there is a difference in the way they behave in the two directions. They stretch much more crosswise than lengthwise and for this reason patterns must be laid as if there were grain lines.

Beneath a transparent blouse an ordinary attractive—concealing—slip will do, but every sheer dress demands a slip of its own. The slip—often of taffeta—may be attached to the dress or not, but should almost invariably be the same color as the dress and should be designed for that dress and no other.

Knitted materials. Jersey presents another problem in pattern selection whether you choose it in wool, silk, rayon, or a blend. Tight garments, especially skirts, should be lined, for unless they are treated in this way, jersey stretches too much and it shapes to the figure too readily. Designs with some fullness are graceful and show off the excellent draping quality of the fabric to advantage. Gathers are good

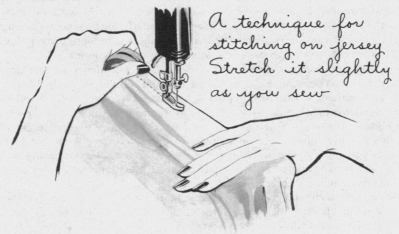

A technique for stitching on jersey Stretch it slightly as you sew

Celanese Corporation of America

and so are unpressed pleats. Fullness of this kind is particularly desirable in skirts because it makes possible the use of rather straight-cut sections in them. Flared and circular skirts are not a good choice because jersey stretches excessively both crosswise and on the diagonal and that means sagging, uneven hemlines except on nearly straight-cut skirts. Orlon and nylon jersey can have pressed pleats permanently set but this is best done commercially.

Making the layout and cutting jersey may confuse you a bit at first. Because jersey is knitted instead of woven, it may come to you in a tubular form or it may be flat. In either case there are no true grain lines, and yet it has to be cut as if there were. Use the wales, those lengthwise lines, as the lengthwise grain, and the courses, the crosswise lines, as the crosswise grain. You cannot tear jersey. You have to cut along the lines instead. Open up tubular jersey only when you have to place pattern sections on a single layer.

There is a trick to stitching, too. Because jersey stretches so much as it is worn, tight seam lines break, causing unsightly rips. To prevent this from happening, stretch the seam lines slightly as you sew. You do this by holding one hand in front of the needle and the other behind it, but do not interfere with the way the cloth feeds under the presser foot. Let the machine take the cloth through.

Nylon. Spun nylon fabrics and fabrics blended with a small percentage of filament nylon usually cause no particular problems during construction. However, fabrics woven of nylon filament yarns, either entirely or in appreciable amounts, are likely to shift yarn positions during wear unless they have been given special treatments during finishing. Some of the other synthetics show this tendency too, although nylon is the worst. Puckered effects and plastic prints seem to bind yarns permanently in place and thus tend to prevent slippage. Either avoid fabrics that shift yarns easily or make them up into loose-fitting garments that will receive little wear and practically no stress on seams.

Despite all of their other excellent qualities, nylon fabrics have still another trait that gives trouble in sewing if it isn't well handled. Stitching tends to draw seam lines and ripple the fabric on either side—particularly long seams on a lengthwise grain. Slanting seams draw or pucker less than others, and therefore a pattern with flared gores cut with bias seams is a good choice for this fabric.

The way you stitch can do much also to reduce this tendency toward drawn and rippled seams. You should use the finest machine needle available (one for size 100 cotton thread at least) and either nylon thread or size A silk thread. Set the stitch regulator to stitch 14 or 15 stitches to the inch. In addition, loosen both top and bottom tensions as much as you can and still produce a good stitch. It's best not to stitch over pins. Either place them to one side of the seam line or remove them as you come to them. Then, as you sew, use the same stretching technique you would use for knitted fabrics, that is, stretch the seam but allow the cloth to feed normally under the presser foot.

Velvet, velveteen, and corduroy. All pile fabrics have a heaviness that should be considered in choosing designs for them. Since part of their beauty lies in the play of light and shadow on their surfaces, velvet and velveteen are particularly attractive when made by a pattern with some fullness or draping. Corduroy is usually made in tailored designs, though in lightweights it gathers very well, also.

Examine the direction of the pile on any of these fabrics. Run your hand first up, then down the cloth to tell which way it is pressed. Then hold the opposite ends of the cloth up side by side. You will notice that one end looks darker than the other. Velvets and velveteens look richer and darker when the pile runs upward and that is the way they are usually cut. Corduroy is generally cut the opposite way. As you must realize, you have to cut any pile fabric by the pattern layout marked "material with nap" and that takes more cloth than usual.

Velvet is very easily crushed and marred. It comes in a special roll as you buy it and that's the way you should store it. Roll it loosely and then put safety pins through the selvage to hang it from a coat hanger. To baste as well as to stitch velvet, use silk thread. For "pinning" it, use fine needles. Velveteen and corduroy are not so fragile.

Seams on any pile fabric shift and slip as you attempt to stitch them. Because of this, you had better hand-baste them before stitching. It will probably save time in the long run. It is difficult to stitch zippers in place, too, because of this shifting. This is a good time to try out that hand-sewn zipper described in technique 17, "Plackets."

Pressing is a bit of a problem too, especially on velvet and velveteen, since the weight of an iron against the pile flattens it. Directions for pressing pile fabrics are given in techinque 12, "Pressing." Even so, a collar or cuff with velvet on both sides is a problem. For that reason as well as for design interest, braid or binding is sometimes used around the edge to give a finished appearance—or one side of the collar is made of taffeta, satin, or faille.

Felt. Felt, sold by the yard, is another popular fabric with a few idiosyncracies. It is fairly stiff and hardly stretches at all and for those reasons it makes up well in simple jackets and sag-proof circular skirts. It resists the cold and the rain and so we use it for hoods and mittens. Then for a bit of fun and gaiety we cut it out— sometimes with pinking shears—in various designs and colors to decorate other garments. We can do this because its edges never fray. There's one precaution though. Don't make it up into tight clothing unless you line it, because it isn't strong and will tear if you do.

Because it has no grain lines and needs so little finishing, felt is the easiest of all fabrics to sew. Its structure is the same in every direction. As you may have guessed, this means that you can turn your pattern in *any* direction. You never have to finish seams, and you can even cut felt off wherever you like without a hem or any other edge finish.

One thing, though, you must watch out for. The more you press felt, the worse it looks and the more it shrinks. Don't press it at all or press it as little as possible.

Twill fabrics. The pattern you select for a twill fabric should have no decidedly bias-cut seams, bias bands which will show on the right side, or similar details. Where bias seam lines occur in this kind of fabric, perfectly cut garment sections seem to be cut off-grain because of the slant of the twill. The reason for this is found in the twill itself, and the more prominent the twill, the worse the effect. Your answer is to select a pattern with relatively straight-cut sections.

Some people wonder if twills have an up and down. Ordinary twills do not and should be cut by a layout marked "without nap." Only a very few uneven twills require the "with nap" layout.

Sometimes it is difficult to distinguish the right side of a twill fabric. If you have this trouble turn to technique 7, "Laying the Pattern on the Cloth."

Bold designs. Any time the design of the material is conspicuous, keep the design of the garment simple. Instead of adding to the beauty of the garment, intricate seaming merely confuses the pattern of the fabric. Plan widely spaced designs so that they fall well on the figure and are not broken by seam lines, if possible.

Plaids and stripes. Since the lines in plaids and stripes are straight, these designs look best when made into garments with predominantly straight lines. Whether the seams of the design are straight or fall along a bias, the effect is usually pleasing. It is only when garment lines are curved or intricately cut that the harmony between garment and cloth is lost. Also, few garment sections are better than many. Two- and four-gore plaid skirts, for instance, are more attractive than such skirts with six or more gores.

If you notice plaids carefully, you will see that some have a definite "up and down," that is, the same end of the cloth must be turned up on all parts of the garment. These same plaids often have a definite "right and left" also. Unless you have infinite patience and skill, you had better avoid this *uneven* kind, the kind with an up and down and a right and left. The only really simple garments to make of this kind of plaid are gathered skirts or scarves where almost no cutting is needed.

Fortunately there are *even* plaids that are not quite so difficult to handle. Either end of these can be turned up and they have no right and left sides. (Don't confuse that with right and wrong sides.)

Stripes, too, are sometimes even and sometimes uneven, and again the even ones that can be reversed are easier to cut correctly.

Planning the layout for plaids and stripes requires care and thought. That is why beautifully cut readymade garments of these fabrics are expensive. Compare the ones you see at school or on the streets and you will notice how much more attractive plaids and stripes are when they are centered on the figure and matched across seam lines than when they are not so placed. Whenever possible place the most conspicuous stripe down the center front and center back lines of all pieces. Then match stripes across seams. This can only be done when seam edges are cut straight or on the same slant. Plan your cutting, when you can, so that conspicuous or dark stripes outline garment areas such as collars, yokes, and hemmed edges. When you can't do that or when matching is difficult, consider turning certain small sections on the bias. Before you do it, though, think of the entire effect. Refer to technique 7, "Laying the Pattern on the Cloth," for help in cutting plaids and stripes. You must realize that you will have to buy extra material when you use plaids or stripes. The larger the design the greater your waste will be.

Geometric prints. The best advice about *printed* checks, plaids, crosswise stripes, and other geometric prints with pronounced crosswise designs is "Don't buy them." They are so seldom printed on a true grain. Then when they are cut perfectly true,

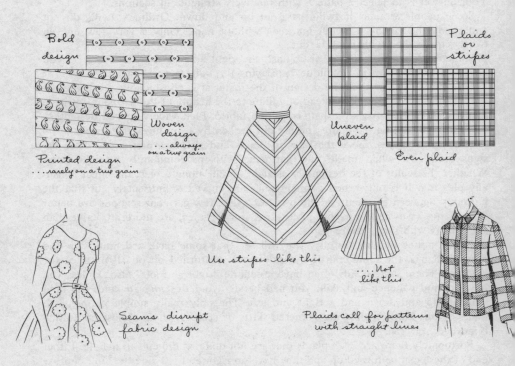

Bold design

Printed design . . . rarely on a true grain

Woven design . . . always on a true grain

Plaids or stripes

Uneven plaid

Even plaid

Use stripes like this

. . . . Not like this

Seams disrupt fabric design

Plaids call for patterns with straight lines

the design makes them seem to be cut off-grain. Once you own such a fabric, the only thing to do is to ignore the crosswise grain and cut the garment with its crosswise stripes squared. The garment will twist on your figure as you wear it, but that is better than having stripes that run in a crooked direction across your figure.

TECHNIQUE 7 *LAYING THE PATTERN ON THE CLOTH*

The first step in laying the pattern on the cloth is to find the cutting diagram planned for the style you have chosen, for the size of your pattern, and for the width of your material, either with or without nap. Encircle that diagram with a pencil line, so that it will be easy to locate as you use it.

You know which style you want and the size is stamped on the pattern. At the time you bought your material you must have known its width, but if you have forgotten, it's time you learned about standard widths. While there are no regulations about the widths of various types of fabrics, there are certain practices which have grown up over the years. Measurements are never exact, however, because the finishing processes often change the woven widths by an inch or so. Here are some of the more common widths of various fabrics:

Dressweight cottons and linens	35 inches
Silks, rayons, acetates, and synthetics	39 inches or occasionally 42, 54, or 60 inches
Woolens, worsteds, and rayon suitings	54 inches or occasionally 60 inches
Net	72 inches or occasionally 36 inches

DETERMINING THE RIGHT SIDE OF THE MATERIAL

Before you make a layout you have to determine the right and the wrong side of your material. Sometimes it doesn't matter. Gingham and chambray, for instance, are the same on both sides. They are made with a plain weave even if designed with stripes, checks, or plaids. Percale, broadcloth, poplin, organdy, dimity, crepes, and many other plain weave fabrics are reversible in plain colors but are not if they have printed designs.

Other materials are sometimes reversible but certainly not always. Even if they look the same at first glance, they may have knots or long threads on the wrong side which would affect their wearing qualities. If you don't see any of these imperfections and you prefer the look of the wrong side, you can go ahead and use it for the outside of your garment.

However, you should know which side is considered "right." There are many clues to go by. Prints are clearer and brighter on the right side. Look at the selvage if you have difficulty because the differences show up more clearly there.

Notice the way the cloth is rolled on the bolt as you buy it. Cotton and linen materials come either folded with their right sides out or rolled on the bolt that way. Wools, silks, and most rayons, acetates, nylons, and other synthetics are folded or rolled in the opposite direction with their right sides in.

The weave, too, gives you many clues. The right side is more perfect and free from imperfections and the selvage is often smoother on that side. Examine fabrics with woven designs for long floating yarns, rough spots and irregularities. These denote the wrong side in most cases. (If some imperfections do appear on the right side of your material, mark them with chalk so you can avoid them in making your layout or return the cloth to your merchant for an adjustment.)

It's simple to tell the right side of dotted Swiss because it has clear dots on the right side with thread ends drawn to the under side. Pinwale piqué has distinct vertical ridges on the right side. Twills are sometimes more difficult to distinguish. Twills run in specific directions in each type of cloth. When you hold up a wool twill against your body, the right side of the material is generally turned out when the twill runs from your left shoulder toward your right hip. Cotton twills commonly run in the opposite direction. There are exceptions, though. You will have no difficulty with fabrics like gabardine because the twill on the right side is raised and much clearer than it is on the wrong side.

FOLDING THE CLOTH

Look at your circled diagram to see how the cloth should be folded. Notice selvages, cut-ends, and fold lines. There are four kinds of folds:

1. Lengthwise center fold
2. Crosswise center fold
3. Off-center lengthwise fold
4. Off-center crosswise fold

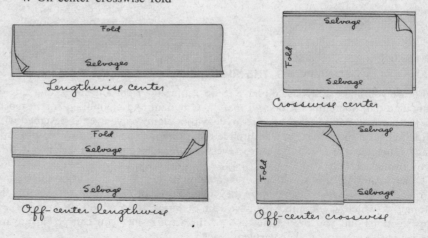

Lengthwise center

Crosswise center

Off-center lengthwise

Off-center crosswise

Some patterns require a combination of these folds, others must be partly or entirely laid on a single layer of cloth.

Always fold the right side of the material to the inside, so that it will be kept clean, and markings can be made on the wrong side. When a single layer of cloth is to be cut, turn the right side of the cloth up.

As you fold your material, keep the grain lines straight. Center folds are no problem because you match selvages and ends. To make an off-center fold on material which is already cut you may have to tear or cut along a thread to get the grain straightened again. Then proceed as follows:

1. Determine from the pattern piece the width of the fold. Its greatest width is the measurement you use.

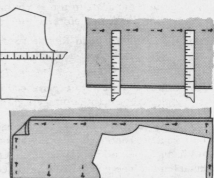

2. Measure this distance from a selvage or a straightened edge at regular intervals. Mark this fold line with pins.

3. Fold along the marked line and pin the fold.

4. Match the edges of the material at the ends of the fold. Pin at intervals to hold the side and the ends of the fold smooth and in place.

FOLLOWING THE LAYOUT

Diagram. Put the layout diagram where you can see it easily and place the cloth as it is shown on the diagram. For instance, if the fold is turned toward you on the diagram, turn the fold of the cloth toward you on the table. A trick to keep the grain lines true is to line up the edges of the cloth with the table edges.

Now starting at one end of the cloth, lay the pattern pieces as they are shown on the diagram. Notice the shape of each and the position of the notches and other details to be sure that all pieces are correctly placed. Here are a few hints.

Make a trial layout before you do any pinning. Place all the pattern pieces on the material tentatively to make sure that you have enough material.

To place sections marked "Lay on a lengthwise fold," first pin the fold line indicated on the pattern exactly on the fold of the cloth. Next, place pins diagonally at all corners, and then place other pins at right angles to the edges in between. Use just enough pins to hold the pattern in place.

To place all other pieces, keep the grain line marked on the pattern parallel to the selvage of the cloth. First place the pattern on the cloth as straight as you can freehand. Then working first at the wide end of the pattern piece, pin that end of the long line marked "Straight of the Material" in place. Now measure from that end of the arrow to the selvage. Note that measurement and adjust the pattern so that the other end of the line measures exactly that same distance from the selvage. Pin that end of the line in place. Then place other pins at corners and along edges as you did above.

Fit pieces close together for an economical layout. The margins of printed patterns may overlap, but allow space for cutting notches outward.

Notice that certain pattern sections are shaded or outlined in broken lines on the diagram. These pieces are to be placed on the cloth wrong side up.

Using a pattern piece once right side up and a second time wrong side up is the way to get a pair when you are cutting from a single layer of cloth rather than from folded material.

When any part of the pattern must be used more than once, it is a good idea to cut a duplicate to use as you make the layout. Substitute the actual pattern for the duplicate before cutting, because the pattern will be more accurate.

If you plan to add to side seams or hems, leave adequate material on the layout. Mark these new cutting lines with pins or chalk after you have pinned the pattern down.

Unless you are very experienced in making layouts, ask your teacher to check your layout before you start cutting.

Making your own layout. Occasionally you have to make your own layout either because there is no layout for fabric the width of yours or because you have altered or changed the pattern a great deal. Try the standard folds until you find the most suitable one. The general rule is to keep the uncut material in as large a piece or pieces as possible. Follow the suggestions above and these extra hints:

Place large pieces at one end of the cloth or at both ends.

Turn the widest part of the pattern toward the cut-end of the cloth, generally.

Re-fold the fabric for narrow pieces that are to be cut on a fold.

Dovetail pieces, fitting the wide end of one piece beside the narrow end of another.

Fit small pieces between larger ones.

Cut pairs, not identical pieces, for the right and left sides of the figure. There are two ways to do this. Either cut both pieces at one time from folded material or cut one piece with the pattern placed right side up and the second piece with the pattern turned over, wrong side up.

Materials that require special handling in making a layout. When you are making a layout, some materials have to be handled in special ways. There's one group that has to be cut by the "with nap" diagram: that is, with all tops turned in the same direction. There's another group that calls for careful placement to get designs well spaced and matched. See technique 6.

Napped fabrics, because they are usually brushed in one direction, are an excellent example of the first group. They even give their name to the diagram designed to handle the problem.

Pile fabrics of any kind also have a definite up-and-down, and must be cut by layout for "material with nap." Most velvets and velveteens look richer when the pile runs upward on the figure. Corduroys are cut with the pile running down. To find the direction of the pile or nap, simply run your finger along the material.

Designs, too, sometimes have to be cut as though the material had nap. This is true of any figured fabric that looks different when opposite ends of the material are held up. Imagine the effect of a dress with horses standing in their normal position on one side and standing on their heads on the other side! Plaids sometimes have a definite "up" end, and so do certain stripes. Differences from side to side puts any design in this same category too.

Going into the second group, bold, widely spaced designs should be carefully balanced on the figure. Consider the placement of the design when you try on the pattern. You might even sketch in on the pattern the best way for the design to fall and try to come as close to that as possible when you make your layout.

Any material with lengthwise designs, such as stripes and plaids, looks far more attractive if one of the prominent lines falls exactly down the front and back center lines of the garment. This means that all center lines on the blouse pattern as well as collars and the like should be placed down the center of this prominent line. Since many of these pieces are cut on a fold, this often means folding the fabric down the center of a prominent stripe before laying down the pattern. If stripes run vertically at skirt center lines, they, too, should be cut in the same way.

Match bold designs across seam lines if you can and match plaids and stripes to form continuous lines across seams or to meet at equal angles. A simple trick for cutting the right and left sides of a garment alike (and incidentally matching center front and center back seams if there happen to be any) is to fold the cloth so that designs match on the two layers. Then cut by one pattern piece at a time and use the garment sections you have cut to place adjoining pattern pieces. Shift the pattern piece on the cloth until the designs match on the two sections at seam lines—not cutting lines. Stripes will match if they are spaced identically at the notches on seam edges that are to be joined—provided you aren't trying to join seams that slant differently. If you cannot cut collars, yokes, or cuffs so that their plaids match those in adjacent garment sections, try them on a true bias.

PIECING

Circular skirts are occasionally so wide that they cannot be cut from the cloth without piecing. When you are short of material you may also have to piece certain sections. Plan piecings in inconspicuous places. Piece along grain lines (lengthwise if possible) and match nap and designs. After you have cut out the whole garment, select a scrap for the piecing. If you can find a piece with selvage you will have a firm edge that won't need finishing. To make piecings along selvage edges:

1. Place selvage edges together with right sides of the material facing. Pin along the edge of the selvage, placing pins parallel to the edge.

2. Open the piecing out flat and replace the pattern.

3. Cut out the piece.

4. Stitch and press the seam, clipping the selvage at intervals to keep it from drawing.

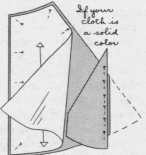

If your cloth is a solid color

When piecing figured materials, follow this method:

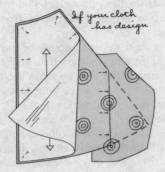

If your cloth has design

1. Be sure the edge to be pieced is cut along a thread or falls along a selvage.

2. From the right side, fold under a seam allowance.

3. Place a scrap of the cloth right side up under the fold. Shift the scrap until grain lines and figures match.

4. Pin, placing pins at right angles to the fold.

5. Replace pattern and cut out the piece.

6. Slip baste along the folded under edge.

7. Turn over and stitch from the wrong side as a plain seam.

8. Trim, unless you joined selvage edges, and press the seam open.

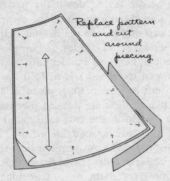

Replace pattern and cut around piecing

TECHNIQUE 8   *CUTTING AND MARKING*

Cut out your garment as soon as you, and perhaps your teacher, have checked your layout. As you cut, walk around the table yourself instead of pulling the material to you. Keep your left hand beside the part you are cutting to hold the material down on the table and to keep the pattern from shifting. Follow the outer printed line on printed patterns or the outer edge of cut patterns. But do not cut slash lines, generally, until you have done some stitching. Use sharp shears and cut with long even strokes. Do not close the shears completely except when cutting to an exact point. Then poise the tips of the shears directly above the point where the cutting should stop and close the shears firmly all the way.

Indicate notches by cutting them out, away from the pattern. Make a short clip into the seam allowance to indicate center lines. Make a similar clip at the top of a set-in sleeve where the symbol appears on the pattern. Use the points of the scissors in cutting these details to prevent you from clipping too far.

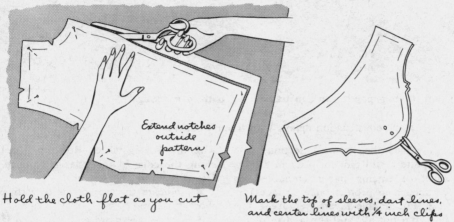

Hold the cloth flat as you cut

Mark the top of sleeves, dart lines, and center lines with ¼ inch clips

MARKING

What to mark. Mark all details, not already shown by notches or clips, which will be needed during the construction of the garment. Sometimes seam lines, especially those along straight edges, are left unmarked and a stitching guide is used to keep seams even. Beginners find traced lines quite helpful. Mark these details:

Seam lines, at least those along curves and corners

Center lines along closings

Darts

Fold lines

Positions for ease or gathers

Positions for pockets

Buttonholes and buttons

Slash lines

Points where a stitching line should stop

Any other special markings used to construct the garment

How to mark. The fastest and most accurate way to transfer construction details from pattern to cloth is with dressmaker's tracing paper or carbon. Use a tracing wheel and have the carbon mounted on a heavy cardboard to protect table surfaces. Details should be marked on the wrong side of the cloth where most construction lines are needed. Use white tracing paper wherever possible, because it is safe. If carefully handled, its mark lasts until needed, and may be almost completely removed by pressing with a warm iron. The pigment in colored tracing paper leaves a more permanent line. It can usually be removed by scrubbing, but ordinary washing methods and dry-cleaning do not always remove it. Test a scrap of your cloth before marking the garment. Garment sections should have been cut with the right sides of the cloth together, or when cut from a single thickness, with the right side up, next to the pattern.

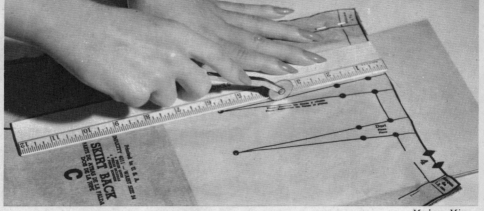

Modern Miss

With tracing paper you can transfer all pattern markings.

To mark construction details with tracing paper:

1. Place the garment section, with the pattern still pinned to it, on a large sheet of tracing paper (mounted on cardboard to protect table surfaces).

2. For double layers, remove a few pins, but not all, and slip a strip of the tracing paper, wax side down, between the pattern and the cloth.

3. Use a ruler to mark straight lines with the tracing wheel. Run the wheel along the edge of the ruler only once. Use a firm, steady motion.

4. Indicate the tips of darts with a short cross line.

5. Curves are more easily marked if the handle of the tracing wheel is slanted slightly inward toward the center of the curve.

Certain lines, such as those for folds and some kinds of pockets and buttonholes are needed on the right side of the cloth. Make the longest machine stitch, called a baste-stitch, along the traced lines on the under side of the cloth. Stitch through a single layer. The basting shows the detail on the right side of the cloth.

White, figured, and light-colored materials that cannot be successfully marked with tracing paper should be marked with tailor's tacks. Use mercerized thread of different colors to indicate different construction details such as center lines and darts. Darning cotton is excellent for tailor's tacks since it clings in place better than glossier threads. Tacks can be made through either one or two layers of cloth.

To make a tailor's tack:

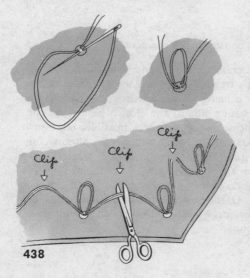

1. Thread a needle with a long strand of thread. Use it doubled, without a knot.

2. Take a small stitch through a perforation or on a printed line.

3. Leave a thread end about ½ to 1 inch long, and take another small stitch beside the first. Draw the thread through to form a loop somewhat shorter than the thread end.

4. Clip the threads to form another end the length of the first. A series of tacks can all be made before cutting the thread ends, but be sure to leave enough thread floating between the tacks for two ends.

5. After all tacks have been made, remove the pattern gently. Printed patterns will need to be slit at each tailor's tack with the point of a needle or pin, so that the pattern can be lifted without being torn.

6. Where the tailor's tack was made through two layers of cloth, separate these gently and cut threads between them. Notice that both sides of two layers of cloth can be marked with one tack.

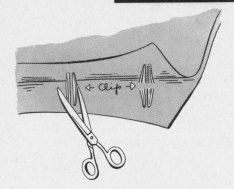

Tailor's chalk comes in white and colors for marking cloth. Again, white is safer than colors. The *wax* chalk is designed for use on wool. On wool it disappears when pressed, but on other fabrics it leaves a greasy mark. *French* chalk and *clay* chalk are for general use. They come in both cake and pencil form. Keep either kind sharpened so that you can make sharp lines. Use a ruler to keep the line straight. Use an entire edge of cake chalk to mark a straight line, not just a corner. Make chalk marks on the under side of the cloth, generally. Test a scrap if there is any danger of injuring your fabric.

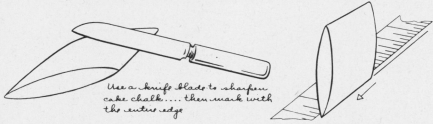

Use a knife blade to sharpen cake chalk.... then mark with the entire edge

Lines of hand-basting may be used for marking certain lines on fragile or easily marred fabric. Silk thread is less likely to injure material than cotton.

Pins, pressed lines, chalked basting threads, and other methods can all be used at times for marking cloth. Avoid the use of a lead pencil where the line will be seen from the right side of the garment, because the mark is rather permanent. A faint pencil mark can sometimes be used on interfacings, or for marking cutting lines for bias strips, and the like.

TECHNIQUE 9 *STAYLINES, INTERFACINGS, AND LININGS*

Staylines, interfacings, and linings might be called the "hidden values" in any garment. They do not show from the outside, but their effects do. Staylines keep seams and grain lines true, and interfacings and linings give crispness, body, and strength where these qualities are needed.

STAYLINES

A stayline is a line of ordinary machine stitching made in the seam allowance of a garment through a single layer of material. Staylines are used to reinforce curved and bias-cut edges, and thus keep the garment in shape. When you make staylines, keep the machine tension well regulated, because a stayline that draws can distort the grain as much as a stretched seam line.

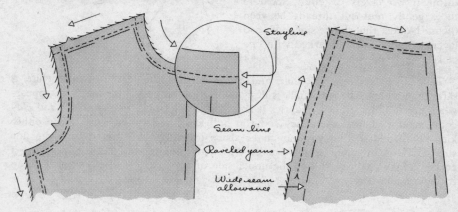

Make staylines with the grain. Think of the frayed yarns along the edge of the material as the fur of an animal. Stitch in the direction in which you would stroke fur. Garment edges cut on the straight of the material need no staylines.

Until you have learned to stitch straight, a stitching guide is a big help in making accurate staylines. Stitch ⅛ inch from the stitching line toward the seam edge. On ⅝-inch seam allowances this would make the stayline ½ inch from the raw edge. However, if you have cut garment side seams with extra wide seam allowances, stitch the stayline ½ inch from the raw edge instead of ⅛ inch from the seam line. Then if the seam must be let out, you will not need to rip the stayline.

INTERFACINGS

Interfacings are used in cuffs, collars, and other garment parts to add stiffness, crispness, or body. They improve the roll of a collar or the way a cuff stands. Strips along center closings reinforce buttonholes and the cloth beneath buttons.

Materials used for interfacing. *Permanent-finished organdy* gives a crisp, light-weight effect, and its crispness lasts through many washings. *Muslin, cambric, long cloth,* and *lawn* are all useful interfacing materials and all will wash if necessary. Lawn is starched more than the rest, but the starch finish is not always permanent. *Acetate taffeta* does not wash, but used inside crepes or soft wool it gives a rustling body that is quite attractive. *Linen canvas* is made of natural colored linen and is rather heavy. *Mohair canvas, tailor's canvas,* or *hair canvas* is used under wool and heavy fabrics in suits and coats. It holds up well, but because its springiness keeps it from lying flat inside faced edges, it requires special handling. *Pellon* and other plasticized fiber interfacings are easy to handle. They come in several weights and are all washable and dry-cleanable. They do not lie quite as flat or roll quite as smoothly, however, as woven interfacings. Instead, they often break into irregular, crackled surfaces—somewhat like paper though softer, of course.

Unless it has already been done, shrink any interfacing material thoroughly before cutting. Always shrink unbleached muslin, for instance, but not organdy.

How to cut interfacings. An interfacing is generally cut on the same grain as the part of the garment it interfaces. It should not be cut crosswise to interface a lengthwise strip, or vice versa. Sometimes bias interfacings are used on straight sections to reduce the chance of puckering. Straight interfacings may be used on bias-cut sections to prevent stretching.

Few commercial patterns include interfacing patterns. When they are not included, you will have to use regular pattern pieces. For instance, use the collar pattern to cut the collar interfacing. Use the facing pattern to cut interfacings for necklines and closings. But when you use the facing pattern, cut the interfacing ½ to 1 inch narrower than the pattern along the unnotched edge. That will prevent it from showing after the edge of the facing is finished.

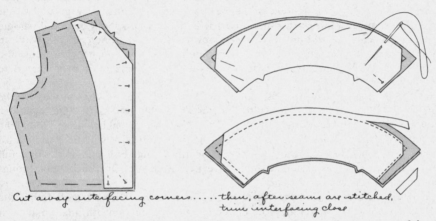

Cut away interfacing corners.....then, after seams are stitched, trim interfacing close

To keep from adding bulkiness to the garment, cut away the corners of interfacings as soon as the interfacings are cut out. Cut across each corner just inside the seam allowance, about ⅛ to ¼ inch from the corner. After stitching the seams around interfacings, trim away interfacing seam allowances very close to the stitching line. This is possible because there will be almost no strain on these edges and little raveling once the raw edges are enclosed.

Attaching interfacings. Interfacings can sometimes be attached as the staylines are being made. Edges where staylines are not needed may be baste-stitched to hold the interfacing in place temporarily. For instance, an interfacing used along a front closing would be stay-stitched at the neckline but baste-stitched down the straight front edge of the closing.

Instead of machine basting, hand basting is often used. Diagonal basting is particularly suitable since it keeps the interfacing very smooth.

LININGS

Many fine dresses, skirts, and blouses of opaque materials are lined, either throughout or partially, to strengthen, protect, and preserve the shape of the garment. Sheer materials, such as net, lace, and marquisette, are lined for these reasons and also to reduce their transparency. Gathered and flared skirts may be lined to increase their bouffant or "stand-away" effect.

Unless you are striving for a crisp silhouette, linings should generally be of rather soft, lightweight material which will not appreciably change the drape and appearance of the dress fabric. Organza (the name given to silk and rayon organdy), marquisette, china silk (a thin silk originally made in China), and flat crepe are suitable lining materials for many silk or wool garments. Stiffened effects may require a lining of taffeta or one of the many weights of Pellon or similar lining materials. Try textures together first and note the transparency and color combination to make sure that you are producing the effect you want.

Test both fabric and lining for shrinkage. Even a little in either one ruins the final effect. Obviously both fabrics should clean alike, too, because they will be permanently united. Drip-dry and other washable materials are usually not lined, but if they should be, select drip-dry or washable linings, too.

To cut linings, use the main pattern pieces for the areas to be lined. You may want to line a skirt throughout, or, if the material is opaque, only partially. The back of any pencil-slim skirt, especially if it is made of a spongy material, should be lined at least two-thirds of the way down—and sometimes all the way. In front, unpressed pleats and pockets often require a lining, too, to give body and strength. The lining may extend only beneath these details or it may extend to the hemline.

For fully lined, narrow skirts, cut the lining to extend to the bottom of the finished hem—that is, a hem-width shorter than the top skirt. (Be cautious, though; it is often better to cut the lining like the top skirt—then, after the hemline is marked, cut the excess away.) Lining and skirt will be handled together so that no hem allowance is needed in the lining. Full gathered skirts fall better, however, when skirt and lining are kept separate. For these, cut linings full length to provide for a hem.

You may decide to line the entire bodice or perhaps you will omit lining the sleeves. With sheer material, you can omit the lining beneath the yoke area for a transparent effect. If you cut away the lining beneath the upper bodice, try the pattern on in order to obtain a becoming line that will conceal the undergarments you will wear with the dress. Allow, of course, for a suitable edge finish—a hem or facing usually—so that the lining can be finished inconspicuously.

You will not use facings on unlined transparent materials—bindings are much more attractive—but where facings *are* used, they are made of the garment material only. No lining is needed. Belts of sheer material must be lined, and so must buckles and covered buttons.

Instead of transferring construction lines to the garment proper, you can often transfer them to the lining only, since the two will be joined prior to construction. For unlined areas, you would, as usual, transfer markings to the under side of the dress fabric itself.

Before starting construction, finish the loose edges of partial linings. Use a hem, fitted facing, binding, or other suitable finish for bodice tops and armholes. Usually, pinking will suffice for partial skirt linings.

Here are directions for completely lining a simple dress with a narrow skirt:

Lining a dress

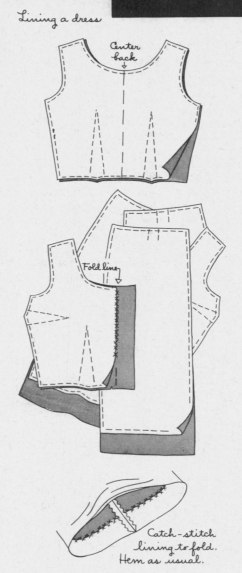

Center back

Fold line

Catch-stitch lining to fold. Hem as usual.

1. Place the bodice back, right side up, over the bodice back lining. Then, with the two pieces spread out smoothly on a table, pin the two layers together carefully and baste around all edges, preferably by hand. Do your basting in the seam allowances.

2. Repeat these same steps for every other garment section that will be lined.

3. While sections are still flat, pin and baste slightly outside all dart lines to hold the two layers together and prevent shifting. Similarly, baste along pleat lines, fold lines, and hemlines.

4. During all construction steps, *up to the hemming of the skirt,* treat the lined sections exactly as if they were single layers; that is, make staylines, darts, seams, and pleats through *both* layers! Of course, you will sometimes be able to trim the lining material away beneath stitched pleats and darts to reduce bulkiness. Hems at center fronts and similar areas should be cut away before hemming, too, just as you do the skirt hem, below.

5. After the skirt hemline is accurately marked, trim the lining away at the exact fold line. Rebaste it slightly above the fold line, if previous basting was cut away.

6. Catch-stitch the bottom of the lining to the fold line if there is danger of shifting.

7. Complete the hem as usual, except that hand stitches should catch the lining only—not the dress fabric.

TECHNIQUE 10   *SEAMS AND SEAM FINISHES*

Seams are the structural lines of a garment. They are used to join variously shaped pieces of fabric to give the style of garment you want. There are several kinds of seams, but by far the most versatile and widely used is the *plain seam,* made simply by stitching two edges of cloth together. Other seams used in particular situations are the *lapped seam, French seam,* and *flat felled seam.*

When a plain seam is used around collars, cuffs, and other faced garment edges, it is called an *enclosed seam,* because the two layers of cloth hide or enclose the seam allowances. Instead of being pressed apart as usual, the garment sections in this case are folded back together so that the seam appears along the outer garment edge.

Simple as seams are, they do have to be made "just so" if they are to look right when finished. Any perfect seam is strong, flat, and smooth. It has no bulky spots, no puckers, no irregular lines.

THE PLAIN SEAM

The perfect seam. There are many devices for achieving the perfect plain seam. Staylines, made before the seams are stitched, keep grain lines accurate. Traced lines or stitching guides keep stitching lines straight and seam allowances even in width. Stitch with the grain and you will find that the material lies flat and doesn't stretch out of shape easily. Slashing and clipping permit seam allowances to lie flat against the garment. Snipping off unnecessary seam corners removes bulk. Seam finishes prevent excessive raveling and strengthen seam lines.

Here are the steps for making a perfect plain seam:

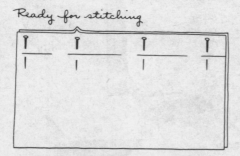

Ready for stitching

1. Place the right sides of the material together, with notches, raw edges, and seam ends matched. Long seams are easier to join accurately when laid on a table. Do not rub or force the top layer into place. Instead, match the ends of the two layers, and then lift them and shake gently to match all parts.

2. Place pins, heads toward the edge of the material, at right angles to the seam, first at notches, next at ends, and then at points between. Use only enough pins to hold the edges in place. If you are using a *flexible* presser foot (one that is hinged), you can stitch over pins placed directly across the seam line. However, the pin heads must be kept inside the raw edges of the material if you are going to use a stitching gauge— but keep the heads out of the way of the presser foot. If you are using a *rigid* presser foot (one that is not movable), either place pins far enough from the stitching line to miss the presser foot, or remove them as you stitch.

3. Basting is not necessary except when seams need to be fitted, or when making seams in difficult spots. When basting is necessary, use long machine stitches, or baste by hand. Baste slightly inside the seam line toward the garment side.

4. Stitch along a traced seam line, or use a stitching gauge.

5. Remove hand-basting by clipping the thread at intervals and pulling it out in short lengths. Never pull a knot through the cloth. A good way to remove machine-basting is to pull and break first one thread and then the other. Tweezers are helpful if you have them.

6. Trim or finish seam edges, as explained later in this technique. Press.

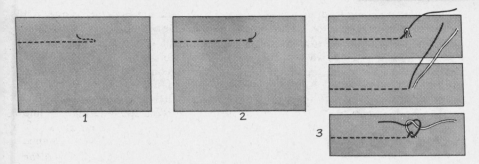

Ending seam lines. As a painless way of fastening the threads, most seams should be stitched all the way to the edge of the cloth even though the pattern does not show them extending that far. Then they are crossed by other seams and caught securely. Some stitching lines, however, end at specific points indicated on the pattern, such as at the end of a placket. They may be fastened in one of several ways:

1. Retrace the stitching line for a short distance. To do this, pivot the material on the needle and stitch backward. (Of course, if you have a machine that sews backward, you need not pivot.) *Or*

2. Hold the material so that it cannot be fed under the presser foot until several stitches have been made one on top of the other. The presser foot may be lifted ever so slightly to facilitate this process. *Or*

3. Draw both thread ends to the same side of the seam, and tie them securely. Naturally, keep the knot on the wrong side of the garment.

Easing one seam edge to another. Directions sometimes indicate *ease* along the back shoulder seam, at the elbow of a sleeve seam, or along other seams. "Ease" means slight fullness in one of the garment sections to be joined. For instance, if your pattern allows for ease in the back shoulder seam, you will find that edge longer than the front shoulder seam to which it is to be stitched.

Ease is usually handled like gathers—by running one or more gathering lines along the longer seam line, then drawing the gathering threads slightly until corresponding seams are the same length. Always distribute the fullness evenly in the material and allow no pleats to form. Stitch the seam as usual.

Stitching bias seams. Seams made along two bias-cut edges tend to stretch, causing the stitching line to break or draw. To prevent this, staylines should be used.

Sometimes, however, it is better to allow the seam to stretch slightly. For example, if a bias-cut skirt seam is prevented from stretching, the material on either side of the seam may sag and the line of stitching is likely to break. To permit just the right amount of stretch along such seams, use one of the following methods:

1. Pin the skirt gores together along the bias seam lines, and hang the skirt from a coat hanger overnight before stitching the seam. *Or*

2. Stretch the seam slightly as you stitch, being careful not to interfere with the feeding of the material under the presser foot. See drawing page 427 for position of hands.

When you are going to stitch a bias edge and a straight edge together, stay-stitch the bias edge first. Then stitch as you do an ordinary seam.

Stitching an inside curve to a straight edge. To stitch an inside curve to a straight edge, you must clip the curve so that it can lie along the straight edge. You would come across this situation, for example, in attaching a convertible collar.

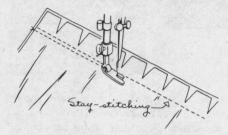

1. Stay-stitch the curved seam line ⅛ inch from the stitching line.

2. Clip through the seam allowance of the curved edge almost to the stay-line. Make enough slashes to permit the seam to open out in a straight line.

3. Pin the curved edge to the straight edge and stitch as usual.

Stitching an outside curved edge to a straight edge. To stitch an outside curve to a straight line, you must clip the straight edge to conform to the curve. Traced lines are more accurate to use than a stitching guide in this case. You would need this technique in stitching the seam over the bust of a princess-line garment.

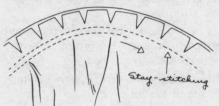

1. Clip partially through the straight cut edge to allow it to assume same curve as other edge.

2. Pin and stitch with the straight edge on top. Keep seam edges carefully matched.

OTHER KINDS OF SEAMS

In addition to the plain seam, there are other seams for special purposes—the lapped, the French, and the flat felled seams. The lapped seam is used to emphasize construction lines and to form points and curves where a plain seam would be difficult to use. French seams are used on soft or sheer blouses and undergarments, while flat felled seams are sturdy enough for sport and work clothes.

The lapped seam. The classic lapped seam, described later, has its particular uses, but here is a mock lapped seam that saves time and looks the same on straight or slightly curved seams.

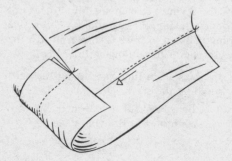

1. Stitch as you would stitch any plain seam.

2. Press both seam allowances in the same direction.

3. Stitch from the right side near the seam line. This line of top-stitching will hold the seam edges back in place and emphasize the seam line.

4. Trim or finish seam edges together and press them together too.

The simplified lapped seam, while fine for straight edges, will not do for shaped edges. If you want a shaped yoke with top stitching, you will have to make a real lapped seam as follows:

1. Stayline the top section barely outside the stitching line.

2. Fold the raw edge of this top section under on the stitching line and press or baste the edge to hold it in place. (When the edge which is to be turned under is an inside curve it must be clipped before turning; an outside curve should be notched at intervals.)

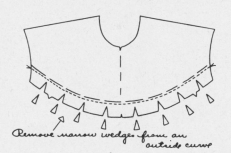

Remove narrow wedges from an outside curve

3. Place this turned-under edge over the other seam edge, both right sides up.

4. Turn to the wrong side, match notches, seam ends, and seam edges from the under side.

5. Turn back to the right side and pin in place.

6. Hand-baste back from the edge about ⅛ inch to obtain an accurate seam. Remove pins.

7. Stitch ⅟₁₆ inch from the folded edge on thin materials. Wool and heavy materials may be stitched ¼ inch or more from the edge, as desired.

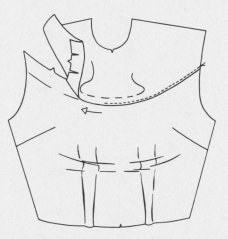

8. Remove pins or basting, finish the two seam edges together, and press. Never try to open up the seam edges of a lapped seam when pressing. Both edges must remain pressed back against the garment.

Sharp points require a special technique. To obtain a perfectly shaped wide-angle point when using a lapped seam is not difficult, but sharp points must be trimmed in a particular way if they are to be accurately shaped. Fold the seam allowance

Avoid extra material at point   *fold point over and trim*   *fold as usual*

across the point exactly at the tip of the stitching line. Cut away material nearly up to this fold—⅛ inch away. The seam allowance can usually be folded as usual after this step, but, if necessary, slightly more material may be cut off along the sides near the point.

The French seam. The French seam is used on sheer fabrics where wide seam edges would show through unattractively. It is also used on children's clothing, blouses, and undergarments to give a seam that is particularly smooth to the touch and durable enough to stand frequent washings. French seams are strong and completely free of ravelings. From the right side the French seam looks like a plain seam; from the under side it shows a narrow seam with all raw edges enclosed.

While excellent for certain purposes, the French seam has limitations. It cannot be used on heavy materials because of its bulkiness. It cannot enclose gathers satisfactorily. It cannot be used on curved seam lines such as armscye seams, or on shaped yokes. Even a skirt seam which must curve slightly over the hips does not fit well when made as a French seam.

A good French seam takes time and skill to make. This is how it is done:

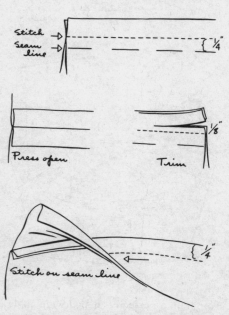

1. Match the seam lines with the wrong sides of the pieces together. (This is the opposite of the way you put them together for a plain seam.) Pin notches, ends, and seam lines.

2. Stitch on a line about ¼ inch or less from the seam line toward the raw edge of the material. (The distance from the seam line that you make this line of stitching determines the finished seam width.)

3. Press the seam allowances open.

4. Trim seam allowances to ⅛ inch in width. Trim both at the same time by holding them together.

5. Fold the right sides of the material together, keeping the fold on the stitched line.

6. Press and baste, if necessary.

7. Stitch on the seam line to give a seam ¼ inch wide or slightly narrower.

A mock French seam is sometimes used for shaped seams where a French seam is needed but cannot be made successfully.

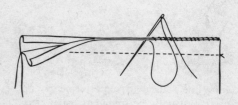

1. Stitch as you would a plain seam, right sides of material together as usual.

2. Trim the edges to ⅜ inch, or slightly less.

3. Turn in each edge about ⅛ inch and crease.

4. Pin or baste the turned under edges together.

5. Fasten permanently with small running stitches or whipping stitches.

The flat felled seam. The flat felled seam is a strong, flat, tailored seam with no raw edges. It is used on sport clothes, shirts, little boys' clothes, pajamas, and work clothes. It is time-consuming to make and is difficult to use on curves, but is durable and comfortable to wear. It is not successful where gathers enter a seam. It should be no more than ¼ inch wide except on heavy materials.

1. Match the seam lines with the wrong sides of the pieces together. (This is the opposite of the way you put them together for a plain seam.) Pin notches, ends, and seam lines and stitch.

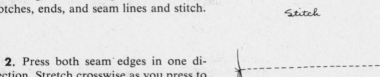

2. Press both seam edges in one direction. Stretch crosswise as you press to avoid pressing in a pleat effect on the under side.

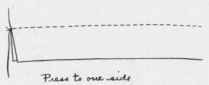

3. Trim the underneath seam edge to ⅛ inch width, and the top one to ⅜ inch.

4. Fold the wider seam allowance over the narrower one, turning it under ⅛ inch. Crease or baste the fold.

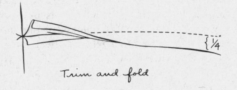

5. Spread the two pieces of the garment apart with the creased edge in position against the garment.

6. Stitch near the fold line.

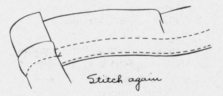

SEAM FINISHES

French seams and flat felled seams are already finished, but plain seams and lapped seams often need further finishing if they are to wear well. You have undoubtedly had seams that raveled until they pulled apart. You may also have had ravelings catch in a zipper. You know how annoying both these experiences can be. Sometimes in the past, to prevent such occurrences, so much effort was spent on the finishing of seam edges that the garment looked half worn out before it was completed.

Today, however, while we know that most fabrics do require some kind of seam finish to prevent such raveling, we try to keep our handling to a minimum in order to preserve the fresh new look of the cloth. We accomplish this by using the simplest and easiest seam finish appropriate for our material.

The easiest materials to finish are those which don't ravel such as jersey, felt, and net. In fact they need no finish. Just cut away projecting notches and even up seam allowances if necessary. Net and felt are so ravel resistant that skirts of these are simply trimmed off to the proper length rather than being hemmed! For materials that ravel slightly such as firmly woven cottons, most wool fabrics and crepes pinking is sufficient.

Loosely woven materials generally require stronger finishes than firmly woven fabrics, and seams on wash clothes must be stronger than those on clothes which are to be dry-cleaned. Try the finishes given below on scraps of material along straight-grain and bias-cut edges. Give the finished edges a thorough rubbing or wash them to determine the finish your seams require.

Remember that the edges of lapped seams are always pressed in the same direction and are finished together. Plain seams used at the armscye and waistline, or where gathers are used are generally finished together. Whenever plain seams are pressed open the edges must, of necessity, be finished separately. The vertical seams in girls' and women's clothing are usually pressed open. However, wash dresses and house dresses may have seams finished together.

Pinking. Pinking is the most popular of all finishes. It is easily and quickly done with either pinking shears or a pinking machine. Used on materials that ravel only slightly it is a good finish, but is not adequate for loosely woven materials which must be washed often. Also it is not attractive when seen through sheer fabrics. Two seam edges may be pinked at one time, even though the seam has been pressed open. Hold the main part of the garment to the left and out of the way as you pink seam edges. This helps to prevent your snipping a hole in your garment. Pink close to the cut edge of the material, unless seam edges need to be straightened or made narrower. Use long even strokes as you do in using the shears. Draw the handles together in a straight up and down movement. Do not twist them as you cut.

Machine stitching. If pinking is not enough, a line of machine stitching about ⅛ inch from the cut edge of each side of the seam allowance may prevent raveling. This machine-stitching finish may be used on plain trimmed edges, pinked edges, or overcast edges (see next page) as needed.

Edge-stitching. Edge-stitching is just like machine stitching except that the raw edges are turned under. This is a heavier finish, suitable only for light and medium weight materials, and for materials on which such a finish will not leave a mark when the garment is pressed. You will find this finish often on fine chambray dresses.

Straight seams are fairly easy to edge-stitch, but bias seams require more time and skill. Press the seam open and turn its edges under about ⅛ inch. Crease and then stitch very close to the creased fold. Push the garment back out of the way and stitch from the top, not the under or narrow side of the folded edge.

Stitching raw edges together. An excellent way to finish armscye seams of dresses and blouses where narrow yet strong seams are needed is to stitch raw edges together. This also makes a sturdy seam finish for school and house dresses which must be washed often. Dress manufacturers use this double-stitched, narrow, smoothly trimmed seam on sheer materials to give the effect of a French seam at a fraction of the cost.

For this finish simply stitch through both thicknesses of the seam allowance ¼ inch from the stitched seam line. Then trim so that there is only ¹⁄₁₆ to ⅛ inch of material beyond this line of stitching.

Overcasting. Overcasting is a hand-finish used extensively on custom-made dresses, but it is found only on expensive ready-made clothing. Although it is time consuming, it does give an almost ravel-free seam. Since it is flat and smooth, it leaves little imprint on the right side of the garment when it is pressed.

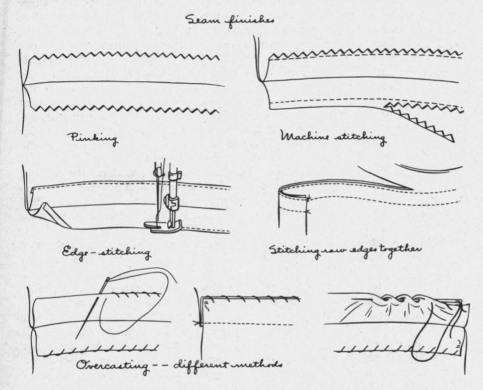

Seam finishes

Pinking *Machine stitching*

Edge-stitching *Stitching raw edges together*

Overcasting -- different methods

Edges may be finished together or each one separately as required by the position on the garment. Do your overcast seams with the grain—the direction in which seams were stitched. A skirt seam, for instance, would be overcast from the hem upward. Trim the edges neatly and overcast from right to left, holding the seam edge up. The stitches should be made about ⅛ inch into the cloth and about ¼ inch apart.

You can take one stitch at a time, but to work rapidly, lift the point of the needle over the cut edge and insert it again and again until the needle is filled before you pull it through. Point the needle toward you and slightly to the left for this overcasting stitch. However you do it, adjust the stitches carefully to give a smooth—never a drawn—seam edge. This means loosening the threads if you used the fast method.

ENCLOSED SEAMS

Almost no part makes more difference in the final appearance of a garment than its edges. Flat, smooth, well-shaped collars, cuffs, and faced areas give a clean-cut, professional look; lumpy, ill-shaped ones give that done-with-fond-and-loving-hands-at-home look. The difference lies in the way enclosed seams are stitched, trimmed, clipped or notched, turned, and pressed.

The way you cut the pieces can often affect the final appearance of enclosed seams. The general rule for fitted facings, of course, is to cut them the same shape and size as the garment area being faced. Although this is the correct procedure for necklines and front closings, it is not entirely right for collars, cuffs, belts, tabs, etc. Perhaps you have noticed that some commercial patterns give you two collar patterns—one top and one under-collar (facing) pattern. If you compare these pieces, you will find that the under collar is slightly smaller than the top one along all the edges *except* the neckline. This is not a mistake, but intentional. Being smaller, the under collar will be hidden beneath the upper one—exactly what is necessary for an attractive edge. If your pattern does not provide smaller facings, you can trim away about ⅛ inch from all the edges of the facing or under layer, *except* the edge that will be attached to the garment. You can stretch the under layer enough to match the top one as you pin and stitch.

Sometimes enclosed seams are made with just two layers of cloth: the garment section and the facing. For well-made garments, however, a third layer, the interfacing, is necessary, particularly where body, crispness, or strength is needed. (Turn to technique 9, "Staylines, Interfacings, and Linings," for kinds of interfacing materials and ways to use them.)

Stitching. Stitch as accurately as possible because your stitching line represents the finished shape. The only trick in stitching enclosed seams comes when you turn corners. Instead of pivoting and making a sharp turn, it is better to take one or two diagonal stitches across the corner: one stitch for thin fabrics, two for thick ones. This makes a thinner, neater corner when it is turned right side out.

Trimming. Next, trim seam allowances to approximately ¼ inch—or narrower if the fabric is firm. This would be much too narrow for an ordinary plain seam, but it is not for enclosed seams as raw edges are protected from raveling and wear.

Layering. On fine clothing made of heavy materials you will find that enclosed seams, instead of being trimmed in the ordinary way, are layered; that is, one seam allowance is trimmed narrower than the other to reduce bulkiness. If you decide to use this trick, trim the bottom layer narrower. The wider allowance will pad the imprint of the narrower one, thus keeping the outside of the garment smooth. Trim the top layer to about ¼ inch in width or wider; trim the under layer to ⅛ inch or wider.

Trimming corners. Trim outside corners, such as those on pointed collars, even closer than you do the rest of the seam. Snip off the corner, leaving only a thread or so outside the stitching line. For very sharp corners cut away a bit at the sides of the point, in addition, to avoid bulkiness. Of course, inside corners, such as those on a square-neck blouse, must be slashed. But reinforce them first by stitching ribbon seam binding or a firm selvage to the facing directly across the tip of the slash line.

Trimming curves. Curves present another trimming problem. Inside curved seam lines, such as neckline seams, must be clipped through almost to the seam line at

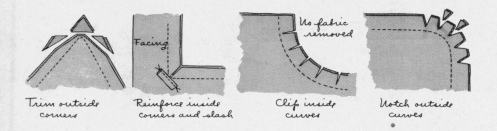

Trim outside corners   Reinforce inside corners and slash   Clip inside curves   Notch outside curves

regular intervals to allow the seam allowance to fold back against the wider curve. Clip far apart on slight curves, closer along sharp curves. Don't remove any material—just clip and be careful not to go into the seam line.

On outside curved seams, such as outer collar edges, you do have to remove some material to get the seam edges to lie flat. If you don't see the reason for this, fold the seam edges back along the stitching line of such a curve. You will notice that tiny pleats form in the seam allowance. Remove material at these points by making narrow V-shaped notches. Do not cut quite to the seam line. More notches are required on sharp curves than on slight curves, of course.

Turning and shaping. After trimming away excess material along enclosed seams, and clipping and notching as necessary, you are ready to turn the unit and shape the corners, curves, and even straight edges.

If there are *outside corners,* they are your first concern after the unit is turned. Points should be gently forced out to shape with a gadget designed for this purpose, an orangewood stick, or a similar instrument. If this is not successful, use a strong needle from the outside to draw the point out. Force the needle deep into the point; otherwise you may pull out yarn ends.

Your next concern, after the unit is turned, is to force the stitched seam out to the edge of collars, cuffs, front closings, etc. Fortunately, there are several ways to control the shaping of enclosed seams. Some are easier than others, and some are suitable for one situation and not for another.

Under-stitching consists of a row of regular machine stitching made through the facing and seam allowances only. It is not made through the top fabric layer and therefore does not show when the garment is worn. Under-stitching is easy because it requires no basting and no pressing before it is done. It is suitable for washable fabrics as well as for those that will be dry-cleaned, for, even after a garment is laundered, under-stitched edges hold their shape. These edges are attractive, too, because under-stitching helps to draw the seam slightly beneath the garment edge and keeps it there so that the under layer of cloth is always completely hidden.

There are limitations on the use of under-stitching, however, for the extra row of machine stitching does make an edge slightly stiffer than it would otherwise be. There are also hard-to-get-at spots where under-stitching cannot be used. You will not want to use this kind of stitching on scarves or on anything else where both sides of the faced edges will be seen.

If you turn to Construction One, "Making a Blouse and Skirt," you will find full instructions for under-stitching. It is shown there on a neck-and-front facing, and also on a sleeve facing.

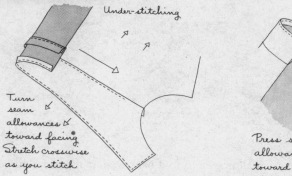

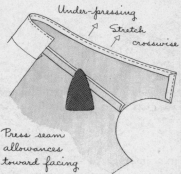

Under-pressing is another quick-and-easy method for shaping enclosed seams. When under-pressing alone is used, it is not as durable as under-stitching, but is usually satisfactory for wools and other dry-cleanable materials where a soft edge is wanted. You can under-press any seam that you can reach easily with an iron. In using this method you have two choices: (1) you can press both seam allowances in the same direction—always toward the underneath layer of cloth; or (2) you can press the seam allowance open.

In most cases, you should press both seam allowances toward the under layer of cloth because this method, like under-stitching, tends to draw the seam slightly beneath the faced edge. An ideal place to try this method is along the front facing of a dress or coat. To underpress both seam allowances in the same direction:

1. Be sure that the seam is trimmed or layered.

2. Open out the facing with seam allowances up. Stretch crosswise as you press seam allowances toward the facing. (When the facing is to appear on top, of course, you press the seam allowance toward the garment.)

3. Fold the facing back in place and press along the under side of the faced edge, being careful to keep the stitching line almost, but not quite, to the edge of the detail.

4. Turn the detail right side up. (Notice that seam and facing are both hidden.)

Pressing seam allowances open—the second method used for under-pressing—tends to keep the seam exactly on the edge of the faced detail. That is the way you want it on ties, scarves, and lapels that may be worn either high at the neck or turned back. Even convertible collars of lightweight fabric can be handled in this way. (Since it is slightly easier to press seams open before they are trimmed, reverse the usual order here and trim or layer seams after pressing.) It is easy enough to press open seams along straight edges. It takes a little ingenuity though to get into corners and ties to press seams open. If you have a pointed seam board, use it for opening up seams near the corners of collars and similar areas. Or, place a tie or collar flat on an ironing board and press one seam allowance back to open up the seam perfectly along the stitching line.

Regardless of which method you use, after seams have been opened, turn the detail right-side out. Now you should be able to sharpen the edge by pressing along it again.

Tricks for pressing enclosed seams in difficult spots

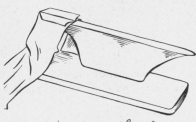
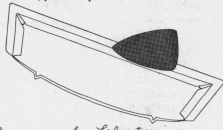

Use a pointed seam board   *Press seams open before turning*

On shaped seams that you cannot press open, you will have to work the seam out to the edge with your fingers and then baste close to the edge through all fabric layers. Next, press the edge lightly, remove the basting, and press again.

Under-basting is your last resort for shaping those difficult spots that you have not been able to shape by any of the preceding methods. Because under-basting does not involve the top layer of cloth, it eliminates any possibility of marring the right side of the garment with the imprint of basting stitches (as may happen when basting goes through all layers). Also, the seam is drawn beneath the faced edge in the same way that it is by under-stitching and under-pressing. To under-baste an enclosed seam, proceed as follows:

Basting seam allowances to facing

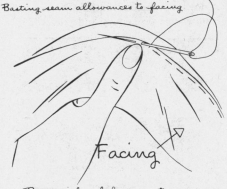

Facing

1. Place the index finger of your left hand inside the collar or cuff or whatever unit you are working on.

2. With the facing side up, stretch crosswise along the seam as you hold the trimmed seam edge against the wrong side of the facing.

3. Baste through the facing and the seam edges, but not through the right side of the unit.

4. Press the unit and remove bastings.

Baste either before you turn the unit or afterwards

If you have followed these instructions, your work now shows gratifying results. However, a facing may still work out as you wear your garment, and it may not look right if all future pressings are not as careful as the first. On garments that will be washed or that will receive excessive wear, edges that have not been under-stitched should be top-stitched.

In areas where one or more rows of top-stitching would be decorative, you can stitch all the way through the faced edge—an excellent idea for tailored things as well as washable ones. Stitch with the right side up and use the presser foot or stitching guide to keep the lines straight.

Hand-picked edges, made with a pin-point back-stitch, are often used on suits and coats. These, too, hold enclosed seams in place and are decorative at the same time.

TECHNIQUE 11   *DARTS, PLEATS, TUCKS, AND GATHERS*

      Darts, pleats, tucks, and gathers are construction details that are usually made before seams are stitched. They serve the purpose of controlling fullness and giving shape to the garment.

DARTS

    Darts are used to shape flat cloth to fit the curves of the figure. They are sometimes wide at one end and pointed at the other and sometimes wide in the middle and pointed at both ends. When they end in a pleat effect rather than a point, they are called *dart tucks*.

    Darts are usually stitched from the wrong side of the material, but for decorative purposes they are occasionally made on the right side of the garment. The first requirement for making a good dart is careful marking including a crosswise line showing the exact length of the dart and ¼ inch clips into the seam allowance at dart lines, unless your pattern shows a fold line down the center of each dart.

    The next problem is to fold the dart perfectly. Unless a fold line is shown, this is not too simple a matter since you can see only one side at a time as you fold it. Follow this procedure and you will have no trouble:

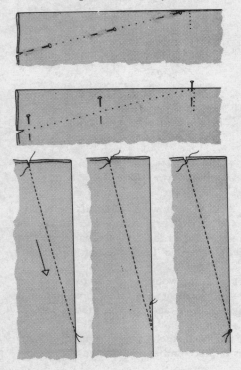

1. Fold the material from the point through the center of the dart. Place pins lengthwise along the traced line through both layers of cloth. Turn the dart over to see that pins fall along the traced line on the opposite side.

2. Remove one pin at a time, replacing each one directly across the stitching line if you plan to stitch over pins. Otherwise, remove pins as you sew.

3. Stitch from the wide end of the dart to the point. Keep the point of the dart sharp, and end the dart exactly where indicated.

4. Cut the thread ends ⅜ to ½ inch in length. These threads at the point of a dart will not need fastening if the point is sharp and the stitch fine and well made. When necessary, fasten thread ends and clip them. On decorative outside darts, draw threads to the wrong side and tie.

A single line of perforations is sometimes used on the pattern to indicate a narrow dart, such as is found at the back neckline, shoulder, or elbow. Directions will explain that you are to start stitching ⅛ or ¼ inch from this line and continue to the point of the dart. To make the dart accurate, draw it on the material before stitching.

Making a dart tuck. Instead of tapering to a point, a dart tuck ends in a pleat. Some instructions tell you to fasten the line of stitching where the dart breaks off, but a far better technique is to pivot the material at a 90° angle and stitch across the dart. This holds it firm. Otherwise match the lines, pin them, and stitch a dart tuck just as you would any other dart.

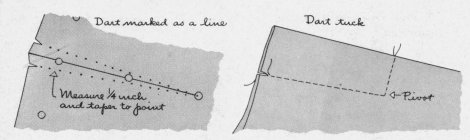

Finishing darts. Most darts require no further steps except pressing; but if the dart is particularly wide, it may be trimmed to ordinary seam width. In very heavy material, the dart should be not only trimmed but also pressed open, except for the tip, which is pressed into a small box pleat, or turned to one side if very narrow. To trim and press open a dart in heavy material:

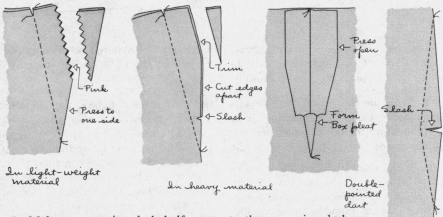

1. Make a crosswise slash half way through the material of the dart, about 1 to 1½ inches from the point of the dart.

2. Trim the wider end of the dart to a regular seam width. Cut edges apart to the crosswise slash.

3. Finish dart edges like other seams.

4. Press the dart edges open and shape the tip of the dart into a small box pleat as you press, or turn to one side.

Darts with points at both ends will not lie flat unless the material of the dart is slashed crosswise in at least one place. Slash at the middle or widest part of the dart, and to within about ¼ inch of the stitching line.

Pressing darts. There are two general rules which will help you to decide which way to turn untrimmed darts. Follow these rules, except where special effects are desired:

1. Press vertical darts, those that run up and down the figure, so that the material under the dart is pressed toward the center of the figure. Front darts should be turned toward the center front; back darts should be turned toward the center back.

2. Press crosswise darts with the material turned toward the bottom of the garment.

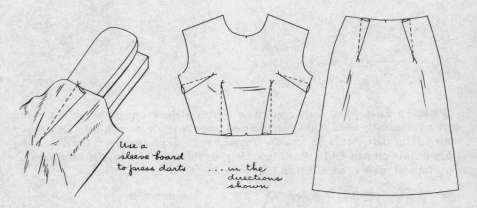

Use a sleeve board to press darts ... in the directions shown

The chief difficulty in pressing darts is in opening the material back completely to the dart line. A pleated effect, or false crease, on the right side of the dart is unattractive. This is the way to avoid it:

1. Press the dart itself flat with material still folded together to crease the dart down the center and flatten the stitching line. Don't press beyond tip.

2. Now, place the dart on a sleeve board with the material of the garment spread apart and the dart turned uppermost. Place the point of the dart close to the narrow end of the sleeve board. (Some people prefer to use a curved surface, such as a tailor's cushion.)

3. Turn the dart in the correct direction and press it lightly, stretching the material crosswise as you press.

4. Lift the dart and check the right side of the garment to see that the material has been completely opened to the dart seam. The material on either side of the stitching line should be smooth and flat, with no crease lines forming a "hiding place" for the stitching line. Press again, if necessary. Don't press so hard that the dart imprint shows on the right side of the garment. Press under the dart if you have made an imprint.

PLEATS

Pressed pleats provide a slender silhouette but break into rhythmic fullness to allow movement of the body. Unpressed pleats add softness and fullness to a garment. A single kick pleat makes walking easier in a narrow skirt.

In larger cities pleating of many kinds is done commercially, and most sewing centers sell devices for pleat-making. However, you can make the kinds of pleats indicated on patterns better yourself.

Your pattern may frighten you with instructions to use many rows of basting to make pleats. A simpler way to form the creases is to baste-stitch to close the pleat, then press, remove basting threads, and your creases are formed.

Making a double unpressed pleat

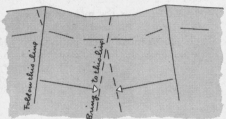

Fold as arrows show

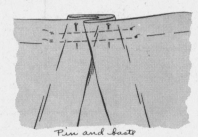

Pin and baste

Unpressed pleats. Unpressed pleats are the simplest of all to make. Use them in *soft* medium-weight, or even heavy, materials. Unpressed pleats may be made on the lengthwise straight of the material or on a bias line. It often improves the appearance and fall of unpressed pleats to line the upper skirt section before making the pleats. Use stiff marquisette, crepe, taffeta, or other suitable lining material.

An unpressed pleat may be made by a simple fold caught into a crosswise seam, or it may be stitched for an inch or so at the top of the pleat like a dart tuck. For instructions on dart tucks, see page 457. In either case, baste-stitch at waist.

Pressed pleats. Unlike softer pleats, pressed pleats should be made of *firm, medium-weight* material. Wool is excellent for pleated designs because it holds a crease exceptionally well during wear and dry-cleaning. The same is true of wool blended with nylon, Orlon, and some of the other man-made fibers. Some crush-resistant materials will not press with a sharp edge, and there are other materials which lose a crease quickly. Washable garments when pleated by the home sewer present a problem because the pleats so often have to be re-formed each time the garment is laundered. But if you do want pleats in materials that won't hold a crease or are washable, at least edge-stitch them to help hold them in shape and guide you in re-pressing them. Fibers which can be heat-set commercially are difficult to set by home methods.

Pleats made along the lengthwise straight of the material look and behave better than radiating or bias pleats. Edge-stitching on any material and any grain will help to hold pleats in shape, and will sharpen creases.

To make a side pleat:

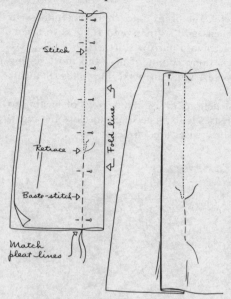

1. Working from the wrong side, match both pleat lines and ends of the fabric perfectly.

2. Stitch the pleat to the bottom of the stitching line. Retrace about ¼ inch to fasten.

3. Baste-stitch the rest of the pleat as a continuation of the stitching above.

4. Turn the pleat in the direction in which it is to go and press lightly while the basting holds the pleat in place.

5. Remove the baste-stitch and press again to remove any imprint of the basting stitches.

To make a box pleat:

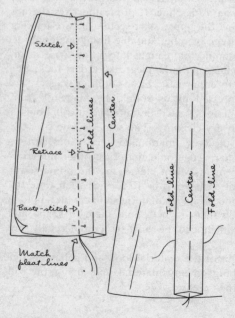

1. Fold on the line that indicates the center of the pleat, wrong sides of the material together. Match the stitching lines and pin.

2. Stitch to the end of the stitching line, retrace about ¼ inch to fasten, and baste-stitch the rest of the pleat.

3. Crease the box pleat accurately on fold lines for the entire length of the pleat, keeping the pleat flat. Pin and baste, if necessary.

4. Press lightly, remove basting stitches, and press again.

A kick pleat requires an extra piece of material inset behind the pleat. To make a kick pleat:

1. Stitch the seam line of the skirt down to the pleat. Retrace about ¼ inch to fasten. Then baste-stitch the pleat closed as a continuation of the seam line.

2. Press the seam open. At the same time, press the pleat open too.

3. Fit the back inset in place beneath the pleat, with the right side of the inset against the under side of the pleat. Pin the two raw edges together but do not pin through the skirt.

4. Stitch seams at the outside edge of inset.

5. Remove basting and press seams. Of course, you will not open the side seams as you press.

6. Finish seam edges.

7. Now, from the right side, stitch across the top of the pleat. You can stitch straight across or you can stitch diagonals from the center of the pleat. If you do the latter, cut yourself a guide from folded paper.

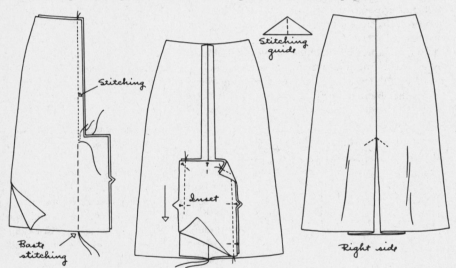

Edge-stitching pleats. After pleats have been made, and the hems of skirts or peplums finished, you may make a row of stitching along the entire crease of each pleat, if you care to. Sometimes both inside and outside creases are stitched. When stitching is not desired on the right side of the garment, the inside edges may be edge-stitched and the outside creases left unstitched. To do this edge-stitching:

1. Stitch through both layers of cloth ¹⁄₁₆ to ⅛ inch from the fold line. Use an edge-stitcher (one of your machine attachments) to keep the lines straight. Stitch from the hem up.

2. Fasten thread ends inconspicuously.

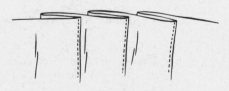

TUCKS

Tucks are attractive on chambray, batiste, and other light or medium-weight materials—especially on sheer materials because of the light and shadow effect they give. Tucks lie flat when made along a lengthwise thread. They are easy to make on materials that crease well. On materials that will not crease, you may have to baste each one before stitching it.

If your pattern does not call for tucks but you would like them, simply use your sewing machine tucker attachment on the material before you cut it.

For patterns providing for tucks:

1. Fold along marked tuck lines, wrong sides of the material together.

2. Use the edge-stitcher, tucker, or the stitching guide to stitch even tucks.

3. Stretching crosswise, press the tucks into position.

GATHERS

Only soft or light-weight materials gather well. Even in such materials gathers which fall crosswise of the material are sometimes quite stiff and bunchy. Gathers are more attractive when the folds fall along the lengthwise grain of the fabric or along a bias.

You can gather by machine or by hand. Two or three rows of gathering threads may be used. One line must always be *on* the seam line or very near it. The other lines can be ¼ inch away on either or both sides of the first one.

To gather by machine:

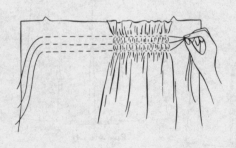

1. Lengthen the stitch as for basting and stitch along the seam line. Leave thread ends about 3 inches long.

2. Repeat, stitching ¼ inch on one or both sides of the seam line.

3. At one end of the gathering, grasp all thread ends extending from the underside of the material and draw up gathers slightly. Do not fasten thread ends.

A shirring foot attachment on the machine will draw the threads as you stitch. If you use this, the length of the stitch determines the fullness, but you can adjust the fullness later if necessary. This attachment is not too easy to use on a second row of gathering, so if you want more than one row and you certainly need two or three for fine, even gathers, it is better to use a long machine-stitch or a hand-stitch.

To gather by hand:

1. Use a knot in the thread end. Make fine hand-running stitches along the seam line. Use double thread for long lines of gathering.

2. Leave thread ends loose and sev-eral inches long.

3. Repeat, ¼ inch on one or both sides.

4. Draw up thread ends slightly but do not fasten them.

Joining gathering. The problem in joining gathering to a plain edge is to distribute the fullness evenly. If the gathered section is to be very long, before gathering divide it into fourths and mark these fourths with short clips into the seam allowance. In a like manner, divide and mark the plain edge into fourths. Match these clips before drawing up and distributing the gathers. For short rows of gathering you can omit this step.

To join gathers in a plain seam:

1. Pin seam lines at each end of the gathered section.

2. Draw threads up so that the gathered material is exactly the length of the plain strip of material.

3. Fasten loose thread ends by winding them in a figure 8 about a pin at both ends of the line of machine gathering or at the unknotted end of hand gathering.

4. Distribute gathers evenly. To hold them in place, insert pins at right angles to the seam line and close together.

5. Baste with fine hand-basting, if necessary.

6. With the gathered side up, stitch along the seam line (center gathering line if you have used three).

7. Remove basting and press with the seam turned toward the plain section. Remove gathering threads or not, as desired. If you leave them in, tie their ends.

To join gathers in a lapped seam, follow the instructions for making a lapped seam in technique 10, "Seams and Seam Finishes." The gathers are always placed underneath and should be distributed as described above.

TECHNIQUE 12   *PRESSING*

Careful pressing done at the right time during construction and afterwards helps to give your work a smooth, professional look. It removes wrinkles and unwanted creases, and helps to shape fabric to the curves of the figure. It can be used to restore the right-angle structure of the cloth. It is also used to shrink some materials, and often takes the place of lines of basting. Thus pressing both improves your work and serves as a short cut in sewing.

SPECIAL REQUIREMENTS OF VARIOUS FIBERS

FIBER	HOW TO PRESS
Cotton and Linen	Will stand relatively high temperatures if they are properly dampened and if the iron is kept in motion. While smooth, light-colored cottons can be pressed from the right side, they often look better when pressed from the under side. Textured cotton and linen materials, dull surfaces, and dark colors should be pressed from the wrong side wherever possible. For touching up the right side of these, use a press cloth to preserve the texture and prevent shine.
Rayon	Will stand relatively high temperatures similar to those used for cottons. Press from the under side or use a press cloth to touch up the right side. For materials that water-spot, use a steam iron or a dry press cloth under a damp one.
Wool	Use a moderate temperature. Wool should never be pressed while wet or damp. Instead, use a steam iron or a damp press cloth on the dry fabric. A steam iron may be placed directly on the under side of wool, but should not be used directly against the right side. Never press wool until it is entirely dry. To do so flattens the material and makes it shiny and harsh. If you find that you have over-pressed wool fabric, press again, leaving steam in the material. Another method to remove shine from wool and give the fabric more life is to hold a steam iron suspended directly above the shiny spot. The steam will lift the fibers unless the damage is permanent.
Silk	Use a moderate temperature. Some silks, especially those called wash silks, can be pressed damp. However, most silks should be pressed with a dry cloth next to the silk to avoid water-spots. Of course, if you have a steam iron, use it on the under side wherever you can.
Acetate, Nylon, Dacron, Orlon, Acrilan, and Dynel	Avoid a hot iron, use adequate moisture, and press on the wrong side. To press on the right side, cover with a press cloth. If the iron sticks slightly or a glaze is formed, the iron is too hot. Don't let that happen because you cannot repair the damages. A very hot iron will even melt a hole in these fabrics. Dynel is the most heat sensitive of all. Use the lowest iron setting and great care. And strange as it may seem, use no moisture. It presses better without it.

SPECIAL REQUIREMENTS OF VARIOUS CONSTRUCTION AND FINISHING PROCESSES

CONSTRUCTION AND FINISH	HOW TO PRESS
Glossy Fabrics	Glazed chintz and other glazed fabrics require little or no moisture and should be pressed on the right side to develop their luster. No press cloth is used. Linen and cotton damask should be moistened and pressed in the same way.

Pile Fabrics	The steam from a tub of hot water will remove light wrinkles. Expose the garment to the steam by hanging it on a hanger and keeping the room closed. Velvet and velveteen may be pressed on a needle board without flattening the pile. Place the pile side down on the board and press on the wrong side. Use a steam iron or a dampened press cloth. When a needle board is not available, pin one end of the velvet wrong side up to the ironing board. Hold the velvet up from the board and gently cross it with the tip of a steam iron. Corduroy can be pressed from the wrong side on a well padded board, and then brushed to raise the pile; but if it is hung dripping wet in a strong breeze, it will need no pressing.
Napped Fabrics	Wool broadcloth and other napped fabrics should be pressed on a softly padded board. Press them on the wrong side or with a press cloth. A scrap of the cloth makes the best press cloth. Handle them carefully so as not to force the nap to fall in the wrong direction. Brush with a soft brush while steam is still in the cloth. Brush "with the nap" on the right side, using little or no pressure.
Creped Materials	The amount of moisture you use and the way you handle the iron will change the size and shape of heavily creped materials. Use steam for pressing them, because they shrink unevenly when water is applied directly. Press with the grain to retain the original shape. Creped fabrics that have been stretched or shrunk in cleaning can be restored to shape and size. Glide the iron over the cloth with pressure to stretch it. Use steam with little or no pressure to shrink it. Press from the wrong side or with a cloth.
Embroidered, Embossed, Textured, and Twill Materials	Use a soft, well-padded board, and press from the wrong side. A plain turkish towel placed over an ordinary board will give extra padding. Use plenty of moisture either from a steam iron or a press cloth.

There are three stages during the construction of a garment when pressing is needed: (1) before cutting, to smooth, straighten, or shrink fabric; (2) during construction, called *under pressing*; (3) after the garment is finished, called the *final pressing*.

No matter what your purpose is, there are certain standards for any kind of pressing:

After pressing, cloth should retain its original texture. Dull materials should remain dull, and glossy ones should retain their sheen. The pile of velvet should not be flattened. Embroideries and rough textures should remain raised above the background of the cloth.

The right-angle structure of cloth should be retained or restored, except where it is deliberately pressed off-grain to shrink or shape the cloth. Materials that have been heat-set are an exception. You cannot change their structure, but even they can be molded to shape.

The right side of a garment should appear smooth. No imprint of darts, facings, and other thick areas should be visible. Wrinkles and creases should be pressed out.

The creases of pressed pleats, hems, and faced edges should be uniformly sharp.

To meet these standards, you need moisture, heat, and a certain amount of pressure.

The use of moisture. Few materials can be well pressed without being dampened in some way. A small amount of moisture will remove light wrinkles; but a greater amount is needed to remove sharp creases, such as those down the center fold of the goods.

Moisture is especially necessary in re-shaping fabrics, although fabrics vary in the amount of moisture required for this purpose. For instance, you may be able to "square up" a piece of untreated cotton cloth without any moisture by merely pulling or pressing it on the diagonal. Wool and some permanently-finished fabrics must be thoroughly moistened before their right-angle structure can be restored.

Materials made of acetate, nylon, Dacron, Orlon, and the like are often heat-set, which means that they are permanently set and cannot have their grain lines changed at ordinary pressing temperatures, no matter how much moisture is used. Some crush-resistant finishes and glazes used on cottons set the position of the yarns more or less permanently, also. Do not attempt to straighten them.

Moisture is applied to clothing in two forms, as water and as steam. You can apply water directly to any washable garment. A wet cloth can be used to dampen cottons, linens, and most other washable materials just before you press them. However, this method would water-spot sized rayon or silk fabrics and give poor results on others. It is generally safer to use steam on any fabric that must be dry-cleaned.

For applying steam a steam iron is excellent and should be used if possible. When one is not available, create steam by doing your pressing over a damp cloth. The damp press cloth can be placed directly over a fabric that will not water-spot. For those that do water-spot, place a dry press cloth directly on the garment and the damp one on top of the dry one. By this method you can press with either the right or wrong side of the material up.

The use of heat. With experience you will learn to gauge the amount of heat to use. The dial on your iron is not an absolute guide. If you are using lots of moisture or are using a press cloth, the iron can be hot. It can also be hot if you are pressing rapidly. Reduce the heat for places difficult to press where you go slowly.

Of course, different fabrics require different iron temperatures for best results. Cotton and linen stand the highest temperature, then wool, rayon, silk, and synthetics, in that order. In the case of a blend, use the lower temperature always.

The use of pressure. With the proper heat and moisture, very little pressure is necessary. Much pressing is best done with only slight pressure and an up-and-down motion of the iron. Napped and textured materials and wools particularly should be pressed in this way to keep from flattening their surfaces. Let steam, not pressure, do the work.

For smoothing surfaces and for changing or straightening grain lines a gliding motion is used. You glide along grain lines to smooth material. You glide on the bias to square it up. The same motion is used to develop luster and to stretch crepe materials back to size.

PRESSING BEFORE THE CLOTH IS CUT

It would be nice if all material were ready to cut when you bought it, but unfortunately it is not, though the situation is improving. For a while yet you may have to press your material for any of three reasons: to straighten grain lines, to shrink it, or simply to get rid of wrinkles. A thorough pressing job will often take care of any and all of these faults at the same time.

To remove wrinkles or shrink cloth, place one end of your material on the ironing board so that it is smooth and its grain lines are squared up. Protect the other end by putting it on a chair or by putting clean paper on the floor for it to fall on. Check the chart pages 464–465 for the particular requirements of the material you are using. With a gliding motion, move the iron parallel to the selvage, or along the lengthwise grain. For squaring grain lines, glide diagonally toward the short corner of the cloth.

UNDER PRESSING

Seams and darts. One of the most important rules to follow for fast, professional work is to press each dart and seam before crossing it with another seam. Most

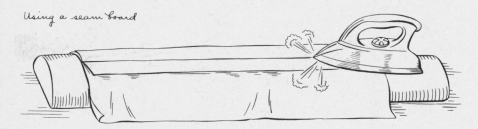

Using a seam board

plain seams are pressed open, but a few have both seam allowances pressed in the same direction. Refer to technique 10, "Seams and Seam Finishes" if you have any doubts. To press a plain seam open:

1. Place the seam, wrong side up, on an ironing board or seam board. Since a seam board is rounded it will prevent the imprint of the seam from showing on the right side of the garment.

2. Stretch the fabric crosswise gently so that it will lie flat against the board. This is done to prevent pleats or false creases on the right side.

3. Open the seam allowances with your fingertips and apply moisture with a damp cloth, or by holding a steam iron slightly above the seam.

4. Stretch the seam lengthwise very gently as you run the point of the iron directly down the center of the seam. Press with the grain, that is, from the hem of a skirt toward the top, etc. Press the seam thoroughly, but do not over-press.

5. Unless you pressed on a seam board, check to make sure that the imprint of the seam allowance does not show on the right side. If it does, run a steam iron under each seam allowance.

When both seam allowances are pressed toward the same side, moisten the top seam allowance instead of the inside layers. Otherwise follow directions above.

The general rule for darts is to press vertical darts toward the center of the garment and horizontal darts down. It is easy to shape them over the end of a sleeve board or over a tailor's cushion. Stretch crosswise as you press. If you have any trouble, refer to technique 11, "Darts, Pleats, Tucks, and Gathers."

Shrinking fullness. Before you ease a full section to a plain edge, shrink the fullness from the longer seam edge. You run into this situation most often in the sleeve cap of a plain set-in sleeve; therefore we will give instructions for that and you can apply them to your particular problem. To shrink sleeve cap fullness:

1. Run one row of machine gathering stitches (long stitches) just barely outside the seam line. Place a second row in the seam allowance about ¼ inch from the first. Leave thread ends about 3 inches long.

2. Draw the underneath threads until the sleeve cap turns slightly but don't draw them enough to gather.

3. Place the sleeve cap, wrong side up, over the end of a sleeve board or over a pressing cushion.

4. Getting moisture from a steam iron or a damp cloth, press from the sleeve toward the edge of the sleeve cap with a gliding motion. Allow no pleats to form. Press a small area. Then move on to the next.

 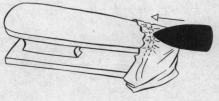

Turning a hem. Pressing the fold line before finishing a hem will result in a more accurate job and an easier one. Circular hems must be pinned or basted, but straight ones can sometimes just be turned as you press. When there is excess fullness, shrink it out after you have pressed the hemline. Do this by gliding the iron from the fold across the hem to the cut edge.

FINAL PRESSING

Garments that have been carefully pressed during construction and hung between class periods need only slight final pressing. Large flat areas can be pressed from the wrong side, but thick areas may be improved by a final pressing from the right side.

When pressing a complete garment, start with the smaller or dangling areas and end with the larger, less intricate ones. You are less likely to wrinkle the finished part as you press, if you follow this rule.

The clapper is especially useful for pressing wool and other heavy fabrics from the right side. It flattens the fabric without the danger of over-pressing. The weight of the clapper against a soft padding imbeds or sinks the heavy areas, thus giving a flat smooth top layer.

To use a clapper:

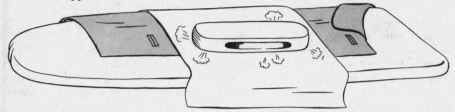

1. Place the area to be pressed right side up on a soft, well-padded ironing board (or use extra padding on top of the regular ironing board).

2. Cover the garment area with a press cloth and press as previously described. Do not press until dry, but leave plenty of steam in the fabric.

3. Quickly place the clapper over the freshly pressed area, holding it down firmly against the cloth.

4. Allow the clapper to remain for several seconds until the steam has left the fabric. Then lift it.

5. Repeat until you have finished the area.

TECHNIQUE 13   *NECK FINISHES*

Necklines are perhaps the most conspicuous part of any dress design and for that reason deserve careful consideration, both as you choose a design and as you carry it out. Select a becoming and comfortable neck style and one suited to the fabric. Then do all you can to give it a smart, professional look.

Some neck styles are suited to one kind of fabric, some to another. For instance, stand-away collars require crisp or firm material. And sheer fabrics are certainly not attractive with facings, interfacings, and seam edges showing through. Bind their edges and you will have enclosed most of your problems.

Most necklines are finished in one of three ways—with facings, bindings, or collars. The choice may seem limited but it isn't really because there is such infinite variety within each type. Regardless of the type, a well-made neck finish should conform to these standards:

Neck edges not stretched out of shape

All seams and edges as thin and smooth as they can be made without weakening the garment

All edges true in shape, with accurate corners and curves

Facing edges, whether beneath a neckline or a collar, hidden from view

Body and stiffness sufficient for the design

Low-necked dresses and blouses slip over the head easily, but closely fitting neck-lines require a placket or slash of some kind for head-room. Many such garments are made with full-length closings, either front or back. Any closing may be fastened with buttons, zippers, or in other ways but a slash only long enough to permit the head through is often left open, or perhaps closed at the top only. Whether fastened or left open, the edges of the closing are usually finished in the same way as the neckline proper—though there are times when this is not done. For instance, with a faced neckline you would ordinarily face the edges of a closing or slash, a bound neckline might call for a bound slash, and so on. In such cases, the facing or binding for both neckline and closing are usually cut together.

Before you start the neck finish, the blouse needs some preparation. Staylines should have been made and, if an interfacing is called for at the neckline or along a closing, that should have been joined to the blouse with the staylines. Shoulder seams also should have been completed. But don't stitch the blouse side seams yet. It is easier to work on the neckline while they are open and the blouse can be stretched out flat.

FACINGS

There are two types of facings; fitted and bias. For the collarless blouse or dress the *fitted facing* is easier to make, lies flatter, and shows less from the right side. The *bias facing* is used for attaching set-on (Peter Pan) collars, and occasionally for neck edges which are to be top-stitched with several rows of stitching, or treated in other decorative ways.

Fitted facings. Facings cut the exact shape of the garment edge they face are called fitted or shaped facings. They are generally cut on the same grain as the corresponding garment section. However, sometimes neck facings are cut in one piece to eliminate the seam on the shoulder. Facings cut this way are generally satisfactory, but may not lie as smooth as if they were cut on the exact grain of the neck edges. Another exception to the general rule is a bias-cut neckline which may call for a straight cut facing.

These are the steps for making a typical neck facing:

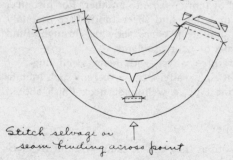

Stitch selvage or seam binding across point

1. Join the front and back facings with a plain seam at each shoulder. Trim the seam edges to about ⅜ inch in width and cut away the corners. Press the seams open. (If you have planned

your work efficiently you have done this as you did corresponding steps on your garment.)

2. Finish the outer edge of the facing while it is unattached and easy to handle.

a. On lightweight materials make a stayline ⅛ inch from the raw facing edge. Turn under the edge just inside the stayline and edge-stitch along the fold. (The stay-stitching makes it easy to turn the edge, particularly on curves.)

b. On firm, heavy materials and those that show an imprint when pressed make a stayline ⅛ inch from the raw facing edge and pink just outside the stayline. This is sufficient finish for fabrics that do not fray easily.

c. On heavy materials that fray easily you have a choice between overcasting and using seam binding. Ribbon seam binding can be used on straight edges but doesn't behave well on curves. If you don't use seam binding, make a stayline ⅛ inch from the raw facing edge and then overcast raw edges, using stayline as a guide.

3. Pin the facing to the garment with right sides together. Match all notches and seam edges carefully; also center lines and shoulder seams. Stitch around the entire neckline and down closing edges, if any.

4. Trim the seam edges to about ¼ inch in width (or, if the material is thick, layer them), then clip almost through the seam allowances of the neck curve at about ½ inch intervals. Snip away corners if there are any.

5. Here's a trick that keeps the facing from showing from the right side of the garment even after it has been cleaned or washed. Stitch the facing to the seam allowances wherever such a line of stitching will not show from the right side of the neckline. Do this with the right side of the facing up and the blouse pushed out of the way so you won't stitch through it. Keep the facing flat and perfectly shaped as you stitch. (If you do not stitch the edges back, you will probably have to baste them back this way by hand to keep the facing hidden.)

6. Turn facing into position; press.

7. Tack the facing to the blouse at the shoulder seams, darts, and any other double areas where stitches will be invisible. Tack by making several small hand stitches quite close together.

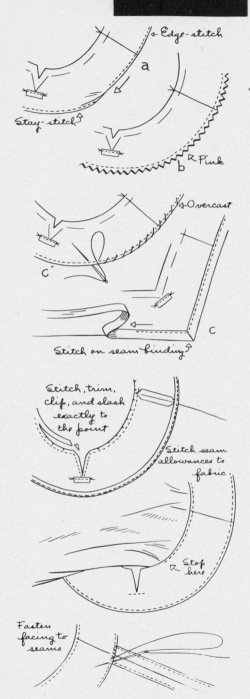

Decorative fitted facings. Decorative fitted facings are made like inside facings, except for two things: The right side of the decorative fitted facing is sewed to the wrong side of the blouse, and the outer edge is stitched to the garment as a lapped seam instead of being left to hang free. To prevent the raw edges of the shoulder seam from showing at the neckline, the shoulder seam of the blouse should be reversed just inside the outer finished edge of the facing. To reverse the shoulder seam:

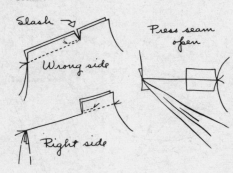

1. Stitch the shoulder seam, right sides together, from the armhole to a point just inside the facing line. Fasten the line of stitching.

2. Slash through both seam allowances all the way to the seam line at the end of the line of stitching.

3. Stitch the rest of the seam with wrong sides together. Fasten the line of stitching at the joining.

Facing a slashed opening. A slashed opening is used to permit you to put your head through a small neckline. It is made as the facing is attached whether there is a collar or not. A faced opening is easy to make, but special care must be taken to make stitching lines accurate at the point of the opening. The only disadvantage of a slashed opening is that the lower end of the opening is weak unless it is reinforced. Top stitching made around the entire edge of the slash after it is finished adds strength. If decorative top stitching is not appropriate, stitch seam binding or a firm selvage to the end of the slash. Stitch it to the wrong side of the facing before that is attached.

Do not cut the slash either in the garment or the facing until the two are stitched together. To make a faced slashed opening:

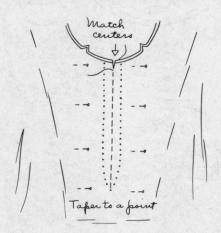

1. Mark the stitching lines for the slash on the garment section. If these lines are not on the pattern, make them ¼ inch on either side of the center line and bring them to an accurate curved point at the lower end of the slash. Stitch binding to wrong side of facing at the exact tip of the slash.

2. Pin the facing to the garment with the right sides together and notches and center lines matched perfectly. The facing should extend at least 1½ to 2 inches below the point where the slash will end. Be sure that center lines are together all the way to the bottom of the slash.

3. Place pins on both sides of the center line and at right angles to it.

4. Baste-stitch along the center line to the end of the slash.

5. Stitch along the marked lines on either side of the slash, taking one stitch straight across the point. Stitch in one continuous line.

6. Slash through both garment and facing along the center line to the exact point, leaving not more than one thread between the end of the slash and the stitching line at the point.

7. Turn the blouse wrong side out and press the seam, turning allowances toward the facing. Then turn the facing to its final position and press again.

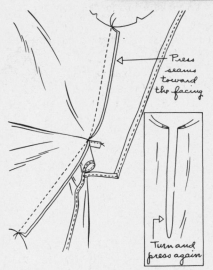

Press seams toward the facing

Turn and press again

Patterns for fitted or shaped facings are usually included in commercial patterns. When one is not, it is a simple matter to cut your own. Pin the edge of the pattern of the piece you plan to face on a sheet of plain paper. Mark along the edge to be faced and along the seams and fold lines adjacent to it, indicating notches where they appear. Remove the commercial pattern and mark the other edge. Neck

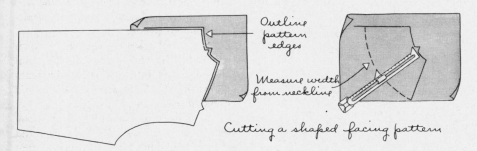

Outline pattern edges

Measure width from neckline

Cutting a shaped facing pattern

facings should be about 2 inches in width when finished, which would mean that they should be cut about 2¾ inches wide. Facings for slashed openings should be cut at least 1½ to 2 inches longer than the opening and the width graduated from the upper to the lower end of the facing. Front facings for buttoned closings should be wide enough to extend well beyond the outer end of the buttonhole. Facings for front and back should be exactly the same width at shoulder seam lines and under-arm seams. After drawing the pattern, cut it out.

Bias facings. Bias facings are made by stitching a bias strip to a garment edge, and then turning and finishing the bias strip back against the garment. Bias facings show from only one side of the garment, whereas bias bindings show from both sides of the garment. Finished bias facing should be fairly narrow. Wide ones draw at the outer edge. For a facing beneath a collar, ⅜ inch is a good width.

To make a bias neck facing:

Stretch outside edge as you press

Pin bias to neckline

Join ends of bias

Stitch, trim and clip neck seam

Baste and hem facing to neckline

1. Cut a strip of true bias about 1½ inches wide and long enough to face the entire neckline. See technique 3, "Basic Sewing Techniques and Hand Stitches," if you don't know how to cut and join bias strips.

2. Shape the bias to form a circle by stretching one edge as you press it. Keep tip of iron along stretched edge. This is called *swirling*.

3. Pin the bias strip to the neck edge, right sides of the material together. Start pinning at one shoulder. Keep the edge of the strip matched to the raw neck edge. Pins should be turned at right angles to the seam.

4. Join the bias strip with a seam at the shoulder. You will have to unpin some of the pins to have room to work. Stitch on the straight of the material—not straight across the facing. Trim and press the seam open, clipping away the corners of the seam allowances.

5. Stitch the bias strip to the neckline along the seam line. Allow the end of the stitching line to overlap the starting point to fasten.

6. Trim the seam edges to ¼ inch in width. Clip almost through the seam allowances at intervals. Turn the seam allowances back toward the facing and press or baste them in place.

7. Turn under about ¼ inch along the outer edge of the bias strip and crease along this fold. If you find that the facing is wider than you want it to be, or if it is uneven in width, trim it before making this last turn. When finished it should be about ⅜ inch wide.

8. Pin and baste the facing in place.

9. Fasten the folded-under edge to the garment with a hand-hemming stitch or make several rows of top stitching as a decorative edge finish. See technique 19, "Hems," for appropriate hemming stitches.

10. Remove bastings and press.

BINDINGS

Bias binding can be used on any medium or light-weight material. In addition to being particularly useful on sheer fabrics where a facing would show through, it is used where gathers originate along a garment edge. A bias binding should be just less than ¼ inch in width when finished and very even. If the pattern wasn't planned for a binding you will have to cut away the seam allowance before you start. Otherwise the neckline might be too small.

To finish a neckline with bias binding:

1. Stayline the neck edge in this case exactly ⅛ inch from the raw edge.

2. Cut a strip of true bias 1⅛ to 1¼ inch in width and long enough to finish the entire neckline. If you don't know how to cut a bias strip, see technique 3, "Basic Sewing Techniques and Hand Stitches."

3. Starting at one shoulder, pin the bias strip to the neckline, right sides together. On inside curves stretch the bias slightly and on outside curves ease it slightly. Turn pins at right angles to the seam line.

4. Seam the ends of the bias strips together on the straight of the material at the shoulder. Trim, clip away corners, and press the seam open.

5. Stitch the bias strip to the neckline along the seam line, overlapping the stitching at the end to prevent ripping. (Seam should be about ¼ inch.)

6. Trim the seam edges—not the binding—to ⅛ inch. This is a time for extreme accuracy because the seam allowance width determines the width of the finished binding. Lay the blouse and binding out flat on the ironing board and press the seam allowances toward the binding.

7. Working from the right side of the garment fold the binding back over the seam allowances and baste it to the blouse. Again keep the width even.

8. Press the binding from the wrong side to crease the neck edge and to give an imprint of the seam line—the seam that joins the binding at the neckline.

Trim seam to ⅛ inch but do not clip

Stretch crosswise as you press

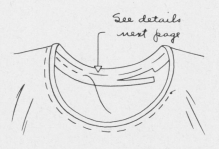

See details next page

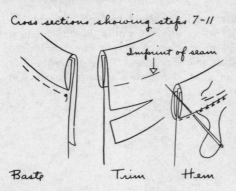

Cross sections showing steps 7-11

Baste   Trim   Hem

9. Trim the binding ⅛ inch below the imprint of the seam line.

10. Turn the raw edge of the binding under ⅛ inch and baste it in place, being careful to avoid diagonal wrinkles.

11. Use slant hemming stitches to fasten this folded edge permanently in place. Put stitches into seam line so they will not show from the right side.

12. Remove basting threads and press lightly from the under side. Do not flatten the binding by pressing from the right side or pressing too hard.

Where binding is not continuous, it must be finished off neatly at each end. Do this by allowing the binding to extend ¼ inch beyond the edge where it is to stop. Then after pressing the seams, turn this ¼ inch to the wrong side and finish the binding as usual.

Binding a slashed opening. A bound opening is stronger at the point than a faced slashed opening, but it is more difficult to make. Again you need markings on the wrong side of the garment. There should be parallel lines about ¼ inch apart, one on each side of the slash line, and there should be a crosswise line to join them at the end of the slash. (But don't cut the slash yet!) Here is the way to proceed:

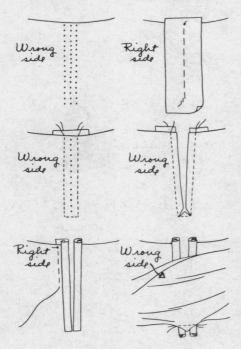

1. Cut a strip of true bias about 1½ inches wide and at least ½ inch longer than the slash.

2. Baste the strip right side down to the right side of the garment directly over the slash line.

3. With the wrong side of the garment up, stitch along the marked lines and across the end in a continuous line.

4. Cut through both layers of cloth to within ¼ inch of the end of the slash lines, then cut exactly to each corner.

5. Follow steps 7 to 12, above, to finish the binding to each side of the opening.

6. To finish the end, start with the right side of the garment up. Then fold the garment back to expose a triangular extension at the end of the slash. Stitch straight across this triangle on the previous line of stitching to hold the triangle to the binding ends.

COLLARS

There are as many varieties of collars as designers can think up. Some are single cut, some are folded double, but most are cut of two layers of fabric, possibly with an interfacing between to give the collar the correct shape or roll.

Collars are generally finished as a unit in themselves before they are attached to the garment. The garment is ready when its neck edges have been stay-stitched, when its shoulder seams have been finished, and when the free edges of any facing or hem extension have been finished. When a facing extends to the shoulder seam but is not joined to another facing at this line, it must be turned under on the shoulder seam line before the collar is attached. Leave the facing free, however.

The Peter Pan collar. Peter Pan and similar collars are usually cut double and interfaced, although they can be made from a single layer of fabric or they can be made double without an interfacing. In any case, the center back line should fall along a lengthwise thread if the collar is to lie well.

There are two tricks you may want to use in making this kind of collar. If your material doesn't show up marked lines well, cut a guide out of heavy paper to follow in stitching the curves around the edge. For this purpose, cut guide by stitching line on pattern—not cutting line. Pin it securely to collar and stitch along its edge.

The other trick is a technique for hiding the seam along the collar edge. Cut the under collar a little smaller than the upper collar (except along the neck edge!) but pin them together with their edges matched. About ⅛ inch or less trimmed away from the under collar is generally plenty. The strain on the material will pull the seam to the under side and out of sight.

To make a Peter Pan or similar collar:

1. When an interfacing is used, place it against the wrong side of the upper collar before making the staylines around the collar edge. (For collars that have a decided roll, baste the interfacing to the under layer.)

2. Trim away about ⅛ inch from the outer edge of the under collar but do not stay-stitch it. (Trim the interfacing also if it is attached here.)

3. Place upper and under collars together with right sides together. Match center lines, notches, and outer edges and pin them together.

4. As you stretch the seam gently, stitch along the outer seam line—not along the neckline. If there are points, take one stitch across each, pivoting at each end of this stitch. Refer to technique 10, "Seams and Seam Finishes," for more detailed instructions on this and following steps.

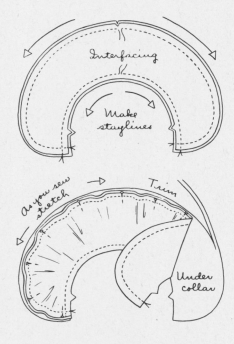

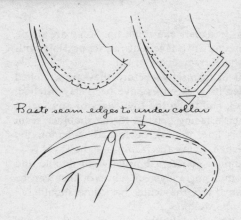

Baste seam edges to under collar

5. Trim the seam allowances to between ⅛ and ¼ inch in width. *Or* layer heavy fabrics. Cut points away even closer.

6. On full curves and in firm material you may have to cut narrow V-shaped notches partially through the seam allowance to eliminate bulkiness. Don't cut wide notches.

7. Turn the collar to the right side. Baste the seam allowances to the under collar. Or, if you prefer, understitch.

8. Press. Remove basting and press again.

9. Pin and baste-stitch the raw neck edges together.

A Peter Pan collar can be attached to the garment with either a fitted facing or a bias facing. Since most patterns call for a bias facing, we will give directions for that. The bias should be cut true and should not be more than ¼ to ⅜ inches in width when finished. To attach a Peter Pan or similar collar:

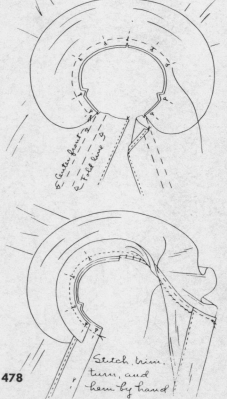

1 Center front 2 Fold line 3

Stitch, trim, turn, and hem by hand

1. Pin the collar to the garment with the under side of the collar against the right side of the garment. Match and pin at center back and notches. Bring each front collar edge exactly to the corresponding center front line of the garment. Keep raw edges matched.

2. Baste the collar in place with machine- or hand-basting.

3. Turn back the hem extension on the fold line along the front closing or attach the facing. The right sides of the material should be turned together in either case. Pin the hem or facing over the collar at the neckline, matching any notches.

4. Place the bias strip around the neckline with its right side against the collar. The bias strip should overlap the hem or facing. Stitch around the entire neckline. Trim, clip, turn, and fasten by hand following instructions for making a bias neck facing given earlier in this technique.

The convertible collar. The convertible collar may be worn open as a V-shaped neckline or may be buttoned high at the throat. To give a finished appearance when the collar is worn open, the front closing facing must extend up to the shoulder seam. The collar is sometimes a perfectly straight strip cut on either grain, but it may have inside or outside curves along the neck edge. Look for notches which tell you which edge is to be joined to the neckline. Sometimes convertible collars are cut as two pieces and seamed together. At other times they are cut as one piece and folded over at the outside edge.

A convertible collar is simple to make. If it is to be folded, you only have to stitch the ends. If it is cut in two pieces, stitch around the entire outside edge but not along the neck. Trim seams, turn the collar right side out, shape and press as you do any enclosed seam, and the collar is ready to attach.

Bias facings are not used to attach convertible collars because these collars roll sharply at the back of the neck, especially when worn buttoned. Hand-stitches and the imprint of a bias facing would show beneath the lower edge of the collar. There are several methods for attaching convertible collars, but only two will be given in this book. The *dressmaker method* is suitable for notched collars of medium- and light-weight materials. Notches are formed when the outside edge of the collar does not extend to the end of the front neckline. This dressmaker method for attaching notched convertible collars is given in Construction Two, "Making a Dress."

The *continuous horizontal-seam method* should be used for convertible collars without notches as it gives a smoother line along the front collar edge. Before attaching the collar by either method, clip the neck edge of the garment almost to the stayline at ½ inch intervals. To attach a convertible collar by the continuous horizontal-seam method:

1. Match the under collar (single layer) with its right side to the right side of the garment neck, pinning only at the center back and at notches.

2. Put your hand inside the collar and pin the opened-out seam at one end of the collar to the fold line of the blouse front closing (or to the seam line, in case a fitted facing is used at the front closing of the garment). Repeat at the other end of the collar.

3. Finish pinning the under collar to the blouse, keeping seam edges matched.

4. Now fold the hem extension wrong side out and pin the facing or hem extension to the upper collar, matching notches.

5. Stitch the long continuous seam around the facing and neck edges.

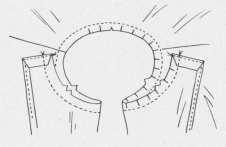

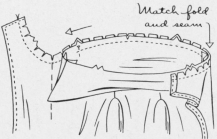

Match fold and seam

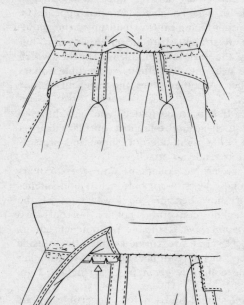

6. Clip the seam allowances as necessary to open up the seams from the front to the shoulder seams. Press.

7. Press the seam allowances at the back of the neckline (from one shoulder seam to the other) up into the collar.

8. Finish the back of the collar by turning the free edge under on the seam line and securing it with slant hemming stitches. Keep the stitches hidden in the layers of the seam.

9. Pin the upper and lower layers of the collar together along the front neckline seam. Place pins lengthwise along the seam to hold the seams together, then turn the facing back.

10. Turn the facing back in order to expose the seam edges which extend below the neckline. Fasten these two seam edges together with a hand running stitch.

11. Remove pins and press.

12. Fasten facing to the shoulder seam with slant hemming stitches.

The mandarin or Chinese collar. The narrow upstanding collar called a mandarin or Chinese collar can be cut as a straight strip, but hugs the neck much better when it is curved slightly. The collar is made like a convertible collar with or without interfacing. Then the finished collar is best attached to the neckline with a fitted facing. The neck edge of the garment and facing must be clipped at intervals nearly to the stayline before the collar is attached. Full instructions for a fitted facing are given earlier in this technique.

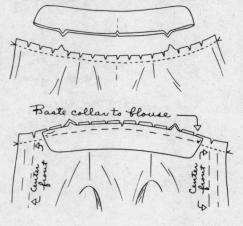

The tie collar. The tie collar is cut as a long narrow strip of material. It makes the best-looking bow if it is cut on the lengthwise grain. It is attached like the waistband of a skirt. See Construction One, "Making a Blouse and Skirt." This collar should not be made before it is attached. However, the neck edge of the garment needs to be stay-stitched and clipped at intervals first.

To prepare the blouse for a tie collar:

1. Starting with the front closing of the garment, turn the hem or facing back along the fold line, right sides together. Pin neck edges together, matching special markings which indicate the end of the stitching line.

2. Stitch from the special markings to the fold. Fasten all thread ends.

3. Slash through both seam allowances to the exact end of the stitching line (special marking).

4. Trim seams, cut away corners, turn, and press these short seams as you do any enclosed seams.

5. Pin the rest of the neck edge of the facing to the neckline of the blouse.

To make and attach the tie collar:

1. Join one edge of the tie collar to the neckline of the blouse, right sides together. Match center backs, notches, and special markings and pin.

2. Stitch, blouse side up, from one special marking to the other. Fasten thread ends.

3. Fold tie ends down the center, right sides together. Match notches. Pin and stitch across the ends of the ties along the seam lines and around to the special markings. Fasten thread ends.

4. Trim all seams to ¼ inch in width, and cut away corners. Turn and finish as you do any enclosed seam.

5. Turn under the inside collar along the seam line. Pin it in place to the stitching line matching center backs.

6. Hem the inside collar to the stitching line with slant hemming stitches.

7. Press.

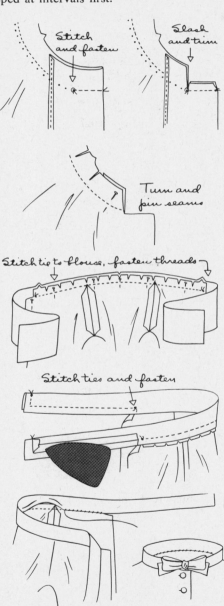

The shawl collar. The shawl collar is not cut as a separate collar but as an extension of the blouse front and nearly always has a center back seam. If it were not for the slashes at the neckline on the front sections and the curved back neckline having to be joined to a straight collar edge, this type of collar would present no special problems. However, the blouse shoulder seam enters into the process, which is not usual.

Before you start work, be sure that seam lines and slash lines are accurately marked. Trace them on the interfacing if there is one. Don't cut the slashes until later. As usual, trim away some of the under collar to prevent it from showing beneath the outside finished collar edge.

To prepare the blouse fronts:

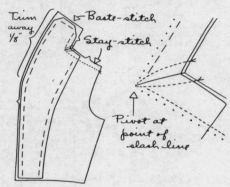

1. Pin and baste-stitch the interfacing against the wrong side of the blouse front and collar extension.

2. Stay-stitch the shoulder seam as usual, then stay-stitch around the slash line at the neckline in a wide V-shape to reinforce the slash.

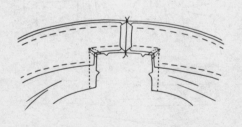

3. Join the two collar extensions with right sides together as you stitch the center back seam of this collar. Trim and press the seam open.

4. Now going to the outer collar edge, trim away about ⅛ inch from both the collar and interfacing edges but taper off to nothing at the point where the collar begins to roll. This point will be even with the top buttonhole marking.

To prepare the blouse back:

1. Stay-stitch the shoulder seam and back neckline as usual.

2. Clip through the neck seam allowance to the stayline at ½ inch intervals.

To join front and back blouse sections:

1. Lay the blouse back on a table right side up. Place the blouse front over it right side down. Match the shoulder seam lines, being particularly careful to match notches. Also, the tip of the slash line on the front must be placed directly over the point on the blouse back where the neckline and shoulder seam lines meet. Pin the seams.

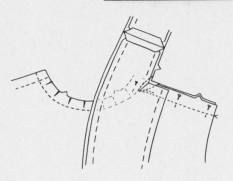

2. With the blouse front up stitch the shoulder seam, ending the line of stitching exactly at the tip of the slash line. Retrace the stitching line for a short distance to fasten it at this point.

3. Cut along the slash line precisely to the point where the line of stitching ends—the one you just fastened.

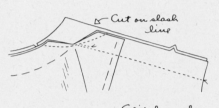

Cut on slash line

4. After both shoulder seams are stitched, fastened, and slashed, you are ready to join the neck seam. Place the right side of the collar against the right side of the blouse back neckline—previously clipped so that the two seam lines will fit. Work with the collar side up. Match center back lines and seam lines as you pin the two layers together. Notice that seam edges will not meet at each side where the slash lines were cut.

Stitch neck seam

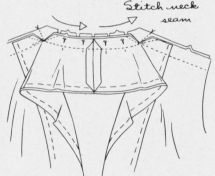

5. Stitch along the seam line, collar side up, in a continuous seam. Be sure to stitch through the exact tip of each slash line, starting before you reach the first one and stitching on beyond the last one to secure the two ends of the stitching line.

6. Trim the neck seam to about ¼ to ⅜ inch, or layer the edges if the material is heavy.

7. Press both neck seam allowances up into the collar. Press the shoulder seams open.

Trim neck seam, press toward collar

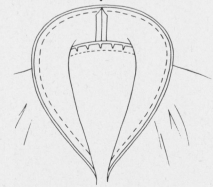

To prepare the facing:

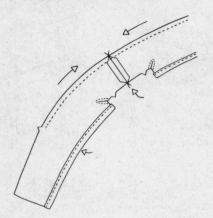

1. Stay-stitch around the slash line in a wide V-shape. Stay-stitch around the outer edge of the top collar area, stitching only to a point even with the top buttonhole position. (The stayline will help you to ease the top collar to the under one later.)

2. Now finish the opposite edge of the facing—the unnotched edge—with edge-stitching, seam binding, or pinking, whichever is more suitable for your fabric.

3. Join the collar extensions as you did those on the blouse fronts. Trim and press.

To attach the facing to the blouse:

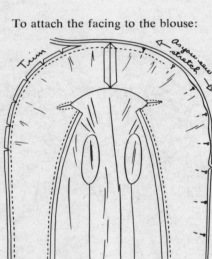

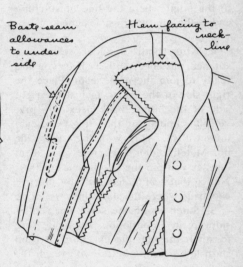

1. Place the blouse, right side up, with the collar and front closing edges spread out flat on a table. Place the facing, right side down, over it. Match outside edges, notches, and center back lines. You will have to ease the facing to the under collar slightly because you trimmed away some of the under collar.

2. Stitch in a continuous line around the collar and front closing edges.

3. Trim the seam to about ⅛ inch or layer the edges if the material is heavy. Notch along curve if necessary.

4. Baste the seam edges toward the under side. This will mean basting them to the garment side through the collar area but to the facing side along the front closing. Or understitch similarly.

5. Press, remove basting, and press again.

6. Cut along the slash line on the facing. Fold under the seam allowances along the neckline. Also fold in the seam allowances at the shoulder seam.

7. Pin and baste the facing in place at the neckline and to the wrong side of the shoulder seams. Then hem it to the garment with slant hemming stitches. Remove basting and press.

Detachable collars. There are several reasons for making collars separate from the garment. Light-colored and white collars must be washed or cleaned more often than the darker dresses they so often accent. Many times a different cleaning method must be used. For instance, a piqué collar should be washed and perhaps starched, while the wool dress it is used on will require dry-cleaning. Even when both are washable, the darker color of the dress might "bleed" onto the collar and discolor it.

Although you plan to use a detachable collar it is wise to finish the neckline of the dress so that it can be worn either with or without the collar.

Separate collars should be made to fit the neckline perfectly. It is usually best to cut them by the collar pattern of the dress. Make the detachable collar as you would any other collar. Bind the inside edge with a bias strip of the material.

The collar may be basted to the garment to hold it in place between cleanings. Do not allow the basting stitches to show from the right side of the dress. Attaching the collar to the dress with snaps instead of basting, makes it simpler to launder and replace the collar.

TECHNIQUE 14   *SLEEVES*

The sleeve line is an important part of the fashion silhouette. One year sleeves may be non-existent, leaving arms bare to the shoulder. Another year, large sleeves may dominate the costume. There are variations without number— some past history, others still to be designed. From the maker's point of view, however, there are two categories: those cut with the blouse and those cut separately.

CUT WITH THE BLOUSE

Sleeveless armholes. Finish the armhole of a sleeveless blouse or dress as you would a collarless neckline. Depending upon the design of the garment, armholes may be finished with either bindings or facings. Fitted facings are more attractive than bias facings, because they do not draw the sleeve edge as bias facings do.

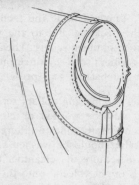 

The only difference between neckline finishes and armhole finishes is that facing edges at armholes must always be hemmed securely to the garment. The neck facings hang in place, but armhole facings must be attached to the garment if they are to stay where they belong.

Kimono, cap, and cape sleeves. Kimono sleeves, and sometimes cap and cape sleeves, are cut as extensions of the blouse front and blouse back. Such sleeves are simple to make. Their edges may be hemmed, faced, or bound. Kimono sleeves may have cuffs. Sometimes these cuffs are made of separate pieces. In other cases, they are formed by turning back a wide hemmed or faced edge.

To make a short kimono sleeve with a hemmed or faced edge, refer to Construction One, "Making a Blouse and Skirt."

Sleeves with gussets. Sleeves which are cut as extensions of the blouse often have inset sections called *gussets* beneath the arm. Gussets may be diamond-shaped or triangular. These extra sections permit greater freedom of arm movement.

The way you stitch gussets depends upon the shape of the gusset you are using. If you are using diamond-shaped gussets, you must stitch the underarm sleeve and blouse seams before inserting the gusset. (Leave the top sleeve-shoulder seam open until all underarm construction is complete—a reversal of the usual procedure.) Triangular gussets, on the other hand, are first set into both front and back blouse sections, and then the underarm sleeve and blouse seams are sewed as one continuous seam right across the gusset edges. Even when your pattern calls for only one triangular gusset, you should follow this order of work.

It is easiest to attach gussets at the underarm with *lapped* seams. Regardless of the shape of the gusset, your first step is to stay-stitch around slash lines on the blouse in order to add necessary strength. You then cut along the slash line, being sure to stop about ¼ inch from the tip—that uncut portion also strengthens the tip of the slash. (For diamond-shaped gussets, this is the time to stitch underarm seams.) Now use the following procedure to inset gussets with lapped seams:

1. Turn under the seam allowances of the gusset (4 sides of a diamond, only 2 sides of a triangle). Shape corners and baste as for any lapped seam. Press lightly. (If you have forgotten how to fold corners, turn to technique 10, "Seams and Seam Finishes.")

2. Bring the folded edge of the gusset to the marked stitching lines on the blouse. (Notice that the seam width is quite narrow near the tip of the slash.)

3. Pin and baste the gusset in place, then stitch around its folded edges.

4. Remove basting and press.

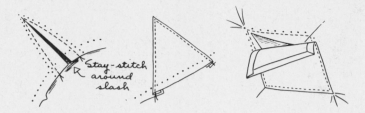

For those garments on which you prefer no top-stitching, gussets can be inset with *plain seams*. A problem arises here, however, because ordinary stay-stitching does not give enough reinforcement to prevent raveling (and sometimes holes!) at gusset corners. One way to prevent this tragedy is to stitch seam binding around the slash. If your gussets are triangular, this is the way to proceed. (You can follow these steps for a diamond-shaped gusset, and stitch the underarm seams at the proper time.)

Reinforcing the slash line:

1. Before cutting the slash, turn the wrong side of the blouse up, with the tip of the slash line toward you. Place seam binding over the left, traced stitching line, as shown.

2. As you make the stayline near the stitching line, catch the very edge of the seam binding all the way to the tip of the slash. (Near the tip, keep seam binding as far to the left as possible to give space for slashing later on.)

3. At the tip of the slash line, stop with the needle down; then fold the binding over crosswise so that its opposite edge falls barely over the other traced seam line.

4. Pivot on the needle and take one stitch directly across the tip of the slash to catch the edge of the folded back seam binding.

5. Pivot again and stay-stitch through seam binding on the second side of the slash line as you did on the first.

6. Cut to the exact tip of the slash line, but do not snip into the binding. (If the gusset is diamond-shaped, this is the time to stitch those underarm seams. Stop each line of stitching at the gusset stitching line and fasten it there.)

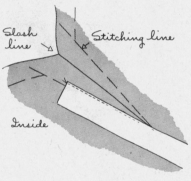

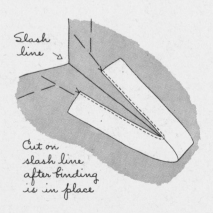

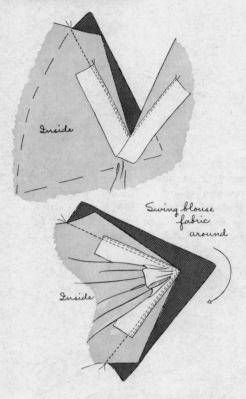

Insetting the gusset:

1. With the wrong side of the blouse up and the tip of the slash toward you, slip the gusset, right side up, beneath the left side of the slash. Match stitching lines. (Notice that the seam width on the blouse tapers to a point.)

2. Stitch to the tip of the slash. Stop with the needle down.

3. Swing the blouse fabric around partially until the fullness falls over the gusset. Pivot and take one stitch across the tip of the slash. Again, leave the needle down as you stop.

4. Match seam lines on the remaining side, pivot, and finish stitching that seam.

5. Finish seams and press them open, or press both away from the gusset.

CUT SEPARATELY

When sleeves are cut separately from the blouse, there is a possibility of error. Beginners so often make two sleeves for one armhole that this mistake has become the theme of many jokes. The sleeves of a garment should form a pair—not be identical.

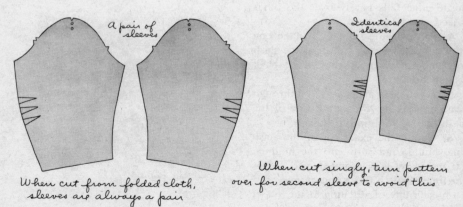

To check your cutting, place the flat sleeves with their right sides together. They should match down to the last notch. Now, if you can tell the right side of the material from the wrong, your chances for error are almost nonexistent. That's simple if you have done your marking with traced lines on the wrong side of the cloth only. If you haven't and the right side is difficult to distinguish, make a chalk mark on the wrong side of each sleeve. Then if you stitch as usual and match notches carefully, you will end up with your sleeves properly made and placed.

Raglan and epaulet sleeves. Raglan and epaulet sleeves have shoulder extensions which make it necessary to join the sleeve to the blouse front and back before finishing the neckline. Blouse side seam and sleeve seam are stitched as a continuous seam after the blouse is practically complete. Certain sections of the seams must be

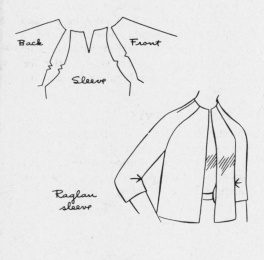

The raglan sleeve, which continues to the collar, gives an attractive loose effect and is often used on loose fitting top coats and men's overcoats.

This sleeve which also continues up to the collar line is named after the ornamental shoulder piece used on military and naval uniforms.

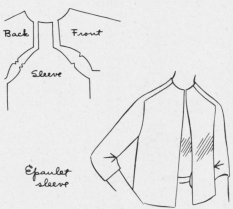

eased. These sections will be indicated on your pattern. Clip through inside curved seam edges and notch outside curved edges. Corners on epaulet sleeves need to be reinforced with stitching around the slash lines.

Regulation set-in sleeves. Full instructions for making and setting in short fitted set-in sleeves are given in Construction Two, "Making a Dress." If you are making long set-in sleeves, an additional first step is necessary: either stitch darts or dart tucks or use long machine stitching where ease is called for at the elbow position.

The lower edges of the sleeves described in construction II are faced. Set-in sleeves may also be hemmed or have cuffs. See directions given later in this technique for just when and how to make these other finishes.

Gathered sleeves. Sleeves that have gathers at the sleeve cap are set into the armscye seam very much as plain sleeves are. Use either machine or hand gathering stitches. Obviously the shrinking process is unnecessary since you want gathers in this case. All other steps are the same.

Deep-armhole sleeves. Sleeves which are to be set into deep armholes are kept flat and blouse side seams are left open until after they are attached to the blouse. There is usually some ease along the top of the sleeve which should be shrunk out before making the joining. Deep armhole seams may be plain or lapped and are finished as are other seams on the garment. Plain seams may be pressed either open or toward the blouse or toward the sleeve. Inside curved seam edges must be clipped; outside curves may need to be notched. Before attaching the sleeve, finish both the neckline of the blouse and the shoulder seam. After the sleeve is seamed to the blouse at the armscye, the underarm blouse seam and the inside sleeve seam are stitched as one continuous seam.

FINISHING THE LOWER EDGE OF SLEEVES

The lower edges of sleeves may be finished with hems, fitted facings, cuffs, or cuff bands. Hems are used on many short sleeves, because their lower edges are usually cut on a true crosswise grain, which makes hemming possible. Fitted facings are used as a simple finish on sleeves that have shaped lower edges, even on those that have their lower edges cut on a slight curve.

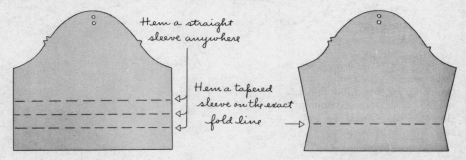

Hem a straight sleeve anywhere

Hem a tapered sleeve on the exact fold line

Hems. Sleeves which are the same width along their entire length may be hemmed at any desired length. Shaped sleeves, those that are tapered toward their lower edge, must be turned back at the exact fold line indicated on the pattern. Notice that the hem section of this type of sleeve is cut to flare below the fold line. This shape is necessary for a smooth hem. (Any alteration in sleeve length should have been made in the pattern above the hem line before the sleeves were cut.)

To hem a sleeve, start with the sleeve still flat. Follow the instructions given in Construction One, "Making a Blouse and Skirt."

Fitted facings. To attach a fitted facing to a shaped sleeve edge, start with the sleeve seam finished:

1. Finish the un-notched edge of the facing by edge-stitching, by pinking, or by applying seam binding.

2. Join the facing ends, right sides together, to form a circle. For a smooth fit, especially in heavy material, make the facing circle slightly smaller than the circle of the sleeve. Press the seam open and trim its edges to ¼ inch.

3. Pin the facing to the sleeve, right sides together. Match notches and vertical seam lines.

4. Stitch and trim seam edges; then shape, and press them as enclosed seams.

5. Fasten the free facing edge to the sleeve with vertical or invisible hemming stitches.

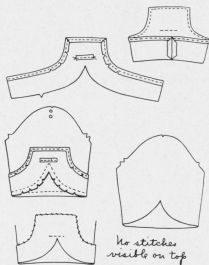

No stitches visible on top

If the sleeve edge is fairly straight, you can use a quicker method of attaching the facing. Refer to Construction One, "Making a Blouse and Skirt."

Cuffs. Cuffs are sometimes formed by turning back a hemmed edge. Faced lower sleeve edges can be turned back in the same way. Many cuffs, however, are first made as complete circles, while others are made flat with pointed or curved ends. They are then attached to an otherwise finished sleeve with either a bias or a fitted facing. A flat cuff is made with all sections flat, just as you would make a separate collar. To make a circular cuff:

1. Stay-stitch around the entire outer cuff. If an interfacing is required, attach it to the under side of this top cuff section with the stay-stitching.

2. Join the ends of the top cuff section to form a circle, right sides of material together.

3. Trim ⅛ inch off the top of the under cuff section and join its ends in the same way. If the material is heavy, stitch the under cuff so that it is slightly smaller in circumference than the top cuff.

4. Trim and press seams open.

Stay-stitch interfacing to top cuff

Seam top cuff

Trim under cuff

Seam under cuff

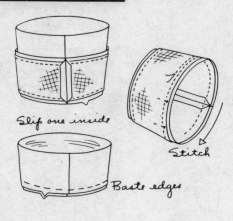

Slip one inside

Stitch

Baste edges

5. Drop the under cuff inside the outer cuff, right sides together. Pin their upper edges together with pins at right angles to the edges.

6. Stitch the pinned edges together, overlapping the beginning of the line of stitches to fasten. Trim seam edges and turn the cuff right side out. Shape and press as you do any enclosed seam.

7. Baste-stitch the raw lower cuff edges together.

To attach a separate cuff to a sleeve:

1. Pin and baste the cuff to the lower edge of the sleeve, notches matched, with the under side of the cuff joined to the right side of the sleeve.

2. If your pattern does not provide for a facing, cut one, following the bottom of the sleeve pattern but keep it narrower than the cuff. Or cut a strip of true bias about 1¼ inch wide. Seam the facing ends to form a circle of correct size. Trim and press the seam open. (Bias facings should be joined on the straight of the material.)

3. Place the facing over the cuff, right side toward the cuff. Pin and perhaps baste in place.

4. Stitch through all thicknesses along the seam line. Stitch inside the circle.

5. Trim seam edges.

6. With the sleeve wrong side out, turn the cuff down. Slip the sleeve over a sleeve board and press the seam allowances and the facing up into the sleeve. Stretch crosswise as you press.

7. Turn under the edge of the facing unless you finished the facing edge before you attached it. Pin the facing in place and fasten it by hand with slant or vertical hemming stitches.

Baste cuff to sleeve

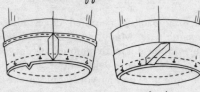

Fitted facing   Bias facing

Stretch as you press

Hem

Cuff bands. Cuff bands, such as those used on men's shirts, are attached to the lower edge of a sleeve after a sleeve placket has been made. The placket may be a faced slit like those used at a neck opening or a continuous bound placket.

To attach a straight cuff band to a sleeve:

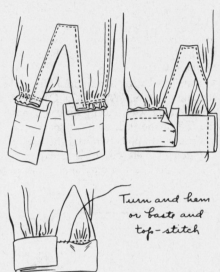

Turn and hem or baste and top-stitch

1. Join the right side of the band to the right side of the sleeve, matching notches, and distributing gathers carefully. Pin.

2. Stitch with the gathered side up.

3. Trim seam edges.

4. Fold the cuff in half, right sides of the material together, and stitch across each end of the cuff.

5. Trim seam edges, turn the cuff right side out, and shape cuff ends accurately as you do any enclosed seams.

6. Turn under the raw edge on the seam allowance and hem it to the under side of the cuff by hand.

TECHNIQUE 15   *POCKETS*

The chief purpose of pockets in women's clothes is to add design interest to dresses, suits, and coats. No smart girl will fill her pockets so full of sundry articles that they destroy her streamlined silhouette. Use a pocketbook to carry all these things. Pockets not only accent the design; they accent the figure. Place them above or below areas of your figure you prefer not to emphasize. It is better to omit pockets than to have them draw attention to an overdeveloped bust or a too-rounded hip line.

Fortunately, there are pocket styles for all figure types. The tall slender girl wears particularly well large patch pockets and pockets that stand away from her figure. The girl of average build and her a-bit-too-plump sister look better wearing flat, inset varieties.

Whatever the style, pockets should never sag in limp, drooping lines. Cut them accurately on true grain lines, mark them carefully, and use interfacings wherever required to give a firm line. Unless the fabric is very firm, reinforce it by basting muslin or other interfacing material beneath the pocket position.

Patch pockets. A patch pocket is made of a separate piece of material. Many patch pockets are unlined but those on suits and coats are frequently lined with light-weight material to add strength and hide raw seams. Before either type is attached to the garment all raw edges must be hidden. The upper ones are enclosed by the facing or hem. Those below are either folded under and basted or enclosed by the lining.

Instructions for hemming, lining, and attaching a patch pocket are given in Construction Three, "Making a Coat." A faced, lined pocket is made and attached in the same way except that you have one more seam to make—the one across the top of the pocket. That seam really simplifies the process because it holds the interfacing in place without the use of catch-stitching.

Patch pockets on shirts and pajamas are rarely lined. Many have top facings with decorative top stitching. Here is the way to make an unlined pocket with a top facing.

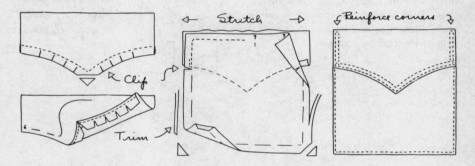

1. Starting with the bottom unnotched facing edge, fold the edge under on the seam line. Crease or baste. For pointed or curved facing edges, treat the edge as you would the top part of a lapped seam. That may mean staylines, clips, notches, and the like. See technique 10, "Seams and Seam Finishes."

2. Trim away a small amount from each pocket side—less than ⅛ inch.

3. Place the right side of the facing against the wrong side of the pocket. Match the notches and raw seam edges. Pin.

4. With the pocket side up, stitch in a continuous seam across the top and sides of the facing. Extend the ends of the stitching line slightly below the facing on each side of the pocket to fasten the facing securely, or retrace clip.

5. Turn the facing into position and top-stitch its bottom edge to the pocket to correspond with the way you intend to stitch the pocket to the garment. See illustration above.

6. Fold under the remaining raw seam edges at the sides and bottom of the pocket. Again shape points or curves as you would a lapped seam. Crease or baste. Press.

Now you are ready to attach the pocket to the garment. Before sewing there be sure that the markings for the pocket position are visible on the right side of the garment. When attaching patch pockets to washable garments, stitch very close (1/16 inch) to the outer edge. Additional lines of stitching may be used. The upper corners at least should always be reinforced with additional stitching. In wool or other firm, heavy fabric you may get a welt effect by stitching ¼ inch or more from the pocket edge. (Curved edges must be faced or lined if you plan to do this but a welt edge on a rectangular pocket is no extra trouble.) Another decorative possibility in a firm fabric is to sew the pocket on with either pin-point back stitches or saddle stitches—widely spaced running stitches done with heavy thread.

The slot pocket. A slot pocket looks like a long piped or bound buttonhole. Made in a slash in the body of the garment, its pouch is hidden from view inside the garment. Each edge of the slash is finished with a strip of material which forms an extension or lip. Sometimes these lips are narrow and sometimes they are wide. You may even see them made over cording.

There are many variations of the slot pocket, but here we are going to describe one with narrow piped edges made by the one-strip method. This method can be used successfully wherever a straight-cut slash is called for. In a garment made of medium-weight material cut the strip of self material. In heavier fabrics the mid-section of the strip—the part that forms the pouch—should be made of lining material to eliminate bulkiness. Piece the strip together, using 3 inches of self material on each end. Self material will form the lips and the lining part of the strip will not show from the right side.

Do not cut along the slash line before you start work on the pocket. There are several things you have to do before you cut. First you will need to reinforce the slash line. To do this, cut a muslin strip about 2 inches longer than the pocket line. Baste it in place beneath the slash line on the wrong side of the garment. Replace the pattern and transfer all pocket markings to the muslin reinforcement so that you will have accurate lines to stitch by later on.

Here's the way to make the slot pocket:

1. Place the pocket strip against the right side of the garment, right sides together with markings matched. Be sure to turn the long end of the strip down toward the bottom of the garment. Pin and baste around the slash with diagonal basting stitches.

2. Working with the wrong side of the garment up, stitch around the slash on the marked stitching lines. Start midway on one of the long sides—not at a corner—and overlap the starting point. Count stitches at the ends to keep the width of the rectangle even. Remove diagonal basting.

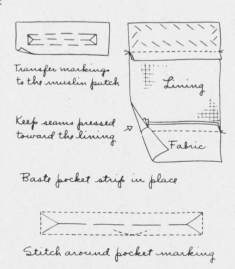

Transfer markings to the muslin patch

Keep seams pressed toward the lining

Lining

Fabric

Baste pocket strip in place

Stitch around pocket marking

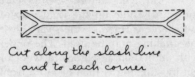

Cut along the slash line
and to each corner

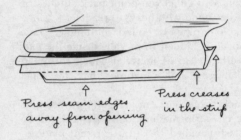

Press seam edges
away from opening

Press creases
in the strip

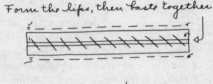

Form the lips, then baste together

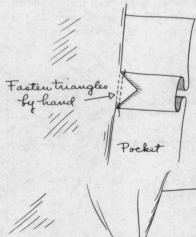

Fasten triangles
by hand

Pocket

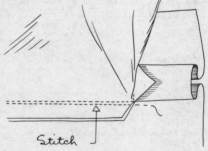

Stitch

3. Now cut along the slash line (the center line) through all layers of the fabric, stopping about ¼ inch from each end. From those points clip directly to each corner of the rectangle. Do not cut through the stitching line but exactly to it.

4. Turn the pocket strip through the opening to the wrong side of the garment.

5. Press the narrow seam edges away from—not toward—the opening. Continue the pressing beyond the ends of the pocket to form creases in the strip.

6. With the right side of the garment up, form a lip along both long sides of the opening. To do this extend the strip out into the opening. Then fold it under, being sure to keep the tiny seam allowances pushed back away from the opening. The lips should barely meet in the center of the opening and they should be exactly the same width. Baste the strip to the garment just back of the lips to hold them secure. Do not baste across the ends of the opening.

7. Use diagonal basting to hold the lip edges together.

8. Fold the garment back to expose a tiny triangle on top of a narrow box pleat at one end of the pocket. See that the box pleat is accurately formed, then fasten the triangle to it with a few hand stitches. Repeat at the opposite end of the pocket. Press. Leave the lips basted together but remove other basting lines.

9. The lower lip has to be fastened in place, but no stitching should show on the right side of the garment. To accomplish this, fold the garment back to expose the narrow seam allowances which extend below the lower lip. Stitch these to the pocket strip beneath them, keeping the new line of stitching on top of the previous one.

10. Fold the bottom of the pocket strip up to form the pouch. Match the raw edges of the two strip ends. Pin them together, catching the narrow seam allowances of the upper lip but not the garment itself.

11. Fold the garment back to expose the narrow seam allowances, then stitch along the previous line of stitching to hold the lip secure and the ends of the strip together.

12. Now you are ready to seam the sides of the pouch. Turn the garment back to expose the box pleat and triangle at one end of the pocket. With these uppermost, pin and stitch the two layers of the pouch together being extremely careful to stitch along the base of the triangle at the end of the pocket. This will mean stitching on the previous line of stitching across the triangle. Repeat, stitching the opposite side of the pouch in the same way. Press.

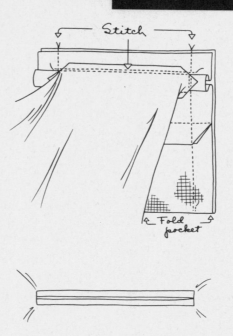

A welt pocket. Like the slot pocket, a welt pocket is inset in a slashed opening. But unlike the slot pocket, it has one wide lip, called a welt, instead of two narrow ones. This type of pocket is usually cut with two pocket sections and a separate welt all of self material.

In thick materials it is better to cut the pocket sections of lining material, but the upper 2 or 3 inches of the pocket back (the longer pocket section) should be made of self material to prevent the lining from showing when the pocket is opened up. It is a simple matter to piece the under pocket together in this way. Use a plain seam, and press the seam edges toward the lining to keep the pocket flat.

Before starting work on the pocket, transfer the pocket position lines to the right side of the garment. Then reinforce the slash line with a strip of muslin as described for the slot pocket.

The next step is to make the welt. Straight welts cut on a grain line can be folded, but other welts must be made like a Peter Pan collar. Use an interfacing if the material does not seem firm enough to stand up well. Stitch around three sides of the welt (the top and the two ends), turn, and press so that the under layer is completely hidden. Baste-stitch the raw edges together. Now, attach the welt and make the pocket. Here is the way to proceed:

1. Start working from the right side of the garment. With the right side of the finished welt next to the garment, place it below the slash line with its raw edge against the lower edge of that line.

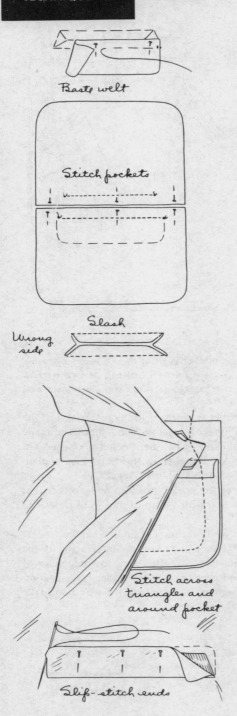

Baste welt

Stitch pockets

Wrong side

Slash

Stitch across triangles and around pocket

Slip-stitch ends

See that the ends of the welt match the ends of the pocket slash. Pin and baste it in place.

2. Place the upper pocket section (the shorter one) right side down over the welt, with seam lines matched. Pin it in place.

3. Place the under pocket above the slash line, right side down with seam lines matched. Pin it in place.

4. Stitch along these two lines. Do not stitch across the pocket ends. Draw thread ends to the under side and tie them at the end of each stitching line.

5. Cut along the slash line but stop about ½ inch from each end. Then, cutting through the garment, but not through the welt and pocket sections, cut diagonally just to the exact tip of each stitching line.

6. Turn the pocket strips through the opening to the under side of the garment. Pull the welt up to cover the opening. Press all seam edges away from the opening. Do not press the triangular projections at the ends of the pockets.

7. You are now ready to stitch the edges of the pouch together. Working with the right side of the garment up, fold the garment back so you can see the triangles against the under pocket. Pin the pouch edges together, being careful to keep the pocket flat, and the triangles extended. Stitch around the entire edge of the pouch and across the base of each triangle. Finish the seam edges and press.

8. From the right side pin and baste the welt in place. Remove pins and slip-stitch each end to the garment securely but invisibly. Press.

TECHNIQUE 16   *WAISTLINES*

The natural waistline is the smallest part of the figure between the chest and hips. It is the line where a cord tied snugly around the figure falls. On the average figure a cord tied in this way dips lower in the back than in the front. There are times when a drooping line at the front or back waistline is favored by fashion, but the standard practice is to keep the waistline of a garment parallel to the floor. Lower the cord slightly in front to make it level with the back line.

In most cases the waistline of a skirt or dress should fall no higher and no lower than the leveled natural waistline. A waistline placed in this position gives maximum comfort, and keeps the garment properly placed on the figure.

If the figure above the waistline seems too long for the lower part of the body, it is sometimes advisable to lift the waistline of a dress slightly. There is always the danger, however, of merely producing the effect of an out-grown, or poorly fitted garment. It is often better to select a design with a shaped inset waistband, or a wider belt than usual to correct the figure proportions. When they are in fashion, Empire waistlines may be used successfully.

When the upper figure seems too short for the lower part of the body, the waistline of the dress may be lowered slightly. It should be worn with a narrow belt, slightly loose. However, a lowered waistline as part of the dress design may be a better way to achieve a pleasing effect.

You will notice that the waistline from side seam to side seam is longer across the front than across the back. The difference on average figures is about 1 inch. However, the waistline of a skirt or dress from center front to center back must be identical in length on the two sides. When plackets are closed they should not change these relationships.

The waistlines of both skirts and dresses should fit snugly, but should not be tight. Loose waistlines on dresses allow the waistline seam to show below or above a belt. On skirts, they allow the skirt to shift on the figure, and blouse tails to pull out of the skirt easily.

SKIRT BANDS

Skirts are sometimes made without waistbands, but nearly all separate skirts and many suit skirts are made with waistbands. These vary in width from about 1 to 1½ inch. A shaped waistband may be several inches wide.

The regulation skirt band is cut on the lengthwise grain of the material, because fabric is stronger and stretches less in that direction. There are times, however, when the waistband must be cut on a crosswise grain to save material. Skirt bands should be longer than the waist measure to allow for an overlap and, of course, should be cut to allow for seam allowances. Skirt bands are usually cut to be folded along the top edge, but occasionally they have a seam along this line.

Unless the cloth of the skirt band is quite firm and stretches little, it is wise to use an interfacing. This can be made of firm muslin, drilling, duck, or similar material.

Shrink the interfacing material, unless you are sure that it will not shrink noticeably. Cut a lengthwise strip the width of the finished skirt band and the same length as the band.

Full instructions for interfacing and attaching an ordinary waistband to a skirt are given in Construction One, "Making a Blouse and Skirt." Here we will just give special cases.

Before attaching a waistband, stitch and finish all skirt seams and darts and make the placket. The waistline of the skirt is supposed to be slightly larger than the skirt band and must be eased to the band. Staylines should have been made ⅛ inch from the waistline seam of the skirt. Clip through the seam allowance to the staylines on curved waistline edges.

Re-marking a waistband when the pattern does not fit perfectly. The fact that your waistline front is longer than your waistline back is what makes it tricky to get a waistband with a side opening placed right. A skirt with a center placket is no problem. After measuring your waist, you merely halve that measurement to get the two sides equal. Just be sure side seams are equidistant from the center points and you can't go wrong.

To attach any waistband to a skirt, you need accurate markings at these points— the side seams and the front and back center lines. As you are fitting your skirt, it is a simple matter to adjust a waistband with a side opening to fit you perfectly if it doesn't already. Just be sure that you have the waistband folded down its lengthwise center and the front end of the band matched at the left side of the skirt as intended on your pattern. Fit the band just the way you would like it to fit and pin it that way. Then proceed as follows:

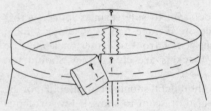

Try waistband on, then mark these points with pins

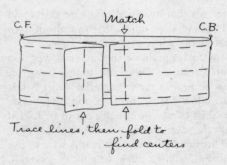

C.F.   *Match*   C.B.

Trace lines, then fold to find centers

1. Place a pin in the front end of the waistband exactly in line with the placket line. Repeat on the back end of the belt directly underneath.

2. Put another pin in the waistband where it overlaps the right side seam line.

3. Take the waistband off and open it out flat.

4. At each pin, trace a line across the waistband on a true grainline. Tracing will put the markings on the wrong side of the material where you want them.

5. To find the center front and center back lines, match the placket markings with the right side seam marking. The center points will be on the folds. Mark these in the same way and your belt is ready to attach.

DRESS WAISTLINES

Blouses and skirts of dresses are seamed together with either plain or lapped seams. The plain seam is easier to use and is satisfactory for joining most dresses. Lapped seams are used along shaped waistlines.

Whether plain or lapped seams are used, seam edges should be turned toward the plainer edge of the garment. For instance, plain gored skirts have seam allowances pressed toward the skirt. A dress with a fitted bodice and a full skirt would have the seam edges pressed up against the bodice. When both edges have fullness, an inset waistband should be used to separate the full edges and define the waistline. In thick materials where there is no fullness at the waist, plain seams are sometimes pressed open.

Full instructions on sewing a tape to the waistline of a dress with a side placket are given in Construction Two, "Making a Dress." To mark the tape for the waistline of a blouse or skirt with a center front or back closing and no side placket, measure the tape to fit your waist and cut it off that length. Fold it in half and mark the center point. Then, against the blouse or skirt, mark the side seam lines. Check to make sure that the side seam marks are equidistant from the center point. Pin the tape in place with the ends at the center front or back lines (not the placket edge) and other markings in place. Stitch.

For a lapped seam joining, turn one edge under along the seam line and join it to the other, as you would any lapped seam. The design of the garment will determine the seam edge to place on top. Follow above instructions for matching center lines, etc. Stitch close to the folded top edge, finish, and press the seam.

An inset dress band. When a dress has fullness both above and below the waistline, an inset dress band is often used to join the blouse and skirt. This double layer of material controls gathers or unstitched pleats and gives a trim fit at the waistline. Because it is strong and will not stretch, no tape is needed. Wide dress bands may be cut with side seams to fit the figure, but narrow bands are usually cut as straight strips. Some inset bands have an interfacing which strengthens and stiffens the waistline of the dress.

Of course, the band must be set into the dress before a placket is made. However, a front or back blouse opening which extends only to the waistband should be completed before the band is attached.

To join blouse and skirt with an inset dress band:

1. Fit the band on your figure to check its size as you are fitting the blouse and skirt.

2. Where waistbands are cut with side seams, join the sections of the top layer together with plain seams, except along placket or closing.

3. Next, join the sections of the under layer in a similar manner.

4. Pin the blouse to the upper edge of the top layer of the band with a plain seam right sides together. Be sure that center lines, notches, and side seams match. (Along a placket the seam lines of blouse, waistband, and skirt should form a continuous line.) Pin the under layer of the waistband to the blouse in a similar way except that the right side of the band should be placed to the wrong side of the blouse.

5. Stitch through all layers with the top waistband up. Follow a traced line for best results.

6. Attach skirt to the lower edge of

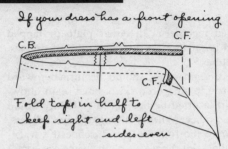

If your dress has a front opening

C.B.   C.F.

C.F.

Fold tape in half to keep right and left sides even

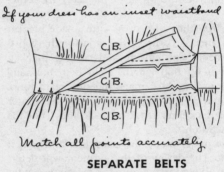

If your dress has an inset waistband

C|B.

C|B.

C|B.

Match all points accurately

the top band in a similar manner. You will have to leave the under band free this time.

7. Trim both seam allowances to ⅜ inch or layer them to prevent bulkiness. Do not trim seams too narrow because of the strain which will be exerted upon them. Clip away the corners, if any.

8. Press both seams toward the waistband, stretching the seam open, as usual. Press the under band down.

9. Turn under the raw edges of the under band on the seam lines at the bottom of the band. Pin the under band to the under side of the top band and hem it in place by hand.

SEPARATE BELTS

Contrasting belts of leather, straw, and other materials may be the decorative note your garment needs. There are times, however, when you want a belt of the same material as your dress. You can make either the soft tie variety or the stiffened type with a buckle.

The lengthwise grain generally gives a better looking belt than the crosswise grain does. Cut the material on a true grain. It is sometimes easier to tear the material to shape than it is to cut it by the belt pattern. (Instructions for making a stiffened belt are given in Construction Two, "Making a Dress.")

To make a soft belt:

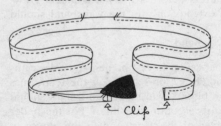

← *Clip* →

1. Fold the belt down its lengthwise center. Match the cut edges, keeping cross grain lines straight to prevent diagonal wrinkles. Pin the edges.

2. Stitch the ends and the lengthwise seam, except for a space of several inches near the middle of the belt. This opening is used for turning the belt right side out.

3. Trim or layer seam allowances. This time they can be trimmed fairly narrow. Clip away the corners.

4. Press the long seam open over a seam board or press one edge back, preferably before trimming.

5. Turn the belt through the opening on the rubber end of a pencil or with an orangewood stick.

6. Work the seams to the outer belt edges. Shape the belt by hand or baste the edges in place.

7. Along the opening turn the raw seam edges in. Baste them together and fasten them invisibly with a slip stitch.

8. Press, remove basting, and press again.

TECHNIQUE 17   *PLACKETS*

Plackets are used at waistlines, necklines, wrists, and other snug-fitting parts of clothing. They should be strong, easy to fasten quickly, and long enough for convenience in dressing. Fastenings should hold securely, and there should be no gaping edges. Unless used as a decorative detail, a placket should be inconspicuous. No placket should be bulky, puckered, or stretched. In fact, a placket should never interfere with the smooth-flowing lines of the design.

Slashed openings serve the same purpose. See technique 13, "Neck Finishes."

Selecting a suitable placket. Zipper plackets are easy to make, and fasten quickly and securely. Since the advent of zippers, other types of plackets have dwindled in popularity. Yet zippers are a bit stiff for some places and materials. A buttoned placket is more flexible and often more decorative. Zippers are seldom satisfactory at the wrist because they are difficult to operate with one hand. In sleeves, faced slashes, for instance, are a better choice. In a gathered skirt, a continuous-bound placket is just as satisfactory and less expensive.

ZIPPER PLACKETS

There are types and weights of zippers for all openings. Many patterns tell you the style and length to buy. Measurements refer to the length of the metal portion, not to the tape. Neck-type fasteners have fine teeth and are light in weight. They come in many lengths. Skirt zippers are usually 7 or 9 inches long and slightly heavier than the neck-type. Dress fasteners for side seams are usually 12 or 14 inches long and are closed at both ends. Select a color which blends with the fabric.

Kinds of zipper plackets. Slide fasteners are usually concealed, sometimes with two overlapping fabric edges and sometimes with one. Either type placket is suitable for skirt, neck, or dress openings. The placket with two overlapping edges, known as a slot zipper placket, is perhaps the simpler of the two to make but the single-lap type covers the fastener more completely. This single-lap placket requires a wider than usual seam allowance—about ¾ inch. However, you can extend the seam allowance if necessary to make this kind of placket. For the princess-line garment, a slot zippper placket is preferable because it will lie flatter. One wide overlap stands away from the figure unless held down with a belt.

Hints for sewing zippers in place. Zippers are easy to insert if you know how. The steps to follow for each type of closing are given later, but here are a few hints to keep in mind regardless of the type you make:

Stay-stitch all seam allowances except those cut on a true grain.

Check placket length. It will always be the length of the metal plus various allowances.

Fasten seams at the ends of the placket openings to prevent holes from developing there.

Baste the placket together whenever possible to keep the sides true.

Press the seam allowances back carefully before inserting the fastener because it is difficult to press the overlaps afterward.

If tape is too long, trim it, but always leave at least ½ inch beyond the metal at each end.

Never permit the lower end of the metal on any zipper to extend below the end of the placket opening because the zipper will tear the cloth if you do.

Be careful not to stretch material as you attach it to a slide fastener; ease it, instead, to allow the fastener to lie flat. Staylines help, of course.

Unless the width of the placket allowance is at least ⅝ inch for slot zipper plackets and ¾ inch for the kind with one overlapping edge, you had better add to them. Extend each seam (placket) allowance by top-stitching a strip of ribbon seam binding to the raw fabric edge. Cut a strip as long as the zipper tape and attach it. On washable fabrics, instead of using seam binding, sew on a bias strip of the dress fabric. Fold under one edge and top-stitch.

To stitch the zipper in place use a special presser foot with only one prong which allows you to stitch close to the metal. The presser foot with the left prong is supposed to be for zippers and the one with the right prong is supposed to be for cording, though either will serve both purposes if you don't mind which side you stitch on. There are adjustable zipper and cording feet too, and with one of these you can stitch on whichever side of the zipper you want to.

Slot zipper plackets. A slot zipper placket should meet these standards:

The fastener should be centered beneath the opening.

The fastener should not show between the two overlapping edges.

The two overlapping edges should be equal in width—each about ¼ inch wide except that the top part where the pull rests may be wider.

Stitching should be straight.

The fastener and the material around it should be flat and smooth.

Full instructions for making a slot zipper placket in a skirt are given in Construction One, "Making a Blouse and Skirt."

A neck slot zipper placket is made the same way you make one in a skirt except that you usually have a neck facing (and sometimes a collar) to cope with. Also, you will probably want to use a hook with a thread eye at the top of the zipper to keep the placket securely fastened. Here is the way to prepare the opening and make a slot zipper placket at a neckline:

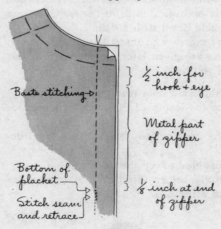

Baste stitching ▷

½ inch for hook + eye

Metal part of zipper

Bottom of placket

Stitch seam and retrace

⅛ inch at end of zipper

1. Find the finished placket length by adding about ⅝ inch (½ inch for the hook and eye, and ⅛ inch at the bottom of the zipper) to the length of the metal part of the zipper. Measure that distance below the neck seam line—that's the stitching line, of course, not the raw neck edge—and mark that point.

2. Stitch the vertical blouse seam to the bottom of the placket (the point you have just marked) and retrace.

3. Next follow steps 1, 2, 3, 4, 5, and 6 given for the skirt placket in Construction One.

4. After the neck facing and the collar (if there is one) are attached, you must fasten the edges of the facing to the under side of the placket. To do this, trim the facing edges slightly, fold them under and attach by hand to the zipper tape near the metal part of the zipper. Of course, you must keep the facing far enough from the zipper so that the pull will glide up and down easily.

5. Make a thread eye (just as you would a thread loop, technique 18, "Fastenings") on the left placket edge above the zipper. It should be about ¼ inch long when finished.

6. Next, sew a small hook of the right color beneath the opposite edge of the placket. Place it so that the two placket edges will be drawn together and the hook hidden from view when the garment is worn. (Refer to Construction One, "Making a Blouse and Skirt," if you have forgotten how to sew on a hook.)

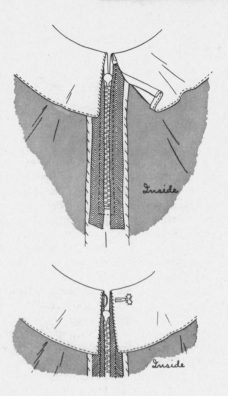

Some instructions for neck slot zipper plackets tell you to face the entire neckline and placket edges before insetting the zipper. This method is satisfactory, especially for long zipper closings that are faced all the way to the bottom. When you use this method, of course, you cannot baste-stitch the placket seam edges together. Just pin the faced edges in place so that they meet over the zipper. As you do so, be careful to cover the zipper completely and keep the placket sides even at the neckline. You will usually have to turn the tape back at the top of the zipper; after you have stitched the zipper in place, fasten it securely by hand.

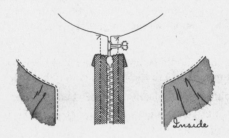

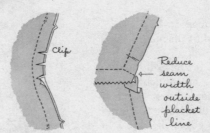

Slot zipper plackets in dresses are made like those at necklines except that both ends of the placket and zipper are closed. However, any dress placket requires special attention before the zipper is inset.

In preparing a dress placket opening perhaps your first consideration should be *waistline curves*. Whether your dress zipper will be inset in a slot seam or with one overlapping edge, it requires special care if it extends above and below the waistline of a fitted garment. Placket edges on such inside curves must be clipped, faced, or let out to allow them to spread enough to fold back smoothly against the garment at the curve.

A few clips near the waistline are usually sufficient for slot zipper plackets on princess-line dresses and blouses, since the two overlapping edges are narrow and the clips need not be too great. However, if you insist upon using the placket with one overlapping edge on such garments, your only solution is to face the wide edge with a bias strip of cloth which will stretch to fit the curve. If you cut the facing wide enough, this method also enables you to add seam width when that is needed.

If you have a waistline seam on your dress, it is an ideal place to let out placket allowances. Stitch that seam only to the placket line and fasten the stitching there. In this way, the placket allowances are free to fold back smoothly as the seam spreads open at the waistline. *Or,* perhaps a still better way is to stitch the waistline seam as usual, but narrow its width rather gradually outside the placket line. If the angle is correct, it will permit the placket allowances to fold back perfectly.

Another consideration in dress zipper plackets is the *length of the placket opening*. Ordinarily, you are told to make it about ¼ inch longer than the metal part of the zipper. However, if you would like to have the pull tucked into a little "pocket" at the top of the closed zipper, you should make the opening the length of the metal or slightly shorter. In that case, the pull rests partially beneath the underarm seam—just enough to keep it from rubbing against your arm.

Zipper plackets with a single overlapping edge. A zipper placket with one overlapping edge should meet these standards:

The overlapping edge should be approximately ½ inch wide and even in width, except that the top part where the pull rests may be wider.

The fastener should be completely hidden when the placket is closed.

The overlap should extend not more than ¹⁄₁₆ to ⅛ inch beyond the edge of the fabric of the underlap.

The fastener and material around it should be flat and smooth.

Before sewing in a dress placket zipper, have:

Placket edges stay-stitched
Waistline seam, if any, sewed
Waistline curve on a fitted garment clipped, faced, or let out
Placket length determined
Side seams stitched to each end of the placket and fastened
Narrow placket edges extended to ¾ inch in width
Zipper foot attached—use an adjustable one because you should stitch from the bottom up at all times, and that means shifting the zipper foot from one side to the other.

To inset a dress zipper with one overlapping edge:

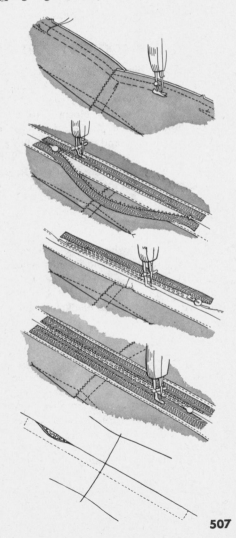

1. Machine-baste the placket edges together, stitching on the placket line. Press the seam open.

2. Extend the back seam to the right —the remainder of the garment, turned wrong side out, is kept to the left. Open the zipper. Place it face down with the edge of the teeth (those on the right hand tape) over the baste-stitched seam line, and the bottom stop ⅛ inch above the bottom end of the placket. Stitch the tape to the back seam allowance, keeping the zipper foot close to the metal teeth.

3. Close the zipper and fold it over to the right so that its face side is up. Fold back the material at the left of the zipper, stretching it crosswise and creasing it if possible. Again stitch the fabric to the tape. (Keep the stitching close to the fold this time.)

4. Now spread the garment out flat —still wrong side up—so that a single layer of cloth extends on each side of the zipper. Turn the zipper face down across the seam. Stretch crosswise and perhaps pin it in place there. Stitch across the lower end, then up the front close to the zipper, and across the top. (Never attempt to stitch over pins with a zipper foot, of course.) Draw thread ends to the under side and tie them.

5. Remove basting and press. Finish any raw seam edges so that raveling will be kept to a minimum.

Use these same steps for inserting skirt and neck placket zippers with one overlapping edge. Of course, there will be minor variations, especially when you prepare the opening. Refer to slot zipper plackets, page 504, for help in preparing the opening.

Hand-stitched zippers. Instead of machine stitching, either kind of zipper placket may be made with a firm pick stitch, a sort of pin-point back stitch. This method requires no sewing machine and no zipper foot; it is inconspicuous and easy to do, but, of course, not as fast as machine stitching. These "hand-picked" plackets are used on some expensive readymade and custom-made clothing. Stitches should be about ⅛ inch apart, evenly spaced, and almost invisible from the right side. Sew with a double strand of thread for added strength. Both edges of a slot zipper placket should be attached in this way. However, attach only the wide, top edge of the single-lap zipper closing with this stitch. Then fasten the underneath fabric edge to the zipper tape with fine slant hemming stitches.

PLACKETS WITHOUT ZIPPERS

Non-zipper plackets are fastened with buttons, snaps, and hooks and eyes, or with a combination of these. For attaching these fastenings, see instructions in technique 18, "Fastenings." Instructions for just the plackets themselves are given here. To insert "Velcro" closures, follow the directions on the package.

Continuous-bound placket. This type of placket is strong but is too bulky for most smooth areas and does not lie flat along curved seam lines. A narrow version is excellent for gathered sleeves and children's clothing. A somewhat wider strip is needed where snap fasteners are to be used, as in a dirndl skirt. This placket can be made either in a slash or in a straight-cut seam.

To make a continuous-bound placket in a slash:

1. Cut a lengthwise strip of material 1¼ inches, or wider, and at least twice the length of the slash. A little extra length doesn't matter since it can be trimmed away after the placket is completed.

2. Place the end of the placket slash at the center of the strip with the right sides of the strip against the wrong side of the garment. Draw the tip of the slash back almost ¼ inch from the edge of the placket strip. Pin the two fabrics together at this point.

3. Match the remaining seam lines except near the end of the slash. To do this, spread the placket edges apart in a straight line. Stitch ¼ inch from the edge of the placket strip with the garment side up. Use special care at the point to avoid pleats, and yet make certain that the garment edge is caught in the seam. Stop at the point with the needle down; lift the presser foot and move the fullness backward out of the way before continuing.

4. Press the seam edges toward the placket strip.

5. Hem the free edge of the strip back to the stitching line to form a continuous binding. Fasten with machine stitching.

6. Press the placket with the binding folded under the top edge and extended from the lower one.

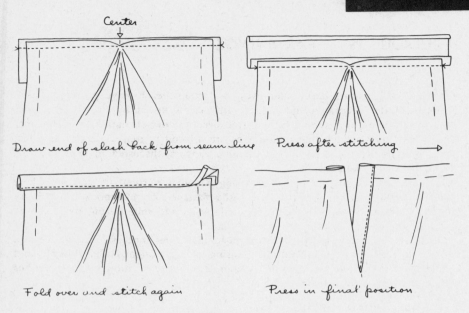

Draw end of slash back from seam line   Press after stitching →

Fold over and stitch again   Press in final position

To make a continuous-bound placket in a straight seam:

1. Cut the strip slightly wider than when making the placket in a slit (step 1, above).

2. After the entering seam is stitched and fastened at the end of the placket, clip straight across both seam allowances exactly to the end of this stitching line.

3. Join the placket strip to the placket seams, with the right side of the strip against the wrong side of the garment. Pin lower end of placket to center of strip. Match raw edges and pin.

4. Stitch, with the garment side up, along the seam line of both placket edges. Move the fullness back as you reach the lower end of the placket. Stitch carefully to catch the material at this point without forming pleats.

5. Trim the seam allowances, press them toward the placket strip.

6. Hem the binding strip back and press it, as described for the placket made in a slash.

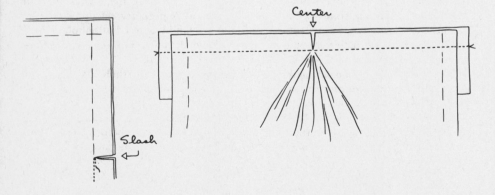

Buttons, hooks and eyes, and snaps, each have particular uses. Buttons are often decorative and are generally easy to fasten, but only certain types wash well. Some kinds should be removed even for dry-cleaning. There are materials that fray so much that buttonholes are difficult to make and on these materials buttons are not a practical fastening. Zippers, discussed in technique 17, "Plackets," are a better choice.

Hooks and eyes give an invisible closing which is particularly suitable where there is crosswise strain, but they are easily flattened or misshapen by ordinary laundry methods. Snaps hold overlapped edges flat and smooth, but will not stay fastened where there is any appreciable pull.

Often a combination of two types of fastenings gives the best closing. A snap, correctly placed, may keep a buttoned closing properly aligned. Tiny buttons and thread loops fasten convertible collars high at the throat and are inconspicuous when the collar is worn open.

BUTTONHOLES

Some buttonholes are finished with thread and are called *worked buttonholes*. Others are made with cloth and are commonly called "bound buttonholes." However, when these buttonholes are well constructed their lips are thin like a piping and therefore *piped buttonholes* is a more accurate name for them.

Either kind of buttonhole wears well if properly made and the choice between them should depend on the design of the garment, the kind of material you are using, the size button, and your skill. Piped buttonholes are more decorative than worked ones, and are often found on "better" dresses. They look particularly well on tailored or semi-tailored garments. But in sheer materials piped buttonholes are unattractive because the layers of cloth show through. Tiny buttonholes had better be worked as it is hard to make small piped ones. All in all, piped buttonholes can not be used in quite as many situations as worked ones can.

Until you have gained some skill, you may want to use machinemade worked buttonholes. You can have them made commercially or make them yourself with a sewing-machine attachment. Once this attachment is properly set up, it is easy to operate and makes a satisfactory buttonhole. Hand-worked buttonholes when skillfully made are better looking than machinemade ones, but they do require patience and practice.

Piped buttonholes can be made by any beginner who can stitch and press accurately. They require more time than machinemade but perhaps less than hand-worked ones.

When should buttonholes be made? Worked buttonholes are made after the closing is finished. Piped buttonholes must be partially made before facings are attached. Then, after the facings are permanently in place, the buttonholes are finished.

Where should buttonholes be made? Buttonholes are made in overlapping edges. In a center closing whether the edge that overlaps is the right or the left one depends on whether the garment is intended for a man or a woman. Women's clothes lap with the right side over the left whether the closing is in the front or the back. Men's clothes lap in the opposite direction. Skirt fronts overlap skirt backs, and the front of a sleeve overlaps the back.

Commercial patterns usually show the positions for buttonholes. Notice the direction in which they run. Most run at right angles to the edge of the closing, that is, in line with the pull. This is always true of snug fitting garments; otherwise the crosswise stress would cause the buttonhole to spread.

Shirts or other loose fitting garments sometimes have buttonholes that run lengthwise along a center line. Buttonholes should always run in this direction down the center of a band closing to give a balanced effect.

Notice the distance from the buttonhole to the edge of the closing. It is usually at least ½ inch, but may need to be more for large buttons, because buttons should not extend beyond the edge of the closing.

You may be surprised to see that crosswise buttonholes on center closings start quite near the center line and extend into the garment as far as necessary. They start about ⅛ inch from the center line toward the edge of the closing because buttons are pulled to the end of crosswise buttonholes nearest to the edge of the garment. When buttonholes are so placed, the buttons will be on the center of the figure.

When you must re-space buttonholes. Sometimes re-spacing of buttonhole positions is necessary. It will be if you have altered the length of your blouse. It is also necessary if you change the depth of the neck opening or if you use a different number of buttons from the number called for on the pattern. You will find that more buttons are required on close fitting garments than on loose ones. Small buttons may need to be closer together than large ones to give a pleasing effect. Remember that a closing with 1, 3, or 5 buttons is often more attractive than one with 2 or 4 buttons, although design and spacing may alter specific cases.

To re-space buttonholes evenly:

1. Locate the position for the upper buttonhole, then the lower one (the two end buttonholes in a series).

2. Measure the distance between the two.

3. Decide how many buttonholes you need.

4. Subtract one from that number to find the number of spaces.

5. Divide the distance by the number of spaces.

6. Measure off the spaces and mark positions of buttonholes.

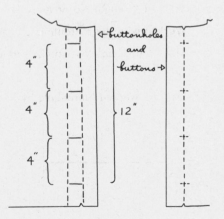

It is even simpler to find the center buttonhole position in a series of three. Fold top and bottom buttonholes together. The crease line will mark the position for the third buttonhole. Continue to fold if five or nine buttons are to be used.

How large should buttonholes be made? The width of the button plus its thickness, plus about 1/16 inch ease gives you the length of the buttonhole needed for any regular shaped button. For unusual shapes, cut a short slit in a scrap of cloth and keep making it larger until the button will just slip through easily without stretching the cloth. Measure the slit and make all buttonholes that length.

Worked buttonholes

Machinemade worked buttonholes. There are buttonhole attachments for sewing machines which make firm, good-looking worked buttonholes. These attachments must be carefully adjusted following the directions which accompany them. Once the adjustments have been made, they are simple to operate. Machines which do the zig-zag stitch make buttonholes without an attachment. If you do not care to make them yourself, you can have worked buttonholes made by machine at shops which specialize in such work.

Handmade worked buttonholes. To make worked buttonholes by hand requires a bit of practice, but they are not difficult to make in firm material. When cut crosswise, or "in line with the strain," they are made with radiating stitches at the end where the button will rest. These stitches are called the *fan.* The other end is finished with a *bar*—extra stitches which hold the edges together. On a vertical buttonhole, as on a shirt, it is customary to omit the fan and put a bar at each end to keep the buttonholes from spreading.

Handworked buttonholes to be up to standard should be:

Accurately spaced

Cut on a grain of the material, unless the design calls for a bias cut

The correct size for the button

Cut "with the pull" except on loose fitting garments

Worked through two or more layers of material

Worked with the buttonhole stitch, not the blanket stitch except on the bar

Made with firm even stitches about 1/16 inch deep and laid side by side, but not crowded

To make a worked buttonhole by hand:

1. Mark the position of the buttonhole, indicating its length. (Do not cut yet.)

2. Stitch with fine machine stitches (about 20 stitches to the inch) around the entire buttonhole, using only two stitches at each end. These stitches must be close enough to the cutting line so that they will be covered as you work the buttonhole. (Very fine hand running stitches may be substituted for the machine stitching, but are not as firm.)

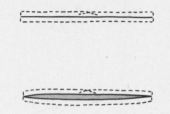

3. Cut the buttonhole with sharp pointed scissors or with buttonhole scissors. When neither is available, fold the buttonhole end to end and snip in the middle. Open out and cut to each end.

4. With the right side of the garment up, hold the cut buttonhole over the index finger of your left hand. For crosswise buttonholes the edge of the closing should be toward the left. You will take the first stitch on the side near you and at the end where the bar is to be made—the end farthest from the edge of the closing. Work from right to left.

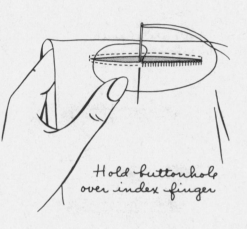

Hold buttonhole over index finger

5. Leaving the thread unknotted— you can cut it off later—bring the needle up even with the tip of the buttonhole and just outside the stitched line. It should be about 1/16 inch from the cut edge.

6. Throw the thread slightly to the right, then up and around to the left to form a circle about the point where you will make the next stitch. Hold the lower edge of the loop in place with your left thumb until you start to draw the stitch up. Insert the needle under and at right angles to the cut edge bringing it up beside the starting point. Then draw up the stitch, pulling the thread away from you. Pull the stitch gently but with firm even tension to form a purl along the cut edge of the buttonhole.

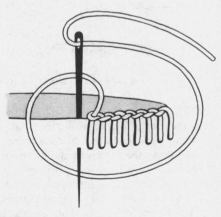

Form the loop, then insert the needle

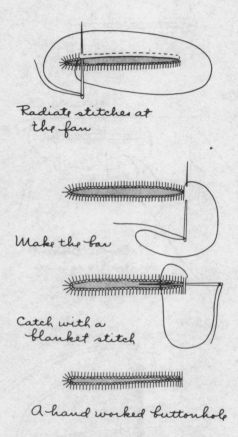

Radiate stitches at the fan

Make the bar

Catch with a blanket stitch

A hand worked buttonhole

7. Continue making stitches along one entire side. Occasionally straighten out the thread by allowing the needle to hang downward, or by twisting the thread in the opposite direction to the excess twist. So doing prevents getting the thread knotted.

8. When you reach the opposite end, begin to radiate the stitches to form the fan. You should take from 5 to 7 stitches in the fan, and the stitches should appear to be the same depth as those along the side of the buttonhole. In order to appear the same length these stitches have to be slightly longer than the stitches along the side.

9. Continue to work along the opposite side of the buttonhole until you reach the end of the slit. You are now ready to make the bar.

10. Make two or three straight stitches from the outer edge of the beginning stitch to the outer edge of the last stitch. These stitches for the bar should go across the buttonhole exactly at its tip and will be twice the length of the regular buttonhole stitches you have made.

11. Take one stitch as shown at the center of the bar and across it, catching the fabric beneath the bar. Take your thread to the under side and fasten it inconspicuously with several stitches. *Or,* for a stronger buttonhole, use closely spaced blanket stitches along the length of the bar, instead of the single stitch illustrated. Fasten and clip thread ends.

Piped buttonholes. These buttonholes can be made of the same material as the garment or of a contrasting material. The extra strips which form the piping or lips of the buttonhole should usually be cut so that the lengthwise grain of the strip runs along the length of the buttonhole. Checks and stripes look better, however, when the strip is cut on a true bias. Strips for corded buttonholes are often cut on the bias, also, since the cords give the strength and firmness that bias strips lack.

The over-all width of piped buttonholes should rarely exceed ¼ inch and sometimes it should be less. This means that the piped edges will be ⅛ inch or less in width on any medium or light-weight material. The lips should never overlap.

They may just touch each other, or a tiny space may appear between their edges. Avoid a wide space.

Remember that a piped buttonhole should be made through the garment section and the interfacing but must not be made through the facing. Make them before the facing is attached to the garment. Later the facing must be slashed and hemmed to the buttonhole. Here are other standards for a good piped buttonhole. They should be:

Accurately spaced and aligned

Made along a true grain, except in special cases

The right size for the button

Square and firm at the corners

Made with piped edges of suitable and even width

Flat because they have been carefully slashed, pressed, and trimmed

Free from any lines of stitching which show from the right side

There are several ways to make piped buttonholes but here we will describe the patch method and the two-strip method. Beginners seem to be more successful with the first method since it provides definite lines to stitch by. On the other hand, the two-strip method is the method usually used in factories because, once mastered, it is quicker. No intermediate pressing and no trimming is required but extreme accuracy is essential.

To make piped buttonholes by the patch method:

1. Buttonhole markings should appear on the wrong side of the garment or on the interfacing if there is one. Mark continuous parallel lines at buttonhole tips to insure that all buttonholes will be the same length. Draw faint pencil lines about ⅛ inch on either side of the buttonhole lines as stitching guides.

2. Cut a strip of material about an inch wider than the length of the buttonholes and long enough to extend about an inch beyond the two end buttonholes. The lengthwise grain of the material should run parallel to the ends of the strip, except when it is cut on the bias. (If you don't have enough material to cut such a long strip, you can cut an individual patch for each buttonhole.)

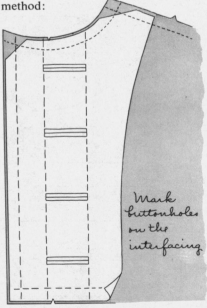

Mark buttonholes on the interfacing

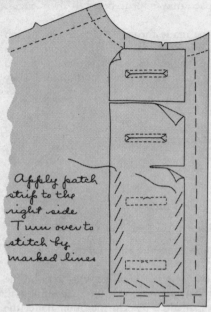

Apply patch strip to the right side. Turn over to stitch by marked lines

Work on the entire series of buttonholes as you go

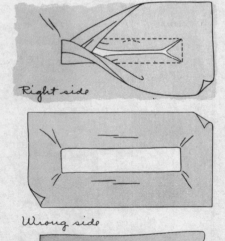

Right side

Wrong side

Wrong side

3. Place this strip on the top side of the garment right side down. Space it evenly over the buttonholes. Keep grain lines aligned. Baste it to the garment section.

4. Set the machine for 20 stitches to the inch and stitch around each buttonhole as follows. Start midway on one side and stitch to the corner. Then as you stitch across the end count the stitches. There ought to be 5. Stitch the other side and again as you go across the end, take the same number of stitches to keep the ends even. Now finish the first side, overlapping the stitching at the starting point. Of course you keep the needle in the cloth as you pivot at each corner.

5. Cut along the center of each buttonhole to within ¼ inch of the ends; then cut diagonally to each of the four corners. This forms triangular tongues ¼ inch long at each end. Do not cut the line of stitching.

6. Turn over, remove basting stitches, and slash the strip half-way between buttonholes to form individual patches.

7. Turn and stretch each strip back to flatten it against the underside. Check to see that buttonholes form true rectangles when the strip is held this way. If not, you did not stitch straight, or have not clipped all the way to the corners. Correct any errors.

8. Now press each side of the piping strip, but not the tiny seam allowances, back toward the center of the buttonhole. Continue the pressing beyond the buttonhole ends to form creases in the patch. Use a steam iron preferably.

9. Fold back the piping strips to form the lips of the buttonhole. Baste in place along each side of the buttonhole, but not across the ends.

10. Long buttonholes, or those made of soft material, should be held together with diagonal basting stitches.

11. With the right side of the garment up, turn back the edge of the closing to show the tongue lying on top of the small box pleat at the end of the buttonhole. Stitch across this triangular tongue by machine on top of the previous line of stitching. Then turn back the garment at the other end of the buttonhole and stitch across the tongue there.

12. Press, and trim away the excess piping strip. The strip should extend about ¼ inch beyond the buttonhole at each end, and about ½ inch on each side.

13. After the facing is attached to the garment permanently, it must be slashed and hemmed to the under side of each buttonhole. To hold the facing in place, baste around each buttonhole before slashing the facing, using diagonal basting stitches. (Not illustrated.)

14. Insert a pin at each corner of the buttonhole from the right side. From the under side, slash the facing as you did the buttonhole. Turn under the facing edges about ⅛ inch and hem the facing to the outer rim of the buttonhole. (If you prefer, just insert a pin at each end of the slash, cut between the pins, and hem the edges under in an oval shape.)

15. Remove bastings and press. Leave lips of buttonholes overcast until the garment is completed.

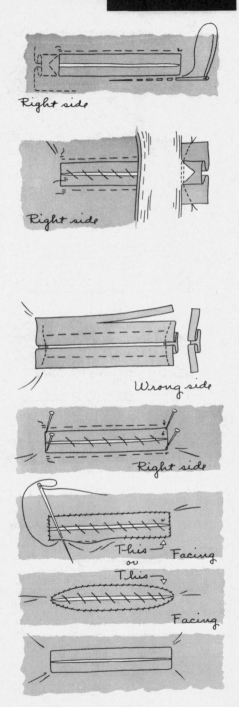

Right side

Right side

Wrong side

Right side

This — or This — Facing

Facing

To make piped buttonholes by the two-strip method:

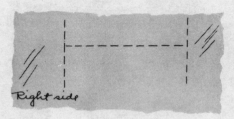

Right side

1. Transfer markings to the right side of the garment with machine-basting stitches. Indicate the tips of the buttonhole positions with continuous lengthwise parallel lines also transferred to the right side.

2. You need two strips for each buttonhole, but it is easier to start with one piece of material long enough for all the buttonholes. Cut it exactly ½ inch wide and be sure that it runs along the lengthwise grain unless you are using a bias.

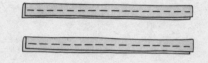

3. Fold the strip down its center with the right side of the material out. Baste-stitch down the center of the folded strip to hold the two layers together. Press.

4. Cut this strip into sections. Each section should be the length of the buttonhole plus ½ inch.

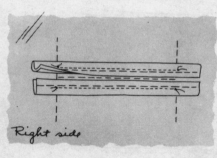

Right side

5. Baste these short strips to the right side of the garment on each side of the buttonhole, with the raw edges turned inward on the line of the buttonhole. The strips should extend ¼ inch beyond each end of the buttonhole.

6. Stitch through each strip along its exact center line, and the exact length of the buttonhole. Draw threads through to the under side and knot them to fasten the ends of each stitching line. Or retrace the stitching lines if you prefer.

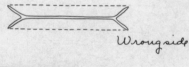

Wrong side

7. Slit the buttonhole down the center to within ¼ inch of each end; then cut diagonally to each of the four corners. Cut only the garment. Do not cut into the strips.

8. Turn strips to the under side.

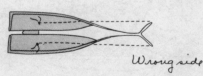

Wrong side

9. Baste the edges of the lips to hold them together. Use diagonal basting.

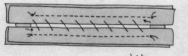

Wrong side

10. With the right side of the garment up, turn back the edge of the closing to show the triangular tongue lying on top of the two tiny strips at the end of the buttonhole. Stitch across this triangle exactly at each end of the buttonhole.

11. Press.

12. Later hem the facing to buttonholes, as described in steps 13 and 14 on page 517. Remove bastings and press.

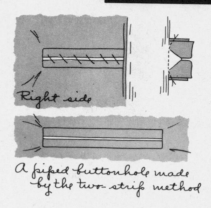

Right side

A piped buttonhole made by the two-strip method

BUTTON LOOPS

Instead of buttonholes, buttons may be fastened with loops. These, too, are made of thread or of cloth. Thread loops are often used singly to fasten a tiny button in a hidden spot or they may be used in series on a sleeve opening. Thread loops are an inconspicuous fastening.

Cloth loops add a decorative touch to party clothes. Because they take so long to fasten, it is usually advisable to use them only on that type of garment. As they join meeting rather than overlapping edges they have to be closely spaced to make an effective closing and it takes many a loop and many a button to close a blouse edge. Make them of self cloth or a contrasting one.

Thread loops. For a thread loop use a single strand of thread that matches the color of the fabric. If you knot it, hide the knot between layers of cloth. The loop should be just large enough to allow the button to slip through easily, and should form an almost straight line.

To make a thread loop:

1. Decide on the position for the loop. Indicate its length with a pin at each end.

2. Bring the needle out from between the layers of cloth at the left end of the loop as you hold the edge of the closing toward you right side up.

3. Insert the needle in the folded edge at the right end of the loop and bring it out again at the left. Take several stitches in this way, keeping them equal in length.

4. Over these long stitches, working from left to right, make closely spaced

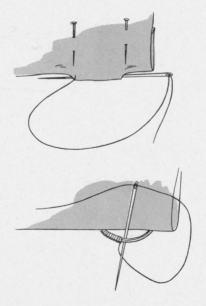

stitches by passing the needle under the loop but over the thread with which you are sewing. Hold the thread down with your left thumb as you make the stitch. Loosen the thread beneath your thumb as you draw the stitch up. These are called blanket stitches.

5. Space stitches close together and when you reach the opposite end, fasten the thread inconspicuously.

Cloth loops. Cloth loops should form half circles along a garment edge and should be spaced so close together that their edges touch. The cording which makes the loops should be firm, round, and as slender as possible. There is generally no overlap on closings where loops are used. There must be a seam along the edge of the closing.

To make cloth loops:

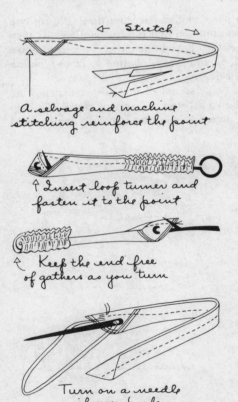

A selvage and machine stitching reinforce the point

↑ Insert loop turner and fasten it to the point

← Keep the end free of gathers as you turn

Turn on a needle if you prefer

1. Cut a strip of bias about an inch wide, and long enough for all loops.

2. Fold the strip lengthwise with the right side of the material in. Baste, if you like.

3. Stitch the desired width—about ⅛ inch on thin materials, but wider on heavy ones—stretching the bias slightly to prevent stitches from breaking later. Keep the width even. The machine attachment, the edge-stitcher, is helpful for this purpose. Stitch one end wider for ease in turning.

4. Turn with a loop-turner, if one is available. Insert the turner, fasten it to the opposite end of the strip, then draw the strip gently back over itself. Instead of a loop-turner, you can use a coarse needle and a strong thread, as shown.

The seam allowance pads the loop and keeps it firm. If the strip is too difficult to turn, some of the seam allowance may have to be trimmed away.

5. To plump and smooth the loop strip, stretch and pin each end to an ironing board. Shoot steam over the strip with a steam iron. Then roll strip crosswise with the palm of your hand. Stretch again and repeat.

To attach loops to the opening:

1. Make a trial loop to determine the size required for the button. The inside width of the loop should be the button width. The depth of the loop should be no more than half of this measurement.

2. On a sheet of paper draw a line to represent the stitching line. Left of it and the depth of the loop away, draw a parallel line. Make cross lines the width of the loop apart.

3. Pick up the strip and shape the loops inside these markings. Stitch each one to the paper as it is formed. Keep the seam line in the cording on the inside of the loop.

4. Matching seam lines, pin this strip of loops to the right side of the closing edge, turning the loops back away from the edge. Baste-stitch it just outside the seam line. Tear off the paper.

5. Pin facing right side down over loops. Turn wrong side of garment up and stitch along seam line.

6. Open the seam allowances and clip the cording between loops to allow the cording ends to flatten out.

7. Turn facing to under side. Loops will now extend from placket edge. Remove basting stitches and press.

BUTTONS

Consider comfort in choosing buttons. Use flat ones on the back of a garment. Large buttons are easier to fasten than small ones. For buttons to go with cloth loops, choose ball shaped or half-ball shaped ones. They are not only easier to fasten, but look right with this type closing.

Where to sew buttons. Patterns occasionally indicate button positions as such. More often, however, just the buttonhole markings are given and you are expected to sew buttons at the intersections of the center line and buttonhole markings.

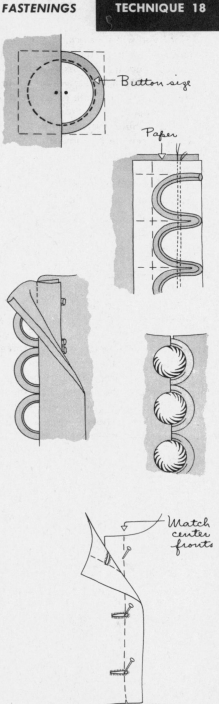

Since you will be working from the right side of the garment, take a few basting stitches at each button position to transfer the markings. Otherwise you must locate the button positions after the buttonholes are completed. To do it then, overlap the closing accurately—center lines should be matched on center closings—and insert a pin or chalk pencil through the buttonhole to mark the button position on the underlap. For crosswise buttonholes, the button will go at the fan end; for vertical buttonholes, the button will go at the center point.

How to sew on buttons. Buttons should be raised above the surface of the garment enough to allow for the thickness of the overlapping edge. Some buttons are made with shanks to give them this lift. Flat buttons and those with too short shanks should be sewed on with a thread shank. Otherwise the buttonhole will be forced to spread and the overlap will pucker between buttons.

A thread shank and different ways to sew on a 4-hole button

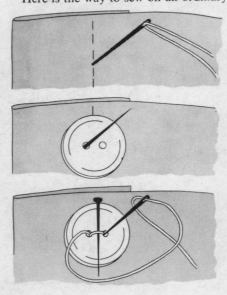

Use either a single or double strand of thread with a knot. The color should generally match the garment, but may be selected to match the button. Heavy thread, especially made for sewing on buttons, may be used where there is excessive pull. You might rub the thread with beeswax before you sew buttons on heavy garments. The wax reduces wear and adds strength.

The most common type of button has either two or four holes running completely through the button. Four-hole buttons are sewed on in the same way as two-hole ones, except that the stitches between holes can form various designs.

Here is the way to sew on an ordinary button and provide a thread shank:

1. Insert the needle through the button mark from the right side of the garment to hide the knot under the button.

2. Bring the needle up through the cloth and through one hole of the button. This kind of stitch is called a *stab stitch*.

3. Place a pin across the top of the button between the holes. For longer shanks use a tooth pick, match stem, or other similar object.

4. Take several stitches over the pin, first going down through one hole to the underside of the cloth, then up through another hole.

5. When enough stitches have been made, bring the needle out between the button and the cloth.

6. Remove pin. Hold the button away from cloth as you wrap thread around stitches to form firm shank.

7. Fasten with several small stitches near the base of the shank or on the under side of the garment.

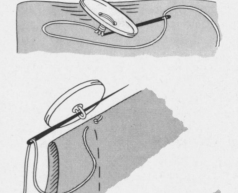

To sew on a shank style button:

1. Take a small stitch from the right side of the garment at the point where the button is to be sewed.

2. Run the needle, with the point turned away from you, through the hole in the shank of the button.

3. Continue to take first a stitch through the cloth beneath the button (needle pointed toward you); then a stab stitch through the hole of the button (needle pointed away from you).

4. When enough stitches have been made to hold the button on securely, fasten the thread with several small stitches as in step 7 above.

HOOKS AND EYES

Hooks and eyes are especially suitable for an inconspicuous closing where there is a crosswise strain. They come in two finishes: black for dark clothing and a whitish-metal color for light-colored garments. They are made in a wide size range, sizes 2 and 3 being for medium-weight fabrics where there is an average amount of pull at the closing. For heavier fabrics or greater strain use larger hooks and eyes, with larger numbers. For finer fabrics or less strain use smaller ones.

There are two shapes of eyes—and usually the manufacturer will give you one of each for each hook on the card so that you may have your choice each time you use a hook and eye. There are round-shaped eyes and straight ones. The round ones are for edges and make a stronger and flatter closing than the straight ones. However, straight ones are needed for places other than edges. Instead of a straight eye, a small thread eye, made like a thread loop, is less conspicuous.

Sew a round eye on before you sew on its hook. The eye should be sewn to the under side of the underlap, or if the closing just barely meets, to the under side of the left closing edge. About half the eye should project beyond edge of closing.

Sew a straight eye on after you sew on the hook. For a straight eye the hook should generally be placed back about ¼ inch from the edge of the closing. Find the position for the eye by closing the placket. The eye should be placed at the tip of the hook.

Instructions for sewing on hooks and eyes are given under "Waistline Fastening" in Construction One, "Making a Blouse and Skirt."

SNAPS

Snaps are rarely used alone—except the sturdy kind on play clothes. Usually they help hold a button or a hook-and-eye fastening exactly in position. The colors are the same as hooks and eyes. The sizes you will use for medium-weight fabrics are 2–0 and 3–0. You will find instructions for attaching snaps under "Waistline Fastening" in Construction One, "Making a Blouse and Skirt."

TECHNIQUE 19   *HEMS*

Hems are used more than any other edge finish because they are flat and because they are the easiest of the edge finishes to make. Hems are made by folding an edge of cloth back and fastening it in place, either by hand or by machine. Popular as they are, however, they do have limitations. Only straight or outward-curving edges can be hemmed successfully. Inward curves and corners cannot generally be hemmed. For instance, you can't hem a curved neckline. (Face or bind it instead.)

A hem should be flat, even in width, and true in line. There should be no bulky areas or diagonal wrinkles and scarcely an imprint of the hem on the right side of the garment. The fullness in hems should be shrunk out or evenly distributed.

Hems on finer clothing are usually fastened with hand stitching because it is inconspicuous and permits the hem to fall softly. However, machine stitching is used for certain types of garments. While a single line of machine stitching does not make a particularly attractive hem, it is strong and quickly done and so is satisfactory for house dresses, aprons, and similar garments. For sturdy sport and tailored clothing several rows of machine stitching give a decorative edge finish.

For the sake of simplicity, we are going to divide all hems into two categories: skirt hems and narrow hems. By skirt hems we mean the hems you see on street-length clothes. These are generally wider than the other kind of hem—the narrow ones you find on ties, scarves, and full floor length skirts. These two kinds of hems, of which there are many variations, are made somewhat differently.

SKIRT HEMS

There are several steps in making a regulation skirt hem. To decide on a becoming skirt length is the first. You may need help in marking the hemline accurately, but once that is done you can mark the width by yourself. Next, you must choose the appropriate way to finish the raw hem edge and to distribute the fullness. Finally, you must select the best hemming stitch for your skirt from a handful of possibilities, and then you can settle down and put in the hem.

If by any chance, you cut off your street-length skirt too short for a regular width hem, don't despair. There are several things you can do to save the skirt. On firm materials, for instance, you might use several rows of parallel machine stitching on the very bottom of the skirt as described under "Multiple-stitched hems" later in this technique. Another way to save your skirt is to face it with either a bias or fitted facing. Use either self material or a contrasting one. You can use a very wide fitted facing and stiffen it to make your skirt stand away when a wide silhouette is in vogue. (You might even plan your skirt that way.) Refer to technique 13, "Neck Finishes," to learn how to cut and apply facings.

Deciding the skirt length. Your build, the height heels you wear, your age, and the prevailing style all affect the skirt length that looks best on you. Tall girls can wear their skirts farther from the floor than short girls. Slightly long skirts will hide large or poorly shaped legs, but they should not be so long as to be conspicuous. You may already know your most suitable skirt length. If you do not, measure a becoming skirt, or try on the skirt you are making when it is almost completed. Before you try on the skirt the garment should be practically finished and carefully pressed. Leave only handwork and fastenings to do later and even these details should be left only if the skirt hangs correctly without them. Ask a classmate to turn the hem up temporarily to find the proper length. If you're sure your skirt is even, mark this length with a pin, then let the hem down and take the skirt off. If the skirt is uneven, and they frequently are, you will have to ask someone to measure the distance from hem to floor and mark the hem all around.

Marking the hemline. Hem markings are always made on one thicknes of material. Never attempt to turn the hem as you mark it.

There are alternate methods of marking hemlines. The method you use will depend on whether you found the skirt to be even in length or not. If the hem edge is even and parallel to the floor, your job is simple and you can just use the hemline indicated on the pattern or mark a line equidistant from the raw skirt edge to make the skirt the length you like. Only straight-cut or moderately flared skirts made of firm material can usually be marked by this method but for straight-cut dirndl skirts especially this method is the only way. (A dirndl skirt should have been adjusted at the waistline as you made it so that it hangs evenly.)

To mark the hemline on a skirt that is already even:

1. Lay the skirt on a table right side up, hem edge toward you. Spread a section of the skirt smooth where you are working.

2. With a gauge measure up from the raw edge of the material at regular intervals. Mark with pins or chalk parallel to the hem edge. Space markings about 3 to 4 inches apart around skirt.

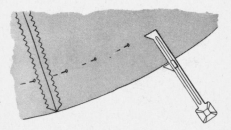

When the raw hem edge hangs uneven there is nothing to do but ask someone else to mark the hemline for you an equal distance from the floor while you model the skirt. Use this method whenever you are in doubt as to the evenness of the skirt. A day or two before you do this, hang the skirt up to allow its bias-cut areas to stretch as much as they will.

Try the skirt on with the undergarments and shoes you expect to wear with it. Be sure the placket is closed and waistband is overlapped just right. Stand with your weight evenly balanced, and keep your hands either clasped, or hanging at your sides.

If one is available, stand on a low platform to make the job easier for your helper. Standing on a table is dangerous. It is preferable to stand on the floor on a large sheet of clean paper. Your classmate can sit on the paper beside you. As she marks the hemline she can move around you or you can turn. If you turn, be careful to balance your figure each time and move only when requested to do so.

The pin-it variety of skirt-marker is easy and accurate to use on any material. The markers that use chalk are satisfactory for fabrics on which a white chalk line will show. (This type marker must be kept close to the skirt to form a clear line.) If you can't get your hands on a commercial skirt-marker, a yardstick or any smooth slender stick will do. It takes a little more skill to use a stick than a commercial marker but it can be done. Mark the hem height on either kind of stick with an elastic band, chalk, or a pin inserted in the wood. You will prevent errors by marking the stick this way so that the hem height can be quickly seen. The person who marks the hem should keep the stick perpendicular to the floor directly beneath the point being marked. The skirt should fall free.

When someone is helping you to mark your skirt, have her:

1. Measure from the floor to the desired skirt length at regular intervals. Insert pins or mark straight across at each point measured. Pins or chalk marks should be about 3 inches apart.

2. Check the hemline by going around quickly a second time and correct any errors.

Folding and pressing the hemline. As soon as your skirt is marked, true up the hemline. No matter how carefully your hem was marked, there are likely to be a few pins or marks out of place. Here's the way to find the offenders.

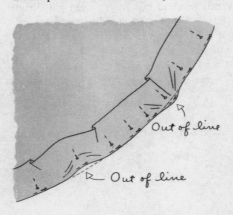

Out of line

Out of line

1. Place the skirt on a table wrong side up. Spread section of hem flat.

2. Fold hem on the marked line.

3. At each place where the hemline was marked, insert a pin at right angles to the folded edge to hold it in place. Keep the pin heads ½ inch from the fold to leave room for the iron to pass as you press the fold later.

4. Check the fold line to see if any pins are causing an imperfectly shaped curve. Change these pins slightly to obtain a smooth-flowing hemline. Beware of making radical changes, however.

Hold this fold line by pressing it. Your mother used to hold it with a line of basting, but pressing is quicker and just as accurate.

After the fold line is firmly creased, remove the pins and press the hem to shrink out fullness. Press from the fold line in toward the skirt. Avoid forming pleats or changing the original crease. Turn the iron sidewise and glide it across the hem slowly. Unless the skirt is quite circular, this trick should eliminate excess fullness.

Press this way to crease the hemline

Press this way to shrink fullness

Deciding how to finish the hem. Although you can't finish the raw hem edge until you have trimmed it, you should decide what finish you will use first because the finish may add to or decrease the width of the hem. Also, if you decide on a pinked edge, you can pink and trim at the same time.

Hems on sheer fabrics and on light-weight washable skirts are usually turned twice; that is, once along the hemline and again ¼ inch or less from the cut edge of the hem. The second fold may be edge-stitched or not, as you like. Turning twice of course decreases the width of the hem.

Heavy materials should never be turned a second time. Instead, trim or pink the edge or apply seam binding to keep the hem flat and inconspicuous. Plain or

HEMMING PROBLEMS

WHERE FOUND	WHAT THE PROBLEM IS	SOLUTION
In flared skirts (*versus straight-cut ones*)	Distributing the excessive fullness	Shrink out as much fullness as possible by pressing. Distribute correctly the fullness left by using gathering stitches. Make hem no wider than 2 inches.
In heavy material (*versus light-weight material*)	Keeping the hem flat and inconspicuous	Pink or use seam binding—never turn under the edge.
In transparent material (*versus opaque material*)	Making the hem edge look neat	Turn under the raw edge and perhaps edge-stitch it. Never use seam binding.
In materials that ravel (*versus firm materials*)	Preventing the hem edge from fraying	Use seam binding or turn under edge and perhaps edge-stitch it.
In washable skirts (*versus those that will be dry-cleaned or handwashed*)	Preventing the hem edge from being injured or from wearing out	Use washable seam binding or turn under and perhaps edge-stitch the hem edge.

pinked edges are satisfactory on heavy materials that do not ravel easily and will not be washed repeatedly. For clothing that is to be dry-cleaned, seam binding of silk, rayon, or acetate is suitable, but these fibers do not stand ordinary laundry practices. Bias-cut commercial seam binding of batiste or lawn is a better choice for heavy washable fabrics that ravel. Any tape adds width to the hem which should be allowed for as you mark the hem width. Refer to the chart "Hemming Problems" to help you decide on a suitable finish.

Marking and trimming the hem width. Next you must decide what width hem you want. Sometimes the narrowest part of the hem will limit your choice. When you have enough material, hems on most street-length skirts should be 2½ inches. Whether the fabric is opaque or transparent, a wide hem helps any skirt hang well. Sheer materials are attractive with even wider hems to hide slip hemlines. Circular skirts cannot have such wide hems because there would be too much fullness to distribute. Make circular hems 1½ to 2 inches wide depending on the flare.

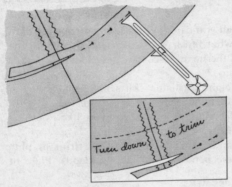

Turn down   to trim

To mark and trim the hem width:

1. Again, place the hem edge flat on the table wrong side up. Turn the hem toward you.

2. Using a gauge to guide you, make marks with chalk or place pins 2 or 3 inches apart around the entire skirt.

3. Spread the hem out flat and trim along the marked line. Trim with pinking shears if pinking is to serve as a finish.

Finishing the hem. After any hem is trimmed to an even width, your next step will depend upon the amount of fullness in the hem and the way the raw edge has to be treated. If after you have pressed and shrunk a hem little or no fullness

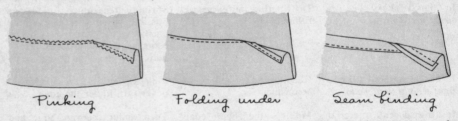

Pinking   Folding under   Seam binding

remains, it is ready for the edge finish. Unless pinking is to serve this purpose, apply seam binding or fold the edge under ¼ inch and edge-stitch it, whichever is required for your fabric. (See instructions for applying seam binding on page 497.)

Greater fullness must be controlled with gathering. Some people use narrow pleats for this purpose, but when the garment is pressed the imprint of the pleats shows on the right side. Gathering gives a flatter hem and therefore is preferable. Make gathers after an edge is pinked or folded under, but before seam binding is attached.

Machine-gathering is easy to use along a plain or pinked edge, but along a folded edge, as on a washable skirt, machine gathers are sometimes difficult to adjust. A shirring foot, which draws the threads as you go, is valuable to use along such an edge. Handmade gathers are easier to distribute than machine-gathers made without an attachment but naturally take longer to do.

Make gathers close to the hem edge with a shirring foot, a long-stitch setting on the machine, or by hand. If you use a shirring foot, adjust the length of the stitch until it gathers the hem just enough to fit loosely against the skirt when the hem is folded back in place. If you use handmade or machine-gathering, adjust the line of gathering with the skirt spread out flat on a table and the hem folded back. Draw the gathering threads just enough so that the hem fits loosely against the skirt. Then adjust the gathers to fall at right angles to the hem edge. This is the time to apply seam binding if it is to be used.

To attach seam binding to a hem edge:

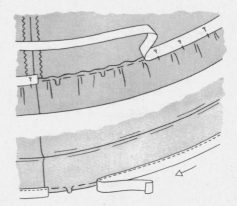

1. Unless you are sure your seam binding will not shrink, steam press it to shrink it.

2. Pin one edge of the seam binding to the raw hem edge or to the adjusted line of gathers. Allow slight ease in the tape. If you make it tight, it will pucker the hemline. Stitch the binding to the hem very close to the inner edge of the binding. Turn the hem down first.

3. Turn under the end of the binding to overlap the raw binding edge where you started.

As soon as any hem fullness has been controlled and the hem edge is suitably finished, fasten the hem in place as follows:

1. Lay the skirt on the table wrong side up with the hem toward you. Smooth out one section between seam lines to work on.

2. Pin the hem in place first at seam lines and center lines, then between them. The seam lines in the hem should fall along the seam lines in the skirt. Center front and center back lines should fall back on themselves, also. Avoid diagonal wrinkles. Place pins at right angles to the hem edge and a few inches apart.

3. Baste the hem in place near the edge. Then remove the pins.

4. Hem with one of the hand hemming stitches described later. The invisible hemming stitch is excellent for a pinked edge; the vertical hemming stitch is best for folded edges. Use either on seam binding.

5. Remove basting and press.

Spots that need special handling

Hems in pleated skirts. Some pleated skirts present no problem in hemming but pleats with a seam along the inside fold must be handled in a special way if they are to fall correctly. This inside seam is pressed together above the hem but must be pressed open in the hem. To make this possible clip through the seam allowance all the way to the seam line at the top of the hem.

Hems at corners. Coat style dresses, skirt slits, jackets, and certain peplums have hems that intersect to form corners. In such cases, the vertical facing or hem should overlap the hem at its lower edge. To avoid a thick corner, trim away extra folds of material at the corner, being careful to leave enough to hide all raw edges. However, do not do this if the garment will need to be lengthened later.

To make a hem at a corner:

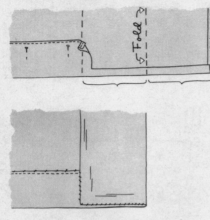

1. Hem the lower edge first. The area beneath the vertical facing (or hem) should be folded and pressed, but should not be hemmed in place.

2. Trim away inside layers of hem and facing at corner, but leave a seam allowance at lower edges and at side.

3. Pin the facing over the lower hem, being careful to turn the facing up enough at the bottom so that it will not show from the right side.

4. Slip-stitch the lower edges together, and hem the side of the facing to the lower hem.

NARROW HEMS

Narrow hems are used on long dresses, ties, scarfs, loose panels, and the like. They should be quite narrow. Usually two folds are used. The first fold or turn is made near the cut edge rather than at the hemline as it is in making a skirt hem. The second turn is gauged by the width of the first and should be made as narrow as possible to enclose it. Narrow hems may be finished by hand or by machine. Hand stitches give the finer finish.

To make a narrow hem:

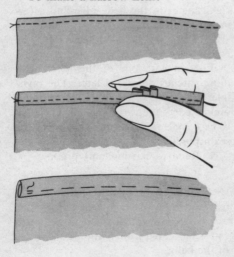

1. Trim away all ravelings.

2. Along bias edges or on material that may stretch, stay-stitch very close to the edge.

3. Turn under the raw edge about ⅛ inch or even less. On material that will crease, pleat and pinch the fold together between your thumb and forefinger to sharpen the crease. On material that will not crease, you must baste.

4. Crease or baste the second fold, checking the hem width as you go to make sure it is narrow and even.

5. Use hand hemming stitches, pages 532–534, or machine stitching to hold the hem in place.

6. Remove basting, if any, and press.

The narrow hemmer, a machine attachment, will do the whole job and is excellent for use on firm materials when hemlines are cut on the straight of the material. Follow instructions which accompany the sewing machine.

Multiple-stitched hems. A different kind of narrow hem, one that is turned only once, is sometimes used on tailored and sport clothes. This multiple-stitched hem is a boon when you have accidentally cut a skirt too short for a wide hem. It consists of two or more rows of machine-stitching done near the hem line. The first row is placed close to the folded hemline; other rows are spaced evenly about ¼ inch apart. Stitch this hem from the right side of the garment. Firm materials can have plain trimmed edges; those that ravel will require pinking or seam binding along the raw edge before the top-stitching is done.

Inside curves and other odd shapes can be faced and stitched to resemble top-stitched hems. For instance, the neckline and armholes of a jumper could be faced and then top-stitched.

Rolled hems. To give a particularly fine finish, rolled hems are used on scarfs, ties, sashes, and the like that are made of soft and light-weight material.

To make a rolled hem:

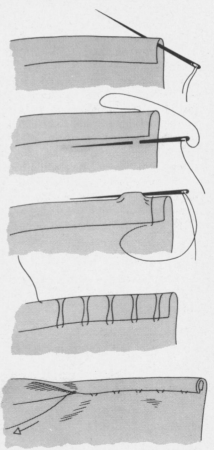

1. Hold the hem over your left forefinger and work from right to left. Fold the hem edge over about ⅛ inch as you go, but do not crease it too firmly.

2. Make a knot in the thread end and pass the needle through the fold to fasten the thread in the hem.

3. Take a tiny stitch directly opposite this point in the garment. The stitch should be parallel to the raw hem edge and close to it. It goes through one thickness of material only.

4. Now directly above this stitch insert the needle into the fold and run it through the fold for about ⅛ inch before you bring it out through the fold.

5. Continue taking a tiny stitch in the garment and then a longer one through the fold of the hem. When your stitches have covered about 1 inch, stop with the needle coming out of the fold. Notice that you have two parallel threads running between the garment and the fold at about ⅛ inch intervals.

6. Now draw the thread up firmly to roll the hem over. The parallel threads will disappear and the hem will be round and only half as wide as you folded it.

7. Repeat until the hem is finished.

HAND-HEMMING STITCHES

Hand-hemming stitches should be quite fine and spaced close enough to hold the hem securely in place, yet far enough apart to be inconspicuous from the right side of the garment. Thread should match perfectly. You will need a fine needle to make the tiny stitches. On heavy materials the stitch should not go through to the right side; on thin materials try to take up only one yarn of the garment fabric. Stitches should be almost ½ inch apart on wide skirt hems, but should be only about ⅛ inch apart on narrow hems and on the under side of bands, bindings, and such.

Hems should be pinned or basted in place before you start the hemming stitches. Basting is perhaps a time-saver in this case, because pins catch the thread as you work and do not hold the edge as securely as basting does.

As you make the hemming stitches, hold the hem in your hands. Do not try to keep it on the table. Turn the wrong side of the garment toward you, with the hem up and the rest of the garment down or in your lap. Hemming goes faster when, after you have completed a little stretch, you pin the end to a padded weight to keep the material taut. Most hemming stitches are made so that you progress from right to left, though there are exceptions. The needle points toward your left shoulder. Before starting to hem, fasten the thread with either a fine knot or several tiny stitches on top of each other. Keep hemming stitches loose enough not to draw the material. Finish off the hemming with several stitches to fasten it securely.

Left-handed people should place a mirror beside each diagram so that they can see the exact position for their hands and work. They should also observe their instructor give demonstrations by peering into a mirror placed at her side.

The invisible hemming stitch. The invisible hemming stitch is the most inconspicuous hemming stitch of all. With practice it can be the fastest too. It is inconspicuous because it does not hold the hem rigidly to the skirt and because the stitches are placed between the hem and the skirt. It can be used on pinked edges or on those finished with ribbon seam binding. It is not satisfactory on turned-under edges, except when they are edge-stitched and even then is fairly difficult to make.

To make the invisible hemming stitch:

1. Fold back, not under, a narrow edge of the hem, about ⅛ inch. Do not crease this as you will want it to return to its original position once the stitches are in place.

2. Fasten thread in hem at fold.

3. Take a tiny stitch first in the skirt, then one in the fold at the edge of the hem. Zigzag them, spacing them about ¼ inch apart.

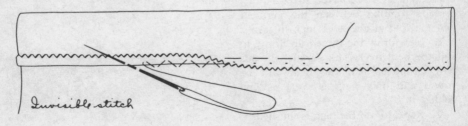

Invisible stitch

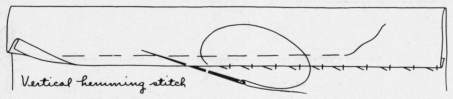

Vertical hemming stitch

The vertical hemming stitch. The vertical hemming stitch can be used on any firm edge, but cannot be used on raw or pinked edges. Use it on edges finished with seam binding and on folded edges whether they are edge-stitched or not. Its particular advantage is that it can be widely spaced and yet the floating threads between stitches are almost completely concealed beneath the hem. It is relatively quick and easy to do.

To make the vertical hemming stitch:

1. Fasten the thread beneath the hem bringing it up through the hem.

2. Take a tiny stitch in the garment parallel to the hem and directly beneath the point where the thread comes up. Now bring the needle up in the hem edge about ⅜ inch away—for narrow hems make stitches shorter—and very close to the edge (⅟₁₆ inch or less).

3. Repeat, always taking a tiny stitch in the garment directly even with the last stitch in the hem. This will give a vertical stitch between hem and garment. Always bring the point of the needle up in the hem some distance forward before lifting the needle. This part of the stitch produces a long floating thread hidden beneath the hem.

The slip stitch. The slip hemming stitch is useful where both sides of a hem show from the right side of a garment, as on a tie scarf, and for holding two folded edges together. It can only be used where there is a folded-under edge, preferably not edge-stitched. Made very much like vertical hemming (except that the thread between stitches is hidden in the fold along the hem), it is more time consuming than most other hand-stitches.

To make the slip stitch:

1. Fasten the thread beneath the hem, bringing the needle out through the edge of the fold.

2. Take a tiny stitch in the garment directly beneath the point where the thread leaves the fold. Make it parallel to the hem and very close to the fold.

3. Insert the needle in the hem, slip it along inside the fold, and bring it out again about ½ inch away. (For certain positions slip stitches must be much smaller.)

4. Repeat the stitch. You will soon learn to take the stitch in the garment and the one through the fold without lifting the needle between them.

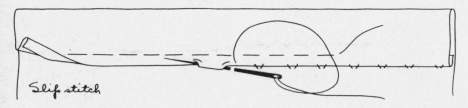

Slip stitch

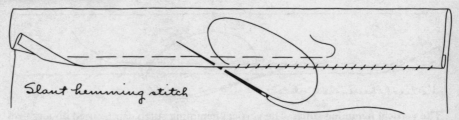

Slant hemming stitch

The slant hemming stitch. This is the simplest of the hemming stitches to make, but it has a limited use. To be at its best it must be closely spaced. Otherwise, its long exposed threads wear and break. When made with short stitches (about ⅛ to ¼ inch) it is strong and holds fabric securely in place. However, so made, it is not particularly inconspicuous from the right side and therefore should be used only where it will be concealed or where edges must be held firmly. Use it for fasten-ing down bands, bindings, collars, and cuffs. Because it is durable when properly made it is excellent for wide hems on little girls' dresses and for narrow hems on scarfs and sashes. It can only be used on folded or quite firm edges.

To make the slant hemming stitch:

1. Fasten the thread in the hem, bringing it up through the hem close to the edge.

2. Take a tiny stitch in the garment slightly forward from the point where the thread came out of the hem. Make the stitch close to the hem and slant it forward to catch the hem again close to the edge.

3. Continue, repeating step 2. Notice that progress is made by the space be-tween stitches and, also, by the slant of the needle. Avoid long floating threads by keeping stitches closely spaced.

The catch stitch. The catch stitch can be used on any single thickness hem edge whether it is left raw, pinked, or finished with seam binding. It forms a crisscross line of stitching which allows plenty of play between the layers it joins. Unlike any of the other hemming stitches, progress with the catch stitch is made from left to right but the needle is still pointed toward the left. This means that you make the stitches backward.

To make the catch stitch:

1. Fasten thread in hem, bringing it up through hem close to the edge.

2. Take a small back stitch in the garment parallel to the hem and about ¼ inch to right of where thread came out.

3. Take a second similar stitch about ¼ inch farther to the right in the hem, through only one layer of material.

4. Continue zigzagging stitches in the hem and in the garment.

Catch stitch

PART VI   CAREERS IN CLOTHING

20. Careers in Clothing

CHAPTER 20

CAREERS IN CLOTHING AND FASHION

Perhaps you are enough interested in clothing and fashion to consider some phase of it as a possible career. The clothing field, whether it is advertising, designing, dressmaking, merchandising, research, or teaching offers unlimited opportunities to women.

Although an art or college education is a basic requirement for many of these careers, it is not necessarily a "must" in all branches of fashion. Some successful designers have learned their art from the "ground up" as apprentices to some fine designer. There are many cases where a girl has advanced in the retail trade from a saleslady to a buyer or a shop executive. The clothing and fashion field is open to all who have ambition, interest, and a dogged perseverance to make good.

The following material will give you an idea as to some types of work that are open to you if you are interested in clothing or fashion as a career. Even though you may not be interested in such as a career, you may want to know what goes on "behind the scenes."

OPPORTUNITIES FOR THE HOME ECONOMIST

Years back, most girls took "Domestic Science" courses in cooking and sewing for the sole purpose of becoming more efficient housewives. Comparatively few girls thought of such training as leading to a career.

The past few decades have brought many changes. Along with the change in name from "Domestic Science" to "Home Economics," the educational program has expanded into the broad area which is called family living. Courses in "Clothing" are no longer limited to sewing; they include instruction in cosmetics, grooming, color, design, fabrics, wardrobe planning, budgets, and consumer education as well as in clothing construction. Such a background in clothing equips a girl to launch herself on a career in one of many fields. Many opportunities are now open to young women who have successfully completed a four-year course in home economics. Let us look into some of the careers that are open to the home economist whose interest is clothing.

Teaching. This is a field which is familiar to you, because your clothing class is taught by a home economics teacher. When you realize that home economics classes are available to approximately nine-tenths of all junior and senior high-school pupils in the country, you realize the number of teachers needed in public schools alone.

The minimum educational requirement for a high-school teacher is graduation from a college or university of recognized standing, with a major in home economics and emphasis on teacher training.

Greater specialization is required to teach in a college or university. College teachers have done graduate study toward a master's or doctor's degree with emphasis on textiles, pattern-making, or clothing construction. College teachers are the ones who prepare home economics majors for careers in teaching, research, and business.

Then there are those specialists who teach in professional or trade schools. Such positions demand a good educational background and actual experience in the trade or art which they are teaching, whether it is costume design, draping and pattern-making, textile design, millinery, or merchandising.

Teaching has gone beyond the bounds of the standard classroom. Courses in dressmaking, coat tailoring, and millinery are offered in many civic adult education programs. The women who teach these courses have had either teaching or trade experience or both.

Home demonstration. Another field closely allied to teaching is that of home demonstration work. Unlike the classroom teacher whose pupils come to her, the home demonstration agent goes to her pupils within a particular area. She teaches rural homemakers about better home management. She organizes clubs for women and 4-H Clubs for girls to instruct them in clothing, foods, and related activities.

Home demonstration work is administered through the demonstration staff of the Extension Service of the United States Department of Agriculture and State Agricultural Colleges. The minimum educational requirement for a county home demonstration agent is a B.A. or an A.B. college degree with a major in home economics. State agricultural and land-grant colleges offer training in home demonstration work. Most states also require one or two years of teaching or of work in some related field.

Research. The word "research" may bring visions of test tubes to your mind. Broadly speaking, research involves all types and methods of observation. In regard to clothing, it includes testing the final product for durability, colorfastness, moisture or crease resistancy. It includes consumer surveys and statistics that may involve house-to-house canvassing, questionnaires by mail, "counting" on street corners, analysis of complaints, comparison shopping for a retail store, and a host of other ways of determining public reaction.

Scientific testing goes on in textile mills, dye companies, dry-cleaning plants, tanneries, soap and cosmetic companies and in most large manufacturing concerns. Technical laboratories are maintained by the government and nonprofit organizations to ensure consumers good quality. The laboratory technician in charge is a highly trained scientist with advanced degrees.

Actually, more home economists are in charge of the research divisions where final products are tested. Such consumer divisions are maintained by

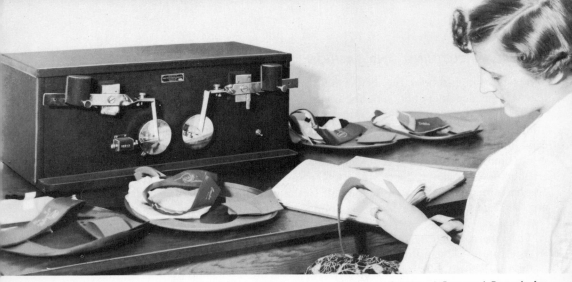

Courtesy of Consumers' Research, Inc.

This girl works for an organization which tests goods and passes the information along to the consumer. Here she is testing the quality of felt used in men's hats.

manufacturers, by the government, by non-profit organizations, by some large department stores, and even by some women's magazines. The seal of approval assures the consumer that the product she buys has been tested by experts for her benefit.

Every large company, both wholesale and retail, wants to know how Madam Public reacts to its merchandise. This is where consumer surveys come in. It is a good field for the home economist. She has the woman's viewpoint; this is important because most shopping is done by women. More important, she has a trained viewpoint—the ability to analyze a product in the light of consumer reactions. She finds out such things as why and how many women prefer low heels to high; fitted hose to seamless; nighties to pajamas; solid woolens to plaids, et cetera. Such surveys are of value to the fashion industry.

Magazines, newspapers, and trade publications also conduct surveys on topics of fashion interest. Many social welfare agencies and the Bureau of Human Nutrition and Home Economics of the U.S. Department of Agriculture prepare detailed reports on family clothing expenditures.

These are all phases of clothing "research." The home economist with a clothing background is admirably suited to the work.

Consumer education. Actually, all home economics work is directed toward educating the consumer to a better way of life. Let us see how consumers can be taught about clothing.

The Textiles and Clothing Division of the Bureau of Human Nutrition and Home Economics issues bulletins on the construction and care of clothing. The instructions are prepared by the Home Economics Staff.

Consumer education in clothing and textiles has also become a tremendously important phase in national advertising. Some banks and finance corporations prepare booklets to help the family with typical financial problems, including information on how to plan, buy, and care for clothing. Manufacturers of fabrics prepare booklets on the use and care of fabrics. Shampoo companies distribute hints on the care and styling of hair. A certain manufacturer of children's garments published a helpful little book on Child Care. Obviously, such educational booklets are excellent advertisements for each firm. These booklets are often prepared by a woman with a home economics background. The work involves a considerable amount of research and writing ability.

There are other ways by which a manufacturer or retailer educates and encourages the public into buying his product. A style consultant in the yard-goods department of a retail store who helps a customer to select becoming fabrics and patterns may be hired by the store or she may be hired by a fabric manufacturer or a pattern company to promote the sale of their product. Stores that sell sewing machines frequently offer beginning courses in sewing to those who buy their machines. A demonstrator may show various operations to a customer. Training in home economics is a good preparation for all such work.

Dressmaking. The woman who is adept with the needle and enjoys sewing for herself might consider sewing as a career. There are possibilities here for the home economics graduate as well as for the girl who was not able to go to college. Advanced courses in clothing could be taken in night school. Many women turn to home dressmaking and alterations to help the family budget. Home sewing has several advantages. Your business can be carried on at home during your free time. You may accept as much work as you have time for. Your income will supplement the family funds without taking you away from home duties. Home sewing can be carried on in any community.

Yet, home sewing is not the only job for the skilled seamstress. Many retail stores employ a staff of fitters and seamstresses to take care of alterations. In larger cities, wholesale garment manufacturers employ "sample hands" and "finishers" to make up sample dresses for their season's line. Retail designing shops that sell directly to the more exclusive trade need seamstresses and finishers in their workrooms.

So far we have been discussing the opportunities for the girl with training in home economics. But the field of clothing and fashion is a vast industry that demands many other specialized skills. Careers in costume design, textile design, fashion illustration, fashion writing, and retailing generally require special training and experience. The following material is a survey of some of the other opportunities in the fashion field.

OPPORTUNITIES IN FASHION DESIGNING

Offhand, you may think of designing in terms of coats, suits, dresses, and other outer apparel. Actually, everything you wear or carry represents an artist's design. Your coat, your blouse, your cardigan, your shoes, your garter belt, your panties, your slip, your gloves, and your hat all are produced by different manufacturers who employ designers to develop new merchandise to appeal to the buying public.

Then consider that the "public" includes several age groups: matrons, misses, junior misses, teen-agers, children, toddlers, and infants. The merchandise for any one age group represents a vast number of designers at work. Then, too, merchandise is designed to suit different tastes and budgets. Not all people like the same thing; nor can all people afford the same prices. This should give you some idea as to the variety of designers needed.

The designing of fashion merchandise is a highly competitive field that demands outstanding creative talent and specialized training. Basic art courses in color, costume design, historic research, and sketching are essential for designers of any fashion merchandise. Later, specialization determines still further training. Designers of apparel need advanced courses in textiles, draping, pattern-making, and clothing construction; designers of millinery study all aspects of millinery, and so on. Such practical courses, together with the more theoretical art background, give a student an understanding of the limits of material and construction.

Perhaps the most important part of a young designer's training is "learning her trade" on her first job. A beginner may not do any actual designing at first; but any job gives her a practical knowledge of her field that can launch her on a designing career. If she wants to become a milliner, she may sell hats or work in the millinery workroom. If she wants to design teen-age dresses, she may start out by selling them or by modeling them. After such general experience, the next logical step would be to work for a firm where actual designing is done. This could be a wholesale house, a retail designing establishment or a pattern house. Here again, the beginning designer may not be entrusted with any actual designing. Yet, her opportunity lies where designing is done. Gradually, she can prove her ability.

Wholesale trade. You may have wondered just how a new line of merchandise is designed and put into production. For the sake of example, let us suppose that Mr. Blank is a wholesale manufacturer of "Hi-teen" casual dresses that retail from $12 to $18. Well in advance of a season, he confers with his head designer as to what fabrics will make up his line. The selection is based on trade reports as to what will be "good" during the coming season.

Miss Roe, the head designer of the firm, is responsible for the designs that will make up the new line. She attends fashion shows, reads fashion and trade magazines, and keeps up with "young" trends in order to create designs that will appeal to teen-agers. Miss Roe sketches dozens of ideas; some are "copies" of more expensive dresses; others are based on standard classic styles; a few are variations of styles that were big sellers the previous season. She then confers with Mr. Blank and his staff to decide which sketches will be made up in sample models. Although Miss Roe knows how to draft a pattern and how to sew, she generally leaves the making of these first muslin models to her assistant-designer. These models are made up in sizes which will be worn by teen-agers at the final showing. When these muslin models meet with the approval of Mr. Blank, the patterns are ready to be made up into the actual sample dresses. The assistant checks the final pattern and cuts the fabric. She supervises the "sample hands" who sew the sample dresses. She also supervises the "finishers" who attend to such details as dress fasteners, trims, and hems.

The sample dresses are modeled before the executives and sales staff of the firm, who check the dresses before they are presented to store buyers when the market opens. An artist or "sketcher" makes detailed drawings of the sample dresses for the use of the firm's salesmen and also as a record of that season's line.

When buyers from retail stores come to the "Hi-teen" showrooms, teen-age girls model the dresses for them. The individual buyers place their orders on these samples in the colors, sizes, and number of dresses desired. If orders on a particular sample are too low to warrant large-scale manufacture, that dress is dropped from the line. After all orders are in, the dresses are put into volume production and delivered to retail stores in time for a season's selling.

From this you see how many steps there are in preparing a garment for large-scale production. One of them might be a beginner's entry into wholesale designing. As a model, as a "sample hand," as sales help in the showroom,

A graduate clothing class on a field trip watches one step in commercial pattern making. The draper is finishing a half-muslin, following the designer's sketch.

Modern Miss

or as a sketcher, she would learn dress manufacture. By proving her ability in one job, she gets a chance to prove her ability in others. All wholesale houses are constantly in search of creative talent.

Retail designing. Whereas a designer for a wholesale garment firm has no direct contact with her customers, the designer of a retail designing establishment does have personal contact with her clientele. Her customers, as a rule, have come to her year after year. They are wealthy women who can afford beautifully made "originals." The designer's collection may include street, sports, dressy, and evening clothes; or she may specialize in one or the other. As customers "drop in," the various originals are modeled for them. Many customers have costumes specifically designed for their individual requirements; some may even have particular fabrics woven for them.

Retail designing establishments, of course, vary in both size and importance. The finest are owned by America's leading designers who help to shape the course of fashion. Yet even the most exclusive designing houses have usually started out on a small scale. So the young designer who has dreams of some day owning her own shop need not feel that it cannot be done.

The first step for the beginning designer is to try to get placed in a good designing shop. Most design schools give their graduates a "lead" as to possible openings. Once hired, the period of apprenticeship begins. Rarely does a beginner have a chance to do actual designing. She makes herself useful in the workroom, sewing on buttons and snaps and generally assisting the seamstresses. Later, she may assist with fittings, which gives her her first contact with the customer. Actual designing comes much later when the routine of cutting, sewing, fitting, and finishing is really clear to her. Then she may attempt to promote her own ideas.

Setting up one's own shop is somewhat of a gamble, even for a talented designer. It takes considerable capital to pay high rentals; to buy materials, sewing equipment, and showroom fittings; and to pay a staff of cutters, seamstresses, and salespeople. Not only must a designer have talent—she must be a shrewd business woman with executive ability and a "selling" personality.

But enough American women have established themselves in such a business to prove that it can be done. A few of them not only run their own shops, but sell designs for ready-to-wear specialty shops as well. An exclusive ready-to-wear retail shop may have a special "designer's room" which features the original creations of one or more top designers. Such originals are beyond the budget of the average customer. Yet, they influence the trend of fashion.

Pattern trade designing. Another field open to the young design graduate is that of pattern-designing. Most pattern companies carry a full range of patterns for several age groups, including coats, suits, dresses, play togs, lingerie, and even some hats, bags, and gloves. Such a range gives a beginner an opportunity to observe firsthand the design, pattern-drafting, and construction requirements of various items of apparel. It may even help her to decide on a field of specialization such as designing lingerie or children's clothing.

Obviously, the beginning designer may not be considered a full-fledged designer from the start. She may assist in the drafting rooms; or if she excels in clothing construction, she may work in the department where models are assembled and tested for the final pattern. Such varied work provides a valuable background to the practical requirements of the pattern trade.

OPPORTUNITIES IN FABRICS AND FASHION

Not so long ago, the textile field was a "man's world." The intricate processes of producing finished cloth from raw fibers and its final sale to clothing manufacturers and yardgoods departments were all considered man's work. Even today, comparatively few women are involved with the technical side of cloth manufacture. However, an increasing number of women are employed by leading fabric concerns as stylists or promoters because mill executives realize that women have a fashion viewpoint that men may lack.

A *stylist* for a fabric house is expected to forecast fashion trends about a year in advance. The designing of a fabric, its sample testing, and its final weaving and finishing take many months. It takes several more months for garment manufacturers to make up their merchandise. Such long-distance forecasting on the part of the stylist means that she has to confer with designers, garment manufacturers, and buyers of leading retail stores as to possible fashion trends. She must know which colors will be promoted and which fabric textures and weights are needed for the coming silhouette. The stylist confers with salespeople to determine customer reaction to the current line of fabrics. The stylist also studies market reports to learn which fabrics are good sellers and which are lagging and *why*.

In all cases, the stylist is the operating link between her mill or fabric concern and the clothing manufacturer or retail yardgoods merchant. Besides being a "go-between" and style forecaster, a stylist has a hand in developing new ideas for a fabric line. If she works for a mill whose output includes woven stripes and plaids, she may be asked to work up new patterns and color combinations. She experiments with actual woven samples. To do this, she must know the fundamentals of weaving. Otherwise, she might develop an idea for a plaid that is not workable on the loom.

If a fabric concern carries a line of printed fabrics, a stylist supervises the selection of the designs. She herself may or may not be a "print" designer. The company generally has its own staff of designers, and the stylist directs the work of these artists. Many companies also buy fabric designs on a piece work basis from artists or from a design studio. The stylist selects the designs which fit into the company's line. She has to have fine critical ability and a knowledge of color printing.

Much of the work of a stylist has to do with publicity—the promotion of goods. Some fabric concerns hire a special person to act as *fashion promoter*. Promotion work includes everything that will help to sell the firm's product: advertising in magazines, trade publications, and newspapers; conferences with garment manufacturers, retail buyers, and pattern companies; educational talks to store employees, to women's groups, or on the radio; reports on sales and consumer reactions in various parts of the country; fashion sales letters to help the company's salesmen.

From this you can see that stylists and promoters are busy! Theirs are jobs that require both mental and physical stamina, an agreeable personality, and a genuine liking for people. A woman's success depends on the impression she makes in her contact with mill workers, manufacturers, designers, retailers, and customers.

Courses in art, advertising, clothing, and textiles in high school and college are a necessary background for such work. Sales experience either in a yardgoods section or ready-to-wear is valuable. Later, a job in a fabric house, even if at first it is a minor clerical job, provides an understanding of production, which is the best training.

We have already mentioned the artist who creates designs for printed fabrics. Art school training, with emphasis on color, textile design, and historical research is required for this field. The first job should be with a fabric concern or a design studio on a full-time basis. Actual trade experience is valuable training for understanding the procedure of preparing art work for textile printing, and knowing what designs are practical and saleable. Later, the designer may wish to sell individual designs to a textile house on a free-lance basis.

Although the technical side of fabric production in a mill is almost wholly left to men, a woman can prepare herself for the field. There are textile schools that offer special training in a detailed study of fibers, spinning, power-loom construction, drafting of pattern weaves, assembling warp threads on the loom for weaving, and various finishing processes. Such technical training, plus actual mill experience, is necessary to become a mill expert.

OPPORTUNITIES IN FASHION ILLUSTRATION

A fashion illustrator may work for an advertising art studio that handles the art work for several firms; or she may find a place in the advertising department of a large retail store that handles its own newspaper or magazine advertisements. She may be employed by a pattern company to draw the figures used on pattern envelopes, in pattern books, or on large display posters. She may be on the art staff of some fashion or trade publication or a woman's magazine. Some illustrators prefer to work on a free-lance basis; that is, on order. A free-lance illustrator may get orders through an advertising agency, but she often makes her business contacts directly. A free-lancer works on her own time and in her own quarters. Her charges are based on the amount of work handled.

Fashion illustration demands art training, *plus* natural talent. As good figure drawing is the basis of good fashion illustration, art school training is generally preferable to that given in most colleges. Although a fashion figure is rather stylized, a thorough knowledge of figure structure is absolutely essential. In addition, the student must learn to handle many types of rendering easily: water color, pen and ink, pencil, wash, and even airbrush. She must know the methods of reproduction—that is, how the drawing is printed.

A student may get some of this basic training in college, of course. But unless she is unusually talented, she should plan on a year or two of more advanced work at an art school that offers special courses in fashion illustration. Furthermore, such schools maintain a close contact with the fashion industry, so that they can refer their graduates to possible openings.

It is generally advisable for a young, inexperienced artist to get her basic training by working for some firm on a full-time basis. Later, as an experienced illustrator, she may wish to free-lance. A successful illustrator generally earns far more as a free-lance than she does on a weekly salary.

OPPORTUNITIES IN FASHION WRITING

Those who have a knack with words, rather than with a needle or sketch pencil, may consider a career in fashion writing. It offers varied opportunities to the girl who has a keen style sense and the ability to write "selling" words.

The catchy phrases and short, convincing descriptions found in advertisements are the work of a *copywriter*. She may work in the advertising department of a retail store or a wholesale firm, or in an advertising agency that handles the accounts of several firms. Her job is actually a combination of reporting and advertising. She must describe merchandise so convincingly that the public is urged into buying it.

What is the preparation for such a job? First of all, selling experience is especially valuable because it provides a contact with the buying public. Courses in advertising, stenography, journalism, and fashion are also recommended—taken either in college or night school.

Fashion reporters write articles for newspapers, women's magazines, fashion periodicals, trade publications, or pamphlets. Such writing varies in style from chatty notes on fashion such as are found in fashion magazines, to the more factual style that is used in some trade publications. In any case, the writer must keep abreast of all the latest fashion trends, for it is her job

The New York Times

The reporter who covers fashion does a lot of traveling.

PARIS DISPLAYING FASHION IN PRINTS

De Givenchy Collection Stems From Lawn or Silk Organdy —Embroideries Stand Out

By DOROTHY VERNON
Special to THE NEW YORK TIMES.

PARIS, Feb. 4—The atmosphere of summer enchantment pervading De Givenchy's collection stems from exquisite lawn or

to keep her public well informed. A good fashion reporter must actually be several jumps ahead of her public. If she works for a monthly publication, her article must be submitted several months before the magazine is released. This means that she must keep in close touch with designers and manufacturers of fashion merchandise. Reporters for leading fashion publications are sent to fashion centers both here and abroad. They attend fashion showings of leading designers; they go to fashionable "spots" where "best dressed" women set the course of fashion.

What are the qualifications and requirements for such a position? A well-rounded basic college education is definitely in order, with an emphasis on history, art appreciation, and literature. She should have advanced courses in creative writing and journalism; she should know shorthand and typing. She should be familiar with as many aspects of the fashion industry as possible. If she writes for a particular product—be it cosmetics, furs, or fabrics—she should know that subject from all angles.

Reporting jobs do not just drop into a girl's lap! Here again, secretarial work in a business or publication office may be the first step. A girl may work her way into fashion reporting if she is "on her toes" and shows news sense as well as style sense.

Of course, the really big positions in the field of publication are those of *fashion editor*. She may be the fashion editor for a magazine, a newspaper fashion "section," or for a fashion column of a newspaper syndicate.

Although a magazine fashion editor has generally risen from the ranks of reporting, she may do little actual writing. Assistant editors take on such responsibilities. The fashion editor is an authority on fashion in every sense. She is in close touch with leading designers both here and abroad. She understands the problems of merchandising and senses fashion trends in all parts of the country. She does a great deal toward shaping the tastes of her fashion-conscious public. She is at the top because she has good taste, a varied background in the fashion field, a sense of organization, and executive ability.

Radio and television publicity provides still another field for writers. Along with the commercials and news items, the "woman's hour" engages in feminine chit-chat about the latest style hints. A girl has to have an audition if she is going to speak or act but the girl who writes fashion scripts has only to know how to write well for the listening public. Occasionally, the commentator writes her own script. Many colleges and universities offer courses in radio writing.

OPPORTUNITIES IN MODELING

To the casual observer, the life of a model may seem like a glamorous existence. But modeling makes great demands on a girl, whether she models clothes in fashion shows, in exclusive shops, in a manufacturer's showroom, or for photographs.

In the first place, a fashion model has to measure up to certain physical qualifications as to height, weight, and general attractiveness. This does not

U.S.D.A. Extension Service

This is a 4-H club meeting. Learning how to attain good posture is of fundamental importance for all girls—whether or not they plan a career.

mean just a "pretty-pretty" face. Rather, a model must be striking and distinctive in appearance, she must have a certain poise and style about her— and grace!

Then, she has to see that she retains all those fine qualities. Her life is a constant routine of keeping fit and lovely . . . a program that involves proper diet . . . plenty of sleep so that she looks fresh at all times . . . an exercise routine to keep supple and graceful . . . and perfect grooming, for she cannot be lax about her appearance ever. This means frequent shampoos, flawless skin, beautifully kept hands, and work at the ironing board night after night. It is a model's business to look attractive always.

Much has been said for and against modeling schools. A few schools have a good rating and make good models out of good "model material." But the best of schools cannot make a good model out of average material. Actually, many of the best fashion models have not gone to a modeling school. If a girl has natural grace, good carriage, poise, spontaneous facial expressions, and gracious unaffected manners, she is model material. Dancing does much to develop grace; dramatic training gives added poise and stage presence; and good setting-up exercises keep a body in trim and encourage good posture.

"Live" modeling applies to those who model clothes in smart retail shops, hotel shows, or in manufacturer's showrooms during the "buying" season. In a wholesale house, a model's size requirements depend on the line of clothing manufactured by a firm. Teen-agers with a natural, wholesome look are quite likely to be used for young fashions; about 5 feet 5 inches in height, 9–10 size, from 100–105 pounds. Most "adult" fashions specify 5 feet 7 inches–5 feet 8 inches in height, 10–12 size, from 115–120 pounds.

The beginner in "photographic" modeling should sign up with a good model agency. An agency requires good, full-length photographs of prospective models to keep in their files, complete with measurements, weight, and coloring. Tall, slender creatures with distinctive features are the photographic favorites.

The agency then provides a model with a list of advertising agencies, fashion publications, and others who need models.

There is a tendency for some "photo" models to become associated with certain types of clothing. One model looks well in severe, tailored costumes, another in sophisticated "after-five" ensembles, another in young casuals. Although this may limit the range of possible jobs, it can be an asset. If Miss So-and-so always makes an evening gown look "like a million," she is called on frequently.

Of course, all photographic models do not necessarily appear in full-length poses. Some model hats or neckwear; others model hosiery and shoes; those with lovely hands may pose for nail polish, gloves, or jewelry; still others model foundation garments.

There is another job in some fashion photo studios or agencies that is open to women. It is that of *stylist*. Her job is manysided. She carries out the specifications of the firm that is advertising the merchandise. She is the photographer's assistant. She prepares the model for the photograph and checks style details before the camera clicks.

A firm may provide its own models or specify the model to be used; it may provide all costume accessories. Many firms, however, bring in only the merchandise to be photographed. Then it is up to the stylist to engage the right model. She must know which models on the studio listing display various types of apparel to the best advantage. A stylist selects accessories that are appropriate for the costume. She helps the model to dress; she adjusts bows, belts, hair-dos, jewelry. In other words, the model is style-perfect when she appears before the camera.

Modeling is often a springboard to other careers in fashion.

Du Pont photo

Television has opened up another possible field for fashion models. It can be a valuable advertising medium because "live" models are more convincing to many people than even a superb photograph. By observing a moving model, a woman will better understand how a garment looks from all angles. Moreover, a woman may sit in her own living room and see fashion shows that once were limited to those who could attend fashion shows in exclusive shops, hotels, or at resorts.

OPPORTUNITIES IN RETAILING

Store work offers varied opportunities to girls. A girl who is interested in store work can find opportunities in small towns and large cities alike.

To give you an over-all picture of opportunities in fashion retailing, we will consider the more specialized work of employees in a large department store. Of course, even department stores differ. Some carry a distinctive, high quality merchandise for the customer of means. Other stores carry goods within the price range of the average or low income group. Such differences influence a store's entire merchandising program. Buyers, salespeople, advertisers, display artists, and others are all geared to satisfy the demands of its particular type of customer.

Anyone who has worked in a large department store knows that it is like a world in itself. It is a complex organization which usually consists of four main divisions, each with a huge staff of specialized employees. (1) The *merchandising* division includes all those who actually buy and sell goods. Each department—coats, millinery, shoes, et cetera—has its own sales force, stock girls, head of stock, assistant and head buyers, and managers. (2) The *general promotion* division includes those who increase sales through newspaper and magazine advertisements or publicity, display, and special promotions. (3) The *financial* division includes auditors, bookkeepers, cashiers, and so on. (4) The *store service* division is just what the term suggests—services and conveniences for the customer. At the top are the executives who control the store's management and shape its policy.

Obviously, the two divisions in which fashion careers are found are merchandising and general promotion.

Merchandising. A girl may enter the merchandising division either as a salesgirl or stock girl. Large stores have a training program by which beginners are taught the general routine and policies of the store. New salespeople learn how to fill out many kinds of sales slips: "cash," "charge," "deliver," and so on. When they are ready to sell, an experienced sales person is on hand to help them.

What are the possibilities for advancement? A capable sales person who knows her merchandise, who has a good sales record, who shows ability to evaluate style trends, and knows how to organize her work may hope to become either *head of stock* or *assistant buyer*. After that, she may become *head buyer* if there happens to be a vacancy. Successful buyers may become *merchandise managers*, although such positions are generally held by men.

A brief description of these merchandising jobs may interest you. More detailed information is found in books listed on page 523.

Obviously, the duties of a *salesperson* are to sell; to make every effort to satisfy the customer. She, of all people in the store, has the most direct contact with the buying public. Therefore, she should be gracious, helpful, unhurried, and pleasing in appearance. A salesgirl should be well-informed about her merchandise and fashion trends in order to advise and help a customer in her selection. As a helpful salesperson is directly responsible for customer satisfaction, she is a vital part of the store's success.

Although a selling job requires long hours of standing, constant alertness, and a certain amount of regimentation, many women prefer it to any other work in the store. Other salespeople use it as a step toward more advanced positions in merchandising.

Another thing . . . sales experience is valuable for any girl who is interested in *any* branch of fashion. A contact with the buying public provides an understanding as to what the public wants and buys.

Head of stock is a job for a woman who is a good organizer. She has to see that there is sufficient merchandise in the reserve stock room to replenish dwindling stock on the "floor." When the reserve stock runs low, the head of stock informs the head buyer what merchandise should be reordered.

The head of stock is the all-around housekeeper of a department. She checks on incoming goods in the receiving room. She sees that all merchandise is marked before it is delivered to the selling section. She supervises the arrangement of stock on racks, on shelves, in cases, and drawers. She sees that salesgirls put away or cover merchandise at night and display it properly in the morning.

As the head of stock works very closely with the buyer of her department, she is in a position to learn how a successful buyer plans the purchase of stock. Such firsthand observation may eventually lead to a position as buyer.

The head of stock has a *stock girl* to run her errands; to help her in the stock room and on the floor. A stock girl in a ready-to-wear department is usually responsible for keeping the showroom and fitting rooms in order. She puts away garments that have been shown to customers. She reports on missing buttons, ripped hems or seams.

Buying merchandise for a store is a big responsibility that involves training and experience in selling, estimation of seasonal stock consumption, and advertising. A *buyer* must have good taste and must foretell what styles will be "good" months before the merchandise is available in the store. To do such forecasting, a buyer reads fashion and trade magazines; she must know what fabrics and colors textile firms are promoting; she must attend fashion showings; and she must know her wholesale market.

Above all, a good buyer must know how to buy merchandise for the type of customer to whom her store caters. She studies her sales records to know what stock "moves." A buyer who miscalculates her stock and buys too little or too much will bring severe losses to her store.

Buyers attend showings of sample merchandise in the manufacturer's or jobber's showrooms months before the selling season. They place orders on the samples. The merchandise is made up in the sizes, styles, and colors ordered and delivered to the store in time for the selling season. Buyers interview salesmen and seek out every possible wholesale market and the best values.

A buyer also co-operates with buyers of other departments to make sure that inter-departmental merchandise is harmonious. Such co-ordination is often under the supervision of merchandise managers or fashion stylists. A buyer also works with the advertising, publicity, and display departments to promote sales. She studies what buyers of other stores are selecting, to compete with them. The higher her department sales, the more valuable she is to her store.

The buyer may have an *assistant buyer* who assumes much of her routine store work. As a rule, the assistant does no buying. Occasionally, she may accompany the head buyer at special showings. Being an assistant to a shrewd head buyer is the most valuable training toward becoming a buyer.

A competent buyer may become a *merchandise manager*. There are an increasing number of women merchandise managers in the fashion retail business. The position commands a high salary.

The merchandise manager supervises the buying and selling of goods. She specifies the budget to be spent for stock by each department; and the price range of merchandise within a department. In one section, suits may sell from $20 to $30; in another, from $35 to $55. She helps to plan the location of merchandise. She also allots advertising space and display areas to various departments. She usually determines *what* should be featured *when* to promote greatest sales. It is a big job that involves knowledge of budgets, buying, advertising, and promotion.

In a large store, several divisional merchandise managers supervise the buying of stock for related departments. One divisional manager directs the buyers of related apparel such as coats, suits, and dresses. Another supervises the buyers of belts, gloves, handbags, and neckwear. These managers are responsible to the general merchandise manager or the chief executive of the store. In smaller stores, the buyers may assume responsibility of buying for their departments and report to one general manager.

Promotion of fashion merchandise. Running a store is not a simple matter of buying and selling goods. A large number of a big store's personnel is engaged in sales promotion. The advertising, display, and publicity departments co-operate to promote the store's merchandise, often under the supervision of a special promotion director.

A *promotion director* co-ordinates the efforts of all departments of a store and its executives to promote sales by means of the most effective advertising and display.

The woman who aspires to such a position must have a well-rounded knowledge of art, costume design, fabrics, advertising, publicity, and all aspects of merchandising. She must have a keen fashion sense, executive ability, and imagination. She keeps up with current events both at home and abroad. Her position of leadership calls for all-around ability and tact.

The promotion director also is in charge of the store's special fashion shows, but engages a *fashion-show director* to supervise it. (A store may have its own director or it may call in someone who plans shows for several stores.) The fashion-show director selects the models and the costumes to be shown. She has assistants who help models in the dressing rooms; others who assist with lighting, music, and other details.

A *stylist* or fashion co-ordinator acts in an advisory capacity in the harmonious selection and promotion of merchandise. She judges merchandise from the viewpoint of customers, maintaining her own standards of good taste. She has the imagination and ability to revamp a lagging department or to create a new one if it meets with customer demands. As it is the stylist's job to "influence people" in the right direction, she herself must be an exponent of good taste.

Training for such a position requires training in art, costume design, and fabrics. To gauge consumer demands and know store management, experience in selling and buying is valuable.

A *publicity director* is in charge of all the writing and photographs that appear in magazine and newspaper publicity articles. She sometimes supervises fashion shows. She is actually a combination of advertiser and writer, and has generally risen from a position as fashion publicity writer. She must write convincingly and with color. Publicity writing often involves research.

Training for publicity includes a good background in art, history, fashion, advertising, and journalism. The first step toward such work may well be a job as secretary. Later she should try to become an assistant to the publicity director.

An *advertising manager* (in most cases a man) is in charge of all printed advertisements that appear in newspapers, magazines, store booklets, monthly bill enclosures, and store display cards for elevators, counters etc. He selects the newspapers and publications in which the store will advertise; and decides on space to be used. He organizes the work of artists, copywriters, and type specialists. Such a position demands training and experience in layout, illustration, copywriting, mathematics, type faces, and general advertising. The entire advertising staff works under terrific pressure, for there are many people to please and constant deadlines to meet. Daily "ads," week-end "specials," not to mention monthly publications, keep the advertising department moving at a hectic pace.

The *art director* in the advertising department is responsible for the appearance of all advertisements. (There are few women who hold this position, but it can be done!) She directs the work of layout artists and illustrators. The layout artist plans the arrangement of the copy and illustration in the ad, and decides on the type faces to be used in the copy. The illustrator then proceeds with the drawings. A director may also hire free-lance artists for some of the work.

An art director must have keen critical and creative ability, and a knowledge of the technical aspects of printing. The position demands a good art background and experience in illustration and layout. A successful layout artist may aspire to a position as art director, if she has creative and executive ability.

The *display manager* (seldom a woman) plans all show window and interior counter and "spot" displays. In smaller stores, an art director is in charge of display, but in large stores a special staff handles it. Window displays can be works of art. Good displays are the work of creative artists who know how to "set the stage" for a store's merchandise. "Window shopping along the avenue" can literally be an evening's entertainment.

Display artists go to no end of trouble to achieve good results. Often, a "set" must be built. A display might require an opera box, a Western corral, or Santa's workshop.

Display work requires a headful of ideas, knowledge of color, arrangement, lighting, and plenty of physical endurance. The building and lifting of props and merchandise is not work for a woman. That is why much of the display work is left to men. Yet, all phases of display do not require masculine brawn! A woman can create ideas for a display and plan the color and lighting just as readily as a man.

The girl who is interested in display should have courses in color, design, painting, stage design, and lighting.

This survey of work in fashion is by no means complete; nor is it descriptive of all kinds of work. But now, you have an idea as to the many opportunities in fashion. There is a job there for every type of girl. Many a successful woman has started her career in one of the less skilled jobs and worked her way up. Perhaps you can too!

ACTIVITIES

For the class

1. **Collect** for the class bulletin board and files newspaper or magazine clippings that deal with women who have made careers in the fashion world.
2. **Invite** a woman who has made good in some phase of the clothing world to give a talk to your class. Ask her to tell how she got started and what training she got along the way.

For the individual

Line up a summer or afternoon job for yourself that might be the beginning of your fashion career.

BIBLIOGRAPHY

BOOKS

Ahern, Eleanor, *The New Wash Day*. New York: M. Barrows & Co., Inc., 1944. A practical discussion of laundry equipment, washing agents, fabrics which need special handling, and ironing techniques.

Bane, Allyne, *Tailoring*. New York: McGraw-Hill, 1958. A college-level text which explains basic steps and professional techniques of custom tailoring.

Bendure, Zelma, and Pfeiffer, Gladys, *America's Fabrics*. New York: The Macmillan Company, 1946. A comprehensive coverage of fabrics as they are being manufactured in America today. Excellent photographs—many in color.

Burnham, Helen A., Jones, Evelyn G., and Redford, Helen D., *Boys Will Be Men*. Philadelphia: J. B. Lippincott, 1942. A high-school text for boys with helpful material concerning their social life, diet, and clothing selection.

Chambers, Bernice G., *Color and Design: Fashions in Men's and Women's Clothing and Home Furnishings*. New York: Prentice-Hall, Inc., 1951. The interrelationship of fashion and taste as it affects choices in clothing and house furnishings.

Davis, Adele, *Vitality Through Planned Nutrition*. New York: The Macmillan Company, 1949. A lively high-school text on good nutrition: what happens if you neglect its principles and what they can do for you.

Denny, Grace G., *Fabrics*. Philadelphia: J. B. Lippincott Co., 1953. An alphabetical listing of fabrics, fibers, and textile terms with definitions of each.

Dessner, C. M., *So You Want to Be a Model*. New York: Halcyon House, Garden City Publishing Co., 1948. This book provides valuable information as to qualifications, training, and opportunities in modeling.

Epstein, Beryl Williams, *Fashion Is Our Business*. Philadelphia: J. B. Lippincott Co., 1945. An informative biographical survey of some of our leading American designers, including the particular contribution of each to fashion.

Erwin, Mabel D., *Clothing for Moderns*. New York: The Macmillan Company, 1957. A general clothing text for college use, with emphasis on clothing construction. Instructions are clear and specific.

Evans, Mary, *Better Clothes for Your Money*. Philadelphia: J. B. Lippincott Co., 1952. Consumer information on how to buy clothing, with specific hints on what to look for in each article.

Evans, Mary, *Fundamentals of Clothing and Textiles*. New York: Prentice-Hall, Inc., 1949. A college text covering clothing selection, a study of textiles, and certain clothing construction processes.

The Fashion Group: Bernice Chambers, editor, *Keys to a Fashion Career*. New York: McGraw-Hill Book Co., 1946. A glimpse into the fashion industry—its demands and opportunities—as told in personal interviews by women who have reached the heights.

Garnell, Helene, *It's Fun to Make a Hat*. New York: Liveright Publishing Corp., 1944. The "hows" of millinery design told in spritely style. Directions are given for making hats of fabric, felt, and straw.

Goldstein, Harriet, and Goldstein, Vetta, *Art in Everyday Life*. New York: The Macmillan Company, 4th edition, 1954. A classic text on the application of art principles to clothing and home furnishings.

Goodman, Bonnie V., *Tailoring for the Family*. New York: Prentice-Hall, Inc., 1951. How to make suits, coats, slacks, etc., by custom tailor methods. Clear, full description of processes with adequate illustrations.

Hardy, Kay, *Costume Design*. New York: McGraw-Hill Book Co., 1948. A helpful guide on drawing fashion figures, on creating original designs, and on rendering a variety of materials.

Hemstead, Laurene, *Color and Line in Dress*. New York: Prentice-Hall, Inc., 3rd edition, 1947. Applying art principles to the choice of lines, colors, and textures in articles of apparel. Combinations and suitability are stressed.

Hess, Katherine P., *Textile Fibers and Their Use*. Philadelphia: J. B. Lippincott Co., 5th edition, 1954. A study of fibers and the way they are made into cloth and finished to produce fabrics. Market information, selection, and care of fabrics are included.

Hollen, Norma, and Saddler, Jane, *Textiles*. New York: The Macmillan Company, 1955. A college text with accurate and pertinent information about today's textiles.

Iowa Home Economics Association, *Unit Method of Sewing*. Ames: Iowa State College Press, 1950. A manual on clothing construction by quick and easy methods adapted from industry.

Kettunen, Marietta, *Fundamentals of Dress*. New York: McGraw-Hill Book Co., 1941. A college text on how to dress artistically, suitably, and becomingly through the application of art to clothing and accessories. Grooming, wardrobe planning, dress for occasion, and other aspects of clothing are discussed.

Lewis, Dora, Peckham, Gladys, and Hovey, Helen, *Family Meals and Hospitality*. New York: The Macmillan Company, 1960. A good guide to nutrition, meal planning, and food preparation.

Mansfield, Evelyn, *Clothing Construction*. Boston: Houghton Mifflin Co., 1953. A college text devoted to the construction of women's clothing for both beginning and advanced students. Has numerous excellent photographs of construction processes. Some short-cut and some custom methods are used.

Marsh, Hattie Marie, *Building Your Personality*. New York: Prentice-Hall, Inc., 1947. A discussion of personality development, poise and correct speech; a guide to clothing selection; hints on health and beauty aids.

Mauck, Frances F., *Modern Tailoring for Women*. New York: The Macmillan Company, 1947. Custom tailoring methods applied to women's suits and coats.

Picken, Mary Brooks, *Mending Made Easy*. New York: Harper & Brothers, 1943. Mending and other types of repair are taken up in detail.

Ryan, Mildred Graves, and Phillips, Velma, *Clothes for You*. New York: Appleton-Century-Crofts, Inc., 1947. A college-level general clothing text.

Schultz, Gladys, *How to Be a Fashion Designer*. New York: The McBride Company, Inc., 1941. An entertaining, informative survey of opportunities in the fashion market which gives the student an idea of how the garment industry functions.

Scott, Jane W., *Easy-to-Make Fashion Accessories*. New York: Woman's Press, Whiteside, Inc., 1953. Tells how to make flowers, bracelets, belts, and other accessories from felt and other fabrics as well as from walnut shells, safety pins, ribbon, and the like.

Scott, Judith Unger, *Lessons in Loveliness*. Philadelphia: Macrae-Smith Co., 1947. A chatty discussion for young girls about good looks and good health, with suggestions for hairdos, cosmetics, and winning manners.

Stone, Dorothy, *Men, Too, Wear Clothes*. Philadelphia: J. B. Lippincott, 1950. An interesting and informative book on men's clothing.

Talbot, Constance, *The Miracle Book for Your Clothes and Home*. New York: Arco Publishing Co., Inc., 1944. Home care of the family wardrobe, including textiles, rubber, and leather. Repairing, cleaning, and remodeling old clothes.

Thompson, Henrietta Mary, and Rae, Lucille E., *Clothing for Children*. New York: John Wiley & Sons, Inc., 1949. Covers the choice of functional clothing and wardrobe planning for children of all ages. Psychological and economic factors are considered as well as design, care, and storage.

Wilson, W. Harmon, and Eyster, Elvin S., *Consumer Economic Problems*. Cincinnati: Southwestern Publishing Company, revised edition, 1951. A basic text in applied economics, financial principles, and personal management.

Wingate, Isabel B., *Textile Fabrics*. New York: Prentice-Hall, Inc., 4th edition, 1955. A college text on all phases of textiles written principally for students in retailing classes.

Wingate, Isabel B., Gillespie, Karen R., and Addison, Betty G., *Know Your Merchandise*. New York: McGraw-Hill Book Co., 1953. Consumer information on what to look for when you buy clothing, furs, leather goods, jewelry, cosmetics, and household articles.

Wingo, Caroline E., *The Clothes You Buy and Make*. New York: McGraw-Hill Book Company, Inc., 1953. A basic text for a college clothing course.

PAMPHLETS

Bureau of Human Nutrition and Home Economics Bulletins and Leaflets, U. S. Government Printing Office, Washington, D. C.: U. S. Department of Agriculture Farmers' Bulletins, No. 1968, "Pattern Alteration"; No. 1837, "Cotton Shirts"; No. 1851, "Women's Dresses and Slips"; No. 1963, "Dresses and Aprons for Work in the Home"; No. 1474, "Stain Removal"; No. 1877, "Buying Boys' Suits"; No. 1778, "Fabrics and Designs for Children's Clothes"; No. 1894, "Coat Making at Home"; No. 489, "Family Spending and Saving"; No. 1925, "Mending ABC's"; and No. 1497, "Home Laundering"; U.S. Department of Agriculture, Bulletin No. 148, "Family Clothing Inventories and Purchases," 1956.

Home Economics Association, 700 Victor Building, Washington, D. C.: "Your Career in Home Economics," "Your Career as a County Home Demonstration Agent," and "Home Economics Teaching as a Career."

Household Finance Corporation, Consumer Education Department, 919 North Michigan Avenue, Chicago, Illinois: "Money Management" and "Better Buymanship Bulletins" on "Cosmetics," "Fabrics," "Furs," "Hosiery," "Shoes," "Soap and Other Cleaning Agents."

Proctor & Gamble, Cincinnati, Ohio: "A Girl and Her Hair."

U. S. Department of Agriculture, Agricultural Research Administration, Miscellaneous Publications No. 688, "Buying Men's Suits"; No. 545, "Make-Overs from Coats and Suits"; and Leaflet No. 271, "Shopper's Coat."

Westinghouse Home Economics Institute, Mansfield, Ohio: "Home Laundering Guide."

AUDIO-VISUAL TEACHING MATERIALS

Many school systems provide audio-visual materials through a special department, or through the school library. State departments of education supply information as to sources and in some instances materials also. Various departments of the federal government, such as the Department of Agriculture and the Department of Commerce, are valuable sources. Also commercial companies often have good films or filmstrips that relate to their products. However, new materials appear and old ones go out-of-date so fast that we are making no attempt to list individual materials. Instead we will note directories and some sources. This is by no means an inclusive list, but it is fairly permanent, representative, and reliable.

Sources of Visual Aids for Instruction in Schools, U. S. Office of Education Department of Health, Education, and Welfare, Washington 25, D. C. Sources of films, filmstrips, lantern slides, and pictures.

A Directory of 2002 16MM Film Libraries, Visual Aids Section, Office of Education, Washington 25, D. C.
(Write to U. S. Government Printing Office)

Educational Film Guide, H. W. Wilson Company, 950 University Avenue, New York 52, New York. Cumulative annual catalogue, with evaluations of each of over 2000 films, original sources, and local distributors or libraries.

Filmstrip Guide, H. W. Wilson Company, 950 University Avenue, New York 52, N. Y. Gives information similar to above relative to filmstrips.

Directory of United States Government Films, U. S. Film Service, Department of Health, Education, and Welfare, Washington 25, D. C.
(Write to U. S. Government Printing Office)

Dale, Edgar: *Audio-Visual Methods in Teaching.* The Dryden Press, New York. An excellent guide to the use and evaluation of all audio-visual aids. An extensive list of sources of teaching materials is included.

Other Sources of Current Information:
Department of Visual Instruction
National Education Association
1201 Sixteenth Street, N. W.
Washington, D. C.

INDEX

559